PLEDGE

The Public Radio Fund Drive

BY DON MERRILL

Printed in the United States of America
First Printing, 2019
ISBN 978-1-7326846-0-7
LCCN 2019906593

Don Merrill & Associates
16101 S. Leland Road, #82
Beavercreek, OR 97004

www.pledgethebook.com

Cover Illustration & Design by Karen Green
Book Design by Susan Bein
Editing by Kelly Luce
Indexing by Joanne Sprott
Author Photograph by Vanessa Menendez

Contents

To my parents, Donald and Mamie Merrill

Acknowledgments

"Writing is like driving at night in the fog. You can only see as far as your headlights, but you can make the whole trip that way."

—E.L. Doctorow, *The Paris Review* Radio Interviews,
George Plimpton, 1963

Thank you to the people and organizations who took the time to answer odd letters, emails, phone calls and tweets that fell on them from the sky.

First, to the more than 250 federal agencies that responded in wonderful detail to help me "perfect" my FOIA requests about money they may or may not have directly granted to public radio stations, groups or networks. Likewise, I am grateful to the state senators and representatives in 25 states who themselves responded, or tasked their aides to respond to my questions about state funding of college and university radio stations.

I am very grateful to all of the reporters, producers, program directors, station managers and development folks who agreed to return my survey, talk with me over the phone or correspond via email and social media. To focus group participants who let me lead them through their feelings about pledge drives, your opinions were invaluable. And I am very thankful to some of the people who were there at the beginning; Bill Buzenberg, Bill Siemering and Bill Kling, who shared some of their history with me.

Locally, thanks to Becky Meiers, who was the development director at community radio station KBOO here in Portland when I started this project. She took the time to help me understand how pledge drives work. She has since moved on to bigger and better things because she represents the best in radio and that's always in high demand. Also, thanks to my friend and former KBOO station manager Lynn Fitch whose stories from the trenches were excellent background for deeper dives into radio; community, commercial and public.

The data I collected on 37 public radio station pledge drives during spring 2016 was compiled by sports statistician, Joe Meyer. His adeptness with the Python programming language took me far beyond the SPSS of my college days and revealed station behavior that helped me confirm things I'd suspected. Thank you to my editor, Kelly Luce. She complimented my writing even as she chopped it, which made for a more streamlined book. Indexer Joanne Sprott showed me the difference between a word list and the tool that an index is supposed to be. Karen Green, a superbly talented graphic artist designed, and then tweaked the cover to perfection. And since a book isn't a book without someone who knows how to lay it out, a note of appreciation to InDesign expert Susan Bein. Like arranging living room furniture, I may know what I like but have no idea where it should go to make sense. Susan employed her typesetting "feng shui" and made this beast beautiful.

To my family; my cousin Julian, who's always been as loving as he's been lovable, gave financial help even as he faced a ridiculous tax bill. To my wife Robin who has been patient and loving though not always at the same time as I cloistered myself in my room for weeks and months on end while deep in the obsession of authorship.

And finally, to my parents, who both died in November 2018 before I could get the book to print. You worked hard your whole lives and blessed me with your ethic; a strong back, a sharp mind and a clear eyed relentlessness to finish what I start. Your gift helped me get *Pledge* over the finish line. I'd give anything for you to see it. Without you Mom and Dad, it would still be papers in a box under the bed. I love you and I miss you. ☎

Introduction

"I've had a come-to-Jesus moment if you want to call it that."

—Former Toronto Mayor Rob Ford

In 2013, the late Mr. Ford was beginning a recovery from drug and alcohol use. He had embarrassed his party and was the target of calls to resign. But his constituency loved him because of his prompt responsiveness to their ordinary concerns, and because they sympathized with his struggles. Ford was an open book and people like open books. They don't like feeling like outsiders. But journalism, not unlike politics, is full of insider attitudes, like those from Nicholas Quah. He founded and writes for the Nieman Labs blog *HotPod*. In 2016, Quah dismissed a Baltimore station manager's concerns over a show he was canceling because he felt it no longer served his audience. Quah used a lot of insider-speak, ending the piece saying, "To everyone reading this who isn't really into the whole public radio thing: Sorry about that." When Public Radio International announced in September 2014 that it was ending *The Bob Edwards Show*, PRI senior VP Julie Yager said, "We have communicated [that Sirius XM is halting production of new episodes] to stations and talked about it at the [PRPD] conference last week, so it shouldn't be a surprise to anyone." But did it surprise listeners?

Attitudes like those, which have called non-public radio insiders "civilians" for instance, is one of the things this book examines. That's why it's not written for insiders. It is written for the tens of millions of regular listeners who love public radio, but hear stuff they don't understand that doesn't always to come with explanations. And it's written for millions more who listen to AM

PLEDGE: The Public Radio Fund Drive

Talk Radio. Compared to the soothing tones of NPR, talk radio is *Smokey & the Bandit's* Firebird to NPR's Bentley. Many lovers of Hannity, O'Reilly and Limbaugh know public radio, in part, because they hate it and want to see it die for reasons they'd call more philosophical than mean. For instance, a taxpayer-supported NPR should toe the government line. That means no contradicting it and certainly, no confronting it. Others say if public radio is so good, it should give up taxpayer money and let the marketplace decide its value. And, many more don't like paying taxes toward what they call liberal opinions they may not agree with. For nearly a century, these remain the key arguments against government support for public broadcasting by many conservatives. Since President Johnson signed the *Public Broadcasting Act of 1967*, defunding calls have only grown.

This book tells listeners on the left of how soft spoken public radio has found itself in some street fights. But good news: it has learned how to hold a knife. Conservatives too get something for their years of public radio angst. Although it isn't the hammer and nails for the industry's coffin it does finally acknowledge some of the right's own suspicions about public radio. In writing this book, I've come to respect public radio more than I already did. But I'm not going to lie for it. And so I've focused on asking how honest it is with you? For years, charges that it compromises its legitimacy with manipulative pledge drive techniques had made some wonder where else is it being less than totally honest; with corporate underwriting, or double standards amongst its ranks or diversity?

Getting answers to those questions hasn't been easy. Though public radio talks a lot, it's careful what it's talkative about. A listener may think they know what's going on in public radio because public radio tells them what's going on in the world. But the two aren't synonymous. Listeners may complain that public radio keeps important information private, such as technical problems,

8

employee issues or detailed financial information. Station sign-offs and programming changes can sucker-punch listeners who didn't see them coming. NPR's own Ombudsman has accused the organization of a lack of transparency. Former KPBS General Manager Doug Myrland confirmed that attitude in 2007 comments re-reported in 2012 by *San Diego Reader* reporter Matt Potter. Responding to questions about the public's need for greater transparency after firing 12 staffers, shutting down popular local programs and collecting an $87,000 pension, Myrland said, "This process doesn't need to be 'transparent.' We aren't elected officials — every budget line item and every personnel decision and every bit of information we collect is not everybody else's business." And he wasn't finished. "Just because you give a contribution or pay taxes doesn't give give you the right to decide — or even influence — what goes on the air and what doesn't." To make the point that it didn't agree, the California legislature cut $200,000 from its appropriation to KPBS in 2012, prompting its next manager, Tom Karlo, to plead for help from the 89% of viewers who weren't giving.

If a listener chooses to search for their own answers, good luck. As abundant as it is, information isn't easy to sort or digest. And after a while, its sheer volume can start to make the search more cloudy than clear. A post on the NPR Extra blog began with, "We want to raise the curtain and explain how we use an algorithm at NPR One." That there is a curtain to be raised implies that there are other curtains that will remain lowered. Government information is especially thick. The FCC maintains dozens of excellent databases if you have the time and patience to search them for ownership information, station infractions, antenna locations or broadcast power. Corporation for Public Broadcasting rules for stations that get federal funds are easy to read, but there are lots of them. Congressional hearings on problems and fixes in public radio's back story can be found with the help of the Congressional Research Service and the Office of Management and Budget.

But other references are buried deep in the congressional record, which itself is submerged in the nearly infinite pages of the Federal Register.

Uncovering grant money not part of the congressional appropriation is doable with the help of websites like USASpending.gov, but tedious. The good news is the IRS 990 shows how stations get and spend their money. And websites like the Foundation Center or Guidestar help users make sense of this information. The bad news is that stations know details of who has given what, but they don't have to say more than what's already in the form. And you can only see one station's financials at a time.

Newspapers, magazine and broadcast reporters do a good job covering public radio. But their stories are buried beneath clickbait. About a fourth of those about public radio made it to mainstream publications like *Variety* or the *New York Times*. The rest appeared in research, government, non-profit or trade publications, meaning most people never saw them. And stations can be slow to hold required Community Advisory Board meetings or provide a record of their behavior in the mandatory public file. They make no secret that the effort costs time and money they could be using converting listeners to members. Almost every public radio station has a Frequently Asked Questions page. But FAQs don't always satisfy. Ombudsman emails almost always include the line, "although we can't answer every question." And listeners trying to pull tidbits about costs or internal goings-on from a pledge break flyover may turn away frustrated.

These issues are prompting hard questions. Is public radio honoring its philosophical purpose? Is it a service or a utility and how does the difference affect how it's paid for? Do the voices in public media reflect the center of the nation as well as big cities on the coasts? Can reporters do objective work or voice personal opinions without losing their jobs? How does an industry that's benefited from the way things have worked to this point adapt to rapid change without imploding? And how does it not just survive, but thrive?

Since the early 70s, the key to public radio's survival has rested with the pledge drive. And for almost as long, at least half of listeners have said they detest these drives. Yet public radio continues to rely on the pledge drive even though 21st-century technology exists that could destroy it forever. Pubcasters say they keep stations connected with listeners and vice versa. But if people knew they could tune in to public radio without having to hear pledge drives, wouldn't that bring more listeners? This book aims to answer these questions and raise better ones. I want to bring conversation about public radio out of the realm of think tanks, listservs and industry conferences and to its almost 40 million lovers and substantial pool of haters.

Do we want to live with the compromises stations make to give us what they think we want while drives change or even disappear as the industry evolves? And is that evolution putting public radio on the verge of its own "come to Jesus" moment? ☎

Chapter 1 - Basics

*"National Public Radio will serve the individual:
it will promote personal growth; it will regard the
individual differences among men with respect and
joy rather than derision and hate; it will celebrate
the human experience as infinitely varied rather
than vacuous and banal; it will encourage a sense
of active constructive participation, rather than
apathetic helplessness."*

—From '*National Public Radio Purposes*,'
1970 by William Siemering, NPR's first Director of
Programming.

In the 1950s, the Carnegie, Ford, Heald and Rockefeller foundations started using contributor money to fund a non-commercial, "public" radio as an alternative to commercial radio with Wolfman Jack and Brylcreem commercials. In 1963, the stars aligned. In the White House was Lyndon Johnson, a horse-trader and street fighter with substantial influence in Congress and a family with broadcast holdings in Texas. When President Johnson signed the *Public Broadcasting Act of 1967* and switched on the Corporation for Public Broadcasting (CPB), the entity that would be the progenitor of NPR blinked in the sunshine of Congressional funding for the first time.

The government had been convinced by big, non-profit voices that America needed to reclaim itself from the "vast wasteland" of mindless game shows and situation comedies. They convinced Johnson of the need for a venue that could reignite American passion for its educational and cultural heritage which was under existential threat by Nikita Khrushchev's launch of Sputnik. Commercial radio, dominating the AM wavelengths, ceded FM, a new, experimental band to educational, religious and "public" radio. Ever since, there has been a debate as to what public radio is or should be. Music or news? Information or entertainment? Is it art interviews and author profiles, or is it radio verité in a war zone, bringing you crying children and exploding houses? Is it an NPR host speaking over the opening music of *Morning Edition*? Is it stories from *The Moth* or the fast-paced, financial reporting of *Marketplace*? Is it nation-stations like WNYC and wall of sound smashes like *Radiolab*? Is it podcasts like *Serial* or 99% *Invisible*? Or, is it local voices doing traffic and weather, encouraging you to be a sustainer and download the station's app to your smartphone?

Public radio may be ubiquitous, but that doesn't mean every listener shares the same radio reality. When Oregon Public Broadcasting's Dave Miller interviewed NPR CEO Jarl Mohn in 2014, Mohn said Portland's listeners had "unusual" engagement with OPB. "Every market in the country should be like this market and this radio station: 'dominating,'" said Mohn. Compare Portland with Highland Heights, Kentucky. State cutbacks and the market forced their folk music icon and NPR affiliate WNKU off the air in 2017. In 2002, the Public Radio Program Directors created a set of guidelines for understanding what it called *Core Values of Local Programming*. These guidelines stated that listeners don't see any event in isolation and expect network and local news to help them connect the dots of the larger picture. So what should they infer about the state of public radio from stories like WNKU's? Are listeners at individual public radio stations seeing that larger picture? Or do they assume that public radio is OK if their local station is OK?

Jefferson Public Radio listener K. Beck suggests, in her reply to a piece by JPR's Valerie Ing, that would be a mistake. "[The

President and the Congress] need to be "lobbied" by every single person who listens to public broadcast radio and TV," said Beck in April 2017. "Otherwise, they will do whatever they want, or are pressured into doing by people who do NOT have our best interests at heart."

But do listeners have their own best interests at heart? Minnesota Public Radio wrote on its website in 2015 that from 2012 to 2014, more than one in five dollars received by NPR were from corporate sponsorships, or "underwriting." MPR said NPR leaned toward this money because stations (and by extension, listeners) "do not provide enough financial support to enable NPR to do its job." Considering how public radio relies on euphemisms like "We're not quite there yet" when missed pledge drive goals keep it from "ending successfully," MPR's directness is refreshing. Some in public radio say to get the audience more involved in the mission of public radio, such truths need to be spoken more openly and more often. But is that something the boards and staff overseeing public radio nationwide even want? Some, like philanthropist and former KPBS General Manager Stephanie Bergsma, say yes to having more grassroots voices at the decision table. Others, like Minnesota Public Radio founder Bill Kling, say absolutely not. ☎

What is a Station?

"If you operate a TV or radio station, you have to have a license. It has nothing to do with fundamental freedom. It has to do with protection of the average citizen against abuses."

—Robert Cailliau, created the original web brower for the Apple Macintosh, *Forbes Global*, Christopher Watts, Oct. 18, 1999

A terrestrial radio station is not complicated. On the supply side, it needs a transmitter, a frequency, an antenna, staff, a building, shows people want to hear and advertisers convinced they'll buy their products. On the demand side, it needs listeners. Regulators have more rules, most notably, that a station needs a license. A license, as Cailliau says, makes a station behave in the public interest. Pirate broadcasters, like WSQT in the nation's capital, ignore this licensing requirement. "WSQT Direct Action Radio currently broadcasts on 88.1 FM into randomly picked afternoon rush hours in Washington DC.," says the station on its website. "We cover news, protest, and militant direct action both inside and outside the US." The FCC hunts WSQT and other mobile or offshore pirates with the same kind of vans the UK uses to catch cheaters of the BBC. Meanwhile, pirates turned activists, like the Prometheus Radio Project, fight the agency on behalf of small broadcasters and challenge it on everything from power requirements to what it considers regulatory bullying. For most listeners, though, a station isn't a station and gets no private or corporate funding without a license. And a license to broadcast is almost worthless without someplace to broadcast from. About a third of public radio stations exist on university campuses thanks to in-kind agreements that let them contribute facilities instead of money. But in recent years, many institutions of higher learning have given up their stations for desperately needed cash. Stations run by communities or other entities may be in a slightly better position by entering into collaborative agreements for space. KCPW in Salt Lake City moved into the cozy Denker's Broadcast Facility which was on a sweeping wing of the brand new main library, built in February 2003 and assisted in part by those in power at the Gothic city hall right across the street.

In some cases, an overseeing entity like a school board or a state government might build a home for its radio station. In others, an existing station might give up its space and opt for a totally online presence. Stations like Boston-based WFNX reap the benefits of such streamlining. These hybrids get their music

from *YouTube* and deliver digital-quality sound over high speed
Internet that rivals the best terrestrial broadcasts. But they have a
limited audience. The problems that causes for advertisers, as well
as lurking digital music rights disputes, can be costly. After losing
its on-air frequency in 2012, WFNX went silent mere months later.
Online-only is no substitute for over the air, at least not yet. The
2016 *Pew State of the Media* report says about 93% of people over
the age of 12 still listen to at least two hours of broadcast radio
every week compared with only 26% who get most of their radio
online.

A big part of defining a station is defining the language that
describes it since a station can have several designations. NPR's
bylaws require its member stations, i.e., "licensees" meet basic requirements. A licensee may be what the FCC defines as a "full service station," meaning one with a staff, a building and a programming schedule that stretches into at least an 18-hour broadcast day.
If licensees receive CPB money, they must also be non-commer-
cially structured and educationally focused. Some of NPR's licensees, in addition to being some of the biggest stations in the country,
are also among the original 80 or so founding members of the
network. In his 2002 book, *Conflicting Communication Interests in
America*, Tom McCourt explains that NPR created station designations like "auxiliary" in 1985 to serve outlying communities. They
tended be in rural areas, and because of that, said McCourt, got a
break on the fees they paid to the network for programming. But
auxiliary stations didn't get exclusive rights to the best shows like
their larger competitors with more listeners or bigger budgets. And
in recent years, the auxiliary discount went away. In a 2016 spring
pledge break, pitchers for Baltimore's WEAA explained how they
must now pay the same price for programming as "the big boys."
Another category, the "associate" member, said McCourt, "consisted of stations that extend [or rebroadcast] the coverage of full-service stations." The FCC calls them "satellites." But licensees may

also operate satellites, which can also be known as "affiliates." WCQS in Asheville, North Carolina and New Hampshire Public Radio both run networks of eight affiliates each. And those stations can be designated as either "translators" or "boosters." Translators are low-power transmitters that rebroadcast a station's main signal to a different frequency. Their call sign heard at the top of the hour is full of numbers; W285AD or K220AA, for example. NPR does not count translators among the more than 1000 stations its licensees operate. But repeaters, which simulcast the main signal on the same frequency with the purpose of spreading it further and wider, are counted. They typically have their own traditional call sign, followed by "FM."

Gemma Hooley, NPR's VP of Member Partnerships, said in December 2017 that NPR had 260 licensees. That number has fluctuated between 263 and 269 since 2014 but it used to be even lower. In the mid-80s, thirteen markets were served by the CPB, and the National Telecommunications and Information Administration (NTIA) concluded that the nation didn't need any more full-service stations since the country could be adequately served by repeaters and translators. NPR disagreed; they wanted to add eighty more stations in larger markets. Because rural America had been adequately penetrated, an NPR researcher, according to McCourt, advised that, "clearly ... if we are to serve more listeners better, we've got to fish where the fish are."

Associate stations (satellites), member organizations (full service licensees) and non-member stations air NPR programs. The Pew report showed that in 2016, 1,072 NPR stations consisted of 726 associates, 264 licensees and 82 non-members. NPR's slightly different 2017 fact sheet showed 1,098 stations, with 838 associates, 260 licensees and 120 non-members. Non-member stations may air NPR programs. But like the bygone auxiliary stations, they may not get the best shows or the best rates.

The last time a list for all of NPR's member stations appeared in its annual report was 2011. NPR created publicly available PDFs for some years, including 2013 which also listed all of its stations and didn't distinguish between licensees, satellites or non-members. The 2014-2015 report was a rare consolidation. By then, the station list seemed to have disappeared. Around that time, the network switched to a dropdown menu that required users to know the station they were searching for. Though convenient for users wanting locally specific station information, the new dropdown menu prevents seeing all stations. NPR declined to produce an updated list although as of this writing, the 2013 PDF is still online, as are some of its older annual reports. The network also said it wouldn't provide a list of its licensees. But, it kind-of did. On the inside front and back covers of its multi-authored book, *"This is NPR: The First Forty Years,"* is a decorative motif of call signs. It is a listing of the network's 263 licensees as of the book's 2010 publication.

McCourt calls satellites "ludicrous" but admits, from his 1999 perspective, they "may become more common as public radio increasingly emulates the practices of its commercial counterparts." By all indications, he was right. The number of NPR stations grew from 695 in 2001 to 1,098 in 2017. Only about one in four stations have staff, programming, and a building; Ms. Hooley referred to the rest of them as "sticks in the ground." It's a reasonable assumption that three-quarters of the network consists of satellite affiliates. So, the next time you hear an announcer reading a long list of call signs, remember most of those are boxes in the middle of nowhere connected to the main station by computer, telephone or microwave link. They make the network sound big, but at most of those places, there's literally nobody home. Though the network sounds impressively large, it is surprisingly small.

PLEDGE: The Public Radio Fund Drive

In October 2017, the FCC was on track to make the number of "local" stations even smaller by eliminating the *Main Station Rule*. Currently stations must have a local presence, meaning the community has access to local staff and local facilities. The agency described eliminating the rule as a move that would help stations better allocate limited resources and the FCC's three member Republican majority voted to scrap it. Activists feel the decision passes off non local programming from non local entities as local. The result, they say, may be even more satellite stations diluting the local flavor of radio. NPR and the National Association of Broadcasters supported the rule and others those activists feel were designed to cripple local and low power radio.

Other requirements a station must meet include being recognized by its resident Secretary of State as a native non-profit organization. Its games and contests may also be under the oversight of a state gaming commission or a consumer protection bureau. It must meet nightmarish tax requirements like the IRS's *Public Support Test*. It must satisfy FCC technical requirements. Even networks like Public Radio International, can impose their own rules on potential members. Lastly and most important, to be a non-profit, a public radio station must have a plan for raising money. Most times, that means pledge drives which means, listeners becoming "members." But commercial radio, which has gotten rich from the kind of advertising public radio can't do, has started asking its listeners for voluntary contributions too. Seth Resler, writing for Jacobs Media in 2016, noted that commercial stations, mimicking public radio, are creating "membership" websites that give listeners access to premium content like past interviews and exclusive contests. In 2009, American Public Media's financial program, *Marketplace* explored that trend. Needless to say, NPR spokesperson Dana Davis Rehm wasn't happy about it. "NPR isn't pleased about the new competition. There's plenty of opportunity for confusion," said Rehm. Reporter Scott Jagow said the network fears the "audience may not discern the differences between public and for-profit operations." ☎

Character and Ownership

"It's not written in the Constitution or anything else.... Congress, just out of the clear blue sky, said the airwaves belong to the people, which means, in essence, that it belongs to Congress."

—Adrian Cronauer, IWCE Conference, Jim Barthold,
March 1, 2005

Workplace relationships between overseers and the overseen can be tricky. When those relationships sour, labor disputes are common. But public radio listeners probably don't think about unions for public radio employees because public radio is so cerebral, reasonable, progressive and intelligent. Why would there be a need for anything as pedantic as labor agreements? Everybody is always moving in the same direction, right? A 2014 statement from the WYPR Organizing Committee in response to station efforts to kill a union vote suggests not. "We are disheartened by management's decision to spend significant station resources to undermine our democratic effort. We hope they will commit as fully to mak-ing measurable improvements to the workplace and supporting the production staff."

In These Times reporter Bruce Vail said the Baltimore station's management broke up the vote with a "notorious union buster." Employees worried that corporate interests were influencing programming standards and wanted stronger barriers between them. And, said a former WYPR executive, they complained about "heavy-handed management techniques and substandard pay levels." Jonathan Rogers, Chair of the WYPR Board of Directors, told Vail that though the board hired the law firm Jackson Lewis, it wasn't to break the union. "We felt it was in the best interest of the station to ensure that the concerns of the organization were heard," said Rogers.

But unions blossomed elsewhere. KUOW Seattle employees embraced SAG-AFTRA in February 2018. WBEZ Chicago ratified its first union contract in July 2015. And the mothership itself, NPRHQ, came within hours of its D.C. newsdesk hitting the bricks in August 2017. They got their contract after flooding social media with #WeMakeNPR. An informal survey I conducted in 2017 found that nearly one in three public radio stations are not unionized. For listeners, that might be a surprise, which can lead to trouble. Development officers like their givers copacetic. Strikes tell them all is not well in public radio land. Labor unrest, stressing givers, can cause station morale to plummet and familiar voices to vanish, both affecting station quality.

Many handle their issues well enough to keep their public volume low. That's saying something, considering the rainbow coalition of entities that can own or operate public radio stations. Education has the biggest chunk of them. WRUC at Schenectady, New York's Union College was among the first college radio stations on the air in 1920. Today, KCRW at Santa Monica Community College, KUT at the University of Texas at Austin or WAMU at Washington DC's American University are among the best known stations. Also known as student radio, campus radio or college radio, they may be entirely programmed by students or serve as a training ground for students enrolled in a broadcasting curriculum.

If college and university stations air NPR, PRX, APM or PRI programming, it means they're receiving Congressional appropriations that make them accountable to the CPB. But that doesn't mean they have to be conventional. Their formats, like those of Astoria, Oregon's KMUN, or the former KUSP in Santa Cruz, California, can range from staid to wildly eclectic. Many proudly call themselves "independent" public radio. But stations are expensive. And sometimes, colleges sell them to NPR affiliates or religious corporations for cash to do their main work of educating students. The problem was big enough to be a topic of discussion during the 2011 National Federation of Community Broadcaster's conference. Some schools, however, are fighting the siren song of quick money. With new collaborations and facilities, Oregon's Jefferson Public Radio, for example, is keeping its program alive by bringing students further into day-to-day radio works.

Religious schools also run public radio stations. Abilene Christian University in Texas operates KACU; Augustana Lutheran College in Rockford, Illinois, also known as Quad Cities NPR, runs WVIK. And Boston University, with its Methodist tradition, owns and operates WBUR. Many religious and non-religious, non-commercial stations began their broadcast lives on the AM band but moved to FM when the FCC began issuing low power Class D licenses in the 1960s. FM is much friendlier to radio signals than AM. Broadcast power can be much lower, meaning running stations can be cheaper. And because of how it behaves in the atmosphere, FM is cleaner with less interference and much higher quality. But its signal is line of sight, unlike AM, which can travel further because it bounces or "skips" off layers within the atmosphere. That means FM doesn't have the range of AM without "boosters." There are about 260 state universities, 27 community colleges and 25 private colleges in the U.S. that operate some form of radio station. Many, though not all of them, are NPR member stations or licensees.

School boards can also own and operate public radio stations. Georgia's WABE is owned by the Atlanta Board of Education. And like campus radio, high school radio has been around for decades, and subject to the same pressures. The costs of running a high school station can force administrators to choose between keeping their stations or not. Schools and their coveted frequencies can be squeezed by commercial signals on either side. They may be tempted to give up their space by offers in the tens of thousands of dollars. Or surrender them due to FCC requirements to increase tower height, transmitter power or equipment specifications. As of 2013, about 22 school boards and boards of education own or operate radio stations in the United States. And as with colleges and universities, not all of them are NPR member stations or licensees.

Community, state and tribal governments hold licenses for most of the 150 or so remaining stations that aren't educational but may have had their start on college campuses like Hawaii Public Radio, Minnesota Public Radio, Oregon Public Broadcasting and WHYY, Inc. These stations are licensed to their communities and as with colleges and school boards, not all of them have public radio affiliations. Without state or institutional support, they must rely more heavily on other money including underwriting, pledge drives, unrelated business income and direct federal grants. West Virginia, Nebraska, Alabama, South Carolina, South Dakota and Mississippi own all public broadcasting licenses in their states. And as of this writing, a handful of native American tribes, including KWRR of the Northern Arapaho (until 2013), KCIE of the Jicarilla Apache (until 2013) and the KUYI of the Hopi Indian Nation own and operate public radio stations in Wyoming, New Mexico and Arizona, respectively. It should be noted that these stations are especially susceptible to proposed changes by administrations hostile to CPB's budget. ☎

Tuning the Dial

*"In the '50s, listening to Elvis and others on the radio in Bombay—
it didn't feel alien. Noises made by a truck driver from Tupelo,
Mississippi, seemed relevant to a middle-class kid growing up on
the other side of the world. That has always fascinated me."* -

—Salman Rushdie, CNN.com, April 15, 1999

It's an iconic image from the 1950s and 1960s: a kid in bed listening to faraway stations on a table radio as their bedroom walls
glowed yellowish-orange from glass amplifier tubes. The parade of
various call signs may have sounded like incantations, spoken by
strange static-filled tongues. Those paying closer attention might
have noticed that U.S. stations west of the Mississippi River began
with "K" while those east of it began with "W." But call signs are
far from being romantic mysteries of youth.

Call signs, like personality profiles, give clues to what new stations value most. The FCC lets a station pick its own as long as it's
not obscene, suggestive or already in use. KBOO in Portland, when
it went on the air in 1967, was allegedly named after a strain of
west coast weed. To this day, and true to form, KBOO continues to
balance necessary professionalism and wild unorthodoxy. KRVS's
call letters have two meanings. One stands for the University of
Southwestern Louisiana, which used to be called the University of
Louisiana at Lafayette. The call sign reflects its new identity as the
Radio Voice of Southwestern. But KRVS, which joined NPR in the
mid-70s, is also a mnemonic for the Cajun French word *ecrivisse*,
meaning crawfish. Baltimore's Morgan State University station
WEAA stands for "We Educate African Americans." Before 1933,
WNKE, an early station of Northern Kentucky University had call
sign WPAY, which stood for "Pay any yodeler." That's because
between 1933 until it was taken over by the university in 2011, it
played country music. Boston's WGBH refers to the location of its

25

transmitter in "Greater Blue Hill." When Seattle's listeners saved KPLU from extinction in 2016, it thanked them with its new call sign, KNKX or "connects." Even WHYY, the moniker of Philadelphia's "*Fresh Air*" with Terry Gross, was initially filed with the FCC to stand for "Wider Horizons for You and Yours." But call signs are not sacrosanct, meaning stations can change them at will. The Gap, Pennsylvania station currently known as WLRI has changed call signs 21 times since 2003.

But call signs may be disappearing. Many stations determined to re-brand themselves into friendlier sounding, easier to remember entities have, over the years, become groups such as New York Public Radio or Oregon Public Broadcasting. Those names are constantly repeated while stations use their legal IDs only when and because the FCC orders them to. Listeners wanting to easily identify a station in west-central Colorado must know, for example, that Aspen Public Radio is actually two stations; KAJX Aspen and KCJX Carbondale. And the traditional way to identify a station may change if pubcasters get their way. The FCC's "Call Sign Reservation System" lets potential broadcast owners know if the call sign they want is available. But even as they ask the government for a new identity, they're petitioning that it be less identifiable. In May 2017, the FCC sought suggestions for regulations to update; removing the "burdensome" station requirement to give IDs at the top of the hour was near the top of the list. Stations argue that they should have the right to identify themselves in ways that fit the local community. They say listeners know to whom they're listening.

It is an interesting point that doesn't seem to apply during pledge drives when stations may repeat a telephone number up to 30 times a minute because they say listeners might not remember it or not have anything with which to write it down. For listeners who only know stations through their taglines, their broadcasting groups or their bookmark rather than their frequency or call sign, the move raises questions of how station accountability might be affected. And it seems to say that making sure listeners send in their support is apparently much more important than insuring they know who they're sending it to.

Most of those stations live on the FM band, which stretches from 87.9 to 107.9 megahertz for all U.S. radio stations. And many public radio stations live below 92, a part of the FM band the FCC calls "reserved." Only non-commercial, non-profit stations can be there. Those stations don't have to pay for their broadcast licenses because they're broadcasting not-for-profit underwriting, not advertising. And because of crowding at the low end of the FM band, the FCC sometimes lets public radio broadcast outside of it. But ironically, those that do must pay for a license. Rome, Georgia's WGPB FM and WNGH FM in Chatsworth, Georgia were both former commercial stations before being bought by Georgia Public Broadcasting in 2007 and converted to pubcasters to serve the ridge and valley Appalachians northwest of Atlanta. They wanted the elbow room near the middle of the band (97.7 and 98.9, respectively, but they were not alone.

NPR's 2013 station list shows about 85 CPB funded stations exist between 92.1 and 107.1. About half of the states have public radio stations outside of the reserved band. And the more remote a state's terrain, the more of its stations are outside this band. But public radio is also on the AM band. That same NPR station list shows at least 56 AM public radio stations. From 2004 through 2009, Salt Lake's KCPW broadcast at AM 1010 as well as 88.3 FM until its AM frequency was bought by Immaculate Heart Radio Educational Broadcasting and re-branded as KIHU Catholic radio.

FM stations may seek AM just to have another presence before another audience. But the trend since 2009 is the reverse; the FCC is letting AM stations simulcast on FM. AM has been losing listeners for years, though sports and conservative talk radio has slowed the exodus. The band enjoyed revitalization in 2013 due to lobbying by the nonprofit Minority Media Telecommunications Council, an advocacy organization which promotes and preserves "equal opportunity and civil rights in the mass media, telecommunications and broadband industries." But AM's higher cost for lower quality has pushed some owners to ask the FCC to throw them a lifeline and let them expand their audiences to FM.☎

Chapter 2 - Major Public Radio Players

"NPR...is not responsible for every show in which polite voic-
es speak in a restrained, earnest manner about the issues of
the day; other players that traffic in such fare include Amer-
ican Public Media, which produces Marketplace, and Public
Radio International, which co-produces The Takeaway."

—*Slate* staff writer Leon Neyfakh in a 2016 article,
"The Fight for the Future of NPR."

D on't forget the Public Radio Exchange, or PRX, which
has a number of award-winning shows like *The Moth
Radio Hour*. But that it was left out says something about
public radio hierarchy. There are other big names;
Wisconsin Public Radio, WNYC, WGBH, KERA and Texas
Public Radio, among others. Stations that can produce and
distribute their content are in a different category than those
stations that serve smaller communities or can't produce
syndicated shows.

Keeping track of which programs are produced by which
stations or affiliates is a recurring problem not only for listeners
but broadcasting peers. On July 14, 2017, Jackie Watts reported for
CNN Money, on the impending strike by 400 NPR employees over
stalled negotiations for a new contract. The story's 2:50 p.m.
version mentioned affected shows that were identified as NPR's,
including *Serial*, *This American Life*, and *Radiolab*. The 6:53 p.m.
update said, "An earlier version of this article incorrectly iden-

tified the producer behind *Serial*, *This American Life* and *Radiolab*. Those programs are not made by NPR."

In 2016, *On Being* (formerly *First Person*, then *Speaking of Faith*) was moved from American Public Media to PRX. Another non-NPR show, the Peabody award winner moved mostly because delivering it via Internet was cheaper for its producer than bouncing it through the Public Radio Satellite System. *This American Life* apparently left APM for similar reasons two years earlier. *Radiolab*, a production of WNYC in New York has also never been an NPR show. And *Serial*, the lovechild of *This American Life* and WBEZ, is also not NPR's. But hey, none of this affects what is public radio's big happy family, right? Not exactly.

"While, of course, I don't have any inside knowledge of the situation," says poster aaronread on the *Radiodiscussions.com* thread from December 2008, "in my uninformed opinion I always thought the creation of APM was a naked power play and made little sense. It antagonized affiliate stations, who now had to pay even more licensing fees to a third content clearinghouse (APM, PRI and NPR) and it fragmented things badly; neither PRI nor APM had any really rock-solid shows that could be viewed by affiliates as 'they're not going anywhere.'" Well, maybe APM had *Marketplace*, but that's no *Morning Edition*, *All Things Considered*, *Fresh Air* or *Car Talk*."

He goes on to describe what looks like a lot of midnight style raids amongst providers in an effort to hold onto audiences or grab new ones.

"This led to all three outlets scrambling to sign new programs (for example, PRI "stole" *Living on Earth* away from NPR, but NPR "stole" *Mountain Stage*, too ... and APM 'stole' *Marketplace*, *American Routes* and *A Prairie Home Companion* from PRI) and also to create new shows (APM's *The Story*, PRI's The *Takeaway*, etc." Aaronread concludes, "These are not bad things *per se*, but I think the feeding frenzy was way too much to be sustained in anything but a boom time, and now we're seeing the painful fallout from that."

Aaronread was referring to the "painful fallout" of budget cuts that public radio was again cycling through while he typed in 2008. A well-trodden path, financial crises came in 1983 and 1994 and would come again in 2014 and possibly, in the wake of the 2017 inauguration of President Donald Trump. For the four general personalities of public radio—NPR news, APM culture, PRI international and PRX innovation & grassroots—threats of painful fallout are not new or necessarily threatening. The greatest dangers seems to be from within their mosh pit rather than from outside it. ☎

NPR

"In reality, NPR is much more corporate than many of its progressive admirers believe, and it is much less liberal than many of its conservative critics assume."

—Michael Arria, *"In These Times"* for *Salon*

In April 2017, the website tracker SimilarWeb said NPR.org was visited by about 84 million people, making it the 180th most visited website in the U.S. With Google being the second most visited site in 2013, and indexing 30 trillion web pages a month, 180 is pretty high. Yahoo was number one. That helps explain why public radio and "NPR" tend to be conflated even though they're not the same. But NPR, being the biggest dog, has less reason than any of its competitors to separate the two since this confusion serves the organization well during pledge drive time.

NPR's history is as much lore as common knowledge. It began
as a collection of mostly hippies from the counter-culture with
few real reporters among them. It broke ground by pushing the
technology of the day as far as it could possibly go; namely, by
sending a new and experimental, 90-minute national program over
telephone lines to a few dozen stations across the country. Robert
Conley, its first host broadcasting its first report—live coverage
of a May 1971 march on Washington—made history. It was just
what National Public Radio's first head of programming, William
Siemering, hoped for public radio. His idealized manifesto, *Public
Radio Purposes*, spelled out roles and responsibilities for the new,
non-commercial alternative in contrast to what he detested: commercial radio.

He wanted to tell stories that lifted the human spirit and "serve
the individual," "encourage a sense of active constructive participation, rather than apathetic helplessness," and "not regard its
audience as a market." But by the early 80s, Siemering was gone.
And though staff was sad to see him go, the increasingly weighty
problems and complicated political landscape in which the network
found itself made his lofty rhetoric seem quaint. It should also be
noted however, that with the advent of big data and website APIs,
especially as they are used in the service of pledge drives, Siemering's concerns about not regarding the audience as a market were
prescient. "The more choices we are giving to the user, the more
information we're capturing about them, the more targeted and effective we can be in asking for membership," said Thomas Hjelm,
WNYC's VP of business development and chief digital officer for
New York Public Radio in a 2013 interview. "There's a delicate
balance there, and one of the more powerful things about public
media is the unique compact and trust we have with our audience.
I don't want to ever cross that line where we become creepy and
invasive." But despite how far some may accuse it of practically

straying from Siemering's goals, public radio would argue it has strained to stay true to its spirit.

Around the time Siemering left, CEO Frank Mankiewicz was building his news operation and while his organization headed into debt. As financial problems loomed, he was approached by the head of upstart Minnesota Public Radio, William Kling, to bring a new MPR program into the NPR fold. The odd little weekend show, called "*A Prairie Home Companion*" was surprisingly popular. Mankiewicz said he was concerned that *PHC's* costs would take away from his news operation. But the bluntness with which he rejected Kling's offer is as significant as the fact that he rejected the offer at all. It showed his well known dislike for Kling and what MPR represented: a threat to NPR's dominance to shape the public radio universe. In retrospect, had Mankiewicz accepted Kling's offer, it's possible some of the financial issues the network faced later wouldn't have been as severe.

By 1981, overspending, a poor and untested accounting system and hopeful but unrealistic schemes to raise cash pushed NPR into a meltdown. It took less than six months to bring the network to the brink of death. Intense negotiations saved NPR at the very last moment with a $9 million grant from CPB. But among the conditions were that CPB hold NPR's Public Radio Satellite System, as collateral to insure the money would be repaid. This led to the first "Drive to Survive," which asked listeners directly, via affiliates, to give NPRHQ money so it wouldn't go away. The next year, another, less popular, network drive took place. Mankiewicz promised to leave NPR as soon as it was in the black. And in 1983, he did. Staff lionized him for his dedication to them and the news they produced. The rest of the industry was not as kind, practically blacklisting him for what it saw as his heavy-handed tactics, especially with other stations and the CPB.

PLEDGE: The Public Radio Fund Drive

Though the emergency drives of 1982 and 1983 helped NPR clear the massive debt, to this day, network drives are taboo. Some say the programs NPR produces are so good, they could coax listeners to give to the network directly. That's called "bypass." When it happens, listeners don't hear the underwriting embedded in local shows that local stations depend on because they're listening to network shows instead. Until the 1990s, that wasn't much of a concern because there was no easy way for people to hear NPR programs without their local station piping it into their clock radios and dashboards. But with the advent of the Internet, digital streaming, apps and now podcasts, many affiliates live in a state of fear as they try to strengthen listener loyalty to the local station. In 2009, the idea of a national pledge drive was again floated by some at NPR, but then-CEO Vivian Schiller, as reported in *Current*, downplayed the idea. "They're not our listeners," she told the trade publication, implying that local audiences belong to local stations. Former *Weekend America* host John Moe promised that if the network decided on a national drive, affiliates would storm the gates of NPRHQ, torches blazing. The subject of programming and who pays for it is at the heart of pledge drives.

The technology of the day, which limited program movement to only one direction along those telephone lines, gave affiliates the uncomfortable feeling that they were under the network's thumb. Until 1979, it insured that NPR but none of its 200 or so affiliates could inject programming into the network. But that year, the Public Radio Satellite System came online, and with it, the ability of affiliates to upload their own shows. Since then, the technology improved further, first with the Satellite Operations Support System in 1994 and later with Content Depot in 2007. Located at NPR's Network Operations Center in Washington D.C., NPR Satellite Services arrange temporary and full time accounts for entities that want access to the public radio satellite. The system manages programming feeds from NPR affiliates, as well as those from

34

APM, PRI and PRX. All programs from all providers can now be on the satellite feed to affiliates. Stations can choose their most popular shows directly from their sources. Satellite distribution is supported by grants from CPB and all networks share it through cooperative agreement.

Douglas Bennett, NPR's next CEO after Frank Mankiewicz, was aware of affiliate frustration with the costs of shows and problems with distribution. He proposed funding for "unbundled" shows—programs sold individually rather than as part of a costlier package—go directly to stations. Until then, CPB funded NPR, who in turn funded its network of stations. But station complaints along with the introduction of PRSS made Bennett press for change. CPB started funding stations directly in 1987. That gave them the freedom to buy whichever shows they wanted from whichever providers they chose. Bennett also responded to station manager complaints that they were losing weekend audiences. The network debuted *All Things Considered* Saturday and Sunday in 1977, *Weekend Edition Saturday* (WeSat) in 1985 and *Weekend Edition Sunday* (WeSun) in 1987.

NPR also worked to match the overseas bureaus of its media competitors by beefing up its foreign desks. It dispatched reporters around the world, putting it on par with network television's foreign correspondents. But even as NPR was growing up, some felt it was losing something. William Drummond, a creator of *Morning Edition*, left the network on the eve of its seemingly imminent shutdown and never looked back. "The network recovered," he said, "but it did so at a tremendous cost." Drummond said NPR was no longer the little network that could. "It began to take itself too seriously," Drummond said. "Middle management proliferated. NPR cut off its ponytail." Drummond called the network unrecognizable. He called it, "Just one more media company, dispensing the conventional wisdom." He said, "In its new headquarters, it resembles an insurance company."

When the network launched *Morning Edition* in 1979, it chose polished voices from commercial radio. But complaints quickly rolled in that they didn't quite capture what "public" radio was about. NPR dropped them and looked inward. One of the two voices that that eventually became *All Things Considered* belonged to Kentuckian Bob Edwards. Edwards joined NPR in 1974, and began co-hosting the show with Susan Stamberg. That year, he was pulled away for a 30-day "trial" as host for NPR's new morning show, *Morning Edition*. He started out with Barbara Hocter, another trial host, but Hocter left in March 1980, leaving Edwards to host the program for the next 25 years. Edwards is most re-membered for chats with baseball's Red Barber, his connection to his listeners, and his legendary 2004 split from NPR. That split, opposed by NPR's Cokie Roberts and CBS's Charles Osgood, ulti-mately generated over 50,000 angry letters and emails.

NPR replaced Edwards with hosts Steve Inskeep and Renee Montaigne to freshen up the *Morning Edition* brand and attract younger listeners. Edwards himself kept a low profile, speaking rarely about the firing. He went on to win many awards and host two shows on Sirius XM Satellite Radio for another eleven years, until 2015. After his 2004 firing, the backlash against NPR was so severe that in later years, it adopted a philosophy that de-empha-sized the individual host or reporter. The thinking seemed to be (and research supported) that the story told should hold universal attributes no matter who is telling it. That way, a generic voice that captures the NPR brand of storytelling with the "NPR sound" accomplishes the mission while avoiding the problem of cult followings. Commenter "Greg" said at *Josh Gerstein*'s blog in 2008, "The host is secondary to the formula, and while I'm sure a bad host could drive people away, it doesn't take a superb talent to mind the store there. People don't tune in to *ME* for the talent. They tune in for the formula." That was part of the thinking behind WAMU's internal process for replacing *The Diane Rehm Show* with *1A* in 2016. Executive producer Rupert Allman said in selecting host Joshua Johnson, WAMU looked for the same attributes that made Diane Rehm such a great host. It was more evidence that public radio was going for a flavor rather than a taste.

In the 90s, some conservative legislators, like Georgia Congressman Newt Gingrich, were no friends of NPR. Gingrich directly attacked federal funding for public broadcasting with his *Contract with America*. It promised, among other things, to reduce unnecessary spending for what he called the "elitist enterprise" of NPR. Much is made of his backing down from that fight. Scott Sherman, writing for *The Nation* in 2005 quoted Gingrich in 2003 comments about his vitriol towards NPR, saying, "Either it is a lot less on the left or I have mellowed." But in 1994, the network was his mortal enemy and his bill was engineered to cut support. Although Gingrich was not fully successful in defunding NPR, funding levels for CPB were frozen in 1995 and a House proposed $141 million cut for 1996/1997 became a cut of $55 million. NPR and its affiliates raised enough grassroots attention to defang much of the measure, but cutbacks in state funding to stations themselves reduced money system wide by about $150 million. With less money, stations bought fewer NPR produced shows. That may have contributed to legendary mid-decade blood-lettings for the network. Twenty jobs were cut, as were several cultural programs, including *E-Town*, *Bluesstage* and the acclaimed *Afropop Worldwide*, which moved to Public Radio International.

Seven years later, on a clear New York morning in September, *9-11* changed everything at NPR. Insiders like former Supervising Editor Ellen Weiss recalled that the network realized on September 11 that it wasn't nearly as responsive as it needed to be to breaking news. "I began to recognize," said Weiss in Susan Stamberg's 2010 book, *This is NPR; The First Forty Years,* "that somehow we had to figure out how to be where we needed to be when we needed to be there ..." Senior VP of News Jay Kernis said to the assembled staff as smoke poured from the World Trade Center, "We're about to go into 24-hour coverage." Until then, Stamberg says the joke at NPR was, "Report it a day late and call it analysis."

Like Weiss, Stamberg realized NPR needed to be more responsive to breaking news. That was despite the fact that in 2001, radio wasn't the way most people got their news. Researcher Dr. Ruth Propper, an associate professor of psychology at Merrimack College in North Andover, Mass., showed that on September 11, most people in her study weren't listening to the radio during the attack. But NPR pressed on. In 2002, the network opened NPR West, a production facility in Culver City, California. Its purpose, said then NPR CEO Kevin Klose, was to "reset how we report on California and the West." But as Kernis later said, "September 11th made it apparent in a very urgent way that we need another facility that could keep going if something devastating happens in Washington." That work NPR put into covering breaking news would be tested in seven more years when reporter and host Melissa Block, while in China for the coming Summer Olympics, would be one of the few newsies on the ground during one of the worst earthquakes in human history.

In 2010, commentator Juan Williams unleashed his own temblor in American culture when he shared his fear of seeing someone in "Muslim garb" board a commercial airliner. But because people still confused NPR with other broadcasters, PBS got thousands of angry letters for "firing" Williams. The flare-up was so big that PBS Ombudsman Michael Getler pleaded, "My interest in mentioning this is simply to remind the vast majority of those who wrote to me or called is to explain that PBS is not NPR, that

Juan Williams does not work for PBS, that PBS did not fire him, and that both organizations, while part of public broadcasting in this country, are separate organizations and separate public media entities." Getler seemed to be saying, "Stop yelling at me!"

The Juan Williams "incident" also redefined what being a public radio journalist meant. Besides sharpening the charge of NPR's liberal bias, a charge the network strenuously denies, a number of high-profile dismissals and reprimands have occurred throughout public radio since the introduction of new ethics standards after his firing. Some of them forbid reporters from participating in political rallies. Others don't let them have personal opinions on their own social media accounts. Public radio managers call this ensuring objectivity. Others, NPR apostates among them, call it "Draconian." But if the incident showed the network could respond a little too quickly to bad optics, the firing of NPR's senior Vice President for fundraising, Ron Schiller and later President Vivian Schiller showed that no one was untouchable. Both were a little too close to the dirty bomb that Brietbart disciple James O'Keefe detonated in revenge for William's firing. O'Keefe set up a meeting between fake donors and the former Schiller to discuss a supposedly large contribution to the network. During the meeting, Schiller said some disputed but unfortunate things that O'Keefe later released in a covert video to the mainstream media. The network continues to struggle to uphold its own standards. In late 2017, NPR dismissed Senior News VP Michael Oreskes over allegations of sexual improprieties.

In 2014, as in the mid-90s, station managers complained that in the hours between *Morning Edition* and *All Things Considered*, listeners deserted in droves. The network again thought a news magazine was the answer and it chose a show produced by affiliate WBUR called *Here and Now*. But to put it on, longtime network staple *Talk of the Nation* and its host, Neal Conan, had to go.

The changes weren't only about programming, however. Months earlier, *The Washington Post* reported that the network was trying to cut its 840 employees by 10% to reduce costs. At the same time, it opened a $201 million headquarters building around the corner from its longtime home on M street. NPR denied there was a connection between financial problems and the format changes. For some, it was reminiscent of a similar purge in 2008, when 64 staff were cut and two shows, *News and Notes* and *The Bryant Park Project* ended.

One goodbye that really stung in the 2014 cuts was Michelle Martin's *Tell Me More*. To people of color, the loss of the show revived ongoing suspicions of the network's commitment to diversity. Martin's was the only show in NPR's lineup that served the black audience. Its cancellation prompted the *The Guardian* to call NPR's predicament "A low level identity crisis." Martin told NPR media critic David Folkenflik, "To be honest with you, I think we've been casualties of executive churn. Every CEO who has been at this network since I've been here — and how many are there now? Six? Seven? – all of them have supported this program, but none of them have stayed around long enough to institution-alize that support." The network subsequently installed Martin as host of *All Things Considered* Saturday and Sunday, no doubt in an effort to bring her professionalism, mass-appeal and personal sensibilities to NPR's core demographics.

NPR has weathered ethics scandals, staff defections and bud-get crunches like the old soldier it has become. But the network's biggest challenges may lie ahead. The first is the ability of lis-teners with smartphones to cherry pick programs they want and avoid those they don't. For the network, that's a problem but for the affiliates, it's a potential disaster. Plus, savvy listerers com-plain that instead of "digitizing," many stations are "digifying," or simply putting existing content online rather than creating digital content specifically for the digital space. Millennials; the coveted demographic that lives in that space, know the difference. They want original, captivating and long-form podcasts. But for many smaller stations, the money to create them is just not there. Meanwhile, shuffles of top people within NPR by CEO Jarl Mohn show his efforts to bring more attention to content rather than platforms (Mohn himself announced in November 2018 that he would step down in June 2019. But the moves sharpen accusations that the network isn't serious enough about tectonic digital shifts. *The New York Times* reported in 2014 that Chief Content Officer Kinsey Wilson, the brains behind much of NPR's digital footprint, was pushed out by Mohn. And in more change to NPR's leadership, former WXPN GM Roger LeMay was chosen as NPR's newest Chair in Nov 2015. LeMay is notable because he also cofounded and was elected chairman of VuHaus, a video distribution platform. With Mohn's pending departure, it will be interesting to see which direction the network takes in the digital space.

Application or "app" wars are also defining the next set of fights. Even as listeners with apps can go looking for content they might like better than what their local stations give them, stations are also pushing their own "native apps" and encouraging listeners to connect to their content through them. But networks have created apps of their own. Listeners can use the station's app to download and listen to local content. But this will also take them to content on other networks; not the local station's preference. Or, they can download killer apps from the Public Radio Exchange's Radiotopia, or NPR One, a vehicle the network released but has avoided talking about very much since its launch. On the NPR One web page, the network says, "NPR One is the audio app that connects you to a stream of public radio news, stories and podcasts curated for you from the ends of the earth to the tiniest corners of your city." For local stations in those tiny corners, that last part is a looming problem. ☎

MPR/APR

"APM is the program production and distribution division of Min-nesota Public Radio. Minnesota Public Radio is part of a group of organizations whose nonprofit parent support organization is American Public Media Group."

—Service Agreement, American Public Media, v. 2007

Minnesota Public Radio was founded in the late 60s. According to the website of its descendant, American Public Media, MPR "began as a single classical music radio station ... on the modest campus of St. John's University in Collegeville, Minn. Since then, Minnesota Public Radio has grown into a 45-station network serving virtually all of Minnesota and parts of surrounding states ..." Those surrounding states include not only its home state, but also adjacent South Dakota, Iowa, Idaho and Southern California. It is vast.

But in 1964, what would become MPR was just a gleam in the eye of Father Coleman Barry, who was about to be appointed President of St. John's college. He'd recently met and was im-pressed by a soon-to-be graduate, Bill Kling. Kling was trying to decide between careers in business and communications. Barry told Kling that if he chose the latter, a job running a radio station would be waiting. Kling did and Barry applied for and got a license for KSJR FM. In 1966, the 24-year-old Kling went to work, first convincing the monastic order of the need for the station, and then, designing and overseeing its construction. In March 1967, KSJR received its license to broadcast. Its weak signal couldn't even reach the 66 miles to the Minneapolis/St. Paul area. And without that audience, it was doomed to underperform. Even though the station managed to grow its power up to 150 thousand watts over the next three years, it was barely enough to reach Minneapolis. St. Paul couldn't hear it at all.

After KSJR signed on, Kling and the college struggled with low funding, a tiny audience and technical problems ranging from errant static electricity to gophers chewing through transmission lines. But when KSJR received a $5,000 check from a lover of the Metropolitan Opera, grateful that she could now hear it in her living room, Kling and Barry realize the potential of fundraising. In 1968, Kling convinced the college to buy another tiny station closer to their Twin Cities audience. Kling used KSJN to start a radio reading service, which supplemented operating expenses, but didn't stop the two station network from bleeding cash. Kling tells "St. John's at 150," a commemorative issue of the college newspaper, "While innovations like that helped, they didn't resolve the financial problem. In 1969 Father Colman, Father Gordon Tavis, Abbot Baldwin and I decided to preserve the concept by giving the assets to a broader-based community corporation, first named Saint John's University Broadcasting, Inc., then Minnesota Educational Radio, and finally Minnesota Public Radio." MPR's main offices eventually moved from the college to St. Paul. That same year, Kling took a temporary job at CPB. There, he met Hartford Gunn, who'd crafted Boston-based WGBH into a regional force with the help of political contacts and corporate sponsorship. That, along with a good look at the top-down nature of CPB returned Kling to Collegeville two years later with an even clearer picture of what he didn't want Minnesota Public Radio to become.

During that time, Kling noticed a young DJ working at KSJN named Garrison Keillor. Keillor hosted an odd little program on MPR called *The Morning Show*. It was an eclectic mix of jazz, pop and marches by John Phillip Sousa. He populated it with odd characters that matched his own eccentric personality. Over time, Keillor and his show had developed a reputation. Kling and Keillor

43

refined *The Morning Show*, which Keillor later renamed after a roadside cemetery he'd passed near Fargo, North Dakota. Growing numbers of devoted listeners were treated to the weekday version, *A Prairie Home Morning Show*. But on the weekends, they got *A Prairie Home Companion*. The first national airing of *PHC* was in 1979, when Keillor debuted its fictitious sponsor, "Powdermilk Biscuits" and the strong men, beautiful women and above-average children of the Utopian "Lake Wobegon." The show became a hit. A big one.

Meanwhile, high-ups at NPR were looking in disbelief at the growing strength of MPR and the growing audience of *PHC*. In *The Trials and Triumphs of NPR*, author Michael P. McCauley describes as "apoplectic" Mankiewicz's reaction to the rise of both. NPR had focused on what it believed were William Siemering's key points: news and information told through stories, but professionally, in a way that conveys credibility and authority. Its managers and board thought its audience wanted serious news talk, not what it considered Kling and Keillor's brand of low-brow humor.

This attitude defined the distinction in philosophy between NPR and MPR, and the atmosphere that led, arguably, to one of the two biggest marketing blunders by NPR in its history.

In 1980, Kling felt *PHC* was ready for syndication. He approached Mankiewicz, offering *PHC* and a slice of the revenue in return for it becoming part of the network's lineup. But Mankiewicz turned down Kling's offer. His argument was if NPR had to pay for *PHC's* production and distribution, (which it would do from its limited federal funds), the show would, to paraphrase Mankiewicz, be starving his network and staff of money they'd need for serious reporting. Kling walked away. But he realized that just because NPR didn't want his show didn't mean other stations wouldn't. That led him to form American Public Radio in 1981, an entity that could apply for the same federal money as NPR and use it to distribute its own shows.

Kling's growing network was very different from NPR. It would be overseen by an independent board of directors while NPR was managed by a CEO, who was in turn responsible to a board of member station managers. This spotlighted the difference between the top-down NPR and the more democratic MPR. Also, unlike NPR, Kling's network would not have a central location where shows were produced and distributed, at least not early on. NPR's shows were fed to affiliates via telephone lines, which gave it near total control of what they broadcast and when. And affiliates complained that the network didn't take nearly as many of their stories for national distribution as it promised. NPR's concentration of production and distribution in Washington meant that NPR was practically supporting the network alone, and that cost a lot of money. Mankiewicz's reasoning that *PHC* was too expensive was true considering how much it already cost to run NPR. But it's also true that he simply didn't like *A Prairie Home Companion* … or Kling.

Another big change in the relationship between MPR and NPR came with the 1984 launch of the Public Radio Satellite System. Kling got CPB to re-envision how the system would allow for the up and downlinking of all public radio programs, not just NPR's, as well as the number of programs the satellite could carry at one time. The changes, including Kling insuring MPR would get its own satellite access, let programs be fed from any of 16 uplinks, live, to any one of 24 channels on the new system. For example, if stations didn't like anything on the NPR channels, they could pick shows from MPR's side of the satellite. MPR had flipped the script by encouraging programming to flow from its affiliates rather than from a headquarters. It reduced MPR's operating costs at a time NPR was struggling with a debt crisis and, some argued, encouraged the kind of creativity and national dialog William Siemering trumpeted in his *Public Radio Purposes*.

CPB also changed how it funded public radio. Until the mid-80s, NPR received the total Congressional appropriation for public radio, which it then used to create the shows it sent to its affiliates. In 1985, CPB started funding stations directly. Although this removed NPR as a middleman, stations had new flexibility in how they spent their program money. Subsequently, NPR and APR decided to "unbundle" their programs. Until the CPB decision, stations were forced to buy unpopular shows to get the ones their audience wanted. Some affiliates hated the package policy because they said it created holes in their programming schedule that pushed listeners away. But for many smaller stations with limited staff or money to produce local shows to fill the gaps, package deals kept the dead air away. With bundling gone and funding opened up, stations enjoyed more power while the relationship between NPR and MPR grew more tense.

In his most direct challenge to NPR's dominance, Kling added news to APR's lineup in the mid-80s. First was news from the BBC. Later, Kling added news from the CBC, the Associated Press, the Pacifica network and finally, the now-defunct Monitor Radio, then a service of the *Christian Science Monitor*. Since MPR wasn't paying a staff to produce these programs, it could deliver excellent journalism while banking the cost savings, something NPR could not do. But Kling wasn't finished. In the late 80s, MPR launched its most ambitious news project, a financial program called *Sound Money*. The show was designed to tell listeners about savings, retirement, markets, commodities and everything else in the world of finance in a way that had never been attempted in radio. Host Bob Potter said he was, "a long time fan of Louis Rukeyser's *Wall Street Week* on public television." Why, wondered Potter, was there no public radio equivalent?

Co-producers James Russell and J.J. Yore brought *Sound Money* to life in 1989. David Brancaccio began contributing to the show that same year, and became senior editor and host of the revamped *Marketplace* in 1993. By the time Potter left MPR in 2000, *Sound Money* was airing on about 150 public radio stations. And, despite that its parent was based in Minnesota, that revamp also included new broadcasts from Pasadena, where *Marketplace* was produced and aired with the help of a grant to the University of Southern California's KUSC, and underwriting support from General Electric, which began in 1991. Listeners to the show can still hear echoes of GE's influence. The original *Marketplace* theme, composed by B.J. Leiderman, was based on a jingle that composers Thomas McFaul and David Lucas created for the company in 1979. Within Liederman's theme was a six-note stinger that corresponded to "We bring good things to life," the slogan of the appliances company from its copyright date in 1980 to 2003. The stinger disappeared in the around 2005, but the rest of the theme remains.

Kling made three shrewd but accurate assumptions about *Sound Money.* First, people who were investing their money would be interested in hearing about how other people made theirs. Secondly, where other than California could one get the best, firsthand information on the biggest deals affecting the fastest, wealthiest lifestyles? Lastly, financial service firms had lots of services to sell, and that meant lots of underwriting opportunities. In 2018, *Marketplace* is heard by 14 million listeners, each with an average household income of $101,000.

Marketplace quickly developed the reputation as a program with "attitude." Timely, smart and sassy, listeners often have to run to keep up. Brancaccio left *Marketplace* in 2003 to work with journalist Bill Moyers and host Moyer's PBS program, Now. Senior editor David Brown became the show's new host, bringing quick wit and a Texas twang to the numbers. In 2005, Kai Ryssdal moved into the big chair and Brancaccio returned to *Marketplace* in 2011 as host and senior editor of its morning catcher-upper, The *Marketplace Morning Report*. The show has seen its share of ups and downs. Between 2012 and 2013, John Dimsdale, Bob Moon and J.J. Yore were let go to cut costs. In 2014, the weekend *Marketplace Money* was replaced with *Marketplace Weekend*. And the show has been at the center of uncomfortable questions of journalistic independence after it fired a transgender reporter for expressing a personal view on a personal social media account.

APR changed its name to Public Radio International in 1994 and split off from American Public Media. Meanwhile, American Public Media became the parent of Southern California Public Radio, which now operates *Marketplace* and is heard on nearly 800 stations including flagship KPCC. The Pasadena station had been student run since its 1957 launch. Around 1995, APM entered into a 20-year subsidiary agreement with KPCC to air APM programs. Kling finally got his NPR-like headquarters when American Public Media became the production and distribution arm for Southern California Public Radio and Minnesota Public Radio. In 1998, all three entities came under the managerial control of the American Public Media Group, formerly known as the Minnesota Communications Group (MCG).

MCG owed much of its financial stability to businesses Kling started in the 1980s to support MPR. He created the Greenspring Company, whose subsidiaries included Rivertown Trading, which published a host of catalogs including two public radio fans know well: *Wireless* and *Signal*. According to Michael McCauley, Rivertown had started to sell *A Prairie Home Companion* posters. And in *Listener Supported,* Jack W. Mitchell explains the catalogs sold public radio swag to three different demographics and were so successful that their UBI, or what the IRS calls "unrelated business income" rivaled what the non-profit MPR itself generated. That was a no-no. In 1998, Rivertown Trading was sold for $120 million. Three-fourths of the proceeds went straight into the MPR endowment. What was left went to Kling and top executives at MPR. But Kling did set aside $10 million, part of which he used to set up the eventual home for *Marketplace*.

The network has also resorted to some belt tightening of its own. In 2015, American Public Media dropped a classical music network it picked up in 2011 and cut 13% of its staff. And in 2017, *Marketplace* created new upper-level management positions with the intention of transforming the radio show into something more cross-platform friendly. Despite these and other changes, the 45-station network MPR created with its American Public Media parent oversees a 24-hour news service called *The Public Insight Network* and a Triple-A (Adult Album Alternative) format music service called *The Current*. In an interview with the author in 2016, Bill Kling reflected on Frank Mankiewicz's decision to turn down *PHC*. "In the end it created competition. Competition is good and it made us all better at what we did and making sure that we were in the lead and that was a plus I think for the stations. It meant NPR got better. They had to. They couldn't just fund anything. They had to fund something that was going to win."

In that spirit, NPR and Minnesota Public Radio collaborated in 2004 to bring the *Marketplace Morning Report* to NPR's audience during the last ten minutes of each hour of *Morning Edition*. An attempt by stations to do something similar in 1992 led to NPR trying to ban what it saw as a brand diminishing "program within a program." After affiliates complained, NPR dropped the ban. Twelve years later, the collaboration was revived in earnest.

Critics complained that Kling was too much of an entrepreneur for public radio. William Siemering wanted public radio to aspire to a higher purpose. That, he reasoned, might require principles to sometimes supersede business forces. But Kling had no such aversions to making money. He created programs listeners told him they wanted rather than forcing upon them programs that were "good for them." Although Kling loves public radio, he is a follower of what's been described as "social purpose capitalism" in that he is able to make the kind of business decisions about public radio that public radio itself has been slow to emulate. By combining for-profit thinking with a non-profit mission, Kling put MPR on steady financial ground in an early, public radio example of "public-private partnerships." It is an attitude some in public radio have been slow to get behind.

That's partly because public radio, in the larger category of non-profit organizations, is often painted with a "poverty mentality" brush. In other words: a non-profit that truly serves the public should be able to operate on a shoestring and as such, project an image of sincerity through austerity. Push back to that attitude came from Amie Miller, Director of Institutional Giving for Twin Cities Public Television. In 2015, she argued that the connection between low overhead and high organizational effectiveness was a myth. Aside from the differing definitions of "overhead," funders want to hear about results rather than operational costs. But ongoing scandals, especially those involving Red Cross allocations of donations after 9-11 and most recently in Haiti, changed the public's trust level. The resulting moves within the charitable industry have tried to address those skeptical givers who feel some salaries are too big and some missions too divergent from what should be core, charitable services.

"You don't [become financially viable] with hundred dollar contributions from satellite or streamed versions of NPR," Kling said in 2017 "You do it by working with stations and cities where there are major donors who were giving seven, eight and nine figure gifts to entities in their community or sometimes national entities that have no greater rationale and sometimes considerably less impact than National Public Radio does. It's just that NPR never set its sights. NPR and the public radio stations never set their sights high enough. Harvard has an endowment of billions. Why is that? Why, except for the Joan Kroc gift (a massive $200+ million donation in 2003) is NPR's endowment in minor millions?"

An anonymous $10 million donor in November 2013 seems to make Kling's point, though it did not stop the network from selling three classical music stations in Florida or prevent the layoff of nearly two-dozen MPR staffers that same year. The fact that Kling leaned in a more entrepreneurial direction for building and guiding Minnesota Public Radio, American Public Radio, and American Public Media, has not disadvantaged those networks. But his relationship with his supporters seems rooted in his understanding of their desire for both command decision-making skills and results.

At the time of his 2006 interview for the commemorative issue of the St. Johns college newspaper, a 64-year-old Kling looked back and marveled at the decisions that led to the public radio leviathan of which Minnesotans seem so proud; a 24-year-old in charge of a new radio station, a Catholic administrator trusting him enough to let him blaze new media trails and a college that essentially put its future in his hands. Could such things happen today? ☎

APM/PRI

"Kling was a founder of PRI [Public Radio International] and American Public Radio [APR] in 1983 as an alternative distributor to NPR. But former executives of the companies say the estrangement [between APR and PRI] began in the early '90s, when PRI began producing programs, sparking fears of competition at MPR [Minnesota Public Radio]."

—Mike Janssen, Digital Editor of *Current* in 2004

NPR was first infuriated, then terrified, then resigned to a public radio universe that it had to share with Minnesota Public Radio (MPR) in the early-to-mid-80s. So it is ironic that the same fears National Public Radio had of MPR, American Public Radio (formed by Kling at MPR) had of Public Radio International (created with Kling's help) a decade later.

Kling and four stations—KQED in San Francisco, KUSC in Los Angeles, WGUC in Cincinnati and WNYC in New York—were miffed that Frank Mankiewicz at NPR had turned down Kling's offer to buy *A Prairie Home Companion*. In 1983, they created American Public Radio to distribute their own programming in cooperation with Minnesota Public Radio. Homespun shows, like *PHC* and others were produced by some stations within the MPR network and distributed to other stations that were willing to pay for them. Kling and his group estimated that carriage fees of more than a quarter-million dollars a year [fees stations pay to broadcast proprietary shows] were possible once APR started distributing MPR (and soon to be Southern California Public Radio) programs. By 1988, Steve Salyer had been named president of APR, and he started hiring from his new location, "a strip mall in Long Beach next to a Merry Maids." The names that populated the upstart entity - Jim Russell and Bob Ferrente among them, may sound familiar to long-time public radio listeners.

APR's name changed to PRI in 1994. Between 1988 and 2005, APR/PRI developed a number of groundbreaking programs and initiatives in addition to *Marketplace*. *Studio 360*, an arts and culture program co-produced by PRI and WNYC, won several awards, including a Peabody in 2004 and a Third Coast International Audio Festival Award in 2007. Public Radio Interactive, founded in 1999, was a forward-looking, web-support company that PRI created and NPR bought in 2008. It was an impressive coup for PRI. But these and other muscle flexes by the Pasadena crew set up a tense relationship between Bill Kling, essentially PRI's founder, and Salyer, PRI's president.

Things got worse when in the same year as the name change, PRI began producing and distributing an international news show called *The World*. It cut into the news programming MPR was already offering. PRI's decision to co-produce it with the BBC and WGBH rather than Kling's Minnesota Public Radio, added insult to injury. The acrimony between Kling and Salyer reached a peak in 2000 when PRI sued to stop MPR from taking *Marketplace*. *Marketplace* was an APR property at the time its name changed to PRI. Six years later, Kling wanted to bring it back into the MPR fold. Salyer's PRI won the battle but lost the war by only managing to keep the program for another year before losing it to Kling in 2007.

Minnesota Public Radio had contracts with PRI to air many MPR programs, including *A Prairie Home Companion*. When those contracts expired in 2004, MPR took the shows back so it could air them itself. Their claw back amounted to up to 40% of PRI's listening audience. Some accused MPR of trying to hurt PRI. It was an echo of the same way MPR had been accused, twenty years earlier, of trying to hurt NPR by adding news programs to its lineup. PRI did manage to retain some headliners, including *This American Life*, *The World*, *Living on Earth*, *Afropop Worldwide*, and *The Takeaway*. In 2005, PRI entered into an agreement with XM Satellite Radio to bring Bob Edwards, recently departed from NPR, to XM and PRI audiences. MPR, meanwhile, called the change a win for its affiliates who would only see a slight rise in carriage fees. Sayler left PRI in 2004. In 2012, it became a subsidiary of WGBH.

In 2003, public radio luminary Ira Glass called PRI, "Simply the best distributor of public radio programs in the country." He continued, " It's more in touch with stations' individual needs than anyone, and better set up in every way to help a producer get his or her show out to the public." Glass, it should be noted, was an NPR alum. In 1996, he pitched his own show, *This American Life*, to the network. But in possibly its second biggest marketing blunder, NPR turned him down. So it was with, as Kara Buckley of the *New York Times* called it, "karmic symmetry" that NPR was one of the biggest bidders for the show when Glass left PRI in 2014 to market it independently.

But the love goes both ways. A year earlier, Jesse Thorn, of *The Sound of Young America* and *Bullseye* also left longtime home PRI, but for new diggs at NPR. Thorn's programs target the younger demographic NPR is hungry for. Thorn was also hungry for simplicity. "There is only one NPR," he told *Current*'s Andrew Lapin in February 2013. "We're excited to be joining forces with the big dogs in public radio, and excited that we'll no longer have to spend like half of every conversation at every cocktail party explaining the complicated square-rectangle relationship between 'public radio' and 'NPR.'"

PRI can't help its alphabet soup lineage. And changes in ownership or distribution can make public radio programming feel like a carnival shell game. For one, Ira Glass is now the sole owner of *This American Life*, which is no longer part of the PRI lineup. Jonathan Goldstein's *Wiretap* along with *Whad'Ya Know* (a younger version of *Wait Wait Don't Tell Me* have disappeared from the airwaves altogether. But PRI continues to thrive and grow a distinctive reputation for being one of the fastest innovators of programming and platforms for public radio.

As of 2018, the network was in the process of conducting 23 crowdfunding campaigns on its Kickstarter page. Its offerings include thoughtful podcasts, weird devices, live performance venues and tools for journalists. At least three former NPR employees who left that network feeling creatively restricted have Kickstarter projects for PRI. In 2002, then CEO Salyer told the *Twin Cities Business Monthly*, "We don't own studios and we typically don't have producers on staff." But according to the article, being able to spot a winner, nurture it and give it the marketing support it needs is where PRI shines. In the same article, MPR's Kling concurred. "APR [PRI] would put all of its time and energy into finding new ideas — talking to stations, international producers, to independent producers — and bringing those ideas from elsewhere to fruition."

And PRI's vision remains undimmed. While NPR seeks to bring a slice of "all things" to an American audience, and MPR's regional powerhouses tap into the country's musical and cultural roots, PRI bills itself as "How America connects with detail around the globe." As proof, while Minnesota Public Radio gets 96% of its web traffic from the United States, SimilarWeb said that in March 2017, nearly half of PRI's web users were from countries outside the United States. In a 2013 blog post on the citizen media website Global Voices, PRI said, "At Public Radio International, we believe sharing powerful stories, encouraging exploration, and connecting people and cultures will effect positive change in the world. By building a deeper awareness and understanding of the world's peoples, conditions, issues and events, we enable others to form their own opinions, share their knowledge and creativity, and take informed actions on issues that matter to them." ☎

PRX

"Before PRX came along, local radio stations had basically two options for programming; produce their own content or purchase a relatively narrow range of programs from networks like National Public Radio or Public Radio International."

—April Burbank in a 2012 article for *Forbes.*

Critics of the pace of public radio innovation might call it an industry struggling to escape the past. The Public Radio Exchange (PRX), created in September 2003, has been called "a taste of the future." PRX was born with help from the Corporation for Public Broadcasting, the National Endowment for the Arts and the Ford Foundation. The Ford Foundation has a long history of nudging the development of public broadcasting. It, along with the Carnegie and Rockefeller foundations, supported research and funding that eventually helped President Johnson sign the *Public Broadcasting Act of 1967* and turn on the lights at CPB. Without it, public radio might not exist.

And without ancestors, there are no descendants. The Public Radio Exchange contains the DNA of every public radio incarnation that precedes it. It has the serious news and analysis voice of NPR, the grassroots, storytelling appeal of Minnesota Public Radio, the inclusive, international sensibilities of Public Radio International and the entrepreneurial spirit of American Public Media. PRX defines itself as a "marketplace" for stories. Differing from the cathedral-like formality of mainstream public broadcasters, PRX is arranged more like a street bazaar, letting stations wander amongst the selection of mainstay programs like *The Moth,*

Livewire and *WTF with Mark Maron*. That flexibility is why PRX stories are often heard on the mainstream networks.

PRX has an impressive reach. In May 2007, PRX had more than 12,000 available radio pieces and 14,500 registered users. The next year, it had 20,000 and 44,000 pieces in its catalog. By 2017, PRX had logged over 19 million downloads per month. This lets the network claim the largest on-demand catalog of public radio programs available for either broadcast, streaming or podcast. But PRX also accepts stories of thousands of individual producers. If a piece is accepted, and a station somewhere opts to air it, that producer gets a royalty payment. This lets PRX be a force multiplier for interviewers, producers and editors to get their work before huge audiences and more importantly, get paid.

PRX also gives producers feedback on their work and statistics for how much interest it's generating. And, submissions can be of any reasonable length. This lets producers end a story when it's finished instead of cutting or dragging it out to meet time. This gives stations the flexibility to fill odd sized holes in their programming schedule. It is doing what many public radio producers have wished public radio would do. Namely, step away from what some have called zombie programming, as *Car Talk* was accused of being, and let millennials reach millennials with shows and voices they recognize.

Since 2007, PRX has opened its marketplace to more producers. In February of that year, PRX and CPB announced an open search competition for new public radio voices and stories called the Public Radio Talent Quest. By May, 1,400 people had submitted entries and 14,000 had registered on the Talent Quest website. The next year, PRX received a MacArthur Award for Creative and Effective Institutions. In 2009, it launched another initiative called the Remix Radio Project (later renamed PRX Remix) which gives producers, stations and the public greater access to its content. By 2010, PRX had received a Peabody award for *The Moth Radio Hour* and its brand of intimate storytelling by everyday people.

PRX's web-based distribution system is, for some, an efficient way to get and deliver that content. In 2014, Chicago's WFMT announced a deal with PRX to leave Content Depot, operated by NPR Satellite Services. According to the Chicago Business Journal, the station moved all of its syndicated programming from satellite to PRX to "keep the fees it charges stations for programming low and affordable." And its reputation to innovate is spreading. *Fast Company*, in 2015, called PRX one of its "Ten Most Innovative Companies in Media." At every turn, PRX has worked to be both accessible to the public and supportive of radio novices and professionals alike. Accessibility includes being added to XM satellite radio in 2009 and introducing a number of apps that let users hear shows like *This American Life*. Support includes a CPB-brokered agreement with SoundExchange that covers PRX for music webcast royalties. This lets producers use music licensed by ASCAP and BMI in their programs for distribution on PRX without violating copyright laws.

Accessibility also looks like the Public Media Accelerator, a joint effort by PRX and the Knight Foundation. Begun in 2011, the project, which focuses on early stage investment, is described by former PRX CEO Jake Shapiro as "in technology startups, providing a mix of financing, mentorship and other support to help launch new companies with the potential for explosive growth." An accelerator, with its networks, planning strategies, logistical support and "demo days" are like a *Shark Tank* for public radio producers. Some ideas are funded. Others are sent back to the drawing board.

PRX has also redefined the podcast. Its biggest and most successful podcast experiment thus far is Radiotopia, described by PRX as "somewhat like a record label" in that it provides fourteen high-octane, award-winning storytelling venues that cover a wide range of tastes. Created by Roman Mars, also the brain behind his own Peabody-winning podcast, *99% Invisible*, Radiotopia began in 2013 with 900,000 downloads per month. By June 2016, that number had skyrocketed to 13 million. *99% Invisible*, a unique treatment of design and architecture, won praise from public radio royalty, Ira Glass, himself. Glass called *99% Invisible* "completely wonderful and entertaining and beautifully produced."

Radiotopia's lineup includes *Reveal*, an investigative journalism podcast. Begun in 2013 and jointly produced with the Center for Investigative Reporting, it is another PRX ground breaker both in terms of impact and medium. Such long form, hour long offerings have become an increasingly popular way for people to listen to complex stories in depth. Contrary to popular belief, our society's hectic pace does not preclude the desire of many listeners to engage with a long, well-told narrative. As a case in point, *Reveal* exposed the VA's role in over-prescribing opioid drugs to returning Iraq and Afghanistan war veterans. The piece put pressure on the agency, which forced it to reform some of its worst prescription practices. Wins like this make producers, stations and networks around the country watch not only what shows like *Reveal* do, but how they're doing it in hopes of catching some of its lightning in their own bottles. That story got PRX its second Peabody award in 2014.

In 2016, a basket of investors including the *New York Times*, the McClatchy News Agency and American Public Media were aiming to make PRX's moneymaking branch profitable in the way that many non-profits create for-profit arms to fund the non-profit mission. By 2018, a second round of investing had begun.

Meanwhile, PRX has given up the pledge drive. In 2014, it began a push for sustaining support from podcast listeners just as terrestrial radio asks for sustainers from its ranks of over-the-air listeners. And because of the deeper relationships podcasts are believed to form with its audience, PRX thinks its work may be a little easier.

In May 2016, Jake Shapiro spoke to listener's desire for hearing a good story well told whenever they wanted. In trade journal *RadioInk*, Shapiro said, "Listeners want to consume audio in a native app that allows them to listen to podcasts and other radio when they're in the car, out of sync with their data connection, or otherwise on the go." Shapiro went on to say he and his team see vast and largely untapped potential in the current base of audio consumers. "Having billions of radios, essentially, in people's pockets," he says, "is an enormous channel for distribution that is still, in many ways, up for grabs." The Radiotopia app in support of the RadioPublic project promises to drop individually curated shows right into those pockets.

PRX's financial supporters, though they are news competitors, are also forward thinkers. "News and entertainment radio is at a moment of profound transition as broadcast and podcast listening moves to simple on-demand digital listening," said *New York Times* Executive VP of Product and Technology, and editor of Innovation and Strategy, Kinsey Wilson. "The Times sees opportunity there." Ironically, Wilson is also the former chief content officer fired from NPR in 2014 over differences in vision with NPR CEO Jarl Mohn regarding innovative content. Then as now, Wilson knows it's all about the mission, the story, the audience, the technology and the money. And not necessarily in that order.

One of the biggest shakeups in public radio in years was when PRI and PRX announced in August 2018 that they would merge. In a joint press statement, the move was described as, "bringing together PRI's award-winning journalism and storytelling with PRX's cutting-edge content and audio distribution technology." It seems that many of the ongoing projects of both entities will continue, and even strengthen. The *Minneapolis Star Tribune* says the combination promises 28 million listeners making 56 million downloads per month. As the audience size (and subsequent underwriting dollars) become more tied to successful distribution of content, the move is the clearest sign yet of how public radio is being disrupted by digital technology. And how the stations will likely lean into the pledge drive even more for financial support to create and disseminate them. ☎

Community Radio & LPFM

"The public broadcasting system has grown since its inception to include a public infrastructure that community media organizations struggle to navigate alone."

—National Federation of Community Broadcasters website

In some ways, community radio is far older and more established than public radio. Just as public radio has its superstar stations and their recognizable call signs, so does community radio. KDNA St. Louis, KFPA Berkeley, WAIF Cincinnati, and of course, the stations of the early KRAB "nebula;" a collection of community radio stations headquartered in Seattle and started, in part, by radio activist Lorenzo Milam. A primer on U.S. community radio can be found in the writings of Lewis Hill, who had a vision of giving voice to the common person. Related to Bill Siemering's goal of telling the stories of outside groups, Hill's intention was even more basic. He believed that the individual had a "right to be heard." Community radio went in that direction.

Community radio is distinctive from public radio in its connection to the "grassroots." For one, it means community radio stations tend to not take big money. Because of community radio's usually leftist slant, there's an underlying suspicion that any money coming from government or big business might be a lever trying to silence its "alternative" voice. Stations do underwrite, but audiences are small compared to larger stations in the same market. So small that community radio stations may not show up in radio ratings services. And since businesses choose stations according to their reach, the sponsorships community stations get usually draw on long-standing relationships with businesses that share stations' political ideology. That makes money, or the lack of it, an ongoing issue for community radio, since, as one insider noted, fundraising for community radio "isn't always super-planned or strategic."

Former KBOO Portland's news director, Zeloszelos Marchandt, said in 2018 that funding isn't the only issue for community radio stations. They also self-censure more than they need to. So when money comes, it can highlight problems rather than solve them. "I've witnessed thousands of CPB dollars meant to go toward syndication be squandered without the project goal met," says Marchandt. "And as someone who got to talk and meet with *Free Speech Radio News* reporters, funding was not the only thing that caused them to go dark. A failure to understand what the public wanted was instrumental. It led to community journalists both in America and abroad feeling less supported, less clear in purpose and less inclined to devote time to growing community media." FSRN was one of community radio's few credible news sources. Its microphones went silent in April 2017 due to funding problems.

The National Federation for Community Broadcasters, or NFCB was begun in 1974 by KBOO Portland, KGNU Boulder and WORT in Madison, Wisconsin with the goal of helping community radio stations navigate technical, licensing, managerial and funding issues. In fact, funding is so crucial for community radio that the NFCB sponsored an effort to coordinate fundraising for about 200 stations to help them hit their fundraising targets in 2016. That's important because some community radio stations do take federal money, which means they have to hit targets set by a complicated CPB formula. If they don't, and don't raise enough cash to continue operating, they face going silent. Consequently, stations must resort to pledge drives. And when they do, they can sound and feel identical to pledge drives conducted by public radio stations.

Because community stations have smaller audiences with less money, they must have more frequent pledge drives that tend to be drawn out for longer periods. But if any fundraising station doesn't understand the limits of what its community can give, goals will always fall short no matter how hard it tries to reach them. With the same needs to upgrade equipment, expand programming and create more community engagement as public radio and commercial radio, it's no wonder that some community radio stations have turned to the feds. And although they may philosophically be "community" radio, by accepting federal money and airing CPB programming from NPR, APM, PRI or PRX, one could ask if they are also demonstrating behaviors of public radio?

Another aspect of community radio is since it exists to serve the community, everyone from the community is invited inside. Volunteers learn the technical, administrative or journalistic aspects of radio, and then go on the air. This is, in some ways, similar to the mission of cable access television. But while public access TV often remains inside the wires of a cable subscription service, community radio broadcasts a signal to the world. This makes community radio trickier because its amateur broadcasters may make mistakes that can put the station's license in jeopardy.

Finally, community radio operates with a kind of grassroots flexibility, rather than the tight organizational structure of public radio. Some stations forgo an official station manager or program director, since this is seen as being too "corporate" and taking power away from the membership. It is that membership consisting of listeners, volunteers and supporters that community radio says it wants as its ultimate overseers. Regular community meetings bring those groups *en masse* to express all manner of complaints, praise, suggestions and criticism. But this often makes the decision making processes within community radio stations agonizingly slow. Stations are reluctant to tinker with the process, however, since it holds true to the spirit of Lewis Hill.

The fact that community radio is run by people from the community has been a longtime source of pride for some and irritation for others. Even within community radio, some think it could be more financially self sustaining and more professionally self-respecting if it adopted not all, but some of commercial radio's attributes. The NFCB thought so too. So in 1994, it filed a copyright for the name of a new initiative that, it thought, would help community radio stations do just that. "The Healthy Stations Project," according to a 1997 article for *Free Pacifica*, was described as "an effort, spearheaded by CPB, which pushed community stations toward commercialization and 'professionalization,' and advocated the use of more paid staff and a reduced role for community programmers and members in decision-making." In 1997, Seattle-based journalist Jesse Walker, in a piece for the conservative Cato Institute, wrote that "the availability of CPB subsidies [such as those buried within the Healthy Stations Project] has grossly distorted the stations' goals. However well-intentioned, CPB rules pressure community radio stations to replace volunteers with paid staff and to abandon diverse, experimental local programming for more bland fare."

For lovers of Salt Lake City's KRCL, this resulted in a 2007 firestorm that led to the firing of long-time volunteer DJs and reorganized programming in what locals ruefully refer to as "The

Change." The Grassroots Coalition, born ten years earlier in response to HSP, was and is "composed of a growing number of stations who have rejected the 'Healthy Station' premise. In many cases, these community stations have had to fight long hard battles to take their stations back." Stations implementing the principles of HSP met fierce resistance. In 1998, industry trade publication *Current* highlighted an HSP conflict at KBOO. Some, like former Pacifica stringer Barbara Bernstein complained that some on the air "can barely do a decent air sound" and wondered how an outside look at station programming might help improve audience and membership. Others, like then NFCB President Lynn Chadwick supported HSP, but suggested CPB weigh KBOO's performance with its history and cut it some slack before cutting its budget.

Since community radio stations rely on volunteers to produce and host shows, stations can have large volunteer pools and tiny staffs. Those shows are plugged into a 1960's style checkerboard, or "crazy quilt" programming schedule that, unlike public radio and commercial radio, changes constantly. Public radio, by contrast, relies on consistent programming to hold audience attention throughout the day. And community radio programming itself can be radical, from space sounds recorded by NASA to Jamaican dubstep to Polish dance music, live-on-tape radio dramas and archived speeches of Angela Davis.

The programming is more evidence that community radio tries to serve diverse needs and unrepresented voices in a communitarian spirit. This makes volunteer programmers protective of their shows and the tiny slivers of time they may occupy on that checkerboard. Even if a station isn't trying to "corporatize" its operation, it may need to make program changes it thinks best serve its audience. But community stations find themselves in a bind with volunteers who, although not employees, keep them on the air with the content they essentially create for free. It gives those volunteers a sometimes out-sized voice compared to station staff and board members who are ultimately accountable to state and federal authorities. Attempts to reign in volunteers have led to some ugly family fights.

This is a good place to mention the importance of those volunteers. Many participate, especially in community radio, without the benefit of shows from which they may draw self-affirmation or on-air credibility. But community radio is notorious for attracting on the left the same type of people AM Talk Radio attracts on the right: passionate and smart, but perhaps financially struggling and feeling outside of the mainstream. These are people who believe no one is listening and, at least in community radio, who go to the left side of the dial (as Lewis Hill intended to be heard. More needs to be done to recognize their effort away from as well as within stations.

Finally, shoehorned into community radio is a subset of relatively new radio called "Low Power FM," or LPFM, also known as "microbroadcasting." Since 2000, advances in technology have helped microbroadcasting, which was born in the 1970s, catch up with the 21st century. The website LPFMDatabase.com, scraped from the FCC's LPFM database, shows that during two open windows in which LPFM applications were taken, 2001 and 2013, a total of 3,299 requests were granted while 926 were either canceled or expired. Of those left, another 477 were revoked for various paperwork problems or rules violations. Those remaining occupy the reserved band.

But an LPFM can be hard to explain. Like community or public radio type stations, LPFMs may have to convince listeners that they're not commercial. Where the benefit is clear or the relationship is long term, the explaining is easy. But for new LPFM stations, getting volunteers or money can be a challenge if listeners have always associated radio stations with advertising and thus, see no need to volunteer or donate. LaGanzie Kale, General Manager of Jonesboro, Arkansas's KLEK-LP said until his station switched on in 2014, his primarily black audience listened to urban stations in Little Rock. The community conversations his station hosts are having helps draw that audience to the new kid on the block. But getting them to see the distinction and the need to support it is a heavier lift.

And LPFMs have enemies: big broadcasters. They have always seen a network of legally licensed, community operated LPFMs as an existential threat to them and their market share. In the late-1970s, the NAB and NPR petitioned the FCC to change the requirements which let LPFM's on the air with one to ten watt transmitters because of charges they caused "interference." Although the FCC limited minimum power requirements for LPFMs to 100 watts as part of a confusing rule making and enforcing process in 1978. The move pushed many LPFMs off the air while giving the NAB and NPR access to the newly vacant frequencies for their own full power translators. But the FCC wasn't fully convinced that LPFMs caused interference and it proposed a study to see. Because the agency resisted imposing the other restrictions, NPR and the NAB did an end-around and got Congress to introduce the *Radio Broadcasting Preservation Act of 2000*. It proposed to give broadcasters the fence they wanted around their own frequencies. And since stations are packed tightly on the reserved band, a DMZ around the big boys threatened smaller stations with quieter voices.

But Congress, like the FCC, also wanted the study. Its results, much to the dismay of NPR and the NAB, found LFPMs caused little interference to big broadcasters and their translators. NPR disputed that conclusion and tried to insure more restrictions on LPFMs. Ironically, NPR and the NAB justified the interference

their new translators inflicted on LPFMs by arguing that they were
more important to the American people. Congress didn't buy that
argument. The *Local Community Radio Act of 2010*, signed by
President Obama in 2011, permanently lifted some of the restrictions on LPFMs and offered them a more hospitable environment.
Meanwhile, organizations like the National League of Cities and
the Communications Workers of America, as well as activists
like singer-songwriter and musician Bonnie Raitt, joined to argue
against "radio homogenization" that many accused NPR and NAB
of wanting. Although LPFM proponents were the underdogs, they
didn't always behave like the good guys either. History shows
some applicants acted like linebackers, ruthlessly plowing the road
for their own side.

This reflects the quandary community radio can frequently
find itself in. Because of its heritage, many station mission statements reflect lofty aspirations. But while striving for diversity,
inclusion and communitarianism, those values are often belied by
the same kind of in-house viciousness, personal attacks and pedes-
trian politics that make outsiders look at the trumpeted goals with
skepticism. Different internal camps, each toting their own
weaponized morality arguments, can make hopes of harmonious
workspaces rare. Because of its grassroots connections, community
radio proponents might consider it the most "sincere" form of
radio. Unfortunately, that is not always true. The medium
must sometimes fight through, and other times embrace, the same
pettiness commercial and public radio frequently endure.

The original visionaries of community and public radio sought
to do something with the medium that they believed commercial
radio never could or would, which was to provide the public with a
true voice rather than a means to consume. Comparing commercial, public and community radio, supporters of the latter would
say it remains essentially untamed, and has had a powerful social

and legislative effect on commercial and public radio. Despite all the problems of community radio, its supporters have never stopped believing that their way is the only true way. ☎

PLEDGE: The Public Radio Fund Drive

Chapter 3 - Is There A Problem?

"[P]ublic radio doesn't have a revenue problem, it has a spending problem."

—Eric Nuzum, former vice-president of programming for NPR.

"Public radio has a revenue problem. It does not have an audience problem."

—Dana Davis Rehm, former senior vice president for marketing communications and external relations for NPR.

"Public radio has an audience problem."

—Paul Farhi, media reporter for the
Washington Post

Audience, revenue and spending. Three elements in a simple formula that is anything but simple in public radio land. Stations put everything they have into presenting a calm, stable on-air and online presence for their audience, but there is static behind the scenes. Station managers, program directors and development officers watch ratings. Ratings agencies have taken fire for confusing numbers, which have forced some stations to hire their own head counters. That's no small problem since the sole purpose of media kits most stations distribute to advertisers (underwriters) is to sell ads. It's an obsession public radio shares with commercial radio, and something those underwriters (advertisers) won't do if those kits show that nobody's listening. It should be no surprise that there has been a fight around how those numbers are collected. Predigital methods of tracking listening habits have been replaced by high-tech, wireless-enabled methods that not everyone feels are fair. But at least the curious can get a basic understanding about the transition from diaries to digital "people meters;" pager like devices that detect electronic codes hidden in broadcast signals (called "watermarks") and use them to report which stations the wearer is hearing.

Higher ratings draw more underwriting money. But it should also spark in stations a desire for brighter, thicker lines between opportunities and ethics. Like promotional announcements, which mean more revenue for operations and building renovations, underwriting helps buy equipment, pay more staff, and create new programming. But if supporters criticize attached strings, does the money help or hurt a station's reputation in the long run? Forty percent of public radio revenue comes from listeners. Shifts in that audience, with boomers listening less while millennials listen more, also shifts how consistently stations get that money.

Misunderstandings or bad practices don't help. Muddled knowledge about spending doesn't help either. Government appropriations are public. Corporate and foundational money is increasingly spotlighted. Pledge drive goals are usually spelled out. Where all of that money goes should be equally apparent. But Mr. Nuzum told the filled room he was addressing, "You are spending money on things that are not in your future. You are spending money on things that are your past." So what is it being spent on instead? More of public radio's big givers want this question answered in exchange for continuing to be big givers. NPR says it does provide consolidated financial information, but upon request. And while services like Guidestar, Charity Navigator and ProPublica's Nonprofit Explorer offer some tax records online, those who don't like doing their own taxes won't likely read the IRS 990 of a public radio station.

Even money well spent can look like it's not, which many an ethics manual warn mirrors an equally dangerous "perception" of impropriety. *Washington Post* media reporter Paul Farhi, when describing NPR's new $201 million building in 2014 said, "It immediately began drawing grumbles from those who see the edifice as far too luxe for a non-profit radio and digital news organization that depends, in part, on taxpayer support." The network signed the papers on its new building (paid for from the sale of its old building, tax-free bonds and donors) even as it was months away from killing programs and cutting staff, resulting from a multi-million dollar budget deficit. That budget is made up of station fees, corporate sponsorships, federal appropriations, philanthropic and individual donations. Around the same time, the network also received a $17 million grant to "expand coverage and develop digital platforms." In the same year, NPR was working with at least three huge pots of money that could not mix in the slightest.

Reports say the old building was too expensive to retrofit, and had simply been outgrown by the network's mission. Perhaps there is never a good time to institute enterprise rescuing austerity measures. And maybe the fact that the network, despite being filled with very smart people, seems to have an unavoidable financial meltdown about every ten years. But the overall optics were bad. Critics and donors, looking at industry averages, can also blanch at the salaries of some public radio hosts. Like other voices with national reach, advertisers pay big money to big names to reach big numbers, whether commercial or non-profit. But as other affiliates have demonstrated, just because an executive or a high-value correspondent doesn't work at a network doesn't mean they won't get big money or that they necessarily deserve it.

NPR is engaging its stations with something called "The Station Compact." It's a plan to better connect with its licensees while becoming less financially dependent on them. This, amidst calls for an audit of public radio. As far back as 2010, Republican House Representative Eric Cantor launched an initiative called "YouCut," which he said was intended to let ordinary people say what they thought should be cut from the federal budget. After the firing of Juan Williams, Cantor spokesperson, Brad Dayspring told *Slate*'s David Weigel, "We're going to conduct a full audit to trace avenues of federal dollars that go to NPR. At a minimum," he said, "we would be including preventing the flow of taxpayer dollars to NPR through the Corporation for Public Broadcasting." Though the program was widely panned as a gimmick, it shows the anger of Republicans for what they consider wasteful, unnecessary programs that are neither in the spirit of American self-sufficiency or freedom of choice. Defenders counter public radio spends its money judiciously.

So which is it: Does public radio have a revenue problem, an audience problem, or a spending problem? ☎

Audience

"As NPR and Public Radio content becomes increasingly accessible on more platforms, each release of Arbitron's broadcast ratings is met with more skepticism."

—Ben Robins, formerly with NPR
Digital Services

Commercial and public radio overlap when it comes to the importance of measuring the audience. That's because underwriters only want to buy into programs that are characterized by high numbers of listeners during specific "day parts." Those times are weekdays between 6 a.m. to 10 a.m. and 3 p.m. to 7 p.m., aka "drive time" when people are in their cars going to and coming from work. It made categorizing them on the basis of employ- ment, education and income easier. But with digital downloads possible from anywhere through any device at any time, terrestrial radio is less dominant. HD radio and streaming are now players when determining a station's total audience size. There is an art of knowing exactly where people are and what stations, songs or programs they're listening to. But the science is not precise. That makes "people like you" more elusive than stations, marketers and researchers like.

The terminology describing that science is spare, but efficient. The number of new listeners over a period of time, usually mea- sured for a week, is called "cume," or the cumulative measure. The number of people who are listening during any 15-minute period is called the "average quarter hour," or AQH. A subset of AQH is the AQH Share, with "Share" being a separate measure of how many people in a specific market who could be listening are listening. And the length of time a listener listens to any one radio station is called "time spent listening," or TSL. AQH and TSL are used together to determine audience size. Advertisers (or underwriters) prefer a station with high TSL and low AQH since the opposite means someone listens to the radio a lot, but is constantly changing stations and would never hear the ads.

A 2010 guide from radio rating service Arbitron (before it was bought by TV ratings company Nielsen in 2012, and re-branded as Nielsen Audio) says there are nearly sixty different formulas that can be used to measure an audience. AQH, for example, is incredibly forgiving. A station need only capture five minutes of a listener's attention in any 15-minute period to get credit for that quarter hour. And the five minutes does not have to be continuous, though all five minutes of listening must occur within the same 15 minutes.

Once stations know how many people listen, that number is compared to the number of people who are within range of the station's signal. That's the station's "potential" audience. AQH is divided by the number of people a station's signal could reach and multiplied by 100 to get the percentage of people actually listening, the "AQH Rating." For example, an AQH of one equals an AQH rating of 1%. New York City's market, which includes parts of New Jersey, Connecticut and Pennsylvania, is the number one rated "Metropolitan Statistical Area" (MSA) in the United States. Its MSA has the most radio listeners. With a population of 16 million, an AQH of one would mean 160,000 people, or 1% in the New York MSA are listening to *Morning Edition* on WNYC at 8 a.m. Beckley, West Virginia, with 66,000 people, is 272nd, making it among the smallest radio markets in the country. According to the FCC, West Virginia Public Broadcasting operates WVPB in Beckley. But if WVPB had a high AQH rating, it could do as well in the ratings with on-air listeners (for its size) as WNYC.

The higher the AQH, the more attractive to underwriters. Unofficial tools like radiolocator.com and official ones like the FCC Propagation Curves Worksheet, used with census and zip code data, tell stations about how many people may be within their reach. That's why it's such a big deal when stations stomp on each other's signal. Other measurements include focusing on specific demographics within a market (called "P1"), determining whether listeners to station A are also listening to station B ("cume duplication" and the amount a station sponsor spends to reach each 1000 listeners ("CPM" or "Cost Per Thousand"). Public radio stations sometimes don't have big enough audiences to show up in commercial radio rating services. NPR has worked to generate its own numbers with the help of research like *Audience 98*, and research firms like Comscore and Gfk MRI. NPR made the importance of audience statistics clear on its website in a 2012 discussion about how Arbitron measures the radio audience. "NPR raises its revenue (almost exclusively) through underwriting and programming fees based on Arbitron broadcast ratings." How those numbers get calculated has changed a lot.

Arbitron used to count listeners to MSA stations using old-school "diaries." Those were paper booklets that listeners used to remember the stations they listened to over the previous week. The system was slow, prone to mistakes and overly subjective. Stations gamed the system by pushing contests on certain days and times that corresponded to diary periods ending or starting. They would endlessly repeat the call sign to make sure listeners heard it and wrote it down.

But in 2007, "people meters" were introduced, first to the Philadelphia and Houston markets, and later to Los Angeles and others. At the time of the switch, Arbitron compared diaries and people meters results in the same market. But the results were so different that critics assumed the diary numbers were inflated. Later, the difference was attributed to quirks in each system's collection and tabulation methods. Critics also seemed to attack Arbitron for throwing diaries, a method it pioneered, under the bus so quickly. "[A]fter three decades of defending the diary methodology, Arbitron seems to have embarked on a mission to destroy the credibility of the diary methodology," said Richard Harker in his *Radio Insights* blog from 2008. Diaries were everywhere, though, and it would take time to replace them with people meters. But Arbitron received criticism for other reasons. In the early 2000s, because of falling household participation, stations and critics accused the company of surveying too few people. The low response rate threatened to make its numbers much less accurate and make advertiser buying decisions less effective. Diaries were not perfect.

But neither are people meters. PPMs cost stations 60% more than the paper diaries. What were they getting for the extra cost? Apparently, headaches. Early use was spotty. Nielsen's entry into radio represented a hope that its numbers were more accurate and would give stations better information. Though also on a near quarterly, 13-week rotation like Arbitron, station data is uploaded each night, giving users instant access to their numbers every day. Mistakes still happen, however. In 2012, PPM ratings were both certified in some markets and decertified in others. In 2011, NPR worried that if Pandora and Spotify were included with Arbitron's measurements of larger stations, the pool of potential underwriting revenue would be spread too thinly and affect the rates it could charge underwriters or member stations for *ME* or *ATC*. NPR didn't want non-radio to be seen by ratings services as radio-like, even though they believed that's how the public was already start-ing to perceive them.

By 2015, stations were complaining that sample sizes were too small, making sought-after demographics like blacks, Hispanics and millennials hard for advertisers to reach. Results of MSA mea-surements, which include some but not all terrestrial public radio stations, are published in what is essentially a regional popularity contest by Nielsen and redistributed to public radio stations by the non-profit, Radio Research Consortium. According to RRC's Summer 2017 rankings, WAMC had the best overall numbers of the 30 top-rated public radio stations nationwide. It scored the second-highest AQH, the top share number, the third highest cume. WAMC's Alan Chartock constantly praises his listeners as being the most responsive in the country. Pledge drives typically drive listeners away.

OPB's Fall 2017 pledge drive ran from Monday, October 2 through Saturday, October 7. In September, the station had an AQH of 9.1. In October, that number fell to 8.0, slowly creeping back to an 8.8 by December. That means in October, 1.1% of the Portland market, or nearly 25,000 fewer people were listening when the station was asking for support. And rebounds can be slow. With newer ways of listening, some users don't return to terrestrial broadcasts after pledge drives.

The type of formats stations broadcast also affects their audience. There are about a dozen different types of radio formats, including Contemporary Hit Radio (previously "Top 40"), Spanish, Adult Contemporary aka, "Soft Rock" and News/Talk. Most public radio stations, like many stations on AM, are in the news/talk category. Stations like WNYC and WAMU push for dominance in their markets. But if some stations aren't top dog, they can at least be top in their format. A station may be ranked 14th compared to all of the other stations in an MSA, but it may be ranked third in its format which gets highlighted to underwriters. Eric Nuzum implied to a room full of radio executives in 2015 that perhaps their emphasis on technology was a distraction to what was really important, which was the listener experience, which some could argue, is represented by a station's format. *Current*'s Tyler Falk wrote, "As a programmer, Nuzum said he stopped thinking of his job as just handling scheduling. He said he saw his mission as: "I create great listening experiences that stay with the audience long after they're done listening."

Dick Taylor is assistant professor of broadcasting at the School of Journalism & Broadcasting at Western Kentucky University. In the same year, he told *Radio Insights* that PPMs aren't the problem. "It's that PPM has taken radio broadcaster's eyes off the ball. The game is programming radio stations with great content. It's hiring great talent. It's crafting commercials for advertisers that get results and don't annoy the listener. It's super-serving the community you're licensed to operate in." In other words, like Nuzum, Taylor says radio is about the listener experience.

To improve that experience, NPR created *NPRListens*. It's an effort to draw millennials into NPR through new media and podcasts like *Invisibilia*. But they have to be properly counted, which ties numbers and technology together in stations' ability to follow you across platforms and mark your engagement. Because the promises of PPMs have yet to be fulfilled however, the science of measurement has yet to be elevated to an art form. About half of radio's nationwide markets still use diaries.

Gerry Boehme, a measurement industry veteran who runs his own consulting company speaks for many when he says, "Radio is being terribly shortchanged by a system that is totally incapable of measuring current broadcast channels, much less streaming and podcasting." But public radio's future depends on it. In 2016, *RadioInk* asked retiring iHeart programmer Chris Kampmeier whether or not he thought people meters were a success. "It's a challenging technology," said Kampmeier, "but whether PPM is better than diary or diary better than PPM, who knows?"☎

Revenue

"The network's multiple sources of revenue, endowments, foundation grants, advertising and individual donors, via station programming fees, are indeed the envy of the media industry, which has been decimated across the board by plummeting ad revenue."

—Bob Garfield, NPR's *On the Media*, April 15, 2016

Revenue is income consisting of cash and receivables. Cash is what a company can spend today. Receivables is what it expects it can spend tomorrow. Sustaining memberships, public radio's best example of receivables, are a listener's promise to pay stations money over future months. Revenue is an asset class, like land, buildings, investments, gear and the dollar value of a station's reputation. Public radio has many revenue streams; individual giving, sales and investments and government appropriations among them. But each one can represent its own set of problems. It's often said non-profits shouldn't make a profit. That's not exactly true. They can make a profit, but they're not allowed to spend it, for example, by paying dividends to shareholders since non-profits aren't allowed to have shareholders. But they can plow every cent back into the operation while using some of it to pay "reasonable" salaries.

Forty-nine nations around the world have some form of public broadcasting service. And they fund them differently. The U.K. imposes a mandatory tax and monitoring vans to make sure people with radios and TVs are paying it. Even if a government provides the bulk of funding, it is the editorial independence of the service that determines how free it is from government control. Nowhere near as draconian as the Brits, Canadians swung the other way and struggle with how much commercialism they should allow into their beloved CBC. But however public radio gets funded, it's an ongoing issue for every society if donations stop being enough.

In 1967, President Johnson provided partial taxpayer support for the Corporation for Public Broadcasting. Intended to reignite American exceptionalism by reconnecting its citizens with their intellect and culture, CPB created a TV branch, the Public Broadcasting Service and a radio branch, National Public Radio. Johnson and his 89th Congress agreed to annually increase appropriated funding to the entity. Over the years, public radio has come to rely less on government support or taxes and more from corporate, philanthropic and individual givers. Federal money supports the umbrella organization known as NPR. But it also supports three other "networks:" the Public Radio Exchange, Public Radio International and American Public Media, along with about 260 key stations and their satellites nationwide. Public radio was never intended to be funded only on the federal dime. And public funding remains a thorn in the side of conservatives who believe it prevents stations that receive public money from testing their value in the marketplace without it.

After a run-in with the Nixon administration and his Assistant Attorney General, conservative jurist Antonin Scalia, public radio realized government support had too many strings attached. It began looking for other sources. It found direct federal grants, in which an agency of the federal government needs help promoting a program and pays public radio the way a client pays a contractor. The money could be for simple underwriting announcements, or they could represent a reporting collaboration with agencies such as the National Science Foundation, the Department of the Interior, Underwriters Laboratories and others. But while grant money can disappear if agency budgets get cut, money from the business community can seem unlimited. With paid sponsorships, business pays public radio to promote its products and services. Strict federal guidelines limit the language public radio can use in these "underwriting credits" since Congress didn't want public radio sounding like or competing with, commercial radio.

The question remains whether public radio is ethically unaffected by corporate money. States can provide money directly to state-owned and operated broadcast licensees. Or they support universities who in turn use state funding for stations on their campuses. But state government never has enough cash, and what funding there is can be as fickle as the political leanings of legislatures and governorships that guide it. In fact, since the 2008 financial crisis, states have cut back on direct and indirect support to pubcasters. Some argue those cuts disproportionately target public radio and TV in states with Republican-dominated leadership. And as universities themselves look for new sources of revenue, some of them choose to sell their stations and frequencies.

Meanwhile, philanthropic giving, like the legendary $235 million gift to NPR from Joan Kroc, wife of McDonald's founder Ray Kroc, is less fraught. But stations can find themselves in a *Catch-22*: If they don't agree to spoken or unspoken terms of big donors, they don't get the money. In other cases, stations may be forced to turn down philanthropy, for example, if its defined use is too narrow. Or if, as a condition to get it, stations must violate their own ethics. Or if stations realize that after the money is gone, they won't be able to keep supporting the infrastructure the money built. Plus, as the emphasis shifts from average givers to so-called "major givers," some accuse public radio of letting the big money direct station programming decisions.

Which brings us to individual giving. Givers are categorized according to how much and how often they give. And although they represent about forty percent of total contributions to the system, they get public radio's most personally directed messages to support it. Stations rely on emotional connections that encourage givers to dedicate themselves to their station's well being. And those givers are sought not just through pledge drives, but advocacy campaigns designed to get public radio past historically stagnated levels of financial support. Marketing efforts within pledge central itself encourage pitchers to call out to friends and family to become members between taking calls from random donors. Stations that can, have generated cash through one-time, "Hail Marys" like selling off their own frequencies. Others resort to crowdfunding or sales of station swag to generate extra income, but those can also attract the taxman. Still others are turning to online programming and its looser federal restrictions that may mean a new way to raise more money. Both the FCC and Congress have looked at tightening profane and indecent language rules for broadcasters migrating their freer speaking content from on-air. Unless they are private subscriptions services, beefed-up underwriting rules too, may migrate as well.☎

Funding Models

"The nonprofit world rarely engages in equally clear and succinct conversations about an organization's long-term funding strategy. That is because the different types of funding that fuel nonprofits have never been clearly defined. More than a poverty of language, this represents—and results in—a poverty of understanding and clear thinking."

—Stanford Social Innovation Review, Spring 2009

Governments know radio's power to paint a unique picture in each listener's "theater of the mind." That's why many own and operate their own stations that broadcast "official" information. The U.S. government operates a number of official, state sponsored information outlets that are designed to expose other nations to American values as a tool of American foreign policy. These are funded by the American taxpayer.

The American Forces Network (AFN), formerly known as the American Forces Radio and Television Service (AFRTS) broadcasts American programming, along with a mix of command information, community relations and public affairs, to U.S forces and their families overseas. Operational and editorial control of AFN rest within the Department of Defense (DoD). Radio Free Europe, Radio Free Asia, Middle East Broadcasting Networks and Voice of America broadcast to parts of the world that the U.S. has determined keep their citizens from a free flow of information. Radio Liberty, directed at the Soviet Union since the 1950s, signed off in 2012. Radio Marti, another such service, is directed specifically at Cuba. Radio Marti's broadcasts have been challenged by the International Telecommunications Union as illegal. Each of those networks (excluding military-related ones) were sanctioned and supervised by the Broadcasting Board of Governors (BBG), the U.S. agency that oversaw all U.S. government international broadcasting services until December 2016. The BBG was replaced by a single administrator in 2017.

Many democratic governments also recognize that a thriving civilian broadcasting industry is essential to principles of free speech. Besides commercial radio, which is supported mostly by advertising, 18 governments around the world provide some kind of financial support for their version of public radio broadcasters. The United States does too, although at between $1.38 and $3 per capita, its support is the lowest in the world. Compared to a nation like Finland, which extracts $180 from each of its citizens to support national broadcaster YLE, America's funding wouldn't be enough to turn on Finland's transmitter. It has come up with several ways to pay for public radio, however. Congressional funding of CPB is one. Over time, public radio has learned to draw on others that add up to more than it receives from the government. But federal money is critical. So despite what has historically looked like spotty support, foreign and domestic public public radio providers have been able to benefit from a "basket" of funding.

Of those other models, a license fee is the first. Like a road tax, a license fee for government supported radio works the same way. In the United Kingdom for example, license fees are paid as taxes by each household or public entity the British government assumes owns and uses a radio or TV to watch or listen to the BBC. In 2014, the UK's $97 per capita fee brought in $6.9 billion to the BBC. However, the BBC has been moving toward a budget reduction of about 20%. In 2010, licensing fees were frozen and remained so until 2017 as the organization continued to review its operating costs. Since the license fee is a tax, not paying it is a criminal offense. The BBC has the authority to conduct surveillance to know who is watching TV or listening to radio illegally. From January through June 2012, the BBC caught more than 400,000 people. Ironically, this makes the BBC one of the leading prosecutors for tax evasion in the UK. Members of Parliament have criticized the threatening letter the BBC sends to its users.

The second option is a dedicated broadcasting tax. The money broadcasters earn is taxed by the government and that tax is put in a fund. The interest-earning fund, like a 401K, is used to support those same broadcasters. The closest American public broadcasting came to such an excise tax was in a late-1960s conversation between Wilbur Mills and President Johnson. As a condition of the passage of the *Public Broadcasting Act of 1967*, the powerful Ways and Means committee chairman forced Johnson to drop two provisions that could have made public broadcasters more financially independent. One of the axed ideas was for CPB to have independent, non-government types on its governing board. But the other was a tax on television manufacturers. Similar to the licensing fee, but applied to TV rather than radio sets, that revenue would've also gone into a fund from which the CPB could draw. As predicted, the National Association of Broadcasters and TV makers lobbied Congress to kill that idea.

A third option is sponsorships, or in the U.S., "underwriting." American public radio listeners know this option well. A major company pays for an announcement about itself in exchange for funding a station program. That announcement can be on the air, streamed online, in the form of banner ads, cash, or in-kind contributions. Underwriting in pledge drives includes endorsements and cross-marketing during challenges, matches, gifts and contest giveaways. Related to underwriting is foundational giving. Non-profit foundations wanting to promote their own missions may, like business and government, have preferences in how public radio spends the money it's given. Joan Kroc's gift to NPR in 2003 stipulated, for example, that the endowment could never fall below its original amount of $235 million. That means NPR may only use the interest the principal generates (5% or about $10 million a year) but never the principal itself. Uses of such gifts can be restrictive. A station's immediate need, like "paying the power bill," as Jim Lewis wrote about foundational giving for *Current* in 2011, "tend to be less compelling than content about topics that matter to [donors]."

The next method for funding a national public broadcaster is the straightforward listener donation. This is the public radio pledge drive in a nutshell. And although other methods of raising money and connecting with its audience exist, American public radio broadcasters continue to rely heavily on the pledge drive, mostly because it remains effective. For example, whenever the public thinks public radio is being politically attacked, donations soar. Pubcasters say listeners rally behind shows they depend on that connect to them through their own values. That's why reactions to threats to public broadcasting can seem so visceral. Wyoming Public Radio programming director Roger Adams echoed this in a 2011 story about WPR's funding. "Our phone volunteers reported that many of the people calling in donations mentioned the controversy or the fear of CPB cuts. We are also receiving many second, and even some third gifts this spring." Plus, Adams said more members than usual were joining in the wake of threats to cut public radio funding in the aftermath of the firing of Juan Williams.

Then, there are past advocacy efforts like *170MillionAmericans, 3MillionGivers, MajorGivingNow,* and current ones like *Protect My Public Media.* These are lobbying proxys for America's public broadcasting organizations. Community radio has *MyStationGiveBig.* Public law prevents public radio from lobbying Congress directly. Office of Management and Budget Circular *A-122: Cost Principles for Non-Profit Organizations* also says federal funds recipients, like NPR, can't get on their own airwaves and pitch for contributions the way local member stations can. But it can, underwriting-style, encourage people to share their stories about the value public radio has played in their lives. The pledge drive is not infallible, however. Although some stations are fundraising superstars, other are not. And powerful mixed messages have muddied the pledging waters.

During the 2011 scandal, NPR's chief fundraiser, Ron Schiller, admitted in a right-wing blogger's sting video that NPR didn't need government money as much as it says it does. NPR CEO at the time, Vivian Schiller, came out strongly denying Mr. Schiller's words. Pledge drive perceptions can't afford such ambiguity.

The final self-sustainability option for a national public broadcaster is subscription fees. For vendors, this guarantees a steady stream of income as long as the customer feels the product is worth regularly paying for. In an informal survey I conducted, participants were asked, "In your opinion, can you imagine a time when all of your station's content is offered for an access or subscription fee?" About 82% of public radio respondents said "no." But much of public radio already operates on a *de facto* subscription fee: sustaining memberships. And even though public radio may not, yet, be ready to start regularly charging for its content, the idea is already embedded. "A voluntary membership model could turn an adversarial relationship on its head," said Matt DeRienzo for *Editor and Publisher* in 2016. "Instead of 'We're putting up this paywall so you stop freeloading,'" he says the conversation could be, "We're partnering with you to keep doing the work you care about." DiRienzo says of the idea, "the NPR model represents Membership 1.0."

A 2016 pitch break from Tallahassee based WFSU said, with no irony whatsoever, "A sustainer is someone who has set up to give a small monthly contribution to WFSU, maybe ten dollars, maybe fifteen dollars a month. You can even pay for listening the way you pay for your cell phone. The same way you pay for your cable or your Netflix." Jason Brown of KRCU in Carbondale, Illinois told listeners, "Maybe consider making a $10 contribution right now. Consider that your subscription to shows like *Fresh Air*, *All Things Considered*, *Snap Judgment*, all those programs you enjoy on the weekend."

Former NPR CEO Vivian Schiller told reporter Jason Pontin at the Beet.TV Executive Retreat in 2013 that people who support public radio, either through taxes or through pledge drive donations, feel as though they own it. And with that sense of ownership can come fury over how that money is spent. Schiller said that's why it would be better for public radio to move away from any government funding and consider a subscription model. But as late as 2009, such mixed-company talk was off the table. Dick Meyer, then Editorial Director for NPR's Digital Media spoke to *Mediate* in response to the questions, "Will NPR.org ever be members only? Will NPR.org ever have a subscription plan?" His response: "We are a public service. That is our dominant goal, not profits, not growth, not market share. We are chartered to give the public free, universal, high-quality news and information and that is what we will do. Repeat – free."

More recently though, when public radio talks about these issues, the reporting seems obliquely engineered to land on the minds of listeners with the impact of a meat tenderizer. In 2012, NPR talked about the growth and benefits of web-based subscription services like Dollar Shave Club. In 2015, PRI's *The World* featured a story, "Subscription is the New Sharing; The Rise of the Membership Economy." Canada's CBC television earned $131 million in subscription fees in its 2013-2014 funding year. Many online newspaper readers are also familiar with the subscription model. The *New York Times*, the *Cincinnati Enquirer*, the *Oregonian* and the publication pointed directly at pubcasters, *Current*, let readers access some content for free but to get premium content,

they must pay to penetrate a paywall. The push for sustaining revenue especially fits public radio's unwilling definition of a subscription fee. But pubcasters says givers are meeting a moral obligation
to pay for what they use, or paying it forward for those who can't
afford their fair share, or helping provide news and information to
the public as a way of building community. Above all, public radio
says members are not forced to give. They choose to willingly, so
their support is not in response to anything like a bill that comes in
the mail. Although these six methods—advertising, licensing fees,
broadcast tax, sponsorships, audience donations, and subscription
fees—represent the basic choices broadcasters have when deciding
how to pay for themselves, it is clear that they vary widely in how
they are mixed and matched to fit changing audience needs and
political realities. ☎

Our Canadian Cousin

*"CBC has a very important mandate to bind Canada together in
both official languages, tell local stories, and make sure we have a
sense of our strength, our culture, our stories."*

—Justin Trudeau, Canadian Prime Minister

Public funding for public broadcasting is compulsory in the
UK, and heavily supported by advertising in Canada. The U.S.
falls somewhere in between. American public radio has taken
many cues from Canada, including from the CBC's calm, professional and often whimsical flagship program, *As it Happens*.
But as NPR knows, flagship shows can't stop budget cuts. And in
2014, the CBC had plans to eliminate 1,500 jobs and outsource
the production of every program it broadcast except news and
public affairs. In the end, *"600 jobs were cut to fill a C$120
million shortfall."*

Supporters of NPR often say the cost of public broadcasting to each U.S. taxpayer is less than $1.36. The 2015 Congressional appropriation to CPB has remained steady for several years at about $446 million. Meanwhile, in 2014, the government in Ottawa authorized an operating budget for the CBC of C$1.34 billion. And in late 2016, the CBC requested an additional C$400 million to counter a reduction in its budget to C$1.03 billion. The CBC said it was trying to recoup money it would've made in advertising had the government not scaled back its ability to do so with the reduced appropriation. When it made the request, Nicole Ireland for CBC News reported that the network said it was operating, "[under] a business model and cultural policy framework that is profoundly broken," while other countries "[reaped] the benefits of strong, stable, well-funded public broadcasters." So the CBC, like public radio in the U.S., isn't necessarily happy with its funding model either. But Canadians seem to be. A 2014 poll conducted by Nanos Research showed that 41% of Canadians wanted funding increased, 46% wanted it to stay where it was and only 10% wanted it cut.

The CBC's ask was part of a plan to stop doing something public radio in the U.S. is loathe to do: sell advertising. And in Canada, it's really advertising, not the masked advertising U.S. pubcasters are forced to call "underwriting." In Canada, the public broadcaster supplements the money it gets from the government with bare-naked ads that were estimated to have brought in around C$350 million in 2016. The CBC also earns C$100 million or so from cable and satellite subscription fees, C$140 million in "other" revenue. Its annual take is closer to C$1.8 billion each year. Plus, in 2016, the CBC asked for C$100 million more to help it deal with the same kind of technology *"disruptions"* around digital content its peers in the U.S. are facing.

That year, revenue from CBC stations increased for the first time in four years. Between 2011 and 2015, they had collectively lost 18% or more than C$60 billion. Broadcast of the Rio Olympic Games boosted the broadcaster's revenue by 20%, according to Regan Reid, writing for *Media in Canada* in 2017. But Reid reports that although digital advertising revenues rose, overall advertising rates and subscriptions related to cord cutting, fell. The network, said Reid, also saw a huge jump in programming costs. Critics complain bitterly that the CBC is wasteful even as most Canadians seem satisfied. And as defenders like Tony Wong of the *Toronto Star* point out, "the Canadian market is a 10th of the size of the American one. But the cost of producing a quality product is the same, with serialized episodes costing in the $2 million to $3 million range."

Since Canada doesn't assess a licensing fee to each and every Canadian citizen as the UK does, supporters argue it must rely on such a mix. But the broadcaster seems to have conflicted feelings about it. In 2000, the *Globe and Mail* reported that the CBC was planning to remove all ads from its website in an effort to better reflect its *"public service"* role. But by 2005, in what looked like a reversal, a *Globe and Mail* headline read, "CBC to Boost Ads in Website Overhaul." ☎

Appropriated Funding in the U.S.

"We are not spending the Federal Government's money, we are spending the taxpayer's money, and it must be spent in a way which guarantees his money's worth and yields the fullest possible benefit to the people being helped."

—Richard M. Nixon

Just before Ron Schiller, NPR's chief fundraiser, was fired from his job for comments he made to filmmaker James O'Keefe in 2011, he said some things that for some, brought into question the whole idea of federal support. Schiller, in seeking fundraising dollars from a fictitious Muslim Brotherhood front group, told his hosts, "Frankly, it is very clear that we would be better off in the long run without federal funding." Jeff Jacoby, writing for the conservative *TownHall.com* said that public radio could use the "come to Jesus" moment to consider that perhaps it needs a little tough love. Jacoby writes, "One of the men posing as a philanthropist asks if NPR would survive, given "all the donors that are available, if [Congress] should pull the funding right now." Schiller, via Jacoby, replies, "Yes. NPR would definitely survive, and most of the stations would survive." Less than a day later, then NPR Senior Vice President Dana Davis Rehm, told *Slate*, "The assertion that NPR and public radio stations would be better off without federal funding does not reflect reality. The elimination of federal funding would significantly damage public broadcasting as a whole."

The Federal government's revenue comes mostly from taxes and interest on individual, corporate and social security income, various fees for services and government bonds. And it spends that money mostly on the military, cabinet level agencies, non-discretionary (sometimes called "mandatory") spending for entitlement programs like Medicare and interest payments on the federal debt. But compartmentalization doesn't stop there. The website Budget. House.Gov says the federal budget is divided into more than two dozen "budget functions." Each function covers all spending for similar efforts across government no matter which agency oversees the work. Function #500, which covers education, training, employment and social services includes CPB's appropriation along with funding for the National Institute for the Humanities, the National Endowment for the Arts, the National Gallery, the Smithsonian Institution and the John F. Kennedy Center for the Performing Arts. Congress was apparently saying if the CPB is ideologically focused on arts and education, that is where the bulk of its support should come from. The *Labor, Health and Human Services, Education and Related Agencies subcommittee* oversaw the $446 million CPB got in 2016. In 2017, Republicans outnumbered Democrats on that subcommittee by 8 to 5. But even among that majority, CPB has its fans. "With public radio I can wake up without someone shouting at me," said Representative Tom Cole, a Republican from Oklahoma. Cole is also the chairman of the subcommittee that handles Function #500 funding.

But an appropriation is not the same as an allocation or an authorization. An appropriation is an OK by Congress to set aside money for spending if it's available. An allocation guarantees that money is available. Authorizations let agencies start spending. Even if Congress is legislatively bound to appropriate $446 million for CPB each year doesn't mean that's the number on the check. Once the President has submitted the annual budget, Congress begins deciding what changes it wants to make to the President's request according to what it thinks the government should spend taxpayer money on. That is the total appropriation, also known in Congress as 302a. After deciding the spending ceiling, Congress divides the budget among the 12 cabinet agencies. Those agencies know those subdivisions as 302b and each of them now needs to hammer out its own 302b allocation. For example, the bill that covers the departments of Labor, HHS, Education and a handful of smaller agencies like the Corporation for Public Broadcasting is called the *Labor-Health and Human Services-Education and Related Agencies* appropriations bill. That group will now divide their respective pieces of the budget pie according to how much they want to give to each of the programs they oversee.

CPB is funded on a two-year appropriation. The schedule was designed to insulate "CPB from politically motivated inter- ference with programming," which is another way of saying that interference happens. And it is something the Congress, despite itself, has tried to keep from doing, but not always successfully. Ellen P. Goodman of Rutgers Law School wrote in 2003 of the *1999 Satellite Home Viewer Improvement Act*. Implemented by a congress that was having an increasingly hard time applying First Amendment rules to growing types of new media, Goodman says legislators "fashioned a copyright benefit." The law allowed Direct Broadcast Satellite (DBS) operators to rebroadcast local television programming in their own market but without copyright restrictions. This was essentially a free-speech benefits subsidy which gave those carriers a marketplace advantage to rebroadcast that content for a profit. Goodman calls this no different than a grant or a tax exemption. It has been argued as an example of government manipulation that uses business forces rather than law.

When Congress faces an impasse, the budget fights can be fierce. Bills are amended or riders are added that protect legislation with poison pills to stop opponents from killing it. Versions of the same bill working their way through the House and the Senate might not survive. Or if they do, they can differ by language and billions of dollars. Both versions may end up in "conference" committees where they also may or may not survive. But if both bills can be successfully meshed into one, it then heads to the President's desk. Presidents can approve or not approve funding for CPB. But if the appropriation is approved and the allocation is granted, then the authorization lets CPB start spending.

In a 2011 piece for WBUR, reporter Jim Zarolli notes that "Critics scoff at the notion that public broadcasting would collapse without federal support. They say PBS and public radio have a loyal, affluent audience that will come to their rescue if funding is cut." And it is true that for nearly 30 years, public radio's own research has shown that not only are public radio listeners more affluent, educated and socially engaged than Americans in general, but that they will give nearly as often as they are asked to support public broadcasting. Republican Rich Nugent, U.S. House member from Florida agreed, saying at the time that losing federal funds would "force stations to reinvent themselves by becoming more community-oriented." Nugent also thinks that access to so much news through technology makes public broadcasting practically redundant. But Zarolli's piece also says that though some believe weaning public broadcasting off public money would yield benefits, many smaller stations depend on that federal support and without it, those stations could disappear. And their audiences could find that some parts of the public airwaves that they own are no longer able to reach them. ☎

Corporation for Public Broadcasting

"A private corporation funded by the American people"

—slogan of the Corporation for Public Broadcasting

There are guidelines for how CPB distributes public radio's $100 million portion of that $446 million Congressional appropriation. They are found within about 40 of federal rules and 88 pages of CPB regulations. CPB itself says, "Applicant and current recipient stations must each year meet a variety of legal, managerial, staffing and operational criteria for Community Service Grant (CSG) funding."

CPB divides its federal appropriation three ways: CSG programming grants for pubcasters, system support, (also known as "six percent" funds) and administrative costs. Those programming grants, classified as restricted and unrestricted, represent money stations get for innovative shows, services or other community benefits. Restricted grants is money stations must use to create programming that provides value to all of public radio, whereas stations can use unrestricted grants to benefit their own audience. When local stations rebroadcast *All Things Considered,*

Science Friday, The Moth, or *Marketplace*, they are using the restricted portion. Likewise, in 2017, WNYC and Minnesota Public Radio ended a collaboration called *Indivisible*, which looked at the similarities and differences between American citizens in the wake of the 2016 election.

Stations across the country likely used some of their restricted CSG money to purchase the rights to air *Indivisible*. CPB has been criticized for how the money stations get is used to pay for shows from NPR, APM or PRI. Detractors say the current system, introduced in the mid-80s, isn't much different from when stations were forced to buy packages of programming at one take-it-or-leave-it price. Stations like the current system a little better because they can choose cheaper programs from a variety of providers. But because listeners love the tent-pole shows that stations must carry to keep them listening, some argue stations have little choice but to continue paying high prices for them, leaving them little money for anything else.

Restricted CSGs account for about a quarter of the money allocated to public radio; the unrestricted portion makes up the rest of the overall CSG. An example of the use of unrestricted funds might be Oregon Public Broadcasting's *Politics Now* podcast, which examines the legislative climate in the Oregon statehouse. Programming grants cover many of the costs of producing such shows, including preproduction planning and development, production such as feld recording and post-produced narration and editing. The shows themselves can range from town meetings to call-ins to educational. So they may need lots of promotion, fundraising support and administrative time, much of which can be covered by such a grant.

Station websites use pie charts, spreadsheets or bar graphs to show what percentage of their financial support comes from where.

But there is no standard format for this representation nor language for describing it. Funding combinations for station A may be completely different for station B. This makes the conflation of terms and dollars difficult for the average visitor to understand. Fortunately, the CPB is more consistent. Its FY2009 *Community Service Grant Criteria*, for example, spells out how stations should report their support in annual financial statements. If applicable, that support should show all seven categories, including first, foundations and nonprofit associations, like the James S. and John L. Knight Foundation. Next, business and industry supporters include companies like Constant Contact or BNSF railway. "Friends of" groups that support stations in ways they may not be able to support themselves is a category, as well as net auction revenue which is money a station may earn from selling off unused portions of its frequency. Another category is net revenue from special fundraising activities including co-sponsorships, contests or cross-marketing with other non-profits. Gifts and bequests represent the recent emphasis on "major giving" from the wealthiest donors. And finally, support from one-time giving, renewing, and "sustainer" contributions.

Each of these types of financial support (not including government) is part of what is called Non Federal Financial Support, or NFFS. Stations qualify for federal, CSG money based on their ability to raise NFFS. Eligibility requirements include the size and racial composition of the audience, station management or board makeup, and the extent to which a station is the main source of news and information for a listening area. Operational requirements include the status of a station's license, operating power, duration and content of broadcast schedule, staffing, quality of facilities and many other data points. Stations qualify for CSGs depending on how each of these criteria rate, resulting in a final score. These requirements mirror those in Article II of NPR's by-laws, which outline how stations can become "members." Stations that have the greatest difficulty meeting eligibility and operational requirements of CPB are internally classified as level A stations. Those most able to meet those same criteria are level D stations. B and C stations are somewhere in-between. Ironically, to receive a CSG means a station is demonstrating its ability to be self-sustaining. Like a first time seeker of credit, getting it depends in part on one proving to the lender they don't need it.

But a CSG is also like a matching grant. If the number of its listeners is growing, stations can keep getting the money they need to add programming or upgrade equipment. If they don't or can't grow, however, the station can begin a downward spiral. This happened to KCSN, the California State University radio station at Northridge. The station was one of 80 on a so-called "Dis-List" that were in danger of losing CPB support. In 1998, CPB eliminated about $150,000 in federal support to the station. At the time, KCSN General Manager Teresa Rogers said CPB stopped funding a number of stations it felt were too small, and "KCSN is one of them." As of 2017, the station, which airs public radio shows like *Le Show*, *World Café*, and *On Point* is still on the air, though it has relied on listeners and underwriting to survive. In 2013, small stations again were put on notice when CPB changed its eligibility formula, and KZUM, at the University of Nebraska at Lincoln, became a target. After missing CPB's goal two years in a row, it was in danger of losing $70,000 in federal support if it didn't hit the $300,000 requirement in 2016.

Together, restricted and unrestricted program grants make up about 95% of the $99.1 million radio gets. What's left comprises what CPB calls the "Radio Program Fund." CPB says the fund "supports the development of new public radio services and series, the production of urgent or timely content, the work of independent radio producers, programming for underserved and unserved audiences and the development of innovative con-tent forms." For example, although restricted funds let stations buy *Indivisible*, Radio Programs Funds helped MPR and WNYC create the show. Other funded shows include *StoryCorps*, NPR's international news coverage and specialty programs for coveted demographics and unique music genres. Restricted and unrestricted community service grants and the Radio Program Fund equal all of public radio's $99.1 million portion of the Congressional appropriation. Television gets $298 million. Radio and TV together represent 89% of the $446 million in federal funds.

The remaining 11% is CPB's "Six Percent" funds and its administrative costs. System support funds CPB's programs and initiatives to bring pubcasters together to solve problems, innovate solutions or just improve communication within public broadcasting. Six percent, or about $27 million goes toward this organizational infrastructure building. System support can mean CPB pays music licensing fees so producers can use music in their shows without worrying about violating copyrights. It can mean providing stations with training to help them improve their financial, management or technical operations. Or, it can sponsor pilot programs that may later be rolled out to all of public radio. CPB also contracts with professionals through the posting of Requests for Proposals (RFPs) each year. CPB announced 58 RFPs between October 2013 and October 2016. Those contracts facilitated consultations with black station owners to help them improve operations and fundraising. Or, they asked professional child specialists to analyze Department of Education award recipients to see if anything they're doing can improve PBS children's programming. Programming grants and system support constitute about 95% of the total appropriation from Congress.

Administrative costs, which is the remaining 5% or $22.5 million of the appropriation, covers operation of CPB itself. Senior staff positions reveal how that money is spent; Education and Children's Content Operations, Education and Community Impact,

System Development and Media Strategy, External Communications, Governmental Affairs, IT, Digital Information, CSG and Station Initiatives, Compliance and much more. CPB says its role in public media is, "to shield stations from political influence and deliver federal support in a way that does not affect a station's ability to operate independently." This, despite the fact that CPB itself has been a frequent target of cries to defund it for biased behavior. Those accusations have made some wonder if stations are shielded as much as CPB claims. Peter Hart and Steve Rendall addressed this in a 2005 piece for the left-leaning media watchdog, Fairness and Accuracy in Reporting, or FAIR. The article, called *Time to Unplug the CPB* argued that congressional conservatives have used CPB as a tool to restrict programming with narrow political limits. They charge that public broadcasting bias is indistinguishable from commercial broadcasting bias. "It's not the innovation engine it claims to be because innovation requires risk but risk threatens funding," they said. It's not the first time opponents to CPB funding on opposite sides of the political spectrum have agreed (if for different reasons to remove it from federal support.

For example, this view was reinforced by a 2005 report in *The Nation* magazine. Former CPB CEO Kenneth Tomlinson, an appointee of President George W. Bush had, in 2003, written a letter to PBS President Pat Mitchell concerning the program *NOW with Bill Moyers*. Tomlinson felt the show didn't "contain anything approaching balance that law requires for public broadcasting." Author Scott Sherman for *Current* said that PBS "worked to accommodate the needs of a more conservative CPB, by 'quietly letting major producers know that it wanted proposals for programs that would add conservative balance to the schedule,'" Despite those letters, and new conservative shows launched the following year, Sherman said at the time that the changes weren't sufficient for Tomlinson, "and his CPB continues to squeeze PBS."

PLEDGE: The Public Radio Fund Drive

Some respected voices in public broadcasting support the idea of breaking away from the federal money once and for all. One of them, David Giovanonni, is a noted public radio researcher. In 1995, having come off of the success of *Audience 88*, a seminal study of the giving habits of public radio users, Giovanonni wrote about ending federal support in an article titled, *Can Public Radio Replace Federal Funds with Audience Sensitive Income?* He says, "Public radio can survive cutbacks in federal subsidies, but only if these funds are reduced no more rapidly than public radio can replace them with listener support and underwriting." He provided a plan to help it get off those subsidies, a three-to-five-year "glide path" to zeroed-out federal support. He warned of fast moving changes to the availability of that funding in the mid-90s. But some calculating shows, considering later research says the average public radio donor gives about $144 a year in contributions (the average American gives $1.38), each of public radio's 2.8 million givers would need to give $159 a year to make up for the $446 million loss. Though supporters are not overly concerned that support will disappear, reductions could be devastating in their own way. Although it is true that NPR receives a tiny amount of its funding directly from CPB (1% in 2015), member stations rely on it much more heavily. On average, one out of every 11 of their dollars comes from CPB, highlighting one of those times when NPR may not want to represent all of public radio. And since these stations may or may not represent NPR, questions about attacks on "NPR's" funding, and who exactly is being attacked, start getting fuzzy. ☎

Public Radio's "*Basket*"

"Because funding for public radio comes from several sources (institutional support, corporate sponsors and individual donors), Ragusea said the industry could be particularly resilient to inter-ference from the government, sponsors or major donors."

—Poynter's Ashley McBride in May 2017, on Adam Ragusea's comments of how public radio deals with threats to its funding.

A Congressional Research Service report said that in 2016, CPB received nearly $3 billion from all of its sources of revenue. That's more than six times the $446 million Congressional appropriation for 2018 through 2020. That support, from corporate, business, state, federal, private givers and "other" makes up the so often referred to "basket" of public radio support. But this money is not as reliable as it seems. For example, state support for public radio as of 2017 had been falling for several years. Consequently, some states use accounting maneuvers to delay, avoid or claw back payments to non-profits.

In 2008, the nation's nonprofits took a collective hit of about $150 billion in lost state funding. And as money from states has dried up, stations are drawn to corporate contributors. Stations take steps to maintain their reporting objectivity, such as by erecting "firewalls." But more than one writer has examined how business contributions can over time, breach those protections. The *State of the Media* 2016 report from the Pew Charitable Trust showed that underwriting grew 14% between 2009 and 2016, from $163 million to $189 million. A bright spot for pubcasters is during the same seven-year period, Pew noted that listener contributions grew 10% faster, from $242 million to $317 million. Public radio researcher Paul Jacobs told 2013 PMDMC attendees that underwriting didn't seem to effect how public radio listeners view its credibility.

He told them, "You have something that money can't buy —
your listeners trust in you so much that that trust transfers to the
companies that sponsor you," This "halo" effect was first noticed
in a study NPR conducted in 2003. Jacobs said positive attitudes of
listeners to corporate sponsors of the network hadn't significantly
changed since 2010.

Institutional support, like that from the Rockefeller Foundation,
funds projects like its 2014 "Reconsidering American Economic
Security," which directs money to issues the foundation considers
worthy of attention. The $1.3 million grant to PRI facilitated
reporting on people still struggling to recover from the effects of
Superstorm Sandy. The foundation wanted stories of "resilience,"
or what it calls "making people, communities and systems better
prepared to withstand catastrophic events - both natural and man-
made - and able to bounce back more quickly and emerge stronger
from these shocks and stresses." This was how they wanted their
money spent. But such directed funds can sometimes be controversial.

In 2016, the Ploughshares Fund gave with the intention to only
support NPR reporting on work the fund was doing in Iran.
Though NPR Ombudsman Elizabeth Jensen said there was no
breach of the journalistic firewall, John Sexton, for the Townhall
Media site, *Hotair* noted, "According to Jensen, the system at NPR
is that reporters are not told if NPR is being paid for particular
reporting, that way they aren't biased by the knowledge of who is
paying." "This," said Sexton, "sets up an absurd situation in which
the person writing the checks to NPR can waltz in and do an
interview which he knows his group paid to support even as no one
interviewing him knows that." He says in this case, "ignorance is
not bliss." NPR's 2014 annual report shows a total of 376
corporate and foundational supporters. The network's much flashi-
er 2016 report split corporate and foundation givers while showing

their total numbers had grown to 619. By then, corporations out-numbered foundations by a more than 2 to 1 ratio.

Finally, there's money stations and networks can generate on their own, like investment income and unrelated business income (UBI). The National Council of Nonprofits says a non-profit has a fiduciary responsibility to protect its assets and may put its money into securities. But the 2008 financial crisis showed that market forces or unethical behavior by financial advisers can destroy any non-profit's portfolio. At the height of the Great Recession, the California Public Employees Retirement System (CALPers), one of the largest and most respected funds in the country, lost 38% or $100 billion. Public radio itself talked little about how it was impacted by the Great Recession. But the Pew 2016 *State of the Media* report noted that listener contributions were at their lowest point in 2009.

NPR's 2014 Financial Report showed $204 million in operating revenue, $14 million of which came from "other" income that was not grants, station dues, underwriting, revenue from the Public Radio Satellite System or distributions from its endowments. By 2016, that same pie chart included an new slice called "Investment Income," which totaled between 2% and 4%. Like the network, public radio affiliates also have a variety of income streams to follow. An NPR pie chart of their overall revenue shows money comes from the government, corporations, foundations, colleges and universities and loyal listeners. Those that include "other" show it as a tiny slice. But that tiny slice in public radio's income basket deserves a closer look.

The IRS defines Unrelated Business Income, or "UBI" as "money generated from any on-going activity of your organization when the activity itself does not directly further the organization's exempt purpose." For example, remember how Bill Kling helped start *Signal* and *Wireless* magazines to sell *A Prairie Home Companion* gift items to Minnesota Public Radio devotees? The IRS had a hard time seeing the connection between a multi-million dollar catalog operation and MPR's charitable purpose, which mirroring its mission statement, was to "Enrich the mind and nourish the spirit, thereby enhancing the lives and expanding the perspective of our audiences, and assisting them in strengthening their communities." And the way the agency sees it, UBI generated that's not directly serving the non-profit's mission is suspicious. So, though not illegal, the IRS tends to bog non-profits down for the ambiguity "other" related income can cause.

The Foundation Group, a Tennessee-based non-profit assistance organization, says the IRS requires a UBI to have its own tax filings, which can double the paperwork burden at tax time. And the non-profit must pay corporate tax on the business even if all of the money it made went to supporting the non-profit's tax exempt activities. Though it may sound unfair, the Foundation Group says allowing a non-profit to make money without paying the same kind of tax a business doing the same thing pays gives the non-profit an unfair advantage in the marketplace. MPR spun off its for-profit catalog company, called Rivertown Trading, in the late 90s. Until then, RTC was bringing in nearly 25% of the MPR's total revenue, way too much UBI as far as the IRS was concerned. That's because public radio stations, as 501c non-profit organizations, don't pay federal tax. And their contributors get a tax deduction for gifts they make to the station. The IRS monitors the flow of money through stations with its Form 990.

Stations with more than $25,000 of income a year must submit one. The IRS uses the 990 to tell whether a non-profit is public or private, which in turn, decides how much tax it pays. Stations may call themselves "non-profit," but the IRS uses several tests for determining the percentage of money they're getting from public contributors or the government to also call themselves "public" radio stations. Those tests are the *Public Support Test* and the *Facts and Circumstances Test.* Of the two types of non-profits, private foundations get less favorable treatment than public chari- ties. That's because Congress, who set IRS rules, considers private foundations that are supported by large endowments or some other non-public income less beholden to the public good than a public charity that depends on a steady stream of public contributions. If, for example, as few as 50 people each gave 2% of a station's total support, that would qualify it as a public charity. It's not that organizations must fundraise to satisfy the IRS, but they must raise money from the public and that is most often through fundraising. To qualify as an "other than a private foundation" (like a public ra- dio station), a non-profit has to demonstrate that either at least one- third of its financial support comes from a mix of government and public money, or that at least 10% of its income from that mix meets various other tests, like having an organizational structure with a board of directors and a fundraising mechanism that is constantly searching for more contributions.

Suppose for example, that radio station X does have some large donors. "And if," says Lisa Nachmias Davis of Davis, O'Sullivan & Priest LLC in New Haven, Connecticut, "given the mechanics of computing public support, the station can't say it gets one-third of that support from 'the public' because 'Big Donor' gives one big $1 million gift while "the public" gives a bunch of little gifts totaling $200,000." Then, says Davis, it fails the test because although the total support is $1.2 million, total "public support" gets calculated as $224,000, which is the small donations of $200,000 plus 2% of total support of $1.2 million. Since $224,000 is less than one-third of $1.2 million, the non-profit fails the public support test. But it may pass the *Facts and Circumstances* portion.

The IRS's *Facts and Circumstances Test* is subjective and objective. The objective part requires public support be at least 10% and that the organization be continuously seeking that support. The subjective part is:

1. One-third support is better than 10%,

2. A lot of little donations are better than a few big ones,

3. Everyone must be asked for money,

4. The organization should have a government sanctioned structure, and

5. Its facilities and programs are accessible to the public.

Returning to the example, the public gives in small but direct donations, $200,000 which is just over 16% of $1.2 million. If all of the other requirements are met, the non-profit passes the *Facts and Circumstances Test* and can call itself a "public" non-profit. David Molnar, commenting on *Philip Greenspun's* weblog in 2009 had a slightly more pessimistic view of the quest for public support. "Still, it wouldn't surprise me if one of the motivations for these pledge drives is to survive an IRS review of the nonprofit status ... the way the law is set up leads to some odd incentives for organizations that force them to do public fundraising even if their "business" model would not otherwise require it."

Public tax records for public radio stations can be found at any of the popular charity watchdog websites, including Guidestar, Charity Navigator and ProPublica's Nonprofit Explorer. But Ms. Davis believes some of the information may be redacted since donors don't have to be identified. And she's skeptical as to how many stations meet the one-third portion of the *Public Support Test.* "In any event I suspect that due to corporate underwriting and private foundations, many stations might not meet the one-third test and that could be an additional reason for pledge drives and fundraising generally. The other reason may simply be the there is never enough money and they can never be sure when the sustainers will stop sustaining." The *Public Support Test* is in Part II, Section C of the IRS Form 990. Ms. Davis calls this obscure corner of IRS nonprofit tax law "tough sledding." Large amounts of publicly disclosed money don't protect a non-profit from scrutiny either.

If a non-profit spends more than $500,000 in a single year, it can be targeted for a federal audit. Jon Pratt, executive director of the Minnesota Council of Nonprofits, commented for a 2005 story about this conflict as it related to Minnesota Public Radio's entrepreneurial success. Speaking to the Stanford Social Innovative Review, Pratt said, "This is the plight of the nonprofit sector today. It is both told to be more businesslike, and then attacked for being too businesslike." ☎

Direct Federal Grants

"If you are going to sin, sin against God, not the bureaucracy. God will forgive you but the bureaucracy won't."

—Admiral Hiram Rickover, *New York Times*, Nov. 3, 1986

Federal agencies can choose to provide direct grants to CPB, regional networks or individual public broadcasting stations. These grants are different from the Community Service Grants that are part of the Congressional appropriation provided by the CPB in that they do not pass through CPB. CPB tracks them though to know a station's NFFS, which affects how much support CPB gives them. Federal agencies give grants to stations so they can tell their stories or promote specific initiatives in the public interest. Although as a general rule federal agencies can't lobby Congress or advertise, they can educate the public on their mission.

PLEDGE: The Public Radio Fund Drive

Federal agencies that give money to CPB and public radio
operate websites that show the public which entities have gotten
money, how much, what for and when. The easiest of these to
navigate is USASpending.gov. Begun in 2008, it shows that as
of late 2016, approximately 21 public radio stations in 13 states
have received between $4,000 and $45 million in direct federal
grants. USASpending.gov is not as detailed as some of the other
federally operated public accountability websites. But it does show
whether a station received a federal loan, a grant or contract from a
federal agency. It also shows the "sub-awards," which is money
stations paid entities with whom the station may itself be seeking
some kind of good or service, like a subcontractor. And it shows
the purpose for which the money was transferred. The total amount
in grants, loans and contracts from federal agencies to all stations
between 2008 through 2017 is nearly $233 million. The public
can also submit a Freedom of Information Act request (FOIA) to
any federal agency to learn if it has given money to a public radio
entity.

Six public radio stations in a single state were the largest group
of federal grants recipients. But in an eight-year period, those
stations together got only $4.1 million. Compare that to a single
station, which between 2008 and 2016, received more than $120
million. And the agencies giving that money ranged from the Department of Energy (DOE) for Pell Grant and work study information, to the Department of Commerce (DOC) and its support of
public telecom facilities, to arts and grants help for the National
Foundation for Arts and Humanities. Other grantors, lenders and
contractors ranged from NASA to Housing and Urban Development (HUD) to the Small Business Administration (SBA). And
from the Department of Health and Human Services (HHS) to the
Department of Homeland Security (DHS).

Speaking of DHS, NPR's Ombudsman, Elizabeth Jensen, has addressed NPR's acceptance of DHS money in light of its controversial searches of passengers at airport security lines, it's questionable treatment of the undocumented at detention facilities, its suspect facilitating of unlawful employment terminations and its illegal detainment of bona fide visa-carrying foreign visitors, and naturalized citizens to the United States. NPR says that acceptance of that money, while reporting on such incidents, only proves its ability to be impartial.

The hazards of relying on federal grants was highlighted in a March 2017 article in the *Columbia Journalism Review*. Co-authors Justin Ray and Carlette Spike said that although NPR and PBS get a relatively small amount of money from federal grants (including the Congressional appropriation), smaller stations and their local news operations are in "particular danger." In 2017 and 2018, President Trump introduced budgets intended to "zero out" funding to the CPB from which many smaller stations get double digit funding. Ray and Spike say that although those cuts aren't likely to happen, "the proposal is still bad news because the White House [Congress] and Senate are all controlled by the same party, giving Republicans a greater ability to pass a final bill that looks like Trump's proposal. This means public radio and television broadcasters are still in hot water." Direct federal grants, in contrast, don't come through the CPB. But as federal agency heads are installed that suit the administration, a fair question is will that grant money continue to flow?

Finally, it's important to mention the cost of doing business with the government. CPB, the overseer of NPR, grants money to stations who must in turn, spend many of those same dollars on NPR programming. Of WAMU's $6 million worth of expenses in 2007, $1.5 million went to NPR in programming fees. In 2016, NPR raised carriage fees by nearly 5%. This change, coupled with growing production, staff and administrative costs, force some stations to operate on thin margins. But a recent change in federal rules now requires federal, state, county and municipal entities that contract with non-profits to reimburse them for services they provide as part of that contract. They now let non-profits be reimbursed if, for example, secretarial services were used to conduct the work as part of the government contract. And that can make a significant difference in how the non-profit's bottom line is affected. ☎

Corporate Underwriting

"Making and keeping your underwriters happy provides you with benefits that go well beyond simply having satisfied customers. Happy underwriters are more likely to send more business your way via referrals, and that's invaluable."

—Gordon Bayliss, writing for Greater Public in 2015

"There have also been some less headline-grabbing incidents of unchecked power that seem almost quaint (but are no less appalling): Billionaires who use their money and power to influence what gets shown, or not, on public television."

—*Bloomberg View*, William D. Cohen, June 10, 2013.

In the United States, public broadcasting has both been called a public service (like a library that anyone can use because everyone pays to support it) and a public utility (like a water bureau that anyone can use but each user must pay to use it). In recent years, however, public broadcasting has had to behave more like a utility to have enough money to operate like a service. As state and federal funding has dropped, resulting in part from a changing political landscape, stations have had to rely on more underwriting. Although some argue that underwriting comes very close to advertising, public radio points to the technical distinction set by the courts, like this one after a 2015 decision denying public broadcasting access to money from political advertisers. "Congress recognized that advertising would change the character of public broadcast programming and undermine the intended distinction between commercial and noncommercial broadcasting."

Corporate underwriting, aka "sponsorships," function by a business giving money to a pubcaster in exchange for announcements that benefit the corporation. That benefit could be promoting its goods and services or longer-term political goals. A 2015 study by the American Press Institute showed that about half of the funding for non-profit news organizations came from entities that also wanted to influence government policy decisions in those same areas of reporting. It helps if the corporation's good or service is something the average listener uses, but it's not always necessary. Hearing an underwriting credit for GE appliances is something many listeners can relate to. A GE underwriting credit for its financial services may be more tightly focused on business. But underwriting about GE in its role as a defense contractor may give the general listenership pause in a "How does this apply to me?" kind of way. Yet it is a major underwriter of public radio. There have been other examples.

In 2008, attorney Patrick Lamb with Chicago's Valorum Law Group questioned the growing number of boutique law firms that were either paying for underwriting credit, or were in-studio with the hosts during pitch breaks. Lamb and other attorneys have asked if the average public radio listener cares that high-end law firms are advertising on their local stations. Still other attorneys say name recognition is what's important, and it can only benefit firms to hear their names on what one 2015 article called, "The hottest auditory advertising avenue of the year." But as stations try to form the deepest personal connections with listeners as they can, Lamb seems to be saying high-powered underwriting pleas can jeopardize those connections.

Underwriting grew quickly in the 1970s after President Nixon attacked public broadcasting for what he considered an unfair exposé by public television on constituent relationships with big banks. In response, pubcasters looked for money from non-governmental sources to insulate itself from political enemies. Corporations and foundations, seeing public broadcasting's increasing audience of loyal, educated and financially well-off listeners, turned their attention to the new market. Though they expected to navigate public broadcasting like they had navigated commercial broadcasting, consumers had different expectations. And despite a provision in the 1934 Communications Act that requires radio stations to identify sponsors, it's how those ads speak to them rather than what they say that can make underwriting annoying to the public radio audience. Although, it's important to make a distinction between network versus local underwriting credits. NPR has found that its listeners don't find its own underwriting credits annoying because, since its listeners trust NPR, they see the underwriting as relatively unobtrusive. In fact, network underwriting is designed to not interrupt programming.

Local underwriting, however, especially when lumped in with pledge drives, is seen as highly intrusive, even rude. That's why, besides getting listeners to become contributing members, pledge drives rely on games of chance, gifts and contests to keep people listening long enough to hear the underwriting and of course, give. Underwriting rules for mainstream public radio can be found in *Guidelines for National Program Service Programs*. Even the feisty Prometheus Radio Project produces a guide that helps stations distinguish between underwriting and advertising.

But all underwriting must follow rules. Among them, it can't have calls to action: there can't be something telling the listener to do something like pick up the phone or visit. There can be no mention of price or cost of whatever the sponsor represents. Underwriting announcements must use flat but specific language like, "Support for this program is provided by ..." Network underwriting credits tend to be in "pods" of up to three at a time. Together, no pod can last more than 60 seconds with no individual credit being longer than 15 seconds. Sometimes, stations stretch local underwriting credits by either stretching the length of pods or separating pods of three or less underwriting credits with an unrelated announcement. These rules were developed to make underwriting sound as little like piled-on commercials as possible.

Guidelines also had to be flexible enough to deal with "fuzzier" language. Examples include the use of official ratings of product quality, like DOE's "EnergyStar" in underwriting spots, or references to company slogans that themselves, sound like calls to action, such as Walmart's "Save Money, Live Better." In 2011, APM's *Marketplace* was criticized by *Bad Seed Blog,* a production of Natural News for underwriting announcements for Monsanto that encouraged listeners to "Learn more at ProduceMoreConserveMore.com."

Public radio stations must sound non-commercial to get the legal and financial benefits, like not having to pay for a station license, being eligible for certain grant programs and not having to pay federal income tax. If stations violate those rules, set out in the *Public Broadcasting Act of 1967*, fines can be steep. At one time, those rules were even tighter. But NPR, PBS and several other entities petitioned the FCC, claiming that the restrictions choked off revenue. They said because the tighter rules made it so that public radio listeners couldn't clearly identify underwriters, companies got no benefit from advertising on public radio and were choosing to not spend their money there.

The FCC in 1981 allowed public radio stations to more specifically identify the names and products of their underwriters. Soon after, the money the stations earned from underwriting soared from $4.2 million to $7 million. And stations reported that another million was sitting in their pipelines. Later, a congressional committee agreed to let looser underwriting guidelines stand because, even in 1981, it recognized that the rate of the increase of federal support was slowing. So the question of "identification v promotion" comes up a lot. And now, as before, listeners aren't convinced that underwriting isn't in fact, advertising.

Listeners to Woodlake, California's KUFW must have been asking themselves that very question when they heard the station, owned by the Caesar Chavez Foundation, "broadcast four different advertisements over 2,000 times between March 2006 through December 2008." For that, the station received a $12,500 fine. In 2016, a pledge drive for Delmarva Public Radio showed this thinking is common even among public radio employees. "And another thank you, as far as I'm concerned," said Hannah Miller, "goes out to all the underwriters who support our programs with their (pause) underwriting, which is NPR-speak for advertising." And during a November 2016 pledge drive break, Columbia, Missouri's NPR station, KBIA, played a 30-second underwriting announcement for the Naught Naught Insurance Agency. Although the phrase "live protected" halfway through could be argued to be a suggestion rather than an action step, the spot was full of unmistakable, jingle-like music. CPB guidelines forbid for-profit underwriting with music since such announcements can sound too much like a "commercial." PRI follows these and FCC rules, but imposes its own as well. It restricts underwriting credits "where the public might reasonably perceive bias in program content based on the public position or interests of the underwriter."

The Corporation for Public Broadcasting deals with this question frequently. CPB's audience feedback section, *Open to the Public*, included a listener complaint that local PBS affiliate WGBH was essentially running "infomercials" for a business selling a treatment for diabetes. For many years, listeners to Pacifica stations, including KPFK, have complained that the underwriting within the station's continuous pledge drives are full of relentless selling and questionable claims. But PBS viewers and NPR listeners too have noticed that public broadcasting pitch breaks seem to contain an increasing number of authors and musicians, physicians and attorneys targeting baby boomers. CPB's response to the comment was a stock answer that could be found throughout the site: "Note from CPB: Please understand that CPB is prohibited from interfering with programming decisions." In other words, CPB claims no responsibility for the underwriting choices made by individual stations. But a series of incidents have raised enough questions for stations that they themselves are trying to reduce their dependence on CPB as a funding source even though, some argue, that is driving them further into the arms of corporate money.

NPR Ombudsman Elizabeth Jensen fielded audience concern with public broadcasting in 2015 when listeners complained that the network was airing underwriting credits from flooring manufacturer Lumber Liquidators. Earlier in the year, CBS News had reported that the laminate covering the material the company installed in people's homes allowed the escape of poisonous formaldehyde gas. The question bombarding Ms. Jensen from all sides, simply expressed, seemed to be, "Why is my NPR taking money from Lumber Liquidators?" Jensen defended the network, saying NPR news followed up on the reports. And at the story's conclusion, Lumber Liquidators was identified as an NPR sponsor.

That oversight had taken previous hits, however. In 2013, Jane Mayer of *The New Yorker* and her piece, *"And Now A Word From Our Sponsor"* examined the repercussions of a program that aired on WNET New York public television that spoke to wealth inequality for people living at opposite ends of Park Avenue. The CPB-funded production, *Park Avenue; Money, Power and the American Dream*, focused on 740 Park Ave, the address of WNET board member and station supported David Koch. Mayer's story tells of how, in an unusual move, the station manager called Mr. Koch to warn him of the show's content and find ways to mitigate any uncomfortable outcomes. Koch was on track to contribute millions of dollars to a station capital campaign. After the program aired, the capital improvement donation was never made. A second program, *Citizen Koch*, an exposé that focused on the conservative Koch Brothers, funded by CPB and also scheduled to air on WNET, never aired at all. Although NPR and public radio are not PBS and public television, they are both under the administrative authority of CPB and have similar ethical guidelines.

Public broadcasting content seeks the same freedom from corporate influence as it does from government influence. NPR's ethics handbook holds network objectivity above the ability of underwriting sponsors to affect news coverage. There are few funders from whom NPR will not accept financial contributions and report on. But the "firewall" often mentioned as the barrier between news and sponsors "isn't an impassable boundary" as the handbook also says, "but rather a barrier designed to contain the spread of a dangerous or corrupting force." "Similarly," it continues, "the purpose of our firewall is to hold in check the influence our funders have over our journalism." It is a confusing definition since it makes one wonder if the "impassable" boundary is passable or not? William Siemering, NPR's first program director, said in an interview that when he was managing a public radio station in Philadelphia, the station received support from Sun Oil, the parent of Sunoco. "I wouldn't even introduce any of the news staff to the person we were working with at that company because," said Siemering, "I did not want them to be influenced by anyway like saying, you know, let's say there was an oil spill. 'I think, well, you know, gee, John was really a nice guy. I better take it easy on this.'"

That was his rule. In August 2012, *Current* reported that WBUR was approached by a hospital seeking to buy some underwriting. But the hospital wanted "a direct role in the editorial process in exchange," as in the hospital wanted to help write its own ad. But program hosts can sometimes be complicit in the confusion. On November 21, 2017, WBUR *Here and Now* host Robin Young interviewed Kym Cantor, president of the faux fur company House of Fluff. After several minutes of conversation, Young ended the segment by saying, "OK, so that was a commercial. But, whatever." Examples like this, as the *NPR Ethics Guide* warns, seem evidence that businesses may get special treatment or do have influence over journalism. The network itself has drawn raised eyebrows with what it calls "embedded underwriting." The aforementioned *Current* article refers to Ally Bank's support for NPR's *Planet Money.* It was enough for the Poynter Institute's ethics expert, Bob Steele, to wonder, "whether this particular bank is getting a special deal for whatever reason."

Such conflicts in public broadcasting are not new. During 1992 Senate hearings on the funding for public broadcasting, children's science show producer Liz Schlick said the PBS children's show *Newton's Apple* had to deal with lots of "behind the scenes influence enjoyed" by the program's sole corporate sponsor, chemical company DuPont." Some things we would want to deal with such as chemical pollution. But [the executive producer] wouldn't let us touch [it]." Though the programming for public broadcasting can be groundbreaking, it can't be earth-shattering. Pat Aufderheide, writing for the *Columbia Journalism Review* around the time of those Senate hearings says it another way. "PBS's offerings are indeed splendid, but they are 'safely splendid.'"

Producers in and outside of public broadcasting acknowledge, the more averse CPB feels to support risky programming, the less support it gives to those producers. Those producers then go to corporate supporters who, although they provide money, may be even more restrictive. Pubcasters have other struggles with corporate underwriting, such as compensation for salespeople who secure underwriting agreements. Many public radio underwriters migrate to public radio from commercial radio, and are used to the same arrangements. But the Association of Fundraising Professionals' *Code of Ethical Principles and Standards* forbids "compensation based on a percentage of contributions" and "finder's fees." The AFP doesn't want it to look like fundraisers are chasing commissions, which can compromise the trust relationship between donors, stations and listeners. Some stations contribute to the problem by compensating their underwriting staff more for new givers than for renewals of existing givers. Unbridled commissions can generate bad feelings in-house, especially between salespeople who may be compensated for underwriting sales versus other staff or pitchers who may not be compensated for helping a station reach astronomical pledge drive goals. But stations that limit commissions can suffer high turnover of underwriting staff. ☎

State Money

"I've enjoyed programming on NPR, but 'we're broke' and therefore all spending must be reduced."

—Jaime Herrera Beutler, U.S. Congresswoman for Washington State's 3rd Congressional District

Direct and indirect state support of public radio is at best spotty although state control, where it exists, is absolute. An example of that ultimate power was demonstrated in 2011, when former Governor Chris Christie of New Jersey declared a fiscal emergency and announced a plan to slash state spending. By June, he had used his line item veto to remove nearly $1 billion from the New Jersey budget. That move coincided with his June 6th announcement to end state support of the state-operated New Jersey Network. The network, which since 1991 served areas of New Jersey not reached by signals from New York or Pennsylvania, consisted of four stations. They were sold to New York Public Radio on June 30, 2011, the day before the end of New Jersey's fiscal year. In 2017, a consortium sponsored by media advocacy group Free Press, introduced Senate Bill S3303 and Assembly Bill A4933 to the New Jersey Legislature. It was an effort to inject $20 million into the state's suffering public media infrastructure. Unfortunately, the twins moved into the state's Higher Education committee, where not voted on, they died when the legislative session ended. The consortium pledged in 2017 to reintroduce the legislation.

About half a dozen states own all of the public radio station licenses of their state-run, non-profit public radio networks. They include the Wisconsin Educational Communications Board in partnership with the University of Wisconsin, the Alabama and South Carolina Educational Television Commissions and the Mississippi Authority for Public Broadcasting among others. These entities are different from, say, Wyoming Public Radio, which although operated by a state university, is not under the direct control of Wyoming state government. In 2001, state tax dollars spent by universities dropped from 23% to 12%. On-campus stations likely felt the hit too.

One in five public radio respondents to an informal, author conducted survey said their station has a lobbyist representing it in the state legislature. But that presence doesn't always result in state support. Stations also depend on in-kind support, like the kind

Montclair University provided to New York Public Radio, purchaser of the four New Jersey Network stations (re-branded as New Jersey Public Radio). The two collaborated to find a new home for the New Jersey news bureaus on Montclair's campus. A university building paid for with taxpayer money could be considered in-kind support since the state is technically providing material rather than a cash donation. And it may be easier for the university to give than cash. But other indirect support, as when a college pulls from its budget to run a campus radio station, can easily disappear if the legislature pulls back on university support.

In June 2016, Geoffrey Mearns, President of Northern Kentucky University (which owned WNKU), announced in an email that NKU will "explore the possibility of a sale" of its radio station in the face of "significant funding cuts from the state." The story, reported by the Northern Kentucky Tribune, also said that in a unilateral decision, Kentucky Governor Matt Bevin announced a 4.5% cut from Kentucky's colleges and universities. That slashed more than $2 million from WNKU's budget. In February 2017, the university's Board of Trustees approved the sale of the station to Bible Broadcasting Corporation. The station, an alternative music leader since 1985, was sold for $1.9 million. WNKU was only one of several stations across the country forced to cut back or shut down when state funding was reduced. In 2016, the Mississippi legislature, which funded 65% of Mississippi Public Broadcasting cut MPB's budget by nearly $900,000. Ronnie Agnew, MPB's Executive Director told *Current* the cuts take the station's budget back to 2006 levels. But in an example of the kind of leatherneck pragmatism that has shaped public radio, Agnew said of budgets, "You know they've been cut over the years. You don't cry. You just pick yourself up and figure out what you can do."

Universities are sometimes forced to sell their licenses to get needed money to fulfill their core educational mission. When

Cincinnati's WVXU sold the licenses of its X-Star radio network in 2005 to the fledgling Cincinnati Public Radio, insiders said Xavier University wanted to use the money to fund construction on campus. If they're lucky, colleges and universities like KUNV, can keep their frequencies in the public radio family by selling them to other public radio entities rather than to commercial or religious broadcasters. In 2014, the University of Las Vegas managed to sell its station to Nevada Public Radio, despite objections from students, volunteers and listeners who didn't want it sold at all. And though religious broadcasters often snap up licenses of public radio translator stations, sometimes, in a rare move, they let go of a station that public radio can then acquire.

Market forces often squeeze state budgets. In 2016, Joseph Lichterman reporting for Nieman Labs, a project of the Harvard School of Journalism, told of how stations throughout parts of Oklahoma, North Dakota, Wyoming and Texas suffered cutbacks because of falling oil revenues to states. As a result, unfilled station positions remained unfilled. Some stations have responded by having public radio employees "volunteer" their time to do work other than what their taxpayer supported station is paying them for. This happened in 2010 when West Virginia's state-run Educational Broadcasting Authority asked if station workers, who are essentially state workers, could help two non-profits that generate funding for West Virginia's public media outlets. Even Governor Joe Manchin's office had to weigh in on the impropriety. These "Friends of" types of non-profit organizations can provide substantial help in supporting government run entities. The "Wisconsin Public Radio Association," for example, is actively involved in fundraising to support Wisconsin Public Radio. But keeping money and responsibilities separate can be an ethical and administrative challenge.

PLEDGE: The Public Radio Fund Drive

In a 2011 edition of *The Atlantic*, Brian Resnick reported on an analysis by Free Press. It looked at cuts in 24 states to public media between 2008 and 2012. During those four years, they collectively eliminated $202 million in support to their public radio and television stations. By 2017, at least seven more states had either reduced (AK, CT) or eliminated (CO, IA, RI, TN, VA) support. Fairbanks, Alaska based KUAC left the Alaska Public Radio Network and turned off its HD FM service after state cuts in August 2017 forced it to function on 22.5% less state funding. I contacted each of the 50 states between April 6, 2016 and June 28, 2016 asking for information about their budgets. Twenty-seven states responded. *Free Press*, news reports and author queries combined showed that between 2008 and 2016, at least 25 of 35 states reduced support to public broadcasting. Reduced tax revenue, loss of industries, increases strain from pension plans or a drop in state investments have forced states to pay for only the essentials, of which public broadcasting may not be one.

But it's worth noting that governors propose their state budgets. Between 2008 and 2012, 15 state governorships oversaw 15 cuts to public broadcasting support of the kind that hit South Dakota Public Broadcasting in 2011. SDPB Executive Director Julie Anderson told the Keloland Media Group that program cuts and up to seven impending staff layoffs were coming. Then Republican Governor Dennis Daugaard asked the South Dakota legislature to slash the budgets of many state agencies by up to 10%, but SDPB's budget was cut by more than 16%. Between 2015 and 2016, another ten states cut their public radio and TV budgets between 5% and 100%. A bright spot is that between 2008 to 2012, and 2015 to 2016, ten states seemed to make no funding cuts to their public broadcasting. Although in some of these cases, legislators were not clear as to whether state budget changes would affect support for state public broadcasting. So it was not certain if those states would or wouldn't reduce funding.

124

Many states that do support public radio and TV distribute state appropriated funds using the same 75/25 split that CPB uses for radio and TV. In some states, a station gets state support if it has CPB certification. In these cases, stations outside either the university or state owned system may still get state support. In others, only stations operated by state institutions can get state money regardless of whether CPB legitimizes them or not. A 2007 report showed that the largest piece of a 20% slice of Minnesota's non-profit appropriations went to education related activities. Of that, public radio and television was included. Funding in Minnesota is relatively healthy. But in other states, the attacks on funding by legislatures seem vindictive. The Free Press analysis said that budget cuts on stations are "disproportionately large when compared to overall budget cuts." Alabama, for instance, decreased overall state spending .2% but cut its support to public radio and television by 38%. *(See appendix)* ☎

Foundations and Philanthropy

"Charity aims to relieve the pain of a particular social problem, whereas philanthropy attempts to address the root cause of the problem."

—Wikipedia.

Government and corporations can tie strings to their financial support. But foundations can also restrict how recipients of their money spend it. And that can create tension between philanthropies that want their money used the way they intend versus the recipient not being influenced by the donor's implicit or explicit wish. In an ideal world, these two are in harmony but sometimes, they aren't. That's when dividing lines become necessary. The erecting of a firewall between major giving and editorial departments at NPR came after the historic Joan Kroc gift. At the time, NPR Ombudsman Jeffrey Dvorkin emphasized, "There cannot be strings attached to the money. If it goes to foreign coverage, for example, it cannot go specifically to Middle East coverage." But Dvorkin also acknowledged the tightrope public radio recipients of large donations like Mrs. Kroc's must walk. "If we're doing a piece that involves a funder, are we being unduly hard on them because we know they are an underwriter, or are we pulling our punches?" Large gifts to public radio are not unheard of, though not that large. But if NPR's CEO, Jarl Mohn has his way, Ms. Kroc's gift will be considered among the smaller donations in a future of what he foresees as full of mammoth gifts.

In September 2014, Mohn spoke with the host of Oregon Public Broadcasting's midday news program, "Think Outloud." Fundraising, he told host Dave Miller, was the most important of all the hats he wore. And when he said he wanted to work with stations to raise even more money, you could hear the hair on the back of Miller's neck stand straight up. "What do you mean, 'working with stations?,'" Miller asked. Mohn said NPR's plan was to help local stations find donor money from individuals who are known in public radio as "Major Givers." These are six-figure or larger givers in a community a station serves that it hasn't managed to find. Then, said Mohn, the network splits that new money with the local station. He said "we" haven't done a very good job soliciting those donors and implied that not doing so was leaving money on the table.

Miller responded with all due respect, that he knew people in the very building in which they were sitting who worked very hard each day to raise enough money to keep their own audience happy. He said he could imagine them saying, "I'm scared. You're going to come in and skim off the dollars and take money away from member stations." Mohn said the initiative is purely voluntary, and that stations had to feel that more money can be raised with NPR rather than without it. Once stations get a few of those big checks,

Mohn said their attitudes tend to change. And when the subject came up about the Kroc gift, which itself was about a major giver giving not only to her local station but also to NPR, Miller said that gift seemed like a "once in a generation kind of check." Mohn replied, "You're thinking small."

Ideally, member stations share their donor lists with NPR, as well as prospects which they have already, or have not yet, approached. List sharing identifies high value donors, their motivations to give and which type of approach might work best. Givers who can give no less than $100,000 and foundations that can give $250,000 are prime targets. According to an article in *Current*, the 2015 arrangement, supported by a 12-station consortium (including OPB) seems to be bearing sweet fruit for stations and the network. NPR's sifting of station lists tends to find between two and ten untapped, high value donors per station with the spoils being evenly split. Through mid-2015, the approach has netted NPR and at least ten stations more than $8.3 million. But the arrangement seems not widely known, or talked about. An informal author survey to people in and around public radio asked, "As far as you know, has your station entered into an agreement with NPR to allow it to mine your membership lists for high value donors?" Nearly 69% of respondents didn't know. The one in three that did, said no. Only about 3% said "yes." Though still not at the level of the Kroc gift, the idea is gaining traction.

Mohn, Ira Glass, Bill Kling and others think the best way to get public radio out of its poverty mentality is to make major givers realize the importance public radio plays in their lives and the lives of their communities. Kling said the problem of being stuck in the poor mode came from the days when radio stations were part of university speech or drama departments. Heads of those "classical" methods of communication felt threatened by the electronic medium and turf battles for school money ensued. Plus, many stations still rely heavily on volunteers because they can't afford staff that could make them more professional. "Some are still like that," Kling said. But once "top flight managers with big visions" came in, he said they made an "enormous difference."

The feeling Mohn and others want to ignite in those big donors is "passion." But within public radio, the other battle cry may well be "freedom" as private donations help it move away from government money's history of influence and corporate money's appearance of influence. And CPB's Major Giving Initiative, shows this is not merely an idea within public radio but throughout all of public broadcasting. At the head of its 2012 *Guidelines for Ethical Fundraising* are 24 fundraising standards. MGI guidelines, which are a collection of best practices developed by stations, advocacy groups and others, try to cover every giving contingency from requiring fundraisers to report illegal behavior to policing donor/prospect interactions. Although large donors may have the right to visit newsrooms and meet reporters, stations can restrict contact to a simple handshake. When Dvorkin mentioned "pulling punches," he's talking about big money influence over reporting.

When the time comes that a reporter reports on something connected to that donor, nobody wants a long list of credibility draining disclosures and disclaimers dragging behind. But, in an effort to get more control over their donations, big givers have turned to restricted gifts, which force organizations to apply them the way donors want, refocusing on the issue of possible influence. And stations are not deaf to donor preferences. In late 2015, Minnesota Public Radio received an anonymous, $10 million gift. The areas where most of the money will be spent, namely classical music and music education are passions of the donor.

The Evangelical Council for Financial Accountability (EFCA), says recipients of gifts can ask for restrictions on the gift while other times, the giver imposes a restriction. And although EFCA emphasizes that donor and recipient manage the restrictions jointly, only donors may impose and remove restrictions, which can range from benign to significant. Also, the EFCA notes that restrictions can be explicit or implicit. Explicit in that they are spelled out in a letter to the recipient. Or implicit to the recipient, "if the circumstances surrounding the contribution make the donor's intended restriction on the use of the assets clear," For example, if during the course of a face-to-face meeting, the donor writes a check to a non-profit's representative while verbally indicating what the donor wants the money spent on. "Although the donor did not indicate the purpose of the gift on a response form or on the check," the EFCA notes, "the specific fund-raising solicitation and the immediate gift constitutes an implied donor restriction." The ask by the non-profit, and the response to the ask by the donor together, determine the intent of the restriction.

Non-profits can be funded by several types of foundations. Which type they are determines how they give and what they can expect in return. For instance, while community foundations pool community money for community benefit, donors within that pool have the freedom to direct their money. In 2012, the Tulsa Community Foundation gave over a million dollars to 44 nonprofits in eastern Oklahoma. The Community Foundation of Boulder County in Colorado funds *The Public Affair*, a news/talk program on radio station KGNU that explores local issues ranging from health to civil engagement. Public foundations, to be considered public, have to meet strict tax requirements that insure a fixed percentage of their income come from individuals, not large entities. Otherwise, they may be considered private, requiring them to pay much more in tax. But public foundations (like many public radio stations) must also have a plan for raising money from that diversity of donors. So public foundations must be very responsive to the needs of the people they serve.

But most probably think of the private foundation when they think of philanthropic giving. The John S. and James L. Knight Foundation, a major contributor to public radio, is one. The Bill and Melinda Gates Foundation is another. These family trusts are more independent and controlled by a relatively small group of people. They tightly focus their efforts on one or a handful of causes. The Nonprofit Legal Foundation says for such a family, a benefit of a private foundation is that it "enables you to pass values on to future generations." And when family foundations put those values to work, it can sometimes be a surprise. The Rockefeller family, founder of Exxon Mobile, also funds the Rockefeller Foundation which, in turn, funded the Pulitzer Prize nominated journalism that resulted in reports on Exxon Mobile for its role in climate change. Public foundations can show impressive integrity. But it's one of several examples of how family foundations and the companies they've founded can be on confusingly opposite sides. The Adolph Coors foundation, created by the family famous for the Adolph Coors brewery, supports gay-friendly policies while the family itself created and supports the anti-gay Castle Rock Foundation.

Charity First, a San Francisco based underwriting and risk management company for non-profits, identifies three reasons why an entity might not want to accept a philanthropic donation. First, it's too small, and there's no extra for any use other than what the donor intended. Next, it's too big, meaning that although it may help create a lavish initial infrastructure, the non-profit might not be able to sustain whatever the money establishes after the gift runs out. No gift is unlimited, just as there's no guarantee that future gifts will match previous ones. The Melville Trust, a long time contributor to NPR, has seen its giving fall from more than a million dollars in 2006 to $300,000 in 2017. Still, underfunded programs caused by such fluctuations can, according to Charity First, make future donors and recipients wary. Third, the money is coming from the wrong source, creating a moral or ethical mismatch. The Girl Scouts of Western Washington turned down a $100,000 donation in 2015 because the anonymous gift was made with the stipulation that none of the money be used to support any transgender children. It was a red line that the non-profit refused to cross. In the aftermath of the anonymous offer, the chapter raised $200,000 in a subsequent one-day crowd funding campaign. In all three cases however, fundraising experts recommend trying to work with donors to find uses for the gifts and preserve the possibility of a long-term relationship.

Though stations depend on major gifts, most staff rarely interact with major givers. But at pledge drive time, pitchers interact with thousands of ordinary listeners, each of whom is deciding where their money can do the most good. They may be new givers to public radio, or trying to divide limited money among several causes they care about. This has led to awkward moments when a pitcher encourages listeners to give to the cause they "get the most from," or "that contributes the most to your life." Nearly 79% of respondents to my survey of public radio professionals felt that encouraging listeners to ignore other non-profits in favor of public radio did not make stations look good. Though probably not intending to pass value judgments on the causes to which people should give their support, or the social value of non-profits that are not public radio, it can certainly come off sounding that way. ☎

Individual Giving

"If everyone reading this gave just $1, we would be finished with our fundraising in an hour."

—Wikipedia founder Jimmy Wales

One problem is everybody reading doesn't give a dollar. Some give more, some give less and some give nothing. Some give, but later. Some don't give because they feel public radio is already getting money they don't want it to have. Some give but to other causes with the feeling that it all supports the community. The other problem is that costs keep climbing. In 2018, Wikipedia banners no longer ask users for $1, but $2.97. The situation is similar in public radio. Public radio researcher John Sutton said that in 2008, the average public radio contribution was $80, but by 2011, had grown to about $144. He says one of the biggest problems for pubcasters is convincing listeners to become givers despite what they may know or not know about how public radio is funded. "Research consistently shows listeners are not clear about public radio's funding sources, despite decades of efforts to educate them," he says. A fundraising principle is that when people listen, they give. And the numbers show they are clearly listening. In 2006, more than 800 member radio stations collected $275 million from individual donors. In 2014, Sutton told *Current* that the public radio economy was built on $432 million in listener contributions. That same year, *Current* reported that 440,000 new givers had been added to public radio's member lists, bringing the total of givers to 2.94 million. Meanwhile, former PRX CEO Jake Shapiro told Mark Fuerst of *Current* in 2015 that the total public radio economy is estimated to be about a billion dollars and that individual contributions account for about $350 million of that amount.

That 2014 influx of givers added nearly $53 million more to public radio's bottom line, but didn't move public radio's base beyond the psychological barrier of 3 million paying members. Breaking that ceiling was the goal of the 3MG.org campaign in 2008. Co-sponsored by NPR and Development Exchange (now Greater Public) the initiative was an effort to raise the number of givers from 2.5 million between 2005 to 2008. In 2006, public broadcasting was so unsatisfied with its progress that the CPB commissioned a study by David Giovanonni called, *Losing our Grip*. It was one of several analyses of the state of membership in his subsequent *Audience 2010* report. Shapiro told Fuerst that he noticed a similar stagnation in public television more than 20 years earlier. In 1995, PBS had a peak of 5 million givers, but in the following years, that number fell to the same 3 million as public radio is at now. Shapiro wanted to know how TV got to 5 million and why did it fall to 3 million? For radio, he expects the rut is because of expansion of the number of ways people can consume public radio. He talks of the difficulty stations have following a listener from terrestrial radio, to digital and back. Without that ability, public radio can only guess how many people are truly using it and consequently, how many people are willing to support it.

Stations are constantly looking for ways help them increase donations without breaking the law. KPBS had such a breakthrough in 2005. Jim Lewis, for *Current* described how KPBS was trying to understand why a certain, high value segment of its audience wasn't contributing as much as it could even though it was getting the science, government and arts stories it wanted. The station's fundraising people realized those programs were too spread out. They worked with station management and the news department to package those stories into eight "content-specific funds" that gave those listeners what they felt they were missing. Big donors could now give to what they cared about most and donations rose.

KPBS CEO Tom Karlo called the idea a "Restricted, unrestricted" grant. It was expected to bring in nearly a quarter-million dollars per fund for the station over three years. But some have asked if the station created the special programming categories as a tool for soliciting money from major donors? And does that put programming decisions in the hands of listeners with the ability to compel stations to adjust them to their wishes?

It's worth mentioning, as Michael McCauley did in his 2003, *Public Broadcasting in the Public Interest* that high value audiences, whether underwriters or listeners, are public radio's target. Although public radio says its shows aim at similar thinking people, not specific demographics, examples of programming that seems tailored to the interests of high value givers are rampant. It may be politically incorrect to say out loud, but as McCauley points out, "Public radio broadcasters cannot afford to waste resources targeting audiences whose financial support is less reliable." Ironically, those tend to be the demographic groups public radio most often says it is trying to reach. *Audience 98* he says, "warned programmers against potential damage to the target audience if public stations adopted a different 'sound' in order to attract these less demographically desirable listeners."

Stations are on a never-ending quest to find new ways to reach existing segments of their market. "Day-sponsoring" is one such idea. Wilmington, North Carolina's WHQR says on its web page that for $180, a personal, non-promotional, non-political, non-event promoting, language specific statement from a contributor can be read up to six times on each of its two frequencies for the day sponsored. For instance, beginning with, "Thank you to our day sponsor ...," a listener or an entity can pay to wish someone happy birthday, good luck or get well, but that's it. Like underwriting language, day-sponsor language is devoid of action steps. It credits the contributor for contributing and nothing more. But as benign as day-sponsoring sounds, it can be its own minefield.

In 2016, Michigan Radio refused to run a day-sponsored birthday greeting to the nation of Israel. According to the story by the *Jewish Telegraph Agency*, Hannan and Lisa Lis paid for six announcements throughout the day. Lis, whose mother is Florine Marks, the CEO of Weight Watchers, Inc., was first told the station needed two months to schedule the announcement. But later, she received a letter that the station would not air the birthday message. Michigan Radio told the couple, "We have determined that this message would compromise the station's commitment to impartiality and that it crosses over into advocacy, or could imply advocacy." The *JTA* story included a link to Michigan Radio's website which explained that the station wouldn't air any announcements, "referencing political campaigns, candidacies, religious convictions or legislation."

Other ways stations find to increase contributions is through a throwback to what used to be called "Family marketing." Namely, stations encourage employees and volunteers call friends and family to get them to become contributors. These kind of call-out programs, familiar to anyone who has worked telemarketing in real estate, insurance or banking, are stations squeezing the last drops out of every opportunity to make their goals or increase needed membership numbers.

In some public radio bullpens, stations have incentive programs for phone volunteers that resemble bingo cards. Fill up the card with X number of calls or sign ups, and get gifts ranging from bumper stickers and bookmarks to lower level premiums like caps or t-shirts. In a YouTube video from 2016, LA based fundraiser Peter J. Heller calls this core group of family and friends at the center of a diagram of concentric circles, the "nucleus." "And over time," says Heller, "you have to figure out how to use this group of people to effectively connect to the people who are somewhat further out." With call-out programs, stations have figured this out. ☎

135

Other

*"If we are to improve public service to local communities through
increased station journalism and digital capacity, we must find
additional, sustainable revenue streams."*

—Dana Davis Rehm speaking in *Current*, July 14, 2008

On the expenses side, the money flowing through CPB helps
public radio stations buy programs, support special projects and
fund CPB itself. NPR's costs are for its satellite operation, programming and music development, digital services, news, engineering and other program-type support. Local stations spend their
money on NPR shows, community outreach, fundraising, member
services and salaries. On the income side, money for everybody
is a combination of federal grants and appropriations, direct and
indirect state support, corporate underwriting, philanthropic giving
and money from "listeners like you." But in many of those revenue pies, a small but not insignificant piece is "other." What is in
"other"?

"Other" income for local stations, which can total tens of
thousands of dollars, ranges from 8% for Wisconsin Public Radio,
to 4% from Ozark Public Broadcasting, to 2% on Nashville Public
Radio's WPLN site, to 1% at Indiana Public Media. NPR averages
it out for local stations to about 7% nationwide. It includes gains
and losses on investments, emergency fund drive type "capital
campaigns" (for big ticket items like transmitters), money made
from side businesses like catalog sales, and "Special Fundraising
Activities" like concerts, fairs and other events. Everett, Washington's KSER said in a 2010 pitch training manual, that 25% of total
station revenue comes from renting space on its tower. Fordham
University's WFUV tells listeners that it makes money when they
shop via the station's Amazon, iTunes and Good Shop links.

WGBH's Media Access Group provides captioning and other services to broadcast programs like the CBS hit *NCIS*. It also captions YouTube videos and transcribes program audio for a fee. In other words, "other" is everything covered by Part VII of Schedule D of IRS Form 990. Part VII is one of twelve sub-parts of the Schedule D *Supplemental Income* section. It includes all assets, including liquid assets that can be spent immediately like cash. And it includes illiquid assets that take time to convert to liquid assets like art, land, buildings, equipment, endowment funds, etc. But there's more than cash being given, like volunteering. It's worth, some argue, needs to be part of the calculus of what stations consider valuable to their cause. Researcher John Sutton says that individual giving, the basis of pledge drives, may be supplemented by other efforts by stations to raise money. "What's likely to happen," he said in 2005, "is that stations will try to develop alternative forms of income such as car donation programs, on-line shopping affiliate programs, and the direct selling of products to listeners."

Crowdfunding has seen the arrival of many self-funding sites including Kickstarter, Indiegogo and Patreon. Changes to securities laws promise to help this interesting way of raising money get free from what had been entangling finance regulations. In response, stations and producers can tap a whole new way of funding that doesn't involve a pledge drive. The language to describe what crowdfunding does, however, is still in flux for some digital executives who struggle to avoid the dirty word, "paywall." Mans Ulvestam, a co-founder of the Scandinavian streaming platform "Acast" talked with Harvard's Nieman Labs in a 2016 interview and didn't sound like a fan. Ulvestam said crowdfunding, "wasn't a business model. That's just begging." But as far as Kickstarter is concerned, that's just so much talk. In December 2016, the Poynter Institute said that the crowdfunding site created a new category specifically for journalism. PRX producer

Roman Mars used Kickstarter in 2012 to fund his successful *99% Invisible* podcast. The program, which looks at hidden meaning in architecture and design, raised more than $170,000 with the help of PRX, which has also been airing segments of the show within another PRX program, the wildly popular *Radiolab*. Interestingly, in 2015, PRX moved away from Kickstarter as a funding platform to create its own. It got 13 of its Radiotopia podcasts to ask listeners to donate on a sliding scale. Then PRX Chief Operating Officer Kerri Hoffman said in 2016 that they made the choice because, "We wanted to build the infrastructure around our own user database, which you really can't do if you use another platform."

Big influxes of one-time money, though a launch pad for new voices, can also silence them when the money dries up. And spectrum sales, a complex version of one time money, is when stations sell a portion of their unused frequency in exchange for cash they need to better serve their audiences. Charges fly that the wrong people are made rich by the sale of those coveted spots on the dial while not diminishing the need for pledge drives. ☎

Sales & Investments

"If wishes were fishes, we'd all cast nets."

—Old Scottish nursery rhyme

And if dollars were pounds, Bill Kling's Minnesota Public Radio made a 60,000 ton profit from the sale of Rivertown Trading, home of *Signal* and *Wireless* magazines, in 1994. Kling drew a new line for bringing in money, though stations had to walk it with care. If their unrelated business income (UBI) got too big, the IRS would make stations pay for-profit sized corporate tax. Kling sold Rivertown to the Dayton-Hudson Corporation, later renamed Target, in 1998. By 2000, the retailer had kept only six titles while folding others into the Marshall Field's catalog which it relaunched in 2002. But unimpressed by sales, Target rid itself of Signals and Wireless in 2004. Both are now owned and operated by Universal Screen Arts, a catalog sales company based in Hudson, Ohio.

Catalog sales of public television gifts remains a respectable portion of revenue. The Direct Marketing Association says that in 2007, 11.8 billion catalogs were mailed, even though over the next six years, numbers stagnated. Signals, which says it's "For fans and friends of public television," promises on its back cover to support program development for WGBH by feeding it a percentage of sales for every item it sells. Though it sells videos and DVDs, its selection is not as extensive as that offered at the PBS.org website. Meanwhile, public radio has the "NPR Shop." And in September 2017, NPR added to its offering by launching the NPR Wine Club. For about $80 plus shipping per year, members get monthly bottles of Malbec, Cabernet Sauvignon and Merlot. They'll even come with paring notes and serving suggestions.

Items on both NPR and PBS sites are public broadcasting branded. To get locally branded "thank you gifts," listeners go to the websites of individual stations. These pledge drive related hats, mugs and t-shirts are tightly aimed at the local audience, often designed by local artists or cross-marketed with local businesses and non-profits. Still, the Quarterly *E-Commerce Report* from the U.S. Census says that online sales represented more than 9.5% of total retail sales in 2018. Though it's not known how much NPR earned from shop.npr.org, NPR's "other" category (which includes sales and investments) made more than $13 million in 2016. That's $2 million more than it earned in 2015.

Some stations separate investments from "Other" revenue. Others combine individual giving and corporate giving in the same slice, but that can make separating them impossible without a financial statement. The rest of "other" investment income found within Schedule D of the IRS 990, includes charitable trust and gift annuities, alternative investments, investments in LLCs, and still more "others." Those can include the cost of fixed assets like land, buildings and equipment as well as their depreciation, or how much it costs to maintain those things over time. And, it shows endowments (large gifts from which stations are periodically allowed to withdraw fixed amounts).

Though the categories themselves fluctuated, revenue within public radio's "other" was a steady until recently. From 2008 through 2014, the amount of money stations, in the aggregate, made from "other" hovered around 8%. In 2014, when CPB's annual *Public Broadcasting Revenue Report* included investments for the first time, there was a noticeable drop in "other" income. It fell from an average of 9.45% between 2011 and 2014 to 6.1% beginning in 2014. Through 2015, that is where it remained. The 3.35% difference is likely the annual revenue NPR's investments have earned it in the three years for which information is available.

Market securities in which NPR or member stations invest is not publicly available. But NPR's 2017 balance sheet showed $412 million of investments. Isabel Lara of NPR Media Relations says the network liquidates securities it receives as gifts from individuals almost immediately. Otherwise it would be trying to manage tiny pieces of thousands of stocks and bonds. Ms. Lara said it makes more long term planning sense to have a policy to sell those gifts at the market rate as soon as possible. As a non-profit, it pays no dividends and has no shareholders. But as a corporation, it does have a fiduciary responsibility. Woods Bowman, writing for *Non-Profit Quarterly* in 2011 said, "The fiduciary duties of non-profits tend to have more of a moral basis. A membership association has a clear duty to its members." Bowman says the investments a non-profit manages are mostly its endowments. According to *Current*'s Mike Janssen, "In 2004 NPR's budget

increased by over 50% to $153 million due to the $235 million
Kroc gift." About 7% of the money was deposited in its endowment, which was $35 million before the gift. Considering the rash
of state cutbacks, falling listener contributions and ongoing attacks
from members of Congress, it's a safe bet that the network intends
to focus more on investments in coming years.

A relatively recent change to NPR's bylaws allowed it to
expand the number of board members to 23. Twelve of those represent
member stations and nine are what it calls "prominent" members
of the public, which include five finance and investment advisory
firms. The network's 2014 Form 990 shows it spent more than
$300,000 on investment services. The remaining two board members
are the NPR foundation's chairman, and CEO Jarl Mohn. Mohn,
NPR's president since 2014, is a seasoned executive and experienced
in fundraising and meeting shareholder expectations. Mr. Mohn has
served as advisor, director, president or CEO of more than a dozen
companies or their divisions, throughout media and entertainment
since 1986. Although he brought more entrepreneurial focus to
NPR's financial independence, and an increased emphasis on sales,
investments and major givers, his November 2018 announcement to
step down in 2019 again spins the network's revolving CEO door
while forcing it to consider a new direction. ☎

One Time Money

"That's terrific Daffy. They loved it. They want more!"

"I know. I know. But I can only do it once."

*—Daffy Duck's ghost explaining to Bugs Bunny why the ultimate
magic trick is unrepeatable.*

"Show Biz Bugs," a Warner Brothers classic, has Daffy drinking
gasoline, nitroglycerin, gunpowder and Uranium-238 to outdo Bugs
onstage. Then, he swallows a match. Spectacular, yes, but one-off.

Likewise, over a nearly 20 year period, many states got a piece of the settlement from the lawsuit against cigarette makers to compensate them for health care they provided to people made sick from smoking. Then, after the attacks of September 11, more states received money from the federal government to upgrade their communications infrastructure so first responders could better talk to each other on emergency networks. And in 2009, "shovel ready" project money flowed into many states in an effort to jump start the economy during the Great Recession. In all cases, it was practically an explosion of cash... but it didn't last forever.

For stations, one-time money can mean money over time but only for a fixed length of time. When that money dries up, the shows and special projects can go away. Here, supporters of these shows aren't just buying a flight of spots for six or eight or ten weeks. Instead, they are putting up money for a year or more with a much deeper, ideological stake in the program. But even those stakes can get pulled up. Some of the programs that lost funding include *Open Source*, a news and public affairs show that aired on PRI and its partner, WGBH Boston as well as the University of Lowell's WUML. Christopher Lydon, also host of WBUR's *The Connection* hosted *Open Source* until it was canceled in 2006 due to a lack of funding. The show lives on as a WBUR podcast.

Justice Talking was a production of the Annenberg School of Communications and hosted by NPR veteran Margot Adler. Noted for its legal debates, it too ceased in 2008 due to a lack of funding. *Common Ground*, an award-winning focus on international affairs, and recipient of the Robert F. Kennedy award among others, went silent in 2004 due to a lack of funding. And most recently disappeared, APM's The *Dinner Party Download*. Described as "an hour-long celebration of culture, food, and conversation," DPD launched as a podcast in 2007 and an on-air show in 2010 with *Marketplace* alums Rico Gagliano and Brendan Francis Newman as its hosts. It was announced in late October 2017 that the show would end because production costs were growing faster than its audience and ongoing funding could not be secured. If the disappearances prove nothing else, it's that nothing in public radio is a sure thing. Ideally, each show would attract sponsor support based on a cost per thousand (CPM formula). That means for every thousand people who'd hear the sponsor's name, the sponsor would pay the show $X. So if producers expect to reach an audience of 100,000 per show, and the CPM is, say, $25, the underwriter pays show producers $2,500 per episode.

Jake Shapiro says some podcasts have CPMs of $100 and may reach millions of listeners. Perhaps, with all four was the hope that they would eventually make the jump to larger syndication and eventual listener support. But they didn't. These shows, often started by staff with a passion, end with pushing their creators into more stable parts of the operation like development, membership or underwriting. Or even out of public radio altogether while teaching the lesson that creativity must be its own reward. "I don't really feel like I have anything to lose," explains OPB's Julie Sabatier who owns and markets the podcast, *Destination DIY.* "If no sponsors are interested, fine, then I won't count on any revenue from this podcast network … I've lost nothing."

Something out of the public eye but hugely consequential to public broadcasters are so-called "Spectrum sales." The concept is simple. FCC issued licenses let licensees transmit on one or more specific frequencies. Joint licensees, those public broadcasters that hold licenses for both radio and television, converted their TV broadcasts from analog to digital in 2008. Many realized they had unused portions of their frequencies that they could sell. Spectrum sales let them sell those unused spots to buyers who would then put them to use. That's the concept. The process, managed by the FCC, can be complicated. Bidders compete, first to underbid, then overbid each other on available frequencies. Businesses and manufac-turers remaining, who have created new products and services that use those frequencies, buy them and then, apply for licenses to use them. Wireless companies like Sprint and AT&T, which already own huge chunks of the spectrum from previous sales wait for new auctions, finding new uses for new frequencies. In 2016, the 600 Mhz block, valuable because of its ability to penetrate walls and travel longer distances, opened up to bidders.

That sale brought the U.S. Treasury, via the FCC, tens of billions of dollars. Since 1994, 87 such auctions have earned the government nearly $60 billion. By April 2017, at least 34 pubcast-ers with valuable, high-demand frequencies, had earned nearly $2 billion. Somona, California's KCRB collected $72 million in early 2017 by giving up its original channel and renaming its call letters for Channel 22. CEO Nancy Dobbs said the change should be "unnoticeable to the public." For many, the rush of cash lets stations pay off debt while allowing others to grow their missions by expanding programming, upgrading equipment or improving community outreach. When it instituted the auction, Congress' goal was the best use of frequencies for the market and for the public. Auctions have not been without criticism, however. Some have questioned such a market-based method of allocating what are sup-posed to be the public airwaves. And for those stations that have sold off portions of their frequencies, it's an opportunity many will only have once. In 2014, NPR did something similar when, accord-ing to its IRS Form 990, the network sold off excess capacity from its Public Radio Satellite System.

Finally, in what some would consider a close call in the "one time money" quest, a December 2013 ruling nixed the possibili-ty of political ads for public radio. For context, when incumbent Barack Obama ran against challenger Mitt Romney for President in 2012, both campaigns raised more than a billion dollars each.

That same year, congressional races raised another $4.3 billion. Wells Fargo Securities guessed that advertising costs alone for the 2016 presidential election would reach $6 billion. Although political campaigns use donations to hire staffers and consultants, fully 80% of all campaign contributions go to TV and radio ads. An earlier 2012 federal court ruling cleared the way for public radio to start airing political ads, and more importantly, getting a significant piece of that ad money. But speaking for the majority in a rare, 11-member *en banc* session of the 9th District Court of Appeals, Judge M. Margaret McKeown said, "Congress recognized that advertising would change the character of public broadcast programming and undermine the intended distinction between commercial and noncommercial broadcasting." That Judge McKeown makes no distinction between commercial and political ads shows how both Congress and the courts felt either could be poisonous. In 2018, political ad revenue could have generated $564 million for radio. Since public radio represents about 1/15th of all radio stations in the U.S., it's conceivable that it could've earned at least $37 million from ads annually.

It's also conceivable that the commercial broadcast industry breathed a sigh of relief from that 2013 decision since it wouldn't have to share that money with hundreds of public radio and television stations. For some struggling pubcasters, the court decision was a body blow that prevents public radio from reaching its potential rather than preserving it. But the decision also blunted a political possibility. Scarborough, a Nielsen reporting service, shows that of the 31% of public radio listeners that identify as democrat, another 14% that identify as independents lean democratic. Those listeners also tend to financially support their local public radio stations and vote in higher numbers than the general public. So denying political ad money to stations whose millions of loyal, wealthy, highly educated and politically aware listeners only listen to public radio must have set the opposition somewhat at ease. ☎

Crowdfunding

"I used the principles of Kickstarter to make 'She's Gotta Have It.' We filmed that in 1985 to 1986. The final cost was $175,000. I didn't have that money. It was friends, grants, donations. We saved our bottles for the nickel deposit."

—Filmmaker, Spike Lee

Crowdfunding can be full of surprises. NPR's *Planet Money* team found that out when, in 2013, they decided to make a t-shirt. The 2008 financial crisis inspired the network to launch the show. It simplified all of the talk of traunches and collateralized debt obligations and did it so well that it became part of the finance curriculum for some schools. Five years later, show producers decided to make a t-shirt to show how labor and supply chains around the world contributed to making this piece of cheap, but ubiquitous clothing.

Planet Money launched a crowdfunding campaign on April 30, 2013 with a $50,000 goal that covered the estimated $41,000 in material costs. What was left over would go into an education program for journalists. The amount of Kickstarter contributions passed NPR's meager goal by May 1, 2013, eventually sliding to rest at $590,000 thirteen days later. NPR was reportedly 'pleased' with the results, but local stations may have been less so since the campaign was, in a sense, an end-around that supported only one specific network initiative. On April 30, NPR sent stations a note saying the campaign wouldn't be promoted over the air, lessening the criticism. Janko Roettgers presciently explained station fear in a 2012 piece for Gigohm: "Radio producers that directly connect with their audience online are circumventing a key piece of the public radio puzzle: the local affiliate. Over decades these affiliates have been licensing shows and paying for them through their pledge drives. Changing listening habits have slowly been eroding

146

this relationship, with audiences increasingly tuning in through podcasts and mobile apps as opposed to the local broadcast signal." Crowdfunding, he says, could disrupt that relationship even more.

But though the network promised to not promote the t-shirt to member stations, it would be promoted everywhere else, including NPR.org. Though not cutting stations and their pledge drives out of the loop, project leader Alex Blumberg was clear as to his hope for the project in a 2013 interview with Gigohm: "One of the reasons why it seemed like such a good fit is that public radio and the NPR model already involve reaching out to listeners and supporters directly, so it seemed natural to blend the two." At the time it ended, NPR's Chief Marketing Officer, Emma Carrasco declined to say what if any effect the campaign might have on future direct listener contribution efforts.

In 2012, *99% Invisible* producer Roman Mars asked Kickstarter donors for $42,000 in support but raised $170,000, and later $375,000. In a comment board post, Mars dismissed its "magical" success, owing it instead to a lot of hard and deliberate advanced work. "The reason why *99% Invisible* hit its initial goal in about 24 hours was because *99% Invisible* had been releasing episodes for a year and a half and built a good following online (thanks in large part to *Radiolab*). That time to grow was a luxury provided by the support of an amazing local station (KALW) and then later a distributor (PRX) who believed in the project and invested accordingly." Mars and former PRX CEO Jake Shapiro, overseeing the creation of PRX's Radiotopia, pulled in another $600,000 from Kickstarter for that project in 2014. As for charges of bypassing stations for direct support, Mars told *Current* in 2012, "I'm not bypassing stations. For the most part, they're bypassing me." It was a reference to the fact that at the time, only ten public radio stations were airing his show. But he's made it clear he doesn't need to turn his podcast into an hour-long, network-style program.

Crowdfunding, also known as peer-to-peer giving, is subject to limitations. Some people want to give but can't give very much. This is where the pay-what-you-can model comes in. Stations will take whatever amount people give, though their systems may not be set up to integrate odd payments in their already established ladder of payment options. Many stations have a minimum gift of $30, though walk-ins can hand over whatever sized gifts they can afford to give. Although the PWYC model has made a name for itself, most notably with Denise Cerreta's One World Everybody Eats nationwide network of community kitchens, no station relies on it completely. And critics say no entity realistically can unless they also have a stream of steady payers. Meanwhile, some stations equate crowdfunding and fundraising. When Montana Public Radio launched its 2014 version of the "Montana Food Bank Network Challenge," MTPR's Fundraising Director, Linda Talbot, told the University of Montana's *UM News*, "Public radio and television stations were the pioneers of crowd-sourced fundraising. We've been going directly to our audience to fund Montana Public Radio since 1976, and they always come through for us."

On the other side of crowdfunding sits longtime public radio observers like John Sutton. Sutton said around the time of *99% Invisible*'s success that if public radio becomes over-reliant on crowdfunding, it ends up focusing shows around only the few thousand people who support them. The implication is that mass popularity may not have the clout of big monied supporters, who can direct the programs they want while ghettoizing the less popular ones. And crowdfunding can be a crapshoot. Capital campaigns for equipment can succeed while appeals for programming can fail. In his analysis of crowdfunding's impact on public radio, Richard McPherson writing for *Current* in 2013 noted that its success depends not on a bunch of small, short-term gifts but rather, building what he calls "a cohesive funding community." Kickstarter campaigns are stories that must be told in support of raising money for

148

telling another story. As such, they must capture the imagination of givers just like public radio programming itself. It's worth noting that in the Nieman Labs piece about PRX's embrace of crowd-funding, even author Joseph Lichterman calls the money it raises "one-off." Apparently, even public radio knows it can't drink from the crowdfunded well too often. ☎

The Cable TV Model

"Because obscenity is not protected by the First Amendment, it is prohibited on cable, satellite and broadcast TV and radio. However, the same rules for indecency and profanity do not apply to cable, satellite TV and satellite radio because they are subscription services."

—FCC Consumer's Guide

Before Janet Jackson's infamous "wardrobe malfunction," the FCC's penalties for indecency, profanity and obscenity were a meager $35,000 per violation. After the 2006 Super Bowl, fines jumped to $350,000 and the enforcement got much stricter. Stations complained that the federal agency, never considered "a creative force in our culture" not only had the power to set technical standards, but now assumed it to set cultural ones too. But government involvement in setting morality standards is a long story. In 1992 Senate hearings on funding for public broadcasting, Senator Robert Byrd of West Virginia successfully introduced legislation specifically targeting public radio and TV, to restrict what stations could broadcast and when. Meanwhile, his colleague, Senator Robert Dole of Kansas, in criticizing a PBS program exploring gay life, asked, "Is this the kind of programming taxpayers and public TV contributors have in mind? I do not think so."

That's also not to say that "sh*t" or the "f-bomb" are essential for gripping storytelling. FCC rules specifically target the casual

149

use of sexual and excretory language. But the freedom print en-
joys, the same freedom that let *Radiolab*'s Jad Abumrad use both
the words "fuck" and "shit" in the same interview with the Guardian newspaper in late 2016, is, to some degree, enviable. A recent
Supreme Court decision allowed Asian musician Simon Tam to
call his band "The Slants." In a brief Twitter exchange in June
2018, I asked Mr. Tan, whether the right to use a racially charged
term contradicts future moves towards social justice. He replied,
"at the end of the day, my social justice work is more than just
this case. I don't care about legacy, I just want to change lives by
empowering the marginalized. At the end of the day, equity is the
goal." The decision, a technical triumph for free speech, guarantees
more creative and horrid band names in the future. All of them potentially blessed by the U.S. Copyright and Trademark office and
the Supreme Court while out of reach of the FCC.

But listeners wanting to hear such language might not hear it
on anything the regulator considers the public airwaves. Behind the
electronic paywall of subscriptions, that's another story. That there
are hundreds of directories to hundreds of thousands of individuals
emoting online isn't what keeps the FCC up at night. Instead, it's
that the FCC doesn't license subscription services like HBO or
Showtime, or distribution channels like iTunes, Stitcher or
Audible. No license means no control. And because the *1996
Telecommunications Act* didn't speak to Internet content, podcasts
are "fully exempt" from the agency's language restrictions.

Independent radio producer Greg Barron recently stressed
the importance of risqué over reserved in holding listeners. And
podcast producers are responding by deftly walking that line. Their
new shows promise more raw, long-form stories. They're guessing,
as Bronwyn Fryer said in a 2014 edition of the *Harvard Business
Review*, people want the tension between "personal expectation
and reality with all of its nastiness," as well as jumps in underwrit-

ing and advertising it may bring with it. The *Public Broadcasting Act of 1967* prohibits public radio from accepting ads. And of course, more sanguine content originally created for on-air public radio, like OPB's *State of Wonder* and WNYC's *Snap Judgment*, remain subject to all of the same restrictions if they move online. But as podcasters start making stuff with that familiar public radio "sound," what kind of surprises could they bring?

The *Chez Risque* Podcast, for one. Described as bringing "BDSM (Bondage, Discipline, Sadomasochism) into a new light," *Chez Risque* had seven airings in 2014 before it disappeared. Producer Master Marc said the show talked about "love, sex, relationships, and good old fashioned kink." And though it didn't appear at NPR or PRX, the program was on the ubiquitous iTunes. *WTF with Marc Maron* famously featured a conversation with President Obama in which he used the "n-word" when describing what he saw as the racial injustice issues facing the U.S. Maron found a way to monetize his podcast by requiring listeners to download a custom app that unlocks the episode and other special content. One of Time's ten best podcasts for 2017 was *Girl Friday*, which included an episode in which its three hosts spoke frankly about why the 2016 Women's March on Washington was important. Said Erin Gloria Ryan to her co-hosts Amanda Duarte and Brianna Haynie, "For the next four years, it's fuck or get fucked. And, I'm here to fuck." It's clear that *Girl Friday* has a strong working knowledge of FCC limits. For gamers, there's *Role Playing Public Radio*, aka *RPPR*. From Dungeons and Dragons to anime to the *Call of CTHULHU*, *RPPR* absolves itself from the language live game players might use with this brush-off: "We are adults, so keep in mind there will be some profanity." Commenter "Griffin" responded in 2011, "'Some' profanity?! Surely you jest!"

Podcast listeners want this kind of content, not re-purposed mainstream shows unaffectionately referred to as "shovelware."

Besides the sharp-edged sophistication, they're openly challenging the dominance of the tone of public radio, first by cloning it and then by exploiting it. But that doesn't make them distinctive or successful, just numerous. And while monsters like *This American Life* might share some of its famous revenue with its WGBH partner, each tiny voice in an ocean of noisy ones needs to tell one hell of a story to be heard, let alone make money.

Support, along with legality, is the other huge issue for podcasts and their public radio distributors. When a listener hears a podcast, to whom should they donate to support it? Listeners to pitchers during public radio pledge drives might hear them say something like, "When you listen to a podcast, you aren't listening to something that's free. Somebody had to create that content." But that's only part of the message. "We here still need your support because if you are hearing that podcast through this station, you need to help us continue to bring it to you." Even when listeners have made up their minds as to where they want to send their money, the directions they get can be inconsistent. Local stations are free to say listeners can hear their favorite shows on a station's own app, a distributor like iTunes, and aggregators like TuneIn. But programs, especially if they originate at the network level, practically never mention NPR's own player, NPR One.

In 2016, the network said it wasn't directing its audience to its own player because, it implied, older listeners might get confused. The more likely reason is that since local listeners are hearing the same shows on their local stations, those stations, who are also paying for those shows, don't want NPR bypassing them by letting those same listeners get those same programs from a different source. But stations can have similar fears about podcasts. An online commenter responding at *Wired*'s *The Long Tail* in 2008 defends the idea of supporting independent producers over the stations that air their podcasts. "My attachments are to individual shows, not to a broadcast station. My engagement with public radio is at a more granular level than the affiliate. I just don't care that much about KQED, and now that I've got another way to get the shows I like, I don't really feel much of a connection to it."

Commenter "garlic" queried *Metafilter* in 2013, asking if, because her money subsidizes WBEZ programs she doesn't like, why shouldn't she just give directly to the producers of the podcasts she does like? Cable TV subscribers have asked this same question for years. But cable providers fight legislation that lets viewers line-item veto specific shows, offering instead "packages" that still manage to cover the cost of shows the audience may consider clunkers. Acast, the Stockholm based podcast platform, lets users listen to a handful of shows on a sliding scale but doesn't make all the world's podcasts available to listeners. Public radio, by contrast, puts that powerful choice in the hands and hearts of its users. Respondents to commenter "garlic" were generally of the view that the money a giver feeds into the system, whether at the producer, station or network level, still tends to flow everywhere. But in light of shows that end because of poor support, designating specific directions of that flow isn't so easy to do. Support can also be lopsided. Stations can end up with piles of money for something popular and nothing for something less popular but just as, if not more, socially relevant.

Also, since podcasts aren't broadcasts, public radio has been experimenting with ways to include ads. But do it in a way that listeners don't find as offensive as the average 14-minute spot loads of commercial radio. In a 2015 article for the culture blog *The Awl*, reprinted from *Ad Age*, Ira Glass said, "My hope is that we can move away from a model of asking listeners for money and join the free market." "Public radio," said Glass, "is ready for capitalism." Technologies like Dynamic Ad Insertion are helping that happen by letting sales departments like those at NPR's National Public Media choose when to drop ads in and pull them out. This method, rather than produced shows in which ads remain forever, became viable after stations green-lighted the process in February 2016. The software looks for quiet spaces in shows, sometimes called "natural breaks" and discreetly inserts the ad. Listener annoyance is minimized while helping networks make lots of new underwriting money. But the real beauty of the technology is that the ads make themselves disappear after being heard by a set number of people, essentially guaranteeing advertisers are getting the number of listens they are paying for. The technology is based on research that shows listeners are OK with ads as long as they're gently inserted rather than packed like sand down their throats.

Finally, language issues happening in broadcast isolation that attract government scrutiny can have wide ranging effects on cable and perhaps, elsewhere. In 2011, Mary Elizabeth Williams wrote the piece, "Jose Luis Sin Censura" for *Slate*. AT&T and Time Warner yanked their support for the long-running Spanish talk show after homophobic comments infuriated the Gay & Lesbian Alliance Against Defamation and the National Hispanic Media Coalition. The FCC fined the show $110,000 in November 2013 for indecent and profane language. But the show, which had been airing for nine years on affiliates in LA, Miami and Kansas, had been breaking those language rules since the beginning. For some reason, ethnic slurs in Spanish on the public airwaves didn't attract as much FCC attention as ethnic slurs in English. After those fines, lawmakers in Congress revisited the idea of expanding FCC restrictions to subscription services. But if that line is crossed, would the agency stop there? The entire episode is a warning to producers. That cohort, representative of the coveted "youthful" demographic public radio pursues, is rewriting what public radio is by ratcheting up the stories it tells. Their efforts promise to keep their audiences riveted, and the courts busy. ☎

Pledge Free Streaming

"I was listening to an NPR show ... and a listener wrote in with a brilliant idea. I have no idea how it could be implemented on a radio, although it could be possible on the Internet. The suggestion was to give listeners some form of key that would "unlock" normal programming once one had contributed. Seems like a good idea to me; they'd probably meet their goals quickly if one knew one could end the pain by pledging at the beginning of the drive."

—Commenter *"Plynck,"* The Straight Dope message board, October 29, 2005

It is a brilliant idea. But Plynck wasn't the first one to refer to it. Commenter Steve Chapman, in a 2003 posting to newsblogs. chicagotribune.com had the same thought. "If the public radio folks want to increase membership, all they have to do is offer contributors a device that lets them block out fund-raising appeals. As I envision it, the station would offer regular programming to anyone who donates, and the gadget would be deactivated once those payments end. I can hear it now: "Join now, and you'll never have to listen to me whine about money again!" In 2011, Tod Robberson, a columnist for the *Dallas Morning News*, followed suit, imploring public radio to come up with a new way to get its money, rather than through "this outdated fundraising technique."

The idea of a "gadget" or a "key" that separates the shows you want to hear from the pledging you don't has been on the minds of ordinary people who have given this considerable thought. Comment boards are full of those who've dreamt of an electronic off-ramp from incessant pledging. But overall, what kind of thought has public radio given it? Turns out, a lot. New Hampshire Public Radio created a Survey Monkey questionnaire for asking its listeners what they thought of the idea. The technology essentially does exactly what it sounds like it does; it lets users hear a stream of pledge-drive free programming in exchange for tying your support to a code that lets your device receive that stream. But to date, a surprising number of public radio stations haven't put it to use.

There has been relatively little chatter about what one would think to be revolutionary technology, either inside public radio or in the mainstream since then. Kelly Williams Brown, writing for the *Daily Beast* in 2014, talked with WWNO General Manager Paul Maassen. "I asked whether there would be a time when those of us who are already members could magically skip the membership drive; it does feel unfair that those of us that dutifully pony up our $12.50 a month have to suffer with all the shirkers." "No such luck," said Maassen. "At least, not yet." But by then, it had already been three years since the technology had undergone its first successful use. So why the delay?

Pledge free streaming has the potential to generate more money for public radio than any of the other avenues discussed so far. Why is because since at least 50% of listeners hate pledge drives, removing them lets listeners hear public radio the way they watch Netflix. Think of it like a sustaining membership but with an Obamacare mandate. And when a reminder pops up on your device, like renewing your car insurance, not paying means no more pledge free stream. The technology, first debuted by San Francisco's KQED in 2011, at WBEZ in Chicago, and later, at New Hampshire Public Radio in 2014, has proven technically feasible. But commenter ERK, blogging on the "educatedguesswork" blog in 2011 noticed something shortly after KQED unveiled its pledge free stream.

The stream was a "gift" that had to be paid for separately and in addition to a pledge. From the KQED website; "Because the Pledge-Free Stream is a separate gift item, you must select it when

156

making your donation. For example, if you'd like to donate $75 and receive the KQED Wave T-shirt, you would still need to select the Pledge-Free Stream and give an additional $45, for a total of $120."

EKG suspects the option to choose a pledge free stream, which diminishes the reach of underwriters, is an accessible, but not necessarily friendly option. "I've been talking as if forcing people who have already donated to listen to pledge breaks was all loss, but arguably it's not. If nothing else, it forces those people to listen to a lot of free advertising for the station's sponsors (and especially to listen to the announcers pimping the various "gifts"). Allowing people to opt out to some extent diminishes the value those sponsors are receiving for funding the pledge drive, and perhaps diminishes their willingness to donate." Plus, as I was told by a giving officer at a public radio station, the technology is expensive for small stations that don't have the bandwidth to host it. Besides, if their sustainer program is robust, he says, stations might not need a pledge free stream.

Digital technology strategist Frank Catalano explains that the fact that it took two more stations three more years to adopt pledge free streaming shows reluctance to try the technology is high. "I think there is fear of losing the one-to-one connection and important info about listeners if there is an easy tech way to bypass pledge drives without interaction." For those who are reluctant to turn so many aspects of that interaction over to algorithms, this is a well-known fear. Vermont Public Radio, in answer to the perennial question of why station pledge drives are necessary said, "We know that VPR has more than 200,000 listeners a week from our 27 stations across the state. However, we don't know who many of those people are, or whether they like what we do. There's no better way to reach our audience and ask for support and feedback than an on-air drive."

157

Catalano says one cure is to "make pledge drives funny and informative. And short." But he also feels a big block to adopting it is generational. "Too many pub media staffers (and many listeners) may believe pledge drives are the castor oil of public media, required and 'good for you,' if unpalatable. Alternatives are suspect if they bend the model too much."

Public media's willingness to wear such a hair shirt is what he calls "the devil you know." But Catalano, a supporter of the technology, has ideas to adopt it gingerly, "like streaming the same stations' drive-less HD streams during broadcast stream drives." He says supporters of pledge drives are OK with saying, "We give," but won't stand for being lectured about giving. "I think, until it's proven to pub media execs' satisfaction that alternatives to long, boring, talky pledge drives work as well as the traditional model, listeners will need to find tech bypasses on their own." And they are, as witnessed by stations that have been trying out different kinds of drives within existing limitations for years now.

Some program directors, like KING Seattle's Bryan Lowe's see pledge drives as programming, not just "breaks in programming," say Catalano. That shift in thinking requires a lot more thoughtful consideration of what they need to sound like in the service of what they're designed to do, which is make money. For its spring 2018 pledge drive, Kent State's WKSU offered a pledge free stream for the very first time.

Meanwhile, WBEZ's pledge free stream requires a minimum, one-time contribution of $250 a year. Membership to its "High Fidelity" club gives access for $180 a year, but that requires a sustaining membership of $15 a month. By contrast, KQED offers pledge free streaming to its sustaining members but non sustainers can get access for a mere $60, one-time donation. But that access is only for an upcoming drive, not the entire year. ☎

Spending

"You're spending money on things that are not your future. You're spending money on things that are your past."

—Eric Nuzum, Former VP of programming for NPR.

According to its IRS Form 990, Public Radio Exchange's total expenses in 2015 were $7.7 million. PRI's operating budget for 2013 showed total expenses for program production, acquisition and distribution, human capital and other operating expenses to be $18 million. In 2014, total expenses for MPR & APM were about $88 million, including $10 million for fundraising. And in 2016, NPR's operating budget shows total expenses of nearly twice that of all four of its competitors combined, or $209 million.

Nuzum, speaking as an executive for Audible, told his peers that stations reaching more listeners wasn't about spending on technology to create podcasts simply to have podcasts. It wasn't about retaining lousy shows that don't engage the audience, or keeping fruitful shows in lousy time slots. Nuzum said those kinds of mistakes rob stations of the cash needed to do truly interesting stuff. It wasn't about how a lot of public radio talent is lured away from public radio to commercial storytellers like Gimlet, Midroll and Audible. And he said these things even as he admitted, "I don't even get paid to say this anymore." These are costly missteps most listeners probably know little to nothing about.

Plus, they may have wrong assumptions about how public radio should behave. First, many Americans have a romantic view that a non-profit's mission should be noble. Though donor money is supposed to be spent in support of a moral rather than a financial bottom line, that message can get lost when news reports tell of how stations use that money to pay high salaries or buy big, shiny buildings. The fact that non-profit stations need to compete with subscription based podcasting companies, both in terms of facilities and talent can be a heavy lift for public radio. It gives the impression that public radio is cash flush.

Corporate underwriting, the number of pledge drives, and the average gift per listener has gone up, while the number of over-all givers has dropped. Listeners get confused when they're told during pledge drives that the money keeps shows they love on the air, and then those shows disappear. In 2006, Detroit listeners responded to that mixed message. Maria Aspan, writing for the *New York Times*, reported that when WDET shook up its schedule by dropping shows and replacing them with newstalk, the station "probably expected some complaints from listeners. "What it got," says Aspan, "was a lawsuit asking for their pledge money back." Listeners sued, claiming breach of contract over shows that were cut just six weeks after the station's pledge drive was supposed to be in support of those very programs. This, in addition to the fact that by 2012, program fees had climbed 28% over 2007 rates.

This brings us to carriage fees. Stations often choose to keep buying national shows that promise to hold local audiences over local shows that might not. In a 2013 commentary for *Current*, Wisconsin Public Radio content director Michael Arnold said, "Most unrestricted funding at networks comes either directly from stations through carriage, affiliate or membership fees, or indi-rectly through money made from radio-related sponsorship. It can be easy to forget how important stations are to network finances, especially when other revenue streams are growing." For example, when PRI's *The Takeaway* started in 2009, it was only on 40 sta-tions. By September 2013, PRI was owned by WGBH, *The Takeaway* was on 214 stations and each of them paid between $1,400 and $3,200 a year to carry it.

Then there are membership fees stations pay to organizations like NPR and others. These are separate from carriage fees for shows and, according to NPR's 2014 IRS Form 990, helped the network rake in more than $8 million from affiliates. And every few years, stations pay it more. A 2016 hike in membership fees seemed to shift more of the burden to wealthier stations, which was good news for smaller, poorer stations. Although 2012 numbers showed that public radio in general earned $3 million more than in 2011, most of it came from the 11% of stations with budgets of $5 million or more. Medium and small stations with smaller budgets didn't generate much cash and actually lost money. Plus, there are fees stations pay to get access to the Public Radio Satellite System. It lets local stations send local stories to the network and delivers network stories to local listeners. Those fees went up for some stations by as much as 4% beginning in January 2017.

Other fees include those imposed by the FCC, along with industry fees from music licensing companies ASCAP, BMI and SESAC. Those payments stations make to play the music of musicians have drawn attention to the fact that music services like Spotify and Pandora only pay tenths or hundredths of a cent to musicians per play. It also highlights how those fees affect commercial and non-commercial public, college and religious broadcasters access to the music. In 2007, NPR came out against the music licensing fee increases while radio stations across the web, in danger of paying the most for digital music rights, protested with a "Day of Silence." When NPR went to the table in 2016 to update a fee structure that had been first introduced more than 15 years earlier, NPR's Membership Development officer Gemma Hooley said, "The network wants to develop a business model that reflects and supports the changing business realities in public media." It's worth mentioning that stations and networks often initiate special projects that are sometimes not connected to buildings, gear or fees.

CPB's "Station Support" or "Six Percent" funds pay for many of these kinds of collaborations, technological innovations, and special projects focusing on programming or reporting. That seed money helps public radio, TV and networks work together, sometimes despite years of mistrust, to build permanent connections in service of the audience. Grants from government, whether from CPB or federal agencies, often require stations to come up with "matching funds" before they can get support. In other cases, grants may be fully funded and require no matching funds. In those cases, it costs stations little to nothing to use them. But when stations pay out of their own pocket for a new gadget or process, that's altogether different. ☎

Programming & Carriage

"He who pays the piper calls the tune."

—John Bell, former VP of Membership for OPB

Until the early '80s, NPR was calling that tune. That's because NPR used 100% of CPB radio appropriation, or about $34.25 million to produce and provide all of the programming for its early affiliates. But after its financial meltdown around 1982, and increased regulation by CPB and Congress, the network was forced to change how it interacted with stations. The *NPR Business Plan*, introduced in 1985, distributed money directly to stations and ended NPR as their funding source. But the network managed to keep taxing "each station a fixed percentage of its total income to buy access to everything NPR produced." Making stations an offer they couldn't refuse, author Jack W. Mitchell, in his book *Listener Supported*, said the network offered no other choices. "It was all or nothing, and since few stations could get by with nothing," says Mitchell, "nearly all stations had to buy all, in effect, leaving the total NPR program package intact and freeing little if any money to buy programming from other producers." Nevertheless, after the implementation of the business plan, the new saying heard 'round the building, according to former NPR News VP and Ombudsman Jeffrey Dvorkin was, "The customers own the company."

But shows remain pricey, with their cost represented in something called "carriage." It is a verb, as in stations carry a program. But it's also a noun, as in a program has high "carriage" on a lot of different stations. NPR, PRI, PRX and APM, and certain key affiliates impose a charge on stations in exchange for carrying their programs. As Michael Arnold, Wisconsin Public Radio's Director of Content told *Current* in 2013, "Those fees also help cover the cost of producing those programs." So the multi-purposed fees keep shows in the pipeline as well. Meanwhile, companies like Information Concepts based in Herndon, Virginia, help networks like NPR develop carriage type systems, which may include not only evaluation and analysis of programs but payment mechanisms. Carriage fees represent some of an entity's biggest sources of unrestricted income. But in 2013, radio researcher John Sutton wrote in *Current* that if NPR could fundraise directly from stations, and those stations didn't fear "bypass," NPR could stop charging carriage fees and offer all of its programs for free. As Arnold points out, station managers liked the idea so much that they started asking out loud why they should even pay carriage fees.

Carriage fees are calculated based on the number of hours of a show a station airs. In an article called "The Cost to Know WHYY," former NPR spokeswoman Jenny Lawhorn told Philadelphia *City Paper* in 2004, that carriage fees are set for each station depending on its size and budget. A formula determines how much CSG money stations can get from CPB to help pay for a show. Another formula decides how much of that money they have to give back to NPR in carriage fees. In a 2007 version of American Public Media's service agreement, affiliates must first enter into carriage agreements before they can air programs. But once they do, they

PLEDGE: The Public Radio Fund Drive

can not only air an APM program, but may also stream the same
program for free on their website. Stations can benefit from a sort
of volume discount, meaning, the more hours of a producer's show
they use, the less they pay for it overall. High quality programs that
are too expensive in time or money for a station to produce itself,
are good candidates to rent. A brochure produced by American
Public Media and the National Endowment for the Arts in 2005
says a small market station may pay $100 to $200 to air a weekly
program for a year; many large stations have seven-figure bills for
their use of the NPR newsmagazines.

For example, an undated pitch guide from Las Cruces-based
KRWG shows the station pays $298 a day for *Morning Edition* and
All Things Considered. KRWG, based at New Mexico State
University has a broadcast power of 100,000 watts. That's significant because it means the station, with its five, 55-watt repeaters
at Alamogordo, Silver City, Lordsburg, Truth or Consequences
and Deming, give it a wide coverage area. Radiolocator.com show
the propagation pattern of its signal includes El Paso, Texas to the
southeast. Though Arbitron ranked the Las Cruces market at 212th
out of 272 nationwide in 2015, the company also ranked the El
Paso market 75th. So, because of its coverage and the number of
its potential listeners, it pays nearly $109,000 a year for four of
NPR's tent pole shows. It also paid $13,000 a year for *Car Talk*
and around $10,000 a year each for WHYY's *Fresh Air* and Min-
nesota Public Radio's, *A Prairie Home Companion*. And after each
mentioned program cost, the guide encourages pitchers to remind
listeners to "engender" contributions. In February 2018, Hawaii
Public Radio General Manager Jose' Fajardo declined to pick up *A
Prairie Home Companion*'s reincarnation, *Live From Here with
Chris Thule*, because there was no guarantee it would draw *PHC's*
audience. "We could not justify purchasing what was in essence
a new show for the same $25,000 we had paid (annually) for the

164

iconic Prairie Home." HPR went with the established *American Routes* and saved $22,000 a year.

Carriage fees are based on a carriage regime, which surprisingly, is a set of standards outlined in the *1934 Communications Act*. It says providers of carriage can't discriminate against providers of content wanting carriage, though courts have questioned whether the law should interfere with the editorial discretion of carriage providers. Even as rules have historically focused mostly on cable companies, increasing attention to the digital space, already enveloping services like Hulu and Netflix, could extend further. When NPR chose to drop *Talk of the Nation* in 2013, Neal Conan wrote in an e-mail to staff members: "I'm proud that we go out on top, with record station carriage and the largest audience in the program's history." In 2004, TOTN was heard on about 200 stations. By 2013, that number had grown, by about 23 stations a year, to 407. But being heard on hundreds of stations and paying the required fees, doesn't protect a show if the network sees a need for change. And though NPR did not make its carriage rates available, PRI's can be found online. The billing formula is based on a combination of station size as determined by its "tier," its ability to generate revenue and the size of the population it serves.

A tier is another way to measure how successful a station may be. Stations receive their community service grant money based on their tier, which range from A through G. CPB, with help from the FCC and audience measurement firms like Nielsen Audio, determine which stations fall into which tiers. Tier A stations have a minimum audience of 5 million potential listeners and no maximum, making them the powerhouse stations in the top radio markets. Their carriage fees are the highest. Tier G stations may be very small and isolated with either a very tiny coverage area, or a very small listener base, or both. Their ability to generate income is limited, and so the carriage fees they pay are relatively small, though they may not seem so to their station managers. For instance, for one of PRI's most popular shows, the newsmagazine PRI's *The World*, tier A stations pay almost $26,000 a year in carriage. Tier G stations pay $1,500.

Radio researcher John Sutton said in 2013 that, on average, stations were spending about 15% of their gross revenue to broadcast NPR shows. Of course, that doesn't include other costs for other shows from other distributors. And this might be a good place to explain a little more about how this process works. Station A pays to rent a show from Network A. That means, after making space for the new show in its own programming schedule, Station A can tap into the feed Network A is sending to other stations when regular network feed time for the show rolls around. Station A can also "timeshift" the show so that it can be heard at a time that's more convenient to its audience. Either way, Station A is now "carrying" Network A's show, and it pays a fee for the program, a carriage fee for the program and a satellite connection fee. But let's say Station A has produced its own show and wants to make some money by distributing it to the rest of the network. It pays the satellite connection fee to Network A for the ability to uplink its show to PRSS. Other stations can now "carry" station A's show and they too pay the satellite fee to downlink it. Those stations also pay the carriage fee and the program fee, of which Station A gets a piece. It's one reason why stations are constantly juggling schedules and testing out homegrown shows. They're trying to reduce spending and increase revenue.

Some programs thrive under carriage. APM's *Marketplace* gets about $18 million of annual revenue with about 25% of that coming from carriage fees paid by the 750+ stations that air it. But for some, programming and carriage fees can be choking. In *Public Radio and Television in America*, Ralph Engelman describes how, Newark's WBGO, in 1992, "indicated its intention to drop

All Things Considered and NPR membership because of its dues." Engelman says the station was paying $144,000 from a budget of $1.6 million. As of 2017, WBGO still does not carry any NPR shows, although it does link to NPR stories through its website. Also in 1992, Philadelphia's WXPN did drop NPR's news and as of this writing does not carry any of its news magazines, though it does offer NPR's music to its listeners. In 1992, Purdue University's WBAA dropped *Morning Edition* and *All Things Considered* and until 1997, replaced them with Public Radio International. At the time, the $60,000 a year fee was too much. Salt Lake City's KCPW dropped expensive NPR programming in 2013 to prevent a financial shutdown. By 2017, the station, after years of struggle, restructured its debt and seems to be in the clear but as of January 2018, it hadn't significantly returned to NPR.

Stations do have choices when it comes to paying for programs, carriage fees and satellite access. *"A Way With Words,"* produced by KPBS until 2007, and independently produced since then, is distributed through PRX, heard on over 100 stations and charges no carriage fees. Planetary Radio, another program available through PRX, airs on 150 stations and is also free. And since at least 2011, Randall Davidson, the Director of Radio Services for Oshkosh, Wisconsin-based WRST, has provided a list of shows that can be downloaded or recorded to CD and mailed. Besides showing nine big name distributors with multiple program options, he also lists 124 individual shows in his, *"Non-Satellite Programming Resources for Radio Stations."* More than 100 are free. And stations are under no obligation to pay for their use. Some are fillers only minutes long, while others are long form pieces covering everything from grassroots music to global newsmagazines. Of course, stations may be looking for specific shows to fit with the overall feel of their station and preferences of their audience. So many of Mr. Davidson's selections may not work for them. And according to an employee at KCPW, some free shows are free only if stations leave the embedded underwriting intact. But the number of shows that stations can use for free point to how, even in this niche market of public radio, market forces still apply and consumers seek out substitutes when their original choices become somehow unattainable. ☎

Salaries

"A fair day's wage for a fair day's work."

—Motto of the American Federation of Labor

Jason Dorsey of the Center for Generational Kinetics, says millennials love things like fast casual dining and emoji, while hating things like lines and big brands trying to be cool. About a third of them also don't like companies that have salary issues, whether that means paying unfairly, or hiding who gets paid what. Public radio is trying to attract that coveted demographic. So it isn't helped by stories questioning if the money for executives and some of the most well known voices compared to the relatively low wages paid to news staff at smaller stations is justified. Some stations pay high fees for public radio membership or programming but may not be able to afford enough reporters to run a newsroom, engage with the public or create locally relevant programming. And when employees themselves question the sense of asking listeners to make pledge donations while their boss pulls down high six figures, it can make for a credibility issue.

Mark Dent writing for *BillyPenn* in 2017, reported that WHYY CEO William Mannzano, earned $842,832 in salary and compensation. In the same story, some of his own employees called his salary, "a slap in the face." Mr. Mannzano's salary has been of long time interest to the people of Philadelphia. In 2007, Philadelphia Magazine's Steve Volk, reported on how Marty Moss-Coane, acting as a sort of unofficial spokesperson for the staff, confronted

Mannzano during an all-employees meeting. "Bill," she began, "one of the reasons morale here is so low is that your salary is so large compared to everyone else's." "I work very hard for my salary," he responded. "So do a lot of people here," Moss-Coane fired back. At the time, Mannzano was getting about $431,000. By 2015, Mannzano, who was by then making $580,000 in salary and deferred compensation, told Jane M. Von Berger with the *Philadelphia Inquirer* that WHYY's 401K plan lets him set aside some of his salary so that when he retires, "you can have a chunk of change." It is the size of that chunk, and whether it is, in fact "change," that is making people question one of the ways public radio is spending its money.

The Atlanta Journal Constitution also investigated the salaries of executives at Georgia Public Broadcasting and Public Broadcasting Atlanta. PBA CEO Milton Clipper, and four other executive staff received nearly $200,000 each in 2009. Teya Ryan, the CEO of Georgia Public Broadcasting, along with three other executives there, also earned six-figures. In 2017, Joe Battenfield reported for the Boston Herald that WGBH, while in the midst of reporting a $38 million loss, "CEO Jonathan Abbott, got an $85,000 bonus in the 2016 fiscal year, boosting his annual compensation to $624,930, according to tax reports filed with the state attorney general's office." Battenfield says WGBH also distributed another $300,000 in "big pay hikes and bonuses to executives and staffers."

And Salt Lake City's KCPW was investigated by CPB auditors in 2006 after reports surfaced of $1.6 million in salary and compensation paid to station manager Blair Feulner and his wife. Sixteen months later, in an effort to break free from Community Wireless of Park City and sister station KPCW, the Salt Lake station formed Wasatch Public Media and took on a $2.4 million loan to buy its broadcast license from its former parent.

After years of negotiation with creditors, time was just about up when, in 2011, an anonymous donor provided the stability KCPW needed to obtain financing for the loan, thus saving it from extinction. The public radio compensation issue was large enough that pubcaster magazine *Current*, in 2015, published a sortable table of top salaries at 85 public radio stations, including the one owned by its American University parent, WAMU. Some stations have even questioned the salaries paid to executives at other stations. On the website for Wesleyan University's WESU, a May 5, 2013 post from the station compared how it survives with no CPB support "when other public radio stations around the country, including right here in CT, have budgets so huge they can afford to pay their General Managers more than twice WESU's entire annual budget."

"There's this assumption that everyone was like drunken sailors passing out money without regard to the consequences or without giving it any thought. That wasn't the case," said Robert A. Profusek, a lawyer with the law firm Jones Day. Profusek wasn't talking about public radio. Instead, he was explaining to the *New York Times* in 2009, how he worked with many of the Wall Street banks who approved large compensation packages for executives even as the 2008 financial crisis raged around them. Some relate it to the "rewarding failure" argument made by Kevin Roose in a 2012 New York magazine piece.

Roose said Wall Street bankers, who helped drive the economy into the ground, shouldn't get bonuses for it. But the high salaries paid to executives is part of a deep calculation in board-rooms across the country. According to a 2012 report from Harvard University, executives, including public radio executives, are paid handsomely by their companies as incentive not only for what they've done, but for the risks they are expected to take to grow the institution. That report also said, however, "executives were fully exposed to the upside of risks taken but enjoyed substantial insulation from part of the downside of such risks. As a result, executives had incentives to increase risk-taking beyond optimal levels."

In their defense, companies say they must offer the high salaries and compensation packages for the best talent, and that such "value maximization" is written into executive contracts. Changing their terms, despite money problems for the company, say defenders, is a non-starter since boards write contracts and contracts can't be changed. But the Columbia University Law School, in 2017, concluded that executives can have significant sway over boards in what their compensation will ultimately be. As hedge fund investor Bill Ackman told *Marketplace*'s Kai Ryssdal in December 2017, "Being a director tends to be a way to make a living when you're a retired CEO. And your willingness to challenge the status quo and push back against the CEO, you become pretty quickly a director that doesn't end up ... on future boards." Another concept, "Rent extraction" lets executives draw personal value from shareholders and proves that contracts can be written in ways that are intentionally more beneficial to the executive than the institution. As the reports says, "Executives, directors, and consultants spend time and effort designing compensation contracts, taking into account unobservable firm, industry, and executive characteristics." Executives who underperform are undoubtedly removed. But for those that meet the institution's goals, regardless of what kinds of financial crises it may suffer, the bottom line is boards tend to continue paying its executives no matter how terrible the optics.

At the network level, when NPR CEO Kevin Klose resigned in 2008, his reported salary and compensation was $1.2 million. When NPR's Jarl Mohn took over in 2015, his salary was listed at $298,884. Although high network executive pay may be more justified than high affiliate executive pay, some kind of message is still getting through. But it may not be trickling down. Affiliates paying their executives network-like salaries don't necessarily pay

their reporters like their network peers. So, the value maximization argument also seems at play when it comes, not just to senior
staff, but on-air staff. When David Brauer, writing for MinnPost
in 2009, asked Minnesota Public Radio to elaborate on the salaries
of notables like Garrison Keillor, he got a crisp reply from spokesperson Christina Schmitt. "We don't discuss staff salaries or other
aspects of their employment beyond what we're required to by
law," said Schmitt in an email. "So I have to decline to expand on
the information in the 990 ... beyond saying our general approach
to compensation is to pay competitive rates for every position we
hire, including our national hosts."

Minnesota Public Radio is the poster child for entrepreneurial
public radio and for keeping salaries close to the vest. The Minnesota legislature was set to give MPR $380,000 in taxpayer support
in 2006 if, in line with a new state law, it would reveal the salaries
of MPR employees. MPR not only said disclosing all of its salaries
would violate employee privacy, but also said it was being singled
out when other non profits didn't have to disclose salary information to the same extent. Republican Marty Siefert, in an interview
with the Winona Daily News, didn't see it that way. "It's tough for
me to justify spending hard earned tax dollars on an organization
that claims to be non-profit and gives its top executives that type of
money," said the former state representative. "No wonder they are
non-profit. There's no profit if it's all scooped up by fat cats." An
MPR spokesperson suggested that the public radio affiliate might
consider asking the Minnesota legislature to change the law.

Sarah Carmichael, talking with author David Burkus for the
Harvard Business Review in 2016 asked him why, at this moment
in American history, is it so hard for companies to talk about salary. "I think that secrecy is the easiest way to deal with the uncomfortable feeling of inequality," said Burkus, author of *Under
New Management*. "So we know that there's inequality, income

inequality in society or pay inequality in organizations, and dealing with it is hard. As we just talked about, it's an uncomfortable conversation. But not talking about it?" he asks. "Well, that's a whole lot easier. So maybe we just go down that route, and we keep it secret." In other cases, on-air staff is cut and replaced with outside programming in an effort to save money.

If it is a given that the salaries and compensation packages of executives are high out of necessity, what about those of aforementioned national hosts and correspondents? Their pay can be compared to the plethora of salary tables for local hosts and correspondents from affiliates across the country. That comparison begins with a rule of thumb that newsrooms with higher budgets tend to pay higher salaries to their staff. The next data point is how is a newsroom job categorized? For instance, does a "special correspondent" make more money than an ordinary correspondent? Does a host make more money than an executive producer? And finally, what amount of public or market pressure if any, do stations face that makes them pay more or less to those reporters relative to the value they deliver from their reporting?

The *NPR Finances* page at the npr.org website, explains the network news budget. "Year to year, our expenses are affected by major news events, particularly those that require extensive reporting and operational support." The network goes on to say that costs can vary depending on the amount of heavy lifting it must do to provide the type of circumstance defined reporting listeners expect. In a 2013 to 2017 projection of operating expenses, the network says news and engineering takes more than four out of every ten dollars it gets in revenue. With an annual budget of around $214 million, that means the news and engineering pie piece is about $88 million. If around half of that, or $44 million, goes to newsroom salaries, compensation packages and logistics, that puts NPR's news budget far above those of other stations identified in national salary tables. Michael Marcotte, a journalism professor at the University of New Mexico, in his 2011 study of newsroom salaries, seems to agree, saying, "Larger broadcast service areas correlate with higher salaries, but not as directly as with higher budgets. That's because you find low budget stations in large markets, and they pay low budget salaries not large market salaries."

No single licensee has the broadcast service area of NPR. Thus, their revenue pie tends to be smaller, meaning, their newsroom budgets and the salaries they pay their newsroom staff is less. This makes the dichotomy between affiliate executive pay and affiliate staff salaries even more confusing. Marcotte's responses, collected from 400 stations and compiled at *InsideNPR*, showed the average salaries for the top four positions in most newsrooms; reporter, producer, news director and host. Generally, reporters find and collect the news, producers help reporters get resources to create and shape stories, news directors oversee the entire process for quality and accuracy and hosts deliver the final product. Marcotte's results showed public radio stations with budgets between $2.5 and $5 million paid their reporters no more than about $58,000 a year. Producers at the same stations received about $55,000, hosts got about $89,000 and news directors were paid about $87,000 a year.

Marcotte also categorizes the staffing strength of newsrooms by what he calls "weight classes." Only seven of the 247 stations he classifies as "heavyweights," with 30 or more full time news people are in the $2.5 million to $5 million budget category. Employer review site GlassDoor.com says NPR reporters get paid about $110,000 and producers get around $62,000. Executive producers and news directors are paid roughly $120,000 each. For hosts, the average seems to be around $335,000. It's good to remember that at smaller stations, a single person is likely performing the jobs of reporter and producer, and possibly, host. But they are likely not being paid three salaries. Job site Indeed.com reports that American Public Media salaries, by contrast, are more consistent with industry averages. For associate producer/producers (the skill level likely needed at most smaller stations) salaries range from $22 to $27 per hour, or about $52,000 annually. Reporters for APM make about $28.30 an hour, or almost $59,000 a year.

Public radio's salary problem is less what they are but more so, how they're perceived. Commercial hosts, some argue, should be paid whatever commercial companies can afford since their revenue stream is entrepreneurial. But since public radio hosts are paid, in part, with public funds, the thinking goes that those salaries should be closer to salary tables for regular reporters since that will make them more like what an average American earns. Others disagree. "The money paid to Siegel, Montaigne & Inskeep is a relative pittance compared to what top radio talk-show hosts make," says commenter Steve Gossett, weighing in on *Josh Gernstein*'s blog in 2008. The comment section in *Current'*s survey of public radio salaries also shows listeners as reluctant to vilify public radio for paying its hosts those high salaries.

Gossett continued, "Rush Limbaugh, for example, makes $35 million a year. His is the most-listened to show in the nation. NPR's Renee Montaigne, on the other hand, makes 1% of that amount co-hosting the second most-listened to show." In the end, there may be nuances in the data, but not many. Stations that can afford to pay their CEO's network level salaries seem also able to pay their journalism staff more, but don't. Meanwhile NPR pays its news staff significantly above industry averages because it can and wants to. "Overall," says Gossett, "I'd say NPR's getting a lot of value for their money." Now, if only more of the public felt the same way at pledge drive time. ☎

Fees

*"The Member and all stations licensed to (or operated by) the
Member and broadcasting NPR programming must pay all dues,
program fees and assessments as determined by the Board of
Directors."*

—NPR Bylaws, 1999

Fees, as opposed to payment for goods or services, might be
for an agreement to maintain that good or service. Or to remain in
good standing with an advocacy group by supporting it financially.
Or to renew a license or permit that gives the holder the right to
keep doing something. The feeling of being nickel and dimed to
death by fees is common. And although fees are among the costs of
doing business, that doesn't mean they're liked. NPR started
preparing its affiliates for higher fees besides carriage, more than
a year before it levied them. By October 2017, member stations
could expect to pay as much as 4.25% more for its newsmagazines, membership dues and digital services while fees for some
non-newsmagazine programs increased by 3.5%. And like everything else in public radio, the increase stations pay depends on a
formula.

Public radio distributors tie those increases to seven, A through
G tiers that are related to those CPB uses to determine station
strength through radiated power, audience size and revenue generation. For NPR, stations earning over $30 million pay the highest
rate while those earning under $500,000 a year pay nothing extra.
Tom Thomas, of the Station Resource Group, told *Current* in 2016
that for *Morning Edition* and *All Things Considered*, stations pay
the average of their average spring and fall AQH ratings for the
previous two years. For shows like *Fresh Air* or WWDTM, Thomas says stations pay according to rate card categories tied to how

much money their stations earn. NPR Digital Services fees, which were implemented in 2013, must be paid along with a station's membership fee. It covers statistics of audience and industry trends, access to features associated with NPR One, website development and revenue and marketing support. Stations can't opt out of NPR/DS like they can when choosing to take some shows and not take others. John Sutton, in a 2011 blogpost, says the fee structure enacted with the creation of NPR Digital Services (formerly known as Public Interactive, before purchased by NPR from PRI) upset stations, because they now had to pay for all of NPR's Digital Services "whether they want them or not. Stations with more money pay more, not because they are receiving greater value, but simply because they have more money." It was a reversal from what had, before 2011, been considered a more fair way of cost sharing.

The *NPR Station Manager's Handbook* also describes Distribution and Interconnection (D/I), which is another fee stations pay every year as their share of the cost for operating and maintaining PRSS. To use PRSS, stations must also sign a contract called the Satellite Interconnection Agreement. The last time NPR raised D/I fees was in 1999. But because of changing economics, the flat fee that had worked so well for stations then was ruled by an NPR interconnection committee in 2016 to be, "not perceived as equitable." In 2017, NPR's board decided to raise fees again. Larger stations were slated to pay more basically because they could afford to. A news release from the NPR Board in 2016 said of the new PRSS fees, "The expectation is that in 2017, no station will pay more than $10,500, that is, the increase will be no more than $1,500 over this year (the current rate is $9,020). "It is likely," said the release, "that about 140 of the smallest stations will pay less than they are paying now." NPR also makes programming available via the Internet for stations that can't afford the extra perks PRSS provides. Stations choosing to take their programming that way pay about half what satellite users pay. PRI doesn't make that option available to its content users. It distributes its content exclusively on PRSS.

Returning to membership fees, in a 2010 station blogpost, Temple University's WRTI told readers, "WRTI pays a small membership fee to NPR to have access to its programming." But the definition of "small" can vary, depending on market size, service area and the amount of NFFS that stations generate on their own, says Nebraska Educational Television in a 2012 FAQ. Former NPR VP and Ombudsman Jeffrey Dvorkin said of the network's fee structure, "It's quite a complicated arrangement and changes almost annually based on regular negotiations between NPR and the stations." Membership fees stations pay shift according to the size of their market and the successfulness of their pledge drives. For example, stations along the Aleutian island chain have a cost sharing agreement with NPR to get their programming from Fairbanks and split the cost of providing it to the communities of Sand Point, Unalaska and the Pribiloff islands. Pledge drives goals for these remote communities can be small. The help, not something the network wants to talk about, shows it is willing to work with stations when necessary.

In 2014, Paul Farhi with the *Washington Post*, mentioned how WAMU, the former home of Michelle Martin's *Tell Me More*, paid an annual membership fee of $12,500. According to its 2017 annual report, WAMU has revenue of about $25 million, and its two annual drives bring in about a million dollars each. In an email exchange, Farhi said, "A big, relatively rich station like WAMU in D.C. surely wouldn't be paying the same fee as a tiny rural one." Before merging with PRI, the Public Radio Exchange had a handy, station membership fee calculator on its website. When WAMU's total station revenue of $25 million is entered, the site says the station would pay PRX $8,700 for a year's membership and get one hour of programming each week for 52 weeks. By contrast, Oklahoma Classical Radio KUCO, said in 2016 that it had annual revenues of $270,000. PRX would proportionately charge KUCO $775 a year. By contrast, annual membership with Public Radio International would cost KUCO $13,000, which doesn't include additional program fees of $7,500.

Radio also has to cope with increasing fees from the FCC. In 2016, David Oxenford with the *Broadcast Law Blog* said when imposed by the government, fees are designed to help it recoup the cost of oversight. But the overseen can also get stuck with over-head costs. Because the FCC's lease for its building was expiring, the price of its move into a new space was folded into some of its highest fees in years. The fees, said Oxenford, "are mandated by Congress to fund the operation of the FCC, so there is not much that the FCC can do about the fees themselves except to make minor changes in how the burden is distributed." Those tweaks are spread out across all of the industries the FCC regulates, not just radio. In 2016, FM stations that served more than 6 million people paid between $15,000 and $17,000 in regulatory fees. Stations that served under 25,000 people paid less than one-tenth of that amount while some classes of stations saw no increases at all. Plus, the FCC charges for, "licenses, equipment approvals, antenna registra-tions, tariff filings, formal complaints, and other authorizations and regulatory actions."

Digital music has been of great interest to public broadcasting. New rules affect not only its relationship with artists but how much it ultimately must pay them to play them. Public radio is depend-ing on music to draw in millennials. Costlier, harder to get music doesn't help that strategy. So public radio has been fighting hard for years to keep those prices, "fair and reasonable." Tables from the Copyright Royalty Board in 2015 show how much players of music have to pay those who license it. Over air broadcasts for non-commercial, college or university affiliated stations with more than 20,000 students will pay music licensing companies ASCAP and BMI up to $983 each by 2023. Stations not affiliated with a college or university pay according to whether or not their population is more or less than a quarter-million listeners. It may be one reason why some of those stations are moving to the news/talk format while many of the music offerings are moving to streams and podcasts where the audience is smaller and the fee structure is much different. Commercial, non-subscription webcasters pay $.0018 per song, per listener. Meanwhile, services like Pandora bypass the CRB and pay negotiated fees directly to licensing companies of between $.006 and $.0084 per stream. Using this formula, the CRB says one million plays would generate $7,000 on Spotify and $1,650 on Pandora. Non-commercial, public radio webcasters pay SoundExchange a flat $500 a year for a measure of station listenership called "Aggregated Tuning Hours" or ATH. Created in 2003, SoundExchange is a non-profit, "designated by the Librarian of Congress as the sole organization authorized to collect royalties." It insures all types of musical performance artists, on all mediums, get paid for their recorded music, lyrics and arrangements. Without it, public broadcasting would have to negotiate each music contract individually. An ATH equals one listener hearing one hour of a webcaster's programming. Stations can't have more than 159,140 listens, or ATH's per month without paying more. Those that do, pay more. Public radio contributes money to CPB for licensing and copyright related payments. CPB sends reports of those payments to SoundExchange.

Fees for playing those short pieces of music between stories can sometimes be avoided if they are what the service calls "brief" and "incidental." Brief, meaning no more than about 20 seconds, as long as the entire piece isn't 20 seconds. Incidental, in that it relates to something else, like as a transition rather than a performance. Almost every public radio program uses music, not only as a segue but to expose listeners to highlighted artists. And with the help of collaborations between public radio and organizations like Spinitron, which publishes playlists of music from any station in real-time, listeners can discover and follow new singers, bands, composers, arrangers and instrumentalists. In 2009, Spinitron cost stations at least $630 a year, though its president, Tom Worster told the Copyright Review Board, "accounting for this as a specific cost of census reporting is not straightforward." In other words, costs can change a lot. NPR Digital Services also charges non NPR stations from $250 to $500 in data processing fees for collecting music usage information, plus an extra $500 if stations send it with wrong formatting. Live performances are different. If NPR, APM or any of their affiliate stations either records a live concert for rebroadcast, or has a musician perform live in a studio, those musicians are paid on site according to rates provided by the American Federation of Musicians. For entities that offer many such performances to their listeners, costs are modest. In 2014, AFM charged $108 for a half hour performance, $132 for a full hour and those rates doubled for single musicians, contractors and band leaders.

Then, there are fees for membership to public radio organizations. Many of them only take individuals as members, not their stations. There are ethics, advocacy and professional development organizations like the Society for Professional Journalists, The Poynter Institute and the Public Radio Association of Development Officers. But others serve institutions and stations. The Public Radio Program Directors, for example, "advocates for high-quality programming and provides resources for public media program directors." Station membership fees are on a sliding scale based on its NFFS. PRPD says no station will pay less than $500 or more than $4,500 annually for membership. The Station Resource Group, created by founders of Minnesota Public Radio, is dedicated to co-operative action, strategic analysis and legislative advocacy. SRG annual station memberships, also tied to a station's NFFS, range from $4,700 to $74,000, with a median of $17,000. Greater Public, calling itself "an industry leader promoting innovative strategies for public media development" bases fees for annual membership on a station's NFFS. In 2017, stations joining will pay no less than $1,995 and no more than $8,595 annually. Finally, membership with the granddaddy of them all, the National Association of Broadcasters, costs $360 per market each station reaches. So if a station's signal overlaps several markets, it pays several times.

There is no doubt that there are those who do not weep over public radio's fees. But if they are even marginally important for an average public radio station to be competitive in its market and amongst its peers, it's easy to see how it doesn't take long for them to pile up. And public radio depends on people like you to help it pay them. ☎

Facilities & Infrastructure

"Escaping its 51,400 square feet of tired but rent-free space scattered on eight floors of the Municipal Building, [WNYC] will make a $45 million move northwest to two and a half floors of a 12-story former printing building at 160 Varick Street."

—*New York Times* reporter Glenn Collins

Facilities, unlike fees, represent the tangible. Even programming, which is more ephemeral than physical isn't in the same category as hardware, buildings and gear. WNYC's new offices, said Collins of the station's 2006 move, increased floor space by half, more than doubled the number of studios, provided street level theater seating for 140, and all under 12-foot ceilings. "Critics," says Collins, "question whether the pricey move will pose an intolerable fundraising burden, jeopardizing the station's independence, forcing it to rely more on corporate underwriters and skewing its audience toward a well-heeled elite."

Facilities are elaborate, expensive and as noted, controversial. In 2014, listeners became aware that NPR had spent $201 million on a new building. Some wondered why, while awash in grant money, it was at the same time cutting programs and firing staff. The cuts, and the money for the building had been programmed into the budget. But the unfortunate timing looked bad. Donors may complain that a station spends on such capital improvements even as there are ongoing problems with programming or staff. Critics say that such expenditures make public radio look self-centered, and it shouldn't be using taxpayer money anyway. But radio stations are practically living organisms; inhaling money and exhaling content. And almost nothing about that process is cheap.

As proof, in 2011, the Department of Commerce, in cooperation with the National Telecommunications Information Administration (NTIA), published a rough guide on the cost of what a station at every level of operation needs. The list includes the prices for transmitters, towers and equipping on-air, production and news studios. It also included prices for Low Power FM, EAS and Radio Reading Service gear. What was recommended for stations depended on how the FCC categorized them into classes A, B and C. Class A stations have the smallest effective radiated power and the lowest antennas. Class Cs have the highest effective radiated power and the highest antennas. Class Bs split the difference.

And while it may make sense that class Cs don't need to be in the middle of a big city, or class As shouldn't be in rural areas, those aren't necessarily correct assumptions. Nancy Murphy, Assistant Chief of the FCC's Media Bureau said, "There is no specific correlation between station class and market size. Additionally, full service stations, including both Class A and Class C, may use translators and boosters to simulcast the content of the parent station in various situations." Finally, there's HD radio transmission requirements, which are in their own NTIA category. It's a reminder that the NTIA's list is only a recommendation.

In 2016, Richmond, Virginia's WCVE completed the installation of a new transmitter and antenna. The old set up, which the station had been using since 1988, no longer met the needs of its changed audience and technology. The switch was made possible by a 2014 ask of its listeners for help, most of which came from an ongoing capital campaign. The final, $345,000 bill reflects FCC information from January 2017 of a new, approximately 774-foot high antenna being fed 10,000 hot, new watts from its shiny HD transmitter. That antenna height, at that power level, makes WCVE a class B station and gives it stronger, cleaner access to the Richmond market, 53rd in the nation and 14 miles west. Likewise, over about a three-week period in September 2016, Salisbury, Maryland's Delmarva Public Radio replaced two, old transmitters which together broadcast 10,000 watts, with a brand new 20,000 watt version.

According to the NTIA's 2011 list, and not accounting for inflation, a 20,000 watt transmitter that broadcasts both analog and digitally cost between $72,000 and $109,000. Plus, to have better signal reach, Delmarva moved its tower at an expense for a class B1 station of about $200,000. That, and all of the little extras, likely puts the total bill for Delmarva's WDSL and WCSL on par with Richmond's WCVE. And listeners to APM's *Marketplace* may have noticed a bit more sparkle in Kai Rysdall's voice after what *Mix Magazine* called, "The Great Marketplace Studio Redesign of 2009-2014." The work included everything from deeper incorporation of IT to improving "sight lines" for better eye contact between co-workers during broadcasts.

Tower and transmitter life are of particular interest to stations, but that's out of necessity rather than choice. When Current's Scott Fybush described station's relationship with their towers, it sounded like a scene from *Law & Order*. "Expensive to maintain, fraught with potential hazards, bounded by an ever growing web of regulations, unloved by neighbors and often inconveniently far away, a pubcaster's tower still serves as the essential link between its program service and its audience."

And in fact, a Google search in January 2018 showed discussions about towers were far more abundant than those about buildings and transmitters combined. Pledge drives can also be a platform for talking about towers. During a spring 2016 pitch break, a pitcher for Gaston College-based WSGE told listeners that just the costs to maintain its tower is over $4,000 a month.

Stations seem both proud and afraid of their towers. Improving a signal often involves nothing more than moving it or raising it as opposed to building an entire building and filling it with new gear. But the regulations around altering a tower can be onerous. Concerns over bird strikes yield conflicting information over how stations should deal with tower lighting, for example. Until 2015, stations posted their own methods for dealing with lighting issues. Then, the FAA weighed in and required new towers to have only flashing lights. Old tower lighting systems could be grandfathered in. Towers can be a station's *Achilles Heel* in other ways. In 2015, commercial oldies station WHPR in Highland Park, Michigan was fined $22,000 because the coordinates of its tower and transmitter didn't match the FCC's records. And as we know by now, the FCC hates wrong paperwork.

Work on the building itself is no less important or pricey than work outside. Since 2010, nearly a dozen public radio stations have launched capital campaigns to either renovate their current building, move to and renovate a different building, or construct one from scratch. They include ambitious makeovers, like Vermont Public Radio's $8 million expansion and renovation in 2015. And more modest ones, like Yellowstone Public Radio's $102,000 work on its three studios and building in 2016. Others include a planned, two-story, 100,000 square-foot home for Colorado Public Radio, Amherst, Massachusetts-based WCFR's 2011 purchase and renovation of the "Fuller Block" ground floor and a 20,000 square-foot addition to Chicago Public Radio's Navy Pier locale.

In 2014, Spokane Public Radio spent $5 million renovating an historic firehouse as its new home. Promising not just new studios, but to become a community broadcasting hub, the station had to raise $1.6 million in matching funds to finish the work by June 2015. Cary Boyce, Spokane Public Radio's general manager told reporter Judith Spitzer, "The math is simple, but powerful. Every private dollar for this project is worth about half again as much." It's the type of language listeners hear often when station administrators are trying to emphasize value over cost. Boyce said that the remainder of the money will be raised from private gifts and listeners. "It's an amazing return on investment dollars and a clear economic impact—all while growing a truly great public broadcast service," he said. Stations like Boyce's, which share the common transportation and communications infrastructure of the contiguous United States can reach their goals much easier than, say, stations that don't.

For instance, Aleutian Peninsula Broadcasting, an affiliate of NPR and member of the Alaska Public Broadcasting Network, requested $140,000 in 2011 for a new vehicle, work on its tower, fixing a translator and renovation of its studios. Though its need was nearly 35 times smaller than that of Spokane Public Radio, it was no less important. The bulk of Aleutian Peninsula Broadcasting's signal skirts the southeast facing edge of the Aleutian Islands, stretching towards Unalaska in the southwest and Kodiak to the northeast. The largest nearby market, Anchorage at over 560 miles away, is itself tiny, ranking 174th out of 272 markets nationwide. Nielsen Audio doesn't even register a market for the 8,100 people served by Aleutian Peninsula Broadcasting's Sand Point Island studios. And its signal, received mostly by fishing fleets in the Bering Sea, and partnered with KUCB-FM in Unalaska, is practically all the radio listeners on that 1,200 mile-long island chain have.

Those stations get *Morning Edition* and *Democracy Now* from KUCB owned equipment installed at KUAC in Fairbanks, in part, because KUCB is too far west to downlink programming from PRSS. Once received, the Unalaska station redistributes it to KUHP on St. Paul Island and to KSDP on Sand Point Island. Competition amongst local radio carriers like GCI and Optimera depends on the ability of their market to support their infrastructure. The limitations of audience generosity are creating a hotbed of innovation, like delivering radio by Wi-Fi more cheaply and efficiently than satellite or broadcast. In the end, KSDP and KUCB must provide a relatively more important service with many fewer resources than stations in the Lower 48. So while similar work in the contiguous states might be considered essential to quality of life, in Alaska it's more akin to activities of daily living.

Station facilities can also include stuff not normally thought of as facilities, like radio reading services, radio broadcast data systems and the Emergency Alert Notification system. RBDS, or RDS for short, is the ability of FM radios to receive text messages including "station call letters, program formats and even alternative frequencies," broadcast by stations so equipped. Radio reading services are primarily for the blind and are mostly a broadcast service of non-profits like libraries and universities. Stations provide it on a sub-carrier to a special receiver where a narrator reads books, magazines, news, weather and sports. NTIA lists the cost for an RRS package at nearly $41,000. An EAS receiver/decoder by contrast, is a flat $4,000 regardless of station class. The system is designed to not only transmit messages by over-riding local broadcasts in the event of a national emergency, but it also can be used manually to inform the local community of impending severe weather and, in recent years, missing children. Systems along the Gulf Coast may have special variations which allow them to alert the deaf and hard of hearing as well.

Broadcasters offering RRS and EAS as part of their public service mission must manage them well. The FCC has a very low tolerance for EAS mistakes. It has fined nearly half a dozen commercial stations since 2010 for broadcasting the activation signal in embedded advertising or failing to even hook up EAS receivers at all. But the system itself is buggy, prone to hacks and human error. As of this writing, the most famous human error to date was a mistaken "Ballistic Missile" alert broadcast across Hawaii in January 2018. Former FCC chairman Michael Powell argued against the system five months after the September 11 attacks, saying, "the ubiquitous media environment" made EAS "slower than *CNN*."

NTIA's list doesn't include a lot of things stations would seem to need like accessories that keep transmitters monitored, emergency powered or cooled. It doesn't include the costs of any building work. And except for the consoles and cabinets to hold the gear itself in office suites, the list doesn't include office furniture or machines. In special cases however, a no may become a yes if they're later judged by decision makers as essential. And the market for buying, building and selling public radio facilities is robust. When an owner decides to sell a station, including the tower, there are companies that can help speed the process. Public Media Company, based in Boulder, Colorado has a track record of helping stations sell critical infrastructure on the open market, or transfer it between owners. The company helped the state of New Jersey spin off the northern part of the former New Jersey Network to New York Public Radio in 2011. It also helped Baltimore's WYPR acquire WJHU from Johns Hopkins University in 2002. ☎

Projects

"Because of the inherently uncertain return on investment, blue-sky projects are politically and commercially unpopular and tend to lose funding to more reliably profitable or practical research."

—Mark Henderson

That's probably true, usually. But although public radio can be accused of a lot, in recent years, being fearful of trying new things isn't one of them. Pubcasters do get support from business, foundations and government to experiment with ways to improve the system. As a 2009 study from the Center for Media and Social Impact pointed out, although "Public Media 1.0" was widely accepted as important, it was, "rarely loved-politely underfunded by taxpayers, subsidized weakly by corporations, grudgingly exempted from being profit centers by shareholders." What it called "Public Radio 2.0," fueled by Internet and social media driven innovation, has morphed its predecessor into a totally different animal. Malak Habback of California State Polytechnic University, in his 2016 study, identified three major "themes" that defined public radio's innovation process. He labeled them "strategizing," "investments and future journalism," and "online strategies." Habback defines strategizing as deeper engagement with content and users, drawing new users to that content and developing new ways to collaboratively share it. Investments and future journalism is about tools and techniques, including podcasts and new ways of storytelling. And online strategies, he says, focuses on distribution. It's in these areas public radio networks and affiliates search for most of its "Blue Sky" project money.

PLEDGE: The Public Radio Fund Drive

Between mid 2014 and early 2018, CPB posted five Requests for Proposals (RFPs) on its website that focused on collaboration. Three of these projects; in 2015, 2016 and 2017, were for public radio stations. Their goals included growing the audience by increasing local content, helping stations become more financially independent, making the most of station resources, improving overall station efficiency and probably most important, building trust. In one case, station grantees received up to $150,000 for each of the three years of the project. In the two others, CPB paid between 50% and 100% of the salaries of key people for up to two years. The two journalism collaborations had the specific goal of creating more newsroom partnerships between regional networks. Money for these and other collaborative efforts comes from CPB's System Support or "Six Percent" funds. It's likely that subsequent projects in the Inter-mountain West, the Ohio River Valley and in the Pacific Northwest benefited from CPB's efforts to bring stations and people together. Laura Hazard Owen, writing for Nieman Labs in 2017, describes six types of collaborations stations can enter into; from loose and temporary to tight and permanent, that best serves their stations and their audiences.

Collaboration happens not only between regions, but within them. In 2015, KUT Austin, KERA North Texas, Houston Public Media and San Antonio's Texas Public Radio received a $750,000 grant from CPB to develop *Texas Standard*. Erin Geisler, writing on KUT's website, said the collaboration facilitated a two-year project to offer, "crisp, expansive coverage of politics, lifestyle and culture, the environment, technology and innovation, and business and the economy — from a *distinctly Texas* perspective" (emphasis theirs to 22 of the state's public radio outlets. Former *Marketplace* host David Brown hosts the hour-long show, which Geisler says serves the Lone Star state the way *Morning Edition* "serves as a platform to connect stories around the country and globe." And collaboration money doesn't just come from CPB. In

2016, Southern California Public Radio teamed up with the Irvine Foundation and its "California Democracy Program" to provide special coverage of statewide elections. The one year, $135,000 grant was also shared with KPBS San Diego, KPCC Los Angeles and Sacramento's Capital Public Radio. Besides election coverage, the project also let stations experiment with ways they might work together in the future. "Inside Energy," a joint partnership amongst stations that see a lot of oil move by rail, formed in 2009 as part of a larger brainchild of Rocky Mountain PBS head Laura Frank, and then CPB head of radio, Brian Therault. Local Journalism Centers, or LJCs were born with their help, plus a CPB advanced RFP which eventually provided $1.5 million to seven stations to focus on their own energy related beats. But their journey has not been a smooth one, as it has been dotted with branding issues and funding cuts.

Habback's first theme also includes gathering new users. For public radio, that means millennials. Though it does that through collaborations such as bringing more of the Triple-A music format to youth and convincing funders to support it, it also does it with projects like NPR's *GenerationListen*. It encourages millennials to get kits that help them plan "NPRListeningParties." An early version of the project, NPRResearch, existed on Twitter and as a blog between 2009 and 2012 until the concept moved beyond its humble beginnings and was shut down. In the new and improved version, subjects for discussion are close to the hearts of those born after 1992, including Women's History, love and relationships, personal growth and the twisted root of politics. Potentially, these parties expose future loyal listeners to the wonders of NPR. But to licensees, this could look like a different kind of "bypass." Those stations may be hoping that millennial excitement over network shows don't make them forget hometown radio as they're punching up NPR One selections on their smartphones.

Habback's "investments and future journalism" theme could also include preserving content. That's what happened in 2015 between PRX's *The Moth* and the New York Public Library. The Knight Foundation offered a grant for a program called, "Together We Listen." The crowd sourced effort asked listeners to help clean up errors in 600 Moth radio stories and over 1,000 stories from the NYPL's oral histories project by gathering ordinary people in-person and online to hear them. Investments and future journalism can also include the work of consultants like Bain & Company. When Eric Nuzum was looking to innovate NPR programming in 2016, he turned to the company and its "Agile Innovations" division. NPR worked with the company to revamp the way shows move around the network clock. The result was so fascinating that PRX's Roman Mars, with the help of Julia Barton, dedicated an episode of his *99% Invisible* podcast to it. Agile also worked with the network to develop a slew of on air and online shows. On its website, the company says, "the network now creates a small number of pilots with a minimal staff and then begins iterating. Show developers gather feedback from local program directors." If those program directors seek the thoughts *GenerationListen* listeners offer, the resulting "quick and dirty" ideas might improve those pilots a lot faster. This savings, according to the company, let NPR, "feed the program to local outlets free of charge for a while so that they can build an audience," but only for a while.

Other investments related to the future of journalism mean projects like New Hampshire Public Media's "dashboard." Working with Public Media Company, a nonprofit strategic consultant, NHPR created a tool that lets it see deeper into PMC's Public Media Database. A beta version, launched in 2015, promised to "create a real time, 360-degree view of audience reach, fundraising success and financial health, designed to help stations not only report on their progress, but provide ongoing comparative data for planning and budgeting." Funding for these and other Public

Media Company projects came from the Public Radio Fund, which its 2014 overview says consists of contributors from foundations, and "other individual investors to 11 different public media organizations." Since 2008, the fund has handed out over $8.9 million, though it's worth mentioning that the Public Media Company website calls them "loans," not grants.

In the spirit of innovative storytelling, *Sonic Trace*, a 2013 storytelling project from Santa Monica's KCRW got $40,000 from California Humanities to tell eight life stories focusing on, among other things, "Latin American immigrants in Los Angeles and across the border." The project included interactive data that let users drill down on statistics and stories. In 2016, the Henry R. Luce foundation gave the *God and Government* series on religion and politics $40,000 as part of its "Religion in International Affairs" project and in collaboration with the Interfaith Voice public radio program. Then, there is Localore, a project of the Association of Independents in Radio (AIR). Launched in 2013, this effort, "attempts to create new types of programs and reach new audiences." A key finding of Localore, according to Chris Kretz of CUNY Stonybrook is that public radio stations show their value "as community hubs, the importance of developing networks within communities, and the power of creating teams of talent to 'throw...like a lightning bolt at a problem or an idea.'" On its website, Localore says it gets funding from CPB, a number of foundations "and AIR's members worldwide."

Habback's last innovation concept for public radio is online strategies. And he says it is strictly about describing new information sources such as, "newsfeeds, Internet channels, blogs, and mobile apps." In other words, online strategies are about how content gets distributed rather than the content itself or the tools that help create it. Minnesota Public Radio and American Public Media crowd sourced the problem in 2017 by asking its interns to think up ways, "to reach new digital audiences - particularly younger people who may not currently listen to APMG programs." One idea, from intern Alex Pardue called "The Lamest Generation" invited millennials to talk with each other about how they felt about particular news items. Another, from intern Mike Rezler, focused on the impact of Voice on Demand technologies like Amazon's Alexa and how millennials interact with public radio content.

Knight Foundation funded projects like PRX's Radiotopia and Project Carbon (now known as NPR One) are some of the best examples of distribution success. Some like NPR's Project Argo, which was designed to build better websites in Wordpress are retired while other digital infrastructure projects continue to mutate. One of them is DAT, a Knight Foundation effort around building new kinds of apps that rely on open communities but secure protocols. With $50,000 from the John S. and James L. Knight Foundation, and another $260,000 from the Alfred P. Sloan Foundation, the DAT project continues to focus on creation of and movement through huge datasets. They may have the greatest benefit for science, but Knight is looking to apply the technology to public media as well. Meanwhile, DocumentCloud is a platform that lets journalists from all over the world upload millions of news and information pieces. According to author Aron Pilhofer, as of mid-2017, DocumentCloud, with the help of a quarter of a million dollars of funding, "hosts 3.6 million source documents, and has been used by more than 8,400 journalists in 1,619 organizations worldwide." High profile stories the project has helped expose to the site's 824 million public views include "*WikiLeaks*, the *Panama Papers*, and the Snowden documents."

Sometimes, an innovation isn't just for stations, or between stations and networks but for networks only, such as when NPR, APM, PRI and PRX created a shared digital tool called the "Public Media Platform." Begun in 2010, and supported with a million dol-

194

lars from CPB, PMP was described as a technological "backbone" for all public media outlets to share their individually massive repositories of content. When fully realized, an NPR press release says PMP will enable, "today's non-compatible systems to connect, allowing for unprecedented access and flow of content." The whole goal of PMP is a seamless listening experience. At other times, innovation has one sole beneficiary. In 2014, WNYC received a $10 million grant from the Jerome L. Greene Foundation, and used it to support the station's development of its, "Discover: Radio on your Own Time" app.

In what looks more like an arms race, "Discover" promises to provide WNYC's listeners with curated, time-shifted and off-line listening, much like major market competitors RadioPublic, NPR One and dozens of other native apps from individual stations. Innovation is at the root of public radio since its purpose is to spread knowledge across the system. That applies not only to content for the audience, but tools and techniques for the practitioners. Stations watch each other for successes to copy or failures to avoid. The projects here represent comets in the universe of public radio's innovative ambitions. Sometimes, stations looking on from the edges, can feel overwhelmed by the pace of change and not know how to keep up. But two truths that seem to remain consistent are, first, because stations are so different, there is no one magic bullet for success.

And second, pubcaster R&D, which may be invisible to the audience, is no small part of the spending pie. It's one reason why in 2011, Beliefnet.com founder Steven Waldman told the FCC public media needed a "technology transformation fund" to help existing broadcasters grow while helping startups blossom. That same year, Eric Newton, speaking at the 2011 Future of Public Media conference in Detroit, said that although pubcasting has access to many sources of funding to try new things, pubcasters may not have that much to spare. "[T]he money involved is a fraction of the operating costs of the organizations involved," he says. "Even the most innovative among them might devote no more than 10 % of their budgets to technology transformation."

But that's still one out of every ten dollars from their budgets. That's why every dollar they get from outside sources to innovate, no matter how small, is important. The Online News Association's "Challenge Grant" program, gives out micro-grants of $35,000 for marvelously innovative projects that range from exploring the effect of so called, "transmedia" journalism on rural and urban communities, to using virtual reality to tell local stories. Scott Hanley, former WDUQ General Manager and former Chair of NPR's D/I Committee said in a 2016 blog post, "Technology allows us to do almost anything. But no one has the time, money or talent to do everything. It's important to make good choices." ☎.

Chapter 4 - Whad 'Ya Know

"The best audience is intelligent, well-educated and a little drunk."

—Alben W. Barkley

It is assumed that public radio listeners like to be smart. Kai Ryssdal, host of *Marketplace* often demands reporters about to tell him a story to "Make me smart." But other assumptions, especially by the audience, are not always accurate. That's because much of what's written about public radio isn't written for listeners. Rather, what's known about the technical, financial and psychological state of the industry and its audience comes mostly from the industry for the industry. The Public Radio Program Directors, National Public Media, Greater Public, the Station Resource Group, Nieman Labs, GfK, the Poynter Institute; these and other research, consultant and advocacy groups are constantly looking for ways to make public radio independent, understandable, ubiquitous and "sticky." And they do it, not always with the audience's full attention or knowledge.

Outside of the genre, there is a spotty flow to mainstream outlets of public radio information written in end-user language. An analysis I did of 1,300 press, academic, think tank, commercial and government pieces about public radio over a 45-year period, found about three-fourths of them were written for insiders, while a quarter were aimed at the general public through mainstream publications. The mainstream pieces tended to focus more on affiliates than the networks. They include big stories about stations changing owners and formats. Or local stations dealing with staff changes or announcing upcoming pledge drives. Media critics, for newspapers that still have them, sometimes break stories about local public radio affiliates going silent or coming online. Occasionally, there was a broad piece looking at the "state" of public radio or TV. But the diet of stories about the networks themselves is thin. Former PBS Ombudsman, Michael Getler, lamented the disappearance of people like him who try to explain the hard to understand stuff about public broadcasting to those who have nowhere else to go. And listeners who do click old links for background on current stories about public media are often subject to "link-rot," when a link goes nowhere and the page displays nothing but an apology.

It's been said that the audience doesn't know what it doesn't know because it doesn't want to. A clich in public radio, apparently attributed to early CBS broadcaster Edward R. Murrow is, "People only care about what comes out of their speakers." It assumes that if they aren't hearing their favorite program from their favorite host at their favorite time, they don't really care about much else. Public radio asks its audience to trust it, not only by believing the stories it tells but by asking it to pay for its successes and its failures; its solutions and its problems. Maybe, in addition to being informed and entertained, part of the caring Murrow addresses includes the public wanting more involvement in the curation of shows or the management of stations. That may be a stretch. But the increased focus in community advisory boards; a requirement handed down to stations getting CPB money that they hold regular open meetings so the community can into see their inner workings, seems to reflect a growing public interest.

But does public radio want listeners that know more to get involved more? Everything in public radio costs stations time, money and people power. And some feel that work is easier if the public isn't in the way. Bill Kling, the founder of Minnesota Public Radio, was adamant, when asked during an interview if public radio does the audience a disservice by not letting it get more involved. "No. Not at all," said Kling, "It would make chaos." He went on to say people only need a cursory relationship with station management except when they're giving money. "They do not need to know the details of what, to whom and why," said Kling. "It's just not workable to have the audience getting into the details of the management of the station. There are notorious examples where that's happened," referring to the discord at Pacifica Radio stations. "They have all underperformed significantly in comparison to those [stations] that had good governance," Kling said.

The most popular message boards reveal that if complaining equals interest, people are interested not only in where public radio takes them, but how it gets them there. There are questions of conflict within the public radio family and how it manages to resolve them while putting on a calm face to givers. There are questions of content, such as why has public radio shifted from classical and jazz to news and talk? And why no sports? There are questions of platforms, or how the public radio sound tries to touch you through all of your devices. It's why NPR's chief between 2014 and 2019, Jarl Mohn, was so preoccupied with turning public radio listeners into public radio "addicts" through that curated sound. And finally, the barges of public radio resources that float toward questions of demographics and diversity.

Stations are getting the hint that being open rather than insular is the way to go. In 2016, *The Washingtonian* described how WAMU borrowed a page from community radio's playbook and reversed a lack of diversity within the station and its programming through more input from the community. Perhaps providing more of those details can help listeners have more support for stations and thus, be more generous givers because they have a better idea what stations are up against. ☎

Time

"Nature gave us time, but mankind gave us the clock."

—Anonymous

When a listener turns on their terrestrial radio, or opens a live stream from their local station, they hear NPR programming like *All Things Considered* and *Morning Edition*. They know that certain stories in those newsmagazines hit certain times every hour, every day. What they may not know is NPR schedules everything listeners hear according to a master programming clock. Producer Roman Mars devoted an episode of *99% Invisible* to the NPR broadcast clock in 2013. Such clocks, used in broadcasting for nearly a century, tell affiliates downstream when to cut away from and return to network programming. They are the glue that makes a network a network.

For the *Morning Edition* audience, for example, that means a preview of the hour's stories at the top of the hour (called a "billboard") that lasts about a minute. Then, headlines of the top stories that may be anywhere from one to almost six minutes long, followed by a network underwriting credit. Then a little music. And after that, a deeper dive into the top story until about 18 minutes after. That pattern more or less repeats three more times before the top of the hour. And after nearly 50 minutes of news and analysis, NPR gives you a break from hard news with something a little lighter, like a conversation with somebody artsy about their newest work. It's designed to leave you feeling that the world isn't so bad after all. It's not only NPR programs that follow the NPR clock. Shows from the BBC, the CBC, Minnesota Public Radio, WNYC and other distributors follow it too. But some of them may have their own markers to meet. The Friday edition of APM's *Marketplace* starts on the half hour with four minutes and thirty seconds of retrospection on the week's biggest financial news. Then a bunch of quick but meaty little stories. Then, somewhere between 17 minutes and 13 minutes till, "the numbers" where *Marketplace* gives the day's stock tally and also where affiliates can cut away if they choose. And finally, just before the top of the hour, some snarky business-related factoid to send listeners on their way for the weekend.

NPR re-engineered its clock in 2014 for a very simple reason. Its several hundred full-service affiliate stations were clamoring for more minutes and seconds to promote their local events, encourage local giving, preview local shows and overall, claim more of the hour for themselves. That's no small thing for a network whose brand depends on spreading as much of itself across that hour as possible. The newer clock shortened some segments previously reserved for stories while lengthening others. It spreads shorter newscasts more evenly across the hour. It increases the overall time NPR itself has to make its own underwriting announcements by about fourteen precious seconds each hour. But among the most important things the new clock does is grow the number of music beds from about five and a half minutes to more than ten minutes. Those transitions are places where local stations can leave the net-work to focus on their local audience and communities.

During pledge drives, stations cut and paste pitch breaks over those musical transitions and around the network clock so as to not dig too deeply into the shows people want. And the changed clock increases "flow," or smoothness in storytelling. That consistency is a key finding of *Audience 98*, a seminal public radio study that became the blueprint for how public radio would gather and satisfy its listeners; people stay tuned when there isn't too much change in whatever they're listening to. In fact, one of the reasons affiliates have such a hard time holding onto their listeners between *Morning Edition* and *All Things Considered* has to do with a perceived drop in programming consistency. But a show in which the transitions are polished, and the stories differ in content but have the same "feel" holds listener's hands gently but firmly throughout the hour.

The old clock also forced some stories to end before they were ready. Like Lucy and Ethel trying to fill chocolate boxes on conveyor belts, the next segment was coming no matter what. So the change was about pace as well as tone by letting stories be of different lengths rather than stretching or chopping them to fit the same space. In a 2016 interview with *Current, Morning Edition* host Rachel Martin explained what she expected from the change. "I think we're going to be more flexible with the clock. If an interview's going really well, we're going to keep that person, and we're going to keep them through the break and bring them back and not be afraid to say that. We're going to be a lot more transparent on the air." In the calculation for support, nothing is accidental. Transparency equals trust and trust, ultimately, means more giving.

But all isn't copacetic in clock world. Podcasts represent a time-shifting problem for affiliates. PEW's 2017 *State of the Media* report shows 91% of people aged 12 and up still listen to broadcast. Podcasts are having an effect however. Though many producers create shows that are a traditional thirty or sixty minutes, a podcast isn't restricted to the time concerns of a bunch of fussy affiliates. So a podcast can be as long or as short as it needs to be to tell the story. Besides, a clock doesn't really mean anything to someone who can get their shows on-demand. As podcasts grow, the relevance of the clock may change, especially as stations not only re-purpose more on-air shows for online, but create more original content that will never see an antenna.

Underlying the ultimate reason for the change is the opportunity for more underwriting. *Audience 98* found that although people didn't like it that they were hearing more sponsor announcements, they trusted businesses they heard mentioned on public radio more. But as proof of the need to adapt to an evolving audience tastes, NPR announced even newer clock tweaks in August 2018 that moved newscasts around again. Among the stated reasons were to help the hour flow better and sound less "commercial" which implies less underwriting. Still, public radio weighs in light compared to the commercial radio industry's spot loads of about 12 to 14 minutes of ads an hour. That the network spends as much effort as it does on its clock reflects the reality that time really is money. ☎

Demographics

"Of course, listeners aren't prey, but we do want to capture their attention and loyalty."

—Audience 98

Despite Bill Siemering's wish that public radio not treat listeners like a market, that is exactly what's happening. Although stations like the University of Pennsylvania's WXPN heads its website with taglines like, "Rhythms, not Algorithms" and "Community, not Commodity," public radio receives plenty of support from companies that do commidify listeners. That's because deep down, NPR, PRX, APM, and PRI want you stuck to their content 24 hours a day. They want to follow you seamlessly from your terrestrial radio to your smartphone to your dashboard to the desktop. They want to know exactly what you listened to, when and for how long so they can know how and how much you may give. It sounds a little creepy, but it can't be creepy because it's public radio, right? Listeners depend on its award-winning news, information and entertainment. So they live with its loving, growing and un-blinking stare. But public radio must survive in a mosh pit of other consumer choices like gaming, sports, shopping and porn among others. Even if it's not tracking steady with the help of big data, it is eying opportunities in bigger business. As Ira Glass said, "Public radio is ready for capitalism."

An industry truism has been that public radio provides service to the community, which leads to support from the community. But public radio's idea of community, like the French republic, is that sameness, rather than difference, is the key to a unified identity. On one hand, this is admirable in that NPR says it aims its content at common likes and dislikes rather than the race or ethnicity of listeners. It has subjected the network to a frequent criticism that its programming stays in the safe, middle lane so as to offend as few people as possible. But public radio is shifting from a sound older listeners recognize to the sound of younger Americans. And while it tells stories about the trials and triumphs of us all, it has always been fixed on listeners who are more monied than not. So its argument that it doesn't target specific groups with pitches or programming can seems somewhat disingenuous. As it pushes the message that content is the great leveler, it whispers the mantra, "Made possible by People Like You." Still, there are supporters who feel left out despite their support.

In 2013, the Media Audit's *National Radio Format Report* described the demographics of the typical public radio listener as being among those who "most often are 67% more likely to earn $150,000 or more in household income, 55% more likely to have liquid assets of more than $250,000 and 80% more likely to be a business owner." "Furthermore," said the report, "those who listen to a public radio station most of the time are heavier consumers of foreign luxury vehicles (39% more likely to own), hotels (25%

more likely to stay 10+ nights per year), and air travel (79% more likely to be heavy domestic air travelers, and 65% more likely to be a heavy foreign air traveler)." Melody Kramer, a former radio producer who, after her 2014 Nieman Fellowship, conducted an in-depth examination of how and why we give, says public radio is service. But follow-up questions include, "Who is it serving and how is it serving them?"

Although public radio's monied donors are often the subject of much of its attention, it's the non-major donors, with their small one-time and sustaining gifts, who carry most of its water. As proof, whenever public radio experiences drops in funding, it's not because listenership falls but because government or corporate support does. Threats to that funding made researchers realize that in times of crisis, masses of ordinary public radio listeners across demographic groups turn to, not away from public radio because it's a source of information they trust. So, to get them to support it with as little pain as possible, stations applied psychology and social science to help public radio craft strategies upon which pledge drives rely today. Prominent among a myriad of techniques are the *Theory of Planned Behavior* and the *Pennies a Day* paradigm. Listeners will hear variations of both of these in pledge drives.

The *Theory of Planned Behavior*, or *TPB*, connects what people do with what they personally believe. It says those beliefs are shaped not only by social pressure to meet certain expectations but personal pressure to conform to them and to "do what's right." Not surprisingly, *TPB* shows up most often in advertising, public relations and people's personal health care choices. The *Pennies a Day* paradigm, or *PAD*, re-frames the impact of large obligations into smaller ones. And because they're now small, *PAD* givers are likely to let those contributions continue, without thought or interruption. This is why stations want sustained giving to happen through checking accounts rather than credit cards. Besides saving stations the transaction fees, credit cards can expire and remind givers they are giving. *PAD* helps givers forget that trickle of support and ideally, everyone benefits.

Pledge training manuals highlight both theories. Puget Sound's KSER and its *Pledge Drive Pitch Playbook* reminds pitchers to remind listeners of how ten dollars a month is only 33 cents a day. Meanwhile, Fort Wayne's WBOI says in its on-air fundraising guide that "only one in ten listeners will ever make a donation. "So," it says, "station support is really 'your job.'" As an aside, Giovanonni and Sutton disputed the oft-quoted low ratio of givers to listeners in 1998, claiming it was much higher. In 1992 Senate hearings on public funding of public broadcasting, conservative columnist George Will offered his own funding solution. In a *Washington Post* piece, he referred to public TV's WETA in Washington D.C., and its 1992 financial statement that showed the average household income of its viewers as $94,583. Will said if everyone who wanted public broadcasting paid an extra $70 a year, the need for federal funding would disappear. So he reasoned, WETA viewers could do so and implied that their household incomes would plummet to $94,513.

TPB and *PAD* are two among many tools stations aim at public radio's broad demographics to get listeners to become givers. But the one to rule them is *VALS*, or *Values, Attitudes and Lifestyles*. A research tool developed in the 70s by Strategic Research Insights, Inc., it is based in part on the work of behaviorist Abraham Maslow. *VALS* became the key to work researcher David Giovanonni released in 1988. He refined those results ten years later in *Audience 98*. That work, to which public radio still refers with the near reverence of a *King James Bible*, spells out exactly who gives and why. Plus, it showed public radio how to tailor its programming so that listeners not only keep listening, but are so affected by what they hear that they will support it almost without question and whenever asked, indefinitely.

Research shows that the more a giver sees of themselves in the asker, the more social effect the asker has on the giver and thus, the more likely the giver is to give. *VALS* breaks an audience down into eight demographic subcategories. But the two of most concern to public radio have historically been actualizers (renamed "Innovators"), and fulfilleds (renamed "Thinkers"). Actualizers are motivated not only by success but displays of it. They're "tote bag" people. Fulfilleds are moved by ideals; they encourage and are encouraged by social change. They're the "Pay it Forward" people. Together, *Audience 98* said both groups account for about one of every three dollars public radio gets from individual givers.

Giovannoni's study informed public radio of the "bait" it needed to catch the attention of its listeners. *Audience 98* says the appeal of its programs generally cuts across race, lifestyle, sex and gender categories generally, but not completely. And although the work continues to be an important reference, public radio supplements it with a 21st century viewpoint. GfK, the largest marketing research institute in Germany and the fourth largest in the world, sells NPR the data it uses to keep pace with its audience.

The network also works with Comscore, an American media company that provides high-octane analytics to publishers and ad agencies. It is significant that Nielsen Audio, the premier audience measurement firm for radio, offers expertise in "Consumer Neuroscience" as a tool for predicting and managing behavior. Bill Siemering might call it service through surveillance. But the effort to wrangle those findings into an Esperanto type world in which everyone listens to and benefits from public radio is an ongoing drain for the industry, mostly because demographics isn't diversity. ☎

Diversity

"My wife and I play a game. Each morning we wake to NPR and listen for about 5–10 min before we get up. We keep track of the number of "news reports" about: (1) Jews/Israel/the Holocaust/ anti-Semitism. (2) Slavery/Minorities/Blacks. (3) Gays/homo- sexuals. On most days, NPR can score at least 2 in 10 min, and sometimes even 3 or 4. Today, we had a perfect trifecta, with all 3 subjects one after another."

—Commenter *"Anonymous"* on the Steve Sailer: *iSteve blog*

The way public radio handles racial, ethnic and gender diver- sity issues are intensely scrutinized. Case in point: the 2016 unrest in Ferguson, Missouri over the killing of Michael Brown. Though some called him a troubled teen, NPR took a liberty that its Om- budsman was forced to defend after former program host Robert Siegel called Brown's behavior "thuggish." Though Seigel's use of the word was deftly explained by the network, not all listeners were satisfied that the NPR's diversity words and deeds lined up. On the day of Siegel's retirement, Metafilter commenter "indubita- ble" flatly asks, "Who's gonna be around on *All Things Considered* to call the next Michael Brown a thug now that Robert Siegel is departing?" "Sio42," also on Metafilter said, "I used to listen every morning until what's his face on morning edition referred to Mi- chael Brown as a thug and it wasn't a quote. I got out of the shower to turn my phone off and have barely listened to NPR since. It used to be different right? It's not just me?" Siegel legitimately asks of Brown's actions, "By the way, what is an appropriate adjective for his behavior in that convenience store?" But starting the question with, "By the way" gives it a sniffy classist taint that could be argued doesn't sound open-minded or diverse.

Big entertainment shows in public radio also draw questions of diversity. SBNation contributor Jon Bois was curious in 2013 about *A Prairie Home Companion* participants over the years. So, he ran a Google search. "There was one racial minority," he said. "This isn't intentional, and I'd imagine that the Prairie Home Companion folks are as egalitarian as anyone." "But," he continues, "listening to this show feels like pressing my face against the bosom of whiteness, clad in the gown of all its stereotypes." Likewise, ethnic groups in the audience can be insulted by poor, entitled humor. During a spring 2016 pledge drive for Salt Lake's KUER, a pitcher, commenting on an NPR story about Spain, said, "And here I thought they were there, over there, taking siestas." Guffaws ensued.

Public broadcasting was created in part to try to bring Americans together under the big tent of a common cultural heritage through "Great Society" politics. NPR, MPR, APM or PRX tell amazing stories of the human condition that attempt to ignore borders, economics and melanin concentrations. But public radio's first slip from economic diversity is in how it relies most on the generosity of a subset of its wealthiest private and corporate supporters. Informing them without offending them and interrupting their giving is one of public radio's balancing acts. That kind of corporate influence came up in 1992, when the U.S. Senate held hearings asking, "How much diversity is America willing to pay for?" Put another way, how willing were corporate funders to support a message different than their own. Public radio and TV show producers told stories of how they were throttled by sponsors for even appearing to criticize the core missions of companies paying for the content they produced. More questions of economic diversity came that same year, when conservative columnist George Will attacked CPB for promoting elitist programming.

PLEDGE: The Public Radio Fund Drive

Twenty years later, the charge was still sticky. But this time, it came from a public radio supporter. Tucker Carlson, editor in-chief of the *Daily Caller* and a member of Maine Public Broadcasting pointed the finger in the April 2012 *Marketplace* blog. "Public radio receives more than $100 million a year in tax dollars," he said. "Teenaged shift workers at McDonald's, every harried single mom emptying wastebaskets at a law firm, lettuce pickers in California are laboring so that you and I -- you in your Prius, me in my Saab -- can listen to a certain sort of educated news and opinion as we cruise in air conditioned comfort to the office each day." It's a different kind of diversity fail and a poisonous indictment. But is it true?

For Arizona's John McCain, those 1992 hearings were a chance to critique what he considered a lack of programming diversity. "All it takes is one week of watching the programs on the Public Broadcasting System to see that there is no adherence whatsoever to the statutory mandate to provide objectivity and balance in controversial programming," accused the conservative McCain. Of 22 PBS special reports in 1992, six focused on dysfunction in the American political system. They also included stories on Wesley Allen Dodd's 15-year sex crime rampage against young boys in Washington State, the Clarence Thomas/Anita Hill hearings and banks redlining a black family in Chicago.

Public broadcasting supporters may have disagreed with Senator McCain that its shows lack diversity. But for like minded lawmakers representing conservative constituencies, an abundance of diversity may mean too much diversity. Fails at the local level may manifest themselves in station manager "gate-keeping" to maintain community standards, as when Alabama Public Television in May 2018, refused to air an episode of the cartoon "Arthur" portraying a same-sex marriage. Other tactics can be creative, like refusing to play diverse political ads because they are not of industry-standard lengths.

Meanwhile, scattered incidents of disrespect directed at the right don't make it easy for conservatives in public radio's demographic to believe it's as politically diverse as it says it is. In April 2016, a pitcher for Birmingham-based WBHM identified as her favorite listener comment a description of her NPR station as, "A morning drive without crank calls and chuckling knuckle-draggers." The oblique reference to AM Talk Radio makes the pitcher's glee in highlighting it, sound closed rather than open minded. Former NPR CEO Ken Stern took a controversial step toward the big tent in 2017, with his book, *Republican Like Me*. In it, he acknowledged that he had become too comfortable and isolated in his liberal hamlet. But the move came years after he had left the network. Stern said in response to criticism of his book that public radio newsrooms can suffer from what he calls leftist "groupthink" or "Balkanization." He says this can make reporters and producers fuzzily work in service of what he calls, "the resistance" in a stick-it-to-the-man kind of way.

Attitudes like those can lead to a belief that convinces one they are of something simply because they are for it. J-Lo and Rachel Dolezal, with their decades-apart missteps to appropriate blackness reinforce playwright Carlyle Brown's thesis. In his play, *Acting Black*, Brown posits that non-blacks, thinking their eyes have been opened may in fact be seeing through eyes wide shut. Such so-called "limousine liberalism" can push a creeping feeling within non-dominant culture of oft-told stories about them served up as a kind of menagerie. And on the privileged side, a sense that the tales are consumed with a *Get Out* like appropriation by those seeking the life without the lesson; the funky without the sweat. *Get Out*, the award-winning, 2017 film by black comedian and director Jordan Peele, tells the story of appropriation lust taken to horrible, mind bending extremes.

Gender, not just politics, weighs heavily in public radio. And reticence around women in positions of influence and power is as mixed as it is age-old. A 2017 *New York Times* story charged that at WNYC, "even as audio journalism has diversified, the station's broadcast lineup remained overwhelmingly white and male." The letting go of three of its stars, John Hockenberry, Jonathan Schwartz and Leonard Lopate in 2017 prompted former producer for Hockenberry's *The Takeaway* to charge, "If you want to be on the air, you're a white male." That left Times reporter David W. Chen to conclude, "men got the shows, women got the podcasts."

People who love public radio say its stories of race, class, income, religion, gender and politics aren't the only work it ought to do on issues of social justice. Some lament that more complex problems exist for public radio that have to do with diversity of thought, word and deed. They say public radio hires brilliant minds but often holds them to a parochial course. They imply it seems to want things both ways, such as when radio seeks grants to open newsrooms to reporters of color, then reports statistics that say the numbers of reporters of color in newsrooms remain inexplicably low. They suggest public radio is "safely" bold. David Oyelowo, who played Dr. Martin Luther King, Jr. in the 2015 film *Selma*, spoke off-set to this cross purpose within American society.

But he could have been speaking directly to public radio. "The only way we are going to get diversity is if the demographics of the decision-makers change. The odd-token bone thrown is not going to do it." Oyelowo is likely talking about skin color or country of origin. But the challenges facing public radio's idea of diversity are much deeper and wider than that. And they're reflected in a brief July 17, 2018 exchange between *All Things Considered* co-hosts

Ailsa Chang and Ari Shapiro. During a mutual greeting, at about 20 minutes past the show's second hour, Mr. Shapiro reminded Ms. Chang that he had just returned from a reporting trip to Zimbabwe. She said, "You came back very tan," to which he replied, "No one can hear my tan on the radio." That kind of chronic hypersensitivity to race, ethnicity and color is not departing the network anytime soon. ☎

In the House

"The best way I can put it is that with PRI and NPR, the kind of programs that they have for us to, you know, kind of choose from or review, it really doesn't, it doesn't speak to our audience."

—An African American Public Radio Consortium member speaking anonymously with the author in 2016.

Former *New York Times* contributor, NPR Ombudsman, and current NPR Public Editor, Elizabeth Jensen is an objective observer within NPR. Her job is no picnic. Like media reporter David Folkenflik, Jensen has the sometimes awkward responsibility of speaking truth to NPR's power. Hired in January 2015, she was the network's third Ombudsman in nine years. Though they fare better than NPR CEOs, the network narrowed the job description in 2014 to allow "fact gathering and explanation, not commentary or judgment." The change came after former Ombudsman Edward Schumacher-Matos questioned network coverage of how Native American children were being managed by South Dakota's foster care system. As Bob Collins implied on Minnesota Public Radio's *Newscuts* blog about the outcome, when questions of stinky network behavior arise, NPR's Ombudsman may no longer say it smells.

Millennials, NPR's sought-after demographic, don't like such mixed diversity messages. Though they tend to be poorer (because

they're not yet professionally established), they are more educated
(though seeking less validation from oldsters around them), under
thirty-five and racially "diverse," meaning not just white or male.
And unlike their baby boomer elders, who were at the center of
public radio's target audience in the '90s, they come with new behavioral preferences. Among them, millennials don't like feigned
conscientiousness. So a brand that doesn't speak straight goes nowhere with them. All kinds of diversity matters. And this is where
the CPB comes in.

The Corporation for Public Broadcasting, as a quasi-governmental organization, supports more than half a dozen media organizations that represent America's federally recognized racial and
ethnic minorities. With that help, blacks, Hispanics, Pacific Island-
ers, Native American Indians and Asian Americans tell stories of
their communities and people. The intention is to try to use their
stories to weave a common cultural heritage. But no matter why
they share them, a 2015 *Chicago Tribune* article says some are no
longer listening to what they're getting back from the network
because it feels diminishing or doesn't relate to them. For example,
some saw the influential Torey Malitia's "advocacy journalism"
characterization of Tavis Smiley and Dr. Cornel West's *Smiley and
West* collaboration as an attack that narrowed program options for
blacks. It's possible millennials saw it that way, too. Some considered another internal attack on diversity to be the canceling of
Michelle Martin's *Tell Me More* in 2014. *TMM* was a program
that focused on news and views of African-Americans, and its
axing was taken personally by black folks. "This represents the
third time," said the National Black Church initiative, "NPR has
canceled a wonderfully produced, nationally recognized African
American radio program." Later installing Ms. Martin at the helm
of both *Weekend Edition* Saturday and Sunday newsmagazines in
October 2015, for example, was a move NPR might have called
successful on multiple fronts.

Mostly, it proved the network was able to pepper her perspectives onto a much larger audience but didn't need an especially focused show to do it. That audience, according to a 2012 Pew Research Center study, consists of conservative (21%) Republicans (17%), moderate (39%) Independents (37%) and liberal (36%) Democrats (43%). That right/center/left pie isn't a totally balanced cross-section, and it leaves out many Hispanics and blacks who are simply not tuning in. But it is much wider than *TMM*'s audience was and makes the network's end-around look like redemptive genius. The move probably earned points with millennials.

So may have others. In 2016, NPR and CPB launched Public Radio Talent Quest, an effort to address charges that the network and its parent don't match enough of their diversity rhetoric with deeds. Years before however, steps taken in that direction were outlined in a 2013 Atlantic feature story, *NPR's Great Black Hope*. At the time, that hope was embodied in Glynn Washington, who became host of *Snap Judgment*, one of WNYC's most popular shows since *Radiolab*.

In 2016, African American host Joshua Johnson took over the retiring Diane Rehm's timeslot with his *1A* from WAMU. David Montgomery, for the *Washington Post*, called the move "bold." Other notable moves include the addition of a relatively new voice to NPR underwriting credits. Senior director of promotions and audience development Izzi Smith told *Current* in December 2016 that Chioke I'Anson's voice will "expand the diversity of voices on NPR,... and create additional 'capacity' for NPR's Programming division."

And here is where the network may have lost points with millennials. If "capacity" means a transparent attempt to deliver a black voice so NPR doesn't sound so white, the move asks a couple uncomfortable questions. First, should people of color sound like people of color? By looking for people who sound like what public radio needs them to sound like, is it stereotyping? Second, how (insert racial minority or ethnicity here) must a voice be to be (insert racial minority or ethnicity here) enough for audiences of color to feel represented? These efforts are valiant. But NPR's longtime, unofficial saying of "you can talk about us without us" still stubbornly floats above good intentions. Today's vernacular would label it racesplaining. Considering the questions directed at the network for diversity fires and misfires, NPR's colors of red, black and blue seem oddly fitting, wedged between rock and hard place.

KQED's senior editor, Queena Sok Kim, in 2015 for its *California Report,* fielded the question, "Why the heck do Latino reporters on public radio say their names that way?" Gustavo Arellano, the author of the surgically sharp *"Ask a Mexican"* column, responded. "In other words," he says, "if I'm talking to you right now in the King's English and I say my name is Gustavo Arellano instead of Goo-STAH-voh ar-ree-YAH-no, why do I do that?" Arellano asks. "Why does Adolfo Guzman-Lopez say his name Adolfo Guzman-Lopez instead of uh-DALL-foh GOOZ-monn low-PEZZ? Why do we have to be so Mexican?"

Such distinctions can also extend to gender. In an April 2018 story on PRI's *The World*, Patrick Cox introduced writer Jack Qu'emi, "a queer non-binary fem" who explained that because masculine versions of Spanish words are considered gender neutral, the word "Latino" is supposed to imply a man or masculine person of Latin descent. But for Jack, who also included "afrolatinx" as part of their nomenclature, that doesn't work. They argued that the "x" serves those who choose to reject gender. Push back comes from other native speakers who say to reject the gender based underpinnings of the language is to reject not just it, but an entire culture. Cox says in a language where every word is assigned a gender, "the only way you can get around that is by inventing stuff that breaks the rules. And once you do that, you really start pissing people off."

In that same conversation, an unidentified YouTuber said *Latinx* sounds like the personal toiletries product, "Kleenix," calling the word, "ridiculous." Others say the debate only seems to be of concern to dual speakers of English and Spanish. Linguist Ron Smyth says the term is almost exclusively used by such bilinguals. "It's fine to butcher another language if you're speaking English," he says. "It just seems to be much more of an English word." Smyth says it's not nearly as much of an issue in Latin speaking countries. But whether the "x" means removing gender or combining genders, the discussion is certainly not over.

In 2016, Sarah Haley Bartlett and Oscar Nn picked the topic apart for the public radio program, *LatinoUSA*. And the show, which bills itself as the longest running Latino-focused program on U.S. public media, isn't the only one weighing in on the debate. NPR's alt.latino arts and music project identifies itself as *Latinx* even if the reasons for such an adoption, according to Ron Smyth, remain generally unclear. "I don't know if speakers in general have come to a consensus about what the X really does; whether it defaces or acts as a variable." Elsewhere, issues of assimilation and exclusion are heavier still. *Codeswitch*, a project to talk race, gender and religion in plain language, has been a major NPR effort since 2015. But Asma Khalid told NPR's *All Things Considered* about how she, a Muslim political reporter for *Codeswitch*, faced bigotry and hatred from people who, she acknowledged, "didn't want to get to know me." Her attempts to talk with people who were fearful of her and who voted for Donald Trump were "frustrating." Within days of her last interview with NPR host Renee Montaigne, Khalid announced she would be leaving *Codeswitch*.

Public radio probably lost more points with millennials in early 2017, when transgender reporter Lewis Wallace from the APM program *Marketplace* was fired. He posted on his personal blog his concern that he might be unable to do objective journalism as a member of the LGBT community in the new age of Donald Trump. "We need to admit that those who oppose free speech, diversity and kindergarten level fairness are our enemies," said Wallace. *Marketplace* executive Deborah Clark, in comments to the *Washington Post*, called Wallace's words "public rejection of objectivity." While with Wallace, the issue was journalistic objectivity versus freedom of speech, it was freedom of association that tripped up former *Soundprint* and former *World of Opera* classical music host Lisa Simione. Simione expressed political views on a personal account in the wake of Occupy-related protests of 2011. *Soundprint*'s provider, WDAV, let Simione go for what may have been suggested to it as a breach of ethics. But in a gangster move, NPR dropped the other program that Simione still hosted, *World of Opera*, while retaining *Soundprint*. North Carolina's WDAV said at the time that it plans to keep Simione as host and that her political involvement had no bearing on her role in the broadcast. The station was also probably betting that lovers of classical music, not disrupted by a Simione departure, will keep supporting WDAV.

When CEO Gary Knell took over at NPR for Vivian Schiller after the 2011 scandal and her resignation, Katherine Fung, in a 2011 piece for the *Huffington Post*, reported that Knell promised to raise the level of diversity at the network. "It's really about fairness and accuracy and honesty in reporting so that our audience can make up their own minds and decide which issues they want to advocate on," Knell said. "That's really the role of public radio." Later, in 2014, Elizabeth Jensen wrote that with the arrival of President Jarl Mohn, NPR's board promised to bring more diversity to the network's 77% white newsroom, and diversify the soundbytes of featured guests. This implies NPR's board knows it needs to do better to, as Jensen writes, "increase the diversity of the audience by age, ethnicity and geography." That NPR is continuing to strive toward that same goal as mightily as it was in 1993 when the same shortcomings were spotlighted by the media watchdog, Fairness and Accuracy in Reporting, is telling.

Progress can be hampered by stereotypes that even the most progressive organizations can hold of themselves. The Chicago School of Divinity wrote after the 2017 resignation of Unitarian Universalist Association president, the Reverend Peter Morales, that the UUA has "served notice not only to liberal denominations but, at this moment, to them especially. There is no place to hide for a group whose language may be "correct," its public pronouncements up-front, but whose pews and letterheads down-home continue to embarrass many Unitarians and Universalists. The same is true for the majority of largely white Protestant bodies. What is most obvious is that there are no quick fixes, no matter how much argument, energy, posturing, and reforming is in evidence."

Public radio, apparently like churches, can get hamstrung by its own hype. Blinded by confidence that they are champions of community diversity, stations may in fact be losing chances to engage with communities other than their own because of unseen biases. A former volunteer at a community radio station, speaking anonymously, talked about how her station ignored asks from the local Hispanic community to help it promote a Cinco de Mayo event. "They have fewer donors, which ultimately impacts the amount of time they spend on air. It goes around in circles," she said. Though community and public radio aren't identical, she says both have had issues boosting for diversity and then blocking their own paths with self-fulfilling prophesies of failure. "I think that diversity absolutely matters when we talk about fundraising," the writer concludes, "because it's not just about pitch breaks. It's also about who gets to say what to which audience." ☎

In the Streets

"I tell people that you're not really in the radio industry until you've been fired at least once."

—Seth Resler, Jacobs Media Strategies, January 26, 2018

A 2017 article on NPR's newsroom diversity used a word listeners may hear in stories about the world, but rarely associate with public radio itself: "frustration." Ombudsman Elizabeth Jensen used it twice in her 2017 piece. "Far more people I spoke to in the newsroom expressed frustration — some even said they were angry — at the slow pace of change," Ms. Jensen says early in the article at NPR.org. Later from Jensen: "[Elise] Hu and others expressed frustration at what they see as problems with the recruiting process." This frustration can be tracked by the number of departures from NPR licensees by formerly well-known names over the last few years. One of the best places to follow up on public radio's departed is LinkedIn.

Libby Lewis was an NPR reporter until 2009. She now works for *Slate*. Margaret Low said she loved NPR "with every fiber of her being" since 1982. But she still left it for a "very enticing offer" at *The Atlantic* in 2014. And Portland, Maine's Megan Tan left her job with New Hampshire Public Radio and created her own podcast, *Millennials*. Tan told Nicholas Quah of the Nieman Labs *HotPod* blog that she made the change "out of a desire for something close to creative freedom, or a space to learn and explore and develop on her own terms."

The non-profit industry has an annual turnover rate of about 17%. Public radio is in the non-profit industry. But for listeners to public radio, that number may seem higher. Typing keywords "former NPR" into LinkedIn reveal several hundred former NPR employees ranging from hosts to reporters, from producers to editors. Daily it seems, Linkedin pings followers of former public radio people with "New Position" notices. Employers certainly have the right to dismiss whomever they choose, just like former employees can search for better career opportunities. But for an organization that depends on audience relationships built on more than just technical skill, a brain drain by former employees not only seeking more challenging ways to connect with listeners but a more diverse environment in which to do it represent not just a departure, but an indictment.

In her book, *Leap Without a Net,* former *Marketplace* host Tess Vigeland says she knows she did the right thing by leaving her eleven-year gig at the flagship financial show around November 2012. But according to Adam Ragusea in a 2016 interview with Vigeland for *Current*'s *The Pub,* she had also "had enough. I've been very circumspect about those reasons," says Vigeland. "People can fill in the blanks based on the fact that I won't talk about it." Vigeland said she just felt like she needed to do something new, but implied her reasons for leaving weren't unlike the "usual" reasons people "usually" leave jobs. That she stopped listening to the show on the day she left and hasn't listened since, Vigeland says, "So you can read into that as well."

In 2016, the *Harvard Business Review* did read into the reasons why people leave their jobs. "In general," the article says, "people leave their jobs because they don't like their boss, don't see opportunities for promotion or growth, or are offered a better gig (and often higher pay)." Vigeland said she practically adored her job with no mention of supervisors. She says her ideas to change *Marketplace Money* into what ultimately became *Marketplace Weekend* were ignored while she was there, but made after she left. And she admits she didn't have anything lined up after she quit, implying that a leap into the fire was better than staying in the frying pan.

But Brian Kropp, who heads HR practice for Washington-based CEB, looks not just at why workers quit but also at when. "We've learned that what really affects people is their sense of how they're doing compared with other people in their peer group, or with where they thought they would be at a certain point in life." The *HBR* article said work anniversaries, midlife milestones, conferences and class reunions are natural occasions where people measure their progress relative to others. "The big realization," says Kropp, "is that it's not just what happens at work — it's what happens in someone's personal life that determines when he or she decides to look for a new job."

In February 2017, Vigeland said, "I haven't talked publicly, except in very broad terms, about why I left, and I'm going to keep it that way unless and until I decide I never want to return to public radio." To date, her fill-in host gigs at KPCC Pasadena, KCRW Los Angeles and at NPR West in Culver City prove she's certainly not there yet.

Unlike a whistleblower that usually loses their job shortly after speaking out about a problem while still employed, Vigeland fell in the category of those who talk more honestly about their former job but only after they've left it. On one hand, ex-employees calling out former employers is understood. In 2013, the newsletter for the *Society for Industrial and Organizational Psychology* quoted two SIOP members interviewed by the *Chicago Tribune*. Robert Rubin of DePaul University said their research showed that in cases where employees quit, other employees agreed with the departed employee that their company practices violate its promise to customers and employees." Stephen Laser of Chicago-based consulting firm Stephen A. Laser Associates seemed to concur, saying that "positive change" can happen when organizations look deep into themselves in light of the criticism "instead of being overly defensive."

On the other hand, employment sites like GlassDoor, rating sites like Yelp and good ole' social media can put huge dents in company brands that weren't possible before the Internet. So much so that J.T. O'Donnell, writing for LinkedIn in 2017, said many employers have adopted non-disparaging agreements that employees must sign to receive severance and other benefits. If they're ever violated, the employee can be sued. O'Donnell recommends however, that "it works both ways," and if employers restrict what an employee can say, the employee can demand that the employer provide good recommendations into the future in exchange.

But losing a job that you criticized can be the result of a self-fulfilling prophesy. As "bunderful" says on *Metafilter*, "Even if you don't get fired, being openly critical of your company and management will tick off the managers and make your peers cautious of being too friendly with you - lest management think they agree with your criticisms. It gets harder to get good assignments and do good work because you've screwed up your relationships. This makes it really easy to create a story - which is not really a story because it has become true - that you're not a good fit. And out you go." A former senior manager at NPR commented on GlassDoor that for most of the time, they loved their time there but sometimes found the bureaucracy stifling. And in a criticism that has defined who is inside versus outside of the network house, they advised it to "Take more calculated risks to ensure NPR remains relevant and operational. Creative ideas don't only come from one are[a] of the company or at one level - listen to the tribe!" ☎

Content

"No matter what kind of news, music or entertainment public radio provides, an important piece in whether or not listeners keep listening is how well it remains consistent."

—*Audience 98*

Consistency means continuing to get what you've been getting. And *Audience 98* makes it clear that consistency is what the audience wants to keep listening and giving to public radio. What it consistently wants is content. Those expectations, in terms of the quality, value, and accessibility of news, music, and entertainment shows are very high. And public radio knows it.

After more than 100 years of broadcasting, news, music, and entertainment are still the primary groupings of content. News, for example, is a self-defined storytelling mainstay. Music, of course, stands alone though some would say certain types of music have long been under attack within public radio. Entertainment is where things start to go sideways, since many of public radio's news and music stories also provide "discussion and analysis." Sports is the stepchild of the public radio family. But relatively new to the traditional lineup are blogs like *The Two-Way* and *Planet Money*. They retell complicated stories in a longer form that's reminiscent of newspapers and magazines. As of this writing, twenty of these are at NPR.org, including one from its Ombudsman. Subgroups to news, music and entertainment include arts, business, comedy, health, music, News & Politics, Science & Medicine, technology and TV & Film. More tabs slice the pie even smaller, with Art & Life and Society & Culture. But the network doesn't have a lock on blogs and podcasts. WNYC, and its *Studio 360* blog, KQED's *Mindshift* and Georgia Public Broadcasting's *"Atlanta*

Considered" are places where local stories are told in old and new ways.

Crossovers are common. News-talk like Tom Ashbrook's *On Point*, isn't the same as the sports-talk of Bill Littlefield's *It's Only a Game* or entertainment-talk from former *A Splendid Table* host Lynn Rosetta Casper. But with so many excellent programs, and only 24 short hours in a day, not even time-shifting lets listeners hear them all. This helps explain why many radio groups have split their programming between stations as some radio stations split their programming between streams. Cincinnati Public Radio has classical music on WGUC while news and information broadcasts on WVXU. Cleveland's *Ideastream* does something similar with WCPN for news and WCLV for classical. Likewise for Minnesota Public Radio and *The Current*.

When WSIU's *Live from Prairie Lights* was canceled in 2008 by Iowa Public Radio after an 18-year run, locals howled. For some, it marked the end of locally produced "subject specific programming" in favor of what blog author and former FCC commissioner Nicholas Johnson called "magazine programming." The state's pedigree as a literary hub, reinforced by a UNESCO designation as a "World City of Literature," supported a program that focused on local writers by inviting the audience into a "virtual bookstore." The decision to pull the plug on the show, possibly motivated by low numbers and high production costs prompted News Director Jonathan Ahi to respond. "I did not unilaterally make a decision on *Live from Prairie Lights*. It was a unanimous decision from IPR's senior team. We did a lot of research, discussed options and made a decision." Ahi's post seemed prompted by a previous poster who accusingly said, "I recall there was a recent pledge drive for Iowa Public Radio. It's interesting that a significant local programming cut was made soon after the drive. I am sure many people pledged to support local programming, but alas it looks like more [o]f it will go to national programming like *Morning Edition*."

The incident shows that local content isn't untouchable. A station must have a goal for its content. Those goals must be spelled out in an annual, CPB required *Local Content and Services Report*. It asks stations to answer a number of not-so-simple questions about how what they deliver to the community enhances the community. Beginning in 2016, stations must make the forms and their responses, due each February, publicly available. But these efforts to ensure local programming meets local needs still encounter resistance from those who feel local support of national programming is the bigger picture stations should be focusing on as well as skeptics who think local shows will never be as good as their network counterparts. In a 2013 commentary for *Current*, Wisconsin Public Radio's content director, Michael Arnold, reminded stations that their fees support the network and a strong network is good for public radio.

Public radio stations answer the questions in that report with no guarantee their shows will get your attention. Screens and their contents, whether *Fortnite* or *Minecraft*, are among public radio's biggest headaches. In 2013, Nielsen reported that although adults spent less than the 6.3 hours teens spent daily on gaming (in 2018, it's 7.8), they spent the most money on games for themselves, meaning that time isn't spent listening to, and that money isn't financially supporting, public radio. And that's just gaming. Nielsen also says Netflix, AppleTV, Roku, Hulu and PBS, took five hours and four minutes of the average adult's time every day in 2013. Meanwhile, the movie industry, suffering from lackluster attendance, fights back with innumerable CGI packed, primary color saturated, decibel busting extravaganzas geared to that 13-year-old boy inside most grown-ass men. It explains why public radio consistently throws at you everything its got and why it wants to

226

be everywhere you and your devices are. They're the few places left it can hook you and your checking account with a news, music, entertainment, sports or a blog-derived "driveway moment."☎

News

"Humans exhibit a nearly universal desire to learn and share news, which they satisfy by talking to each other and sharing information."

—Wikipedia

The origin of the word "news" is evolved from the Medieval Latin word "nova." Its singular root means "something new." Though at the joint Defense Information School (DINFOS) in 1981, the training ground for military journalists, it was also defined as an acronym for the need to know, moving like lightning, from the "North, East, West and South."

Public radio's reporters do carry news from the four corners of the earth. And since its first May 1971 broadcast, NPR has striven to create and deliver news through its more than a dozen on-air and online programs. As of this writing, on-air news offerings by NPR include *Morning Edition*, *All Things Considered*, *Weekend Edition Saturday*, *Weekend Edition Sunday*, *Weekend All Things Considered*, and *Here and Now*, co-produced with WBUR in Boston. Online news programs include the *NPR Politics Podcast* among others.

NPR news also distributes half a dozen or so programs produced by its member stations that cross over into the fuzzier area of "public affairs." In broadcasting, this term means not just focusing on topics of immediate concern to the community like "spot" or "breaking" news. Public affairs give a more in-depth treatment of politics and public policy, i.e., decisions that affect people's day-to-day lives. Its creation was predicted by David Giovanonni as far back as 2004, as an emerging "news and public affairs" cohort. Although distinctive from entertainment shows like *Car Talk*, Giovanonni and others found that listeners listened to public affairs programs for almost exactly the same reasons they listened to *Car Talk*. This demonstrates public radio's reliance on people sharing values, attitudes and lifestyles, rather than content for demographic groups defined by race, age or gender.

In most newsrooms, reporters work with producers while both are overseen by editors, senior editors and news directors. Each turnstile tries to catch problems the one before missed before the final product reaches the listener. These layers are reproduced in the network news bureaus that dot the earth. Bureaus can report, or aid network reporters parachuting in to report local stories with national importance. When added to the collection of musicians, bloggers and librarians, these 483 people create NPR's news.

The debate continues as to whether local news adds to or detracts from the local audience's willingness to keep listening after network programs end. But that isn't stopping local and regional efforts to create interesting and engaging programming. *Texas Standard*, launched in 2015 by KUT and its partners is billed as telling "local, national and international stories from a Texas perspective." The show supplements rather than supplants NPR by retaining the local flavor. But local content isn't always a recipe for success. In 2016, the managers at the ten stations of the Virginia Public Radio network agreed to cancel *Virginia Conversations*, a weekly news and public affairs program that featured interviews with newsmakers and politicians. They opted, instead, for the network to produce more in-depth stories that they could use wherever they were needed rather than a show that they couldn't break apart. Even though they agreed it was excellent programming, it was sacrificed for the good of the Virginia stations.

Public radio is also trying to figure out how to serve audiences categorically. In 2009, NPR, CPB, the Knight Foundation and 12 affiliates launched "Project Argo." In a throwback to old-school reporting, stations were assigned "beats" or areas of reporting expertise. It intends to develop expert reporters with the best journalistic answers for hard social questions. The project also sought to increase collaboration between stations. But its overall goal was as a "test of concept" for whether such sharing could work technologically. If it did, the means to put it to work, starting with an API, could proceed. API, which stands for "application programming interface," is an infrastructure developers create that helps programmers build more user-friendly software programs. Along with an algorithm that not only learns user preferences but allows the different content databases to talk to each other, users can create and curate their own channels of content. The technology arose in part because of accusations that the news business wasn't as responsive to its listeners as it needed to be.

In a 2016 article for the *Columbia Journalism Review,* Jim Brady accused pubcasters of coasting on the "fat and happy" years between the mid-seventies and 2005. Emphasis on "engagement" and the "user experience" is a relatively new focus for stations Confident that only they had the keys to their content, broadcasters didn't see that new digital platforms were undermining their control of not only content but distribution, analytics, reportage, and most importantly, revenue generation. John Sutton told *Current* in 2014 that as digital options accelerate stations losing their exclusiveness as the only place their listeners can hear their favorite shows, stations potentially lose more money because of underwriting credits not heard. He says that's why the emotional connection stations form with listeners is key to station survival. That emotional connection, and the local loyalty it generates, called "a sense of place," isn't lost on the market. Jennifer Brandel is CEO and founder of Hearken, a company that helps media, including public radio, create relevant content to hold listeners in place. "With audiences increasingly promiscuous about where they get their news," says Brandel, "media outlets need to be creating original stories the public finds personally relevant and shares to make popular."

As late as 2012, shrinking budgets were forcing stations to choose certain audience preferences over others. *LocalNPR* is a project of Michael V. Marcotte, a Knight Fellow and professor at the Reynolds School of Journalism at Reno, Nevada. He looked at newsrooms with annual budgets between $50,000 and $750,000 while examining sixteen types of local programming and the resources stations used to create them. He wanted to know the strength of the relationship between stations and listeners. He found that the ways stations felt best connected to their audiences, such as through interviews, newscasts, features, and breaking news, also took many station resources. Marcotte found that other means of outreach, including public service announcements, town hall meetings, live broadcasts, on-air magazines, documentaries, and commentary took up fewer resources, which meant stations were less committed to these methods of outreach. Overall, he found that about half of the stations spent money on local shows that connected with their audience need for sense of place. For the other half of stations in the survey, this was a luxury, as a 2016 survey of newsrooms for the Watershed Media Project showed. It found that the lower a newsroom's budget, the less they were able to engage. Although the number of respondents was smaller than Marcotte's, and represented a narrower range of newsroom budgets, its conclusions were similar. Namely, that the kind of engagement that requires money is "simply beyond the reach of smaller organizations." And as we already know, if stations don't engage with listeners through emotionally connected, sense of place techniques AND give them the legacy programs they want, they go elsewhere.

Stations debate whether to counter drains on their revenue by focusing even more tightly on local news. But they can get in trouble if they cut too many corners. A cautionary tale involves the *Chicago Tribune* 's use of a news service called "Journatic." In 2012, *This American Life* and later, NPR media critic David Folkenflik, explained how the company, using an algorithm to provide local news to dozens of markets across the country, was distributing sloppily written stories under fake bylines. When confronted, Journatic freelancer Ryan Smith said, "I don't know those communities, and I have no stake in them. And so it didn't matter to me that I found out all the information and I got it right." Journatic's CEO Brian Timpone called the use of the fake bylines a mistake. By outsourcing the writing of some of Journatic's stories overseas, and only pretending to offer local news, they and the papers that used them violated the public trust. Although newspapers contacted by Folkenflik, *TAL* and the *Chicago Tribun* e didn't talk about why or for how long they'd been using Journatic, many of them severed ties after the stories aired. It's not known if any public radio stations repurposed those substandard stories into their own newscasts.

Legitimate news-writers have another form of threat to deal with; software that writes news copy. Listeners might never notice companies like Automated Insights or Narrative Science's Wordsmith is writing their weather, sports or stock market story, and that's the goal. In 2012, a *Wired* headline asked, *Can an algorithm write a better news story than a human reporter?* Because an algorithm misses the subtleties of human syntax, pronunciation, tone, pacing and inflection, *Wired* suggested the answer was a categorical, "At least not yet."

In 2015, the magazine revisited the question. But this time, the headline was, *Now this news-writing bot is free for everyone,* acknowledging several depressing realities for the news business simultaneously. Users upload a spreadsheet full of data. And in what author Klint Finley describes as "mad libs meeting mail merge," the software takes the numbers and sets rules for which words can be used when and how often. In moments, it generates something flexible enough that every time the spreadsheet changes, a new "story" can be written and fired off to the company blog. The earlier *Wired* story wryly notes, "this potentially job-killing technology was incubated in part at Northwestern's Medill School of Journalism." These synthetic snippets appear in *Forbes* and other places, which the article says are keeping their identities hidden. In 2012, the software created 400,000 paragraph-long stories. By 2013, their number was expected to double.

In a Casey-Jones-versus-the-steam-drill type contest, NPR's White House correspondent, Scott Horsley, raced WordSmith in 2015. Who could write an earnings report based on the first release of numbers from the Denny's corporation faster? Scott wrote his story in seven minutes. Wordsmith did it in two. Narrative Science's co-founder and Chief Technology Officer, Kristian Hammond said that by 2027, he expected 90% of all news stories to be done by software like his and within five years, his software could write something worthy of a Pulitzer Prize. At the same time, he told *Wired* that journalists had "nothing to worry about."

Tight budgets can also force stations to bypass lucrative niche markets. LPFM stations and their "hyper" local content represent what the *New York Times* called "yet another wake-up call for local NPR news radio stations." Although public radio programming focuses on touching the core beliefs of large groups, LPFM stations target a narrower aspect of much tinier groups. Their more than 1500 stations nationwide reach niches that many public radio stations, through a reliance on network programs and automation, miss. The National Federation of Community Broadcasters, an advocate for community radio, applauds the convergence of LPFM and news. It is sweet revenge for those who remember a consortium, led in the 70s by NPR and NAB, that petitioned the FCC to restrict the entry of LPFM into the broadcast market to avoid this exact kind of growing, grassroots competition.

Other lower key challenges to the news mission not fully known by listeners include calls by staff for more training. A 2007 report from the John S. and James L. Knight Foundation (a major supporter of public radio) says on its first page, "Journalists need training. They know it. Their bosses know it." Reporters want to be more adept in areas that range from law to social media. But as many as 27% of radio stations in the report provided no training while the 73% that offer "some training" only grade the quality of that mostly in-house training a "C."

The need is so great that as late as 2015, former NPR editor Jonathan Kern created a block of journalistic instruction that deconstructed the story of "The Three Little Pigs." "One of the under-appreciated challenges in putting a radio report together is ensuring that the story has a logical structure," explained Kern. Although the need for even the most basic training is ongoing, the report did show that new media training, such as social media and Internet use, was increasing. And more emphasis was turning to distance learning programs, like the Poynter Institute's "News University," as stations looked for higher quality, lower cost ways to help reporters and stations better serve their communities.

More news challenges center on how journalists themselves can affect the news mission, which in turn, can affect how listeners contribute. NPR, in a 2012 revision of its ethics policy, requires staff to hand over personal social media passwords so it can see all comments and contacts. This, the thinking goes, reminds journalists of their impartiality while not letting the network itself be dragged into questions regarding its own. Ultimately, pubcasters

want such moves to dampen listener uncertainty of whether controversy should make them put their financial support elsewhere.
But journalists aren't necessarily happy about it. A 2014 study by
the Indiana University School of Journalism reports that reporters,
in general, are "less satisfied and have less autonomy," though the
study finds that as a group, they are still dedicated to more in-depth
coverage of government, more unpacking of complicated issues for
the public and more dedicated to getting stories out quickly.

With regards to social media and the relatively recent emergence of "Public Insight Networks," a 2006 creation of Minnesota
Public Radio, the crowdsourcing of news is nearly complete. These
type of newsroom/community collaborations ask the community
to not just find stories, but tell them. "Social journalists are accus-
tomed to thinking about engagement as likes, retweets, shares," said
Aron Pilhofer, editor of interactive news at the *New York Times*.
"Those are all important, but we need to go beyond Facebook and
Twitter to look at ways people can participate in a story." In this
way, Public Insight Networks help strengthen listeners' emotional
connection with the station by hearing stories that have a root
within their hometown.

Reporters are also using social media to help them stay more
connected to their communities through "social listening." Search
tools, like from Chicago-based Geofeedia, Facebook's reporter
specific, *Signal* and Nieman Labs' Neighborhood Buzz help journalists find content and then, using embedded geolocation, zero in
on sources, photos and situations that may have been impossible to
find without them. A study by newsroom software provider Cison
in collaboration with George Washington University, also found
however, that 89% of reporters didn't entirely trust the reliability
of social media as a primary source of information.

Nearly half of social media, said the study, suffers from "lack of fact checking, verification and reporting standards." Editors and reporters, although users of social media, deferred to more "old-school" journalism, the report notes. Reaching out and talking directly with organization spokespeople, finding experts, asking questions and putting answers in perspective is the essential job of the reporter, and is a reminder that sometimes, in journalism, there's no school like old school.

"Engagement," says KPCC's Kim Bui, associate editor of social media, "is really getting to know your audience." That could be through live chats, real-time tweet-storms or via Peri-scope, Skype or Facebook Live. But for reporters, making contact is only half of the work. The rest of it involves seeing what those personal relationships, anchored to good journalism, do for how those stories are received in the community. The aforementioned, co-authored study found that reporters do indeed use software to measure the impact of stories. But it noted, "Less-experienced journalists use online and social media metrics to measure the impact of their stories more than experienced journalists. "Man-agement however, does use social media to watch their reporters, not just the beats they cover. Managers may use the metrics to see the value of reporters and make in-house choices for higher pay or more responsibility.

The public radio news business also faces a number of large, low-tech problems. Among them, job uncertainty. In July 2017, Michael Arria reported for *In These Times* that more than 400 NPR employees nearly struck in reaction to moves by NPR management to gut health care and overtime pay for temporary workers, and create a two-tiered salary system. The strength of SAG-AFTRA's representation of news organizations like NPR, says Arria, is why the union is making a comeback. That's something else not com-monly known. In 2014, author Bruce Vail wrote of Baltimore's

WYPR and its loss of the right to unionize despite help from the SAG-AFTRA. Staff members complained the station was run by a board that "didn't understand public radio."

In the wake of hiring a so-called "union-busting" law firm, Jonathan Rogers, Chair of the WYPR Board of Directors, did not seem supportive in recognizing a union at the station. According to *Current*, Southern California Public Radio, and dual licensee KPBS in San Diego joined WYPR for union representation between 2012 and 2014. Such negotiations can be further complicated if higher paid staff in development and underwriting speak against the organizing efforts of lower paid staff in engineering or the newsroom.

Public radio's news rides sanguine upon the undulating tones of soothing voices. Public radio's news business does not. Changes which can seem almost invisible to listeners may feel very personal to staff. In 2013 *Morning Edition* "with little fanfare" stopped giving its team the small perk of running through some of their names at the end of each week. Research showed "it was a turnoff to the audience." ☎

Music

"Not sure if it was mentioned earlier on this list, but today is the last day of daytime classical music on WWNO in New Orleans. Not sure if anyone is keeping a list of which stations have changed format, but you may as well add ours to the list."

—WWNO jazz host Farrah Hudkins in a May 2012 Facebook post

Public radio owes much of its sound to its funkiness. And it owes much of its funk to its music. As early as 1978, a CPB study noted, "When listeners are asked on a closed-end basis whether each of nine possible reasons for listening helps to explain their own use of the medium, music programming is the reason most frequently given." A poster child for music's allure, New Jersey-based WFMU, featured on NPR's *Weekend Edition Saturday* in 2014, was described as a veritable "hot mess" of music. Renegades like Montana-based KUFM, with their eclectic mixes, have gathered an intense following. Public radio has long been the place where new artists have the best chance of debuting their music. Elizabeth Chernosky, in a PhD dissertation for Columbia University, called Bill Siemering's vision of NPR as a place for "sonic experimentation" the reason the NPR audience allowed "new music" to become "American experimental music." But whether talking about new music or traditional pillars like classical, jazz or opera, the relationship between public radio and music has been intimate, as evidenced by NPR's music muses, Don Voegeli, Stef Scaggiari and B.J. Liederman. Voegeli created NPR's *All Things Considered* theme song. Scaggiari penned *Weekend Edition* Sunday's. And Liederman composed themes for Morning Edition, *Weekend Edition Saturday*, *Car Talk*, Marketplace, and *WWDTM*.

But *Audience 98*'s key findings regarding public radio's more traditional music forms was this: "Local classical music is widely heard but not as highly valued. While it generates about a quarter of the listening to public radio, it produces a fifth of all listener support." In 1996, *LA Times* writer Judith Michaelson quoted USC's VP of External Relations, Jane Pisano who said of classical music at KUSC, "The fundamental thing was that our audience was basically falling away from us . . . and we weren't attracting a new and different audience." Perhaps it's because a change was happening at NPRHQ. Between 1998 and 2008, NPR CEO Ken Stern and President Kevin Klose tried to erase what they considered "musty" classical music and stations followed suit. In 2002, the *Washington Post*'s Paul Farhi reported that NPR underwent a massive examination of its music programming, including an "extensive review" of jazz, opera and classical. An internal strategy paper said that *Jazz from Lincoln Center* and *Billy Taylor's Jazz at the Kennedy Center* as well as the cultural staff within NPR that provided them, could "disappear." Farhi noted the review seemed to follow a move by many commercial stations that had also dropped those formats. "These preferences mirror trends in commercial radio," he said. "Public stations have, over time, moved toward news and talk formats because they draw higher ratings, and thus bigger donations during pledge drives." Washington D.C.-based WETA left the format in 2012, but returned to it when WGMS, the only other station in town to play classical music, dropped it. Southwest Florida's WGCU in 2008 and MPR's Classical South Florida stations in 2015 are two among many that left the format and didn't return. In 2007, KUOR ceased rebroadcasting jazz from KKJZ in Long Beach. Purchased by Southern California Public Radio, the satellite station now rebroadcasts KPCC's NPR news programming.

Frank Dominquez, general manager of Charlottesville, Virginia's WDAV doesn't disagree with the data. When he came to the station in 1995, there was a concern that the station's audience was dying off. "That concern has never changed, but the demographics have never looked better," he said. "Yes, half the audience is over 55 years old, but a quarter of it is under 35." The other difference is that in 2017, Nielsen Audio ranked WDAV the number one classical music station in the nation. The station gives its audience up to 22 hours a day of locally produced classical music, delivered by recognizable voices that its listeners know. "Part of it is probably the times we live in," says the 23-year veteran of the station. "It causes people to seek an oasis that they might not have sought two years ago. Everyone needs an oasis to decompress or recharge." Another reason might be that in 2015, the station stopped running NPR newscasts that it had carried since the mid-90s. WDAV's audience represents an odd reversal of the public radio truism that news sells and classical doesn't. Listeners to WFUV were likewise

delighted when it dropped NPR news in 2013 for three more hours
of its *Music Mix*. The move was described by Program Director
Rita Houston as "an opportunity to fill a real need in the New York
market, and we're excited to offer a music mix that's uniquely
diverse, eclectic, and true to our public radio values."

It's too simple to say greater attention to what the audience
wants will save a flailing station format, however. In late 2015,
University of Massachusetts at Amherst's WMAU fell more than
30% short of a $40,000 pledge drive goal after its entire lineup of
jazz hosts for six programs quit over personnel issues and programming inconsistencies. Such hits to a budget can affect the
extra content stations want to provide. Internal stresses, all but
invisible to a listener, can have a huge secondary effect on station
stability. A LinkedIn discussion from 2016, titled *When Classical
Music Programmers Go Bad*, was created by a group of public
radio professionals who were warning their colleagues to resist
burnout, laziness and boredom when playing the music.

The mutual threat to classical and jazz is not discreet. The Jazz
Audience Initiative's 2011 *Segmentation Study* said classical music
was valuable as a gateway for jazz listeners to become exposed to
jazz. "Jazz has entry points from other musics (classical, rock, blue
grass) so booking jazz bands with other ensembles playing in
different genres is a way to attract otherwise disengaged
audiences." But the study also seemed to indicate that jazz was
age exclusive. "Demographically, jazz ticket buyers across the 19
communities are middle-aged, predominantly male, and very well
educated. On average, only 17% are under age 45, and 80% are
white." These results parallel a 2009 report by Walrus Research
that found the audiences of stations that played jazz were aging at a
faster rate than all stations in general while classical music had the
oldest audiences overall. These audiences were also not growing.

PLEDGE: The Public Radio Fund Drive

"Public radio's jazz stations have been less successful at raising money from listeners," the report said.

Audience 98 also identified problems when a network is delivering jazz to a nation of local audiences. "It is futile to talk about the appeal of 'local jazz' or 'local classical,'" the study points out, "when the same genre appeals to an older audience on one station, a younger audience on another, a racially diverse audience on another, and so forth." These demographic and financial reasons seem enough for understanding why jazz and classical have been on decline. But some in public radio suspect that others are on a mission to get rid of the music simply because they feel it doesn't belong in a newsy world. As *Weekly Standard* contributor Andrew Ferguson noted in a 2004 study on the shift in music tastes, "researchers wrote in their report, with unseemly enthusiasm: 'Local classical music just sits there, while NPR news-talk races ahead.'"

Two stations dealt very differently with threats to their core music. In 2011, another Charlottesville-based station, WTJU, was in crisis. A previous general manager had made changes months earlier that led to DJs threatening to quit and a listenership up in arms. Nathan Moore took over that year and addressed the chief complaint by audience and staff of not enough folk music. Moore brought more folk as well as roots, world and specialty music to the playlist. People have rewarded the station for the changes. Moore says that a study by the University of Virginia Center for Survey Research showed that about 30,000 new listeners hear the station. It's also getting an extra $70,000 a year in pledge drive contributions.

Contrast that with the former WNKU, Northern Kentucky University's folk music standard bearer since 1986. This story started out happy. In 2011, WNKU bought two stations with ambitions of spreading its trademark sound from Dayton, Ohio to Huntington,

West Virginia. The next year, despite meeting a record fund drive
goal and increasing listeners by 50%, costs began to outpace revenue. By February 2015, the station announced a staff shake up and
a format change away from its traditional folk music to alternative
music with an emphasis on rock. By the next year, however, university management, responding to an "exponential" jump in costs
as well as cuts in state support to the university, sold the station to
Bible Broadcasting Corporation. A $5 million counter-offer from
Louisville Public Media was not enough to change the minds of
the University's Board of Regents. The sale was finalized in 2017
and the folk music voice in Cincinnati and Northern Kentucky was
silenced.

Some see homogenization as another way of getting rid of the
music. Dennis Owsley wrote in *St. Louis Magazine* in 2012 that
boring and indistinctive music looks and sounds like "pablum." As
host of the 25-year running *Jazz Unlimited* on St. Louis Public
Radio, Owsley said that jazz music has fewer and fewer places to
call home. "There are only 400 jazz DJs on the air," and "only one
jazz disc jockey for about every 775,000 people in this country,"
he said. Owsley says the DJ is one of the three legs that supports
musicians and musical styles. The other two are the record industry
and public broadcasting. "Remove any leg from this stool and it
falls. And it may be that the most vulnerable leg is that of the disc
jockeys." Owsley believes that local programming is being assim-
ilated by what has been called "anemic" syndicated programming,
both in commercial and public broadcasting. "So if the public
broadcasting of jazz goes that way, the real creative music will be
lost."

For some, that means local stations, to save money, drop locally produced programming and turn to classical or jazz services
provided by networks. Such competing music services set MPR
and NPR at each others throats in the eighties. The new climate

also forces DJs to conform to new music rotation schedules. Larry Monroe, a former long-time host on KUT moved to KDRP in 2011 when the former instituted such a rotation. Monroe described how he played four tracks from new CDs as well as three "core artists" each hour and any two tracks from the "new" rack. "Nine of the 12 or so tracks I played each hour had station fingerprints on them. There was no way to do artistic radio with that format," Monroe told the *Austin American-Statesman*.

To some, the purpose of separating music from the mainstream is to segregate it from on-air. That's what loyal listeners of Houston Public Media saw when University of Houston station KUHA 91.7 was sold to Christian broadcaster KSBJ. At the time of the February 2016 sale, KUHA Associate VP and General Manager Lisa Shumante said she was "excited" that it opened up new opportunities for the station to commit even more to other formats, including classical music. But it meant that some lovers of the music could no longer hear it on the public airwaves. That required a new radio, or a device with which to download an app and create an online account. This is another occasional complaint regarding jazz and classical music in public radio; it's only online, though it's not a new idea.

As far back as 2002, NPR was considering moving classical music to an Internet "stream," which is significant considering that Apple released iTunes 1.0 in January 2001. But putting on-air music online is a solution National Association of Broadcaster's president Gordon Smith has never liked. Smith, a former Utah legislator, is no fan of satellite or Internet radio. He sees them as direct threats to terrestrial broadcasters. In a 2011 speech to the Radio Advertising Bureau and the NAB, he said, "Radio has remained successful by remembering our core mission: We keep our citizens connected, informed and entertained - anywhere they are, and always for free."

NPR has maintained that providing "free" programs is part of its mandate. But researcher David Giovanonni asked, if by giving airtime to classical and jazz rather than news, were pubcasters fulfilling their public service mission? The question came in the same year the network opened NPR West, the $13 million back-up headquarters in Culver City, California. It was also shortly before the historic $235 million gift from the widow of McDonald's founder, Ray Kroc. So it's reasonable to wonder if the NPR review was initiated, in part, to examine paying for content that was returning little value. At the time, both Senior VP of Programming, Jay Kernis, and CEO Kenneth Stern said the proposed changes were not about "financial and ratings pressures alone," indicating however that they were part of the equation. Decades later, Giovanonni's question remains politely unanswered while network classical and jazz programming survive. They include *Marianne McPartland's Piano Jazz*, *Jazz Night in America*, hosted by jazz legend Christian McBride, and *Songs We Love*, an eclectic mix that includes jazz and classical. And new music continues to be introduced. In 2014, NPR's *Tiny Desk Concerts*; intimate performances by musicians while chatting at the desks of reporters, invited listeners to share new artists and music.

The effort to bring new music isn't just for the ears. With the added push toward video, and its adoption even by alternative music mainstays like *Afropop Worldwide*, music lovers are discovering VuHaus, public radio's video channel for new music. Six public radio stations across the country, and founding partner Public Radio Music, find and introduce performances of "music discovery" in a direct appeal to a format designed to catch the ear of younger listeners.

Re-engineering formats for younger audiences, while giving a nod to the composers of the baby boom generation, also seems to be having some success for stations. Colorado Public Radio's

Music Forward offers up younger composers like Arvo Part, John Corigliano and John Adams while acknowledging influences from greats like Shostakovich. Meanwhile, Matt Weisner said for CPR's website in 2016, "younger artists like Missy Mazzoli and Mason Bates are redefining music once again, bringing everything from rock and folk influences to electronic beats to the concert hall."

Besides the renewal of classical and jazz in some places, a shift from news talk to a commercially familiar music format has taken some in public radio by surprise. According to a Nielsen Audio report from 2013, the Triple-A (Adult Album Alternative) format has become public radio's "most popular music format" with about one in ten public radio listeners. The *New York Radio Guide* says stations adopting the format, described as appealing more to adults than teens, play mixes of longer, album-oriented tracks as well as extended play singles. "Stylistically," says the site, "such stations may play rock, folk-rock, country-rock, modern rock, blues, folk, and world music." Ironically, playing more music leads to paying for more music. So there are moves to cut costs to the bottom line.

In 2015, NPR was a member of a coalition fighting a piece of legislation called the *Fair Play Fair Pay* act. It helped ensure that terrestrial, satellite and Internet stations paid performers each time their music played. Numerous efforts to pass it were defeated by lobbyists and the radio industry, including by the Music, Innovation & Consumers (MIC) coalition that NPR joined. But its membership in MIC deprived artists like Cassandra Wilson and Elvis Costello the right to be fairly paid. NPR countered that the higher CRB fees not only cost it more but push smaller stations unable to pay them off the air. The conflict was summed up by Adam Ragusea, a staff writer for *Current*. "At least the way I figure it, [a non-profit's] loyalty should be to your institution's mission, not to the institution itself. And yet I often see public media institutions,

244

mostly in little ways, doing things that serve the institution over its mission." NPR withdrew from the MIC coalition in July 2015.

Another issue for stations and artists isn't always complete songs, but pieces. Joel Meyer and Spencer Weisbroth of the Public Radio Program Directors addressed this in 2013. Snippets listeners hear between news stories, whether it's *Marketplace*'s *Juicy* by Mtume, or *This American Life*'s go-to tune, *Rumble* by Link Wray & the Ray Men don't cause much problem, in part, because they are such standards. But music licensing firms accuse smaller, lesser known artists playing their own original work of having copied something similar enough to something the licensor owns that the artist must pay a royalty fee to perform it. Artists, without the deep pockets to fight, often relent even if that likelihood is low. Though CPB does provide stations protection by paying the licensing fees to BMI, ASCAP and SESAC, newer artists don't always have that protection. Stations without proper music rights can be forced to cut music out of interviews and programs to avoid legal action.

How music affects giving depends on who you ask. Paul Resnikoff is the founder of *Digital Music News*, which describes itself as "The leading authority for music industry professionals worldwide." Resnikoff says he's given over $10,000 in the past decade to public radio stations and considers himself a very loyal listener. But, he admits his listening habits have waned. "One day," he said, "I realized that I wasn't listening to KCRW and KUSC that much anymore. I stopped turning on KPCC in the shower." But he says he's still listening to hours of music every day. "What's going on?" he asks. He's listening to music services. "Spotify playlists and podcasts almost non-stop. And half the time," says Resnikoff, "the podcasts don't have any music in them!" Other services like Rhapsody, Pandora and Apple Music chip away at public radio's music dominance. But WDAV's Dominguez has little fear his listeners will turn to a music service. "It's a curated experience you can't get from Spotify and an experience you can't match in the local area," Dominguez said. "We want to be the connection between the listeners and the classical music of the region."

Public radio has not abandoned the music. A 2013 Nielsen Audio report showed a 40% increase in classical music programming for pubcasters, although the increase included streaming, not just broadcast. Award-winning songwriter and musician Nellie McKay acknowledges the increase, telling the *Huffington Post* in 2015 that public radio was "the last oasis of free and independent music." She said that musicians not falling into a single category "would be lost without the local and national support of NPR and public radio stations around the country." But the slow squeeze on classical and jazz has been undeniable. In 2004, the Association of Music Personnel in Public Radio, a group of public radio stations that plays classical music, held its 42nd annual convention. The room, an attendee noted as he wearily waved his hand, was almost empty. As of this writing, AMPPR's Facebook post of June 2018 was only its ninth since August 2013. It may be proof that the audience that built public radio in part with classical and jazz music, may be dwindling away. ☎

Entertainment

"Listeners generally value entertainment over news."

—Audience 98

What is entertainment? PRI's *To the Best of Our Knowledge* has the tagline, "If ideas are entertainment for public radio listeners, then *To the Best of Our Knowledge* is here to deliver." What about the yuck fest that was *Car Talk*? Did it pencil out to be worth more than *Morning Edition*? Public radio implies that news is the driver of the audience and people can't start their day without it. Or that listeners flock to on-air and online music as a way of understanding the world by growing their personal musical tastes. But *Audience 98* said the content pecking order is first music, then entertainment and then news. News and music have been covered. So what is entertainment?

Amusement, understood to include fun and laughter, is strongly associated with being entertained. But entertainment can include everything from satire to ceremony. Its goal may be to distract people from life's stressors, but it may also serve to educate society about culture through display and performance art. Problems in definitions can arise, however, when education tries to be entertaining or vice versa, spawning hybrids like "infotainment." And entertainment, like news or music, can have an air of exclusivity. Public radio might argue that since it works to bring its entire audience up to the same level, all regular listeners would have the same information and context, and therefore, should be able to enjoy the entertainment programming equally.

A random visit to the "Arts and Entertainment" page on the npr.org website shows a listing of interviewed fiction and nonfiction authors and a preponderance of theater, film and music reviews. The "Arts and Life" page breaks down by books, movies, pop culture, food, art & design, performing arts and photography. However, on this particular day of scanning the Internet, the site also featured a story on the U.S. Government's secret plans to survive a nuclear war "while the rest of us died." That sounds more news and public affairs than art. And in fact, that story was a featured conversation between the story author and *Fresh Air*, found under NPR's "news and conservation" category. APM's entertainment offerings include variety shows for each end of the age demographic; the *Dinner Party Download* for young listeners (which ended in October 2017) and *A Prairie Home Companion* (since renamed *Live From Here with Chris Thule*) for their parents and grandparents. And there's *It's Been a Minute*, by NPR's Sam Sanders, a 2017 addition to other talky, fast-paced ramp-ups for millennials. Plus, because cooking and eating can bring joy and laughter, there's *The Splendid Table*. Public Radio International's current site doesn't use the word entertainment, but categorizes what might be thought of as entertainment on its "Arts, Culture and Media" page with "stories that range over music, dance, the visual arts, design, books, media companies and much more." An older version of PRI online, InfoSite, does separate content by genre.

Local stations tend to have a more basic approach to entertainment. First, because they promote local concerts, festivals, speaking events and exhibits, they can help connect their community to these types of shared experience events. Second, because they can associate themselves with the same shared experiences, listeners connect the stations with the community. That's very important for station identity and later, successful pledge drives. Stations sometimes use their websites to highlight network events. Only during underwriting credits do network events get more local space. But stations, when faced with programming changes from the network, have to scramble to re-engineer a schedule that holds listeners in place. This happened to University of Oklahoma's KGOU in 2009. Because of the canceling of the NPR show *Day to Day*, and costs associated with other shows the station was airing, it reworked its entertainment schedule, according to Program Manager Jim Johnson, so that listeners would have the chance to catch second airings of its biggest moneymakers, *Car Talk* and *This American Life*.

Game shows occupy a special place in the hearts and minds of public radio listeners because they encourage the audience to see itself as funny, cultured and smart. The oldest of these was *Whad'Ya Know*, a Wisconsin Public Radio game show hosted by Michael Feldman and distributed through PRI. After the death of show announcer Jim Packard in 2012, and a handful of key staff changes in late 2015 and early 2016, the show ended production in March 2016 though archived episodes remain available online. At the time, Wisconsin Public Radio's director, Mike Crane said, "We are truly grateful for all that Michael and this program have done for WPR." Another long running game show, WGBH's *Says You,* is billed as a show of "wit and whimsy." *Says You* invites players and the audience to solve obscure references to history, culture and language. The show's originator and host, Richard Sher, died in 2015. But after a nearly two-year search, Greg Porter started hosting in April 2017. Next was *Wits*, a production of Minnesota Public Radio, and intended to be a *Whad'Ya Know* for a younger audience. The show was canceled as MPR was also cutting eleven staff positions in a money saving move and coincidentally, within a week of Garrision Keillor announcing he would leave the network's *A Prairie Home Companion.Ask Me Another*, NPR's public radio game show property launched in 2012 as a co-production with WNYC. It's a mix of puzzles, brainteasers, music and "rambunctiousness."

But if the list seems light, it's because public radio's 800-pound gorilla is missing. W*ait* W*ait Don't Tell Me*, launched in 1995, is a weekly trivia game show designed to mainline NPR's weekly news highlights back into its audience. It's hosted by the shameless Peter Sagel and was co-hosted first by longtime NPR newsreader Carl Kasell, and most recently, by newsman Bill Kurtis. The show bullies, teases and shocks both listeners and guests with the help of a rotating panel of comedians and pundits. Though *WWDTM* is the most risqué of the game show crew, and collects regular com-plaints on its irreverence, it has remained among WBEZ's biggest moneymakers. If public radio entertainment has one purpose, it's to provide a vantage point from which listeners can see themselves reflected. Where that reflection was refracted to the point of distor- tion seemed to be in the aftermath of a 2015 *WWDTM* appearance by Kim Kardashian.

Perhaps it was because Ms. Kardashian, besides displaying her ample knowledge of geopolitics, was also promoting her book. *Selfish* was a 448-page tome consisting almost entirely of photos of herself. In public radio world, such self-absorption is a cardinal sin, equal only to talking during a driveway moment or in any way disparaging Scott Simon. Charlestown, West Virginia's Gary Miller, in comments to NPR's Ombudsman, said of Ms. Kardashian, "She has no business in any civilized forum." Elizabeth Jensen admitted, tongue-in-cheek, that hundreds of these fumings represented people who didn't know how to take a joke. More than anything else, however, the complaints give insight into how public radio listeners see themselves. "Many listeners seem willing to laugh until the comedy is turned on something that touches their own lives or sensitivities," Ms. Jensen said. Peter Sagel's news-based, intellectual satire is clearly superior to what was seen as Ms. Kardashian's low-brow, cultural "kitsch." No matter that she got right two of three questions about the North Korean regime in the "Not My Job" segment, a playful test of a guest's knowledge about something the host and the producers assume they know nothing about.

Ms. Jensen, in thinking out loud to her readers, included a comment from Emmanuel Hapsis' *Pop Blog*, KQED's take on culture. "People leaving these incensed comments or posting about how they wish Kim would just go away on their Facebook pages are also maintaining some idea of themselves that they want to project or would like to believe about themselves. Kim puts beauty first, others lead with intelligence, but in the end, it's ultimately the same thing: a facade." Peter Sagel's regular characterization of public radio listeners as "snobs" hasn't lowered his carriage fees. In fact, public radio nurtures this attitude in its own form of navel-gazing, ranging from NPR onesies to tote bag cachet. But how did the dozens of people who threatened to stop giving ultimately affect giving? "If the NPR 'holier-than-thou' complaints had to be written on the backs of contribution receipts, well I'm sure the complaints would just trickle in," poked Lawrence Caring of Houston, Texas. And it proves that entertainment in public radio is not just about fun and games.

Slate's technology writer, Farhad Manjoo, talked with then *All Things Considered* producer Christopher Turpin about the flaming mailbags the network gets, especially when it does a story that falls in the entertainment interest of anyone under 40. Turpin says, "The first wave of letters tends to be the people who are grumpy about what we've done, particularly pop culture," says Turpin. "They feel very strongly that they don't want us getting into the gutter." But the second wave is people who are grateful that the network is trying to wrestle down its stodginess. Summing up that cultural stenosis, Manjoo says, "Oh, I hate them, hate them, hate them. Every time one of their narrow-minded, classist letters makes it on the air, I contemplate burning my tote bag in protest. The problem for me," he says, "isn't just that some people don't like some things NPR covers. It's that these reflexively snobby pseudo-intellectuals see NPR as their own—a refuge from the mad world outside, a 'safe,' high-minded palace that should never be sullied by anything more outré than James Taylor (whom, of course, they love). Not only do these letter-writers perpetuate the worst caricature of public radio, but their views don't track with what you hear on the air." As of this writing, Manjoo is 39. The average age of the NPR listener he's flaming is 55.

Whether it's the changing audience that affects show shelf life or shows themselves get stale, public radio knows the list of new shows isn't as long as it needs to be. A new visitor might be impressed by the list of on-air programs and the swelling list of podcasts. But to loyal listeners of any age, the list can look a little bare. In 2015, *Current* contributor Michael Arnold said so in his bluntly titled piece, *Public Radio needs more Weekend Hits, and Fast.*

Arnold said Audience Research Analysis, the company founded by David Giovanonni, identified just three weekend public radio programs that have an audience of more than a million listeners. Only those shows, said ARA, deliver what it called "positive power," which is an industry term that measures how strongly programs attract new listeners. Since the weekend lineups of many stations are lighter than during the week, they are less likely to be news and more in the "entertainment" category. Even though Peabody Award winners like *This American Life* and *Radiolab* have audiences of a million-plus, the research firm says neither show has the appeal of drive-time legacy programs.

Arnold says the quality of the new shows that could fill older shoes is not high enough or their storytelling ability strong enough. It's harsh, but it's a critique heard of entertainment across the public radio industry. Arnold calls it "vibrancy," and to bring it back, he tasks program directors to look more realistically at their lineup and make the changes that need to be made, rather than relying on long-time, low hanging fruit. He also challenges stations, groups and networks to create programming "tailored" to the new audience rather than serving up what has been called, "digifyed" or "shovelware." Those are on-air shows dropped in the digital stream "as is" on the assumption that because it's online, it will attract young people. And finally, Arnold warns stations to not ignore the power of broadcast to make their podcasts hits. Big names bring credibility to up and comers. The proof of concept (in addition to the great stories and production values) includes WNYC airing early episodes of *Radiolab*, which was the solid fuel to the Krolich-Abumrad rocket.

WBEZ, not only giving a boost to *This American Life*, but helping *TAL* debut the first episode of the hit podcast *Serial* is another famous example. According to researcher Mark Ramsey, WBEZ used *This American Life*, co-produced with Ira Glass (who helped created *Serial*) to promote a show on a medium that was not on-air radio. The first episode of *Serial* aired to a huge terrestrial audience. The next episode was a podcast. Its audience, hungry for the second installment, shifted online like a landslide. This was a kind of station versus station in that, according to Ramsey, WBEZ's goal seemed to be to attack the entire public radio system of terrestrial stations. It did that by drawing audiences to a different platform with a new kind of storytelling. And the funding model moved along with it. Listeners could now support specific programs, not just the stations that air them. Now, those stations had something new to worry about. Not only did they have to keep their eye on NPR's designs in Washington, they also had to watch hundreds of producers buzzing around, any one of which could create the next blockbuster that could leach more of their listeners away from their antenna. In November 2017, Lizzy O'Leary reporting for APM's *Marketplace* told the first of a two-part story about the ingredients in peanut butter. After listeners were hooked with installment one, she told them they must subscribe to the podcast to hear installment two. Michael Arnold seems to be asking, what do producers have to lose by taking such chances? And he says NPR should pay more attention to its ace in the hole, which is affiliate creativity. To paraphrase former Supreme Court Justice Louis Brandeis, stations could be public radio's "laboratories of creativity."

Understanding what entertainment is consumes stations. Northeast Indiana Public Radio's WBOI posted a Google Docs survey to its listeners in May 2017 asking fourteen questions about two programs. Both, according to their marketing, appeal to that under-40 audience. The first, *Bullseye* (formerly *The Sound of Young America*) with Jesse Thorn, and the second, now-departed *Dinner Party Download*, the brainchild of Rico Gagliano and Brenden Francis Newman. Questions tried to tease out how, when and if the audience might be interested in hearing the shows. Both are categorized as Society & Culture, presumably under the Arts & Culture subcategory, which by definition is not news, music, sports or public affairs. The survey asked if listeners used the programs to:

1. Stay informed,

2. help them understand the news,

3. follow financial happenings,

4. hear well-told stories,

5. expand their understanding of society and culture, or

6. be entertained.

WBOI said on its website that each week, as part of a program called *WBOI Listens*, it would post questions about two or three shows it might consider adding to its programming schedule in an effort to "shape future programming based on your tastes and interests."

This is the kind of language stations use not only to sell new shows, but eliminate beloved ones. An angry listener can become a former contributor if their anger isn't soothed. Such was the case in September 2016, when Birmingham's WBHM eliminated both *A Prairie Home Companion* and *Car Talk* from its lineup. In exchange, the station added an extra hour of Weekend *All Things Considered*, as well as investigative journalism program *Reveal* and WNYC's dramatic storytelling venue, *Snap Judgment*. In a statement, WBHM program director Michael Krall told listeners, "We are excited about bringing our listeners these new, fresh, and relevant programs as well as extending the reach of some of the programs that are already well-loved."

In some ways, this demonstrates how the entertainment calculation is no less pragmatic than any other content. It makes conveying "excitement" the only option for stations balancing the entertainment wants of their audience against changing demographics and unforgiving budgets. And audience acceptance of those changes can hinge on something as fragile as how their station protects their self esteem. As Centennial, Colorado listener Max Planck told the NPR Ombudsman as he forgave his public radio for allowing itself to be polluted by the likes of Kim Kardashian, "I'll forgive you this time but don't do it again." ☏

Sports

"Covering sports for NPR is a bit like covering motor oil for Martha Stewart Living — misplaced resources."

—Commenter Roger Moore on the Romenesko.com website, where former NPR sports reporter Mike Pesca's farewell email was re-posted, February 11, 2014

Sports is such a popular topic that when ESPN suspended Bill Simmons for his podcast tirade against NFL Commissioner Roger Goodell, fans of his *B.S. Report* helped make the #FreeSimmons hashtag trend on Twitter. But sports is not anywhere in the famous public radio study, *Audience 98*. Likewise, a 1978 CPB study on audience and programming said, "Miscellaneous programming, including sports, religion, drama, etc., each requested with insufficient frequency to report separately." Looking over the eight *VALS* subcategories and the publicly available analytics from GfK MRI, no combination of attitudes screams organized sports to any significant degree. So why, over nearly 40 years, has NPR had at least five sports guys on its air? Six, if you count Red Barber from the days of Bob Edwards. The other five have been Mike Pesca, Stephan Fastis, Tom Goldman, Frank DeFord and Bill Littlefield.

PLEDGE: The Public Radio Fund Drive

On the surface, public radio's general indifference to sports is hard to understand, since its own research shows 64% of listeners are fitness oriented. But, for every few dozen or so stories about news and entertainment, there are only a few about sports. Even online, the eleven podcasts at NPR.org dedicated to sports sit small in the shadow of hundreds of podcasts about science, art, politics, music and culture. Public Radio International also has a sports blog. But public radio, in general, doesn't seem to do sports because it made the early decision to focus on news. It continues to carry that view as it marches down the field. So, do public radio listeners care about sports? And does that have any bearing on whether or not they give to pledge drives?

According to search tools on NPR.org, between June 2016 and June 2017, the term "basketball" returned a total of 69 stories heard on air. Of those, 23 were about actual play. The rest spilled over into NPR's propensity for "analysis," including politics, labor disputes and community projects by athletes. The treatment of proportional numbers were similar for other sports: 20 of 133 for football, 17 of 82 for baseball, 4 of 54 for soccer, 5 of 19 for hockey and 5 of 27 for tennis. Only NASCAR and volleyball talked more about scores or the event itself.

And since 2016 was also a Summer Olympics year, about 13 of 119 Olympic related stories were about actual results and competition, not the Zika virus, political protests, substandard venue conditions, or the Russian doping scandal. Those subjects, like their domestic counterparts, seemed to be more analysis than recapping. But even after adding Olympic stories of games played, won or lost, from June to June, sports-only stories appeared about once out of every 144 overall, while any story with a sports reference showed up about once in every 39 reports. So why doesn't sports have a larger presence?

"That is a good question," said Bill Siemering. "and I don't know the answer to it." The NPR founding father thought part of the network's avoidance of sports might be because there tends to be a lot of commercialization connected with it and that sports is usually a local story. "You root for your own team, and that is where your passion is. You don't always care, you know, if you're living in Philadelphia, you're fascinated by the Eagles. But the Seahawks or the Buccaneers, maybe not so much." Newspaper and wall-to-wall broadcast, cable and satellite coverage makes sports not that common on public radio affiliates either. Back in the day, Siemering's goal was to do what the commercial stations do, but do it better and more intelligently.

He thinks that in the beginning, public radio's intellectualism didn't mesh well with the sports climate at many of college campuses where it incubated. He admits that the market has changed even as public radio makes a turn toward a commercialization of its own. "Sports is a huge moneymaker for universities," says Siemering. The number of university presidents whose salaries are eclipsed by university coaches is evidence of that. "I would think it would behoove local stations to be covering that more." It's a good point that asks, could stations make a little extra in underwriting by covering local teams? The odds of that happening aren't necessarily low and outside. WBUR, for instance, covers sports extensively. And Hartford's public TV and radio stations have covered Lady Huskies games.

Kevin Draper, posting on the basketball blog *The Diss*, summed up NPR's sports coverage. "NPR is the perfect venue to, rather than see sports as apart from the rest of society, use sports as a lens to better understand the world around us." It is a decision that the BBC seems to have made as well, rather than compete with sports networks that do it better. Draper sympathizes with NPR, understanding that structurally, it can't do much else. "There are two main constraints limiting interesting NPR sports programming: the audience and the medium." Besides, the segments being so short leave little time for depth.

Draper says NPR's demographics skew toward more "serious" subject matter, which makes its sports sound like its news; calm and monotonous. "I talked to blah blah, Professor of blah blah at the blah blah University of blah blah," pokes Draper. That tends to lead to the other category of NPR sports stories that he calls, "whacky shit." For example, he says, "like a segment on trash talking Bhutanese archers." *Slate*'s podcast, *Hang up and Listen* is what he says NPR sports could sound like. Fast-paced and engaging with long form conversations and features on sports is what drew its contributors Stephen Fatsis and Mike Pesca.

Mike Pesca has been in or around New York City sports since he was ten. In 1997, he got his first job in radio. He hosts the *Slate* daily podcast *The Gist* while also contributing reports and commentary to NPR. He's also done podcasts and won two Edward R. Murrow awards. One of them was about the genius behind getting Cracker Jacks into a line of the song sung in the seventh inning at every major league stadium in the country since 1934, *Take Me Out to the Ballgame*. Pesca also has some thoughts about baseball and public radio. "Super shows; *Morning Edition* and *All Things Considered*, know that they don't have to do anything and they would be inundated with the travails of the world," he said. "This is what NPR is structured to do. To bring you stories from all corners of the world and do a little bit of comforting the afflicted and maybe a little less of afflicting the comfortable." "But," he admits, "there's not so much lightness in there." Pesca also says lightness is lacking in the category of actual, non-fiction news that people listen for. "A good sports story does that for people," he says. "I really think the producers who ran the shows knew that a well executed sports piece for three and a half minutes was really valuable to the overall flow of their show."

Pesca says the numbers he's seen show that the public radio audiences like sports just as much as the American audience in general, though there are regional differences that he thinks skew toward large populations in the North and Northeast. "They like hockey more than most Americans, and they like participating in winter sports. Maybe this is a whiteness thing or a class thing. They definitely aren't as into the NFL as the rest of America, but they're into the NFL." So he knows the NPR audience isn't a bunch of rookies and doesn't need explanations of rookie terms like "three-pointer." In fact, he has even doubled down on that sophistication at times. "Since I know who the NPR audience is, I would always feel free to make analogies to the arts, or if I were to talk about a certain running back, I would not shy away from talking about force equals mass times acceleration." But, as Pesca told *Slate*'s Farhad Manjoo in 2011, affection for sports amongst NPR loyalists is not a given. "You can't mention sports without someone saying, 'Why are you covering sports? It's just a bunch of Neanderthals, it's just a bunch of fascists!'"

Pesca, upon leaving the network in 2014, wrote a goodbye note to his NPR colleagues peppered with speed and change but little regret. "I have always wanted NPR to be a wee bit more ambitious or daring, to be willing to take risks outside our comfort zone. So I'm leaving to do a daily podcast about things other than sports, though sometimes sports, because I like sports." And he snarkily included his new Slate email so he could give his NPR pals "some idea of where I'll be working." He said when he left in 2014, there were two full-time sports reporters (he and Tom Goldman) and now, "there are half of that." As to how much sports, either from NPR or its affiliates, weighs in at pledge drive, Pesca repeats the talking points that permeate pledge drive training manuals. "People listen to NPR because it's enjoyable, but people give to NPR because, you emphasize, 'it's their civic responsibility, that they're doing important work, their contributions support our work when other organizations are canceling them.' They give because you appeal to their more high-minded notions." But he also adds a little color commentary when asked, "Would the audience consider NPR less appealing if sports wasn't there?" "I think so," he says. "You know what I think it is?" he asks, pausing. "It's the second and third olive in the martini. Which, maybe you don't think to ask the bartender for three olives, or if he's good, he'll ask you. But once you get the second and third, you really like it."

If NPR can keep taking risks and getting listeners to give more while dishing out those "whacky shit" sports driveway moments, it's a "hat trick" for sure. ☎

Blogs

"Like, radio is closer to a Tumblr, or a blog, or Twitter, than it is to television, I think."

—Ira Glass, *The Grid,* Abby Ohlheiser, *Slate,* Jan 14, 2013

The number of blogs has grown exponentially since they were first introduced in the mid 90s. In early 2011, there were over 156 million blogs worldwide. By April 2017, social media site Tumblr reported it alone had 345 million blogs while blog plat-forms Wordpress and Technorati reported 76 million and a million and a half blogs, respectively. But all of this writing doesn't necessarily mean it's good writing. For instance, blogs can't blather and have value, though they can be a cathartic release for their author. Blogs don't often last beyond a few years because blogging is a lot of work and many bloggers underestimate the amount of time it demands. Also, new blogs bring in little money because it takes time to build an audience. But the biggest killer of a blog is the writer loses their passion for their subject. If authors do keep blogging, its because they've kept that passion.

A blogpost on Hubspot, called *Four Statistics every Blogger should know about Word Count,* suggests that the most popular blogs contain posts of approximately 2,400 words each. And it says sites with between 16 and 20 such posts a month generate four times as much traffic as those sites with many fewer posts, in large part because people trust blogs with longer content. Like public radio's most popular blogs, posts with lots of checkable information tends to contain the answers readers expect to find, which also instills confidence both in the writing and the writer.

Public radio, torn between getting to the point which is fast, and building trust which is slow, relies on staff and professional bloggers to blog about programs and policies of public radio. But even their efforts aren't always successful. On July 2, 2014, NPR's Anya Kamenetz tweeted on the micro-blogging platform about how she, as a blogger on the network education team, "reach out to diverse sources on deadline. Only the white guys get back to me." Listener tumult followed. Six days later, Supervising Editor for Standards and Practices, Mark Memmott, sent a very long memo to the news staff. And drawing deeply from the *NPR Ethics Handbook*, he reminded them that, "If you wouldn't say it on the air, don't say it on the Web."

As of April 2018, NPR has 18 blogs; nine for news programs one for opinion, one for art & life, five for music shows and two for housekeeping (including the Ombudsman's). That's down one news and one music blog from June 2017. American Public Media has one, which seems to be about happenings within APM-like program changes and personality profiles, but no blogs riding shotgun with programs as with NPR. Of Public Radio International 26 programs, only five have blogs. PRI's website seems to have no blog at all although the PRX blog, which published until 2016 and was hosted on a PRX website, moved to publishing platform Medium in May 2017. Medium lets users curate their own newsfeeds as well as surround their posts with supporting images. But, as a commenter noted, moving one's content to a site one doesn't control can open that content to being poached or "share-cropped."

Like music journalism from *Spin* or *Rolling Stone* and arts and entertainment journalism like *TMZ* or *Entertainment Tonight*, public radio uses blogging to help it more deeply cover its content. But respect for blogs has been slow in coming. A 2003 article from the Harvard University's Nieman Foundation was critical of bloggers even as it recognized their importance. Author Paul Andrews noted that bloggers follow stories that the mainstream probably should. The 2008 voting touchscreen controversy is a later example. Only the persistent nattering of bloggers moved the mainstream to focus on potential problems with Diebold and other voting machine technologies. At the same time, Andrews indicts bloggers for knowing "little about independent verification of information and data." He criticizes them for not having the "tools and experience" to dig as deep into stories as professional journalists. And because they don't know how to fact check, Andrews says, "Calling a typical blogger a journalist is like calling anyone who takes a snapshot a photographer." "If journalism is the imparting of verifiable facts to a general audience through a mass medium," says Mr. Andrews, "then most blogs fall well short of meeting the standard."

But by 2014, the U.S. Ninth Circuit court had flipped that script. Robinson Meyer reported for *The Atlantic* a complicated confluence of case law that eventually led to the decision that bloggers are in fact, the same as journalists. Judge Andrew Hurwitz, in writing for the court, said that previous rulings showed how the court has historically refused to give greater First Amendment rights to news organizations over "other speakers." And, he noted that in one case, the Supreme Court specifically said, "We draw no distinction between the media respondents and a non-institutional respondent." As the court warned, "With the advent of the Internet and the decline of print and broadcast media . . . the line between the media and others who wish to comment on political and social issues becomes far more blurred." For public radio users, blogs, like other forms of content, are measured by how much value and trustworthiness they have for the audience. Heavy blog users tend to be heavy consumers of traditional media, including radio. But since bloggers now have the credibility of journalists, they are competition. This is especially true as bloggers add podcasts to blogs and vice versa. The mainstream counters this pull toward blogs by doing more blogging of its own. In a 2006 *NYT* survey, about half of 303 newspapers in 42 states said they had incorpor-rated blogs with their regular coverage. That represented a 100% increase from the previous year and a move by "established" media to reclaim some of the territory it must have felt it had lost.

A 2010 study from Harvard's Berkman Center for Internet and Society showed that public radio blogs tend to invite more partic-ipation from readers, which may be another reason public radio seems to like them. The study's results, on MPR's *Future Tense* blog, said that conservative blogs tend to feature the voice of one person and don't have a lot of other writers or responders. Liberal blogs, said the study, are more likely to include lots of voices and encourage people to get active in a cause or an event. Arts reporter Marianne Combs of Minnesota Public Radio blogged about what it means to blog about art in 2009. She and her small but growing klatch of specialized "peers" like blogging because it lets them share information with readers and colleagues in a more personal voice than that of a reporter. And since a blog lets people respond, Combs says she can do her job as a reporter better by being more plugged into to how people feel about what she's written, not just what she's reported. Lee Rosenbaum, aka "CultureGrrl" for the Wall Street Journal's *Art Beat*, told Combs that blogging gives her more freedom, "because I felt I had a lot to say and no place to put it. I can only write so many articles for the Journal but I have ideas every day that I feel like sharing." Digital Media Manager Jeremy Blevins at the Rockefeller Foundation, speaks about the value of blogs from the intersection of business and non-profit. "Blogs are fantastic for highlighting issues and content that you care about, and establishing your organization as a leader and thought leader in the space," he says.

But blogs can also deliver bad news. When Monterey-based KUSP was in imminent danger of going off the air in 2016, it used its blog as part of its *Maidez Maidez* campaign. Not connected to anything as light as arts or entertainment, the station was trying to rally the community to come to its financial rescue to the tune of $300,000. Sadly, that attempt failed and the station slipped into bankruptcy. In 2014, NPR told *Radiolab* co-host Robert Krulwich that it could no longer support his four years running *Krulwich Wonders* blog. The network cited the need to cut costs and by all indications, Krulwich was gracious to the end. In his blogged explanation, he marveled at how NPR itself was a long shot in the early 70s when it decided to reach out to people in a new way from "the parking lot of radio." He compared the chance given to him by the network to have a blog with the same amazement. "And then, ridiculously," he said, "[I] asked if I could serve the Radio Gods by writing multi-weekly posts and drawing pictures." Krulwich shows the power of a blog ultimately rests in the ability of its author to share his or her passion with the joy of kids running through a lawn sprinkler.

And although big print names like the *Wall Street Journal* and the *New York Times* continue to shutter blogs, public media keeps using them to supplement content and solicit listener support.

Most public radio stations, and especially those that use the NPR API, include blogs in their websites. They've become mouthpieces of station managers and development directors for talking about pledge drives, station events, programming changes or diving deeper into stories. Meanwhile, *Protect My Public Media*, an advocacy website directed at the national audience, encourages listeners to encourage state and federal representatives to keep funding public radio. Though listeners will rarely if ever hear a public radio story about PMPM, its blog posts, on every possible aspect of public radio, permeate the site. Perhaps as Mr. Glass pointed out, this is how the printed word from the 15th century roots itself in digital streams of the 21st century, thus bringing its legacy full circle. ☎

Platforms

"If you look at the entire chain of entities – studios, networks, stations, cable channels, cable operations, international distribution – you want to be as strong in as many of those as you can. That way, regardless of where the profits move to, you are in a position to gain"

—News Corporation president Peter Chernin as quoted by Robert McChesney, in *Alternative Radio*, November 1999

The Internet was only about a decade old when Peter Chernin made this statement. So no mentions of podcasting, digital radio or streaming. But the virtual real estate of platforms has become equally important. In this respect, public radio has borrowed pages from commercial broadcasting's playbook. And some people don't like it. In 2016, public radio station WBAA dropped the popular program *This American Life* because the show had plans to also run on the music service Pandora. Station manager Mike Savage said that the move by the show to a competitor of public radio was, as he saw it, "not complimentary nor friendly to public radio."

It's another example of stations upset that they pay carriage fees to producers of shows that they feel use those fees against them. Pew's 2011 *State of the Media Report* says that even though nine out of ten people still listen to AM and FM, "they take the medium for granted." Pew also said Americans "report listening more to online only outlets like Pandora or Slacker Radio than they do to streams from AM/FM stations." It and other technologies, says the report, are what listeners say have more "impact" on their lives than over-the-air broadcasts.

Public radio's foundation is terrestrial radio. But names of other programming languages, systems, companies and algorithms like Drupal, StationConnect, Midroll and Core Publisher are increasingly common. And there's no escaping pubcaster satellite broadcasts and time-shifted podcasts. Then there's the push for public radio in your car, on your phone, and via aggregators like TuneIn, Streamfurious, Soundcloud, Rhapsody and Spotify. The combination of these delivery systems represents an unbroken content stream tying you to public radio no matter where you go. And that's the way public radio wants it, because only by knowing when and how you are listening can it and its sponsors know how effective it is at reaching you and your support dollars. But cross-platform tracking isn't necessarily a panacea. Some of those digital platforms that depend on revenue from ads are finding that consumers hate the ads and use ad blocker apps to avoid them. Still, public radio wants to provide access to these platforms on its terms. And though it doesn't tell you not to use other apps, it does push its own. Users respond with technology that gives them access to their favorite shows while bypassing much of public radio's marketing.

Publicradiofan.com, for example, is a website run Kevin Kelly at MIT. The site shows when Sirius XM's satellite is rebroadcasting programs that are being fed from NPR's public radio satellite system. These are the original broadcast times and different from when local stations may schedule the same shows. For satellite users, that can be hugely convenient. For broadcast users, the site can also take you directly to any of its more than 2,000 terrestrial stations worldwide, including to hundreds of public radio stations. Meanwhile, the places where podcast lovers can go to get compelling podcasts continues to grow. Podcastdirectory.com lists several thousand shows in each of its sixteen categories. Podcast 411, established in 2004, lists nearly 200 different podcast directories, including well-known names like Stitcher and iTunes.

The fight for your phone and your car, two more platforms being pushed toward the cloud, is raging as well. Former NPR President Vivian Schiller, in a poke at public radio's tendency of innovative talk but conservative action, famously warned in 2011, "The monopoly advantage of the radio tower will begin to fade." The outgoing Schiller, in her conversation with Nieman Labs, was not gentle with terrestrial broadcasters. "New digital-only startups will enter the marketplace in audio, and you will find yourselves longing for the days when the competition was that public radio station that overlapped with your broadcast signal," she said. Gordon Smith, President of the National Association of Broadcasters, doesn't like that. Mr. Smith is on record chafing at the shift of radio to online. He's pushed the mobile phone industry and the FCC to turn on FM chips that are already inside many models of phones.

Meanwhile, providers like Verizon are against the idea because, in a complaint familiar in public radio, the company said, "it is a step backward in cellphone innovation that will have harmful effects, such as shortened battery life." Besides Smith's claim that on-air is more reliable than online, the move lets listeners hear broadcasts for free without the need of an account with a provider like Verizon. Mr. Smith also isn't a fan of Internet radio in cars. But that didn't stop NPR and Chevrolet from unveiling a collaboration at the 2014 Las Vegas Consumer Electronics Show. According to a blog post from the Public Radio Programs Directors, Chevy planned to include an NPR news app as part of the in-dash "AppShop." "The app," available on cars equipped with Chevy's MyLink, "uses the vehicle's GPS system to connect to the nearest local public radio station. It includes direct access to some 25 individual programs and more than 80 music streams from NPR and member stations." Though this is a win for public radio. CNET says the AppShop, with its touchscreen, icon-based interface, makes choosing any other source just as easy as choosing public radio.

Until now, audio, images, video and text have tended to remain in their own stovepipes. But in 2015, that began to change with an effort that coalesced in the Public Media Platform. "PMP" was formed as a non-profit organization consisting of NPR, APM, PRI and PRX. Its goal is to "build public media's first cross-platform digital distribution system." Thanks to a common content management system, any partner will be able to distribute their fare to the entire audience from one common, virtual location. And as it is better able to follow users across platforms, it lets all of public radio keep better track of them. So whether a program is from an independent producer on PRX, from a network like PRI or from a collaboration between WNYC and the BBC, consumers can find it easily. Derek Thompson said for *The Atlantic* in 2014, "Content is king, but distribution is the kingdom."

All of this represents a relatively new word in public radio: disruption. For some, it's a call to arms. Public radio, they say, needs to get off the fence and innovate faster because they see these alternatives as eating public radio's lunch. Others, like the so called "NPR apostates," are leaping from the staid safety of conventional ledges into the chaos, wearing only the wingsuits of their imaginations. Stephen Henn, former technology correspondent for NPR, left the network in 2016 for reasons that, among his ilk, are common. "The digital radio I want would make it easier to support great work. It would help public radio break out of the white, upper-middle class ghetto it has created for itself. It would be personalized. It would be global. It would be social and ubiquitous. It would let the audience talk back. My ideal digital radio, it would listen to the audience." Henn seems to be acknowledging that platforms aren't only what holds a listener. As researcher John Sutton told *Current* in September 2015, "All that matters is whether the listener associates a high-quality listening experience with the station brand." And that brand is not only how they hear but what they hear. In other words, what holds a listener is still, and only, the storytelling ☎.

Satellite

"Too many radio stations, all they do is syndicated programming, it's just piped in from some satellite someplace, and they don't have much of a connection to the community."

—David Shuster, *Mediate*, Tommy Christopher, April 3, 2012

Platforms support things. A launch platform, for example, supports a rocket as it carries a satellite into orbit. The satellite itself is a platform that supports the ability of satellite radios to downlink programming that is being uplinked to the satellite from providers back on Earth. NPR is such a provider. Its public radio satellite system receives programming from the network itself, other networks and a web of public radio licensees across the country. Ideally, satellite radio owners select one of those channels to hear the shows they want from whichever provider they choose, bypassing their local station's programming schedule. But the average satellite radio owner can't dial up the PRSS like they can Sirius XM Satellite Radio. Six months after Bob Edwards was fired from NPR in 2004, *The Bob Edwards Show* popped up on XM Satellite

Radio. Listeners, finding him there, got all of his familiarity with none of the NPR drama. Edwards was heard by only a fraction of his 13 million strong *Morning Edition* audience. But, according to a 2014 article in *Current*, to Edwards' surprise, "the quality of the guests willing to appear on *The Bob Edwards Show* did not fall off."

Sirius, America's first commercial satellite company, was conceived in the early 1990s, but the FCC didn't make it easy to be born. Sirius founder and funder David Margolese spent about eight years raising money and launching rockets before getting permission from the FCC to give it more than $83 million in license fees. In the late 90s, American Mobile Radio Corporation, later renamed XM Satellite Radio, paid nearly $90 million for the same privilege. Similar to terrestrial radio, in that a signal is sent to antennas on Earth's surface, satellite broadcasting is also significantly different. While, for example, the signal of the University of Missouri's KAUD has a modest 18-mile broadcasting radius, a satellite could send the same signal to the entire continental U.S. Reception is limited only by the angle of the satellite to the curvature of the earth's surface.

Over their mutual existence, both Sirius and XM spent more than $3 billion to develop, expand and deliver satellite radio technology. But, it eventually became clear that there was only room enough for one. In July 2007, Sirius and its 110 channels agreed to merge with XM's 137 channels. The next year, the FCC approved Sirius' request to purchase XM for $13 billion. Despite criticism that the agency, by allowing the two industry leaders to combine, was creating a monopoly, the merger was still green-lighted. The FCC's argument was that Internet streaming, though a different platform, was a sufficient digital competitor to satellite, which also distributed programming digitally.

In 2010, the *Pew State of the Media* report noted that the new Sirius/XM mashup showed single-digit drops in subscribers that the company itself expected to continue for another three years. As of this writing, NPR programming can be heard on Sirius XM Channel 122, one among the provider's 15 other "News and Issues" channels, and its 993 other music, sports and entertainment channels.

NPR's satellite can only be picked up by NPR stations, not by domestic U.S. satellite radios. NPR programming is also beamed via the French-owned Eutelsat operated constellation of "Hotbird" satellites. But because of their orbit, those signals are only heard in Europe, North Africa and the Middle East. So again, domestic NPR listeners can't pluck *Morning Edition* live from the sky and bypass their local station's underwriting credits.

On Fiona Ritchie's Celtic *Thistle and Shamrock* website, another satellite provider also offers some access to NPR shows. The site says "NPR is available for a few hours a day on SKY Digital via our partners in London, the World Radio Network." But those also can't be heard stateside. NPR and WRN began collaborating to deliver worldwide news in September 1998. The partnership has since ended.

A comparison of May 2017 schedules for NPR Now on Hotbird and NPR Worldwide on Sirius XM shows curious similarities and differences. What stands out first is Hotbird sends *Morning Edition* to European, African and Middle Eastern early risers at 11 a.m. Central European Time. In the spring, that's six hours ahead of the U.S. start time of 5 a.m. Eastern. Likewise, *All Things Considered* begins for East coast listeners at 4 p.m., while simultaneously being heard in the Eastern hemisphere at 10 p.m.

So, at least with the book-ended news shows, Hotbird users seem to get exactly what domestics NPR listeners get. By contrast, SiriusXM users don't get either *Morning Edition* or *All Things Considered*. But U.S. listeners do get four shows at the same time as Hotbird listeners: WAMU's *1A*, WBUR's *On Point* and *Here and Now*, and APM's *Marketplace*. What's left is a mix of different shows that share no broadcast times.

As far back as a June 2004, a *Doc Searls* blogpost asked about NPR on satellite radio in his blog. A reader responded that among the reasons the offerings were so limited was because, "NPR doesn't let Sirius carry its "A-list" programs, like *Fresh Air* (weekdays), *All Things Considered* and *Morning Edition*." Since then, Sirius XM has begun carrying *Fresh Air*. But it still doesn't carry the newsmagazines.

Many satellite digital video broadcasts (DVB in the U.S. are so-called "Free-to-Air" (FTA), meaning they can be seen by anyone with the equipment. Louisiana and Montana Public Broadcasting can be viewed through domestic receivers, though the technology by which they are transmitted requires a commercial-sized dish to see them. Even when viewers can see some satellite broadcasts, providers sometime scramble signals once they realize they are being viewed. NPR's system, known as Content Depot, also sends programs as Internet streams, files or packets. There is no FTA for satellites serving the United States that lets users hear public radio.

But it's drivers, not people at their kitchen tables, that public radio is targeting with satellites. The market is lucrative. There are about 20 million satellite radio subscribers in the U.S. SiriusXM radios are available for nearly every make and model of car. And dashboard head units with a docking station let users connect and remove portable satellite radios, increasing the convenience factor.

Satellite radio isn't the only way drivers can hear public radio, however. Advances in Internet technology are turning cars into rolling hotspots that can receive crystal clear audio streams through cell phone companies or free community Wi-Fi like Utah's "UTOPIA." It shows that perhaps the FCC was right all those years ago when it made the argument that the Internet was a competitor to satellites. ☎

Internet

"What is radio? Is that like a podcast?"

—Comedian Pete Davidson

Content is to the Internet as trucks are to a highway. And though it's the news, music and entertainment that most agree matter most, the technology does make it fun. New apps, like Anchor, promise to make podcasts simpler (your mobile phone's talk button creates a podcast) and more compelling (Anchor lets users, for example, live broadcast live phone calls). Although podcasting, on-demand and streaming are integrated into how web users get their content, that content rather than the delivery system has always counted more.

Content needs places to live, like servers that belong to services like Dropbox or Soundcloud, until users can get to it. RSS technology tells them new content, organized for the user by subject or date, has arrived in their in box. And that content can be accessed from network, group or station apps, from iTunes or via apps from the Google or Microsoft stores. But these main roads don't include the many side roads people can use to get to that same content. Radio's issues with these other paths to their content are similar to those for other media. When Ariana Huffington built, and then sold the *Huffington Post* for $300 million in 2011, some in the media called it the end of journalism. But Huffpo, along with *Gawker*,

273

BuzzFeed, The Daily Beast, Salon and others, thrived because they ushered in a new logistical model for finding, gathering, warehousing, and disseminating the news. As they learned with funding, social media and music, disrupters used the Internet to crowdsource the process of journalism. Even though Google dropped its *Google Reader* service in 2013, *Feedly, Flipbook* and *Fark* have picked up the slack, showing that even the leader doesn't lead forever.

Streaming is the keystone of public radio's delivery system. But even though NPR spends tons of time and money obsessing over its various downloadable players, it still upgrades listener experience from the old school npr.org website. And the fact that NPR's Scott Stroud apologized if regular users hadn't noticed new options and features says much about how important the web continues to be. Changes the design team made were apparently new and improved over what existed mere months before. The upgrades allowed access by the multitude of screen types the site might be visited on. But more importantly, said the network, "It must offer audio and visual sponsorship to support NPR financially (without annoying our listeners)." The idea of avoiding annoyance shows how smoothly programming must go down to successfully mask underwriting. The design process for NPR's website upgrade seemed more elaborate and extensive than the upgrade itself.

And then, there are devices with which to access much of that content through downloads or streams: the car radio, various types of console radios, smartphone apps, computers, personal assistants (Google, Cortana, Alexa, Siri, etc). These outputs are public radio milking terrestrial, satellite and Internet technology for all they're worth. But in recent years, focus has narrowed on the latter. You see that in how distributors offer multiple ways to send users back to essentially the same place, the web. Internet radio, a misnomer at first glance, includes not only directories of hundreds of radio stations that also stream online, but has come to mean stations that only exist on the Internet, like Northridge, California's KSBR.

It lives solely online, without a transmitter, a music library or a building. The economic efficiencies of the Internet even reached NPR's own Content Depot. This iteration of PRSS gives member stations the cheaper option to receive programs in packets online the same way viewers might get their Netflix. When Peconic Public Radio's WPPB took a lightning strike in June 2017, their satellite dish was fried. According to PPR President Wally Smith, one of the temporary fixes was NPR letting the station receive its programming via the Internet.

Before NPR was ready to connect its greater public on the Internet, companies like Livio were selling innovations like a tabletop Internet radio on Amazon in the around 2005. Meanwhile, tech savvy listeners who love playing with NPR source code have been ahead of the mass of NPR's listeners for years. The network has a history of letting those ultra-early adopters beta test technology before rolling it out on a larger scale. In 2009, Daniel Jacobson, writing for the *Inside NPR* blog said, "Other users in the general public have created fantastic mashups including NPR Addict (for iPhone), NPR Backstory, code wrappers in [programming languages] Ruby and Perl, as well as many other mashups and widgets." This stuff public radio lovers can't do with broadcast or satellite, which helps explain how their access to it affects their adoption of it and their devotion for it. That same year, David Silverman wrote for *Chron* that the release of the new "Public Radio Player" from PRX, with its ability to access and schedule hundreds of public radio programs, "may put local stations at risk."

But users who aren't Internet-savvy, or who don't have a device with which to access it, can be at risk too. National Association of Broadcasters president, Gordon Smith, has been hammering on that point for years. He argues the American citizen should be able to get everything she wants over the public airwaves, or at least, through Smith's collective of broadcasters, rather than through closed channels that must be paid for to be accessed. Cable companies, satellite providers and ISPs, in defense of their business model, disagree. With 274 million people in the US having access to the Internet in 2016, the cost of a device or an account doesn't seem to be a barrier. But Smith has an eye to the future as well. He hopes that FCC changes to how NAB members can access the Internet, including changes to a new TV broadcasting standard, can help old-school broadcasters learn hi-tech tricks.

For users that access their content through a station website, public radio researcher Mark Fuerst came to their aid in comments to the Station Resource Group in 2010. Fuerst talked about the poor quality of station websites, decrying, "only a handful of stations that have anything resembling a serious 'web presence.'" That weak presentation, he said, and the "the obvious futility of the 'everybody do your own website' approach," damages the ability of public radio to deliver news. That seems to be changing. In 2016, I visited every NPR station with a stand-alone website. Only about 207 of them were uniquely designed, meaning there were about 693 clones. Of the more than 900 websites found, the majority of them used the same page layout, based on the same Core Publisher platform. Core Publisher, NPR's content management system, was introduced in 2010 by NPR Digital Services. Its purpose was to try to meet the digital needs of many different types of stations. To some extent, it has succeeded, but NPR believes it is nearing the end of its service life.

That's why, the network will roll out a new platform that gives locals access to the "good stuff" that they see on the npr.org site that they haven't had access to, including more local content on the network site and more flexibility for the local site. It doesn't mean public radio encourages a corporate look. But it can make one wonder if the quasi-governmental CPB, by hiring a federal contractor to design public radio websites, sees efficient uniformity and customer friendliness as going hand-in-hand. After all, the federal government does like its corporate branding campaigns. More likely, stations paid for the functional upgrade in exchange for being relieved of the worry of totally creating and managing their sites themselves.

Within Core Publisher is the Chartbeat API. Chartbeat, an audience and analytics company, develops tools for clients to measure customer engagement online. Its API, or application programming interface, lets different elements within a software program talk to each other. This means stations using the same API can also talk to each other, and can borrow, share and exchange content. With "responsive design," a technology that lets the API know what type of device you're using, it optimizes what users see to give them the best interactive experience possible. In proudly talking about a long-awaited website upgrade for Yellowstone Public Radio, pledge drive host Ken Siebert explained APIs this way during a 2016 pitch break: "What that allows us to do is pull content both from NPR nationally and other member stations," he said. "Let say, for example [KEMC reporters] do an extractive story on coal. Once you're done reading that story and listening to that, there will be others populated on that page that will give you the opportunity to find out what's happening with the coal industry in Virginia, in Wyoming, across the country and really fill in that context for you. It's a great opportunity for us to bring more of the world to you." The API also lets NPR see what is piquing the interest of stations' local audiences, which helps it find local stories with national interest. And the technology lets stations use data bounced back to them from the network to tweak their web pages in real time and adjust to audience tastes on a near minute-by-minute basis.

Audio research firm Nielsen said in 2016 that on-demand streaming grew by 93%. Those streams, to desktops, laptops, dashboards and smartphones, floated 317 billion downloaded songs in a 15% increase over 2014. And news delivered via the Internet got a big boost that same year when NPR and iHeart media announced a streaming collaboration. NPR gets distributed to iHeart's 85 million registered users and iHeart gets to add NPR's newstalk content. The partnership gives both players what they want: deep penetration into a new market. How iHeart's 2018 bankruptcy announcement affects that partnership is unclear. But behind the scenes partnerships, like NPR's contract with digital company Triton, have low profiles and big impacts. The agreement, for Triton to handle web streaming, audience measurement and dynamic ad insertion for some of NPR's member stations, is more proof that public radio is taking seriously its need to adapt to the challenges of the Internet. Those challenges are massive. Among them, the demand for on-demand content.

In 2016, *RainNews* reported that podcast listening grew by 24% over 2015. In 2017, *Forbes* said Amazon's personal assistant, Alexa, has been turning millennials into NPR listeners "since early on." NPR's National Public Media COO Bryan Moffett told the publication that tens of millions of people get flash news updates from NPR with the words, "Alexa, give me the news." Other personal assistants that stream asks and answers over the Internet, like Apple's Siri and Google Voice, will also call up local affiliates just by users asking for them.

Content players have also been an increasingly single-minded focus of public radio. In 2012, contributor Audrey Mandavich wrote on the PRX blog that the network was "going mobile" with the release of its new HTML5 player. Though early versions were marked with complaints that the app was "buggy," that player, which became PRX's RadioPublic, connects listeners to more than a quarter-million podcasts. Public Radio International's content can be heard through its custom player at the Google Store as well as its own website. Minnesota Public Radio, in sync with how *The Current* divides music and news, has separate apps for streaming its on-air broadcasts and separately, its newscasts. American Public Media, by contrast, seems to not have its own player but instead, relies on RealPlayer, a cross-platform media app, developed in 1995. Though widely available on Windows, OS, Android and other platforms, it has been heavily criticized as a vehicle for spyware. Dozens of public radio stations conceived, built and host their own native apps at iTunes while others were barn-raised by app developers like publicmediaapps.com.

It's difficult to talk about public radio apps without again talking about NPR and a longtime problem that highlights the tightrope relationship between distributors and their affiliates. In 2007, the network was doing its first stories on Internet technology for the car. By 2009, NPR was rolling out among its first efforts to incorporate content with the web even as it had an eye on Apple's move to dominate in-car players and their access to radio, including public radio. By 2011, in the equivalent of throwing spaghetti against the wall to see what sticks, NPR's tech team released Infinite Player. Michael Yoch, NPR's director of product development at the time, spoke of the difference between an engaged versus a distracted listener. A distracted listener is someone who has the radio on in the background but can't tell you what's on. Infinite Player was designed to engage by compelling them, through their listening choices, to keep making the decision to listen. Kinsey Wilson, NPR's former manager of digital media said it had a learning algorithm, but the player part of Infinite Player wasn't very sophisticated. "It's not nearly as baked as something we would launch even as a beta project," he said. "But it's a way to do some rapid innovation and see if we're even close to the mark and how people react to it." To repeat NPR CEO Jarl Mohn's goal in a 2014 interview, the only way to make people react to it well is to make podcasts more appealing, or "stickier." And that means making it ridiculously easy to find public radio content everywhere you turn. Infinite Player was followed, a few years later, by Persistent Player. Then the aforementioned Public Radio Player. Improvements included the player's ability to stay with whatever content the user was listening to, even if they were clicking through different content on the website. The player would stay put, in other words, it was "persistent." But even these didn't represent the best rabbit in the NPR hat.

It's been scrambling to create a one-touch, one source, one-ring-to-rule-them type app since the early 2000s. In 2010, Nate Anderson wrote for *Ars Technica* that the Public Radio Exchange had developed two iPhone apps. One, a general "Public Radio Player" app, and the other specifically for its leading on-air partnership with *This American Life*. The app, which cost $2.99 to download, was hoped to attract half a million downloads. Instead, it drew 2.5 million. In 2009, the other big dog in the world of apps and players was NPR One. Isabel Lara, of NPR's Media Relations, told Shan Wang for Nieman Labs in 2016, that use of the app/player was growing about 9% per month or as Wang figured, "about 280% growth per year." NPR One, the ultimate Internet life-form, gives the option of letting people donate while curating the news and entertainment they're hearing.

The app is the network's best effort thus far to make you see the player, your content and the online world as one. After it app figures out where you are, it creates a playlist that includes stories from your local station, news from NPR and a customized listening experience based on what you tap in response to what you hear. Over time, what you get becomes more refined than what you got. According to *RainNews*, more than one in three millennials said they've used the NPR One app within the last week.

The app, which is generations ahead of the stone knives and bearskins of Infinite Player, continues to improve. But its exposure, let alone its release, has repeatedly stalled. So if functionality and popularity aren't the problem, what is? Essentially, a unit that can deliver broadcasts and podcasts on demand is a hand-held radio station. For all of the station managers operating full sized versions, this is not necessarily a good thing. In that 2007 report on how terrestrial radio was being affected by satellites, Internet and HD formats, Alex Cohen said, "NPR and other radio broadcasters have started offering content that you can hear on your cell phone or by dialing in on one of those old tiny corded phones." For all of the pubcasters who depend on reaching listeners through the air, the words "cell phone" probably sound less like English and more like a cannonball whizzing across their bow. That's why in 2016, two years after NPR One launched on the down-low, NPR finally spelled out how it would promote it.

It wouldn't. That the decision was published in a update to the *NPR Ethics Guide* sent plenty of confusing signals on its own. Was the network saying it was unethical to undercut member stations by promoting a product that could siphon listeners and their ability to hear station underwriting credits or pledge pleas? Joshua Benton wrote for Nieman Labs in 2016, "This is not in any way about ethics; whether or not to promote podcasts is not a question of journalism standards." Benton went on to say, "the platforms that are pretty clearly NPR's future—NPR One and podcasts—are in conflict with NPR's present—broadcast distribution and local station structure." By July 2017, the network had gingerly decided to give its app more exposure. But to affiliates, the issue instills fear that listeners will like what they get from NPR better than what they get from their local stations. And many local stations, without the ability to produce their own listener grabbing shows, end up feeling like pass-throughs for network content. They resent paying program fees for technology that makes it easier for the network to reach their audiences than they can. But if they don't innovate with their own apps and podcasts, they may die and therein lies the dilemma. And though the revenue model of podcasting is flooding the network with cash, its not necessarily flowing everywhere. Meanwhile, some podcasts absolutely cannot be promoted because they come from business. And in those cases, promoting business products is a big conflict of interest.

Back in 2008, Jesse Thorn, the host and producer of *Bullseye* talked about former NPR CEO Ken Stern being canned by NPR's board. Consisting mostly of member stations, Thorn said, it fired Stern in part because he wanted NPRHQ to reach out more aggressively to listeners and promote network content. This, despite the fact that it is the affiliate stations that buy most of NPR's programs. When the Public Radio Exchange developed its similar Public Radio Player in 2009, then PRX president Jake Shapiro diplomatically admitted to a "certain anxiety" among stations when big national shows like *Morning Edition* could bypass stations to reach audiences. But that anxiety has slowed neither movement nor direction of the trend. Kinsey Wilson, another app advocate, was let go when Jarl Mohn, openly sensitive to affiliate concerns, became CEO. For stations, it was a move to help ensure that the present would not be overtaken by the future too quickly. For those who wanted to see NPR continue moving in the direction Stern was pointing, it was a disappointment. But NPR One isn't exactly a secret. And in 2016, *AdWeek* announced that NPR, "increased podcasting ad sales by ten times in 2 years." Opponents to disrupters like Uber and Airbnb, critics say, are only delaying the inevitable. Likewise, if NPR One and others like it are as good as they seem to be, something will eventually give. And as former CEO Vivian Schiller implied, apps and the Internet may well become the future of radio. ☎

Terrestrial Radio

"It's not true I had nothing on. I had the radio on."

—Marilyn Monroe, *Esquire Magazine*, Bennett Cerf, 1953

First, some good news. The 2018 *Pew State of the Media* report says that 91% of people over the age of 12 listened to at least an hour of over-the-air radio once a week. That includes public radio. And when they listened, it was mostly on mobile devices. That's more good news for radio, according to mobile and on-line fundraising solutions firm MobileCause. It shows stations how to make money with smartphone fundraising, and stations seem to like it. Meanwhile, connected billboards transmit information on the number of cars passing those roadside ads in what's known as Out of Home (OOH) measurement. It's another way radio can measure mobile impacts on its ability to raise money. The term "mobile" is often used describe wirelessly connected vehicles and the portability of smartphones. But providers, whether they create apps for phones or cars, do sometimes use the same word for both since neither is intended to remain stationary. At least, that's the view of Hans Vestberg who, from 2007 to 2009, was the CEO of Swedish telecom giant Erickson. He says people expect smartphones to do a lot more than they're doing right now, including stuff from the car for the car. Auto manufacturers, of course, want to keep this space. But if the popularity of smartphone GPS over in-dash is any indication, they're going to have a hard time. In several years, that percentage of terrestrial listeners has only fallen by a point or two. The bad news for public radio is that it's slowly falling, not growing. And although smartphone listeners were listening to public radio, many of them may not have been listening to local public radio, or listening to it through phones capable of receiving a broadcast signal. It prompts the industry to wonder, as former NPR CEO Vivian Schiller predicted in 2010, if the radio tower will eventually lie in pieces on the ground. Satellites are pointed at cars. The Internet is in everyone's pocket. Where goes the broadcast signal?

For the nation's approximate 1,000 public radio stations, it's a question they address each time a microphone opens. Because it's another chance for them to prove their value to their local listeners. They do it through news, traffic and weather reports that matter to people heading into, around or out of town. They do it with local takes on national stories and national connections to local stories. They do it by highlighting local people doing things that reinforce the local character. But throughout their broadcast day, the consistent theme is you connecting with your neighbors, your community, you, you, you. Is that, however, what listeners really want? And is terrestrial radio the best way to give it to them or does it need to sunset as is already happening elsewhere? In 2015, the government of Norway decided to end all FM broadcasts by 2017. As of 2018, the same idea was being discussed in the U.K. When *Christian Science Monitor* reporter Lisa Suhay subtitled her piece, *"Will U.S. follow?"* it focused the threat 20th century-era terrestrial broadcasting faces from satellites and the Internet as a content delivery system in the 21st century. In other words, although users may support public radio, do they support public radio broadcast stations?

Public radio is mostly on FM. And though some stations do exist on AM, that band has never been more than a placeholder for public radio. Stations experiment with AM as a way of attracting listeners to the genre, but less than 5% of all public radio stations have an AM presence. And sometimes, owners decide a signal on both bands is redundant. Plus, AM signals suffer from technical problems like atmospheric interference, overlap from other stations and the inability of AM to penetrate structures. These annoyances, plus the fact that the gear required to push the signal through them was getting both expensive and rare, contributed to crippling AM. It's not known how much in pledge drive contributions stations get from just their AM presence during drives. But most public radio stations on AM call FM home. AM has tried to better itself, most notably with the short-lived "AM Stereo."

Around since 1961, the technique of splitting a mono signal into left and right channels was adopted by many AM stations in the mid to late 80s. But the technology was hamstrung because radio manufacturers didn't see a future as rosy as broadcasters did. The technology in most radios of the day didn't let users receive AM in stereo. And although AM gave more bang for the buck because of its ability to travel great distances, FM was growing in popularity because of how much better music and news/talk sounded than on AM. AM became the domain of sports, conservative talk radio and religious broadcasters, none of which required high fidelity. Its capture of national audiences was helped after the 1987 repeal of the *Fairness Doctrine* that required broadcasters to balance views with opposing views. This, argues media historian Kathleen Hall Jamison, led to the rise of talk radio and its own definition of "balance" as a political force. With benefits of FM outweighing drawbacks of AM, many stations considered AM Stereo unnecessary. By 2005, stations that were using AM stereo had either begun to flee the band or remove the defeated technology from their racks. In recent years, the FCC has given AM stations, if they choose, the option to grow their presence on FM.

There's AM, FM, and then there's High Definition or "HD" radio. Adopting stations say the technology combines what they see as the best of both bands: AM's ruggedness and FM's clear sound. HD radio also adds to the primary signal, but unlike AM stereo, it embeds a digital stream upon which a station can transmit other programming or text. Stations on both bands can use it, and radios with HD capability or after-market head units, can tell listeners in their displays the station, the name of the artist and the song they're listening to. These ways of placing information on or near the primary signal aren't new. They also aren't necessarily secure, as Michigan Public Radio learned in 2014 when a hacker sent profane messages to the radio data system (RDS) of HD radios tuned to Michigan Public Radio.

In 2001, Jeff Jury, the president of iBiquity, a seller of one brand of this embedded-type technology, told *Forbes*, "Radios will become two-way devices that let you request additional information about, say, daily traffic or a current weather report." Though that hasn't happened yet for terrestrial platforms, *Radioworld* did report in 2009 that iBiquity claimed total HD radio sales of more than a million units since 2006, with 2009 sales having doubled to three-quarters of a million units over the previous year. And a number of public radio stations, including Minnesota, Wisconsin and Nevada Public Radio, Georgia Public Broadcasting and others installed HD radio systems. In early 2010, a study conducted by Linfield College's Department of Mass Communications identified 1,800 stations broadcasting with HD technology. Listeners listened to HD stations 78% of the time. Even NPR's Alex Cohen, in a 2007 report on how radio was changing, asked, with apologies, if the network could "toot its own horn" about how many of its outlets were broadcasting over HD radio.

Across the pond, *The Guardian* reported in 2013 that although one-third of people listen to digital radio, sales of the gear was flat and nearly six in ten were unsure they'd buy any within the next year. That same year, Pew's *State of the Media Report* concluded, "AM/FM's beleaguered attempt to draw people back to radio through HD did worse than ever. For the first time since 2004, when HD radio receivers became available for retail sale, more radio stations dropped their HD signal [in 2012] than adopted the technology." Later iBiquity CEO Bob Struble disputed Pew's results. "We believe we know the source of the data error and are working with BIA and Pew to try and correct," he told *RadioWorld* in 2013. But by 2016 *DIYMedia* reported that iBiquity had been bought twice, first by circuitry and algorithm leader DTS and later, by chipset designer Tessera. Some stations, like New England Public Radio, removed the FAQ page on HD from their website.

Gwendolyn Fortune, an educator, radio enthusiast and author of the blog, *Keeping the Public in Public Radio* called HD radio a scam that siphoned millions of dollars away from "local concerns and existing programs." Apparently, former FCC Chairman Michael Copps agreed. He called the HD initiative "all about giving the broadcast industry more avenues to make money rather than improving radio from the perspective of the listener." And there have been accusations that, because HD radio expands the width of the main signal, stations wanting to obliterate the signals of smaller stations need not even program those side channels. The white noise from their mere existence stomps the neighbors. A 2008 agreement between NPR and iBiquity, billed as a way to increase HD radio signals, was precluded by concerns from NPR's own NPR Labs that the boost in power of HD broadcasts could bleed onto adjacent stations as well as vital, radio reading services.

Ironically, a 2010 Pew report said HD radio sales stalled as broadcasters "look for new technologies" like, getting FM chips in cell phones turned on. In 2015, suggestions by two U.S. Senators to do just that were "rebuffed" by the FCC. But by 2017, the agency had warmed to the idea of turning on already installed chips in hundreds of existing models of phones. Even NPR teamed up with the NAB to petition the FCC on behalf of the chips. "If someone has decided that their phone is a better way to get information than their radio, we're not going to change their mind," NPR's former news director, Michael Oreskes, told the *Washington Post* in 2015. "So our goal is to be there for them, wherever they are." Critics have charged carriers didn't turn chips on because they wanted users to incur data fees by listening to the Internet streams of on-air stations or aggregators like TuneIn. Carriers countered that they saw no demand from consumers to turn the chips on. But the cell phone manufacturers, supported by advocacy websites like, "free-radioonmyphone.org" continue pushing for a different kind of universal access.

And this argument has translated into court fights over whether those chips will be activated in smartphones so users can listen to radio without a data plan. In a 2017 report, the NAB found that 44% of smartphone chips had been activated. But how long connectivity for radio will survive in phones resting on dashboards, according to Mr. Vestberg, "will orchestrate a lot of things." Free radio, at least in the same pocket as the Internet and satellites, gives terrestrial broadcasters a fighting chance to be "everywhere you are." Will the rising wave of content rushing at terrestrial radio like a digital tsunami deposit a new foundation for a new type of listening experience while dragging radio as we know it out to sea? In a 2016 conversation with Andi McDonald, senior director of content for WAMU in Washington, *Current*'s Adam Ragusea asked if the station was preparing for a future in which terrestrial broadcasting was "not its core business."

"Yes," she replied. ☎

Conflicts

"Attack yourself."

—George Bailey, Walrus Research

Not literally, of course. But what Mr. Bailey, of public radio's Station Resource Group was telling his peers in a 2010 CPB sponsored report titled *Grow the Audience*, was that disruption is coming. And to rely too much on the way things are as a strategy for the future is a plan to fail. There are many within public radio who feel it is, in fact, challenging itself and making terrific progress.

Critics point to other examples within public radio, however, where it seems it is attacking itself like an immune system gone haywire. Sometimes the attacks are good-natured, as when *This American Life* and *Radiolab* took to social media to see which listeners loved best. But other examples are less playful. There's the tension between public radio stations and their public radio distributors. Public radio station managers are on a board that determine where NPR goes and what it does. While they're looking out for their interests, NPR as the entity sitting at the end of that conference table, is thinking about its board and its mission. But it's also thinking about all the new ways it can make money that doesn't necessarily involve them. Both sides are obliged to be on the same team but that doesn't mean it's always easy. Dissent can be as simple as who decided how much grinding change listeners should hear coming out of their speakers, and how often. That's one, not so positive way public radio may be attacking itself.

Others involve local versus national programming tensions. Listeners want local shows with their own identities. They complain when beloved, long-running local shows are canceled. But they also want the national glue of high-quality network programs. Maine Public Radio probably shares little with stations of the African American Public Radio Consortium that are scattered throughout the Deep South. And those likely sound nothing like public radio grant recipients serving listeners along the Alaskan frontier. But for a few hours a day, they all sound like Nina Totenberg or Ira Glass or David Dye. That mismatch often raises branding issues stations and the major public radio distributors struggle to deal with.

Neighboring stations that can't get along can also frustrate the listener. In the endless search for more audience share and revenue, smaller stations can get choked off from their traditional, niche audience by a bigger station that moves in because it can. Tom McCourt, in his 1999 book, *Communication Conflicts in America* describes a nasty fight between two Colorado based public radio stations over land and autonomy; KPRN in Grand Junction and KCFR in Denver. Citing that Denver's concerns mattered less to the Grand Junction audience 250 miles away, KPRN expanded local programming in 1986 but dropped it several years later. By 1991, KPRN said it had merged with KCFR to build the former's audience with the help of the latter's strength. However, while KPRN management approved the deal, KCFR's Community Advisory Board did not, and it tried to stop the transfer with a petition to the FCC. The transfer was granted. Later, Tom Thomas, a member of the Station Resource Group said, "if you can provide a service and people use it, do it. If it hurts another station, that's their problem, and it probably means you're doing a better job."

Such a *laissez-faire* attitude, even within public radio, can make such fights look a lot more like a quest for market domination rather than a community of listeners being served by a "family" of stations. Sometimes, a station gets so out of touch with listeners, its mission and itself that it ends up off the air due to the equivalent of a self inflicted gunshot wound. Finally, there are those unknown unknowns. Conflicts not with government, other networks, other stations or even internal dysfunctional. These attacks, both physical and cyber are anonymous and may or may not be political. But as to their destructiveness there is no doubt. The 2018 revelation that the Russian government created sleeper local news sources solely for growing a trusting audience to one day, confuse with fake news, shows adversaries invest in the long game. ☎

Station vs. Network

"I've always been a firm believer in local news, because it's an opportunity to connect with the community where you live."

—David Shuster

NPR, like PBS, was intentionally given a "federal" structure in which authority is shared between the network and the local stations. The framers didn't want a centralized network becoming a politically powerful mouthpiece for government. Much of NPR's subsequent history has been a three-way battle between stronger, richer stations, weaker and poorer ones and the central authority. The big ones, represented by the NPR board of directors, win many of those wars. In 2016, they won a delay on the distribution of the NPR One app. But other sovereignty fights, like redistributed funding and unbundled programming have happened throughout network history. Ironically, critics say such changes have contributed to a decline in innovative, less local and experimental programming. Local stations were supposed to be closest to the public and thus, serve them best. However, some of them seem to have minimum accountability to their community advisory committees while having become increasingly professionalized in their management. The strongest entities have set up networks and affiliations that now dominate NPR's programming. Instead of fostering local service, the decentralized structure, say some, has diminished it.

But for entities like Minnesota Public Radio, it's a two-tiered fight. In 2012, Greta Kaul and Andrea Schug reported for the *Minneapolis Post* on a legislative quirk that ended up taking money that was geared for small public radio stations and channeling it, instead to behemoth MPR. State republicans, reticent to fund public radio, changed the grant funding model that, in the past, had equally divided state support between Minnesota Public Radio and the Association of Minnesota Public Educational Radio Stations (AMPERS). Inadvertently, legislators reduced the ability of AMPERS stations to meet the new deadlines. This contributed to adding $168,000 to MPR's $1.15 million budget while forcing AMPERS stations for fight amongst themselves over a pot that was nearly $75,000 lighter. It could be argued that in their effort to throttle the public radio voice in Minnesota, lawmakers made it both stronger and weaker at the same time. By the next biennium, AMPERS had successfully lobbied the legislature to return to the previous funding model. But the possibilities of how different the world could be provided a wakeup call.

An example of how a single show can affect an entire network involves Ira Flatow, *Science Friday* and the for-profit, ScienceFriday, Inc. Between 2009 and 2011, funds from the National Science Foundation, intended to expose younger listeners to science via NPR and social media platforms, were alleged by the government as having been misused. Mr. Flatow and his company settled with the feds, while admitting no wrong doing, and paid $145,000 "to resolve allegations of misuse." The program was also restricted from receiving federal funds, including grants and contracts, until September 2015. The year before, Flatow told *Current* that although the grant process is complicated, his program had improved its record-keeping. Later, he told the publication that he felt targeted for the federal action despite the fact that other stations had also been penalized for similar behavior. He said an independent producer told him some considered such fines the cost of doing business with the government. And he speculated that the NSF pursued the action because it was under pressure from Congress to recoup monies from the federal education budget.

Although listeners heard little about the penalty, several years earlier in 2012, Flatow had entered into negotiations to move the show from NPR to PRI. Around the same time, NPR stopped

producing *Talk of the Nation* while continuing to distribute
it. Coincidentally, Flatow's company also produced the Friday
version of *Talk of the Nation*. NPR's decision to cancel directly
affected the carriage agreements between stations and *Science
Friday*. Flatow later said of the new PRI/*Science Friday* relationship, "At PRI, they understand radio. They understand what we
do," which implied that NPR, SciFri's patron since 1991, did not.
NPR's Ombudsman addressed the issue in 2010. And although the
keywords, "Ira Flatow," "NSF," and "ScienceFriday, Inc" bring up
scores of related stories on Google, *Current*, in other mainstream
publications and on NPR affiliate websites, none of the 37 results
on the NPR.org website specifically address the controversy or the
subsequent split. PRI aired the show for four years. *Science Friday*
is now produced by the non-profit Science Friday Initiative and is
heard on WNYC.

Individual shows and producers aren't the only source of
potential pain for stations. The network can hurt their ability to
raise money by offering up perception problems, such as when
NPR was rocked by its own ethics fueled management shakeup in
2011. Reporting for the *St. Louis Business Journal*, Angela Mueller
said the budgets of three Missouri stations were in danger of being
"pinched" because of bad network optics. KWMU, KETC and
KDHX faced a crunch and KETC President Jack Galmiche wasn't
quiet about how network fumbling wasn't helping. "We use that
funding to support the services we provide and to help us raise additional funds from the community," said Galmiche. "It's important
enabling dollars for us."

Station accountability to the network also gets hurt if it looks
like they're "going rogue." What that means, according to a 2005
article in Baltimore's *City Paper*, is "some NPR reporters believe
that their organization's credibility is undermined by inconsistent
journalistic standards at the radio stations that broadcast—and rou-

tinely edit, alter, and add to—NPR programs." Their shining example is WAMC president and CEO Alan Chartock. Mr. Chartock has held the dual power positions at Northeast Public Radio since 1981. In 2005, he was heard on at least six programs including being a regular pitcher for WAMC pledge drives. By 2019, Mr. Chartock was down to hosting four shows; "Capital Connection," "Medical Monday," "Vox Pop" and "WAMC in Conversation with." His face is all over the station's website. Though he serves his audience passionately, some say he walks a narrow line between public service and political activism.

Even though his on-air pronouncements are never enough to warrant sanctions, his blog, which used to be hosted on WAMC's website, regularly criticized the far-right. NPR's news and ethics policies encourage affiliates like WAMC to be "fair, unbiased, accurate, honest, and respectful of the people that are covered." But the *City Paper* piece noted that although many stations getting WAMC's programming benefited from its strongly local emphasis, its tone pushed some unnamed NPR purists and even some of Chartock's supporters to the edge. Frederick Stafford, commenting on *The Rational Optimist* blog in 2013, said "I enjoy listening to Alan Chartock. I certainly do not always agree with him but he makes good points in the progressive vein. He has called people names that should be beneath him, and I don't like that. I think Alan has drifted away from a real commitment to freedom of speech while on the public dime." Since assuming his role at WAMC, Mr. Chartock's view is that his station is no more out of line politically than any of the many conservative AM talk-radio hosts. His 2016 opinions regarding New York Governor Mario Cuomo and his 2018 commentaries on the pluses and minuses of legalized sports gambling show his fire seems to have cooled little. But his free speech counterpoint is one that NPR, CPB, the IRS and the FCC, through their inaction, seem to accept.

Network versus local station conflicts happen, it seems, when a local voice violates such spoken or unspoken rules and how that can affect perceptions or support. This has been happening with increasing frequency since NPR's own ethics train wreck between 2010 and 2012. For *Soundprint* and *World of Opera* host, Lisa Simione, the consequences of her passion for causes she personally supported would soon hit with the force of a pink slip. According to a *ThinkProgress* article from October 2011, Simione, had been "taking part in and serving as an informal spokeswoman for anti-war protests in Washington, DC known as 'October 2011.'" That protest, separate from the "Occupy" movement, focused on efforts around the world by nations seeking more democratic reforms. Right leaning news organizations called Simione an NPR employee and pointed to NPR's ethics rules that forbid employees from, "engag[ing] in public relations work, paid or unpaid." Though she was not an employee, and so, didn't violate then CEO Vivian Schiller's new ethics rules, the article said NPR "reacted sharply" to conservative criticism. It probably didn't help that many stations were engaged in a fall pledge drive, and the negative publicity could be bad for contributions. In a 2011 *Current* article, former NPR spokesperson Dana Davis Rehm spoke to how the network was trying to manage the optics. "It's not just about the content. It's also about how people perceive our organization and the level of trust they have in the organization. It has to touch on content and the activities that people undertake outside of their work." Later, it was announced that Simione's true employer, North Carolina-based WDAV had, according to *ThinkProgress*, folded under network pressure and fired her.

NPR's Mara Liasson was slated to speak to a lobbying group called the Oregon Business Alliance in October 2015. But because Oregon Public Broadcasting President Steve Bass complained, NPR abruptly canceled the engagement. In this rare instance, the scale tipped in favor of the station, though OPB isn't exactly a minor player. The move probably prevented Liasson from being in technical violation of the same trap that snared Simione. Simione complained to *Soundprint*'s Moira Rankin, on the verge of being fired from the show, that NPR's biggest names often speak for compensation. And there is a feeling by some that public radio bestows privileges to certain of its "mothers" over others. "During her trial in the blogosphere, Simione pointed to exceptions made for Liasson, Scott Simon and Cokie Roberts to express opinions on news of the day," said an article in *Current*. Sleuthing done by Oregon's *Willamette Week* discovered other NPR luminaries, such as NPR science correspondent Shankar Vedantam had been paid to give a speech in 2014 to the same organization Liasson was scheduled to meet. *WW* found six other instances of speeches given by Liasson to lobbying groups. "When presented with evidence that Liasson had previously made other speeches to lobbying groups, and assertions that OBA had a signed contract with Liasson," *WW* said NPR refined an earlier response that it was Liasson that declined the request by OBA to speak to its assemblage. But the firings of transgender reporter Lewis Wallace from *Marketplace* for criticism of President Trump, *The Takeaway* reporter Caitlan Curran for being photographed holding a protest sign and WUTC reporter Jacqui Helbert for offending members of the Tennessee legislature all show the long fingers of overseers have firm grips on local station's throats.

In 2003, the Station Resource Group, building on the work of the Public Radio Program Directors, assessed the tilt by some in public radio to more local news. The SRG's seven-station task force concluded, "Standards for locally created content must be as high as for any other type of programming." That sounds benign enough. But considering that *Audience 98* found that high network production quality contributed to the higher value listeners placed on it over local programming, local stations had a problem. The SRG warned that local content could not afford to "under-perform." That under-performance could have many causes; poor quality equipment, inadequately trained personnel, weak writing and speaking styles. But in the defense of many small stations that lacked good gear and better people, such resources must be backed up with cash. For stations that barely have a news department (nearly 10% don't), or a budget, they can do little. CPB funding formulas can be especially harsh to struggling rural stations. The Station Resource Group noted that though station managers may know the cost of national shows, they may not have a clear handle on how much it costs to produce local shows, and that can further strain budgets of small stations that try to push forward and create them. Consultant John Sutton says, "Local programming which typically generates less audience at a higher cost than national programming."

Audience 98 advised that to keep their audiences (and contributions) high, stations should focus on shows that held the largest group of listeners for the longest period of time. Similar network programming playing through all of the nation's local stations sounded darkly similar to the "Healthy Stations Project." Designed to improve audience numbers while bringing more professionalism to community radio, it was criticized for destroying the flavor of some community stations. In public radio, the push for a kind of uniformity met with a little more acceptance. In a 2007 article for the Washingtonian, former West Virginia Public Broadcasting's CEO, Scott Finn said, "Over the years, as NPR grew in popularity, it came to dominate the public-radio airwaves and erase the home-grown, eclectic flavor of local stations. Hundreds of stations, like Washington's WAMU, ditched the locally produced shows that gave them their identities and hitched their fortunes to the NPR brand. Public radio—once a smorgasbord of music and cultural programs—today carries a steady stream of news and talk shows, most of them nationally produced."

PLEDGE: The Public Radio Fund Drive

The prevailing wisdom seems to be that since people listen to shows that satisfy their own needs for their own reasons, the smartest thing for local stations to do is continue airing network shows that deliver them. When a local program, with different messaging, rhythms and character drops into that steady stream, the research says it can be jarring. Jarring enough that listeners may turn off and even, stop giving. That's not to say the local programming isn't quality programming. But it can be sufficiently different to interrupt the listener experience. Stations that want to inject more local issues have a hard time breaking away without losing some of that clamored-for NPR programming. So, they find themselves locked into paying carriage fees for shows they can't afford to let go.

In 2008, blogger Ralph Graves reminded listeners that when they stop giving, for any reason, they hurt their local stations far more than they hurt NPR or public radio in general. But for stations, aware of listener unhappiness but unable to give up network programs that keep them listening, it can be a vicious cycle. *Audience 2010* reinforced earlier findings; the drive to "go local" in a swing away from the national voice hasn't changed the overall conclusion that localism hurts stations and the public radio "brand" more than it helps. As if demonstrating the fierce power of that brand, NPR in 2015, launched the "Spark" initiative. In an effort to increase *Morning Edition* 's audience, nine of ten NPR stations aired up to a hundred promos for *Morning Edition* during a six-month period. Results were mixed. By April, 32 of 57 stations showed up to 20% increases in listeners, while the rest showed decreased listening of more than 20%. In June, CEO Jarl Mohn announced that between July and December, the network would do it all over again, but this time, focus on *All Things Considered*. Research presented during the Public Radio Program Director's conference that September showed listener numbers were still sliding. Again, the blame was laid at the weak local programming aired by stations between the tentpole shows.

Former NPR news chief Michael Oreskes told Poynter in 2017, "The more dire development in journalism in recent years is the destruction of local journalism." However, it could be argued that NPR has been trying to help, not hurt local stations for decades. In the late 90s, the network collaborated with American Public Media to try to strengthen station websites in an effort to help strengthen local news. The experiment offered stations the chance to have their websites upgraded so as to draw more online traffic. Back then, the fear from managers was that the strategy was a ploy to siphon listeners away from local content. But local stations push forward with their local news with and without network help. Although it examined news rather than public affairs or entertainment programming, MVC Consulting, in research it conducted between 2010 and 2012, found nearly 40% of more than 3,000 survey respondents said newsroom staffs either have, or were expected to grow. Those new hires would do substantially more reporting, producing and editing of local news. Stations also planned big on-air and online increases in local newscasts and features. And when compared to NPR, more than 65% of stations were either satisfied or very satisfied with the quality and substance of their on-air news.

MVC's analysis points to government, advocacy groups and industry supporters working to increase and improve local news. Other programs seem to face more difficulty, which suggests that it's easier for stations' news to sound like network news, even if it's locally focused, than for their locally produced entertainment to sound like network entertainment. In 2008, *Denver Post* reporter Joanne Ostrow explained Colorado Public Radio's blunt view of network efforts to increase listeners through growing diversity. CPR's president Max Wyseick considered many NPR shows a "poor return on investment." CPR diverts dollars that at other places go to *Marketplace* or *The Takeaway*, to CPR's news department. Wyseick's effort to focus on local news and local tastes had a name; "NPR takes a Back Seat."

A loud local station complaint that gained strength in the 90s was that many of the voices in stories from *All Things Considered* and *Morning Edition* came from Washington, D.C. Congressmen, cabinet officials and "K" Street lobbyists were dominating a voice that presumed to represent the whole country. In the early years that was a strategy. Frank Manckewicz, named NPR president in 1977, was a player in Washington. He was Bobby Kennedy's press secretary, George McGovern's campaign manager and worked for two of the most influential public relations firms inside the Beltway. He famously said, "I know everyone in Washington, and half of them owe me something." In many cases, they may have repaid the debt with interviews or punditry. By 2005, that desire to be associated with the network hadn't changed. "They want to be on NPR; it's a big deal for them," said NPR Pentagon reporter, Tom Bowman of military officials, also in Washington, wanting to speak. National listeners also heard well-worn call signs and reporter outcues at the expense of voices and stations never heard.

Melody Kramer, a 2015 Nieman Labs research fellow, referenced this in a footnote to her piece, *Putting the Public in Public Media Membership*. Kramer said an NPR report found "that 58% of NPR's go-to sources were either politicians, government officials, journalists, or professors—pools of people whose racial demographics don't reflect the rest of the country." The network and local stations have made moves to shift that historic "diversity desert" imbalance with the goal of creating a more diverse news voice by hearing from places that haven't historically had much of a place in the "national" conversation. The plan is to organize 200 or so stations in the network around "hubs" rather than the current, 17 national bureaus, The goal is to connect stations with each other and mutually cooperate on regionally important stories that might not otherwise make it to the national audience. At least, that was the plan of then NPR News Chief Michael Oreskes. His efforts were likely cut short when, in November 2017, NPR reported he resigned over allegations of sexual impropriety.

Public radio researcher Kim Grehn says whether a public radio voice is telling a local or national story shouldn't matter as long as it aligns with listener values. And Kramer, after asking readers of her newsletter about the importance of local news in 2015, found that reports of the demise of local news may be a little premature. National values are not necessarily local values. Of the dozens of comments she heard, themes stand out. The desire of smaller communities to not be assumed to be interested in the same things as bigger, nearby communities, was a major sentiment. Members of the community who can understand, sustain and improve local news was another. Local people holding local people accountable for local problems and solutions was another. Like KUNC's *Colorado Sound*, the need for locals to know what's happening in their community doesn't go away simply because they live on the outskirts of a larger one. Wrapping local concerns in a regional perspective, said one commenter, "won't hold your city council-members accountable. It won't do deep dives into your local school districts, or talk to interesting people in your area. It'll instead focus on vague things that vaguely apply to everyone … simply because that's where the hive mind exists." Among the scores of remaining reasons was how local programming captures and preserves the cultural history of a community. It engages its members in larger conversations and, in some cases, even teaches them how to use media to make more.

Acting Managing Director for NPR One, Tamar Charney told *Current* in late 2016 that data from the app shows people are likely to use it to hear local news. That's great news for NPR. But for stations wanting listeners to return to the dial or a native app, not the

network player, maybe not so much. Aware of the changing draw
of local news (and despite the decades old research), NPR tried a
month-long experiment in 2012 where it tested adding hyper-local
news content to its npr.org website to see how many of its web
users would visit the websites of affiliate stations. NPR One pur-
posely includes local news in its search parameters. But Andrew
Phelps, reporting for Neiman Labs in 2012, summarized the effort as simply, "Another way for NPR to throw a bone to stations,
many of whom produce news on a shoestring and can't compete
with NPR's shiny digital products and national brand power."
Public radio historian Tom McCourt was more blunt. In *Conflicting Communications Interests in America; The Case of National
Public Radio*, he says, "The contemporary structure of National
Public Radio differs radically from that envisioned by its founders.
Rather than reflecting localism and diversity, stations increasingly
have adopted a business model in which listener support and business underwriting correlate with the size of a station's audience
in general and the audience for specific programs in particular."
"Audience awareness," says McCourt, "is driven by the threat of
declining subsidies and the desire for institutional growth and organization prestige. As a result, the future structure of public radio
will be characterized by regional consolidation, national "super-
stations," greater use of syndicated programming and formats, and
commercial ventures."

Fortunately, some stations do benefit from well told hometown
stories that consistently attract national attention. St. Louis Public
Radio stumbled on that formula with it's *We Live Here* podcast.
Launched six months after the 2016 death of Michael Brown in
Ferguson, Missouri, the show "has gone viral" according to the
website "All Digitocracy" with over 100,000 streams. The community in which it originates has only 20,000 residents. At the start
of the show's second season, producer Kameel Stanley wanted to
know if the audience for the show had grown during a hiatus. "It

had," he said. Though one-in-five listeners were from the St. Louis Metropolitan Area, the audience is also spread amongst New York, Washington, D.C., Chicago, Los Angeles and listeners in the San Francisco Bay area. Stanley says of the show, "There's a saying that content is king. In this realm, context is king." The secret sauce of *We Live Here* is it looks at problems in St. Louis with an eye to the reality that the same types of situations exist elsewhere. Other cities hear their own problems and possibly, their own solutions. It's a great example of how the best storytelling finds a way to make people in one place feel known by people everyplace. ☎

Station vs. Station

"The Strong do what they can and the Weak suffer what they must.

—Thucydides

A station manager who wished to remain anonymous said, during the 2015 Public Media Development Marketing Conference (PDMDC) in Washington, D.C., that neither NPR, CPB or the FCC necessarily care that their station is being forced out of their own market by more powerful signals from their neighbors. And they said the same thing is happening in markets all over the country.

"So public radio isn't one big happy family?" I asked, incredulously. That manager just looked at me.

These kinds of fights are all about gaining or losing audience share. If a station is the larger one, turf battles like this are tolerated because being the larger station has benefits. For one, if a listener is used to listening to station A, but station B is suddenly easier to get and has a lot of the same programming, who is the listener going to give their pledge dollars to? One might assume it is the station with whom the listener has formed a personal relationship. But according to this manager, that's not a given.

For another, bigger stations may garner more political support because they may have the loudest voice. The result, according to this station manager and probably shared by other stations in the same predicament, is reduced fund drive pledges.

"We have not had nearly as good membership drives as we used to," said the manager. "And I think some of it, not all of it, but some of it is because there are so many more options. When you have a very strong signal providing NPR programming, for a certain listener, that's going to attract them and then, they're going to stay with that station. So one of the things I've had to do is look at my schedule and reformat it to try to win that listener back." "But," they continued, "I don't have the same resource as some of the other stations that are news and information stations. One of the things that I wished had happened is if they had approached me, I would've said, 'Maybe we'll look, maybe we can work together. Maybe we can collaborate.'" Efforts to improve collaboration don't always result in collaboration, however. And many of the fights between stations never come to the public's attention until they do. Stations don't like to admit their problems. They especially don't want the trouble in the family to make listeners question their sustainer status. In many cases, by the time it becomes public, it's pretty ugly.

When a radio station broadcasts a signal, that signal can make a specific shape as it leaves the antenna. Sometimes that shape looks like a bow tie. Other times, it can look like a heart. But if it's a strong signal, (which inevitably means a big signal), and on a nearby frequency, it can overwhelm every smaller signal in its way. In November 2013, *The Atlantic* magazine published a fascinating interactive map of public radio propagation patterns. It was created by Seattle-based photographer and graphic designer Andrew Filer. It depicts hundreds of overlapping circles that represent the propagation patterns of public radio stations across the country. Closer looks at those shapes, found at websites like radiolocator. com, explain details like signal power, tower height and transmitter location. In many cases, Filer's map shows big shapes partially cover small shapes. In other cases, the small shapes are covered completely. But this is not a discussion about geometry. This is about encroachment, overlap and power; both the political kind, and the kind found in the electrical formula, watts equals volts times amps.

In December 2015, public radio consultant and researcher Kim Grehn wrote on LinkedIn about the problems stations have when trying to work together. He said a group of stations wanted to improve service to their collective audiences between the Canadian border to New Haven, Connecticut. "Despite honest efforts," says Grehn, "it never came to pass as stations focused on their own issues without drawing on the experience of others." He continued, "The collaborative spirit was replaced by competition and distrust." But this doesn't have to be the inevitable outcome. Grehn says CPB has been instrumental in successful collaborations in other parts of the country. In some cases, collaboration may not be happening because bigger stations are completely unaware that they're walking on a small station's signal or slurping up their critical audience. Or they know and simply don't care. Or maybe, it just looks like they don't care, but they are in fact, hogtied.

When Adam Ragusea of *Current* interviewed the general manager of Seattle-based KUOW, Caryn Mathes in July 2016, they talked about its silence between the time the station approached Tacoma's Pacific Lutheran University, owner of KPLU, and the time the news of a sale of the latter to the former was announced. The station, already the target of criticism after eliminating much of its locally produced programming, was caught in a firestorm months later when KPLU listeners learned of a proposed sale.

This eventually led them (the station's call sign is now KNKX) to raise $7 million in a "Save KPLU" campaign that stopped the sale. But Ragusea, upon learning that KUOW couldn't talk about the sale because of a "non-disclosure agreement," said something that many public radio devotees feel when they're hit with surprises like this. "But maybe what you learned is, don't sign a nondisclosure agreement. Here's the thing: I'm a guy who's worked in the system, I had never worked at your level, I have no idea how these business machinations work — and I think a lot of my listeners are like me in this respect." He continues, "Why can't it be that you guys have a meeting with PLU, and then you say, OK, now let's say something public. Let's say, 'Hey, guys in the public, we're thinking about maybe doing this thing. We haven't really done much work on it but this is a possibility. Weigh in.'" Why, Ragusea seemed to plead, "do you think it can't be like that? Why can't it be that open?"

Mathes answered that the station was bombarded by false narratives that distorted the proposal and interfered with day to day operations which were based, in part, by not being allowed to fully disclose what was going on. And in a sign of the height of emotion at the time, at the bottom of a November 2015 story on KUOW's website about the sale, is this; "Editor's note: To help us cover this story accurately and fairly, we received editorial assistance from our partners at Oregon Public Broadcasting." Stations often acknowledge partnerships in covering stories. But rarely do they say they needed editorial help to insure they're covered, "accurately and fairly."

How can something like that affect a station that's losing audience share? Getting initial money as a small or isolated station is easy. Continuing to get it is the trick. NFFS is all of the money not coming from government. In turn, it decides whether or not stations meet a CPB threshold to get federal money. If however, stations that have been getting CPB money don't or can't reach the targets set for them, it can begin a funding death spiral. CPB watches not only a station's audience numbers, but the revenue that audience is helping the station raise. When audience and revenue falls, stations receiving CPB money based on NFFS get a warning from CPB to bring their numbers back up. But if a larger station is siphoning away the audience of a smaller station, there's not much it can do. And if there is no structure to protect small stations from large stations doing this because of what the PMDMC manager called a "wild west" attitude, they are destined to die without the kind of community rally that saved KPLU.

Listeners everywhere watch as stations are engaged in existential struggles to survive at the hands of their neighbors. Sometimes, what looks like a takeover is a technical snafu, as when listeners thought WCQS had been supplanted by WYQS in September 2014. "The reason WYQS was broadcasting the WCQS programming was purely a byproduct of a technical issue," said president and CEO Jody Evans. "We did it on purpose — a short-term inconvenience to troubleshoot a complicated broadcast problem." Sometimes, ownership negotiation deals are friendly. In 2014, the University of Washington and the Friends of KEXP agreed to keep their station in Seattle while the station got $4 million in on-air and digital underwriting/advertising over 10 years. But sometimes they're not and can be messy. When Georgia Public Broadcasting announced a two-year deal with Georgia State University in 2014 for access to campus station WRAS, complaints were strong from Louis Sullivan, president of Atlanta's sole NPR provider. Until the agreement, GPB covered all of Georgia except Atlanta. The arrangement brought direct competition to WABE in a deal the station says might have been subject to more scrutiny had the process been more transparent.

PLEDGE: The Public Radio Fund Drive

When WBGH absorbed WCRB, classical music fans mocked the slogan "Accountability and transparency are two of our watch-words" on the WGBH website. They lamented that WGBH, in their view, was trying to match Baltimore's WBUR in news cover-age by cutting back on the classical music for which WCRB was known in Greater Boston. Seven years earlier, WBZ began to catch up with WBUR in news coverage. By 2012, WBZ and WBUR had come to a power-sharing agreement that seemed to make most Bostonians happy even if WBUR was quietly not. But what some call a takeover, others call a rescue. When Kankakee Communi-ty College station WKCC was in danger of going silent in 2015, Chicago Public Radio's WBEZ rushed in. On WKCC's final day of broadcasting from KCC's campus, Heather Clayborn, in an inter-view with Kankakee Community College president John Avenda-no, and Wendy Turner, VP of Operations for Chicago Public Radio, asked Ms. Turner why CPR was interested in WKCC. "Well, you know, when we hear about a public radio service that is in jeopardy of no longer serving a community, we feel a sense of mission to look at whether we can help in that situation."

Of course, its motives may have been business and humani-tarian. The college, like so many others before it, cited "budget constraints and other educational priorities" among its reasons for shutting down. President Avendano told Ms. Clayborn that the college didn't have enough money to fund operations while it waited to see if a buyer would step up. After announcing the shutdown, and at a price tag of a mere $400,000, WBEZ scooped up the since rebranded WBEK in December. Listeners used to a strong local signal and a spotty WBEZ were relatively sanguine at the news. Said commenter Ken Kesicki at Chicago media ob-server *Robert Feder*'s blog, "While WKCC has some very good programming BEZ has access to much more. I was saddened when I heard WKCC was going off the air but this gives me some hope. If they simply simulcast BEZ's programming it would be OK but it would be nice if they could incorporate some of our community's interests, perhaps running it like an affiliate station and drawing on BEZ's program resources too. In any case I hope they can keep public broadcasting alive in our community."

Sometimes, the issue isn't a direct takeover as much as it is an encroachment. In 2011, managers of smaller stations complained at how Colorado Public Radio augmented its on-air fund drive with direct mailers. That wasn't as much the problem as that those managers also got that marketing, which meant that CPR's KUNC was targeting their listeners as well. "What I find really distasteful about it is that their official response is usually, 'Oops,' and I have a hard time believing that this is a mistake," said Sally Kane, general manager for KVNF public radio in Paonia. Her station's signal reaches Grand Junction and Montrose, both less than 75 miles away. "It seems like a really stinky tactic to just milk people when they're not aware of it." CPR's response was that all stations are doing well despite the problems with the economy and the mailings were unintentional.

The anonymous PMDMC manager says bigger stations make the tongue-in-cheek argument to smaller stations that they move into the smaller markets not to gobble up their tiny audiences, but to capture vacationers. They say visitors from elsewhere wanting to stay connected with NPR would appreciate a strong signal rather than trying to hunt for a weaker one, even if they don't realize that strong signal is contributing to making the weaker one weak. A fix that has been suggested by some managers is that if a larger station moves into the territory of a smaller station, the larger station essentially forfeits the portion of its CPB funding equaling the amount of money a smaller station would spend to keep those listeners it loses. This would act as a disincentive to keep larger stations out. Partnerships between smaller stations are also a survival tactic some are using. If they can coordinate outreach, fundraising and programming initiatives, they have more collective strength and they don't have to enter into their own "Melian Dialogue" to survive. That dialogue, a 4th century debate between a group of small, independent city-states and superpower Athens, resulted in their destruction because they wouldn't submit to its power. Ironically, smaller stations tend to have the rural and minority listeners public radio often says it is trying to reach. And if the smaller stations go away because the bigger stations absorb their coverage areas, "public radio" will still get them.

In response to a question about whether consolidation hurts or helps stations, WUOW's Caryn Mathes told *Current*, "I believe that of the top 20 public radio entities in the nation, 60% of them have done something similar to this. They've acquired an additional frequency or frequencies." Those consolidations, she went on to say, helped those stations expand their service and serve more audiences through differentiation of program streams. But even if the public is brought into the conversation, and even if the projected benefits are clear, there is absolutely no guarantee people will buy it, especially if they love what they've already got. ☎

Station vs. Itself

"Can't anybody here play this game?"

—Casey Stengel

Writer Jimmy Breslin quoted Stengel, manager of the Big Apple's newest expansion team, the New York Mets, after losing 120 of 160 games in the 1962 season. His frustration could be summarized as how, in a baseball town, could this baseball team not know how to play baseball? Looking at those times public radio trips over its own feet, a variation of it; "We learn more from our mistakes. So why don't we talk about them?," seems applicable.

That plea came from former West Virginia Public Broadcasting CEO, Scott Finn in a 2015 conversation with *Current*.

Finn wasn't specific about those mistakes, but reading between the lines gives clues. A fear of experimentation was one. The damage done by ignoring the importance of local programming in favor of network cookie cutting was another. "See a need, take the lead," an attempt to encourage more small scale collaboration rather than going it alone or following edicts from on-high, was another suggestion from Finn. Also, despite their best intentions, Finn seemed to be saying that cash-sucks can sneak up on managers who can find themselves trapped by drops in funding caused by events beyond their control. His advice was that they needed to be even more strategic. But such contemplating takes time that stations can't always spare in their day-to-day effort to simply stay on the air. And sometimes, the contemplation itself is just too hard. When St. Louis Public Radio took over operations of KMST in June 2017 from Missouri S&T, a news release cheerily noted the regional network was expanding on its own success by assuming KMST's "programming and operational duties." Nowhere in that release was mentioned the "extremely challenging" financial position KMST found itself "in light of significant budget reductions" which forced the management turnover. That information was in an FAQ near the top of the page of the fifth item in the third drop down menu on St. Louis Public Radio's website. And during its spring 2016 pledge drive, KMST made oblique references to its survival but practically all stations do during their drives. Few probably knew that it was on the verge of being absorbed.

In 2015, Montana Public Radio's William Marcus, director of MTPR's Broadcast Center, admitted that during an effort to raise awareness of MTPR's financial deficit, his station may have done too good a job of shielding listeners from station realities. "Over the winter, MTPR's senior staff went on a listening tour to meet with our constituents in Helena, Kalispell, Butte, Great Falls, Hamilton and Missoula. One of the things we learned is that there is very little awareness that the station is facing any financial pressures. I acknowledge that we should have done a better job at communicating our situation to our audience and donors." It's reflective of an old problem for public radio. Like Christmas letters or Facebook posts, public radio tends to want to tell its best stories while barely mentioning big, hairy problems everybody on the inside can see but nobody wants to acknowledge. West Virginia Public Radio's Finn seems to be saying that creating a safe space amongst peers makes for a friendlier and more supportive atmosphere to tackling them. "These stories can serve as powerful warnings," he says. "They can comfort the rest of us when things go wrong. They give us permission to take risks and admit when they don't turn out as planned." But stations also expend a lot of energy to make sure things not seen stay unseen. When KQED was the victim of a ransomware attack in 2017, it's political reporter Marisa Lagos told the *San Francisco Chronicle* the extent the station went to hide the problem. "What listeners don't know is that people have been doing really crazy things to make sure no one notices that anything is wrong," she said. For example, Lagos said the next morning, she and other reporters were told to come in at 5 a.m. to rerecord a segment lost in the ransomware attack. Like KROK, KBIA and KMUX, it refused to pay the ransom of about $3,700 per machine, totaling more than $27,000

Lots of station operations can go wrong, but the biggest problem is when one goes silent. KUSP's slide into bankruptcy in late 2016, and its later purchase by a religious broadcaster, is among the most recent examples of that. But listeners might be surprised to know that going silent isn't all that uncommon. In 2009, the *Broadcast Law Blog* looked at the number of commercial TV and radio stations off the air. When a station, for whatever reason, stops broadcasting, the FCC gives them one year to resume. If they don't, they lose their license. In those cases, some stations coming up on those deadlines employ some creative ways to broadcast without actually broadcasting. Pumping out test patterns or tone rather than actual programming (called "stunting") is one. The FCC seized licenses belonging to Equity and Clear Channel Broadcasting groups when they allegedly used the tactic to manipulate upcoming deadlines. Extreme shutdown stories also circulate. According to *Engineering and Radio*, Florida station WDVH went silent in 2000 when "the county sheriff knocked on the door during the morning show with a warrant to seize the transmitter and automation system for back debts. He was nice enough to allow the announcer to inform the audience what was happening. The station was dark for 10 months until they bought a new transmitter."

In fact, stations go off the air so often that the FCC maintains an ongoing obituary called the "Silent Station List." It's actually two lists, one for AM stations and one for FM stations. Updated twice a month, both lists only show stations that have been off the air more than 60 days. It does not show all stations that have ever gone off the air. And it makes no distinction between stations that are absent because they're getting a new call sign, temporarily gone for some other reason or gone forever. Because the FCC only tracks the disappearing, not the disappeared, the real number could total hundreds more. The July 20, 2017 list, for example, shows 167 translator stations and 326 full service stations had gone away within the previous 60 days. Private organizations, like the National Radio Club, do maintain their own lists of stations that have gone silent. But although Editor Wayne Heinen explained that the NRC shows nearly 1,500 US and Canadian commercial, public and religious stations that have gone silent since 1991, it is only for AM stations. FM is still a mystery, as are all of the AM stations before 1991. Sometimes however, reports of a demise can be premature. For example, summer 2015 was a big wildfire season in Washington state. So big that on or about August 28, fire destroyed a transmission line connecting the feeder cable between tower and transmitter for KOMQ, Omak and KPBG, Oroville. Once off the air, the station was required to tell the FCC it was down for repairs. Both signals went back up about two weeks later, but the information never got to the agency. So, as of April 2016, the FCC showed both stations as silent. Chief Engineer Jerry Olson said in an email that his stations were "very much on the air" and that they were dispatching the station attorney to set things straight.

But in other situations, fault is a perennial bumper crop. And often, it spawns from neglect. For example, some college and university public radio stations may not excel at keeping their paperwork accurate or timely. This was highlighted in the 2012 newsletter edition of NACUANOTES, a publication of the National Association of College and University Attorneys. Their five-page warning, titled *FCC's $10,000 fines against college radio stations; Playing bad records may be legal; keeping bad records is not,* outlined the biggest mistakes stations make and how they can avoid FCC fines. For example, some might assume that because college stations are essentially run by kids, they aren't held to the same standards as "grown-up" stations. But those stations, say the NACU, aren't getting a pass just because they are student or volunteer run. The FCC, by saying student-run stations aren't lemonade stands, is making ignorance of the law no excuse. Bearing the same weight as flagships, such stations are subject to the same fines for the same mistakes.

Besides problems of technology or technique, college stations are also forced into big-boy pants for staffing problems that get in the way of insuring that paperwork is correct. And fortunately or not, stations often expose their administrative issues when applying for license renewal. Since renewals happen about every eight years, it's during those windows when the public tends to see the FCC issuing the most fines. An especially active penalty period

314

was 2003, when the FCC fined 28 stations for not complying with public file requirements. The next period saw WTXR, the Toccoa Falls Christian College station in Georgia's Blue Ridge Mountains, fined $10,000 in 2010. The forfeiture order, reflective of the agency's disdain for sloppy paperwork, was for "failing to maintain the public file." For the FCC, that meant that from 2006 to 2010, the station had not included necessary quarterly lists outlining issues and programs relevant to the audience. The station appealed, arguing that the omission was not intentional as the FCC claimed. But in 2012, the decision was finalized when the appeal was rejected.

WKCR, the Columbia University station, and simulcastor of WWFM's "The Classical Network," was fined $10,000 in 2012 for missing 29 such pieces of public files documentation. WESM, the station for the Eastern Shore campus of the University of Maryland, was missing 32 pieces and was punished in 2012 by being given a four year, rather than the standard eight year license renewal option. WPPB, a service of Peconic Public Broadcasting was fined $10,000 by the FCC in 2016, for its failure "to put into the file a required list of issues the station had covered in the previous quarter." But that failure actually stretched over 13 quarters. The station asked for the fine to be reduced, but gave the FCC no reason why it should do so. NACU says such fines are considered consistent in response to what the FCC calls "a lack of candor" on the part of the stations in their record-keeping.

Some argue that these kinds of mistakes don't warrant the punishments they draw. The *CommLawBlog*, published by the media law firm of Fletcher, Heald and Hildreth, takes issue with what it considers FCC heavy-handedness in dealing with relatively minor flubs by college stations. Pete Tannerwald, a partner with the firm and author of a pointed prequel to the NACU's assessment, *Student-Run College Radio: A Species Endangered by FCC Fines?*, is an ex-officio member of the community council of American

University's WAMU. He accuses the FCC of plowing the road for commercial radio by beating down poorer, volunteer-run public radio stations. By loading them up with fines, Tannerwald says the agency makes already skittish college and university boards more willing to dump stations rather than deal with the federal hassle. For the NACU, whose job is to protect those boards and the stations they run, the takeaway is clear and repeated often: preventive maintenance. "For colleges and universities," it says, "whose stations are not in compliance with FCC regulations, the most likely sanctions are monetary fines or forfeitures, but other possible, more severe sanctions include special reporting conditions, short-term license renewal, and in the very extreme (and very rare) case, possible loss of the station's valuable FCC license." Though the FCC can be lenient, as in the 2015 case of Framingham's WDJM receiving a $1,200 rather than a $10,000 fine due to its public file violations, they are on a strictly case-by-case basis.

Stations that don't pay attention to what the government considers basic requirements may find no mercy within the FCC. The agency's new aggressiveness to cite is matched only by the steepness of its penalties. That's in part because of a 2015 law that, for the first time, lets federal agencies assess fines that catch up to where they "should" be and then, adjust with inflation. Back during the aforementioned 2003 purge, the average maximum fine was $3,500. After the law, it was estimated that the government could expect an additional $1.5 billion extra over the next ten years. The new attitude was best summarized by David Oxenford, publisher of the *Broadcast Law Blog*. In describing the astronomical fines the FCC has begun imposing on stations for violations, he concluded a recent post by saying, "This is not your father's FCC." It's a reminder that if stations plan to field a team with the intention of playing ball with the government, they better know the rules. ☎

Station vs. Anonymous

"We had a lot of people call up and ask us what's going on...you know if we're still in business and all that."

—Station Manager George Hochman responding to public concerns over January 2017 vandalism at his Hawaii stations.

In addition to the fistfights stations have with networks, meanness they may visit on each other, and unwitting blunders they force on themselves, that's not all. Though physical beatdowns on facilities still happen, the ones and zeros version can't be ignored for the extensive damage they've also done to stations.

Old school attacks, like stealing, breaking things or setting stuff on fire are still popular, according to the Texas-based *Victoria Advocate* newspaper. Reporter Sarah Eddington speculated in 2011 that an increase in attacks might have been spurred on by legendary turmoil at NPR. "NPR has come under increased scrutiny since activists caught an executive on camera deriding the tea party movement," said Eddington, "and saying NPR would be better off without federal funding." She thinks they were vindicated in their beliefs about public radio and attacked specific stations in retribution. For example, according to the *Arkansas Times*, KUAR was struck by an arsonist in the early evening of Saturday, April 3. The fire, discovered by a staffer, brought Chief Engineer Tom Rusk running as smoke poured from the transmitter shed. But a new lock stopped Rusk from getting in. Firefighters arrived, broke the lock and put out the fire. KUAR was off the air for several days while the standby transmitter was readied. But attacks on radio aren't new. In 2009, Everett Washington station KRKO discovered that an on-site Caterpillar excavator had been used by activists to try to bring down the tower. They didn't realize it was the bed of concrete, not the guy wires, that held it in place. And in 2010, Paul Thurst, writing for the blog, *Engineering Radio*, said that stations needed to protect themselves from attacks as ordinary as wire thieves trying to steal station copper.

But the computer and the Internet have caused their own share of problems. Vulnerabilities in old software can leave systems open to malicious attacks. Stations scraping by with gaps in IT staffing might not get around to the latest updates. Or the updates can come in not quite the nick of time. In April 2018, Portland's KBOO suffered a cryptocurrency related attack that had the station's servers acting like they were being defibrillated. These types of attacks want computing power, not money. It took more than a month for the Mighty Boo to get the virus under control. An update that could've prevented the hack had been released just two days earlier. But KBOO was in good company. The National Labor Relations Board, UCLA and tech giant Lenovo were bit by the same bug.

Meanwhile, stations still using Windows XP (Windows stopped supporting XP in July 2015), are asking for pain. In 2015, Redmond Magazine reported that 6% or 15 million U.S. users were still using the outdated platform. Then there's socially engineered "phishing" attacks designed to spread malware within a system A slew of such cyber attacks against radio appeared in mid-October 2014. *DIY Media* reported that staff at a handful of stations, including Louisiana-based commercial stations KROK and KMUX, arrived one morning to find themselves locked out of the station's computers. Later, they got emails demanding they pay hundreds of dollars for passwords to release frozen automation and music library software. The stations refused to pay and instead, contacted local law enforcement. The decision cost the stations thousands more as they "rebuild their systems from scratch." Less than a week later came more attacks on stations in Arkansas and Virginia as well as news that September attacks had ravaged stations in Michigan.

These ransomware attacks can scramble computer systems and turn their data into garbage without attacker-provided "keys." Attackers want payment with the untraceable digital currency known as Bitcoin. In 2014, Missouri's KBIA was attacked by CryptoWall 2.0, an early version of later, Bitcoin motivated ransomware attacks. These hacks, as opposed to the one that hooked KBOO, do want money and KBIA's hacker demanded $500 or else. Patrick Neelin, chief engineer of the University of Missouri owned station, shut down the station's computers to try to figure out how the virus got in and what damage it had done. Ultimately, all except two weeks of station's files were saved in part because of a lucky quirk in its backup system.

According to Joseph Lichterman, writing for Nieman Labs, the station had two backup systems. "And while the first system backed up the corrupt files, the second did not because it could only backup files it could read - and since the files were all corrupted, it couldn't read them." The Society of Broadcast Engineers followed up the attacks with new warnings to radio stations to "Know Your Systems, Defend Your Network, Protect Your Equipment and Use Common Sense with Email and the Internet."

Other types of intrusion involve radio data system (RDS) technology. It uses software that let stations and networks show car occupants, through in-dash radios with special circuitry, the name of the station, song and artist they're hearing. This system showed its vulnerability in 2015 when the RDS for Houston-based KBXX had its digital display of station IDs, artist names and CD titles replaced with the "N-word," followed by a picket fence of exclamation points. The hack, discovered by KBXX's parent, RadioOne, was denounced by Vice President of Communications, Yashima Azilove. "Our mission to inform, inspire and entertain our listeners will not be compromised by haters."

PLEDGE: The Public Radio Fund Drive

A larger and potentially more serious hack was when automation for Montana's KRTV cut into *The Steve Wilkos Show* and activated its EAS system. The system, designed to warn the public of national or weather emergencies (and in some communities, of Amber Alerts), can't be triggered by the station, only by county, state or federal authorities. So staff and viewers alike might have thought the notification was a periodic test, that is, until the announcement told people to take cover for an impending "Zombie Apocalypse."

In 2015, Rear Admiral (Ret.) David Simpson, chief of the FCC Public Safety and Homeland Security Bureau, told *Insider Radio* that broadcasters need to harden their software against a growing wave of cyber attacks. He said that fences and locks are security solutions for the 19th century while it's passwords and cyber keys that stations need now. And he reminded his audience, both of how ISIS managed to bring down a French television network earlier in the year, as well as the Sony hacks that were suspected to originate in North Korea. CBS Senior Vice President of East Coast operations, Robert Ross agreed that broadcasters will have to play more defense. And he didn't sound optimistic. "There are thousands of guys who want to get us and they work 24/7 – so they're ahead of us and they always will be."

These attacks are not the kinds of things stations want to talk about. Desperate to show a brave "continuity of operations" face, public radio can have a maddening "Nothing to see here" attitude when it's clear to their intelligent audience that something is seriously wrong. Public radio must not feel it needs to go it alone and instead, follow the example of other public services. In the face of their own overwhelming circumstances, fire, police and emergency management often turn to the public, not just each other for understanding, patience and help. Surely, public radio can do the same. ☎

320

Chapter 5 - Big Pimpin'

To pimp is to advertise (generally, in an enthusiastic sense) or to call attention in order to bring acclaim to something; to promote."

—The Urban Dictionary

When NPR CEO Jarl Mohn spoke to the Los Angeles Times in 2016, he began by talking up the meaning of the increase of listeners to some of the networks more popular, over-the-air broadcasts. Listening, said Mohn, was up 16% over previous years. Unsaid publicly but widely known on the inside, the jump helped affiliates be less suspicious of Mohn's aspirations for world domination since stations are still (for now) key to how NPR programming is distributed. But Mohn also used the interview to explain the importance to NPR of digital in general and podcasting in particular.

Mohn wants listeners, especially younger ones, to know that creaking they hear isn't the network rocking chair, but new capabilities, like transforming robots, shape-shifting into something they find useful. "This is a real additive product," Mohn told reporter Stephen Battaglio. "We're seeing some very encouraging signs that younger people are coming into NPR that previously haven't listened. They get excited about a podcast and then start listening."

That likely got the affiliates all worked up again. Especially since NPR would like nothing better than for those young people to be discovering those podcasts through NPR One. But as Jason Dorsey told *Business Insider* in 2015, "Millennials also aren't going to download your mobile app just because you made one." Dorsey, with the Center for Generational Kinetics, says unless an app solves a problem, young people are not going to want it. So a question public radio seems to be constantly asking is do millennials see it as offering enough solutions in their lives to attract them? "People know how to find podcasts," NPR spokesperson Isabel Lara told *Current* in 2016. The network's assumption is when enough people realize the convenience of the app, there will be nothing anyone can do to stop its wholesale introduction into the market.

Mohn has promised he wants broadcasts and podcasts to share a lot of the same sticky attributes and he doesn't seem interested in throwing antennas under the bus. He wants younger listeners to be attracted to the podcasts and their parents (and grandparents) to keep listening to network moneymaking mainstays, *Morning Edition* and *All Things Considered*. That means exposing millennials to a style of delivery their elders already know and love. But the big question, is do younger listeners want any of their parent's public radio, or do they just want what they want removed from the greater NPR as one crusts a piece of bread? Public radio may be shifting to sound more like the youth they are trying to attract. But this tweaking of the sound doesn't sit well with oldsters who, because they helped build the network into what it is, may be grumpy that the network is turning into something they don't recognize or like.

What public radio sounds like, though, is only half of the pitch youth are hearing. The other is its attitude, and public radio has sometimes been accused of having a slightly snotty one. Millennials aren't drawn to attitude problems. A 2017 article by *Host Merchant Services*, a subsidiary of Wells Fargo Bank, talked of the failures American Express was having attracting young adults to its plastic. "Membership may have its privileges, but American Express is finding out that members of the millennial generation do not consider feeling snooty as a privilege." The piece went on to say that symbols of wealth that have come to be associated with the legacy company are the very values millennials are avoiding like bad sushi. "As a credit card and as a symbol of refinement by means of wealth, American Express has long been associated with the monied class and the jet set, and this association can be explained by the company's marketing and branding efforts over the last few decades. Unfortunately, this marketing image seems to have backfired in relation to appealing to millennials."

Likewise, so many of the ways public radio talks, such as in its traditional news programs, seem bypassed by younger listeners for less-filtered and more personal types of storytelling, found in long form podcasts. The "snob" factor weighs on how younger listeners equate public radio with the sins of their parents. Accusations of condescension, is one. Sometime hints of insincerity and pretension in dealing with victims and tragic situations is another. And more traditional and enduring types of paternalism that occasionally whisper, "I know more than you" is another. These attitudinal attributes of public radio may not be as acceptable to millennials as they were to their parents. But this talk of how and what people are getting is secondary to what public radio really hopes ensues through their employ, which is "engagement."

Public radio is in a debate over what the word means. Is it giving money? Is it volunteering time? In Mr. Mohn's best-case scenario, some do both. But "some" is the operative word. Only between 5 and 10 of every 100 listeners give. And though their average give is around $144, and though their collective giving adds nearly half a billion dollars to public radio's annual congressional appropriation (in 2001, listeners gave $200 million), many public radio stations can still find themselves in a financial hole as overhead continues to rise. Meanwhile, stations at every level are aiming for sound so crisp and clear that, like mountain spring water, people come to drink deeply and often. Making that happen isn't cheap or subtle. As former KERA Vice President Susan Harmon told the *New York Times* in 1995, "Everyone knows we need to support our habit." ☎

The Public Radio *"Sound"*

"Mentholated"

—*The New Yorker* reportedly describing the sound and speaking cadence of the *NPR voice.*

That was then. And to some extent, older public radio's voices represent the last dominant "voice" of public radio. From the days of Edward R. Murrow through NPR's Robert Siegel, that deep, resonate and authoritative voice was associated with radio. As Bill Bradley said in a 2010 *Vanity Fair* article, "Every self-respecting snoot in America knows the exact timbre of Carl Kasell's voice." But when the baton was passed, that voice retired. In its place came more recognizable styles of speaking for a new generation, whether it was the nasal of Steve Inskeep, the syncopation of Kelly McEvers, the staccato of Michelle Martin or the roller coaster energy of Ira Glass and Michael Barbaro. As Farhad Manjoo noted in his 2011 *Slate* piece, *"We Listen to NPR Precisely to Avoid this Sort of Stupidity,"* he makes mention of that energy. "As close listeners of NPR know, the hosts draw upon a wide vocal range to signal a story's emotional tone."

The cadence and pitch of some network speakers might remind hardcore Star Trek fans of the therimin, which like public radio voices, can be sing-songy. Heather Radke, in a 2017 article for the *Paris Review*, recounts Charles Bowden's opinion of the NPR sound. "That fabled NPR voice, produced in some secret kitchen where ordinary Americans are dipped in tubs of soy milk, white wine, and herbal tea until their vocal cords lose all sense of desire, familiarity, or place." Bowden was not a fan. Of course, the 2015 comparison by the *Associated Press* of NPR to Al Bayan, the radio network of the Islamic State, didn't exactly win hearts and minds either. Peter Sagel of *Wait Wait Don't Tell Me* blasted the radio network on hearing that news. "Thank you, ISIS. Yes, we're very flattered. This comes as no surprise to you NPR listeners, who, a couple times a year, get pledge-boarded by your local station."

The public radio sound includes not only the public radio voice but a particular style of storytelling. *Audience 98* said it appealed to people who fall into one of two general categories; those who care about society and want to be involved in changing it for the better, and those who are more interested in material wealth and public displays of that wealth. These two groups tend to be upper to upper-middle income earners, well-educated and white. Together, both groups represent more than three out of every ten pledge dollars to public radio. These people recognize the public radio voice because, according to the NPR Ombudsman in 2015, they and it came from the same colleges and universities of the east, Northeast and Midwest. Baby boomer listeners to public radio may well have been descendants of listeners to educational radio in the 1930s and 1940s.

Besides being the historical homes of classical music pro-grams with their cultivated upper-crust, journalism instructors at many of these same colleges and universities told their students to lose any hint of their ethnicity or regional accent if they wanted a career in media. But some listeners might like that voice to have a little more regionalism. Commenter "ochona" on *Archinect.com* forum in January 2007 said, "It would be great to hear an accent from south of the mason-dixon line every once in a while. It bleeds down to even the austin affiliate, where you can go weeks without hearing anyone who doesn't sound like they emigrated to austin from new york. If they wanted me to give money, they'd say "y'all" more often" Ochona has possibly never heard the Texas twang of John Burnett, David Brown or Wade Goodwyn.

NPR's most valued demographic is precisely targeted. But public radio says it attracts listeners that benefit from public radio's brand of storytelling. And that, it says, isn't dependent on the age, race, gender, income or education of the listener. Instead, public radio says its stories are geared to a type of listening preference. It's someone who wants smart, informative, personalized and engaging stories that keep them informed of events in their community, their country and the world. That type of listener, says public radio in its defense, is not necessarily college educated, straight, wealthy, middle-aged or white. It says those listeners want "long form journalism," a relatively new style of storytelling researcher Kevin Barnhurst began noticing in the late 1980s.

Back then, Barnhurst saw that unlike commercial spot news, public radio stories were getting longer. But he also observed that stories got more focused on the opinions of the reporters rather than the content of their pieces. Barnhurst said this can elevate journalists above their stories and call credibility into question. In some cases, as with former NPR *Morning Edition* host Bob Edwards, an audience can raise a personality to the level of a cult figure. It was a mistake the network worked to avoid in the future. But it shows how personality and voice are of ultimate importance.

Longtime NPR producer Jonathan Kern addressed that importance in his 2008 tutorial on NPR audio production, *Sound Reporting*. A technique for giving every network voice its famous moderation, says Kern is, "When speaking into a microphone, one trick is 'Count down from three, lowering your voice with each number,'" Kern said. Since people tend to talk at a higher frequency when they're reading, deep breathing while consciously bringing the voice lower relaxes the reporter, which can relax the listener. And what the reporter can't do, the editor can. "Fixing it in post" is an expression that means tweaking something to perfection before airing it. John Solomon reported for NPR's *On The Media* in 2005 that NPR makes what's called media sausage "by cleaning up and tightening sound-bites through editing out all the 'uh's' and 'um's' from correspondents and interviewees." "*Fresh Air*" with Terry Gross also reportedly hones the program to aural perfection before releasing it in broadcast and podcast. Although production values may be exceptional, critics say the richness that comes from mistakes and spontaneity may be somewhat lacking.

Other technical tricks which constitute the NPR sound include the fact that unlike commercial stations, NPR and many of its member stations tend not to use as much audio compression in broadcasts. This allows the full dynamic range of music and the human voice to be heard, which can make both sound richer. This audio benefit was one of the results of the network's switch from its first generation of PRSS to Version 2. Known inside as the Satellite Operations Support System, Version 2 "not only provided high-quality digital audio for NPR and other program feeds, but provided automatic tuning as well as recording control for audio servers in radio broadcast automation systems." NPR has also gone to a lot of trouble tailoring their sound to drivers. Road noise is in the 300 hertz and below range. NPR's sound engineers tune out everything below 250 hertz, so instead of rumble on rumble, what riders get are the higher, sharper and crisper frequencies. Finally, for the audiophiles, while many stations' stock microphone is the Shure SM-7B Dynamic, NPR is known to use the Neumann U-87 Cardioid Condenser. That the Neumann is ten times more expensive than the Shure doesn't necessarily mean it is ten times better in quality. But as one reviewer said, "When I need clarity in the mids (midrange frequencies, where the human voice is), the U-87AI is a far better choice."

Public radio's individual voices form its "collective" voice. Whether female or male, foreign or domestic, that voice is recognizable as calm, friendly, knowledgeable and slightly snarky in that you suspect thinks it knows more than you. Followers of the *Dune* trilogy might associate how public radio uses its words in the same way science fiction writer Frank Herbert's mystical *Bene Gesserit* use "the Voice" as a subtle tool of mind control. Teddy Wayne, in a 2015 *New York Times* piece, derogatorily likened the public radio voice to "poet's voice." Wayne, who heard it throughout NPR news, music, entertainment and public affairs defined it as "the practice of poets reciting verse in singsong registers and unnatural cadences." Ira Glass said people want to hear stories from speakers that sound like them. But Wayne says the preponderance of ordinary speakers flooding public radio has led to loosed elocutions like uptalk and vocal fry running buck wild. Uptalk is the tendency of a speaker to end statements with what sounds like a question mark. Uptalkers are accused of not sounding confident, with criticism of women who uptalk being harsher than against men.

Marybeth Seitz-Brown said in a 2014 article for *Slate* that men, like former President George W. Bush, who uptalk aren't accused of sounding unsure. "Think uptalk makes women sound less authoritative?" she asks. "Maybe that's because women are constantly robbed of agency and authority, and we view anything they say or do as less powerful." As Jennifer Barrett noted in her 2017 Wake Forest University thesis on female voices in public radio,

"These conceptions of voice are reinforced through the practices of 'verbal hygiene' by public radio listeners and the emphasis on sounding 'authentic' within the realm of public radio, as this places female reporters and announcers in a double-bind, as they cannot both sound like themselves while maintaining a perceived, gendered standard." Female voices, says Barrett, "are likely to receive more criticism when heard in the public sphere through an authoritative medium, as they are expected to maintain 'ladylike' qualities within their role as 'language guardians.'"

Vocal fry may be considered the opposite of uptalk. It is the tendency of a person to speak in their lowest register when trying to emphasize a key point of conversation. At this low register, the voice may sound gravelly with the intended effect of giving the speaker more "authority." In 2015, NPR's Sam Sanders explained why, for some just starting out in public radio, this way of speaking is so easy to adopt. Sanders looked around and saw lots of others, "try[ing] to sound like other people we've heard on the radio, or the person who is training us." He continues, "Not to mention, the Ira Glass factor," Sanders says. "I hear a lot of people trying to talk like Ira Glass on air. For one, his voice really only works for him. For two, just do you, people!" And although conservative William F. Buckley's West coast, upper-crust speaking style was rife with vocal fry, most of the harshest criticism against it is again directed at women. "Uptalk," "Sexy baby voice," "breathy voice," "slack voice," "creaky voice" and vocal fry are speaking styles that, whether natural or adopted, are increasingly common on public radio.

Such vocal characteristics are targets of scorn because interviewees often sound nothing like hosts and the difference can make the latter sound pretentious. Some, like William Krause commenting on a *Chicago Reader* article about public radio, don't accept it. "The local NPR announcers … are even more offensive than the national personalities. Normal conversational mid-western American English is the broadcast standard, but our locals feel it [necessary] to abandon natural speech and adopt the same affected hyper-inflected patronizing whine that's apparently used throughout the whole network. How and why is this? If these people just spoke with the accent and inflection natural to people in western Pennsylvania, northern Ohio, and parts of Indiana they could—with absolutely no effort—be world-class in their presentation."

In a nod to Mr. Krause's complaint, a Nieman Labs essay called that voice he laments "what some people consider accent-less and others know to be a distinct, specific accent: a white one." For many years, one of NPR's iconic voices belonged to Betsy O'Donovan. She voiced most of the networks underwriting credits. Then with much fanfare, in October 2013, New Yorker Sabrina Farhi became the new "perfect" voice of NPR. Less than two years later, WAMU alum Jessica Hansen took over for Farhi, coincidentally after complaints that Farhi's voice contained too much vocal fry. It was a charge NPR denied. Hansen's strong, clear, near perfectly articulated voice, is practically devoid of accents or regional mannerisms.

But even perfect voices are not loved by all. "When I hear Jessica Hansen (I looked up her name) announce the underwriters I turn off NPR,' says commenter "espresso" in 2015 at the *Washington Post*'s comment board. "Her warm smiling voice talking about cancer treatments (and everything) are like fingernails on the chalkboard of my brain. (I have even written NPR to complain)." And although jokes have been made about the dizzying array of ethnicity in the names of reporters working for public radio around the world, the network has long sought non vanilla flavored voices. For example, for years, Frank Tavares's rich African-American voice covered the network underwriting credits for NPR. Most recently, the first male voice since Tavares, Chioke I'Anson, has been added to the underwriting line up. I'Anson, a black instructor at Commonwealth University in Virginia and a producer of *Backstory* with the American History Guys and *Unmonumental* became NPR's other underwriting voice in November 2016. ☎

Snob Factors

"If All Things Considered didn't exist, the staff would have to create it."

—Susan Stamberg, from *NPR: The First Forty Years.*

Francois-Marie Arouet, known by his pen name "Voltaire" said in 1768, "Si Dieu n'existait pas, il faudrait l'inventer"—"If God didn't exist, it would be necessary to invent him." He couldn't have guessed that 214 years later, his sentiment would come to represent how public radio feels about itself. Public radio listeners enjoy being smug is no surprise to public radio. It's one of the reasons public radio pledge drives so often hammer listeners with the same dual messages; commercial radio is garbage, and you are smarter, better people because you listen to us. Pledge drive guides remind pitchers to keep telling listeners how wonderful they are in ways that can sometimes seem outsized from simple appreciation. To the uninitiated, these messages seem to contradict the humble, inclusive and understated persona that public radio screams.

But public radio does some things very well. For instance, the public radio sound and voice, like a smoked ham, has been long-seasoned before it's ready to be shared with the public radio palate. So while mentholated is what public radio might sound like, curated is the taste that palate is expecting. The word comes from the 17th century Catholic church. A "curator" was an assistant to the priest, whose job was to watch over the souls of the parish. A better job description for public radio could not be written. Public radio listeners, as described by *Audience 98*, have a set of values that they expect to hear reflected back to them by public radio. And though, because of this expectation, they are known to be slightly snooty, the qualities they assign to themselves (which are the ones public radio strives to reflect) are quite reasonable, respectable and deliverable.

Public radio listeners expect mental, emotional and spiritual stimulation as well as a high quality experience. Mental stimulation means a willingness to think, a desire to learn and a hunger to better understand what they already know with deep storytelling dives. Most public radio listeners wanting that mental stimulation, trust that what they hear is truthful and neither sensationalized or fake. The emotional/spiritual experience is all about what makes them laugh, cry, hope and gives them faith in the rest of us. Story quality is not just about how it sounds or makes them feel, but its long-term impact. In other words, what power does a story have to motivate them feel, speak or act, long after it's nothing but a memory?

In part, that's why in NPR's 2008 guide to audio journalism and production, *Sound Reporting*, author Jonathan Kern takes a shot at "the hackneyed phrase, 'Only time will tell.'" This, along with other cliches, Kern argues, isn't stimulating. So while public radio might not call itself *bourgeois*, it is aiming at a level of sophistication. Reporters and producers at every public radio station know there are only so many combinations of words, techniques, sentiments and phrases. But they are constantly challenged to arrange them in new and interesting ways. The goal is to create the kind of excitement that keeps listeners believing that they're always making the right choice with their time and money in their support of public radio. Tried and true methods can get threadbare however, such as when hosts ask a complicated question with only seconds for an answer, hosts equalizing points of view from un-equally qualified spokespeople, hosts immediately repeating to the guest a just asked question as if it was a "new" question, or hosts inserting their own 20-second analysis at the end of a conversa-tion (which can sound a lot like an editorial) rather than a simple "Thank You." This type of massaging, or curation, happens in de-grees. But there are more major and notorious ones. Among them:

Lifesplaining - Hosts often take time to explain things that public radio listeners likely already know. This has legitimate roots. Back in the 70s and 80s was when Americans were just starting to hear about how their school students didn't know state capitals. And that got news organizations worrying that Americans didn't know basic geography. So they started using more graphics and maps, and taking more time to explain a story's basic, internal connections. Google and Wikipedia have since taken up that mis-sion. But broadcasting stills feels responsible to spell things out. When *Marketplace* host Kai Ryssdal, was talking with *Wall Street Journal* reporter Maureen Farrell in July 2017 about angel investors and market valuations, he casually referred to the "S&P" in the course of the conversation. Listeners to a program about stocks and bonds know the "S&P" is shorthand for the "Standard and Poors" index, one of the four major market measures. But Ryssdal, almost out of reflex, instantly reiterated the reference with the more formal, "Standard and Poors." But more obscure refer-ences can go unexplained. On April 11, 2018, *All Things Consid-ered* host Mary Louise Kelly was talking with *Wired* correspondent Casey Chin about Facebook founder Mark Zuckerberg's definition of his company. Kelly mentioned in passing that the social network is *sui generis*. *Sui Generis* is a legal term that means "in a class of its own." But it was not explained. And though the reference is much more obscure than S&P, the example shows a frequent lack of consistency in the public radio talk space.

PLEDGE: The Public Radio Fund Drive

Not a Duck - Related to "Lifesplaining," this is the tendency of public radio to give the benefit of the doubt to subjects, that from the standpoint of the intelligent public radio audience, may seem frustratingly obvious. In August 2017, President Trump, while in a press conference about the opioid epidemic sweeping the U.S., responded to a *National Intelligence Report* that North Korea had successfully miniaturized a nuclear weapon, which could now fit atop its new ballistic missile. "[North Korea] would be met with fire, fury and frankly, power, the likes of which this world has never seen," warned the President. To an average listener, that could easily mean that he was threatening to use America's nuclear arsenal as a "not off the table" option to stop Kim Jong-un's march toward deployment. But when asked by *BBC Newshour* host Tim Franks if that's what Mr. Trump meant, the BBC's Washington correspondent noted that the Trump administration has sent conflicting signals on a variety of issues and perhaps, the White House was merely returning bellicose language to Pyongyang. "We don't really know what he means," said the correspondent. The follow-up interview with a representative from the Union of Concerned Scientists, however, was not so tentative. He expressed clear concern that the language was a dangerous game of chicken that meant exactly like it sounded like it meant.

Likewise, when Freddie Gray suffered a "spinal injury" as the result of his arrest and transport by Baltimore police in 2015, Charlie Rose of *CBS This Morning* was among a small handful of newspeople to use the words "broken neck" to refer to the injuries Gray received. He died shortly thereafter from what public radio tended to describe as everything from a neck injury to a spinal injury to a partially severed spine. But it's also an example of the opposite tendency of public radio, which is what some call "sanitizing" upsetting language that is so clear and painful that it needs softening. Public radio might say, as it did during the "torture" versus "enhanced interrogation techniques" debate that descriptions speak for themselves or "official" language supersedes listener assumptions or listeners can assign their own value to terms.

Stove, Hot! - Public radio likes to warn adults of how adult stories and situations on an adult news program about real life might be upsetting. Though children are sometimes waved off from inappropriate content, public radio seems as concerned with film and TV spoilers as with tragic or violent reporting. Although some adults appreciate the heads up, saying generalized news is not as unpleasant as an in-depth feature could be, the conflict of how to tell such stories is reflected in one of NPR's central reporting tenet: "We report the news, good and bad," says *Guidance on the Use of 'Disturbing' Videos and Audio"* from the *NPR Ethics Handbook*. This policy, however, can feel brutally enforced by hosts who ask permission from guests or victims to revisit graphic details of horrendous situations, (in the interest of providing context) but proceed whether that permission is granted or not.

Like, for example, when host Robin Young of WBUR's *Here and Now*, said to the family of murdered Marine Corps son, Raheel Siddiqui, "We know from accounts, and they are terrible, and I hope you don't mind if I repeat some of them …" Guests often do choose to avoid details of their choice. But when a family like the Siddiquis have a public statement they want to make, that is often not the same as horrendous recapping they may not want to hear. Though story leads do the heavy lifting in preparing the audience for violence or tragedy, *NPR's Ethics Handbook* implies this is not enough, by asking and answering: "Are we treating the audience like children? Some will say we are. We believe we're making editorial judgments."

The Talkover - The "I know more than you" milieu is a kind of knowledge paternalism public radio demonstrates most often during interviews. Talkover is the tendency of public radio hosts to bulldoze guests trying to add more context to an answer they're in the process of providing. Social convention lets people familiar with each other or who are mutually excited about a topic talk at and over each other simultaneously. When hosts do it, however, it can turn from a facsimile of friends chatting to the host sounding rude or ignoring what the guest is trying to say. Commenter "Triscut" on Yahoo! Answers says, "I totally agree. It's very frustrating when the host asks the guest a question and then cuts them off before they've had a chance to complete it. I want to hear the answer to the question!" And although public radio hosts frequently interrupt, they don't suffer much interruption. They often ensure their sentiment, whatever it is, is expressed like a tank driving over a string of parked cars. While the guest struggles to keep time with their own thoughts, the host can grind on until theirs is the only voice.

Sincerely Yours - Public radio's efforts to sound sincere are often heavily criticized. Pitch training guides say, "sincerity is everything." Some call the trend, following the shift from boomers to millennials, menschy or confessional. But its manner has reached such ubiquity that, as Teddy Wayne pointed out in his *New York Times* piece, "consumers (and voters) are ever skeptical of faux sincerity." He accuses public radio hosts of acting rather than newsreading by injecting pretentious stutters designed to show listeners that announcers are "just like them." Or pregnant pauses implying personal processing but instead, may only be about adding *Who Wants to Be a Millionaire* type drama. But real sincerity can be felt as keenly as the fake stuff. When OPB's Dave Miller talked with author Sally Tisdale in June 2018 about the subject of death, callers sharing their own experiences of caring for dying loved ones seemed to have a noticeably humbling effect on both host and guest.

Public radio is capable of such empathy. In many cases however, unless a host has personally reported a story, or been intimately involved in its production, their first contact with it may be mere minutes before the on-air light comes on. In *Sound Reporting*, Jonathan Kern said that hosts have to be brought up to speed by the reporters they're about to interview on-air so as to strike the right tone. A mismatch can sound glaringly insincere. It is a technological miracle for someone sitting in an air-conditioned studio in Washington to talk with a Syrian refugee while bombs can be heard falling in the background. But the larger miracle may be if the former can have true empathy for the latter that extends beyond the next pod of underwriting credits. It is a core flaw in news presentation that forces hosts to switch emotions as one scans for cable channels. But aiming to win the sincerity wars is nothing new. After all, it was vaudevillian and early radio star George Burns who said, "Sincerity is everything. If you can fake that, you've got it made."

All of these "techniques" developed as part of how public radio has come to sound over nearly half a century. But some of them may be aging out as far as millennials are concerned. On Valentine's Day 2018, NPR senior correspondent Jeff Brady was on his way to the shooting at a high school in Parkland, Florida. In his LinkedIn post, he used well-worn descriptives like "tragic," "terrible," "evil," and "heartbreaking" to describe it. The next day, 23-year-old *Palm Beach Post* reporter Lulu Ramandan told Kelly McEvers on *All Things Considered* how difficult it was to tell such a familiar story in a new, compelling way. "It's easier in that I've done this multiple times," says Ramandan, "but harder because you have to do it over and over again, you know, harder because it's the same question and sometimes the same response but you know in the back of your mind that this is just an entirely new situation."

As boomers die off and millennials step in, how different listening choices are made is changing. "Today, radio consumption is frictionless," says Steve Lickteig in a 2016 article for *Slate*. He produced Weekend *All Things Considered* for four years, and he says younger listeners don't stroll for content like their parents did. They just want what they want. "The curated magazine show is dying," SportsCenter's Steve Olbermann told Lickteig. And in its place, for example, is a generation that will talk to their radio like they do a drive thru speaker. "Voice recognition technology," says Lickteig, "will kill *All Things Considered*." Even though shiny NPR One, the prototype for self-curating content, is packed with stories, "you're still being force-fed stories by people who think they know what you want," Lickteig says. Considering the coming technology, it's safe to say the future is not your parent's liner notes. As *On the Media* co-host Brook Gladstone told OPB's Dave Miller during a November 2017 stop for her book, *The Trouble with Reality*, "It's up to everybody now to curate for themselves." Curation and the self-righteousness that comes with it is fading away. "Tell a bunch of 19 year olds that it should be up to the professionals to determine what news is most important," Lickteig says, "and they'll laugh until their earbuds fall out." ☎

Engagement

"Stations need to stop thinking that they're in the radio business. They're in the audience-engagement business."

—Paul Jacobs, Chairman of Greater Public

Links between public radio and business makes listeners suspicious. Practically all public radio user agreements say stations don't sell donor information. Many of those same agreements also say public radio may share donor information with certain "third parties" who may, in turn, share that information with other parties over whom the station has no control. Though not "sold," as that promise of secure user information moves further from stations, listeners may wonder if it remains true. "I haven't dug into it, but I believe that the reason that public radio stations are still running fund drives is that that's how they get the subscriber lists that they sell in order to make the real money," says Dan Lyke on *Philip Greenspun's* weblog from 2009. Old suspicions die hard.

Although stations speak of engagement like a relationship, they tend to use engagement like a wrench. And that gives it a dual meaning. Most times, it's a verb as in to engage or make contact with listeners and encourage them to holler back. It enlists iconic public radio voices to move listeners by praising their local stations. That version is a gentle encouraging that's softened with warm, fuzzy testimonials and sincere pleas to help stations meet their pledge drive goals. It's about reaching out to listeners, heart to heart and convincing them to emotionally connect with the station through their checking accounts. It's about paying it forward. It's about community. But engagement is also a noun and a process as in the mechanism of engagement. Like a military campaign, public radio deploys armies of canvassers, telemarketers, platforms (like WGBH's RedPoint) and algorithms to find people consuming its content. Its apps, players and APIs hang in the cloud like Predator drones mapping pathways and relationships. They tie it all together so each user's movements, and thus their willingness to pay for what they hear, can be logged, tracked and stored. So in a nod to the Reagan administration, whereas definition one is about trust, definition two is about verification.

Media research firm Coleman Insights, in a 2017 report explains why public radio needs such a take no prisoners attitude when it comes to engagement. Although public radio may claim nearly three million contributing members and 40 million weekly listeners, "Fewer than one in four radio users can call to mind any public radio station," says the report, "while almost all listeners can recall a commercial radio station." The report says that although public radio is correct when it says it is not viewed as overly "boring, old or biased," it suggests that awareness of public radio may not be high enough to capture a greater pool of opinions. The remedy, says the report, is to beef up branding, which will grow awareness and, by extension, engagement.

Melody Kramer understands the engagement problem. In 2015, Ms. Kramer joined Nieman Labs at Harvard University for eight weeks as a Nieman Fellow. Her mission was to rethink what engaging with public radio means in the digital age. Focusing on the membership model rather than branding, she later wrote, "The existing membership model for public radio is largely based on a single assumption; that people who want to listen to the kind of high-quality programming that public radio provides will eventually find and then listen to public radio — on the radio, in the car, or on a mobile device. But the assumption that public radio provides a particular type of listening experience may no longer be accurate." In her 2015 work, Kramer said when stations work to build relationships with givers, doors open to the various ways listeners and stations can work together.

"This model," says Kramer, "is based not on the pledge drive (or on cultivating sustaining donors or large donors, as many stations seek to do), but on building an infrastructure that allows community members to contribute to their stations in a variety of ways, including non-financial means. It takes as its starting point the understanding that building relationships with potential donors leads to their sustained support — in the form of time, money, and advocacy on behalf of the station." In other words, neither stations nor listeners should assume that money is the only thing that needs contributing, or that giving cash qualifies them as sufficiently active. This new thinking makes defining engagement trickier.

Stations have historically measured engagement as a marker of financial support. The more a member of the target demographic hears the ask for support, the thinking goes, the more likely they will give. So stations use every means at their disposal to connect, since connection means engagement and engagement means contributions. There are still the traditional ways; pink colored letters in windowed envelopes, email blasts, reminders to give between program breaks, and old school "membership appreciation" events like open houses and barbecues. But more and more, stations are following user engagement to the cloud. In 2007, Ann Phi-Wendt, Marketing Communications Manager for Public Radio International said in a PowerPoint presentation that "E-mails/e-newsletters and podcasts can be used to increase listening to public radio; there is good potential for outreach through blogs and social networks to test impact on listening." That same year, CPB published a guide for broadcasting stations that contained six templates for radio fundraising letters, and six templates for TV fundraising letters. Though those letters have not gone away, one thing stands out from Ms. Phi-Wendt's 2007 conclusion. Nowhere in her presentation was there any mention of any form of outreach that wasn't web based. Social media, website visits, electronic forums and email were the preferred methods. No barbecues, no fairs.

But that's not to say up close and personal ways of meeting and greeting potential givers have gone the way of the rotary phone. Surprisingly, door-to-door fundraising is being adopted by public radio membership and development directors. More than one IRS Form 990 shows a station has hired a canvassing company to explore this old mine for new gold. For instance, Donor Development, based in Denver, shows on its homepage its relationship with more than a dozen pubcasters, including KERA in Dallas and WHYY in Philadelphia.

PLEDGE: The Public Radio Fund Drive

Wisconsin Public Radio says on its website that it launched its "Door to Door Membership Campaign" in April 2016 by sending professional canvassers into south-central and southeastern Wisconsin neighborhoods. Considering that there are 20 or so counties in that portion of the state, it might be more helpful and straightforward to say that canvassers probably blanketed the region's 25 wealthiest communities by zip code. Those boil down even further to a relatively small triangle connecting Oshkosh, Madison and Milwaukee. The effort lets Wisconsin Public Radio "personally convey the importance of public radio and quality programming to thousands of people every week." It also gives WPR "an opportunity to thank current members, rejoin lapsed members, and gain new members" by getting right on their welcome mats. But door-to-door canvassing is small compared to the reach of all things web. And as time passes, even some of those technologies get supplanted by others.

NPR's elimination of its own comment board in August 2016 is a good example. The network dropped it in part because it discovered that by steering listeners to more ubiquitous social media, it could capture more comments where they already were. However, many public radio stations still encourage listeners to comment at in-house message sites as a way of refining their own knowledge of listeners. Those stations may mine their boards for story relevant comments. They may use them to find good candidates for future stories. And they use them to let people feel like they are being heard by the station. But conversation isn't always the intention or the outcome and it is questionable as to whether comment boards hurt or help journalism and public engagement.

Often, general interest programs take live callers. But callers can be volatile. That's why stations need kill switches that let hosts cut them off if they have to. Kill switches have been criticized in that they prevent those from the community with unpopular views from being able to fully contribute to the conversation. In response, many general interest programs have stopped taking as many callers and have moved to comments posted online. This way, they can get the same public engagement by cherry picking the best responses without the fear of being surprised. These programs can get so many however, that they don't even have time to include most of the condensed responses they get on social networks. Plus, since some of them rebroadcast their daytime programs in the evening, those programs have been encouraging people to "join the conversation" throughout the day. Not the on-air conversation necessarily, but a conversation about the on-air conversation.

Critics complain that defaulting to social media can sometimes feel like passing the buck on the obligation to give people a live, or live-on-tape opportunity to engage on a particular issue. What people want is to ask the expert, which is why the program invited the expert. Instead, what some shows do is give participants who use comment boards the less than ideal substitute of engaging each other. This can let people see that listeners of the same program can have widely differing opinions. But relying on comment boards can lead to the worst kind of troll-laced cruelty. Comment boards for publications like the *Huffington Post* have ended anonymous comments and now force users to use their real names. Forums like those for *Wired* magazine ended altogether.

Popular Science closed its comment section because research showed that even a small number of people who post wrong information can skew the perception of the entire group. As a publication dedicated to science and research, suffering the ignorant minority at the expense of the innocent majority was something *PS* could not stomach. Some see heavier moderation as the solution to better engagement on comment boards. Others pin their hopes on software that strains obscenities and polices syntax to remove flamers. But some reporters and journalists say comment boards are true forums for public discussion and the poisons injected by trolls is the price we pay for free speech.

Newsrooms, as well as development directors, understand the importance of engagement. In fact, in an October 2016 survey by Watershed Media, a majority of responding newsrooms supported so called, "engagement programming." This included "social media and outreach campaigns to promote their coverage," directly polling the audience for "tips, feedback and story ideas," annual "listening" events and heavy emphasis on investigative journalism as a way of connecting with the community by addressing its concerns. But engagement as a line item under newsroom operations can be pricey. Survey results show thirteen respondents expressed a desire for more engagement programming. But tight budgets stretched their news missions, let alone engagement efforts. Despite those limitations, pubcasters are working hard to get more personal with their users. In 2017, Neiman Journalism Lab reported on a trend where newsrooms "attempt to insert themselves into consumers' lives via daily newsletters, apps, or texts that ask for feedback in the form of stories and/or data." And all in the spirit of greater engagement. "But," it warns, "engagement producer beware; There is no blueprint for these sorts of projects, because they are built on personality and trust. One size does not fit all. They require building a content feedback loop that requires dedication and resources."

That feedback loop seemed missing, according to nonprofit leader and syndicated journalist Antionette Kerr, writing for *Kivi's Non-profit Communications Blog* in 2016. She was referring to an emptiness on the part of NPR, and called out *The Two-Way* specifically. *The Two-Way* was a network initiative to deliver the first news of the day in blog/podcast form. It ended in June 2018. Kerr found the site, which implies visitors can "engage" with NPR on the site's content, lacking. "I couldn't find a place for a genuine exchange or interaction on its website. Are NPR loyalists supposed to email support staff to get in touch with their innermost feelings?" But the site did offer Twitter and Facebook links. And a "contact" button at the bottom of the page sent visitors to NPR's main contact menu that lets them send webmail to particular NPR departments, programs or the NPR Ombudsman.

Kerr also criticizes what she considers "regurgitated" content. "The digital audience is looking for something a little more dynamic and interactive," suggesting that if millennials find such dynamism lacking from the site, the site will find itself lacking millennials. To draw them in, *On The Media* producers Alex Goldman and PJ Vogt created, *TLDR*, which is millennial speak for "Too Long; Didn't Read." The WNYC team created the blog to drive traffic to the *OTM* website. It was an engagement success as traffic to the site jumped by 33% after the blog was launched. That happened in part because producers encouraged longer stories and, in a move antithetical to a journalism program, made them not always be about journalism. For example, *OTM* co-host Brook Gladstone had a series of extended interviews with singer Cyndi Lauper about music, not news.

Engagement for public radio means getting people to move from passive listeners to active members. But bestowing distinction through segregation isn't necessarily in the spirit of public radio inclusiveness. In an unscientific survey I conducted, nearly 40% of respondents answered "yes" to the question, "In your opinion, does the distinction between 'active, sustaining members' and 'passive listeners' risk alienating those listeners who are not members?" Another 35% said "no" while one in four said, "maybe." No one answered, "I don't know." Engagement is a new word for an old concept: building relationships. Despite decades of public radio equating a person's commitment with their willingness to give, marketing professor Americus Reed of the Wharton School, identifies a new paradigm. What he calls "The act of giving time" passes on psychological benefits that giving money doesn't. Echoing the findings of Melody Kramer, Reed says though giving money is easier, it's the clock that ticks off one's life. He says that makes time something people give with much more thought and intention. That's not to say a parking lot full of volunteers equates to a balanced station budget or money for new programming. But letting people give the best that they are with the time that they have gets them thinking about their moral and mortal selves. And that has the potential of opening material and spiritual ways of giving that they and their stations never expected. Yellowstone Public Radio pitcher Ken Siebert said it best during a 2016 pledge drive when talking about a station volunteer, on the phones, who had also just made a contribution. "Thank you so very much. And, you know what? That's a perfect model right there. There's somebody who is not only giving their financial support but is giving of their time to come in and answer phones." ☎

Chapter 6 - Drives & Elements

"The pledge drive has everything going against it as broadcasting. It's repetitive. It's ad-libbed by people who can't ad-lib. It's about asking for money, which is something nobody wants to hear, even from their own relatives."

—Ira Glass, *The AV Club*, Nathan Rabin

Although about three-quarters of stations tell listeners a pledge drive is coming, about one in six don't. So listeners sometime complain about feeling ambushed. And public radio seems truly conflicted about how it wants drives perceived by an audience it needs to accept them. In a 2009 blog post, Jeff Brooks vented suspicion over the utility of drives. Mr. Brooks operates the blog, *Future Fundraising Now* and wonders if their awfulness is one reason why they're effective. "But I have a sneaking suspicion that one of the reasons the pledge drive sucks is the people who run it think it sucks. They hate it so much that they've actually turned everyone's mutual hate for the pledge drive into a fundraising hook!"

Walrus Research, in 2004, conducted a study called, *"Annoyance with Fundraising."* It said that although annoyance was difficult to track, some things about how people disliked pledge drives were clear. Among them, that fundraising would be more effective if stations moved away from pledge drives and telemarketing, and more toward direct mail and underwriting. As a tool for increasing contributions, stations routinely contract with telemarketing companies. But the upselling tactics they use don't create warm fuzzy feelings for listeners. John Sutton advised stations about telemarketing in 2008, warning "You can't pick and choose what you want to believe about what listeners say. To say, 'We trust listeners when they talk about our local music host but not when they talk about telemarketing' is irresponsible." Suspicions of how the money raised barely pays for the money raising effort itself are also rampant outside and within public radio's listenership.

In public radio, it's the development officer that works with membership to figure out ways to make pledge drives successful. Development watches the audience trends, attends conferences on fundraising, creates outreach programs, staffs open houses, and generally, raises a station's visibility in the community. Ultimately, development officers help send a lot of money to NPR. But APM, PRI, PRX and NPR don't hold pledge drives. And while the networks don't host them, they pull out all of the stops to support them, ranging from playing up how they can be hilariously fun times to siccing network luminaries like Ira Glass on non-givers. As a consequence, network hands stay clean while affiliates do the wet work of keeping the money flowing through the system. And it explains why local underwriting credits say support "comes from our members" while NPR's underwriting credits say support "comes from this station."

But although NPR has only ever had two pledge drives of its own, that doesn't mean it hasn't thought about more. In 2009, NPR was in bad enough shape that a couple of its "mothers" reportedly pushed then CEO Vivian Schiller to consider a third one. That ultimately didn't happen, although some in public radio believe such direct fundraising is inevitable. A pledge drive goal may buy a year's worth of programming, or successive mini-drives pay for capital improvements like studio remodels, transmitter upgrades or website overhauls. Meanwhile, new stations periodically enter pledge drive world for the first time. Norfolk State University's NPR member station, WNSB held its first-ever pledge drive on April 1, 2016. Before that, the station existed primarily on university support.

Other choices aren't complete solutions either. In a 2016 promo for its "Quiet Drive," Larry Voydko, for Pittston, Pennsylvania's WVIA said, "If we can hit our goal over the next few weeks, then we'll not have to conduct the traditional fundraising campaign with those long pledge breaks which, frankly, nobody likes." Researcher John Sutton agreed with Voydko that drives are disliked in 2007 on his *RadioSutton* blog. In 2016, University of Oklahoma station KGOU went where few stations dared go and asked its listeners outright, how they feel about pledge drives. Fifty percent said they don't like them, while 33% said they did and 17% didn't like the choices. By contrast, Market Trends Research helped Wisconsin Public Radio conduct a listener survey in 2013. The online survey asked visitors to rate their news consumption, their use of social media and how they saw their place in the community among a battery of other question. But nowhere in the 30-screen questionnaire did it ask them their feelings about pledge drives.

Defenders of drives often say people continue to listen even though they don't like them. But there is plenty of support for the idea that drives actually push listeners away. So stations rely on gifts to keep people in place. And though goodies haven't been conclusively proved to spur giving, because there can be so many pledge drives in any given year, and because when stations ask their asks, they may encounter donor fatigue, they continue to sweeten pots with giveaways. They do it by stirring up friendly competition between big community names with matches and challenge grants in which they practically dare each other to give. Or, pitchers do it with what's known as "premiums" that include concert seats, wine tastings, wireless speakers, iPads and plane tickets. In other words, promotional items given in exchange for "valuable consideration" like an underwriting credit, or maybe, a bunch of underwriting credits.

Those are served up several times an hour in "pitch breaks" that last about six minutes each. Not counting those just after news, or those just before the legal ID, stations can have as many as four of them an hour, up to twelve hours a day for as long as ten days in a row. They appear in place of the regular program breaks that normally happen about every 12 minutes. But because local stations must more than quintuple normal break size so that pitchers can say everything development directors want them to say, listeners may notice that their favorite shows are between one-third to one-half shorter per hour. In response to listener complaints, stations have tried shortening drives, quieting drives and specializing drives. And though technology for eradicating drives has existed since 2011, pledge drives endure.

Even as many stations run their pitching staff (usually a mix of reporters, on-air hosts and executives) through a battery of training in advance of drives, pitching can still end up sounding awkward and sometimes questionable. Stations aren't shy at experimenting with ways to hook listeners. Those hooks can range from puppies to liquor. They can be a pair of pitchers declining into madness, or describe an Onion-style news break of a pledge drive inspired fake mass shooting. And in an industry struggling to escape orthodoxy, what stations do including what they allow pitchers to say, is equally unpredictable. Though many stations subscribe to services that provide pitch scripts like PledgeDriver, it's what pitchers say in the segues between scripts that can get iffy. While enthusiastic station cheerleaders whip their verbal pompoms, mistakes can happen when people get tired because the drive has dragged on longer than planned, and pitchers start feeling the public isn't responding. It can get personal.

Plus, it raises the "moral hazard" issue of "free riders." It's a central problem to the success of donor centered giving, not just for public radio, but all nonprofit organizations. "Why should I pay for something I can get for free?" non-givers ask. A bulletproof response doesn't exist for the 80% to 90% of listeners who remain listeners rather than supporters. NPRHQ, though forbidden to conduct pledge drives at present, does run promos when local stations are running their drives to encourage people to call their local station, "If this is a program that you value." On the other side however, there are those givers who will give however much and for however long. But they want more information about where their money goes in exchange. As GuideStar president Bob Otterholf told a gathering of public radio pros in 2003, "When [some high powered donors] don't see the results they hoped for, they take action."

Otterholf said donor expectations were changing. "They are more discerning than ever before. They're looking at more than just tradition and reputation. They're demanding transparency. They want to know details—where their money is being spent and why. They're demanding accountability: Prove to us that our donations are being spent wisely." In 2010, KUOW Seattle listeners discovered the station was on the brink of another pledge drive while also enjoying a $1.3 million surplus. Setting aside complaints of low salaries, former longtime staff member Ken Vincent asked, why was information "such a closely guarded secret?" Only when KUOW's then General Manager Ken Roth helped listeners find budget information, which explained the surplus and the ongoing need for drives, did things settle down. But some listeners were resentful that the station wasn't clearer earlier on. "We're not stupid," said Seattle resident and donor, Brian Grant.

Those listeners, if they finally give, are "encouraged" to move in some directions over others. One-time gifts are better than none. But sustaining gifts, like those where a giver hands over a credit card, or a checking account number that can be debited forever, is golden. The lilt in pitcher's voices when talking about sustaining membership is absent in talk about any other type of listener giving. "Easier for you, easier for us," pitchers like to say. And keeping track of that money with certainty happens with elaborate pledge drive software. They follow contributions not only from phones, keyboards and apps but from walk-ins, after hours answering services and good ol' checks in the mail.

Internet outreach to younger groups of donors who may not want contact in more traditional ways is a modernization of the quarterly letter. But some nonprofit experts think the trend pushes fundraising into uncharted territory because the high-tech ask may interfere with cultivating the relationship at a deeper level. And this can cause less attention being paid to donors. Engagement, through listener comments, partially addresses this mismatch. Though not an antidote for under performance, listener comments, if sprinkled like sequence throughout pitch breaks, can be a critical ingredient of the pledge drive recipe. Full of praise for news, programs, stations and staff, they lift the moods of pitchers and momentarily divert listener attention away from pitches. They reinforce the truism that programming quality equals listener loyalty. But in situations other than drives, listener comments often get treated like the red-haired stepchild. And stations with much more important things to do are sometimes accused of placing them, ever so gently, on the back burner.

Pitchers are quick to say that the drive will be noticeably shorter if givers give a lot, quickly and often. But one of the oldest complaints listeners have against pledge drives is that even after they've done as they're asked, the drive continues because so many others have not. "Pledge-driving me nuts" was what Sarah Bunting titled her blog post at *Tomatonation.com* in 2007. While lost in an enjoyable interview from her beloved WNYC, a pitcher interrupted to, she says, "tell me some shit about how everyone listening to him right now who doesn't cough up some money is basically going to hell, like, 1) don't mess up the flow of a perfectly good segment, and 2) I GAVE YOU THE MONEY ALREADY." Kelly Williams Brown, writing for the Daily Beast in 2014, talked to Paul Maassen, General Manager of WWNO in New Orleans. She asked, "whether there would be a time when those of us who are already members could magically skip the membership drive; it does feel unfair that those of us that dutifully pony up our $12.50 a month have to suffer with all the shirkers."

When pitchers imply that "your gift can get us over the finish line," it's not mentioned that the line may be six, eight or ten additional days thick. "Extended" or "stretch" goals, where stations push past their stated ones, can also be a surprise to listeners who had expected pledging for an hour, a show, a day or a drive to end when they were told it would. And while technology exists that would end pledge drives, stations are hesitant to use it. Meanwhile, since talking dollars can be a turn-off, some stations have shifted from dollars to raise to numbers of new members to sign up. With average contributions per member being what they are, stations know that by focusing on the people rather than the cash, if they hit their new member number, they'll hit their financial target as well while sounding a little less gauche.

When drives have passed the halfway point and the asks get more urgent, the phrase "ending successfully" starts sounding less like a triumph and more like a concession. Guilt, what *Slate*'s June Thomas described in 2009 as one of public radio's nine "cunning" ways to get listeners giving, joins altruism, flattery, proofs of devotion, and more. According to my informal survey, about 30% of stations ended at least one of their drives from the preceding year when they promised. And one in six ended all of their drives on time. But more than a third of stations couldn't even remember if their drives ended on time, while 7% admitted that none of them did. That's pretty spotty for an industry that constantly says of pledge drives, "This model works." To be fair, stations can only guess what giving mood their listeners are in. They may use past drives at home, and an aggregation of giving data across the country to guess their success, but they can't be sure. The one thing they know is costs are always rising, so they leave their options open, to listener dismay. ☎

The Long & Short of It

"Even as more stations experiment with less on-air fundraising, they should consider possible drawbacks."

—Jay Clayton, speaking with *Current* in April 2016

Some people could listen to pledge drives forever. Others associate them with tooth extractions. That's why pledge drives, some would argue, are best taken in doses. That's getting harder for listeners, however. As the ability of a station to generate each pledge dollar requires more work, in part because fewer people are listening as frequently as they used to, stations are having longer pledge drives. Though many pledge drives have modified banker's hours, some continue in a "brute force" kind of way, long after the commute is done and the kids are tucked into bed. During its spring 2016 pledge drive, Southeast Missouri State University station, KRCU included days of live pitching that stretched well past 10 p.m. And many stations played promos or read readers reminding givers to give into the wee hours. Many drives, which start as early as 5 a.m., are only one of several that some stations hold in a year. Smaller stations, with smaller staff, may only be able to mount a couple such efforts a year. Tighter budgets and the money saving measures they require means they don't have a lot of cash for local or network programming. This makes them heavily reliant on free shows.

Bigger stations are a different story. Their financial needs, driven by their massive networks of repeaters, multiple programming streams, thick news departments and top tier program lineups can cost millions of dollars a year. For them, two, three or more high-value drives each year are a must. And stations have used consultants to respond with a drive for every need. But no drive is a one size fits all proposition. Besides the various drives stations can choose to run, they also tweak them a lot to find a recipe that they think has the most effect with the least impact on their listeners. The menu stations have to choose from is a long one. They include:

Traditional Drives - These can be anywhere from 5 to14 days long, and seem to bring stations the most consistent money. Many of them, including KUER in Salt Lake City, and Oregon Public Broadcasting in Portland, tend to do their heaviest pitching in four, six-minute sprints that begin about 12 minutes past the hour and continue throughout. Some pitchers use the time to tell stories of how they got involved in public radio, or reflect on the quality of a piece they may have just heard. They may only sometimes mention the station's phone number, website, drive goal or premiums. That type of chatter isn't necessarily connected to any of those money making pitch elements. More experienced pitchers may repeat the phone number and the website up to forty times, leaving little room for pontification. These pitchers seem to assume that anything else you need to know you'll get once you pick up the phone and call. Kansas Public Radio modified the traditional drive by compressing all of the asks into 10 to 15 minutes of each hour, but the allowed regular programming for the rest of the hour.

The six-minute breaks within traditional type drives are flexible. That means if goals are behind targets, pitchers may stomp into a program while reminding listeners, "You know how this works," with the tone of a loan shark slapping his palm with the fat end of a baseball bat. But the traditional drive can hit a wall though, as it did for Rhode Island Public Radio's WMVY. In January 2013, the fundraising effort, targeting the South Coast and Cape Cod concluded ... after 59 days.

Make up Drives - A make up drive is what a station does to meet a goal it missed during its regular drive. WCQS, a service of North Carolina's Blue Ridge Public Radio, told listeners on May 24, 2014, that it was having a one-day drive that day. That's because the regular drive, which ended the previous month, missed the needed goal by $10,000. "It is essential that we meet our goals in order to continue to provide the programming you rely on every day," said station spokesperson Michelle Keenan on the station website. Though WCQS had already raised around $310,000 from its 2,600 new members, and had only missed the goal by about 3%, the appeal shows that for many stations, the bottom line doesn't move, not even a little bit.

Quiet Drives (aka "Silent") - Alaska Public Radio's KSKA, along with Texas Tech's KTTZ, ran relatively quiet pledge drives in Spring 2016. Pitch breaks for both stations, like the Weather Channel, tended to be on the nines and last only about a minute. But while KSKA's sanguine breaks consisted mostly of a network voice encouraging giving with a local voice following up, KTTZ's pitching was local, fast paced and information heavy. It reminded listeners of drawings, obligations and deadlines. The quiet drive was dreamed up as a compromise between incessant asking and no-asking, which left it up to listeners to do the right thing. Stations that do well with a one-day drive may choose to cancel a subsequent drive. Between the identicalness of their message and the automation like regularity of their placement, quiet drive messaging can be like a mosquito that one forgets about until it's back in your ear. There may be another reason why some stations have moved to having more quiet drives. Patrick Emerson wrote in the *Oregon Economic Blog* in 2010 about how many universities begin their drives in what he calls a "quiet phase." He says they "don't go public with them until they have made substantial progress toward that goal. Rightly it turns out since people respond more when they think the goal is obtainable and realistic."

Buy Down Drives (aka "Warp") - In 2016, Public Radio Tulsa, like many other stations, participated in a pre-drive drive, sometimes called "Buying it Down." The thinking is that by reminding listeners, quiet drive style, that a traditional style drive is looming, the audience will choose to fully fund the station's goal as a way of avoiding a week or more of pitch breaks. Because so much of what's needed can be raised before the "real" drive starts, this type of fundraiser is nicknamed after the propulsion of the USS *Enterprise*. Northeast Indiana Public Radio's WBOI announced its first ever warp drive in September 2016. After successfully raising 60% of the $200,000 goal before the drive started, the station reduced its scheduled drive to five days, while announcing another warp drive for Fall 2017. Listeners to Columbus, Ohio's WCBE heeded the station's request to "mess up" its planned fund drive, and killed three days of scheduled pledging by raising $28,000 a day during its own warp drive.

Multi-Day Drives - Stations looking to tweak the length of time of the traditional drive may choose something less than a week but

357

longer than only a few hours. In 2012, Vermont Public Radio ran a three-day "mini" drive with a goal of more memberships. That same year, California State University's Capital Public Radio launched its "Four Day Drive," which had a goal of $400,000. The drive was stopped however, on Friday, December 14 at $144,000. The news department took precedence because that was the same day as the Sandy Hook school shootings in Newtown, Connecticut. Stations often, without question, stop drives when local or national breaking news happens.

One-Day Drives - "Super Thursday" has been a long-time staple of the stations of Northwest Public Radio. NWPR is essentially two networks under one umbrella, serving news and classical music needs of listeners from Tacoma, Washington to Lewiston, Idaho. Noting that many pledge drives are at least twice-a-year affairs, NWPR decided to "try a different approach" in 2008. That first one-day drive netted $271,000 from 2,400 supporters in 24 hours. The method continues to deliver. In 2014, nearly 2,100 listeners gave NWPR $268,000. Bangor Maine's Public Broadcasting Network held a one day drive with a goal of $150,000, but raised $165,000. The*Bangor Daily News* said "Pledge phone lines were manned starting at 5:30 a.m. with the pledge drive officially concluding at midnight."

Power Hours - Used by Nebraska Public Broadcasting, Capital Public Radio, KWBU Waco and Spokane Public Radio among others, these fast drives can raise between $10,000 and $500,000 in a few hours or less. It's another way stations try to get what they need while annoying listeners as little as possible.

End-of-Year Drives - These give givers a last chance in the current tax year to claim a deduction for contributing to their public radio station. For Salisbury University's Delmarva Public Radio in 2015, the end of their fiscal year prompted them to ask for "a little more." But they can also be a gimme for stations that may look at a last drive in the last week of the year as a "why not?" kind of proposition. People are already in a giving mood and some non-profits can get more than four out of ten of their annual dollars in December. Becky Chin for Greater Public noted in November 2015 that "People expect a little boldness from organizations at the end of the year." She says slightly pushy campaigns, focusing on "tax benefits" and "holiday spirit," should be light, tight, direct and emotional. These types of campaigns, says Chinn, "will get results."

Capital Campaigns - This can sound exactly like a traditional drive. But depending on the goal, it can differ by orders of magnitude. Capital campaigns pay for big but doable asks like transmitters and building renovations. In April 2014, Minnesota's KMSU asked its listeners for $50,000 worth of help to replace its 25-year old transmitter. But, at other times, the ask is both broader and much deeper. In 2004, Minnesota Public Radio's capital campaign intended to more than double the floor space of its 52,000 square foot offices. The $46 million ask was also intended to expand MPR's Public Insight Network, invest more in music, culture and the arts, and launch a digital archive project. In 2017, Northeast Indiana Public Radio began a $4.5 million renovation to turn a formerly burned-out church into sparkling new studios.

Specialty Drives - Stations may be involved in special causes where they feel they must contribute to a social effort in their community. Such was the case with Colorado Public Radio in 2009. Its "Instrument Drive," as the station said on its website, "promotes music education and appreciation throughout the Colorado community." Vermont Public Radio, as well as seeking more members in a 2016 drive, also used its specialty drive to support anti-hunger and nutritional education programs. "For every pledge VPR receives through noon on September 8, the Vermont Community

Foundation will donate a bag of groceries for Hunger Free Vermont's Learning Kitchen program," VPR said on its website.

Cooperative Drives - For some stations, winning the pledge drive war means suspending the audience share battle and cooperating with rivals. For example, in many communities with more than one public radio station, station A may plan its pledge drive in concert with station B. Such a tacit agreement might have the possibly unintended effect of giving the listener nowhere to go and thus, helping both of drives end sooner. This happened in Utah around 2007, when the pledge drives of KCPW and KUER would coincidentally overlap. Listeners in other parts of the country have noted the same tendency. In community radio, stations in a single market may indeed work together during what's called "Coordinated Fundraising Week."

Responding to a critique about PBS pledge drives, current NPR Ombudsman Elizabeth Jensen wrote in the *New York Times* in 2011 about how the "official" PBS pledge drive was coming to an end on March 20 (although local stations may schedule their own independently). Later, Mary Helen Stotlz, in a 2016 piece for Missouri S&T, mentioned how KMST's membership drive had been moved up five weeks, to begin on March 19, "to coincide with National Public Radio's fundraising period." It's worth remembering that by June, whatever KMST had done would not be enough, as the station was taken over by St. Louis Public Radio because of its financial woes.

Existential Drives – KMST's example is a good segue to Monterey based KUSP's disappearance from the airwaves in August 2016. Its refusal to bombard its eclectic music listeners with pledge pleas during its spring pledge drive months earlier, forced it to stagger beneath a $300,000 goal. Though, when it did have its periodic pitch breaks, they were star-studded. Nikki Silva of the iconic Kitchen Sisters pleaded with the audience to allow itself to be turned on to the kind of music she herself had discovered through KUSP. "If you know an angel," said Silva, "please, get them on board." By angel, Silva was probably talking about the financial kind. And when the station did make its asks, they were simple, sincere and direct. "If you can donate a thousand dollars or more, we can use your gift to inspire other listeners," said host Alex Burke. Absent were the promises of drawings, challenges, swag or anything else that so often accompany pitch pleas. And though first time givers, sustainers and renewers may have held importance at other times, the station's *Maidez Maidez* campaign needed givers at the thousand dollar level. But still, not at the expense of the music, which continued to occupy no fewer than eight out of every ten minutes an hour. It shows that even when facing extinction, some stations continue to hold the love for their listeners and the content above all.

Greater Public, an industry advocate for public broadcasting, says that although some stations have had some success with modified versions of the traditional drive, reducing the fundraising message ultimately forces stations to "leave money on the table." But also, says author Jay Clayton, shorter drives deprive listeners of education they need to understand the importance of drives, and that the public service component of public radio requires public support. Compared to public television pledge drives, which can last for weeks, public radio listeners should consider themselves lucky. ☎

Breaks & Pitches

"Chug every drop in your possession if an announcer tacks on the word "bitches," as in, "Call 314-516-4000 to donate now, bitches! And donate one year's salary—winner!"

—From *Drinking with St. Louis Public Radio, Riverfront Times*, March 20, 2012

Hosts use pitches to get listeners to do something, whether it's to convince them to give money, enter a contest, volunteer or learn about a thank-you gift. Pitching takes place during pitch breaks. But since a pitch within a break is occupying a space that would normally be filled with other programming, pitch breaks themselves are programming. And stations spend a lot of time and resources to make that "program" as important to you as *All Things Considered*. But that may not be how listeners see it. Fundraiser Jay Clayton, in a 2008 study on listener giving by the Station Resource Group, said it's not that listeners don't like pledge drives. What they don't like is how they're asked.

Clayton says stations tend to ramble about everything except the ask. Forgetting that they may have all the time in the world while listeners don't, he says pitchers don't get to the point. Also, he says listeners don't want to be given something to do if it's obvious that nobody else is doing it. "Often the request is tied to the station's need to meet a goal—dollars or donors—by the end of the hour or to call because there's nothing happening in the room where volunteers are waiting to answer the phones. Asking me to call because no one else is calling," Clayton says, "is not a winning approach." Neither is the ask that can come dangerously close to sounding like begging. Marketing strategist John Moore, on his blog, *Brand Autopsy*, warns, "Begging is not becoming of a brand that appeals to the highly educated and the highly paid." And of course, public radio brags about its appeal to both.

The pitch break is composed of elements. More than a hundred separate catch phrases have been engineered to grab your morality, guilt, sense of grandeur, or some other psychological ring and make you give. And because they're repeated, they could be seen as simply intended to wear the consistent listener down. Indeed, in *Annoyance with Fundraising*, one of four 2007 public radio tracking studies by Walrus Research, listeners commented that they return to their public radio station when they think it's "safe to listen." But because listeners listen inconsistently, repeat messaging may also be legitimately reminding those returning to the programming after a few hours of peace, why they should give, and that they have yet to do it.

A 2017 analysis I conducted of 37 public radio pledge drives showed that the average five-minute pitch break included two nods to underwriters, three acknowledgments of volunteers, four reminders of the goal, seven reminders to become a sustainer, 14 mentions of thank-you gifts, 20 mentions of the station website, and a whopping 35 repeats of the phone number. Although the average number of elements per break was one every 11 seconds, some speed demons like KTTZ in Lubbock, Texas pushed out 25 elements in two minutes, or one about every 4.8 seconds. Based on those results, I determined that pitch pleas are divided into no less than eight categories. They include:

1. Straightforward, noun-verb asks that are full of action steps. "Pledge now; give whatever amount is right for you; pay it forward; let's get those phones ringing; step up and do your part."

2. Pitchers using clairvoyance to speak the listener's mind. "You've been wanting to do this; we know you don't want to let us down; do what you know you should."

3. New listeners that are hand-held through their first contribution. "If you're new to public radio, you might not know how this works; it only takes a couple minutes; someone is here to walk you through the process."

4. Frequent reminders of what you get out of the deal. "These programs are important to your life; support programs you love and depend on, the content is addictive and you know you can't live without it."

5. Reminders of your obligation to the station and the community. "We are mutually obligated; we work hard for you; our volunteers are here on the weekend to take your calls."

6. Compliments to listeners for their superior choices. "You are smart, you're special, the tote bag lets you show off as a public radio supporter."

7. Lessening your anxiety to give ... after raising it. "There's still time for you to give but it's running out; you don't have to be embarrassed for not giving to this point, we don't want you to miss the chance to donate; as a sustainer, you can feel good knowing you don't have to stress about your payment."

8. The consequences for not giving at all. "We have to do this to keep the station on the air; if we don't make our goal, we may have to cut programming; we don't want to go silent."

That last one is a threat that at least one station made good on. When KPBX, the precursor of Spokane Public Radio, was trying to upgrade to become a larger, better NPR licensee in the late 70s, a friend of David Schoengold (who had taken the station over from originator George Cole), told him that it would be easier to raise money for the changeover if the experimental station went off the air. After signing off in 1977, and several years of fundraising and delays, KPBX signed back on January 20, 1980. And listeners, probably remembering what they had missed, gave until their public radio was returned to them in the form of a newer, more powerful station.

Stations are encouraged to use pitch scripts to keep the message from wandering. When, for example, a pitcher is promoting a thank-you gift, there may be specifics about the gift itself as well as promotional information about the provider. Both may be arranged into talking points that are more conversational, along with positive comments from previous recipients. Though they may sound like a lot of work to prepare, mostly gone are the days when stations have to write their own. Those that can afford it now turn to companies that provide templates, software or consultants that analyze stations and their market to create customized scripts that can be easily tweaked by need, location or season.

This frees stations to spread thin staff over a broadening list of duties. Still, freelance rates for advertising copy writing range from between $45 to $100 an hour. Pitchers may read several scripts each break from a binder or screen of dozens of different, drive-specific scripts. As a member of Greater Public, stations can get access to a repository of scripts they can use at year's end for last-minute fundraising pushers. PRI offers its affiliates a wide range of development tools for underwriting and fundraising, including scripts from companies like Minnesota based OnAirFundraising and its script service PledgeDriver. PRI also provides host bios, show highlights and listener comments.

The size of the station, its pledge drive goal, the type of drive it's deploying and the audience may decide how long the breaks are. For instance, WFUM tries to avoid pitch breaks, opting instead for interstitial announcements that don't sound much different from their regular underwriting or PSAs. This works for the University of Michigan's public radio station and its audience, and is one of the strategies stations across the country have refined and adopted to try to prevent drives from wearing listeners out. By contrast, Oregon's Coast Community Radio, during a Spring 2016 pledge drive, followed a 10-minute pitch break with a three-minute song and a 12-minute pitch break.

Small stations have to work harder to get their audiences to engage. And although they are the station's bread and butter, they can wear pitchers out too, as commenter "bluedaniel" noted in a November 2003 post to *Metafilter*. "No one specifically likes a pledge drive. As a matter of fact, if you think it's difficult listening to one, imagine pitching one. There is a reason we all take vacations immediately following a drive, and it's not because the Autumn foliage is ripe, or the Spring air is calling our names. It's exhausting, grueling work to go on air for several hours at a time, appealing to the listeners the value of public radio and how it needs, not wants, needs their support to continue, quarter by quarter, year by (fiscal) year."

John Sutton, on his *RadioSutton* blog about public radio, runs through a list of things pitchers shouldn't say. They include some well-worn staples that anyone who has ever listened to five minutes of any pitch drive, anywhere would recognize. Sometimes however, even when pitchers should be fresh, the anticipation of being worn out pushes through. During the opening seconds of Yellowstone Public Radio's April 11, 2016 pledge drive, News Director Jackie Yamanaka, along with co-hosts Kathleen Benoit, Mark Parker and Chuck Hingle opened their microphones wide. With sparkle, Ms. Yamanaka said, "We're in the studio this morning because today is Day One of our spring ..." But she was stopped cold by a mournful, off mic groan by Hingle. "Oh don't," the News Director rushed in to say. Reactions around the table sounded like triage for heresy.

After several more seconds of awkward silence, Ms. Benoit blurted out, "We need to raise $200,000," with all of the cachet of a soapy washcloth hitting the bathroom floor. So much for segues. Station pitch breaks are above neither disdain nor threats. Melbourne, Florida's WFIT told listeners that if they didn't contribute, the station would be forced to begin airing "standardized programming." Their weekly schedule shows only four public radio mainstays: *Democracy Now*, *Morning Edition*, *All Things Considered* and *World Cafe*. The rest of it is full of local and avant-garde music. The Space Coast station seemed to be darkly promising that a lack of support meant less original stuff and more of something akin to a diet of TV dinners.

Pitchers sometimes need to get themselves psyched up for a pledge drive. Valerie Ing, a program coordinator for Jefferson Public Radio, writing for *aNewsCafe.com* in 2015, describes how her husband prepares her for pledge week with a shoulder massage, a good breakfast and hot coffee. "You need to get powered up, baby. You've got a big day," he says. "I want you to be energized because I know this week is going to take it out of you." Pitchers need lots of positive reinforcement and support, including during pitching itself. Though they're often part of a tag team, they sometimes pitch alone.

A 2016 recommendation in the *Goalbuster*'s pitch manual for public radio stations reminds them that, "When pitching with another person, think of the microphone …as a third person in the conversation," and "pitching is a relay sport." When the light comes on, the first pitcher takes off and runs for as long as they can before handing the microphone off to their partner. And sometimes, when a duet unexpectedly becomes a solo, the terror is palpable. One pitcher, upon realizing he was by himself in the studio, said, "I'm kinda wondering where my good friend got off to. Uh … sittin' here in the pledge room on my own … uh, doing what I can here …" When his partner returned, you could hear the joy: "Oh, there he is!" When stuck, the manual says, "If you find yourself running out of things to say, use these elements to fill; phone number, pledge level, method of payment, information about the program, benefits of membership, premiums, —or hand it off to the next person." That is of course, if there is a next person.

Stations that split their programming into news and classical music streams, like KHPR Hawaii Public Radio, and *Ideastream* at Minnesota Public Radio, present pitches on those streams very differently. The news stream, full of traditional newsreading and reporting, is where the hard-core pledge pitching is heard. But on the classical music streams, the pitches are softer and infrequent, no doubt because classical music pieces can stretch for many unbroken minutes. On those streams, pledge pleas tend to be short, pre-recorded testimonials from listeners and spot break like re-minders, quietly sprinkled amongst movements and tone poems. ☎

Goals

"When it is obvious that the goals cannot be reached, don't adjust the goals, adjust the action steps."

—Confucius

"The campaign goal should be chosen reasonably. If it is higher than the community's pledging capability, then the campaign goal will never be met no matter how the organizers design and ma-nipulate the campaign process which will always converge to a specific lower limit."

—Jijun Zhao, Ferenc Szidarovszky and Miklos N. Szilagyi,
University of Arizona, Tucson.

Public radio likes to say the difference between it and subscription services is they tell you what you will pay while public radio listeners tell public radio what they will pay. That is technically true. When asked if they could ever foresee their station providing content as part of a subscription model, 82% of public radio respondents in an informal survey I conducted said no. But while public radio may say it gives listeners the freedom to decide how much they will contribute, it is constantly reminding listeners of their obligation to do so during pledge drives. That, plus the fact that it suggests sustaining memberships over one-time donations at a nearly 3 to 1 ratio, and listeners feel pressured to give specific amounts at specific times.

Stations are under the gun to raise money. CPB grades them, NPR charges them and research firms track them. This makes goal achievement a kind of crucible. Reminiscent of Oral Roberts' famous "God will take me home" if you don't support the ministry, in 2014, the *Salt Lake Tribune* reported KCPW staff people saying if the station didn't raise the $42,000 it needed to pay six months of arrears to creditors, it would likely go dark. Station Manager Tyler Ford later told *Current*, "While we hated saying we were going under, it was effective." So stations can't be ashamed to ask for what they need nor burdened by ethical issues of how they need to ask for it.

But listeners also aren't afraid to ignore those asks when stations behave in ways they don't like. In May 2008, donors to St. Louis Public Radio's KWMU tried to thwart the station's $12 million goal by slashing pledges to a capital improvement fund for a new building. That came after management fired long-time station manager Patty Wente. Though Ms. Wente raised the station's profile to the delight of listeners, some staff said she was abrasive and unpredictable. Plus, the station noted certain alleged "deficiencies" that prompted the internal investigation which led to Wente's firing. Mary Strauss, one of the major givers who cut her $100,000 contribution in half said, "I thought the way they handled this was in very poor taste and very poorly done." UMSL Chancellor Thomas George and interim general manager Kevin Dunn had no choice but to minimize big donor cutbacks. "Hard decisions were made, and we're moving on," said George, noting that only a few donors had reduced their pledges.

Other stations shoot for much more modest amounts, like the $30,000 tiny WMSE in Dallas, North Carolina, was seeking in spring 2016. For them, the money was especially important since they had just lost an important funding grant. For other stations, like KOPB, part of Oregon Public Broadcasting, $40,000 is what it might minimally expect to raise on an average day of an 8-day drive. OPB's goal for each of its three annual pledge drives is typically around $320,000. Honolulu-based Hawaii Public Radio, by contrast, conducts two drives a year and is famous for raking in over a million dollars during each. But HPR has a chain of islands to support. So the narrowly focused objective is always to get as much money as possible.

Even the 2008 financial crisis was something some stations couldn't afford to let get in the way of pledge drive goals. In 2009, the *Washington Post* published a piece titled *Public Radio Fundraisers Dial it Back*. Staff writer Steve Hendrix reported managers at WAMU were reigning in the usually bullish, high-dollar fundraising language. "For years we've had $50 as a suggested minimum," said Walt Gillette, the station's director of development. "That's out the window. It's going to be 'Every dollar makes a difference, and any dollar is welcome.'"

Stations keep track of who has given in previous drives and hit those people up if they haven't given by the time stations need them to. But goals aren't just about money. In spring 2016, Northwest Public Radio told listeners they were aiming at a target of 1,800 new members, rather than the approximately $220,000 that number would generate. Stations experiment with which type of pitch goes down more easily. More than half the time, pitchers mention a specific dollar amount they're trying to reach. But about a quarter of the time, they ask for a certain number of calls per hour instead.

Station managers and development directors sometimes downplay the fact that a station has missed its goal. One reason is that stations routinely overestimate how much they really need. A 2003 article for Plainview, Texas-based *MyPlainview.com* explained how Wichita Public Radio's then Development Coordinator, Liz Willis, wanted $100,000 in pledges but station officials "only expected $85,000." Stations review past drives and look at the results of drives at stations of similar size and demographics to see what is possible. Plus, according to John Sutton, the cost of raising that money has to be taken into consideration. "You need $200,000 in new revenue," Sutton says. "How much money do you need to raise every year to cover this new expense? The answer," he says, "is $300,000." He estimates every dollar a station raises through fundraising costs it about 33 extra cents.

It's interesting when a station tells the public it missed a goal. Development directors sometimes talk about not meeting a specific amount by the technical end of a drive. But would a station tell a public it had missed a goal if it was still expecting cash to get there? Apparently, yes. When Kansas Public Radio announced at the end of its October 2015 pledge drive that it had missed its $250,000 goal, it was only $23,793 away—less than 10%. But it raised $42,000 more in challenge grants after the drive ended. So did it miss its goal or not? Though the final goal may not include challenge grants or other fundraising campaigns that were finished before the on-air drive began, most times, stations end up hitting their real target. And sometimes stations miss them, then not only hit them, but exceed them the next time around.

Stations have found that if they announce the goal or how close they are to it, some listeners will feel they don't need to give since they may assume others will take the station across the finish line. Many in the audience think their $30 a year contribution couldn't possibly help their station pay the hundreds of thousands of dollars for the NPR shows they enjoy. They must be constantly convinced that their support matters. Some listeners frustrated by such public radio messaging might take their money and go home. Other listeners may hesitate to give for other reasons, like because they might feel some salaries are outsized.

Although Glassdoor shows NPR salary ranges to be somewhat ahead of industry norms, Tim Graham reported in a 2013 piece for the Media Research Center's *Newsbusters* that compensation for executives and luminaries at some public radio networks (and stations) give small donors pause. In July 2017, *Marketwatch* reported on how public radio is becoming "corporatized" in how it pays some of its top executives. Sutton says that the only thing that extracts more from a station's budget than program fees are salaries. And program fees can average 15%.

A related perception problem is managers may try to hide flagging drives by not being clear about the gap between where drive totals stand and what the final goal is. While 25% of my casual survey respondents either said their stations didn't do that, or didn't know if their stations did that, nearly 50% agreed that, yes, their stations did avoid talking about missed goals. Research says stations that constantly repeat the goal and give a running total of givers will likely see giving go up. And when they've reached a goal, it is not uncommon for a pitcher to celebrate by saying that, "Yes, we're glad we've met that goal and thanks to everyone who helped us get there. But for all of you who have yet to give, we have a new goal and we need you to give, now." There is no sentimentality in a pledge drive. Public radio can be precious, but not when it comes to raising money.

Enter the "stretch goal," which is when a pitcher says that although the defined goal has been reached, "We're going to just keep going." The genius of stretch goals is they take advantage of obvious momentum. Stations that have famously raised thousands of dollars in the last seconds of an hourly deadline, for example, may opt to drag that support into the next hour. Stretch goals can be tricky, however. Kickstarter says the practice emerged on its funding platform and has helped creators "make cooler stuff" by giving them an injection of extra cash beyond what they'd hoped for.

But stretch goals should be considered with care. "Stretch goals can make a project more difficult to complete," says Kickstarter, partially because a bigger ask might require a subsequent cost increase to deliver rewards to givers. Considering the issue stations have with premiums, that concern is legitimate. In addition, how stations tell their audience that goals have changed needs to be thought through. "Take the time to explain your intentions, your motivations, and your plans," warns Kickstarter. "Simply proclaiming, 'New goal!' without recognizing what you've achieved together can rub backers the wrong way."

Language

"It depends on what the meaning of the word 'is' is."

—Bill Clinton, during his 1998 grand jury testimony on the
Monica Lewinsky affair

When WBUR changed its website in early 2016, as the station called it, to make audio "a first class citizen online," the Executive Editor for Digital, Tiffany Campbell, bristled at calling it a "redesign." "I've tried to be really disciplined about not calling this process just a redesign," said Campbell to Nieman Lab's Shan Wang in February. "We built a new platform."

Likewise, Gwendolyn Fortune on her blog, *Keeping the Public in Public Radio*, posted a comment from Leslie Warshaw, a WGBH producer for over 30 years and now retired. Ms. Warshaw noted that "the station constantly spoke in her day of "mission." Gradually it changed from "mission" to "service" and then, she noted wistfully, to "business." When President Johnson signed the *Public Broadcasting Act of 1967*, it was only for public television. Then, public radio supporters muscled their way into the bill and it became about public broadcasting. Later, public radio, epitomized by National Public Radio, became "NPR." And when former NPR producer Jay Kernis wrote about this title shifting in a 2006 memo to producers and reporters, he called the digital storytelling they would eventually do as part of "public media." Re-branding language is not only an American public radio phenomenon. After the CBC's Jian Ghomeshi was fired in 2015 for accusations of sexual impropriety, the interview show he hosted for years, was re-branded from "Q" to "q" in an effort to distance the property from its longtime host. The effort is reminiscent of an Ogilvy marketing campaign for *Shreddies*, a company that for years had sold wheat snack crackers as squares and, in a stroke of insight, re-branded them as "diamonds."

This kind of thing goes on constantly within an industry where the power of the word is absolute. But in a world where their meaning changes with the context, the wordsmiths sometimes employ the dark arts to compel, encourage, motivate or even manipulate the listener to "believe" and thus, give. And judging from the clichés and battlefield metaphors pitchers use during drives, all options for raising money, including psychological operations, are on the table. Even when talking about something as simple as the gifts listeners can get, public radio's conception of what to call them shifts. "We used to call them 'premiums,' says a station manager. "Then, realizing we were the only ones who knew what that meant, we started calling them 'incentives.' Most recently, we felt 'thank-you gift' seemed a little warmer." "Rewards" and "collectibles" also cycle in and out of the mix.

Drives themselves may be called pledge drives, fund drives, membership drives, or benefit drives. That matters because, as researcher John Sutton asked in public radio's earlier days, "Pledge drive or Fund drive? That is - is the main purpose of this drive to get donors or money?" In 2016, KMST called its drive an "investment" drive. Likewise, stations have gone from "listener supported" to "member supported" because stations wanted to make clear that givers were more important than mere listeners whether the latter felt excluded or not. John Bell, Director of Development and Marketing at WSKG in Binghamton, New York, often pitched at a blazing speed of 280 words per minute when at OPB. And he frequently said during those breaks, "He who pays the piper calls the tune."

Then, the vernacular changed again to "community supported." This was a not-so-subtle acknowledgment that stations were getting as much, if not more money from underwriting than individuals. NPR underwriting credits often say, "Support comes from listeners that also contribute." That is far friendlier than the more common, "Support comes from our sustaining members." Somewhere in the latter is "If you're not a sustaining member, you're a terrible person," though defenders of the language might blame one's guilty conscience instead of the wording. Stations don't seem to be shy about making the distinction. In 2016, Miami-based WLRN held a "Members Only" call-in where the virtues of membership were extolled to the 85% or so listeners who weren't members. KUT Austin uses "recurring gifts" over "sustaining memberships," while the differences between becoming a "donor" and a "member" often must be explained.

Language used by public radio is divided into positive and negative language. Positive language is about making the listener feel empowered, connected and responsible for the success of their local station. Positive language doesn't draw attention to things that might make the listener uncomfortable. It is woven throughout much of what stations say but it's most obvious during pledge drives. Subaru's "Love ..." campaign isn't about the car, but about the emotions people feel when they think about how the car takes care of them and the people they care about. Likewise, stations use emotional touchstones to remind its audience of their feelings for public radio. "Intimacy," "passion," "personal," and "reassuring" are some of the words stations use to bring listeners to a safe place in their memory while, at the same time, making them feel smart and confident enough to move forward and change the world with their donations.

Examples of positive language in action during pledge drives include saying the phone number slowly and more than once, explaining that listeners might not have anything to write with when they first hear it. Stations say listeners consider this friendly. Although many listeners are seniors, they like their millennial counterparts, like smartphones. So, repeating the number so they have time to "write it down" may be somewhat of an anachronism. Meanwhile, speaking in the active command voice, "Pick up the phone and call now," is based on research that shows some people tend to do what they're told if it's said to them directly and persistently.

Negative language, by contrast, can dissuade. This was especially apparent during a seminar at the 2015 Public Media Development and Marketing Conference in Washington, D.C. It's an annual gathering that brings together many in public media to share practices, trends and gossip. One speaker discussed the importance of referring to listeners as "you" rather than "you-all." You all, the speaker explained, tells the listener they are not alone. In other words, the listener can assume, even if subconsciously, that the announcer is not speaking only to them. In the world of radio, the microphone isn't really a microphone but the ear of that solitary listener. Stations shouldn't remind listeners that they are not the sole focus of the messenger's message. The listener must feel their relationship with the station is special. Collaboration is another tainted word over which public radio has debated. Because even though political context defines the word as meaning different interests working within a range of options toward a common solution, many conservatives feel the word is a proxy for weakness. And since those folks make up a sizable chunk of the public radio listenership, the political climate helps dictate its use. The rules for what pitchers can and shouldn't say during drives fill pledge guides and training manuals. They include:

1. Don't use the word "if," as in "If you love public radio" because it sows doubt in the listener's mind; "I do love public radio, don't I?"

2. Don't tell listeners goodbye or "have a good weekend" since it's the same as saying "go away." They create a "seam" and you want listener's experience to be "seamless."

3. Don't say "phones are ringing." Saying "Our phone lines are open and our wonderful volunteers are ready to take your calls" is much more inviting.

4. Don't say "You out there," "the listeners" or "they," which, like "You all" implies that the pitcher is talking to someone other than "you."

5. Don't say, "We want," "We need" or "You should" when asking givers to give. Saying those things to listeners doesn't motivate them. Instead, say, "You'll get," "You'll feel" and "You'll make a difference."

6. Avoid conditional calls to action, as in "If you value what you're hearing, then you should call." Assumptive calls to action are more positive, such as "Because you value ..."

Stations can only maximize contributions by taking the temperature of givers. During the 2008 financial crisis, pitchers for Washington D.C.'s WFPW were told to pay attention to the language they used. "People do react to certain words: credit card debt, unemployment," said Ron Pinchback, station general manager. "When they hear these, they have a tendency to think twice about donating. We don't have list of banned words," said Pinchback, "but we do tell our programmers to acknowledge the economy without dwelling on it."

Some negative language is intended to compel a positive reaction. And if there seems to be more negative than positive language during drives, there's a reason. When stations send letters and email blasts that ask listeners, "What would you do if you couldn't hear *Morning Edition* or *Fresh Air* anymore?" they are turning to studies that indicate people focus much harder on a message of potential loss than one of gain. That's why pitchers may have to beg to get listeners to give during pledge drives, but threats to government funding of public broadcasting cause donations to skyrocket, though it can take a while. In 2004, KCSB office manager Ted Coe blamed part of the reason why the station missed its $37,000 goal by nearly 20% on the recent presidential election. " … a negative public mood slowed the drive," he told UC Santa Barbara's *Daily Nexus*. "Things started slow, and after the election the public mood wasn't favorable for a fundraiser," he said. "My impression was people were dazed from the federal election. Things started slow but picked up and surged near the end."

Another form of negative language might include things pitchers say as they're getting fed up. Every profession has ways in which its tools, normally used for a higher purpose can be used for a lower purpose. This dual-use dichotomy goes all the way back to *The Republic*, as evidenced by the famous back-and-forth between Plato and Polemarchus:

Plato	"Is not he who can best strike a blow in a boxing match or in any kind of fighting best able to ward off a blow?
Polemarchus	Certainly.
Plato	And he who is most skillful in preventing or escaping from a disease is best able to create one?
Polemarchus	True.
Plato	And he is the best guard of a camp who is best able to steal a march upon the enemy?
Polemarchus	Certainly.
Plato	Then he who is a good keeper of anything is also a good thief?
Polemarchus	That, I suppose, is to be inferred."

Likewise, are not they who are skilled communicators also able to wield words like knives? ABC's Robin Roberts has a reputation as one of the nicest journalists in the business. Her calling, "Bye Felicia" after a fuming Omarosa Manigault was "escorted" from the White House in December 2017 shows how even she can throw the occasional elbow. "Bye Felicia" is a dismissive meme that first appeared in the 1995 comedy "Fridays." It's most often targeted at a person with little social value. But bigger guns have come out. Also in 1995, NPR Legal Correspondent Nina Totenberg implied that Senator Jesse Helms, an opponent to AIDS funding, should worry about divine retributive justice, but not exactly in those words. Showing how language can passive-aggressively extend to pledge drives, WHQR's Cleve Callision offers another example. In a March 2017 *Friday Feedback* response to an anonymous complainer about the station's pledge drive, Callision said, "And finally, I feel Anonymous's pain if a couple of hours of fundraising ruins a show. Having to take it off the air because we can't raise enough money to pay for it would kinda disappoint a lot of people also, I think. Thanks for writing."

Co-opting the language of haters as a way of defanging them, WMPG called their own fall 2014 pledge drive a "begathon." Some stations repeat listener comments "Mean Tweet" style, reminiscent of *"The Tonight Show with Jimmy Fallon."* Others poke fun at themselves. "I say to my colleagues that I've got a future in panhandling when I retire from this business," said WAMU talk show host Kojo Nnamdi of the skills he has perfected over countless fundraising campaigns. Sometimes, pitches come very close to not only asking people why they aren't pledging, but judge them because they haven't. Near the top of the hour of a 2015 pitch break, KCLU news director Lance Orozco sneezed, and then said he was "allergic to slackers." Should pitchers and the managers that support them get the occasional pass to be outright mean considering how often they are attacked with outright meanness? Who knows? But public radio stations are staffed with people who love and believe in what they do. Occasionally, they hit back.

Nearly 47% of respondents I surveyed said their stations conduct pitch training. And pitchers, though they likely sat through it, can reach a point in the drive where what they say becomes, as June Thomas wrote for *Slate* in 2009, "loopy." She recommends listening to the last day of a pledge drive, "and not just because it's almost over. The staffers are so slap-happy," she says, "they start to mangle the phone number they've repeated thousands of times, and the unintentional comedy that results can be highly entertaining." But stations can cash in on even this unintentional comedy, says Thomas. "Public radio listeners are sensitive people, the thinking surely goes, perhaps they'll take pity on these poor souls and call in a pledge to spare them further embarrassment."

Sometimes though, the plea is so straightforward that you just want to reach through the radio and hug the pitcher with a fistful of checks. Such was the strong case for a guileless ask by Dallas, North Carolina-based WSGE during a spring 2016 pledge drive. "We've been telling you about this grant that we lost," said a member of the Beach & Shag crew during a post-*Morning Edition* break. "It kinda like, wiped us out. What little bit of funding we did get, that's gone. So we're really coming to you begging." He continued, "We're really not trying to make anybody feel bad. Believe me, that's not our goal. It's not. I mean, you don't have to give a single penny. But the ones that do, we appreciate it." Although research warns stations to not beg, the human aspects of the pledge drive are built on human connections made through human feelings. Pitchers must be believable and listeners must believe them, and sometimes, only telling the naked truth will do. ☎

Listener Comments

"Statistics suggest that when customers complain, business own-ers and managers ought to get excited about it. The complaining customer represents a huge opportunity for more business."

—Zig Ziglar

A staple of the pitch break is the listener comment. These are moments when pitchers stop talking about the station long enough to talk about listeners who are talking about the station. Dana Davis Rehm told *Current* in July 2008, "We rely on listeners' letters, calls and financial contributions to tell us how well we are fulfilling our mission of public service." That willingness of listeners to communicate (and possibly contribute), according to Walrus Research, is at least partly in proportion to how annoyed they may be with different fundraising methods stations employ. They may want to give, but aren't thrilled about how they're asked to do it. Underwriting, surprisingly, annoys them the least. More annoying is direct mail. Walrus says the pledge drive is number two on the list of the top five things listeners hate most. The top spot belongs to telemarketing, or rather, companies hired by public radio to make solicitation calls. Thirteen stations analyzed all shared the same level of listener annoyance. That annoyance is higher than the median and led the study to say the "vast majority" of public radio listeners say fund drives are becoming more prevalent and harder to listen to. Even if "vast" isn't quantifiable, at fifty percent plus one, majority is.

Listener comments from "people like you" take up at least a few of the precious pitch break minutes. An examination I conducted of the pledge drives of 37 stations show one in four read anywhere between one and four comments per average six-minute break. Stations use listener comments mostly to improve programming, gauge listener willingness to pledge, improve station performance, and build contact lists. It's hard to know exactly how many comments a pledge drive gets. There is evidence that not only are some listener comments recycled from drive to drive, but that script services also provide listener comments, which may be fresh or also recycled. But some listener comments never make it to the airwaves for at least two possible reasons. First, for as balanced as public radio tries to be, it doesn't necessarily want to hear bad stuff about itself more than it has to. And secondly, comments about how people hate pledge drives don't play well when local stations are trying to get people to give during pledge drives.

Both categories of comments can be found in a CPB repository called *Open Public*. Begun in 1993 as *Open to the Public*, it's congressionally mandated to collect thirteen measures of how the public sees public media is doing its job. Back then, comments came by letter or telephone. In 2001, the quasi-governmental agency fielded 42 letters, 128 phone calls and 982 emails. Meanwhile, NPR's one-year-old Ombudsman position logged over 15,000 listener comments. By 2018, CPB was also gathering comments from blogposts and social media. Between January 2012 and November 2017, its archive collected 687 written public comments about NPR and PBS, ranging from concerns to complaints to compliments to threats on subjects including political correctness, programming changes and pledge drives. To quote Mr. Zigler, they represent a "huge opportunity." Is public radio capitalizing on it?

How stations are affected by public comments has been evolving. NPR deleted the comments section of its website in 2016. The mostly news network said social media was a much more efficient and cost-effective way to provide a forum for facilitating engagement with listeners, as well as collecting better information about them. But criticism was fierce. "And while those are all excellent additional avenues of interaction and traffic generation, it's still not quite the same as building brand loyalty through cultivating community and conversation on site," said Karl Bode for *Techdirt* in 2016. "By outsourcing all conversation to Facebook, you're not really engaging with your readers, you're herding them to a homogenized, noisy pasture where they're no longer your problem. In short, we want you to comment -- we just want you to comment privately or someplace else so our errors aren't quite so painfully highlighted and we no longer have to try to engage you publicly." Other news agencies followed suit. *Reuters* told Nieman Labs in 2016 that it got rid of comments because, "it was a fraction of our traffic or engagement."

Amanda Zamora, an audience engagement expert, wrote for the Poynter Institute in 2016, "For a long time, I think comments were an easy answer for news organizations looking to check 'engagement' off their list." But how the network dealt with news-related comments wasn't exactly the same as how its licensees did. In 2011, Christopher Turpin, Executive Producer for *All Things Considered* told Farhad Manjoo of *Slate* that NPR tends to not air very complimentary letters because the network doesn't want to give the impression that it is patting itself on the back. But the network is very different from local stations, which tend to push the nice comments out front. Ideally however, they're not about praise, complaints or any of the eleven other ways CPB says listeners react and interact with public radio. Instead, they're are mostly an indicator for measuring how the monolith of public radio reacts to its listeners. Though there is limited information on what that indicator is measuring, there is some.

Bill Reader, in a 2007 article for the *Journal of Broadcasting and Electronic Media* said that all media, including NPR, have a history of what he called "gatekeeping" listener comments. Reader says that media organizations form views about what their communities are (or should be), which he calls "imagining community." They then try to fit those communities into their "imagined" views of them. This kind of tailoring is influenced partly by how news culture dictates reporting and partly by how the community might want to see itself. Reader says the latter leads to communities seeing themselves through the opinions and beliefs of the reporters rather than their own. For example, if an organization wants to see its community as supportive of something (like a pledge drive), it's reasonable that despite efforts to be objective or include opposing voices, stations will present more positive than negative views of pledge drives to the community. Gatekeeping or "framing" like this, whether it's journalists deciding what is newsworthy or news organizations subjectively reading some listener comments over others, is not new or unique to radio.

The FCC requires stations to divulge a boatload of information to the public. The full list can be found in the 2008 FCC pamphlet, *The Public and Broadcasting*. Though all of it is important browsing for listeners, for this chapter, the most relevant is entitled, *The Local Public Inspection File*. This is a collection of information all radio stations, including public radio stations, must make available whenever anyone wants to see it. Many stations have part or all of it online (thanks to the *Paperwork Reduction Act*), and they may also have paper files that can be inspected at the station during business hours. Inside is information about its license, public notices, applications it has made for upcoming changes, and maps that show where its signal reaches.

Other information includes who owns the station and where its main office is located, requests for broadcast time from politicians and retransmission agreements, like OTA (over-the-air) signals on cable channels. Something public radio stations must have that commercial stations don't is a list of all financial donors. That can be handy for discovering who has been underwriting station content thought it doesn't have to say how much each donor gives. Although my informal survey shows 40% of stations say their public files are online, just as many say they keep all of the public comments they get even though there is no federal requirement for them to do so. Some stations, as part of a university system like WVAS at Alabama State University, may be required to maintain online files according to state rules.

In light of attacks at Virginia and Baltimore TV stations, FCC Commissioner Michael O'Reilly pushed the idea that because some visitors could be security threats, stations should eventually stop maintaining a paper version of the public file in favor of an online only version. A 2018 shooting at Madison, Wisconsin community radio station WORT may add momentum to that push. Stations, by contrast, were concerned that putting the letters on the Internet revealed too much information about their writers in too public a manner. But others feel that social media gives a much better measure of station performance than the rarely reviewed paper version of public comments. "And it is not as if these letters from the public are important documents that are important to the general public," David Oxenfeld writes for the *Broadcast Law Blog*. Oxenfeld says that "Keeping letters from the public in a portion of their public file has never been required of noncommercial broadcasters, and there has never been any outcry that such stations are not responsive to their audiences." He says, "That is the very essence of the business of broadcasting – responding to their audience's needs and desires. Getting rid of the requirement that these random letters be kept for public inspection simply recognizes that the FCC does not need to mandate that broadcasters listen to complaints from their customers."

Research suggests this might suit media organizations just fine. In 2002, Karin Wahl-Jorgensen discovered that staff at a San Francisco newspaper didn't hold reader's letters in high regard.

"The editors speak of the 'idiom of insanity,'" she said, "which plays off the idea that contributors to the section – the members of the letter-writing public – are insane or 'crazy.'" And she found that newspaper staff used their low regard for the comments as a way to distance themselves from their work on the comments. In more recent years, media has been accused of a different kind of impersonal. Bill Reader, in his 2015 book *Audience Feedback in News Media*, refers to how what used to be human involvement in listener comments has slowly been turned over to automation. Though the expensiveness of people may have influenced the shift to the cheaper use of machines, he suggests cost may not have been the only motivation. Since media organizations get waves of mail, they may over time have come to take its volume for granted without paying much attention to its tone.

"Today, those procedures," says Reader, "have become largely automated and impersonal in nature via Web-based applications like submission forms, automated replies, server-side language filters, and online registration systems for writers." Also, he refers to various ranking-and-reporting buttons, like Facebook "likes" that readers can use to praise or condemn specific comments, or even to flag them for removal. He says that although large organizations spend a lot of money developing these systems to manage the public, in the end, "much of that effort seems only like so much traffic control." Worse, unless public comments have substance, rather than being rants, there is little chance they will have any effect on a policy change.

Local public radio stations are presumed to manage that feedback. But how it's perceived by stations may be very different than how they were intended by the audience. An excellent example of that was Public Radio Tulsa's *Kudos & Brickbats* segment, which it posted in the aftermath of September 2014 and April 2015 pledge drives. The word "brickbat" according to the Collins

English Dictionary, has two meanings: a missile and an uncomplimentary remark. The station highlighted 110 written listener comments from 2014 and 125 from 2015. Five of the September comments and eight of the April comments were not glowing praise, but none of those thirteen of 235 comments ranked especially high as either projectiles or insults. If these were the brickbats, it can make one wonder about the editing process or the thickness of public radio's skin, or both.

Writing for Nieman Labs in 2015, Google Journalism Fellow Madeline Welsh talked about a report by Jay Rosen that countered the long-held view that listener comments were negative. "With the rise of 'the people formally known as the audience,'" Welsh says, "there was a belief that readers would change journalism through their participation in its production." The study found that was true. "The increased scrutiny was generally considered to have led to stronger, more rigorous working practices. All this leads to a rather rosy picture of comments — at least in comparison to the usual doomsaying."

There is a corollary in the federal government. Federal agencies with an environmental footprint for example, must collect public comments as part of their process towards completing a federal action like cleaning a toxic waste site or building a dam. And agencies must read the comments so they can be compared against existing alternatives to see if they contain new information that makes the agency reevaluate its course. These agencies can't move forward until they have properly "read the room" and understand the local politics. But, they must also secure permits for water, antiquities, easements and overflights from partnering agencies before the process can check them off. Public comments, at least in some parts of the federal government, have real power.

Public radio prides itself on its ability to get listeners to connect with both content and stations. During pledge drives especially, it is quick to validate itself with what can sound like cherry-picked listener comments. There may be good security and economic reasons why the curation of those comments has been removed from human contact. Perhaps it's a reflection of what stations and their reporters increasingly complain about, which is a distancing of sources from media organizations. "There was a belief [among journalists] that despite the ubiquity of social media, getting in touch with both experts and journalists is harder than it used to be," says Welsh.

Reporters are being forced through press officers while some bureaucrats no longer pick up the phone. In other words, says Welsh, "information is much more tightly controlled than before." Are stations passing that gated community attitude along to listeners? NPR Media Critic David Folkenflik charged in a 2001 piece for Harvard's Nieman Reports, "Journalists ask questions, then refuse to answer them." It's an issue worth discussing since, in the end, listener comments aren't meant to be simply pushed around by algorithms. They aren't just sugar pills for stations to convince people to feel good about giving. They're more than rants. And they aren't the ignorable scribblings of the great unwashed. ☎

The Human Touch

"The pledge drive is a love fest. So, enjoy it!"

—albionwood, October 3, 2007 at publicradio.livejournal.com

If pledge drives were as universally loved as stations wished they were, there wouldn't be so much effort to quiet them, sweeten them or shorten them. But that effort is everywhere. That means pledge drives have to be more than techniques, elements and science. They're more than games and algorithms. They're even more than money. What pledge drives are, primarily, is people. Stations know that people attract people, and so pledge drives are really this aural spectacle. As the author was once told by a season ticket holder to the Cincinnati Ballet, "People love the acrobatics, but also they want to see how close dancers come to falling. And if they do, how they get up." So, that means pledge drives really are about the human drama of trying to compel people to do something they may not want to do. Commenting on the *Philip Greenspun blog* in June 2009, "Gabo" suggests "competitive fundraising" to amp up the drama even more. "You can donate money either to save a program or to kill it. Like American Idol. Vote a show off the air with your money. I'd give $100 bucks if I could 86 *Sound and Spirit*, and I might donate twice if I had to." "Gabo" didn't have long to wait. Within a year, WGBH's *Sound and Spirit* was off the air.

For people who have only heard a few stations in their listening lives, they might be stunned at the variety of station personalities. Even the normally staid hometown station can enter a kind of manic, obsessive compulsiveness at pledge drive time that a new listener might not recognize and a long-time listener might flee from. This is even more true depending on when in the drive a listener arrives. Early on, everyone's calm and hopeful. Just past the middle, when a station may realize it's behind its goal, the pleas get more urgent. Near the end, with the clock running out, pledging can sound downright panicked. Some stations, years into the effort, are still finding their comfort level with pledge drives. For them, you can hear it, mostly, in the awkward silences that aren't easily recovered from. These pitchers aren't necessarily well practiced. That's not to say they haven't had pitch training, or that their station doesn't have a playbook. Their technique is just a little rough around the edges. These drives also tend to not have a lot of pre-produced spots or promos, perhaps because the station budget doesn't allow them or perhaps because straight talk is easiest to focus on. Those pitches consist mostly of staff and guests doing all of the talking, with most of the talking unscripted ad lib.

Other stations can also be mostly talk, but their delivery is smoother perhaps because their stations subscribes to a script service, or because they might be a little bigger, their confidence level is a little higher. When some of their asks turn urgent, it's a more syncopated mix of humor and ease with a touch of necessary firmness. These stations may also include testimonials from long time listeners or network promos from recognizable show hosts. Still other stations add in music, sound effects and sometimes, full-on vignettes. These drives, which combine a collection of pitchers that sound more like a ensemble of friends with an obvious gift of gab, can feel sincerely "fun."

Montana Public Radio at the University of Montana's KUFM, during its spring 2016 pledge drive, bridged a light-hearted break between pitching with Aretha Franklin's "Call Me," and its prominently repeated line, "I Love You." Elsewhere in the Big Sky state, Montana Public Radio's KGLT took flight with its home-grown Captain Willard sound-alike in a pledge drive-geared *Apocalypse Now* parody. It and other voices, adapting the hunt for Colonel Kurtz to why station support is the real mission, was creative craziness at its best. Meanwhile, with Jamaican music pulsating in the background, pitchers for African American themed WEAA's pledge drive talked not just of commitment, but a covenant between listeners and the station with the joyfulness of a Sunday service. Whether drives are technically perfect, yet devoid of warmth, or full of flubs but charming, they are what stations shape them to be in an effort to be what they think their listeners will respond to. What works for one audience might be very wrong for another. But that range helps explain how, when some people give reasons for loving pledge drives while others hate them, both points of view can ring true.

PLEDGE: The Public Radio Fund Drive

The networks produce generic promos for stations to run
before, during or after their own local pledge drives. Sometimes,
they're recognizable voices simply reminding listeners to support
the reporting they've become used to. But other times, their stories are much more personal. For example, NPR political reporter
Tamara Keith told of how, during the 2016 Iowa caucuses, she was
trying to read the *Very Hungry Caterpillar* to her 3½-year-old son
via Facetime. It was part of a promise she'd made that no matter
where in the world she was, she would connect with him every day
at 7:30 a.m. Eastern Time. So, she's waiting for Hillary Clinton to
come onstage, while trying to read to her son over an incredibly
loud auditorium. "And these security guys see this totally pathetic
reporter with a copy of the *Very Hungry Caterpillar* in her hand.
And they pull me over and they're like, 'Go in there.'" Keith continues, "It was this little kitchen they were using as a staging area,
but it was quiet. And so, I'm standing in this kitchen reading the
Very Hungry Caterpillar with five or six burly security dudes, just
watching me." How is that not a cute story?

Learning something about Tamara Keith and her life makes
both matter more to listeners. These tiny vignettes, popping up
in the clock between local and network breaks tell quick stories
about the storytellers, and is a relatively new technique to get the
audience connecting with public radio. But more to the point, NPR
uses them to remind listeners not only of the work it does to keep
them informed, but also to convey a sense of responsibility that the
human touch costs money. And that those listeners need to pay
their local stations for what they're listening to. ☎

Cheerleading

"Yeah, I said it."

—OPB Host April Baer on Twitter

What Ms. Baer said, during a 2016 pledge drive, was that OPB had the best news station in the country. And when she was informed that other public radio stations also had excellent news departments and might she be interested in adjusting her sentiment ever so slightly, well ...

This is a little thing, but it's worth mentioning. Public radio stations cheerlead in part to rally the troops on both sides of the microphone and in part because public radio stations do remarkable work telling stories. Occasionally, they want to puff out their chests. And no doubt many stations will say they absolutely understand what Ms. Baer is saying because they do the same thing. Donations don't go to meek stations that can't convince their listeners that their money will help them deliver the best news, information and entertainment that audience has ever heard. Pledge drive guides tell pitchers in training, "Never apologize for drives. Listeners want what you have to offer." But the listeners, if they listen to only one station, don't necessarily have a broad view of the public radio universe. They may have a broad view of the world, but they may not know how good a neighboring public radio station really is. Why should they? So like any sports fan, they may come to see their local station as the best. On one hand, stations drool over that kind of loyalty. But every station has cheerleaders, thus making every other station second string and straining the greater public's empathy for local differences, as message boards reveal:

"To be honest, I've never heard an NPR affiliate station pledge drive in any other city but where I live. The one thing we never do is harangue people or guilt them. Our drives are civilized and friendly. I'm sorry for you folks who live in a city where the drives are annoying and the pitchers badger you. "

—fishbicycle on *The Straight Dope*, October 2005

"If you lived in the northeast and listened to WAMC, you would love the fund drive. They raise about $600K twice a year to run the station. It never takes more than a week. They have incredible on air people and give away great stuff and are so entertaining. WAMC is a treasure. I've driven in different parts of the country and heard very lame fund drives though, so no wonder it takes so long for some. "

—starfish on *Metafilter*, April 2008

"Having moved to Western Mass from the Boston area a couple of years ago, I YEARN for the shorter WBUR pledge drive. Oh, how I miss it during the interminable, apparently months-long WFCR pledge drive. "

—mskyle on *Metafilter*, October 2012

There are half a dozen lists of what some consider to be the "best" stations floating around. It probably doesn't matter except maybe a teeny, weeny bit to KUER in Salt Lake City, who puts on a pretty darn good newscast of their own. That was the other "excellent" news department reference that prompted OPB's Valkyrie to ride to the defense of the Pacific Northwest. Everybody laughs it off, sorta. Then again, dissing other media may just be baked into the public radio cake. In 2009, Jon Friedman of CBS *Marketwatch* was talking with former NPR CEO Vivian Schiller. He asked her why, with all the problems NPR was experiencing at the time, would she leave a prestigious post at the *New York Times* to be the radio network's new head? "You can count on one hand the number of really important news organizations in this country," said Schiller. Friedman suggested "that the newspapers, magazines and broadcasters who didn't make Schiller's private cut might be a tad offended." Schiller, doing some cheerleading of her own, was possibly remembering her four previous employers from an earlier conversation with *Fast Company*'s Anya Kamenetz; the *New York Times*, *The Discovery Channel*, *CNN & TBS*. But on the other side, when I asked people in and associated with public radio, "As far as you know, are pitchers encouraged to say their station's programming is better than the programming of any other public radio station?," 61% said no.

And the last word on cheerleading? In late January 2017, the Twitter team account of the Portland Trailblazers made fun of an airball by Chandler Parsons of Memphis during a Blazers-Grizzlies matchup. Portland's C.J. McCollum piled on by telling Parsons, "We hit the lottery by not signing you." Less than two weeks later, the NBA sent out new non-dissing rules for social media. Sure it happens in the stands amongst the fans. But the NBA at least seems to be saying to the players, it's not good for the game. ☎

The Money Shot

"Most public radio don't have ads, just a bunch of sponsor messages that are barely distinguishable from ads. Nevertheless, if approaching public radio stations with your message, you should use the right language. Many people at non-profits sometimes feel a bit dirty about the marketing process."

—Commenter 'Sunburnt' on Metafilter, March 11, 2018

Despite all of the hard work to get givers to give, there are people who have reached the point where they just don't want to anymore. People like Chelsea Shannon. And Shannon, an LA-based blogger is just fine with that. "I'd be jamming along my day, feeling really great, only to hop in my car and get a painful play-by-play of the latest human rights violation and the terrible economic forecasts and in an instant, any positive vibes were straight up annihilated." It is a criticism public radio has heard before. "Lately I've been participating in this fascinating psychological study that tracks when and where I'm the happiest." The study to which Ms. Shannon is referring, called "Track Your Happiness" was, according to its website, "created as part of Matt Killingsworth's doctoral research at Harvard University." The project, now including an app, tracks one's mood and shows changes over time. Although she loves NPR, it has helped Ms. Shannon curate her own stock of podcast episodes for her news fix, "so I can fill my brain with the good stuff and skip the depressing." And she's chosen Spotify for her music and notices, "by the time I get to work or school I'm much more likely to be in a good mood."

Besides the change of mood that can reset listening habits, a political awakening can also make one stop giving. Well-worn conservative arguments against giving eventually became self-evident to Tony Award nominee and Pulitzer Prize winning playwright David Mamet. He told the *Village Voice* in 2008 that even though he had lived within the hopeful expectations of liberalism since his youth, he realized one day he'd been calling NPR "National Palestinian Radio" for years. He stopped listening. It's unknown whether his contributions stopped too. Listeners might also end their support simply because they feel NPR doesn't need their money because they feel it's already awash in corporate and foundational contributions.

Public radio, in turn, spends lots of time on tools and talent to secure that support. Pledge drives, and their enticements including gifts, premiums and "leverage" appeal to givers that also want to get. But the importance of giving gifts to get money has been a hot topic in public radio. The industry wonders if the gift infrastructure is costing stations too much and cutting into pledge drive revenue. And it worries that people are giving because they expect to get stuff rather than because they believe in public radio. Drives also entice members of the community to compete against other givers to see who can give the most. Challenges and matches are precision tools that stations use sparingly depending on how they read the mood of the listeners on any given day of the drive. A successful challenge or match can be a nitrous oxide booster for an already hot pitch break. Failed efforts, by contrast, can sour a pitching staff and throw cold water on a drive that may take hours to recover from. Games also must be used sparingly. State and federal regulations impose rules on how stations operate lotteries and contests, which are not the same.

Enticements are only part of the story. Who chooses to give and how is much more important for stations to know. The "who" falls within a life cycle which stretches from young adults to the middle-aged to seniors. Likewise, the "how" can range from new and renewing givers, to sustaining members willing to be upsold, to major givers making plans to bequeath their estates to their station's future. These fit into a matrix, which along with behavioral research, help stations target each group to get them to give as much as they can for as long as they can. And communication channels that lead to those givers have morphed over the years. From face to face and door to door to algorithms, stations are increasingly relying on apps and social media to sell the story of how public radio tells the story. But circling back to supporters who leave, a bigger problem for public radio is non-supporters who stay. Free riders and the moral hazard they inflict bring new urgency to the *Tragedy of the Commons* problem public radio has faced since its beginning.

Lastly, in the equation of people equals money, a key component is often left out. The volunteer adds incredibly to a station's bottom line. A volunteer at pledge central or staffing a table at a public event is often the first physical contact a listener may have had with the station. Volunteers help produce stories, work on gear or file paperwork. But unfortunately, they are often overlooked and frequently mistreated. Volunteers, interns and temps, may do what they do for stipends, contacts and experience. But both stations and companies that use them have found themselves in court for treating them unprofessionally. Behaviors are changing. And that's a good thing. ☎

Gifts, Premiums & *"Leverage"*

"The most significant finding from the data appeared to be that although listeners received gifts and premiums, these perks were not important in the decision to renew membership. It is not known how honest respondents were in their devaluation of station gifts and other rewards."

—Public Radio Listener Data Analysis: Mass Communication Research Course Student Projects, University of Nebraska at Omaha, Winter 2001

Pledge drive gifts are so embedded in popular culture and at the same time, so perplexing, that the topic is part of a *GMAT Critical Reasoning* mock test. Test takers were told that anyone making a pledge was given a free gift and that the retail cost of the gift would be equal to the amount of the gift. The test asks the taker to explain why, at the end of a pledge hour, the amount of money a station raised was greater than what the station said it paid for the gifts that accompanied each pledge. Seven pages and nineteen answers later, respondents are all over the map.

Gifts have become an increasingly dicey topic of conversation in the public radio community. Commenter "Paul P," writing on *Philip Greenspun's* blog in 2009 complained of how, after he

gave his station a $1,000 contribution, he received a tax receipt
for $700. "I was really upset, called the station, their logic was
that I personally got '$300 worth of benefit' from having my name
broadcast as a supporter ('once every 4 hours, for a full day!').
Furthermore, the Kent State "School of Accounting" had deemed
this 'fair/reasonable.' I was furious," he said. But follow-up commenter "Andrew" responded to Paul P., saying he was just on the
wrong end of an accounting rule. "Having your personal name
mentioned is of no value to you, but having your business name
mentioned might have been." Andrew said non-profit 501(c)3s like
public radio stations must subtract any "value received" in exchange for a giver's gift from the deduction value. "This includes
gifts for personal use (mugs, tote bags, etc too, but," as Andrew
reminds Paul P., "in your case your pledge probably looked like a
corporate donation ($1,000 is much higher than most personal
pledges), so it got lumped into wrong category."

Donors are eligible for certain gifts if they reach a certain donation threshold. Even though a giver may become a member with
a one-time donation at the $30 basic level, in some cases, they may
need to give at least $50 a year before they are eligible to receive
the bottom tier of thank-you gifts. Cincinnati Public Radio tells
givers a $100 pledge or more gets them a thank-you gift. As a com-
ment in a 2002 public radio industry report on fundraising noted
about small gifts and low contribution levels, "We're not exactly
giving away refrigerators and BMWs here."

A flexible rule of thumb for stations is that the overall cost of a
premium should be no more than 8% to 10% of the pledge level.
Travel icon Rick Steves explains, "That means the gifts they offer
at any level should cost them around a tenth of the money they
are raising (for example, a DVD gift for a $60 contribution should
cost the station $6). That's a challenge," he says. "I need to make
some money providing the gifts, the station needs a huge mark-up,

and viewers need a good value, too." But Steves says while some stations are very aggressive in marketing their swag, others worry that people are more focused on the gifts than supporting their local station.

Consequently, listening to the distinction of who gets what according to what they give during a pledge drive can remind one of the ETrade commercial with its tagline, "First class is there to remind you you're not in first class." That attitude is reinforced by a 2004 Walrus Research study. *Heavy Givers*, or those who consistently gave $100 or more, represented 16% of all givers, but nearly 50% of all contributions. The study concludes, "The findings would strongly encourage public radio development professionals to segment their givers by levels of amount given and treat those segments differently, in accordance with marketing principles, to maximize the station's income from listeners." Nevada Public Radio, for example, tells visitors to its website that basic membership starts at $60, but the option to receive a thank-you gift comes only with a donation of $100 or more. For now, there is no private channel that high value givers can switch to for their-ears-only offers at their contribution level. So across the country, givers at $30 a year get bumper stickers while they hear $1,000 givers getting lunches with the artistic director of the local ballet company. It might not be classist to experience, but it can be jarring to hear.

Then there is the question of whether contributors receive a gift at all. Astoria, Washington based KTCB and KMUN reminded listeners they didn't have to take a gift during their spring 2016 pledge drive. "You could choose not to receive a gift," said host Kathleen Morgain, during a Day 6, *All Things Considered* pitch break, "and put the full value of your membership to work for Coast Community Radio. It's up to you." Donors to Northern Arizona University's KNAU can see a web page where the selection, "No Thank-You gift for me" is at the bottom of a long list of donation levels accompanied by hoodies, calendars and tote bags. "If no gift is selected," says the site, "your full contribution will support programming." This seems to suggest that the move to include "no gift" as a choice is the newest way stations are trying to make money by saving money. This option may eventually provide definitive evidence as to whether givers like this trend.

All of the talk about gifts is really about how much power those gifts have to compel people to give. That power is what John Sutton calls "leverage." Though listeners aren't bothered much by underwriting announcements, they're aware of how stations push stuff (tickets, trips, coffee mugs, hoodies, cash, etc.) in ways that sound like commercials to get them to give. Sutton says some stations even offer early bird discounts on "premiums" (another word for stuff), where the amount givers pledge in exchange for premiums starts out low rises as the drive progresses. Research shows this helps stations reach their goals faster. The public radio audience probably recognizes this "dynamic pricing" aspect of pledge drives. Indications are they don't necessarily like it. Even so, "More than 90% of people who pledge are likely to contribute even if no premiums are available," says the aforementioned study, presented by PRI. These are public radio's true believers.

But although public radio is full of true believers, what about givers who give simply because they want that stuff? What's the effect of leverage there? It turns out stations have been upping the number of premiums they offer during pledge drives for years. Premiums, say that same study, tend to generate something called "lift." Lift compels a listener to donate more than if no premium was being offered. And the concept is such a staple in fundraising that there's a rule of thumb for it. Every $50 of contributions generates $10, or 20% of lift. But as listeners get more finicky, stations are finding they have to offer more and more premiums to keep listeners giving. Running parallel to that trend is the worry among stations that at some point, they'll hit a wall of diminishing returns. During a fall 2014 pledge drive, Oregon Public Broadcasting was offering 23 different gifts simultaneously. Sutton says some stations are in danger of the stuff they're offering collectively costing more than the drives themselves generate. He recommends guiding ratios between what stations want to raise and what they want to offer, to keep them in the safe zone. But long-timers in public radio warn stations to not spend a lot of time collecting a few gifts since the effort can waste staff time that could be spent getting more premiums for a larger segment of the listening audience.

Collaborating with other entities is a way stations can get more bang for their development buck. Although they can't fundraise for another non-profit, stations can cross-market. They may not have similar missions, but they likely have similar demographics and ideologies, meaning cross-marketing can double the reach by hitting the audiences of both organizations. This desire of non-prof-its to help promote each other's causes is also known as "Cause Marketing." In 2010, Wisconsin Public Radio asked listeners to tell it what they thought about such marketing efforts as part of a national survey about charitable giving in public radio. "During these times, which are both economically challenging and envi-ronmentally focused, public radio stations around the country are partnering with other nonprofits, such as food banks and plant-a-tree organizations, to raise money for both the station and another worthy cause. We'd like to know how you feel about such a part-nership," said the WPR website. It's obvious that stations were thinking about how such relationships affected giving.

It seems bigger fish in the public radio pond were too. In 2012, Greater Public surveyed 100 public radio stations with a total donor base of nearly one and a half million contributors. It asked stations how they felt about such non-profit partnerships. Nearly 40% of stations had partnered, mostly, with "food banks and hunger relief services." A little less than half of respondents, or about 18 stations, said a partnership was important to the success of their fundraising effort. WAMU in Washington, and WFDD in Winston-Salem, both engineered fundraising drives that also fed people. WFDD's 2015 campaign generated 800 backpacks full of food for needy kids while raising $20,000 for the station. WAMU's 2016 fund drive raised $1.4 million for the station while helping a local food bank provide about 77,000 meals. Southwest Florida's WGCU explained a similar relationship between itself, the Harry Chapin Food Bank and Walmart. Stations can't accept money on behalf of another nonprofit, but other businesses can match donor contributions to the station and then, pass those donations to the partnered, non-profit. Or, food banks can donate food to families paid for, indirectly, with thank you gifts listeners decide to not take. Inventory paid for but not distributed for Event A saves the station money that can be used later at Event B. But it can also be confusing when those relationships aren't clear.

Blogger Joe Waters talked about one such confusing relationship between NPR and Urban Outfitters in 2011 on his non-profit giving podcast. He wondered why an NPR branded tee sold at shop.NPR.org generates $20 for the network while the same tee sold on the Urban Outfitters website for $24 did not. He doesn't dispute Urban Outfitters free-enterprise right to sell the shirt. He questioned the lack of a disclaimer that the latter gives no proceeds to the former. "It's totally confusing for consumers. If a consumer buys the NPR tee on the Urban Outfitter site they're probably thinking that a portion of the purchase is supporting public radio."

How such confusion can interfere with giving is seen in a comment Waters found on the company's website. A happy child had given the tee to their parent because the parent loves supporting NPR. Except, they weren't. NPR is full of savvy people and they must have known what they were doing. Perhaps the association with Urban Outfitters was enough and the network didn't require them to share a percentage of sales. "In some instances, the company drives the conversation and the partnership. 'We plan to do this, but not that…' Waters later said on Twitter. "The nonprofit thinks: '50% of something is better than 100% of nothing.' Just a theory." But by not making that clear, Water's seems to say buyers end up deceived by UO's marketing, which he calls "slimy."

Stations, on the other hand, can't afford to leave cash on the table, especially with a huge moneymaker like t-shirts. When San Francisco Bay's KSCM partnered with Goodman Marketing Partners in San Rafael, California in 2009, the purpose was to give listeners something cool that didn't compete with thank-you gifts the station already had. It came up with a set of five tee templates that combined the names of jazz legends with about 40 different donors each. By creating 200 unique t-shirts, "We were able to personalize it and keep the cost low," said company president Carolyn Goodman. KCSM made money. At the same time, the station reached out to nearly 9,000 lapsed members with a bigger than normal ask to renew in exchange for the shirt. The 577 that responded helped the station raise more than $42,000. The campaign's return on investment (ROI) was over 200%.

But t-shirts aren't the only things stations give as incentives to join. In 2009, the Lyons, Colorado based non-profit branding company "ViaABILITY" released a set of rub-on public radio themed tattoos. The idea, hatched in the mind of Ira Glass in the late 90s, led to stations distributing more than 70,000 of the *This American Life* themed henna tattoos. By 2013, the idea had resurfaced and this time, included eight of public radio's top shows, including *On the Media, Fresh Air, Morning Edition* and *All Things Considered*

Between 2007 and 2017, a handful of stations had decided to join a Valentine's Day fundraiser that started in the 1990s at Kent State's WKSU. The partnerships offered discounts of "up to 25% on flowers delivered to someone special" while proceeds went to the station. Although NPR left the partnership in 2017, Susan Seligson of Boston University's *BU Today* told of how the university's WBUR joined a nationally coordinated effort that has since generated over a million dollars for the station. But although some listeners loved getting flowers that were representations of both intimate love and public support, others didn't. "Every morning I wake to NPR begging me to send a dozen red roses to my sweetheart," says Thorpe on the *eNotAlone* message board. "Their pledge drives are annoying, but doubly so when they tempt me to express my 'love' for the ex." Indeed, other posters commented on how public radio's ability to turn anything into a moneymaking opportunity was one reason why they were cynical about public radio. "Remember that all their talk about love is really about making money!" says BeStrongBeHappy. "If they find a hook to make money, they use it."

Whether it's CD of the Month Clubs like collaborations between WXPN Philadelphia and KPLU Seattle in 2014, or WHYY's Passport program that gives special access PBS's library of programs, anything with the potential to raise money for public radio gets a fresh look. At the same time they have been introducing all of these new gifts, stations are getting methodical in how they're managing promotional programs. For profit and non-profit partners are offered "bonus packages" for station placard placement, inclusion in partner events or promotional tickets. Packages themselves mirror weekly promotional schedules that identify how many times an hour a station promotes an entity and how much the station charges them to do it. As stations move into the driver's seat, they've also gotten more serious about how and when they offer these packages or accept new clients to promote. Some have imposed deadlines on promotional requests, limits on who can be promoted and minimum participation amounts.

In the end, a gift from the organization matters to the recipient only as much as the experience of belonging to the organization does. If a giver believes in it, they want to let everybody know. T-shirts, coffee mugs, bumper stickers and tote bags, as low tech as they are, are still the biggest draws because they make the largest public statement about one's values. But as the audience shifts with technology, which shifts with demographics, and the pledge drive slowly declines in effectiveness, new ways of attracting a new cohort of members must reach beyond premiums and touch the emotional heart of not just engagement, but involvement. ☎

Challenges & Matches

"Two of the relational giving patterns often used by charities are "challenge gifts" and "matching gifts" These tools have the potential for great benefit, but also for great misunderstanding, both to charities and to donors."

—Evangelical Council of Financial Accountability

A challenge grant, sometimes casually called both a challenge and a match by public radio, is when someone sets aside a certain amount with the intention of matching every dollar that other givers give related to that match. For example, Donor A promises to match all contributions up to $1,000. That means if Donors B, C, D and E give the station $250 each, Donor A will match those gifts and the station gets $2,000. But Donor A is only giving $1,000, no matter how much anybody else gives. If Donor B wants to give $5, Donor A will match it to $10. But if Donor B gives $2,000, Donor A is still only giving $1,000.

Sometimes, the match may be not just 1-to-1, or 2-to-1, but even 3-to-1, which on the surface, seems like it should be a win for stations and givers. In his *RadioSutton* blog, researcher John Sutton talks about such "force-multiplier" type giving. "Unlike a sweepstakes which the listener may or may not win, there is an instant benefit to responding. The listener gives and the station gets even more instantly!" But Sutton says matches can hurt stations' ability to raise the most money. In 2008, *New York Times* economic writer David Leonhardt summed up the work of University of Chicago economists John List and Dean Karlan on matches this way. "The economics are simple enough. A matching gift effectively reduced the cost of making a donation. Without a match, you would have to spend $400 to make your favorite charity $400 richer," says Leonhardt. "With a 3-to-1 match in place, it would cost you only $100 to add $400 to the charity's coffers." Also, research conducted in 2004 from 50,000 direct mail solicitations shows that although matches do increase the amount of contributions a station gets by increasing giving by up to 30%, 2-to-1 and 3-to-1 matches don't compel a giver's willingness to give any more than a simple 1-to-1 match. This makes stations hesitant to rely on them. In fact, my analysis of 37 public radio pledge breaks during spring 2016 showed only nine, or less than 25% of stations, engaged in matches.

Challenge donors tend to have a long history of giving to the station, but that doesn't mean the arrangement isn't formalized. A challenge gift may include stipulations like, "at whom to target for the challenge, when the donor pays (up front or when the challenge is met), and how the challenge will be advertised or marketed." Fundraising departments seek out donors who are willing to offer challenges, and work with them to engineer those challenges to meet a particular purpose. And when a fundraising department looks for those folks, they tend to follow a hierarchy, starting with the station's board of directors, or the board president. Then, any committee member that happens to have been involved in shaping fundraising policy. Then station trustees (people responsible for making financial decisions or managing assets in the name of the station), and finally, major givers in the community. In each case, the goal is to find people who resonate with the station's mission such that they are not only ready to give, but able to give big.

As an aside, the boards of many large and small non-profits have historically (and anecdotally) consisted of people with little to no experience of how to be on a board and even less able to be a financial resource for the organization. The IRS has no requirements for the qualifications of board members to non-profit organizations. But the organizations themselves have begun to up their professional game. Requirements for board membership at an increasing number of non-profits now often include that members have prior board experience, technical or specialized expertise, the ability to donate significant amounts of money to the organization and extensive contacts in the community to raise even more money if needed.

In many cases, an organization may not make its challenge grant public until at least 50% of the challenge has been matched. This helps protect the integrity of the challenge by unveiling it as a success already in progress. And after money is raised, it's held until it can be used. Colorado Public Radio says its challenge funds go into an escrow account, where they sit until the end of the drive, when they can be applied to station needs. Because challenge grants are usually most effective in the short term, stations may find themselves in a dilemma as to when to use them. Though a challenge applied during a flagging drive could juice overall giving, how much more cash could it generate during a stronger drive that overall, has been more successful? Stations don't want to waste the potential of challenges.

Researchers at the University of Arizona, Tucson discovered that consecutive challenges are more effective than challenges scattered throughout a drive. "A boost or a jump in a single challenge period cannot have long term effect because the process will return to the track of the similar process without any challenges," concluded the research team. Something else that the challenge agreement between giver and station needs to address is anonymity, which some professionals recommend non-profits discourage. Tony Poderis, Director of Development for the Cleveland Orchestra until 1993, and author of *It's a Great Day to Fundraise* tells organizations, "Publicly herald the Challenge Grant and the generosity of its donor in every possible mailing and publication your organization produces. Should the Challenge Grant donor wish to remain anonymous," says Poderis, "comply with her or his wishes. However, try to dissuade anyone from anonymity, as people more favorably respond to real people, rather than to those who remain anonymous."

The other thing about challenges is that they're time sensitive. Employing the tool of urgency, pitchers often plead with listeners to help them meet a challenge, lest the money will disappear by the deadline. Questions over whether a station gets the money if a challenge grant isn't reached circulate within the audience. June Thomas in her 2009 *Slate* article, *Let's Get Those Phones Ringing*, noted that although some may stretch throughout much of a drive, others may only last for hours or the length of a single program. To not lose the potential money, pitchers may urgently steer each and every call to it before the clock runs out.

"These matches engender skepticism in public radio haters," says Thomas, "who believe the challenges are bogus — the super donors are going to give a set sum come what may — and suspicion in even the most loyal listener." In the agreement between giver and the organization, Lawrence Pagnoni for *Non-Profit Quar-*

terly recommends that this contingency be spelled out. "What happens if you don't meet the entire challenge? In the best case you can get your challenge donors to still give their gift, but remember that they are certainly under no obligation to do so. I recommend you ask up front."

Commenter "carmicha" on Metafilter in 2012, shared her suspicions about how stations use challenges, which she also calls a match. "Regarding matches, for several years, Mr. Carmicha and I have made a pretty sizable gift during the pre-pledge drive period that's designed to decrease the length of the fundraising campaign's interference in regular programming. We've then gotten a call from the station asking if they can frame our gift as a match because it helps drive donations. This tactic made me wonder whether there is ever any real risk that the station won't receive the challenge money when they offer a 'matched' donation opportunity." Consequently, stations like Arizona's KJZZ regularly tells listeners on its website that it only gets the challenge grant if, "we successfully meet the goal you set."

Pagnoni suggests organizations plan for the contingency of a giver who may want their gift returned if their challenge isn't met. "In your drive, state that if the minimum challenge is not met by a certain date, your donors' contributions will be returned to them. Your appeal could read, "By May 1, we must raise an additional $10,000 to match the donor's $10,000 challenge; if we fail to raise that full amount from you, our supporters, we will not be able to open the new environmental justice program for our teens, but we will refund your donation promptly. Please help us achieve our goal." More than once, an hourly challenge is announced with fanfare at the top of an hour. But as minutes tick by, with listeners and pitchers realizing it won't be met, it's mentioned less and less. By the top of the next hour, listeners don't know if the previous hour's challenge was met because it is never mentioned again. That may be frustrating for challengers and disappointing for staff, but it can also be supremely annoying to listeners.

The employee match, also known as a matching gift, is another popular type of giving. Here, an employer matches the contribution of their individual employees up to a certain amount. The Committee Encouraging Corporate Philanthropy reported in 2012 that 83% of companies it surveyed offered at least one employee match program. High business participation suggests it is by far simpler than challenge matches and thus, much more popular with stations. All businesses can match, and non-profits except sports teams, political organizations and religious institutions can receive matched money though, different companies have different policies.

The non-profit Pew Charitable Trust, will match money for any religious institution, for example, while DirecTV, a corporation, "will match gifts to qualified institutions affiliated with religious organizations, but will not match gifts made directly to religious organizations … which fulfill tithes, pledges or other church related financial commitments." Public radio, being in the public service, educational or arts and cultural categories, can receive matching funds without restriction. The program is so fruitful that stations ask employees to learn if their employer participates in an employee match program throughout the year, not just during pledge drives. Research shows employees like the employer match too. When employees learn that a company match is available, they tend to give 22% more often. And when they do give, they give about 20% more money.

Challenges and matches are a staple on the public radio menu of giving options. During pledge drives, stations push the responsibility of listeners to become members to enjoy the content, meet the financial need, support the philosophical mission, or guard against political threats. And they offer listeners many ways to take responsibility: sustaining memberships, vehicle donations, bequeaths. But, stations also rely on what's known in the literature as the "imperfect altruism" of "warm glow" thinking. In other words, the desire of people to give not for any particular reason other than to feel better about themselves. Challenges and matches let them do that. From the station's standpoint, it may not be the ideal motivation, but it'll do. ☎

Games

"Marketing is a contest for people's attention."

—Seth Godin

On October 9, 2012, *Reuters* reported that a Florida man died after taking part in a roach eating contest. It was sponsored by Ben Siegel Reptiles of Deerfield Beach, Florida. Thirty two-year-old Edward Archbold was trying to win a python for a friend, and over the course of about four minutes, ate twenty of the bugs, which were likely members of the Blaberidae family of giant cockroaches. For reference, each living, full-grown insect was about three and a half inches long. Minutes after the so-called "Midnight Madness" event, Archbold "collapsed in front of the store and was taken to a hospital, where he was later pronounced dead." Siegel's lawyer, Luke Lirot, wrote that the insects eaten were "safely and domestically raised." Further, Mr. Lirot said, "All participants in the contest were entirely aware of what they were doing and that they signed thorough waivers accepting responsibility for their participation in this unique and unorthodox contest." The most important part of that story to other contest planners, including those at public radio stations, was likely the "signed thorough waivers" part.

Public radio pledge drives are full of DVDs, trips and concert tickets that hinge on listeners participating in games to win them.

But the two main types of games stations conduct are not as simple as they seem and have gotten more than one station in trouble with state and federal regulators. The first is a game with randomly awarded prizes, called a sweepstakes. In a sweepstakes, participants don't have to do anything to win except enter, although how they enter can be an issue.

When a station says it will give tickets to someone who's name has been pulled from a jar of names, that is a sweepstakes in that they are randomly considered to be in it by virtue of mailing in their entry. Sweepstakes are tied to "consideration," or costs for entry, and can be complicated. At one time, Florida viewed entry into any state contest via the Internet as having a "consideration" element that cost entrants more than it was worth to them because a computer and an Internet Service Provider were necessary. Florida has since changed its position. But consideration is a big factor in the perceived fairness of contests. Games that require a purchase as a form of consideration, for example, must also provide an Alternative Method of Entry, or an AMOE, that is equally available.

Some stations call their sweepstakes "drawings" but they're really a form of "lottery" or a "game of chance." As of 2013, seven states didn't have a lottery. All games of chance must have official rules, which in public radio is the contract between the station and the participant. The randomness of winning is what should make their fairness unquestionable. But pitchers can still strike flat notes that can make heads tilt. During a 2014 pledge break for Oregon Public Broadcasting, a host said of a sweepstakes prize, "If by some odd chance, you don't win this Apple iPad Air …" It is a strange thing to say since it is a statistical certainty that all listeners except one did not win that Apple iPad Air. Of course people can hope, but pitchers can't change distribution curves with offhand comments.

Other games award prizes based on some kind of competition. A contest, as opposed to a game of chance, requires the entrant to submit something that demonstrates skill. Public radio stations run all kinds of contests, from those for t-shirt designs to photographs to which public radio station will broadcast *American Idol* -style, listener-produced radio stories. Intelligence-based contests can't have questions that are too hard or easy. Meanwhile, measures of evaluation for items submitted, like cooking recipes or bumper stickers, must be objective and based on things like originality or technique versus subjective opinions. Contests also must have official rules and judges must be qualified to judge entries from both types of games. Once rules are made public, they must be followed and can't be changed except under extraordinary circumstances that must also be made public. Both types of games are fundraising incentives to get people to listen, give and hopefully become members. But neither game can determine winners with a combination of skill and chance, such as if a tie for a contest is broken by the flip of a coin. It must be one or the other. And because sweepstakes and contests can generate a ton of questions (and problems), state authorities scrutinize them and the stations that run them.

Public radio stations must also adhere to a set of federal requirements since federal money supports them and congressional rules say they can't behave like commercial stations if they want it. The FCC says it is unlawful for someone, with the "intent" to deceive the listening or viewing public, to help contestants cheat, force them to under-compete, rig the game or help anybody else conspire to do any of the above. The agency's web page for contests provides an interesting list of enforcement actions taken by it between February 2000 and October 2014 (the last time the list was updated). The site shows forty-six violations of federal law, which are categorized as *Notice of Apparent Liability* or *NAL*, *Forfeiture Orders* and *Order and Consent Decrees*. But those violations don't apply to contests that the agency says weren't contests by licensed stations, weren't broadcast or advertised to the public, didn't ask or let the public participate, or were contests by a non-broadcast entity of the licensee.

Only one public radio station was on the list. WNCW, a service of Isothermal Community College in Spindale, North Carolina, was issued an *NAL* on November 13, 2003. Among the list of violations, the affidavit says the station broadcast a raffle during its spring 2002 pledge drive "that failed to make clear that consideration was not required to participate in the contest." In other words, it didn't tell listeners that they needed to pledge to be entered. Isothermal, according the affidavit, also failed to air the rules for the raffle. Isothermal contested this, saying the rules were very simple, and "anyone who called and asked to be entered was entered, whether or not the caller pledged membership." The FCC pushed back against the station's claim. Besides contest rules appearing on the site two months after the contest ended, the agency essentially said radio shouldn't need the Internet to notify listeners of contest rules. It's flat response, "[t]he material terms should be disclosed periodically by announcements broadcast on the station conducting the contest," was accompanied by a non-negotiable, $4,000 dollar fine.

By 2012 however, Matthew Lasar was reporting for *Radio Survivor* that many radio companies, including NPR, were demanding that the FCC stop making them explain contest rules over the air. Though they all but agreed with WNCW's argument from nearly a decade earlier, Lasar said a rule change might help precipitate a huge "bait and switch." Stations drive eyeballs to their sites, where visitors find the online details of a promised game aren't nearly as exciting as the on-air hype. Meanwhile, online visitor data can be harvested. The rule did change in February 2016, allowing stations to post contest rules on their websites and spare them from reading them in their entirety. And as for the raffle, the commission noted that WNCW did not violate North Carolina state law. "North Carolina state law appears generally to permit lotteries conducted by non-profit organizations such as Isothermal." So, on at least two counts, Isothermal probably felt somewhat exonerated, though it was too late to matter. But the flexibility to post online has since given stations lots of options. Iowa Public Radio uploaded more than 100 pages of rules for all of the contests the station has conducted since fall 2016. Other stations limit their rules to current contests, or have a single template that applies to all contests. Because contest rules can be online, stations have a responsibility to insure those rules account for all contingencies. For example, if a contestant wins a prize, but can't claim it, the rules need to spell out how the station will select another winner. Likewise, if winners don't want to give too much personal information, or prevent the use of their image or voice in future promotions, rules need to be flexible enough to address those issues too.

Lauren Lynch Flick writes in the *CommLawBlog* that just because the federal government streamlines its requirements, state law holds ultimate sway for domestic, non-profit organizations, like public radio stations. Since about 43 of 50 states operate games of chance, whether in the form of horse racing, casinos, or drawings, their gaming commissions monitor contests to insure they don't run afoul of gaming laws. Legislatures grant them the authority to enforce the rules they establish. States and their Attorneys General, also enforce consumer protection laws which prohibit any prize or contest related advertising that isn't legit. Large conglomerates which run national contests tend to use generic language acceptable in all 50 states. But they may also insert the phrase, "void where prohibited" as a catch-all which is blanket protection in states where parts of the contest may conflict with state law. In those states with gaming commissions, contest language used by contest holders can also be similar, though there are standouts. In Rhode Island, any entity that wants to run a contest where the prize is more than $500 must file a statement with the Secretary of State. The $150 filing fee imposes an extra burden on non-profits, including public radio stations. This might explain why prizes offered by Rhode Island public radio are $500 and below.

In 25 states without gaming commissions, including 18 others like Alabama which also run games of chance, contests can vary in part because there is no single authority to standardize rules. The state has been exploring the idea of a gaming commission for several years. Entities running games as simple as bingo parlors, for example, must notify the sheriff in their respective counties with numbers on games and prize winnings. But the *Birmingham News* reported that even that basic law is being widely ignored. Alabama Senator Hank Sanders complained in 2008, "Ours is probably the only state in the nation that has legal gambling without state regulation." As a result, contest rules among Alabama radio stations vary widely. Issues of consideration, as well as the necessity of clear and transparent rules, may be relatively invisible to the audience. But they continue to be a challenge for radio stations in general, and public radio stations in particular, that insist on playing games. ☎

People Like You

"Give, but give until it hurts."

—Mother Teresa

How public radio asks for money from listeners is a big part of what this book is about. But before this chapter looks outward, it's worth it to consider how other non-profit organizations may ask for money from their own employees. One would assume that every employee of every non-profit knows that they are in the giving business. So giving a little out of their own paycheck to help the cause for which they labor should be a given, right?

PLEDGE: The Public Radio Fund Drive

In July 2015, the *Guardian* published an anonymous commentary entitled, *I'm fed up of being asked for money by the charity I work for*. It was one of a series of such commentaries from a project called *Confessions of a Charity Professional*. The writer explained that although he understood times were tough for non-profits everywhere, including his own, he was sick of the near-constant "nudges, hints and barefaced requests from colleagues to donate to our cause." And although he seemed grateful to have a job that lets him pay bills, buy food and keep a roof over his head, the same organization he cares about demands much of him; unpaid overtime, irregular work hours and pop-up events that suck the life out of what should be off time. "It shouldn't be assumed," says person X, "that because I fully support the charity and promote our work, devoting my time and energies to it, that I am so able to support the organization financially."

Whether or not there are public radio professionals on this side of the pond who feel the same isn't known. An informal survey of public radio professionals I conducted in 2017 found that although 43% of respondents did not expect employees to also be contributors to the cause, one in three did. And as station employees relentlessly ask the listener to become members, renewing members, sustaining members, bigger givers, major givers and then to "remember us in your will," loyalty as translated into giving is not a small concern.

Setting aside the motivations for what makes people give, the mechanics of how stations get someone to become first-time members is a straight-up numbers game. For example, some stations brag that they haven't raised their minimum membership fee for many years. But the low entry to public radio likely has a strategic purpose. A $35 minimum membership functions like a loss leader. Retailers use loss leaders; products that sell for less than their retail price, to get the buyer in the door. The store bets that once inside, shoppers will spend much more. Likewise, the administrative costs of managing that $35-a-year membership are probably more than the less than $3 per month revenue stations get from it.

That's even more true if people pay with a credit card rather than letting the station debit their checking account, since a debit has no credit card transaction fees. But stations could be betting that as new members get added to its database, they can be moved up the "giving ladder" at which point, the investment begins to pay off. Appeals to first-time givers are different from those people who have already given, and different still for people who are being asked to commit to a schedule of giving. And chances of that increase as listeners come into contact with the multi-layered ways in which they're solicited, including broadcasts, podcasts, email, direct mail and social media. These ways of reaching out to listeners will only increase.

Then there's the goal of renewing "lapsed" members. Reestablishing contact with lapsed members, like couples in counseling, can be all about reminding them of what attracted them to the relationship in the first place. Renewal letters, for example, tend to explain why the coverage public radio offers is important to them while reminding them of how fundraising works. This at least helps remind lapsed members of what they've been missing. Larry Myler, writing for *Forbes* in 2016 quoted what he called a "worrisome" statistic from global management consulting firm, Bain & Company. "Sixty to 80% of customers who describe themselves as satisfied do not go back to do more business with the company that initially satisfied them. How can that be?" he asks. "Often it's due to a lack of connection." Consultant John Sutton in 2006, noted that new, renewing and lapsed donors are the ones that give public radio its stability. "Public radio," he says, "depends on on-air drives to acquire or keep 900,000 [in 2017, nearly 3 million] names on the annual membership roles. These names are essential

to the $148 million [in 2017, more than $300 million] per year stations raise through the mail, email, telemarketing, and major donor
efforts. This is an essential point."

Then there are sustainers, or givers who've agreed to make regular, often automatic payments. The shift toward them by stations,
because of their financial stability, has been massive. But they are
not a panacea. Deb Ashmore, a senior fundraising executive for
South Carolina based Target Analytics, told *Current* in 2016 that
new members, not just sustainers, are important to a station's pipeline. She said a station with mostly sustaining members loses about
30% of them each year. If they're not being replaced with new
members who are eventually converted to sustainers, stations can
have problems. "Even sustainers do eventually cancel," she said.
If sustainers don't make the change from credit card payments to
automatic debits from their checking accounts, stations may send
reminder emails. If listeners still don't update their payments, they
are contacted by a telemarketing firm on a monthly basis, and via
snail mail packed with "urgency." Before sustaining memberships
was a thing, letters asked for simple, annual renewals. Now, holding people and their credit card information in place as sustainers
is so important that some in the industry call it "recapturing."

Upselling is a dirty word to utter in polite public radio company, but it's a tactic the business of public radio uses just like any
other tactic used by any other business. It's not openly called
upselling, because upselling implies manipulation, which is something public radio would never say it does. There does exist within
pledge drives however, a persistent suggestion (if you can afford it,
of course) to add to your existing contribution, or consider one
larger than the one you gave last time. The thing about upselling
is people know when it happens. And when it happens, they tend
to react by moving away from the message. What that looks like
is a drop in listening and money. But the party faithful who advise

both business and non-profits are undeterred. Lorman Educational Services, a sales training company, tells prospective clients,
"Your customers have many needs - that they know about and that
they've yet to discover; immediate problems and future needs.
Luckily, you have solutions for each. Your key: the ability to upsell
and cross-sell! If you're not upselling and cross-selling you're
actually delivering bad customer service!"

The push to drop larger and larger wads of cash into the maw
of public radio ties in with its new-found appetite for major givers.
A major giver is generally defined as someone who contributes
$1,000 or more. But in the many years since the $235 million Joan
Kroc gift, thousand-dollar gifts have become pocket change. Doug
Eichten, president of Greater Public, told *Current* in 2017, "Many
public media contributors have the capacity to contribute at much
higher levels—including at the $10,000 threshold that educational
and cultural institutions often set for major donors—and more stations need to focus on building personal relationships that can lead
to five-figure gifts." Meanwhile, new agreements between NPR
and member stations promise mo' money for both if the latter will
just turn over all of its donor lists to the former.

Public radio giving seems to follow a life cycle. Babies in NPR
onesies becoming pre-teens strapped into seat belts force fed
Morning Edition is indoctrination. Poor young adults focused on
building families and careers give some. But as they get established, they may want to make up for all of the listening they did in
earlier years without paying more. Then, around retirement, if they
are willing and able, they might generously support a station
they've come to love. Love so much that some of them include the
station in their estate planning. Bequests, the umbrella under which
much "planned giving" happens, can include annuities, insurance
policies, stock, real estate and much more. With the passing away
of the baby boomer cohort, capturing its significant financial

legacy is turning out to be an important piece of a station's revenue pie, and rounds out the profile of the ideal, individual public radio giver. ☎

New & Renew

"Depending on which study you believe, and what industry you're in, acquiring a new customer is anywhere from five to 25 times more expensive than retaining an existing one."

—Amy Gallo, writing for the Harvard Business Review in 2014

In 2012, Vermont Public Radio announced that it would stop offering memberships at the basic level. For decades, the basic level has been the low cost entry point for millions of listeners to legitimately enjoy public radio's content while supporting the stations that provide it. But *Current* reports that while some stations are rethinking the value of a category that may be outliving its usefulness, others are torn. The problem, in an age of rising costs for programs, rising fees from government and institutions and decreased state and federal support, is where should the price of the basic membership be set? As of 2012, the median basic membership across public radio was $40. Some stations have rates as high as $75. Spokane Public Radio tells listeners, "An electronic funds transfer can be as little as $3.75 per month ($45 a year)."

Public radio membership rates are in three main groups: basic or "individual" givers at between $1 to $249, mid-level or "transactional" givers at $250 to $999 and major givers at over $1,000. Most stations give generous discounts to students and seniors. Individuals tend to be people, but they could also be businesses offering matches or groups of individuals pooling their money for challenges. Transactional giving, as defined by fundraising consultant David Allen, is giving in which "what is being given is very closely tied to what the donor receives in return." Although it could be something as simple as a t-shirt, the problem with this type of giving for stations, says Allen, is that the gift may represent something the giver wants in exchange that has nothing to do with supporting the organization's mission. And this runs counter to the entire mentality stations wish for members. The transactional giver, for example, may give for the tax benefit. But the tax reform measures passed by the 115th Congress doubles the standard deduction, thus reducing the incentive for taxpayers to itemize and, as a consequence, contribute to nonprofit organizations. Alan Chartock, CEO and president of WAMC is one of public radio's staunchest supporters, but even he has concerns about the consequences of the change affects giving. "I think there are some places that are really going to get hurt here, but I'm hoping we will not be punished because of this bill," he said.

The idea of seeking new members may be necessary, but it doesn't seem popular. South Carolina based Target Analytics, examined 42 public radio stations and estimated that in 2011, donors contributing $50 or less were about 20% of the public radio's total membership. It went on to say that "because so many stations have converted donors to sustainers, [stations] must try even harder to bring new members into the fold." Proof of that is how, in 2011, San Francisco's KQED offered discounted memberships through Groupon. In a 2015 article for Greater Public, Becky Chinn tells stations, "when it comes to new single-gift members joining the station, a central challenge to achieving healthy growth is the fact that typically only 30% or fewer of a station's new on-air-acquired single-pay members will return for a second year of membership."

These members, say Chinn, can be more costly since recapturing them may require extra costs like telemarketing or premiums. And though stations are more interested in recruiting new members, they want them as new sustainers rather than as basic members. As a veteran public radio consultant told visiting Nieman Fellow Melody Kramer in 2015, "There's been a major shift toward sustainable donors." It's a move that's evident on many station websites, where it's difficult for people who would like to give a one-time gift. "They're less welcoming to the $25 to $50 dollar donor," said the consultant. In 2011, Target Analytics also found that 31% of new members were signed up as sustainers. By 2014, new members as sustainers had jumped to 44%. By 2015, it was 52%. Stations like financial consistency for which they can budget. A 2013 study by Greater Public showed that "sustaining members are typically worth up to four times more than traditional donors to a station."

Meanwhile, the effort expended on renewing members has public radio's attention for entirely different reasons. A 2008 report from the Station Resource Group, building on the work of David Giovanonni, Barbara Appleby and others, said that listeners who listen consistently tend to give consistently. But when listeners tune in every eight to 14 days, rather than listening every day, they fall out of the weekly cumulative measure, or "cume" and become what the industry calls "lapsed cumers." Stations use weekly cumulative measures to determine overall audience strength. A lapsed cumer, says the report, isn't happy with some aspect of station programming. It recommends that stations simply fix the problem, and they will return.

A lapsed donor is a little more complicated. They're someone who gives every 14 to 20 months and routinely misses annual renewal periods. That same SRG report said that while the lapsed cumer needs only better programming to return, the lapsed donor, (who hasn't stopped listening, but isn't giving) needs the station to have a better fundraising program. Thus, stations spend slightly more time and energy "re-acquiring" them than trying to obtain new donors. One in four stations specifically asked listeners to consider renewing their membership. New givers were important, but the report said that stations "had to prioritize by first keeping current donors, getting lapsed donors back, and then acquiring new givers." Portland, Oregon-based Lewis-Kennedy Associates also weighed in on renewing memberships. Among the conclusions in their 2008 look at 55 public radio stations, they noted, "All key renewal rates were down; first-year renewal is a particular problem." That's one reason why, in its recommendation, the report advised stations to not "set the bar too high" during pledge drives. Since any contact is better than none, two out of three stations practically beg listeners to just "pick up the phone and call" for any old reason.

And in those conversations, Greater Public's Jay Clayton advises stations to not just ask donors for money, but to "Take time to thank them! Let them know how much you genuinely appreciate their generosity and show them how their dollars are working to keep what they love on the air." He says, "Just adding a few touch points throughout the year shows your donors that they made a wise decision when they invested in your programming. Welcome the conversation!" The odds of getting a re-commitment from someone who was a steady giver, has lapsed, but is on the line now is much better than getting a new giver from scratch. Also, not mentioning their delinquency while chatting them up on the phone was recommended for the best chance of a successful renewal. ☎

Sustain & Upsell

"I once did phone fundraising for a regional public radio station whose brilliant idea was to call up people who had donated, about a month after their donation, to ask for another one. Needless to say we got a lot of screaming, grunting, and "Well NOW I'm never gonna give you guys money EVER AGAIN" and so forth."

—commenter AugieAugustus on Metafilter, October 1, 2012

A sustaining donor is one who gives to their public radio station on a regular basis. Public radio adopted the model of sustained giving around 2012. Since then tools, studies and graphic aids explaining it have popped up all over the Internet. Public radio researchers Barbara Appleby and Valarie Arganbright provide stations with an online calculator that shows the difference in value over years, of sustainer vs. non-sustainers. Jacobs Media shows which of public radio's music formats are most popular with sustainers. Sustained giving has also changed how stations say thank you to their audiences for their support. Since 2012, it has mutated from thanking listeners, to thanking members, to thanking "sustaining" members. And the ask seems to get bigger and bolder as the circle of substantial givers seems to get smaller. Vince Patton, during an October 2014 pitch break for Oregon Public Broadcasting, said to listeners, "Perhaps you can afford a thousand dollars. Not really all that much money."

Consultant John Sutton warns stations to not be overly focused with $1,000 pleas. "Too much emphasis on $1,000 donations in on-air drives not only suppresses contributions from people who might give less, it also sends the message that your station doesn't need all that many supporters to succeed." For those small givers who have been concerned, (as the research confirms) that their two-digit contributions don't matter much in the bigger picture, such comments don't help. Neither do articles like one headlining the Village Voice in 2014, *NPR Doesn't Need Your Money: NY Public Radio Announces $10 Million Grant Barely A Week After Pledge Drive Ends.*

But public radio isn't the only place where the sustaining model has gained followers. In 2015, Johanna Ginsberg with New Jersey Jewish News told of how synagogues have decided to abandon dues in favor of sustaining memberships. Nick Levitin, Temple Shomrei Emunah's president sees the similarity of the new fundraising model to public radio methods, even mirroring the language. "We depend on your support and please remember how much we provide to you in so many ways." "It's a two-way street," Levitin concludes. "Your membership sustains us and we sustain you." That language becomes more common as non-profits lean into the model. During a spring 2016 pledge drive, KERA co-host Eric Oesen told listeners, "Today is Tuesday. It's also Ten-Dollar Tuesday. We're encouraging you to contribute at whatever level is comfortable for you and your family's budget. Lots of folks are joining us at the $10 a month level on the sustaining membership plan." More than a quarter of stations said this or some version of it to listeners during a pitch break; how much you give is your choice alone. But Oesen's co-host then followed up by equating a $10 a month contribution to a $125 a month, $1,500 a year contribution. This pushiness shows how the plea to give when and what's right for you can quickly morph into a suggestion of what's best for the station.

Patrick Emerson, writing in 2010 for the *Oregon Economic Blog*, referred to a Texas study about how stations "suggest" an amount even though they are constantly encouraging people to "give whatever amount is comfortable." That study gave people an average donation of $75, an above-average ask of $300 and a way-above-average ask of $600. The results showed people didn't want to be average but also didn't want to be way above average. So, with the $300 dollar suggestion, people seemed to upsell themselves. "It also turns out that we don't just give for altruistic reasons, we give because it makes us feel good about ourselves as well," says Emerson. Some people connect with the higher amount not because it necessarily is more doable but because they want it to be more doable. This kind of giving, known as "impure altruism" is giving with a personal benefit and not necessarily out of selflessness. "This is a bit self-serving," he says, "but not really a bad thing – I am giving after all." That not-quite-perfect form also generates in the giver something researchers call the "warm glow," or the good feeling of knowing one has just done something for someone else, even if it wasn't entirely for someone else. If giving is all about altruism, Emerson asks, how can this happen? It happens, he says because people, "like being a 'sustaining member' not just a 'member.'" And stations know this.

They also know that the sustainer model, as much as it turbo-charges contributions, has significant issues. Over-reliance on it by stations reduces the effectiveness of the traditional pledge drive in at least three ways. First, according to John Sutton, "The pool of donors who might renew their membership during the drive is smaller because many of the most loyal donors are now sustainers." Becky Chinn, writing for Greater Public in 2015 says, "We're already seeing some of these effects as a number of stations with high percentages of sustainers on the file are having a difficult time reaching on-air revenue goals that were previously achievable." And Sutton says that add-on gifts are more work for pitchers, "since part of the sustainer pitch is that the listener is already supporting the station every month."

But the biggest problem sustaining memberships cause for stations, oddly, is the same thing that makes them so attractive, which is the regularity of the payments. For example, let's say a new giver gives the station a one-time contribution of $240. The station now has $240. But what if that giver is a sustainer, and gives $240 over twelve months? On paper, the station still gets $240, but now, only in increments of $20 a month. For the membership and development departments, that's a win. For the accounting department, that's a receivable, not revenue. Yes the money's there, but in the future and no good to a station right now. In response, stations try to compensate by increasing the goal of the drive, which confuses listeners who know stations have a bunch of sustainers, which should mean fewer drives. Instead, stations now need to have more drives with higher goals to make up for the spreading out of sustainer payments. A rule of thumb, Sutton says, is "the more successful a station is with sustainers, the less reliant it must become on fund drives for cash flow." But that sometimes doesn't happen. Sustainers can create a tidal wave of cash tomorrow that is just beyond reach of stations trying to pay salaries and bills today. More than one non-profit has gone under, essentially clutching a fistful of IOUs.

In a Greater Public article called *The Hidden Cost of Sustainers*, Ellen Guettler and Jay Clayton say that besides the cash-poorness for stations that have moved to sustainer programs, members who become sustainers require more care and feeding, which translates into more station employee time. And they warn, external events like the Target department store security breach in 2014, "can cause large numbers of donors to change their cards, creating an enormous and immediate financial impact on stations with a large sustaining donor base." Hence, the push by stations to move givers from credit cards to checking accounts. As to the success of sustaining memberships, Greater Public reported in a 2016 study that less than half of 93 stations have converted more than 40% of their members to sustainers. The rest converted less than 40%. Major market stations have been the most successful converting members to sustainers. Smaller stations, not so much.

PLEDGE: The Public Radio Fund Drive

So how do stations get the machinery of their membership departments online to get sustainers onboard? One way is snail mail. Since an average sustainer has been a giver for a while, sustainer letters, unlike letters to renew, don't focus much on why a giver started giving. They may begin with the clear, simple and bolded suggestion at the top to switch from credit cards to electronic funds transfer. Then appreciation for giving, followed by some version of the question, "Can we count on you?" And near the bottom, after the signature is usually a postscript. A tactic of effective letters, the p.s. is the one part of the letter research shows people almost always read. Here, the overall message is repeated. Other stations go so far as changing the color of the paper upon which pledge letters are printed, for example, from white to pink to reflect the increasing urgency of each subsequent reminder. But stations may not coordinate their efforts, even to the same giver. A peer said via text, "A friend of mine from church posted a photo of five identical donation-request letters from public TV ... obviously she's on multiple lists of theirs, but they didn't merge those lists at all before mailing."

The Public Radio Exchange launched an effort with 13 of its Radiotopia podcast brands in 2015 to introduce their listeners to the concept of sustaining membership with a first of its kind, sustainer rather than pledge drive. The month-long ask, monstrous compared to the six-day average run of terrestrial drives was chosen, said PRX Chief Operating Officer Kerri Hoffman, "because all of [PRX] shows run on different schedules — some are weekly, while others only come out every few weeks — and it wanted to make sure the hosts on every show could promote the campaign to their listeners." Although it's giving away swag like t-shirts and tote bags, it's also offering perks for contributions of up to $15,000. Then PRX head, Jake Shapiro told *Current*, "We feel that so much is hinging on how engaged audiences are, and this form

— it's an early experiment of it — of direct support will be a pillar of the business model going forward."

PRX alums already have a pretty good track record of making money. But it isn't as simple as sticking a "Pledge Now" button on a homepage. Shapiro said PRX will build its own community of support with the help of its own community of producers. And he says, those that can afford to sustain a $300 a year contribution, will have a say in pilots Radiotopia might be eying for distribution. That's the kind of engagement and forward thinking that makes casual listeners into loyal givers. But all that matters if, and only if, you listen to podcasts.

My survey asked public radio participants which of the following answers did they most agree with; "Pitchers have the responsibility to encourage listeners to give as much money as they can to support the station," or "If pitchers say they don't upsell, they don't upsell." Respondents could also choose, "I don't know." One in five chose that. Seven percent agreed with number two and 72% agreed with number one. In other words, pitchers were expected to say whatever it takes to get givers to give more. But this is not what pitchers tell listeners during pledge drives, and not what stations say pitchers do. In a review of 37 public radio stations pitch breaks during spring 2016, only one in ten specifically suggested that listeners increase their contribution. If some pitchers are supposed to upsell, they didn't appear to be doing it.

So, where is the disconnect? Could it be in pledge central? One of the breakout sessions of the 2015 Public Media Development Marketing Conference, entitled *Clarifying the Sustainer Message for TV*, asked attendees to consider, "What are our best "upsell" strategies, and how do we best train our phone volunteers to use them when taking pledges?" So could an upsell message be delivered but not so much by the on-air staff? Granted, TV is not radio.

431

But a 2016 article by Tyler Falk of *Current* suggests that public TV and radio stations are sharing more procedures and infrastructure. This may be even more true at those stations which are joint licensees. And Hawaii Public Radio's script for phone volunteers includes the ask of people who are not sustainers, "With your pledge of $_____, may we make you a Sustaining Member?" It appears the process of the upsell may apply to pledge drives, pitch scripts and what phone volunteers say as well.

Software too can be deployed for the upsell on the down-low. SteadySales.com, a sales training company in Williamsburg, Massachusetts, contracted with WFCR, Western New England Public Radio, to help it meet yearly revenue targets. The station, according to company president Sheldon Snodgrass, was spending too much effort on less than optimal assumptions and less that fruitful donor prospects. He said his company "Achieved group buy-in to a 'new way' of selling that left sales reps with a higher degree of confidence, excitement about getting out and selling more, and the tools necessary for goal setting, and self-accountability." That "new way" focused on more naturally sounding scripts that helped generate more return calls from prospects and move more quickly through the underwriting sales process. By helping the station focus on the upsell, underwriting grew by 33%. Is anyone else besides underwriters being upsold?

Radio sales and development people don't call what it does, which is asking listeners to give as they can while suggesting higher amounts (usually corresponding to a thank you gift), upselling. However, there are several definitions of the term. One, according to KBOO Portland's former Development Officer, Becky Meiers, is to convince folks to purchase an item they wouldn't have considered purchasing in the first place. Another, opposite example, is described by Dave Blancharski, author of *Superior Customer Service*. He says grocery store discount cards precipitate the upsell by tracking what you buy and reminding you to buy something you normally would buy at some point anyway. "If for example," says Blancharski, "you buy three jars of peanut butter each week, the store could program the computer to print out a coupon for jelly and bread at the point of sale (that's upsell again!)." Seasoned public radio veterans might recognize this as, "You know you're going to become a member eventually. Why not do it today?"

The question for public radio is, which one do listeners hear? The distinction between how retail does it versus if non-profits do it centers on whether or not it's legitimate, philanthropic behavior. "The use of the term can put one on a slippery slope as it applies to nonprofit development," says Meiers, which is why listeners rarely hear it. But they hear it sometimes. In response to a question about upselling, a representative from OPB's member services department said in an email that she "didn't know what was meant by the question of whether or not OPB upsells the membership." She also likely didn't know that during an October 2014 drive time pledge break, while talking about the benefits of a pint glass, OPB's April Baer told listeners that when they called to pledge, "Seriously, it takes 90 seconds. There's no upselling." But, said the representative, "If you are called by a telemarketer working for OPB they may start at a level a little higher than your last donation or your current donation level."

So, although the industry definitely knows what it is and does, why should it matter what it's called? Public radio's underwriting versus advertising argument provides somewhat of an answer. The suspicion that underwriting, though it has legislative restrictions to not sound like ads, walks right up to the line of that distinction has been a long-time source of frustration for listeners who feel like they're being had. And graduate students from Pennsylvania's Wharton School of Economics say customers in general don't like the conflation. In their 2015 study, they found that "Empirical evidence suggests that upselling is negatively correlated with customer satisfaction." "Negatively correlated" is an academic euphemism for people turning off their radios and leaving the room. That's because even if upselling, in the mind of the person asking, translates into more revenue for the cause, that doesn't mean the same kind of positive connection is happening in the mind of the customer. The study found an increase in the success of upselling led to a drop in customers patronizing the company.

In addition to making customers not feel honestly served, upselling, say the authors, can give customers buyer's remorse. That can affect long-term loyalty. For some listeners, it may even be a question of message integrity. This helps explain why station counter-messaging is constantly tying contributions to benefits the listener receives. Yes, stations may upsell, but the extra stretch on one's purse or wallet is worth it. "We give you more," said NPR's Michelle Martin, in a ubiquitous 2017 network promo. All sorts of digital tools can support the upsell, including coincidentally, one introduced by NPR Digital Services in August 2016. "Marketing Forms" is touted as secure, flexible, data integrated and full of features for user stations, including one called "the pledge challenge bar" and another one quite simply called "Sustainer Upsell." The feature wasn't called, "Give Whatever's Right for You." ☎

Major Giving & Bequests

"People first, then money, then things."

—Suze Orman

Major giving is defined in philanthropy as when a donor contributes $1,000 or more. But when McDonald's heiress Joan Kroc gave NPR $235 million in 2003, that put major giving on another plane of existence. During his tenure, NPR CEO Jarl Mohn made clear that Ms. Kroc's gift is small compared to what he hopes gifts could be. His plan to mine the donor lists of local stations and split the booty down the middle represents new and needed possibilities for public radio. The charge throughout the industry is that major gift fundraising is hampered because the seeking out of these givers isn't done that well.

In 1996, the Station Resource Group measured the ability of 32 stations to generate major gifts. At the time, the concept was new and few stations were doing it. By a 2008 follow-up, SRG concluded that 20% to 30% of stations were taking advantage of the pool of available money, while "70% of the dollars that are on the table are not being effectively pursued by stations at this time." Even in recent years, there are those within public radio who still resist the idea of major giving. As Deborah Turner, Vice President of New Hampshire Public Radio said in a 2015 article for Greater Public, financial success sometimes requires political alignments. "Find an advocate on your board. If there are nay-sayers either on your board or among your staff," she says, "be sure to respectfully explain the benefits of a planned giving program."

There are even ongoing discussions as to what, exactly, qualifies as a major gift. Stations with limited resources can't afford to pay the same attention to a $1,000 giver as they do to a $100,000 giver. Regarding underwriters, Gordon Bayliss, in his 2015 article for Greater Public, *The Right Words When Rates Go Up* tells stations to "play favorites." He said stations should make sure their biggest corporate contributors know before anybody else to expect a jump in the station's expectation so as to "soften the blow." It's conceivable that big individual givers get the same consideration.

Consequently, planned giving, or the money a donor promises to leave through a will, can't be considered all those givers can give. Development officers are turning their attentions to contributions including vehicles, insurance policies, jewelry, artworks and retirement plans. Stations are trying to not leave any local financial stones unturned, even as the ecosystem of public radio gets churned. For instance, station strategizing probably wasn't helped by the sacking of NPR's chief fundraiser, Ron Shiller, in the aftermath of a 2011, right-wing sting. But the *Major Giving Initiative*, which is a project of the CPB, exists to remind major givers that systems are in place to show the system is trustworthy. The initiative includes not only guidance on how to reach high value donors, but a set of best practices for everything from donor privacy to editorial integrity, and from underwriting to avoiding conflicts of interest.

Development officers don't just oversee pledge drives. They also report to the financial officers, who report to the board, about the success of all fundraising efforts, including major giving. Those responsible for securing such gifts, also known as gift officers, are under pressure not unlike that of bank lenders or real estate agents. All must have a robust pipeline of potential customers. And they must constantly work to get new givers into that pipeline while plans for distributions from established givers are being set. Development departments must also be flexible. Some major givers may want to offer "restricted" gifts, directing the money to be used specifically, rather than generally as stations would prefer.

In some cases, negotiations between the giver and the station can achieve an "if this, then that" compromise. But in other cases, stations may be forced to turn down a specific gift while hopefully leaving the door open for another gift from the same donor in the future. Jim Lewis, writing for *Current* in 2011, says stations must walk a tightrope. "If they doggedly pursue general, unrestricted gifts, they risk getting fewer and lower gifts. If they accept too many gifts with restrictions, they risk letting donors determine the station's direction." John Sutton tells of some stations, "that must forever keep certain types of programs on the air because of a large gift accepted from a single donor." Lewis says stations need to avoid such "mission creep."

All this makes matching money to mission important. Development officers need systems that not only help them find good prospects, but understand their likes, dislikes and passions. The word passion comes up a lot in public radio, especially when it comes to major giving. That's because only passion for the community, the programming or for their own personal legacy is strong enough to compel a donor to hand over an estate of personal wealth representing a lifetime of sacrifice and hard work. So finding and connecting with potential big money givers is serious enough business that it relies on technology called "Prospect Pipeline Management," a universal tool of high dollar, high volume sales professionals. Face-to-face contact is key in helping a development officer feel out a prospect and close the deal. But the technology also helps that development officer not waste anyone's time on a fruitless pursuit of support.

Stephanie Bergsma, a former general manager for KPBS turned philanthropist, says of tepid givers, "If they are philanthropic, their underwhelming generosity either reflects their stronger interest in other causes or a lack of interest in what you are presenting. You must lay the groundwork by developing relationships with people so that you can understand their needs, interests, and desires." Deborah Turner agrees and promotes the use of technology to keep development officers out of the weeds. "In addition to databases and research, you must also have internal processes that support major gifts fundraising," she says. "You must track prospects, develop strategy for each prospect, and develop a system of progress checkins that help keep you on track with each individual major prospect."

But sometimes, that doesn't happen. Lisa Napoli, author of *Ray & Joan: The Man Who Made the McDonald's Fortune and the Woman Who Gave It All Away*, recounts a legendary goof along those lines. Joan Kroc was looking for a place to bequeath her fortune as she was dying of brain cancer. After several calls to PBS, she remembered a meeting years earlier with NPR president Kevin Klose. They met, papers were signed, and the rest is public radio history. But for the fact that no one at PBS returned a simple phone call, Ms. Kroc's bequest could have easily gone to public television instead of public radio. It drives home the point that one-on-one contact with major givers is the secret sauce of a successful relationship between donor and development. As amazing as it is, givers sometimes don't get thank-you calls either, says Bergsma. In a 2015 article, *The Major Donor Checklist*, she told Greater Public that those calls "almost never happen." And as a major giver herself, she would know. "Two months ago, I contributed to a special investigative news organization. During a follow-up lunch, I told them I would make another gift after the beginning of the year. I haven't heard a peep!"

But as a station manager, Bergsma's also been in earshot when staff dogged major givers who weren't, in their opinion, being major givers. "For example," she says, "in the course of reviewing potential majors donors to an event I chaired, there were comments about how a couple had a multi-million dollar income but they were only personally donating $10K with $15K from a family foundation." That disparaging probably stayed in the building, but so do other poisons. "The worst thing I have encountered (unfortunately somewhat frequently) is the sense of entitlement that some development people have." Stations and staff are passionate for their work, and have their own opinions about what major givers should do.

But the smart money is on understanding that donors give on their own schedule and for their own reasons. "There are two things you should always remember," says Bergsma. "No one owes your organization anything. They will only contribute if they truly feel engaged and empowered to make a difference." Bergsma says the other rule is to never talk negatively about donors. "It becomes a dangerous habit especially if you start sharing your thoughts with staff and volunteers." She warns to never underestimate the power or speed of gossip. A bad remark said to Donor A about Donor B can find its way through the grapevine and stations end up suffering. Besides, not respecting donors violates a set of promises established by the philanthropy industry in 1993, called the *Donor's Bill of Rights*.

And when it's time to receive a major gift or a bequest, stations should understand that it won't solve existing revenue problems. The bloodletting at NPR in 2014 came on the heels of $17 million worth of grants for expanded coverage and new media platforms months earlier. Though money rolled in from heavyweights like the Bill & Melinda Gates Foundation, and the John S. and James L. Knight Foundation, NPR spokeswoman Anna Christopher Bross made clear that money would not stop coming layoffs or fill a $6 million budget hole. "These grants do not erase that deficit by any means, because they're funding discrete projects," she said. Stations also suffering the loss of programs or staff because of a missed gift, or a bequest that can't be planned because the giver hasn't yet passed away, is less about the money and more about the station's own financial infrastructure. Says Sutton, "it shouldn't be so critical to the station's bottom line that failing to get one or two gifts undermines the station's ability to provide its core service."

The last key for major giving success is what Turner calls "A station-wide culture of philanthropy." All aspects of the station must be programmatically plugged into the work of the development department. Turner says it's important for everybody with a story to tell about how their programs have interacted with donors, to share it. "Yes, we are all grateful for the support of our donors; but is everyone at every level of the organization able to articulate not just what your station does, but why you do it?" This time, it's the passion of the people in the building that needs to flow out to the community and give it reason to trust and give. ☎

Keeping Track

"What counts is what you do with your money, not where it came from."

—Merton Miller

Public radio stations would beg to differ. As people diversify their listening habits and their devices, public radio stations follow. How listeners connect is almost synonymous with what they connect to. It's how listeners learn of program changes, transmitter maintenance and of course, upcoming pledge drives. And when listeners look for ways to give, tip jars, drop down menus and pledge pages pop up. "Donate Now" buttons on public radio web pages have been a hot topic, and got *Non Profit Times* writer Robert Ford's attention in 2005. He reminds public radio webmasters that they can't "slap a 'donate now' button on their websites and expect the money to roll in."

The revenue websites can draw, says a former program director at New Mexico-based commercial station KGUP, can be surprisingly low. "It really depends on how much your site gets organic traffic. If it's a popular website, the conversion is probably less than 1%." But although a website's contribution can be modest, it's not working alone, nor is conversion even its main purpose. Websites don't convert as much as they educate. They do so by not only keeping listeners connected with stations, but informing stations about listeners. So when it's time for a multi-phased fundraising campaign, success is higher since whither go devices, go give buttons. They get more notice because they're in more places, get pressed more often and attract more money.

Whether on low tech, multi-colored carbon paper or with high tech pledge drive software like Simple Pledge or Donor Manager, stations knowing how the dollars are adding up is just as important as the fact that they add up at all. If donors want a human touch during their giving, they can call in. But pledge drive pitchers often tell callers "you don't have to talk to a human being if you don't want to." So, many of the ways to give bypass humans completely. If stations would just adopt it, pledge free streaming could eliminate pledge drives and pesky human interactions once and for all.

People-powered efforts like pavement pounding, survey distributing, listener calling and result tabulating has, to some extent, been supplanted by players and apps that take listeners directly to online forms. Meanwhile, algorithms tabulate listenership and adjust the listening experience automatically. Becky Chinn, writing for Greater Public in 2015 said, "There are nearly as many approaches to the details of an effective membership program as there are public media stations. But one thing stations with top-performing programs have in common is that they apply the full array of identified best practices when it comes to membership strategy and technique." Those best practices boil down to at least ten high and low-tech ways stations ingest money during pledge drives. But Chinn emphasizes that a holistic approach, rather than operating each aspect in isolation, is the key to overall fundraising success. Finally, as much as is possible within station capabilities, listeners need to be tracked across giving streams. That includes not just off the shelf social media platforms, but radio traffic software that follow peak listening periods. Those peaks, which traditionally align with the most popular shows, determine when pre-recorded pledge promos and reminders to give get used.

Frank Berry, writing for *npEngage*, said in 2016 that online fundraising was up 7.9% year over year, to more than $2.6 billion. And different donors responds to different types of fundraising efforts. But as federal and state support drop, and higher value donations are sought, broad-based efforts to scoop up more money from fewer givers through other means are taking shape. In a best practices bent, *Non-Profit Quarterly*'s Aine Creedon advises non-profits to make the pitches less about themselves, and more about what is of importance to the donor. She says 74% of stations surveyed ineffectively focus on the former rather than the latter. And targeting younger groups of donors through social media is, in some ways, a modernization of the annual fundraising letter and can be beneficial.

But this may result in less attention being paid to larger and repeat donors. Chinn says, "All things being equal, a membership program that effectively has all channels of fundraising in play will ultimately be the most successful." Katie Hawkins-Garr, writing for Poynter in 2015 probably spoke for many media organizations when she said, "When it comes to audience engagement, in which social media plays a key role, it's difficult to determine where to focus your efforts. There are no pre-written rules to follow, which can be equal parts exciting and daunting." Regardless of the new ways stations use to reach listeners, the recurring themes of fundraising methods, whether old or new school remain few, timeless and simple; storytelling, repetitive, attention getting, personal and measurable. ☎

Old Dogs

"In a time of transition for journalism all around the world, it's reassuring to know that some of the old ways endure."

—James Fallows, *The Atlantic*, March 4, 2013

The thing about old school is it's often the restore point when modern ways and means get too crazy. And though electronic communication is the rage, emojis and other substitutes for conveying emotion and making connection don't do it very well. It's one of the reasons why stations aren't quite ready to give up the pledge drive. But while they weigh the effectiveness of old methods over the efficiency of new technology, they continue to march with what they know works right now, including:

Face-to-Face - In this old-school category are walk-ins and door-to-door solicitations. Some stations encourage people to bring their donations in person since it's a chance for them to form personal connections with listeners and give listeners a chance to see the building, the gear and the faces surrounding familiar voices. But fears of violence against staff by outsiders has helped dial that back a bit. NPR Washington invites visitors as part of supervised tours. Jennifer Waits describes for *Radio Survivor* her 2014 trip to KEXP Seattle as a participant in the College Broadcasters Inc. conference nearby. But by and large, stations encourage people to visit their website rather than their street address. Door to door, by contrast, is much more robust. Companies like Denver-based Donor Development, as well as public radio powerhouses like WHYY, KERA and Wisconsin Public Radio have sent door knockers proselytizing for public radio. In 2013, Georgia Public Broadcasting tried a door-to-door effort and sent at least 22 volunteers into some of GPB's core listening area. Although canvassers may have gotten an earful from listeners chiding or defending their beloved WABE, such is the occasional messiness of human contact. *Current* says the nearly two dozen or so public TV stations that have embarked on D2D have gathered nearly a quarter million new givers who have given about 14 million new dollars. Canvassing is not cheap, however. For Donor Development to execute a year-long effort can require nearly a quarter-million dollar commitment by a station.

Pledge Central - Landline telephone use has been falling for years. And though Internet telephone services like Skype and Google Voice are growing, they are dwarfed by the explosion of text messaging. Meanwhile, companies like Vonage show drops in both calls made and voicemail messages retrieved and point to the slow decline of voice to voice conversations. But stations show no sign of giving up on the telephone. Practically every public radio station schedules volunteers to answer phones in shifts between two and six hours long. Arriving volunteers usually find a whiteboard, a shift supervisor, a floor manager and bunches of tables with banks of phones. Calls, when they come, tend not to arrive between pitch breaks, but rather flood in as soon as pitchers start talking. This is the *"Pledge Central"* that pitchers often refer to. It's the line of friendly volunteers *"ready to take your calls."* Cheers go up as hourly goals are met, and the room falls silent when they aren't. Those volunteers read scripts from binders or off computer screens that walk them and callers through the donation. And pitchers are correct when they say the process is quick. If a caller is already in the system, it takes less than a couple minutes to take their pledge, offer them a gift, ask them for their comments and move onto the next call. If they're not in the system, that takes a little longer. But trusting callers, intent on supporting the station, make even longer calls go faster with their good humor and willingness to update their personal information.

So far, the telephone continues to be how stations expect to make first contact. I found that the average 5-minute pitch break has dozens of separate pitch elements (mentioning of gifts, reminders to become a sustainer, etc). But on average, more than one-in-four are just the phone number. Meanwhile, many stations rely on a bit of theater, in the form of a loudly ringing phone, prominently off-mic, that sounds straight out of a 1940s Spencer Tracy movie. As June Thomas captured in the title of her 2015 article for *Slate*, *Let's Get Those Phones Ringing,* that big ole' honking phone, probably black, reminds pitchers when it doesn't ring to remind listeners to make it ring. Thomas calls deployment of such genius by stations *"cunning."*

Inbound Telemarketing - Nineteenth century technology also survives with the help of a 21st century business model. Stations contract with companies like Lubbock, Texas based Stenocall to take overflow pledges when phone volunteers are too busy, or after hours calls when pledge central is closed. They may also relieve stations of a day of on-air pledging to give staff a mid-drive breather. The company says on its website that, "Stenocall has been the innovator in providing call center services to numerous public broadcasting stations. We were the first with real time web pledge reporting." But the main job of companies like Stenocall is to provide inbound telemarketing. That's where people call into the company rather than outbound telemarketing, which is where telemarketers call you. When this happens, a caller might not know whether they're talking to a station volunteer, or a contracted someone else somewhere else. *Current* Digital Editor Mike Janssen, in a quest to better understand the pledge drive, was prepared for the romance of pledge central. But, "after a few phone calls and emails, I learned that unfortunately, it's not that simple." Janssen says, "the wrinkle is there may not be any actual call centers to visit."

But inbound telemarketing companies, in the business of collecting money for public radio, can steal from them too. In January

2018, Ohio-based InfoCision was fined $250,000 by the Federal Trade Commission for keeping money it should have been handing over to its clients, including unnamed public radio stations. That fine was the result of a multi-year investigation that began with a 2012 *Bloomberg* report by David Evans, and subsequent follow up stories by numerous public radio stations. According to Evans, "InfoCision brought in a total of $424.5 million for more than 30 nonprofits from 2007 to 2010, keeping $220.6 million, or 52% according to state-filed records." But the deception isn't limited to big companies. Earlier in 2005, a disillusion came in the form of $400,000 of disappeared fundraising money. Nancy Kruse, allegedly an alias for someone named Delany Anderson, persuaded 40 public radio stations over the course of 16 months to let her "help" them be more successful. Although a multi-station auction, as *Current* reported, was apparently just that, Ms. Kruse could not explain to stations the status of the money they were expecting except to say, "There was a business. The business failed." She says her family lost hundreds of thousands of dollars in personal wealth, and the business she took over had been failing from the start. Questionable, prior businesses as well as non-existent school credentials and fellowships behind her *"Nancy Kruse + Partners"* however, were possible but ignored warning signs. Stations and former employees alike blame themselves for being swept up by her charisma. *"Her powers of persuasion were legendary,"* said the speaker who wished to remain anonymous. *"Everyone was hoodwinked."*

Direct Mail - An anonymous public radio station was able to convince 1,300 direct mail recipients to convert from credit cards to automatic deductions from their checking account. And overall, those givers also increased their contributions by between 20% and 25%. These people already had a relationship with the station, so converting them to sustaining memberships was not so hard. In 2015, WOSU in Columbus, Ohio split 30,000 direct

mail asks into two groups with two different options for joining
the station. Group one got a letter for a sustaining membership at
$60, a discount from the regular $85 price tag. Group two got one
that said they could join for, "whatever they believed membership
was worth," but had to give at least $5. Although the second group
gave an average of only $28, there were a lot more of them. And
when it was time for renewals, most of those people renewed very
near the $60 rate. Direct mail, despite the hype around sustainer
programs, continues to be the sleeper. Chinn says that direct mail
helps maintain the steady state for fundraising, over and above the
effect of pledge drives. "In fact, as we compare the basic retention
curves of monthly giving between direct mail and email versus sin-
gle-pay donors to on-air drives, it is clear that the retention path of
direct mail and email acquired donors is a positive path." Five
years later, she says, donors gained through mail outpaced donors
converted to sustainers.

And about that conversion, Melanie Coulson, in her article,
The Seven Habits of Highly Effective Mail Campaigns, tells public
radio peers to use every square inch of that pitch letter, including
reminding recipients of their favorite shows on its back-side. Older
readers need bigger font, and the font should be spelling out
positive language. "Yes! I want to help fund my favorite programs
on WXYZ!" or "Here is my contribution to support more great
radio on WXYZ!" she recommends. Paper needs to build
anticipation in ways that are much easier for electronic media. So
Coulson also tells stations to space their direct mail campaigns
about two weeks apart. And she says that they should include strategic "teasers." That might be an initial letter reminding recipients
how important their contributions are, and a follow-up in "pink"
envelopes marked "Second Chance," that reflects more urgency.
Because direct mail campaigns can be daunting for some stations,
Coulson says that as with emails, Greater Public has ready-made
fundraising letters stations can use that are pre-targeted to specific

audiences and regions. All that's needed is a name and an address, and the letter does the rest.

Text - Text messaging and emails are the newest of public radio's old school fundraising methods. In 2012, text messaging turned 20 years old, while email hit its 40-year anniversary in 2015. But stations continue to rely on them. WVXU, a former service of Xavier University (Now Cincinnati Public Radio), entered into an arrangement with fundraiser MobileCause in 2011 to solicit donations via text message. The company, through its "text-to-give mobile option," encouraged users to text $10 throughout the 3-day drive. It also sent says it sent out hourly calls-to-action to generate new revenues and donors. The advantages were two fold. Givers that couldn't meet the minimum gift of $60 a year could still give. And, because the ask was sent to a mobile device that the user was likely carrying, more givers could give. Jeremy Koenig, Head of Marketing for MobileCause, said WVXU generated about $10,000 in extra revenue with texting. In 2014, Derek Thompson told the Atlantic that texting was three times more popular than phone calls among 7,000 teenagers he asked. That's probably why, in March 2017, KPFK Los Angeles inaugurated its text-to-give program with a tweet. But it's a sure sign that the station was aiming its text giving program at digital millennials and younger, rather than at analog boomers and older.

Coincidentally, Illinois-based Peoria Public Radio used the same 41444 text number as did KPFK. That number traces back to MobileCause and it shows up in dozens of places. Western Illinois University used it to give givers the choice of 14 separate campus departments to support during a campus-wide fundraiser. One of the drawbacks of text-to-give programs, though, as WNYC discovered in 2016, is the method delivers money but not listener information. "We weren't able to renew those donors, and we couldn't turn them into sustaining donors, which is really important for us to be able to do," said the station's digital fundraising strategist, Michael Chaplin. They modified the ask so that givers were sent to its online pledge form. But mobile isn't a panacea, according to Ross Yaeger. Writing for Greater Public in 2015, Yaeger warns stations that although full of opportunities, mobile fundraising brings two problems, lower prices per ad and what Bayliss calls "fake news ads that look like the news copy around them that are actually ads for a product or service." He says mobile ads have helped stations find a new way to reinforce underwriting messages. Native advertising he says, if done responsibly, can be quite beneficial to station bottom lines.

Email - In January 1997, *Investors Daily* said this of email: "Forrester Researcher says 15% of the U.S. population now uses e-mail, up from 2% in 1992. And they predict that within five years, that number will rise to about 50%." Although email is now on the other side of its popularity, it is still a critical fundraising tool for public radio. During pledge drives, stations often send out E-blasts for maximum effect. Opening the email reveals a simple message reinforcing the ask with a link that take visitors to the station's webpage. Becky Chinn, writing in 2015 for Greater Public recommended that stations should send "At the very least, a set of two or three e-appeals, about two weeks out, one week out, then the final day of the year can help secure new supporters and revenue." Emails can even have embedded "Donate Now" buttons, which take users directly to a Paypal account. For year-end giving especially, Chinn recommends a series of on-air fundraising spots about two weeks before the end of the year, followed up on with email campaign. One station started a 2014 campaign to get people to shift to EFT from credit card giving. They sent email, snail mail and posted the instructions for switching on their website. Over 7,000 visitors to the webpage, as well as 150 email recipients, changed their giving from credit card to EFT, bringing in nearly a million and a half more dollars. Coulson says Greater Public, in addition to helping stations with direct mail scripts, also helps stations with ready to download, email campaigns that can match the format of any public radio station.

Although direct mail, email and text messaging are not face-to-face mediums, they have been around longer than social media, algorithm directed apps and players. Thus, people are a little more comfortable with them. But at her *People Communicating* blog, management and IT consultant Imelda Bickham says of inter-personal ways of communicating, "Face to face communicating still remains the best and most complete way of getting our message across." ☎

New Tricks

"Digitization is certainly challenging the old ways of doing things, whether that's in publishing or politics. But it's not the end. In many ways, it is just the beginning."

—Heather Brooke

People can misconstrue each other because human-to-human communication is messy. But old school methods can lend them-selves to fewer mistakes because at least the connection is direct. Technology, though it's great at sorting facts isn't all that great conveying emotion. It's an improvement for stations in that it collects a lot of personal information that in simpler times stayed personal. But as budgets and staff are stretched by increasing de-mand, stations are more reliant on ways that speed up interaction without necessarily improving it. It makes some ask whether the purpose of ubiquitous algorithms is to connect with the audience or merely sort and track them. Stations say the new platforms let them do both personally and technologically. And the new generation of methods are a reminder that times have indeed changed. They include:

Websites - Websites are the oldest new trick stations have to
keep you connected to their content. But web 2.0 has moved them
far beyond email, text messaging and static webpages of the 1990s.
Station websites collect lots of personal and anonymous information. It's used internally to improve communication between
members and non-members, and shared with networks to help
them better understand how listeners are consuming network content. When visiting the "Contact Us" page on the NPR website, for
example, if a user entered their zip code, the call sign of the station
it assumes they're listening to pops up. And, with improved targeting, your station appears automatically along with a box asking if
the information you're seeking can be shared with the local station.
This "opt-in" lets the network share your consumption habits. But
in other cases, websites may collect your computer's IP address or
browsing history, for example, in ways from which visitors may
not be able to "opt-out." These data points are used to hone the station's ability to not only identify you and your behavior, but target
fundraising appeals. With all of the other avenues available however, are websites still important to pledge drives?

Gordon Bayliss, vice president of sales and marketing at
WNED/WBFO in Western New York and Southern Ontario suggests website utility is high for stations recognizing that their audience is online. He says it can help underwriters reach them with a
well-managed web presence. Stephanie Theisen, writing for commercial broadcaster Leighton in 2016, says advertisers (and public
radio's "underwriters") benefit from what she calls "listener/
reader/viewer" base that media websites offer. Because of their
multi-functionality, Theisen says, "Display banners on a media
website are far and away a better investment than display banners
on non-media websites." For stations with a desire for a large
Internet presence, but no ability to maintain it, Heather Mansfield,
writing for Greater Public in 2015, says stations should focus on
their websites. Then, if they are able, focus on one or at the most,

451

two social media platforms. For smaller stations, Mansfield says the benefit of a small social media presence is outweighed by that of a well-managed web page.

In 2014, Nicole Leinbach-Revhle told *Forbes* that websites help convey a good first impression about a company, and let people better browse said company's merch. But she also said that while having no website was bad, having a bad website was worse. "If you can't proudly promote the website you have currently live and available for the world to see online, take it down," she said. With new social media platforms saying "Hello World" every day, will websites continue being important? Carol Gauger, an executive with Hertz Rentals, told LinkedIn in 2017 why social media will never find the success of the plain old website. For one, she says customers will go to a company website for information about a business. Although websites may need to adapt to changing technology, a web page is going to be the starting point in any relationship between customers and the goods they seek. "The media has a historical obsession with predicting the end of various technologies," she says, "but ultimately, websites are no different than movie theaters and newspapers. Social media will never destroy the need for autonomous business websites."

Social Media - In 2017, content marketing and social media company Dreamglow examined social media use. It said over two billion people used Facebook (and its messaging app, Whatsapp) each month. Three-quarters of that number use YouTube. About half of YouTube users were on Instagram (also owned by Facebook). Less than half of Instagram users use Twitter. Barely a third of Twitter users use Google+ or LinkedIn. Nearly half a dozen other platforms, including Kik, Periscope, Meerkat and Foursquare weren't even on the list. In October 2018, Google announced it was shutting down its consumer version of Google+ and shifting its use to enterprise only.

Meanwhile, public radio's loudest praise for social media is during political coverage. NPR hailed Facebook during the first 2016 presidential debate as proof that traditional and digital users were finding both the platform and its content invaluable. Reaching the audience in this way, with enhanced social media, has become the new normal. But some stations can afford neither budget nor staff for a beefed up social media presence. Considering the trends, that can be a disadvantage.

Heather Mansfield said in 2013 that two out of every three stations were trying to implement their own social media, but of those stations, "less than 2% invested more than 21 hours a week." And assigning the job as a "collateral duty" is a bad idea. That's why she says it's essential for stations to have a media manager overseeing the effort since social media's demands can be significant. Mansfield says if stations have a blog, the writing, responding, and researching alone can take a minimum of four hours each week. She says Facebook, Twitter, Google+ and LinkedIn, if thoughtfully done, each require no less than four more hours a week. Stations using Facebook, for example, need to provide users several updates a day since the site ranks postings according to content and when posted. She said Instagram, Pinterest and Tumblr each add three more hours a week.

Understanding what draws users to a station's social media platform is not nearly as simple as just launching one. Planning grids, similar to editorial calendars in print publishing, may be necessary for development and marketing people to map out which media is capable of what, and by when. Campaigns are built around spreading the 'give' message to as many listeners and as far in advance of a drive as possible. But not overextending a presence to the point that it can't be maintained in all of its many places is critical. Facebook adding a "Donate Now" button to the pages of non-profits in 2015, was a gift to public radio stations looking to monetize their presence on the platform, but only partially so. The button isn't connected to any pay infrastructure but sends the clicker to a station's pledge form page.

As Facebook's VP of Project Management told Patricio Robles for *Ecoconsultancy* in 2015, "Fundraisers are dedicated pages that allow non-profits to 'tell their campaign story, rally supporters, collect donations and visibly track progress toward a goal for year-end drives, themed campaigns and special projects such as building a clean water well or funding a clothing drive.'"

As with Facebook, Mansfield says of Twitter use to remember to engage with users on Saturdays and Sundays rather than during the week, since that's when people use it most. From focusing on the storytelling to making sure your screen fits attractively on whatever device it sees, Mansfield advises stations to pay close attention to what they look like on whatever social media they're using. "Facebook pages should be your first priority and entry into social networking. But to stand out from the other 50 million pages regularly active and all vying for likes, comments, and shares, you must excel at Facebook." And Jess Horiwitz, from Minnesota Public Radio advises stations to keep a positive online presence and not feed trolls by responding in kind to their comments.

Mansfield lays out some basic best practices across platforms. Focus on well-designed avatars, upload photos rather than links, and use a platform's buttons generously in email and on station websites. Instagram users, says Mansfield, demands "graphic design skills necessary to embed text and graphics upon images." Consumer users of Google+ learned in October, 2018, that another of its social media experiments was ending. But for enterprise users, she says to post at least every other day and experiment with animated GIFs, which she says are making a comeback. Public media consultant Kim Grehn says, "the best time to post to LinkedIn is Tuesday through Thursday during working hours. Nobody is checking LinkedIn on a Friday." Tumblr, says NPR's Tumblr intern Sara Peralta, encourages users to, "Be gentle when others make mistakes and be generous when others shine. Be determined to be gracious."

Social media's ability to influence giving was documented in the 2006 book, *The Science of Giving*. David M. Oppenheimer and Christopher Y. Olivola examined the connection between how much a donor gave to how big they said their social network was. Nearly 600 people who called to donate to their local station's pledge drive were randomly selected by the researchers at the anonymous station. About two-thirds of the callers were asked about the size of their social network before they gave. The remaining third were asked at the end of the call. Not surprisingly, people who were asked before they gave were larger givers while people who weren't asked until later were smaller givers. But in a twist, the researchers discovered that those asked beforehand said their social network was nearly seven times larger (20:3) than those asked afterwards. Although Oppenheimer and Olivola didn't speculate on the result, it mirrors political polling data that suggests people tend to give an answer they think the researcher wants to hear that reflects positively on them. And in this case, more is better. Those answering at the end of the call may have been more truthful because they had already fulfilled the purpose of their call and had nothing to prove or lose. The researchers suggest that for stations wanting to increase contributions, they selectively "manipulate" callers in this way to extract maximum contributions.

Apps/Players - Facebook Live is an example of a streaming player/app crossover that's embedded in a social media platform. Its content, which pops up as an autoplay, is sometimes criticized as one of the ways the company assimilates the journalism of other "legitimate" news organizations and redistributes it as Facebook content. Considering four out of every ten Americans use Facebook as their go-to media source for everything, the takeover may well be complete. *Inside Radio,* when discussing the 2016 release of the tool, says that even as the feature expands the competition of voices, revenue opportunities may be possible but not completely clear. "Radio stations need to proceed carefully," says the article, "with advertiser involvement in their Live Audio streams, however, as the social media network has restrictions for sponsored and branded content on its platforms, including live video." NPR deployed it several times a day with movie reviews, discussions of the film industry and a page "devoted entirely to live video." News staff are encouraged to remember it during breaking news, but the transition has been bumpy. And yet, there was a time the network didn't give that much love to streamed, digital video. It may get even less in the future. The platform was implicated as a purveyor of fake news from Russian bots during the 2016 presidential election. In response, Facebook will focus more on person-to-person contacts within groups and less content from outside sources including NPR.

My survey found that only 7% of stations do not deliver content through any kind of app. By contrast, nearly 61% of single stations deployed their own app, and 25% of stations shared an app through their group of stations or used something like TuneIn, Stitcher or NPR One. A review of pledge breaks from 37 public radio stations showed that pitchers rarely if ever mentioned a station's app during a pitch break. It suggests that the option isn't yet fixed in the minds of pitchers as securely as phone numbers and websites.

NPR is working to change that. In 2017, it launched a pilot program in four U.S. cities and the United Kingdom that will let listeners donate directly to the network through NPR One. Depending on the rollout's success, the network will expand the program to other cities. But given the historical tension around raising funds directly from listeners, NPR's Chief Digital Officer Thomas

Hjelm legitimately calls the sell job to those stations, "a great deal of heavy lifting." Apps and players, whether germane to stations or networks, are designed with the utmost simplicity. Their effectiveness is an increasingly frequent question for stations as the number of apps, players and the content they distribute keeps growing.

Paywalls - For some, this is the epitome of a subscription in exchange for content. And though public radio hasn't gotten there yet, podcast platforms like Scandinavian based Acast, have been moving in that direction for years. In 2016, Steven Perlberg, writing for the *Wall Street Journal*, reported on Acast's upgraded subscription service as well that of Midroll Media. For $4.99, Midroll gives users access to podcasters like Marc Maron's *WTF.* The success of Maron and others led to a wave of producers and flooding the Internet, lured by the promise of big bucks. But Perlberg says potential revenue for the podcast market is limited because "many podcast ads are from direct-response marketers who promote coupon codes and are more easily able to track their return on investment than large brand marketers."

Amazon-owned Audible is also experimenting with an HBO-like offering of shorter content for a subscription fee. Dozens of mainstream newspapers like the *New York Times*, the *Guardian of London* and the *Columbus Dispatch* erected paywalls, requiring readers to subscribe before getting access to the main paper. *Current,* public media's own publication, asks for support donations like many public radio stations. Its American University parent gets the tax benefit. And contributors who gave $2,500 to beyond $50,000 got a tax deduction. But in February 2016, *Current* told readers they would soon have to subscribe to its content. By May 2017, the publication had begun testing its "Wallit" paywall. In July, the green (now blue) curtain had come down, leaving mostly grayed-out content after a threshold of free articles had been crossed.

And by November 2017, an updated presentation with distinct giving levels, was firmly in place. ☎

Freeriders & Moral Hazard

"Social scientists of all ilks have examined why individuals make charitable contributions and voluntarily provide public goods."

—Rachel Croson and Jen Shang

In 2003, Denise Ceretta opened a pay what you want community kitchen in Salt Lake City, Utah that fed gourmet meals to people who didn't have money. One World Everybody Eats has since expanded to 70 kitchens and garnered Ms. Ceretta a coveted James Beard award. In 2008, the band Radiohead debuted its double-Grammy award winning album, *In Rainbows* by giving it away for free on the Internet. And in 2016, some residents of the Dutch city of Utrecht became part of a social experiment where they received money for no work to see how they would use it to live their highest, best purpose. These examples of a good provided for free represent a model public radio lives with but has never been able to afford. Fortunately, surveys consistently show that most public radio stations enjoy pledge fulfillment rates of 85% or higher. However, only about one out of every ten people listening give. To fight such low numbers for such high rates of what it considers as stealing, public radio deploys the big guns: guilt and shame.

When talking about guilt and shame in the context of pledge drives, it's important to first define free riding and moral hazard. Free riding is exactly what it sounds like, which is enjoying the benefit of something without paying for it. Moral hazard is what victims of free riders suffer from. It means exposing oneself to the chance that bad things can happen while trying to do good. Public radio, by being available to all, technically at no cost, encourages free riders. Ideally, thieves suffer remorse. But just in case they don't, public radio has learned how to leverage guilt and shame with the deft of a Sicilian mother. Guilt is feeling bad knowing you've done something to someone else and you want to make amends. It doesn't define you in the long run. Shame, by contrast, is guilt internalized. It can be painfully eye-opening that, through something done or said, one sees that they have not lived up to their own image of themselves and that they may be no better than that awful thing they did.

The whole idea of "alleviating" the guilt of not contributing to public radio is only an effective strategy if listeners first accept that they have a duty to feel guilty. In the best of all public radio worlds, it comes at the end of a long indoctrination that starts with choosing to listen to the station's content. Then, by buying into any one of the more than half-dozen or so core justifications to support the station based on that choice to listen. Findings indicate that fundraising appeals have at least three dimensions: altruism/self-interest ("Pay your gift forward for those who can't" or "Look at what public radio does for you."), rational/emotional ("You become a more informed citizen." or "This is news you care about."), and reinforcement/trigger ("You can feel superior knowing you support public radio." or "Pick up the phone and call now."). Then, accepting that goods and services absorbed must be paid for and not doing so violates a social and moral code. Wisconsin Public Radio pitcher Caryl Owen said, during a Spring 2016 pitch break, "Anybody can listen, but it takes a special person to be a listener-supporter, a listener-contributor, a listener-member to Wisconsin Public Radio," she said. "Members make what we do possible."

And finally, by refusing to honor that code, comes an unspoken indictment as a "passive listener" rather than an "active sustainer." Writing for *Chron* in 2012, Robert Zaretsky, a listener to Houston's KUHF, broke this dynamic down. "When I listen to commercial radio, a contract of sorts is implied: I can choose to listen to the ads or I can switch stations. Nowhere in the contract though, is there an obligation to buy a mattress in order to support the station. Yet, with public radio, the contract is rewritten." Zaretsky continues, "As with commercial radio, I can either switch stations or listen to the interminable list of KUHF underwriters. Of course, there is no moral obligation to use the services of these underwriters. But there seems to be an implicit obligation for the listener to join their ranks." Zaretsky concludes that those who keep listening without contributing are, by association, freeloaders.

In his 2015 book, *Seducing Strangers*, Mad Men show runner Josh Weltman writes, "The job of any good persuader is figuring out what people want and what motivates them to make the choices they make. In other words," he says, "finding whatever urge that lies within and poking it to wake it up." Thing is, the urge to give is in some people, but the urge to not give exists just as firmly within others. The obligation to recognize public radio's *Quid pro quo* however, is the basis upon which everything else in the pledge drive is built. During KNPR Las Vegas' spring 2016 pledge drive, a pre-recorded listener comment explained the guilt she felt for years of listening without contributing. "It's wonderful because now, when the pledge drive starts, I don't (pause) have that feeling of guilt." She concludes, "Wouldn't it be great to join me as a member and get rid of that guilt?" The co-pitchers followed up with, "Alright, we admit it, you can get rid of the guilt when you make a pledge. If you're reached that critical mass of guilt, you can let it all out." Stations seem to be saying, "First, we make you aware of the pain you should feel by not donating. But hey, now that you feel it, we can also help you make it go away."

Guilt is not the whole story, however. Shame also plays a role in getting people to give by focusing on how they appear to others. Psychoanalyst Carl Jung called shame, "A soul-eating emotion" which stations leverage. Guilt requires one to be able to see a wrong of theirs as a wrong. But shame, a recognition either in ourselves or by those around us that we didn't meet our own ideals or standards, can be much more powerful. Public radio is intensely interested in shame. New Hampshire Public Radio's *Word of Mouth* program from 2015 featured an episode called, "The Shame Show" where it looked at everything from Internet trolls to the degradation of women to "perp" walks. In 2016, Anne Strainchamps and Steve Paulson examined shame on an episode of Wisconsin Public Radio's *To the Best of Our Knowledge*, which asked if there was a re-birth of public shaming. And *Mortified*, a podcast from PRX, regularly focuses on whipping up extraordinary stories of shame from ordinary people. *USA Today* called it "Funny and horrifying." Research shows that if people know other people are giving, they are more likely to give, partly out of a desire of association, and partly to not be the one not giving. But when people are called out, are they more likely to do anything to avoid not being seen as at least as good as everybody else? A 2008 blog post on MPR's *Newscuts* described how the Minnesota Department of Revenue collected over $100,000 owed it by naming the delinquents. The entry was titled *Shame Works*. So, since shame is all about making someone feel the pain of public eyes on their real rather than their desired self, has public radio ever weaponized it to get people to give?

Oh yeah.

In her book, *Is Shame Necessary: New Uses for an Old Tool*, Jennifer Jacquet described a specially produced *This American Life* for the 2011 pledge drive season. Shame, or "lack of honor," was what made *TAL* creator Ira Glass ask listeners to "turn in their friends, family and loved ones who listen a lot to public radio, but have never pledged any money." And after getting some of those names, Glass called them on-air to ask them why they hadn't contributed. June Thomas highlights earlier versions of the calls in her 2009 Slate article, *Let's Get Those Phones Ringing*. She described this technique as one "Only a secret policeman could love." "As someone who grew up with the scary ads for the BBC's TV-license detector vans, I find these spots thoroughly creepy," she said, "though I'll concede that they're memorable and almost certainly effective."

Steve Friess, a Knight-Wallace Fellowship recipient, blogged about the technique in 2008. "I do wonder, though, how a non-giver would actually react to such an admonition. These pledge appeals don't ordinarily wander into blatant 'You're a BAD person if you don't give' territory. They just encourage giving by positive reinforcement and, yes, some carefully worded guilt. This went beyond that motif into shaming people." But some in public radio like it when non-givers squirm in the broth of guilt and shame. Carol Gentry, of Florida-based WUSF, said in a 2011 station blog post, "I actually enjoy it when they bring on Ira Glass of *This American Life*." She says, "He knows how to make listeners who never donate feel guilty."

When staff at stations have had enough of the whole moral hazard thing, frustration can push itself out through their pores and into their production values. "Basically, by listening, they're costing us money," says Lamar Marchese, the president and general manager of KNPR and KCNV in Las Vegas." "They ought to be ashamed," said his then Development Director, Melanie Coulson. "They've got us tuned to No. 1 or No. 2 on their radio dial, and they're letting grandma on a fixed income make three pledges for them." In an April 15, 2016 pitch break, a pitcher for Paonia, Colorado's KVNF said, "We're not upset that you haven't been a member up to this point," which not only implies that getting upset is a possibility, but that their patience has a limit. What would crossing that limit sound like?

Maybe, it would sound like a promo aired during a spring 2016 pledge drive for Montana based KGLT. The station aired a Mr. Rogers sound-alike talking up the moral benefit of giving while delivering a slap across the face of moochers. "Did you know KGLT is having its annual fund drive?," the promo begins. "Did you know that? Did you know they have to raise some money? Sure. Sure. Have you called in with your pledge? No? You haven't called?" "Well," it concludes, "we have a new word for you today. Can you spell 'freeloader?' Can you spell that? Freeloader. Sure." Stations argue that pushing the envelope, especially during pledge drives is something all listeners understand as "funny." KGLT general manager Ellen King-Rogers, in responding to a question that asked if such pushing is comedic or condescending, replied, "That is said in jest. The fund drive promos are funny and people enjoy them. It is done with love and good humor."

Setting aside the emotional component and looking at public radio consumption as strictly cost-versus-benefit, why would anyone pay for something that they could get for free? That's a question three researchers, writing in *Information Technology for Economics and Management* at the University of Arizona tried to answer in 2005. They used previous research and computer modeling to identify types of givers, factors determining whether a giver gives and eight motivations of givers. Each one's willingness to give was measured through combinations of all factors. In other words, complicated. But the model was close enough to real life that it could essentially be a "Predict the Success of your Pledge Drive" How-To. And after a lot of lever pulling, the study concluded that for drives to be successful, stations must "manipulate" elements like time, rewards, goals and surprise, guilt. ☎

Interns, Volunteers & Temps

*"We have pointed to the seemingly basic logic that volunteers are,
by their very nature, not workers. But this is unlikely to be the end
of the story."*

—Vince Scopelliti, CEO & Managing Director, LKA Group Pty Ltd.

Interns and volunteers sign what are essentially code of conduct agreements before coming to work for public or community
radio. Prairie Public Broadcasting in Fargo, North Dakota makes
volunteers acknowledge that they will be exposed to privileged information like station operations and possibly, contact and financial
information of donors. It describes that information as confidential,
and then defines confidential as meaning if it was learned in the
course of the work, it cannot be disclosed. Disclosure results in
termination.

Minnesota Public Radio's confidentiality agreement consists
of two parts. One that makes volunteers accept, with their signature, being subject to temporary restraining orders and preliminary
injunctions if they disclose any of MPR's confidential information. The other lists in detail general behaviors, including expectations of the station when representing the station, distributing
promotional material, attendance at scheduled events and attitude.
And MPR's agreement is enforceable in perpetuity. Though not
full-time employees, stations entrust volunteers and interns with
the privilege of entry and access, so it's only reasonable that they
expect them to behave. Consequently, this makes volunteers think
about contributors a lot more than contributors probably think
about volunteers.

So, other than hearing them occasionally mentioned during a
pledge drive, or having infrequent interactions with them on the
phone when pledging, why should listeners care about station

volunteers? Because how an organization treats its low-paid or un-paid is a reflection of its character. Volunteers of America has high expectations of its volunteers, but it conveys much responsibility and respect on them in return. And as they come from the community, if volunteers feel disrespected, that can trickle down to the community as a whole, with negative consequences. Jennifer Fray, reporting for the *Washington Post* in 2004, said that for a time, Washington DC-based WAMU contracted phone workers during pledge drives to a Texas company, leaving long-time volunteers, as Fray described it, "out in the cold."

Around the same time, former interns and volunteers were protesting the station for what they said were improprieties in the station's budget based on a questionable relationship between it and its university overseer. After American University's president fired the station's executive director, its new ED reached back to its volunteers, calling their exclusion "detrimental to fundraising." "People will give what we ask them to give if they have the means and if they feel involved," said Walt Gillette, WAMU's director of individual giving. "And that's what we're trying to do now, is rebuild the trust." Glenn Ihrig, a 30-year fundraising volunteer at WAMU said after the fight at the station settled into calmer times, "We were upset and concerned. By the same token, we gave our opinions and obviously we've been heard."

Writing for Greater Public in 2015, Stephanie Bergsma tells stations to "communicate with volunteers often and make them feel like insiders." That can be good advice since a sense of investment may be one of the few perks volunteers get. But whereas WAMU's volunteers essentially "saved" their station, stations that rely too heavily on volunteers risk giving them an outsized sense of power. And that can lead to struggles between staff who need them but must manage them, and volunteers who know their strength while feeling less obligation to follow state and federal rules that staff must follow. This is a particular problem for community radio. Community station KBOO in Portland, Oregon for example, has ten full-time staff and 400 volunteers. Those volunteers produce and host almost all of the station's approximately 117 separate news, music, entertainment and public affairs programs.

In 2012, the normally laid-back station was rocked by new policies, recommended by a law firm, that all employees be fired as part of a re-structuring. They could later re-apply for their jobs. Volunteers had to adhere to rules establishing basic professionalism and conduct. In response, "Some show hosts told us, 'F-you'," said Lynn Fitch, KBOO station manager from 2012 to 2013. "We aren't participating in the pledge drive because we don't want to," she was told. They didn't want to, said Fitch because programmers, some of whom had held show times on the checkerboard schedule for decades, believed they also held a special status and didn't want any intrusions on their autonomy. "Some of the shows were terrible, with maybe three listeners," she said.

Programmers pushed back, saying the station's free-form serves the under-voiced and audience size shouldn't matter as much as artistic free expression. "But," says Fitch, "KBOO costs $90 an hour to run. That doesn't sound like a lot, but it adds up for a community station." So, as a way to raise revenue, and bring more order to the programming schedule, Fitch tried to establish rules for shows, including mandatory participation in pledge drives. After less than a year of tumult, she left. The story, and a similar one at community station WJFF in Jeffersonville, NY illustrates the problems stations can have with volunteers. At WJFF, the controversy revolved around a popular program that was removed after a volunteer host used an expletive on-air. Likewise, KBOO was assessed a heavy fine (later rescinded by the FCC) when in 2000, a volunteer played a song with a string of expletives and sexual depictions. Pacifica, the flagship for community radio, has also had its problems with volunteers. As Matthew Lasar said of the network's volunteers in a 2015 piece for *The Nation*, they can be notoriously "difficult-to-supervise."

Though these sound like community station problems, other stations can suffer them too. While non-professionals take pressure off the station's bottom line, a lack of training can lead to problems that can scare stations. Like when, as reported in Swarthmore College's *The Fix,* in November 2017, student host Brandon Albrecht was yanked off University of Minnesota station KUMM after using the word, "tranny." The student station manager said Albrecht had violated FCC rules with his use of the word and removed him while live. The university board later said that although Albrecht hadn't crossed the FCC's language threshold, it considered his use of the word to be hate speech and accused him of programming violations. I unscientifically surveyed people in and around public radio to learn the ratio of volunteers to staff at their stations. Nearly 40% said they didn't know how many volunteers their station employed. Seven percent said their stations didn't use them. Of the rest, 25% knew there were more than three times as many volunteers as staff. Ten percent knew there were three times as many staff as volunteers. The rest considered the balance about equal.

It's important to note that certain classes of interns and volunteers can afford to give their time and energy to their internship or volunteer experience. Bergsma talks of stations that encourage donors to become volunteers, who in turn, solicit their monied peers to do the same. She herself is a major giver. "I even recruited one of my friends to join me on an advisory board and she immediately matched my $2,500 gift. Now, we have agreed to underwrite a table at a fundraising event together with a contribution of $7,500. She and her husband are contributing $5,000 to be on the honorary committee of the event I am chairing.

Another friend is also contributing $5,000 to that event in addition to matching our gift to KPBS to support a reporting fund." This is truly a manna-packed nirvana for stations; volunteers that can not only afford to work but can afford to give while bringing other workers and givers with them.

JoAnn Fritz, writing for the personal finance website, *The Balance* in 2016, references two studies that strongly advocate for nonprofits treating volunteers like donors. *"The volunteer experience a nonprofit offers is more important than one might think,"* she says. A study by Fidelity Investment showed that slightly more donors gave first before deciding to become volunteers. And about 45% of those gave 50 hours or more a year to the cause of their choice. The other study, by the Corporation for National and Community Service, found that in 2015, 75% of Americans volunteered for some organization. Their contributions, whether skilled or unskilled, contributed 7.8 billion hours and $184 billion to the non-profit community, including public radio. That, by the way, pencils out to about $24 an hour, or more than three times the current federal minimum wage. Though younger people volunteered more frequently, older volunteers gave more time. Working mothers and parents with children had the highest volunteer rates overall. A follow-up study, called *Volunteering and Civic Life in America* found that volunteers were likely to give to their charity twice as much as people who didn't volunteer. As Fritz concludes, *"What a bargain! Most volunteers actually pay charities to volunteer by giving back. Some savvy nonprofits even place their volunteer coordinator within the development department."*

But there is another class of radio volunteers not so well off. They may be looking for work. They may hope a volunteer gig at a radio station gets them a foot in the broadcasting door. But in the meantime, they're trying find transportation and health care. And overall, they have a story to tell and believe volunteering at the local station, with its regular call for help, might give them their shot to tell it. Commenter Hypatia addresses the pluses and minuses of volunteers who may be in this situation. On *Metafilter* in October 2016, she replied to a station manager dealing with a difficult volunteer who was possibly suffering from deeper problems. *"If you are meant to provide opportunities for people to produce radio, then a volunteer who makes it impossible for other people to produce radio is in conflict with your mission."* Commenter stormgrey agrees. *"The best way to handle this IMO is to manage volunteers like employees and have very clear expectations and job descriptions. This makes their performance easier to manage and even describe. So it's not, 'you are difficult' it['s] that 'you aren't meeting expectations.'"*

Ultimately, stations must be responsible for who they let in the door, but advocates for volunteering like Melody Kramer strongly believe service needs to be part of the contribution community members can make to their stations. As a Knight visiting Neiman Fellow in 2012, Kramer shook up public radio land with her central thesis, *"a new model of membership within public media that will complement already-existing forms by offering membership to people who may not be able to donate financially, but would like to donate a skill or their time to their local stations."* She encourages stations to let people give generously of both which, she says, can represent a huge cash savings. For public radio stations that have been cash centric ever since the Nixon administration, this represents radically new thinking. *"My goals for the project,"* says Kramer, *"are to see whether people who contribute code, time, or a skill to a station feel more invested in the station's future — and derive benefit from the experience themselves."* That part, whether the experience is personally beneficial, manifests itself in ways that have been of keen interest, both to the news business and the courts. This interest has extended not just to volunteers, but interns as well.

Andrew Lapin, writing for *Current* in 2013 said, *"Recruitment of interns for little or no compensation is commonplace in public media, an institution composed of mainly community-based non-profits that have long relied on volunteers."* Ironically, public radio is constantly under fire for what some accuse as having outsized compensation for its executives. Lapin says, *"Nearly every station, production company and distributor in the system has some form of an internship program that's designed to offer training and experience, but not necessarily pay."* The problems public radio has experienced with volunteers and interns are the same throughout the non-profit and for-profit worlds. NBCUniversal, ClearChannel (now iHeartRadio), Conde' Nast, SiriusXM and Viacom have all found themselves punished by federal rules they either didn't know or ignored. Meanwhile interns, with the help of serious legal muscle, have led the charge against some of the largest institutions in the country to be properly trained and adequately paid for time they've given in exchange. New York based law firm Outten and Golden, LLP, in explaining the provisions of a possible class action on behalf of interns explains, *"Unpaid interns are becoming the modern-day equivalent of entry-level employees, except that employers are not paying them for the many hours they work."* The firm says employers are classifying employees as interns to avoid paying wages, to their peril.

In 2014, New York Mayor Bill DeBlasio gave unpaid interns working for the city the right to sue and filled a hole in the city's civil code. Before then, interns could be fired even if they'd been harassed or discriminated against. Previous suits were thrown out because since interns weren't paid, they weren't employees and therefore, didn't have *"standing"* to bring such a case to the courts. DeBlasio widened the definition of the law. Broadcasting and media interns seem especially fearless, with interns for Fox Searchlight pictures and *Gawker* suing each in 2011 and 2013, respectively. *Gawker* interns sued for the insult of not being paid. Fox Pictures interns sued for the injury inflicted by the company in the form of menial jobs, like making coffee or mopping floors, that were completely unrelated to the professions they pursued. According to Alex Footman, one of two plaintiffs in the lawsuit, "The only thing I learned on this internship was to be more picky in choosing employment opportunities."

After several high-profile incidents, some potential interns for public radio may be thinking the same thing. In 2013, three interns for the American Public Media program *Performance Today* were told their positions would revert from paid to unpaid, effective immediately. Though APM also cut three staff positions, it didn't immediately release the interns. After their time was up, APM did readvertise its search. And this time, it specifically sought unpaid "volunteer" interns. A year earlier, then (now former) PBS property, *The Charlie Rose Show*, was forced to pay a quarter-million dollars in a settlement with show interns that stretched all the way back to 2007. The plaintiffs, including lead plaintiff Lucy Bickerton, received back payment representing intern wages at $110 a week during summer internships stretching over several consecutive years on the show. All told, her salary nearly equaled the federal minimum wage. The next year, PBS began paying all of its interns working all of its programs, whether the work occurred in spring, summer or fall. Before 2012, both PBS and NPR only paid interns who volunteered in the summer months.

Though the six federal guidelines for what qualifies as paid versus unpaid internships are clear, some stations follow them in letter but not in spirit. Until 2016, for instance, public radio flagship WNYC did pay those it accepted into its intern program. But, says *Nation* reporter Natalie Patillo, the station paid them

$12 a day. The station said the $12 a day stipend was for travel to the station from wherever in the metropolitan area the intern may have been staying during the internship. Ryan Kailath, a full-time intern at the station was able to network himself into a job reporting for WWNO in New Orleans. But he brought with him a full scholarship from CUNY and enough of a savings to carry him through a summer. Other intern wannabes can afford to pay search firms thousands of dollars to find them plum internships. Christine Trudeau, another WNYC internship *"winner"* wasn't so lucky. Although she tried to negotiate with the station to supplement her income, Patillo said, *"eventually she was forced to decline the of-fer because she couldn't survive on the $12-per-day stipend."* But that wasn't the end of the story. Former interns uploaded a petition to Change.org, where they expressed their love for the station but said the travel stipend excluded potentially great people from ever getting the chance to work for WNYC. Coincidentally, it was seen by WNYC alum and producer Alex Goldman, who took the station and all of public radio to task. "There is always talk about how public radio wants to represent a diversity of voices, and there's no doubt that its producers are talented, but this hurdle to entry shuts many voices out of the conversation. Paying your interns will make the content WNYC `produces, and the experience of working at the organization, much richer." Gradually, the public grew aware of how little interns were paid. By fiscal year 2017, WNYC promised to began actually paying its interns.

Christina Couch, writing for *Get in Media*, a blog of Full Sail University, reports that *This American Life* hires two interns each year. Among the perks is one-on-one lunches with each of its award-winning producers. Production manager Emily Condon talks of the benefit interns get. "We have things like cutting exercises that [interns] do, which are exercises that we've created where they're really learning a lot about hands-on cutting audio." Condon says interns, Master Class style, sit with either Ira Glass or *TAL*'s executive producer and, "talk about what worked and what didn't [with audio edits] and why." Despite the possibilities of face time with public radio royalty, and Condon recommending up front to those seeking a *TAL* internship apply for paid ones first, the reputation of spotty internships persists. A casual scan of dozens of public radio websites show many of them offer unpaid, volunteer-type internships. And in light of the problems public media has had, many of them work to distinguish themselves from the bad old days by spelling out duties and highlighting opportunities. That effort by the industry to turn the page is epitomized by Miami's WLRN, which said of its own internship program on its Facebook page, "These are not coffee making internships."

Interns and volunteers have fought bad treatment because in some ways, they're freer to stand up for themselves than temporary workers. Temp workers have no guarantee they'll be hired for full time work. James Essey, the president and chief executive of The TemPositions Group of Companies, a large New York-based staffing firm, told *Forbes* in 2012 that he's seen nearly 70% of temp jobs turn full time. But that didn't happen for Julia Botero. She was highlighted in Paul Farhi's December 2018 *Washington Post* story on the plight of temporary employees at NPR. She told him that at the end of each temporary contract, she had to persuade her manager to re-hire her until it became exhausting. She left and went to work for an affiliate station.

Because temporary workers may have to follow strict codes of conduct imposed by both the temporary agency that referred them and the company for which they work, they may be in constant fear of ruffling a feather or breaking a rule. Low salaries, inconsistent schedules and "collateral duties as assigned" force temp workers, as Farhi described, to "face a workplace of anxiety and insecurity." He said that between 16% and 22% of NPR's 483 news employees are temporary workers. After years of what they felt as unfair treatment, Farhi says their frustration peaked in the last half of 2017 with allegations of sexual harassment by since departed news chief Michael Oreskes. Other complaints coagulated into an internal, May 2018 report. Although a month earlier, management agreed to move 26 temps who had been there at least a year to permanent jobs; 70 temps remain temps.

Every business wants to get as much as it can out of its workers at the lowest per unit cost. NPR is a business. So it shouldn't be surprising that during 2017 labor negotiations, it tried to cut overtime pay and health benefits for temporary workers and institute a two-tiered pay system. #WeMakeNPR, fired into every social media platform like a signal flare, was the staff response. SAG-AFTRA defended the staff, but unions don't always support non-union workers. In 2014, the Vermont state employees union complained that the Governor's office was using too many temps. VSEA's Michelle Salvador, said that temporary workers, "have become stand-ins for positions formerly held by fulltime government employees," thus cutting union strength. The union lobbied the legislature to limit the number of private contracts the state can implement as well as the hours temps can work in a year to about 20 hours per week.

Interns, volunteers and temps publicly struggling to survive can get an organization thinking about its image. David Giovanonni's research found that public radio listeners are also moral creatures. Since about one in ten of them donate to public radio, how might they react to what Mr. Farhi had to say? A casual review of the thirteen hundred comments that followed Farhi's story showed that about one in eight defended NPR in particular or public radio in general. Some argued that the network must save money and temporary workers let it do that. Others spoke up solely for the quality of the programs, thus avoiding the stickier ethics problems. Problems, that Bob Collins of MPR's *Newscuts* blog called, "the sausage making process of public radio." But while only about 4% of listeners were mad enough to stop listening or giving, a whopping 20% scolded the network for its treament of temps and tied it to what they saw as the deteriorating enviroment of the working world at-large.

That larger group also felt that the decline has led to a generally lower quality of public radio. Other respondents addressed related and specific annoyances, like false equivalency bias in stories, over-giggly announcers and diversity fails in hiring and represenation. NPR reporter Sam Sanders said on Twitter that although he applauds the network for facing the mess, "my employer still fails to address some of the systemic issues, like temping, that continue to hurt the org's diversity." One in ten didn't see any employer issues, however. They were self-described realists that told temps that's simply how the world works. "The solution; gain experience and go elsewhere," said commenter Silver Laker 2. They and others pointed out that temporary workers, getting a salary significantly above minimum wage, with benefits, skills and career contacts, have little to complain about. And they told temps to take responsibility for themselves and use their time at NPR as a stepping stone to something else.

Meanwhile, the largest block of comments; 33%, were more off-point in that they either devolved into personal attacks, were unrelated to the subject or unclear in what they were trying to say. Several nostalgic mentions of Bob Edwards, for example, were interesting but irrelevant. So were about one half of 1%, who said that public radio and its "liberal" agenda shouldn't be employing anybody since it shouldn't exist. Rounding out the comments were calls for more transparency and financial accountability, stronger unions, the redundancy of public radio in the Internet age, back and forths over salaries, and the hypocrisy of media organizations that throw stones at each other from inside their glass newsrooms.

In 2012, the *Harvard Business Review* declared, "The surprise may be not that top talent is looking for 'permanent temp work' but that anyone who has a choice would want a traditional job." But the world of such work has turned out to be anything but rosy. Career coaches tell workers that they can always complain or ask to be reassigned if they feel unfairly treated, though research shows that can hurt their chances at future work. NPR said it is studying results from that 2018 internal survey. So at least there, the climate is improving, though at a glacial pace. Meanwhile, the WashPo story, along with high profile court fights by interns and volunteers, is plowing the road for non-full time workers in their quest to prove that low cost doesn't mean no value. ☎

Conclusion

"I noticed that it sometimes happens that you start out very mad at something. And in the course of writing it, you then see it as funny and then see it as somehow rather lovable and pathetic at the same time that it's vicious, funny, stupid ..."

—Poet Howard Nemerov talking with Studs Terkel, December 5, 1960, from WFMT's *"Studs Terkel Radio Archive"*

In 2017, author Mark Russell wrote a contemporary version of the Bible called *God is Disappointed in You*. Explaining his treatment of the Christian scriptures to Oregon Public Broadcasting's Dave Miller, Russell said, "I think what people respond to is that it's obviously not an assassination attempt on the Bible" He went on to ask why a writer would write about something if they didn't have some degree of affection for it. That sort of explains one reason why I wanted to write about the public radio pledge drive. Cindy Sheehan is the other. In August 2005, Ms. Sheehan, the mother of U.S. Army Specialist Casey Sheehan, killed in the Iraq War, began a campaign of protest at the George W. Bush family compound in Crawford, Texas. Though she was attacked for her anti-war views by many who considered them anti-American, she eventually made a run for Congress and founded Gold Star Mothers for Peace. Cindy Sheehan is an archetypal example of someone who loves their country but doesn't love some of the things it does. Likewise, I love public radio land. So, as a supporting citizen, I claim the right to protest within its borders. And like some protesters who get tired of writing letters or boycotting products, I decided I wanted to try and stop some traffic.

When I was exposed to my first fund drive in the early '90s, I was undone when I realized the people in my radio wouldn't stop talking no matter what I did. I could turn it off, but my shows also went away. I could try to ignore the prattle, but prattle, like cigarette smoke, gets everywhere until it's impossible to ignore. I could pledge. But my pledge didn't seem noticed at all, despite me being hammered with the message, "Your gift matters." Or I could plot my revenge, a book about how dreadful pledge drives are. I wasn't quite as furious as Sylvia Kronstadt, author of the 2014 public radio screed, *The Beggar Wears Prada*, but I was close. As I wrote, and talked with people, and read, and listened (on purpose) to dozens of pledge drives however, that changed. Over time, I started feeling empathy for a system stuck on a moving sidewalk of history, technology, politics and demographics, with all of it orbiting *Planet Money.*

The wave of change rushing toward the system, in some ways, looks like what Téa Leoni faced in that near final scene of *Deep Impact*. While some are trying to get out of the way, others are standing on that beach with their surfboards. But the other part of the problem is the system coming to a consensus with itself about trust. In 2014, Suzanne Perry wrote in the *Chronicle of Philanthropy* of a meeting Greater Public president Doug Eichten tried to have with station representatives and management at NPR. Perry wrote that Eichten "recalls serving a few times as 'sort of a Jimmy Carter' during talks between NPR and stations on the issue [of fundraising]. He says they spent more time working out the 'rules of engagement' than they did building trust." This is a common problem in public radio.

Though the article mentioned how things seem to be improving, the mistrust that has existed between stations and NPRHQ has been the burnt popcorn smell in the room since the earliest days. The aircraft carrier of public radio turns slowly. But the problem with the pace of its course correction is that it's racing to get young people giving before too many of their parents and grandparents die off. So, while it's morphing before everyone's eyes, the transition seems neither smooth nor pretty. And it reminds me of the sound of *American Werewolf in London* actor David Naughton's bones breaking and reforming as he changes from human to wolf. Public radio's accomplishments, compared to the BBC for example, shows that despite being underfunded, it punches way above its weight while struggling to live up to its own values. It is modernizing, innovating and disrupting at a pace that would be scary if it wasn't so necessary.

And since this has been an examination of the pledge drive, the ephemeral nature of radio itself is the last part of how pledge drives annoy. Unlike letters, email and social media, much of what it says in-between news, music and entertainment shows is forgotten. Listeners recalling something inappropriate or wrong that was casually tossed off by some host, have no way to confirm it. Pledge drives are full of things that pitch guides insist pitchers should never say but things listeners consistently hear. Not all of it is forgotten, however. Comment boards reveal that listeners have long memories for things they didn't like that directly affect what they do today. Staff, stations and networks would take care to remember how smart those smart people in their audience are. They don't like baits and switches. They don't like double-talk or condescension. They don't like feeling taken for granted. As Maya Angelou famously said, "I've learned that people will forget what you said, people will forget what you did, but people will never forget how you made them feel."

PLEDGE: The Public Radio Fund Drive

The bottom line about this book is that it's not just about the pledge drive. It's about how public radio is huge arteries and little capillaries. The big stations are on the trunks. Many people listen to them and so, many people think that public radio is OK because *Fresh Air* is OK, or *All Things Considered* is OK. Or KERA is OK. But the tiny stations on the tips of toes, like the ones up on the Alaskan Frontier, or way out near the Atlantic coast or somewhere in Appalachia, or down in Arizona Indian country; some of those are starving. People should be aware that public radio isn't just about what public radio tells you. It's also about a lot of the stuff public radio would prefer to keep to itself.

Stuff like mistakes and parochialism that waste time and cost big money. Stuff like how corporate cash is eating away at public radio's honor. Stuff like nasty, cross-border, signal stomping, audience slurping family fights that public radio tries to keep quiet behind smiles. Stuff like how public radio seems overly concerned with keeping its hands clean while deep in the dirty work of manipulation, big data and upselling. These are things only talked about in trade journals or at conferences and rarely make it to the *Atlantic* or *Buzzfeed*. Public radio certainly needs your money. Whether it wants to admit it or not, it also needs your oversight and your understanding. But it needs a "get in its face" kind of understanding. Because the imperfect knowledge the listener has of public radio has led to lopsided support, and that is going to kill it dead quicker than any bunch of "starve the beast" conservatives or "limousine" liberals ever could.

In fact, in a "kill to save it" argument, public radio insiders Melody Kramer and Betsy O'Donovan, writing for the Knight Foundation, radically suggest PBS and NPR be spun off to "live or die on their own." The two public radio pros say both entities have had nearly half a century to try to get it right, and both apparently feel each entity has failed. CPB and the values of public broadcasting could be saved they say, by relaunching it as an entirely new unit that focuses exclusively on public broadcasting devoted to children. It's a reversal of arguments from those on the left that public broadcasting is a sacred, unassailable monolith that must remain separate from the evils of the market for the sake of western civilization. And, it's a rattling concession to the views on the right that say it's time for PBS and NPR to see if they can live outside of their protective bubble of public money and tax breaks. As Kramer and O'Donovan say at the start of their piece, "We have to blow this thing up and start again."

In the interim, it's one of the reasons that explains why I, like some other public radio listeners I know have "fallen away" from the faith, so to speak. What about public radio that used to be so representative of me has become less me. The industry measures it in cumes and loyalty. But I simply shift my consumption of news, information and entertainment to other sources I consider more relevant as public radio becomes a less primary and a more supplemental source. Commenting on *Metafilter* in August 2016, "mudpuppie" says "NPR was a good fit for me in my 20s and 30s because it fueled my political idealism. It was a more hopeful new report in a way, because it reported on the really ugly truths in our country from the perspective of 'this thing is shitty, but here is what people are doing to fix it.'" "Now," he says, "the reporting is more along the lines of, 'this thing is shitty, and this is how it's going to get shittier, and here are the reasons why no one can do a damn thing about it.'" I don't know if I'll come back to where I was in terms of public radio consumption. But fortunately for public radio, the youthful energy of the millennial cohort may grow to match the loyalty and passion of their parents and grandparents.

Whether or not they take up the challenge will depend in part on them accepting responsibility for what they want public radio to eventually be. Pubcasters have been doing their best to make their listeners happy. That's why stations, for instance, often careen between trying to create local shows their audience says it wants while struggling to pay for national shows that same audience says it needs. Boomers have always wanted it all, but the generation is pock-marked with examples of how what they say they want vs. what they're willing to accept and commit to hasn't always lined up. Millennials will hopefully have a clearer eye and understand that the system has limits that may be negotiable, but must be respected. That will help public radio perform a little better because it can breathe a little easier.

One evening near the end of the writing of this book, I was watching PBS Newshour. During the closing credits, after the names of supporters had come and gone, there was the final screen identifying the Corporation for Public Broadcasting. I got misty-eyed, and started clapping. I realized that as an American who believes in the vision of the foundations and politicians that gave life to public broadcasting decades ago, I was a little choked up. In learning about what CPB, PBS and NPR have tried to do, I've come to respect their failures, their struggles and their successes. When I can, I give them my time and money. And I, as should we all, continue to watch them like hawks. Why?

Public Law 47 U.S.C. 396 dictates how public radio must handle underwriting. Seven times throughout the 2011 document's subchapter on the CPB is the phrase, "National Public Radio (or any successor organization) ..." It's jarring to think circumstances could ever necessitate a "successor organization" to NPR. Congress however understands that nothing lasts forever. Witness the disappearance of "Air America." Listeners have the power to help public radio (including NPR) last as long as it will, but only if they strive to be an "active" audience, not just "passive" consumers. ☎

Appendix
Public Radio Funding
State-by-State

"Why does one never hear of government funding for the preservation and encouragement of comic strips, girly magazines and TV soap operas? Because these genres still hold the audience they were created to instruct and amuse."

—John Hoyer Updike

In November 2011, author Brian Resnick reported in *The Atlantic* magazine that between 2008 and 2012, many states had restricted or were reducing funding to their public radio stations [https://www.theatlantic.com/national/archive/2011/11/chart-states-squeeze-funding-for-public-media/248518/]. Twenty-four states experienced cuts to their state funding of between 5% and 100%. In 2013, *Current* reported that even as public radio's donor base grew, federal and state support remained flat or fell, respectively [http://current.org/2013/06/gains-losses-spread-unevenly-across-pubcasting-stations/]. While small and middle sized stations suffered a combined drop of nearly 5 million dollars in revenue, large stations saw nearly an 8-million dollar increase. On May 30, 2016, I sent letters to all fifty state legislatures and the District of Columbia requesting information about funding they may provide for public radio. Fourteen legislative representatives responded by letter and 11 responded by email. Their comments are below.

When *Current* began visiting state budgets on a regular basis [https://current.org/state-funding-guide/], its most recent look as of this writing (2018-2019 budget cycles) found six states lost [ND, MS, ID, OR, WV, WY] and four states gained [MN, PA, DE, UT] funding by 10% or more. Seven states got increased funding by 1% to 10% [FL, OK, KY, IA, MD, SD, WI] while two lost [OH, NE] funding by 1% to 10%. Four states have either lost [GA, LA, NC] or gained [AL] approximately 1% or less of state funding while 14 states [AZ, CA, CO, CT, HI, MA, MI, MT, NH, NJ, RI, TX, VA, WA] receive no state funding and 13 states [AK, AR, IL, IN, KS, ME, MO, NV, NM, NY, SC, TN, VT] show no change in funding.

Alabama did not respond to the author's query. *The Atlantic* report showed from 2008 to 2012, the state had cut funding to its public broadcasting stations by more than $5.3 million or between 40% to 99%. Current's most recent analysis shows a .08% increase in funding.

Alaska did not respond to the author's query. The Atlantic report showed no reduction in state support from 2008 to 2012. In 2015, there were widespread reports of deep cuts to Alaska Public Radio including to KSTK, KUAC and KCAW. Current's most recent analysis shows no change in funding.

Arizona did not respond to the author's query. The state does not fund public radio.

Arkansas did not respond to the author's query and did not appear to show any reductions in state funding through Resnick's analysis. Current's most recent analysis shows no change in funding. .

California did not respond to the author's query. The state does not fund public radio.

Colorado did respond to the author's query [Letter dtd July 11, 2016, Joint Budget Committee, State of Colorado]. The state does not fund public radio. Amanda Bickel, Chief Legislative Analyst for the Joint Budget Committee for the Colorado General Assembly told me her staff is not aware of any funding that supports public radio stations in Colorado, i.e., no line item in the budget.

Connecticut did respond to the author's query [Email dtd April 19, 2016, Amanda Zavagnin, Legialative Aide to Connecticut Senator Michael A. McLachlan]. *The Atlantic* report showed no reduction in state support from 2008 to 2012. The Comptroller's Office of the Connecticut Public Broadcast Network received $1 million dollars in bond bill, Grant-in-Aid support from the legislature. But Amanda Zavagnin, aide to Connecticut Senator Michael McLachlan, said this amount was originally proposed to be $3,300,000, but was reduced by the finance committee before approval. Current's analysis shows the state does not fund public radio.

Delaware did respond to the author's query [Email dtd April 7, 2016, Michael Morton, Controller General, State of Delaware]. The Atlantic report showed no reduction in state support from 2008 to 2012. Michael Morton, an aid for Delaware Senator Karen Peterson told me her state provides support to two of the state's six public radio stations; $175,000 to WHYY, which operates out of Pennsylvania, and $5,800 to WSCL, one of the three stations that are part of the Delmarva (Delaware, Maryland and Virginia broadcasting group). Current's most recent analysis shows a 25% increase in state funding.

Florida did not respond to the author's query. The Atlantic report showed from 2008 to 2012, the state had cut funding to its public broadcasting stations by more than $7.8 million or 100%. Current's most recent analysis shows a 1.6% increase in funding.

Georgia did respond to the author's query [Email dtd April 6, 2016, Georgia State Senator John Albers]. *The Atlantic* report showed from 2008 to 2012, the state had cut funding to Georgia Public Broadcasting by $6.3 million or between 20% to 39%. Elizabeth Laparde, the CFO for GPB told Georgia Senator John Alber's office in April that they can't easily say where much of the $14.99 million allocated by the Georgia legislature to GPB's 14 stations goes. But the Senator's office told me that although none of that money can be programmed to go to reporters or radio programming, bond proceeds can be used for infrastructure improvements to towers and transmitters. Current's most recent analysis shows a .3% decrease in funding.

Hawaii did not respond to the author's query. The state does not fund public radio.

Idaho did respond to the author's query [Letter dtd May 4, 2016, Idaho Legislative Service Office, Budget & Policy Analysis, State Capitol]. *The Atlantic* report showed from 2008 to 2012, the state had cut funding to its public broadcasting stations by more than $378 thousand or between 20% to 39%. Chet Herbst, Chief Financial Officer for the Idaho State Board of Education told me that, unlike public television, the State of Idaho, does not provide direct appropriations to public radio. However, indirect support to the 8 public radio stations operated by Boise State University and the one station operated by University of Idaho does come through those institutions from the Idaho legislature. *The Atlantic* report said the state faced threats of multi-year phase outs of all state funding. Current's analysis shows a .22.3% decrease in funding.

Illinois did respond to the author's query [Letter dtd October 11, 2016, State of Illinois, House of Representatives, Michael J. Madigan, Speaker]. *The Atlantic* report showed no reduction in state support from 2008 to 2012. However, Michael Madigan, Speaker of the House for Illinois said the state is facing an "unprecedent-ed budget deficit" which has greatly impacted funding for higher education and thus, the ability to adequately provide state funding for the state's 11 public radio stations. He said only a handful of universities managed to continue their radio programs during the budget impasse. The Illinois Arts Council also reduced support to these programs by nearly $2 million for FY 15. And FY 16 allocated only $90 thousand to eight public TV stations. Current's most recent analysis shows no change in state funding.

Indiana did respond to the author's query [Letter dtd May 20, 2016, State of Indiana, House of Representatives]. *The Atlantic* report showed from 2008 to 2012, the state had cut funding to In-diana Public Broadcasting by nearly $2 million or between 20% to 39%. Mike Brown, legislative assistant to the Indiana State Senate for Senator Randy Head, said that Indiana's bi-annual budget allocated $525,000 to be equally split amongst the state's 18 FM and one AM public radio station. *The Atlantic* said the state faced threats of multi-year phase outs of all state funding. Current's most recent analysis shows no change in state funding.

Iowa did respond to the author's query [Email dtd April 7, 2016, Iowa State Senator Brad Zaun]. *The Atlantic* report showed from 2008 to 2012, the state had cut funding to Iowa Public Radio by more than $2.1 million or between 20% to 39%. Iowa Senator Brad Zaun was on the Iowa Senate Education committee until January 2015 and said he wasn't aware of any state dollars supporting any of Iowa's public radio stations. Current's most recent analysis shows a 1.8% increase in funding.

Kansas did respond to the author's query [Letter dtd April 18, 2016, Kansas State Library]. *The Atlantic* report showed from 2008 to 2012, the state had cut funding to the Kansas Public

Broadcasting Council by nearly $1.7-million or between 20% to 39%. The Schedule A for the Kansas Public Radio flagship, KANU-FM showed that in 2014, the station and its four station network received $136,000 in direct appropriations from the State of Kansas and indirectly, about $1.13 million via Kansas state colleges and universities. In 2015, money from the state had fallen to nearly $100,000 while money from the university had increased by more than $150,000. *The Atlantic* report said the state faced threats of multi-year phase outs of all state funding. Current's most recent analysis shows no change in state funding.

Kentucky did respond to the author's query [Letter dtd April 29 2016, Kentucky Legislative Research Commission, State Capitol]. *The Atlantic* report showed from 2008 to 2012, the state had cut funding to its public broadcasting stations by more than $2.3 million or between 5% to 19%. The Deputy Director of the Kentucky Legislative Research Commission, John Scott told me that there is no line-item in the budget bill appropriated for public radio stations by the Kentucky General Assembly. Mr. Scott also said public radio stations affiliated with universities may receive a portion of funding from their university but the General Assembly does not maintain that data. Current's most recent analysis shows a 9.3% increase in funding.

Louisiana did not respond to the author's query but was included in Resnick's analysis. The Louisiana Educational Television Authority experienced a $2.5 million cut in public radio funding from 2008 to 2012. Current's most recent analysis shows a 0.9% decrease in funding.

Maine did respond to the author's query [Letter dtd April 20, 2016, Maine State Legislature, Office of the Executive Director]. *The Atlantic* report showed from 2008 to 2012, the state had cut funding to its public broadcasting stations by more than $2.3 mil-

lion or between 5% to 19%. Becky Morris, legislative aide
to Maine Senator Andre Cushing told me that the Maine Public
Broadcasting Network has received $245 thousand in state support
for the 2014-2015 biennium. That money supports a network of
seven public radio stations and five public TV stations. Grant
Pennover, the Executive Director of Maine's Legislative Council,
provided a review of MNPB appropriations since the 2007-2008
biennium. It shows a steep drop in state support amounting to
three-quarters of a million dollars, or nearly one-third of the network's state appropriation in seven years, including an approximate 10% cut in 2015-2016. *The Atlantic* report said the state faced
threats of multi-year phase outs of all state funding. Current's most
recent analysis shows no change in state funding.

Maryland did not respond to the author's query. Resnick's analysis showed that from 2008 to 2012, the state reduced funding to
its public radio stations by $245 thousand. Current's most recent
analysis shows a 3.2% increase in funding.

Massachusetts did not respond to the author's query. The state
does not fund public radio.

Michigan did respond to the author's query [Email dtd April 15,
2016, Michigan State Representative Mike McCready]. The Atlantic report showed no reduction in state support from 2008 to 2012.
The state does not fund its eight public TV stations and 29 public
radio stations. Representative Mike McCready said that the state
does provide appropriations to each of its 15 public universities.
However, he said that because of the various revenue sources, it is
difficult to determine how much revenue a station receives can be
traced directly back to the state, so an appropriation dollar amount
is hard to come by.

Minnesota did respond to the author's query [Email dtd May 4, 2016, Minnesota State Senator Bill Weber]. *The Atlantic* report showed no reduction in state support from 2008 to 2012. The state of Minnesota allocated around $476,000, or 5% of Minnesota Public Radio's total funding. Senator Bill Weber told me this number from the legislature has been falling as the majority of funding comes from member donations as well as grants including the Minnesota Legacy Amendment's Art and Cultural Heritage Fund, which the legislature also funds. For fiscal year 2015, the fund provided MPR and its 42 radio stations nearly $1.5 million. Although Senator Weber said how much the fund receives from the state varies by fiscal year, it is forecasted to receive $40 billion in 2016. Current's most recent analysis shows a 10.7% increase in funding.

Mississippi did not respond to the author's query. The Atlantic report showed from 2008 to 2012, the state had cut funding to its Mississippi Public Broadcasting by more than $4.2 million or between 40% and 99%. Current's most recent analysis shows a 11.7% decrease in funding.

Missouri did respond to the author's query [Email dtd May 2, 2016, Myra Rosskopf Wolfe, Legislator Assistant to Missouri Representative Jeanne Kirkton]. The Atlantic report showed no reduction in state support from 2008 to 2012. Senator Joe Keaveny of Missouri told me that $1,010,000 of his state's $27 billion budget would be allocated as grants to the state's one public television and 13 public radio stations. This money flows from a special tax on non-resident athletes and sports teams, through the Missouri Public Broadcasting Corporation Special Fund, to the legislature and into state public radio and TV stations in the form of operating and basic service grants. Current's most recent analysis shows no change in state funding.

Montana did respond to the author's query [Letter dtd June 29, 2016, Linda MuCulloch, Secretary of State, Montana State Capitol]. *The Atlantic* report showed no reduction in state support from 2008 to 2012. Fiscal Analyst Micaela Kurth of the Legislative Fiscal Division of the Montana Legislative Branch told me that the State of Montana and the Montana University System provided the three stations that make up Montana Public Radio $636 thousand dollars in fiscal year 2015. However, Montana Public Radio said because of the loss of a federal grant, and reductions in university support which began in 2012, the station needed an additional $300 thousand annually, raising its annual total from $1.2 to $1.5 million. Current's most recent analysis show the state no longer funds its public radio stations.

Nebraska did not respond to the author's query. Resnick's analysis showed that from 2008 to 2012, the state reduced funding to its Nebraska Educational Telecommunications Commission by $577 thousand. Current's most recent analysis shows a 1.2% decrease in funding.

Nevada did respond to the author's query. [Email dtd April 7, 2016, Democratic Senator Richard (Tick) Segerblom]. The Atlantic report showed no reduction in state support for its two TV and four public radio stations from 2008 to 2012. Senator Segerblom said he didn't believe the state provided any funds for any of Nevada's nine public radio stations. He said their support was a combination of federal and local money. Current's most recent analysis shows no change in state funding.

New Hampshire did not respond to the author's query. The Atlantic report showed from 2008 to 2012, the state had cut funding to its public broadcasting stations by more than $2.9 million or 100%. Current's most recent analysis shows the state no longer funds public radio.

New Jersey did respond to the author's query [Letter dtd May 6, 2015, Office of Legislative Services, New Jersey State Legislature]. *The Atlantic* report showed from 2008 to 2012, the state had cut funding to its public broadcasting stations by nearly $3 million or 100%. The New Jersey Office of Legislative Services sent me the complete 2016 Budget for the State of New Jersey. In the appendix of Section 4, Schedule 2, Dedicated Revenues, Department of Treasury, the budget shows the state allocated $517,000 to public broadcasting services in 2014, and projected $2,220,000 in 2016 but actually allocated $1,200,000. Governor Chris Christie sold four public broadcasting stations of the New Jersey Network in 2011. The state no longer funds public radio.

New Mexico did not appear to show any reductions in state funding to its three university stations through Resnick's analysis. The state did not respond to the author's query. Current's most recent analysis shows no change in state funding.

New York did not appear to show any reductions in state funding to its none public TV stations and 17 public radio stations through Resnick's analysis. The state did not respond to the author's query. Current's most recent analysis shows no change in state funding.

North Carolina did not respond to author's query. *The Atlantic* report showed from 2008 to 2012, the state had cut funding to its public broadcasting stations by nearly $3.7 million or between 20% and 39%. Current's most recent analysis shows a 1.0% decrease in funding.

North Dakota did respond to the author's query [Letter dtd May 8, 2016, North Dakota Legislative Council]. *The Atlantic* report showed no reduction in state support to Prairie Public Broadcasting from 2008 to 2012. Representative Gail Mooney of the North Dakota legislature sent a copy of Senate Bill 2015; a list of appropriation from the Governor that had been vetted by the appropriations committee. In it, $1.7 million is budgeted to the nine radio and nine public TV stations of Prairie Public Broadcasting. This represents roughly .00029% of the state budget. Current's most recent analysis shows a 29.4% decrease in funding.

Ohio did not respond to the author's query. *The Atlantic* report showed from 2008 to 2012, the state had cut funding to its 45 public broadcasting stations by more than $2 million or between 20% to 39%. Current's most recent analysis shows a 3.0% decrease in funding.

Oklahoma did not respond to the author's query. *The Atlantic* report showed from 2008 to 2012, the state had cut funding to its public broadcasting stations by $1.3 million or between 20% to 39%. Current's most recent analysis shows a 3.6% increase in funding.

Oregon did not appear to show any reductions in state funding to OPB or JPR through Resnick's analysis. The state did not respond to the author's query. Current's most recent analysis shows a 33.3% decrease in funding.

Pennsylvania did respond to the author's query [Email dtd April 14, 2016, Pennsylvania State Representative Mike Regan]. *The Atlantic* report showed from 2008 to 2012, the state had cut funding to its public broadcasting stations by nearly $13.5 million or 100%. "The Commonwealth does not provide funding for public radio," according to Pennsylvania State Representative Mike Regan. Elizabeth Rementer of Senator Rob Teplitz's office said that grant funding for public TV was scaled back from $7,500,000 to $900,000 in FY 2009-2010 and has since been eliminated. Since then, some stations may have received other competitive grants, for specific purposes, through other state programs.

Mr. Regan did say that then Pennsylvania Governor Tom Wolf was proposing a new, $4 million funding item for public TV, although none of this is projected to be for public radio. Current's most recent analysis shows a 200% increase in funding.

Rhode Island did respond to the author's query [Letter dtd April 29, 2016, State of Rhode Island and Providence Plantations, House Fiscal Advisory Staff]. *The Atlantic* report showed no reduction in state support from 2008 to 2012. House Fiscal Advisor Sharon Reynolds Ferland said "no state funds are appropriated to support public radio in the Rhode Island state budget." The state no longer funds public radio.

South Carolina did not respond to the author's query. *The Atlantic* report showed from 2008 to 2012, the state had cut funding to its public broadcasting stations by more than $12 million or between 40% to 99%. *The Atlantic* report said the state faced threats of multi-year phase outs of all state funding. Current's most recent analysis shows no change in state funding.

South Dakota did not respond to the author's query. *The Atlantic* report showed that from 2008 to 2012, the state had cut funding to its nine public TV and 11 public radio stations of South Dakota Public Broadcasting nearly $520 thousand dollars or 5% to 19%. Current's most recent analysis shows a 1.1% increase in funding.

Tennessee did respond to the author's query [Email dtd April 8, 2016, Tennessee State Senator Becky Massey]. *The Atlantic* report showed no reduction in state support from 2008 to 2012. Item 27 of the Governor's 2016 Budget submitted to the Tennessee Legislature is a single sentence which proposed nearly $2.8 million in support of state public television stations. Public radio isn't mentioned anywhere in the budget. State Senator Becky Massey specified that there are no funds appropriated to public radio, just public TV. Current's most recent analysis shows no change in state funding.

Texas did not respond to the author's query. Current's most recent analysis shows the state does not fund public radio.

Utah did not respond to the author's query. *The Atlantic* report showed that from 2008 to 2012, the state reduced funding to its Utah Education and Telehealth Network by $300-thousand. Current's most recent analysis shows a 14.4% increase in funding.

Vermont did not appear to show any reductions in state funding to Vermont PBS through Resnick's analysis. The state did not respond to the author's query. Current's most recent analysis shows no change in the single dollar of state funding the state legislature provides.

Virginia did respond to the author's query [Letter dtd April 20, 2016, Virginia Senate Finance Committee]. The Atlantic report showed from 2008 to 2012, the state had cut funding to its public broadcasting stations by more than $4.7 million or 20% to 39%. Elizabeth Daley, the staff director of the Finance Committee for the Virginia Senate told me that in 2008, the State of Virginia provided financial assistance to public radio that totaled as much as $628-thousand. Of the 40 public radio stations in Virginia, 15 operate out of state universities. She said that as of the 2012 session, support for public broadcasting was eliminated and was not restored. It is not known if funding has been increased to state universities. Current's most recent analysis shows the state no longer funds public radio.

Washington did not respond to the author's query. Current's most recent analysis shows the state no longer funds public radio.

West Virginia did respond to the author's query [Email dtd April 11, 2016, West Virginia State Senator Dave Sypolt]. *The Atlantic* report showed no reduction in state support from 2008 to 2012. West Virginia Public Broadcasting, along with its three public TV stations and 17 public radio stations received $5.5 million for 2016. Senator Dave Syplot told me that support comes to about 0.1% of the state's $4.5 billion dollars budget. Scott Finn, former CEO of West Virginia Public Broadcasting told *Current* in 2015 state support was reduced, in part, because of what he called "the collapse of the coal industry" Current's most recent analysis shows a 22.1% decrease in funding.

Wisconsin did respond to author's query [Letter dtd April 19, 2016, Wisconsin Legislature]. *The Atlantic* report showed from 2008 to 2012, the state had cut funding to its Wisconsin Public Radio and Wisconsin Public Television by nearly $1.2-million or 5% to 19%. Senator Chris Larson of Wisconsin told me that the state's Legislative Fiscal Bureau estimate of funding for Wisconsin Public Radio included funding from the Education Communications Board and the University of Wisconsin Extension Service. In total, WPR's 33 public radio stations received $7.1 million in the 2014-2015 biennium and $6.4 million in the 2015-2016 biennium. According to Mr. Larson, this represents a six-thousandth of a percent drop for the total Wisconsin state budget but a 10% drop for WPR. Current's most recent analysis shows a 3.8% increase in funding.

Wyoming did respond to the author's query [Letter dtd April 23, 2016, Wyoming State Legislature, Legislative Service Office]. *The Atlantic* report showed no reduction in state support from 2008 to 2012 to Wyoming PBS. Wyoming's Legislative Service Office said that Wyoming Public Radio may receive state funding for operations of capital construction, e.g., tower enhancements. But because it is housed within Wyoming State University and because the University receives a block grant from the state, it isn't known by the legislature how much money the university provides in support of Wyoming Public Radio. Current's most recent analysis shows a 17% decrease in funding.☎

PLEDGE: The Public Radio Fund Drive

498

Bibliography

"When I'm sniffing around new territory, I often choose, rather randomly, one general book and then follow its bibliography and notes to other, more specialized works and to the primary source material."

—Andrea Barrett, American novelist

Introduction

Charney, Tamar, et al. "The Secret Sauce Behind NPR One: An Editorially Responsible Algorithm." NPR, 21 Dec. 2016, www.npr.org/sections/npr-extra/2016/12/21/505315422/secret-sauce-npr-one-algorithm.

Cockrell, Joe. "State of the News Media 2013 · Joe Cockrell, Expert Consultant." 1 Apr. 2013, joeprguy.com/2013/03/20/state-of-the-news-media-2013/.

Carnegie, Dale. Dale Carnegie Quotes." BrainyQuote, Xplore, www.brainyquote.com/quotes/dale_carnegie_156635.

Flaxman, Fred. "Keeping the Public out of Public Radio." Mountain Xpress, mountainx.com/opinion/050708_keeping_the_public_out_of_public_radio/.

Fund Drive nets $19,000," Carey James, Homer News, v31, n22, June 3, 2004, http://homernews.com/stories/060304/new_060304new005001.shtml

Kalish, Jon. "SiriusXM Cancels 'Bob Edwards Show', but Weekly Public Radio Show Will Continue." *Current*, 27 Oct. 2016, www.current.org/2014/09/siriusxm-cancels-bob-edwards-show-but-weekly-public-radio-show-will-continue/.

Kaplan, Joel. "NPR's Lack of Transparency." CPB, 21 Mar. 2016, www.cpb.org/ombudsman/nprs-lack-transparency.

Potter, Matt. "Naming Rights, Anyone?," San Diego Reader, 23 Nov. 2016, www.sandiegoreader.com/news/2010/mar/24/under-the-radar-2/.

Quah, Nicholas. "Nieman Journalism Lab: Pushing to the Future of Journalism." Nieman Lab, www.niemanlab.org/author/nquah/.

Station Resource Group," Individual Giving, Resources, http://www.srg.org/funding/IndividualGiving.pdf, pg. 14

Basics

Bergsma, Stephanie. A Major Donor Checklist. Greater Public, 23 Feb. 2015, go.greaterpublic.org/blog/2015/02/a-major-donor-checklist/.

Bjerg, Greg. "The Tragic Birth of FM Radio." Damn Interesting, 12 July 2015, www.damninteresting.com/the-tragic-birth-of-fm-radio/.

Collins, Bob. "Debating NPR Underwriting Announcements." NewsCut, 20 Apr. 2015, blogs.mprnews.org/newscut/2015/04/debating-npr-underwriting-announcements/.

Dent, Mark. "WHYY President Got a Massive Pay Raise Last Year: It's 'a Slap in the Face'." Billy Penn, 6 July 2017, billypenn.com/2017/07/06/whyy-president-got-a-massive-pay-raise-last-year-its-a-slap-in-the-face/.

Ing, Valerie. "Mistress of the Mix: Put Your Money Where Your Ears Are." Anewscafe.com, 7 Apr. 2017, anewscafe.com/2017/04/07/redding/mistress-of-the-mix-put-your-money-where-your-ears-are-2/.

Kling, William, phone conversation with author, November 16, 2016

National Educational Radio Network (NERN), NPBA–National Public Broadcasting Archives, 25 Jan. 2011, web.archive.org/web/20120623133418/http://www.lib.umd.edu/NPBA/subinfo/nern.html.

Public Radio Programming Performance." *Grow the Audience* for Public Radio," May 2003, www.srg.org/program/pgmperf.html.

Rothman, Lily. "Newton Minow's Vast Wasteland Speech: How It Changed TV." Time, Time, 9 May 2016, time.com/4315217/newton-minow-vast-wasteland-1961-speech/.

Silva, Ernesto. "President Johnson's Remarks." CPB, 30 Jan. 2015, www.cpb. org/aboutpb/act/remarks.

Sabatier, Julie. "A Conversation with NPR's New President and CEO." Oregon Public Broadcasting, 9 Sept. 2014, www.opb.org/radio/programs/thinkout-loud/segment/a-conversation-with-nprs-new-president-and-ceo/.

Shafer, Jack. "How Lady Bird and Lyndon Baines Johnson Came by Their Millions." *Slate* Magazine, Slate, 16 July 2007, www.slate.com/articles/news_and_politics/press_box/2007/07/the_honest_graft_of_lady_bird_johnson.html.

Siemering, William. "Bill Siemering's 'National *Public Radio Purposes*', 1970." *Current*, 22 Feb. 2017, current.org/2012/05/national-public-radio-purposes/.

Venta, Lance. "WNKU's Final Piece Signs Off." *RadioInsight*, 29 Sept. 2017, radioinsight.com/headlines/119977/wnkus-final-piece-signs-off/.

What is a Station?

A Trump FCC and Pirate Radio: Prepare for Struggle." DIYmedia.net, diymedia. net/a-trump-fcc-and-pirate-radio-prepare-for-struggle/8617.

AFFILIATION." PRI InfoSite, STATION TOOLS, www2.pri.org/infosite/sta-tiontools/affiliation_primer.cfm.

Barthel, Michael, et al. "Public Broadcasting Fact Sheet." Pew Research Center's Journalism Project, 7 Aug. 2017, www.journalism.org/fact-sheet/public-broadcasting/.

Blake, Casey. "Answer Woman: WCQS Ghost Stations, Men in Dresses." Citizen Times, The Citizen-Times, 5 Sept. 2014, www.citizen-times.com/story/news/local/2014/09/05/answer-woman-wcqs-ghost-stations-men-dresses/15157743/.

Caillian, Robert. "Robert Cailliau Quotes." BrainyQuote, Xplore, www.brainy-quote.com/quotes/robert_cailliau_516421.

Conflicting Communication Interests in America: The Case of National Public Radio," Tom McCourt, 1999, Praeger, pg. 96

Court Opinion – "Prometheus Radio Project v. FCC." Federal Communications Commission, 29 May 2018, www.fcc.gov/document/court-opinion-pro-metheus-radio-project-v-fcc.

PLEDGE: The Public Radio Fund Drive

FM Translators and Boosters." Federal Communications Commission, 6 July 2017, www.fcc.gov/media/radio/fm-translators-and-boosters.

Hooley, Gemma. NPR VP Member Partnership, email correspondence Nov. 20, 2017

Halonen, Doug. "FCC Republicans Strike down Studio Rule That Had Mixed Support from Pubmedia." Current, 25 Oct. 2017, www.current.org/2017/10/fcc-republicans-strike-down-studio-rule-that-had-mixed-support-from-pubmedia/.

Lasar, Matthew. "NPR's War on Low Power FM: the Laws of Physics vs. Politics." Ars Technica, 27 Apr. 2008, arstechnica.com/uncategorized/2008/04/nprs-war-on-low-power-fm-the-laws-of-physics-vs-politics/.

Mason, Allen. "NPR 'Voice of Reason' Important for Our Times, President Says." Bowling Green Daily News, 29 Apr. 2016, www.bgdailynews.com/news/npr-voice-of-reason-important-for-our-times-president-says/article_1b02512d-6d29-594f-8d74-4f2a266c1ccb.html.

Nal, Renee. "FCC Shuts down Three Radio Stations, Seizes Equipment." Liberty Unyielding, 19 Apr. 2014, libertyunyielding.com/2014/04/19/fcc-shuts-down-three-radio-stations-seize-equipment/.

NPR Annual Report 2001. NPR, 16 Dec. 2002, pg 22-24, www.npr.org/about/annualreports/npr2001.pdf.

NPR Fact Sheet, 30 Mar. 2018, PDF pp. 1-1, https://www.npr.org/about/press/NPR_Fact_Sheet.pdf

NPR Stations, June 2013, PDF pp. 1–4 http://www.npr.org/stations/pdf/nprstations.pdf

Quinn, Garrett. "Boston Radio Station Touch 106.1 FM Raided, Shutdown by FCC." Masslive.com, 17 Apr. 2014, www.masslive.com/news/boston/index.ssf/2014/04/boston_radio_station_touch_106.html.

"Repeaters–What They Are and How to Use Them," 21 Mar. 2001, PDF pp. 1–6. , http://www.arrl.org/files/file/Technology/tis/info/pdf/repeater1.pdf

Resler, Seth, "Can Your Radio Station Generate Revenue with a Membership Website?" Jacobs Media Strategies, 29 Oct. 2016, jacobsmedia.com/radio-station-generate-revenue-membership-website/.

Smart, Paul. "Can a Commercial Radio Station Also Be Listener Supported?" Hudson Valley One, 30 Mar. 2017, hudsonvalleyone.com/2017/03/27/can-a-commercial-radio-station-also-be-listener-supported/.

Staff. "Commercial Radio Doing the NPR Thing." Marketplace, 20 Apr. 2009, www.marketplace.org/2009/04/20/business/marketplace-scratch-pad/commercial-radio-doing-npr-thing.

Stocking, Galen. "Digital News Fact Sheet." Pew Research Center's Journalism Project, 7 Aug. 2017, www.journalism.org/fact-sheet/digital-news/.

"Unattended Operation of Radio and Television Stations." Federal Communications Commission, 11 Feb. 2016, www.fcc.gov/media/radio/unattended-operation.

WEAA timestamp 16 Apr. 2016 1516 EST

"WFNX Lives On ... Sorta." All Access, 10 Apr. 2013, www.allaccess.com/net-news/archive/story/117276/wfnx-lives-on-sorta.

WSQT Direct Action Radio's Programs A-Infos Radio Project."–http://www.radio4all.Net/, www.radio4all.net/index.php/contributor/4140.

"You'll Want To Visit This Astounding Library In Utah. Only In Your State," www.onlyinyourstate.com/utah/astounding-library-in-ut/.

Character and Ownership

Ahtone, Tristan. "Tribal Radio Stations May Go Dark under Donald Trump." Al Jazeera, 14 Feb. 2017, www.aljazeera.com/indepth/opinion/2017/02/tribal-radio-stations-dark-donald-trump-170212093921927.html.

Cronauer, Adrian. "Adrian Cronauer Quotes." BrainyQuote, Xplore, www.brainyquote.com/quotes/adrian_cronauer_408851.

KCIE Radio, www.kcieradio.com/history/.

KMUN timestamp 15 Mar. 2016 1515 PST

KUSP 15 Apr. 2017 1558 PST

KUYI 88.1FM Hopi Radio." KUYI 88.1FM Hopi Radio, www.kuyi.net/.

KWRR 89.5 FM. Facebook, www.facebook.com/kwrr895/.

Marklein, Mary Beth. "College Radio Stations Fear Budget Cuts Could Silence Them." USA Today, Gannett Satellite Information Network, 10 Oct. 2011, usatoday30.usatoday.com/news/education/story/2011-10-10/college-radio-stations-being-sold/50723728/1?csp=34news.

Merrill, Donald, "MyData," GoogleDocs Public Radio Survey, June 2017, Portland, OR

Nonprofit Media." 29 Sept. 2011, pp. 314–333., https://transition.fcc.gov/osp/inc-report/INoC-31-Nonprofit-Media.pdf

"Saving College Radio Stations Panel at NFCB Offered Tips for Stations in Peril." *Radio Survivor*, 16 June 2011, www.radiosurvivor.com/2011/06/16/saving-college-radio-stations-panel-at-nfcb-offered-tips-for-stations-in-peril/.

Sinclair Broadcast Group. "JPR Plans Major Expansion." , MailTribune.com, www.mailtribune.com/article/20151218/NEWS/151219606.

"Station Highlights & History." Who We Are, www.wbur.org/inside/highlights-history.

Tuning the Dial

Aeschliman , Lesley. "What Is Simulcasting?" Bella Online–The Voice of Women, 2018, www.bellaonline.com/articles/art171369.asp.

Arave, Lynn. "AM RADIO. WHEN WAS THE LAST TIME YOU." DeseretNews.com, Deseret News, 10 Feb. 1989, www.deseretnews.com/article/34207/AM-RADIO-WHEN-WAS-THE-LAST-TIME-YOU.html

Associated Press. "In Well-Mannered Public Radio, an Airwaves War–The Boston Globe." BostonGlobe.com, 4 June 2017, www.bostonglobe.com/metro/2017/06/03/well-mannered-public-radio-airwaves-war/4tmVpry-89f7ZN1RFwNwjJO/story.html.

"Code of Federal Regulations." Title 47 Telecommunication, Federal Communications Commission, 1 Oct. 2007, www.gpo.gov/fdsys/pkg/CFR-2007-title47-vol4/xml/CFR-2007-title47-vol4-sec74-1201.xml.

"Commission Policy on the Noncommercial Nature of Educational Broadcasting." Federal Communications Commission, 15 June 2017, www.fcc.gov/media/radio/nature-of-educational-broadcasting.

"Culture." University of Louisiana at Lafayette, 8 Mar. 2013, www.louisiana.edu/about-us/lafayette-acadiana/culture.

FCC. "Call Sign History." FCC INTERNATIONAL BUREAU, 25 December 2017, licensing.fcc.gov/cgi-bin/ws.exe/prod/cdbs/pubacc/prod/call_hist.pl?Facility_id=135143&Callsign=WLYH-LP,

FCC. "Call Sign Reservation System." FCC INTERNATIONAL BUREAU, licensing.fcc.gov/prod/callsign/main.html.

Georgia Public Broadcasting, www.gpb.org/.

Goldfarb, Michael. "NPR Responds." The *Weekly Standard*, 13 Feb. 2009, www.weeklystandard.com/article/27801.

Kiley, Brendan. "KPLU Renamed KNKX (Pronounced 'Connects')." The Seattle Times, The Seattle Times Company, 12 Aug. 2016, www.seattletimes. com/seattle-news/kplu-renamed-knkx-pronounced-connects/.

Lee, Jasen. "Donors Mobilize to Keep NPR Affiliate KCPW Local." DeseretNews.com, Deseret News, 30 May 2008, www.deseretnews.com/article/700230205/Donors-mobilize-to-keep-NPR-affiliate-KCPW-local.html.

Merrill, Donald, "MyData," GoogleDocs Public Radio Survey, June 2017, Portland, OR

NPR Stations" June 2013, PDF pp. 1–4 http://www.npr.org/stations/pdf/nprstations.pdf

"Radio Station History, in Portsmouth and Scioto Co., Ohio." Henry Radio Engineering LLC, 21 Jan. 2015, www.portsmouthinfo.net/radio-station-history.html.

Rushdie, Salman. "Salman Rushdie Quotes." BrainyQuote, Xplore, www. brainyquote.com/quotes/salman_rushdie_580330.

Sefton, Dru. "Pubcasters Ask FCC to End Station ID Requirement." *Current*, 6 July 2017, current.org/2017/07/pubcasters-ask-fcc-to-end-station-id-requirement/.

"The History of KBOO." KBOO, 7 Aug. 2018, kboo.fm/history-kboo.

WRFI Community Radio." PRX–Public Radio Exchange, exchange.prx.org/ station_accounts/1011-wrfi.

Zurawik, David. "WEAA Goes Back to Its Educational Roots amid Major Change, Controversy." Baltimoresun.com, 13 Oct. 2017, www.baltimoresun.com/entertainment/tv/z-on-tv-blog/bs-fe-zontv-weaa-radio-20171013-story.html.

Chapter 2 – Major Players

aaronread. "Thread: Cutbacks at NPR: Will The Economy Also Impact Local Affiliates?" Radio Discussions, 19 Dec. 2008, www.radiodiscussions.com/

showthread.php?548814-Cutbacks-at-NPR-Will-The-Economy-Also-Im-
pact-Local-Affiliates%2Fpage5.

AP. "NPR BOARD VOTES ON CUTS." *The New York Times*, 26 May 1983,
www.nytimes.com/1983/05/26/arts/npr-board-votes-on-cuts.html.

Buckley, Cara. "Ira Glass's 'This American Life' Leaves PRI." *The New York
Times*, 2 July 2014, www.nytimes.com/2014/07/06/arts/ira-glasss-this-
american-life-leaves-pri.html.

Collins, Bob. "NPR Cuts More Staff, Programming." NewsCut, 20 May 2014,
blogs.mprnews.org/newscut/2014/05/staff-cuts-at-npr/.

"Cutbacks at NPR: Will The Economy Also Impact Local Affiliates?" Radio
Discussions, www.radiodiscussions.com/showthread.php?548814-Cut-
backs-at-NPR-Will-The-Economy-Also-Impact-Local-Affiliates%2F-
page5&styleid=2.

Farhi, Paul. "Economy Forces Staffing Cuts at NPR." The Washington Post, WP
Company, 11 Dec. 2008, www.washingtonpost.com/wp-dyn/content/arti-
cle/2008/12/10/AR2008121002064.html.

Korte, Gregory. "The 62 Agencies and Programs Trump Wants to Eliminate."
USA Today, Gannett Satellite Information Network, 17 Mar. 2017, www.
usatoday.com/story/news/politics/2017/03/16/what-does-trump-budget-
eliminate/99223182/.

Mills, Ken. The Ken Mills Agency. "BEHIND KRISTA TIPPETT'S MOVE
FROM APM TO PRX." SPARK NEWS, acrnewsfeed.blogspot.
com/2016/04/behind-krista-tippetts-move-from-apm-to.html.

Molotsky, Irvin. "One Tough Bird, After All; How Public Broadcasting Survived
the Attacks Of Conservatives." *The New York Times*, 27 Nov. 1997, www.
nytimes.com/1997/11/27/arts/one-tough-bird-after-all-public-broadcast-
ing-survived-attacks-conservatives.html.

Neyfakh, Leon. "An Antiquated Business Model. A Horde of Upstart Competitors. Does NPR Have a Future?" *Slate* Magazine, 10 Apr. 2016, www.slate.
com/articles/news_and_politics/cover_story/2016/04/the_fight_for_the_fu-
ture_of_npr_can_public_radio_survive_the_podcast_revolution.html.

"The Corporation for Public Broadcasting: Federal Funding and Issues." Congressional Research Service, 3 May 2017, fas.org/sgp/crs/misc/RS22168.
pdf.

Wattles, Jackie. "NPR Radio Workers Threaten to Strike." CNNMoney, Cable News Network, 14 July 2017, money.cnn.com/2017/07/14/media/npr-workers-strike/index.html.

NPR

Arria, Michael. "NPR Workers Just Showed Us Why Journalists Need to Organize." *Salon, Salon*.com, 26 July 2017, www.salon.com/2017/07/27/npr-workers-just-showed-us-why-journalists-need-to-organize_partner/.

Beaujon, Andrew. "With Hosting Changes, NPR Displays Commitment to Diversity." Washingtonian, 9 July 2015, www.washingtonian.com/2015/07/09/with-hosting-changes-npr-displays-commitment-to-diversity/.

Block, Melissa. Earthquake Rocks China's Sichuan Province. NPR, 12 May 2008, www.npr.org/templates/story/story.php?storyId=90371578.

"Bob Edwards Forced out of '*Morning Edition*'." NBCNews.com, NBCUniversal News Group, 23 Mar. 2004, www.nbcnews.com/id/4586432/ns/business-us_business/t/bob-edwards-forced-out-morning-edition/.

Briggs, Tracey. "CPB Awards Grant to NPR to Help Public Radio Stations Improve Emergency Messaging." CPB, 26 Sept. 2017, www.cpb.org/pressroom/cpb-awards-grant-npr-help-public-radio-stations-improve-emergency-messaging.

Cerullo, Megan. "NPR's Michael Oreskes Placed on Leave amid Sexual Harassment Accusations." –Nydailynews.com, New York Daily News, 1 Nov. 2017, www.nydailynews.com/news/national/npr-michael-oreskes-accused-sexual-harassment-article-1.3602691.

Chuh, Patricia M. "The Fate of Public Broadcasting in the Face of Federal Funding Cuts," Mar 25, 1995, pg 1-16, http://scholarship.law.edu/cgi/viewcontent.cgi?article=1048&context=commlaw

CPB's Appropriation History, pp. 1–2., www.netadvisor.org/wp-content/uploads/2012/10/2012-00-00-CPBs-Appropriations-History-1969-2012.pdf.

"Customer Support." For Stations, PRSS, www.prss.org/customer-support.

DeBenedette, Sue. Media Advisory. Arizona Public Media, 1 July 2013, uaatwork.arizona.edu/sites/uaatwork/files/here_now_daily_radio_news_program_to_debut_on_npr_89.1_on_july_1_2013.pdf.

Depp, Michael. "WNYC Retools Digital Efforts Around Personal." Internet and Web Industry News–Business, Content, Advertising, Mobile, Social–Net-NewsCheck.com, NetNewsCheck, 26 July 2013, www.netnewscheck.com/article/27694/wnyc-retools-digital-efforts-around-personal.

Drummond, William, Former NPR News Correspondent, email conversation with the author, Jan. 9, 2018

Dvorkin, Jeffrey A. "Bob Edwards Reassigned: Ageism or Just Change?" NPR, 28 Apr.2004, www.npr.org/templates/story/story.php?storyId=1854657.

Edsall, Thomas B. "DEFUNDING' PUBLIC BROADCASTING: CONSERVA-TIVE GOAL GAINS AUDIENCE." The Washington Post, WP Company, 15 Apr. 1995, www.washingtonpost.com/archive/politics/1995/04/15/de-funding-public-broadcasting-conservative-goal-gains-audience/a3cc8e3e-f975-4995-b841-2d2a8186464b/?utm_term=.2b103c9feb40.

Engelman, Ralph. "Public Radio and Television in America," Sage Publications, 1993, pg 123

Farhi, Paul. "NPR Considers Rare on-Air Pledge Drive despite Ban." The Se-attle Times, The Seattle Times Company, 28 Mar. 2009, www.seattletimes.com/nation-world/npr-considers-rare-on-air-pledge-drive-despite-ban/..

Farhi, Paul. "NPR's New Headquarters Refuels Funding Debate." The Washing-ton Post, WP Company, 21 June 2013, www.washingtonpost.com/lifestyle/style/nprs-new-headquarters-refuels-funding-debate/2013/06/21/bb53a64a-da00-11e2-a016-92547bf094cc_story.html.

"First NPR 'All Things Considered' Broadcast Inducted Into Library of Con-gress." NPR, 29 Mar. 2017, www.npr.org/about-npr/521410406/first-npr-all-things-considered-broadcast-inducted-into-library-of-congress.

Fisher, Marc. "On Satellite Radio, Bob Edwards's Orbit Keeps Expanding." The Washington Post, WP Company, 19 Feb. 2006, www.washingtonpost.com/wp-dyn/content/article/2006/02/17/AR2006021700423.html.

Folkenflik, David. "NPR To End 'Tell Me More,' Eliminate 28 Positions." NPR, 20 May 2014, www.npr.org/sections/thetwo-way/2014/05/20/314256024/npr-to-end-tell-me-more-lay-off-28-people.

Folkenflik, David." NPR Ends Williams' Contract After Muslim Remarks." NPR, 21 Oct. 2010, www.npr.org/templates/story/story.php?story-Id=130712737.

Gamerman, Ellen. "Public Radio's Existential Crisis." The Wall Street Journal, Dow Jones & Company, 16 June 2016, www.wsj.com/articles/radios-existential-crisis-1466111586.

Gerstein, Josh. "Josh Gerstein." NPR Salaries: Raw Data, Dec. 2012, joshgerstein.blogspot.com/2008/12/npr-salaries-raw-data.html.

Getler, Michael. "The Mailbag: No, Virginia, PBS Is Not NPR." PBS, Public Broadcasting Service, 26 Oct. 2010, www.pbs.org/ombudsman/2010/10/the_mailbag_no_virginia_pbs_is_not_npr.html.

Johnson, Peter. "Edwards Ousted as 'Morning Edition' Host." USA Today, Gannett Satellite Information Network, 23 Mar. 2004, usatoday30.usatoday.com/money/media/2004-03-23-npr-edwards_x.htm.

Kane, Sally. "Public Radio's Distribution Superhighway: the Public Radio Satellite System." NFCB, nfcb.org/public-radios-distribution-superhighway-the-public-radio-satellite-system/.

Koetsier, John. "How Google Searches 30 Trillion Web Pages, 100 Billion Times a Month." VentureBeat, 16 Jan. 2018, venturebeat.com/2013/03/01/how-google-searches-30-trillion-web-pages-100-billion-times-a-month/.

Laskowski, Amy. "NPR to Take WBUR's Here & Now National."| Bostonia." Boston Hospitality Review RSS, 2 Apr. 2013, www.bu.edu/bostonia/2013/npr-to-take-wburs-here-now-national/.

Lewis, Dannika. "Foreign Correspondents in a Modern World." Elon University, 13 Mar. 2010, www.elon.edu/docs/e-web/academics/communications/reseach/lon.edu/docs/e-web/academics/communications/reseach/12LewisE-JSpring10.pdf.

Lichtenstein, Bill. "NPR Gets in News Staff's Facebook." The Huffington Post, TheHuffingtonPost.com, 25 May 2011, www.huffingtonpost.com/bill-lichtenstein/npr-gets-in-news-staffs-f_b_324698.html.

Lieberman, David. "NPR Seeks To Cut Staff By 10% As It Faces Operating Deficit." Deadline, Deadline, 13 Sept. 2013, deadline.com/2013/09/npr-seeks-to-cut-staff-by-10-as-it-faces-operating-deficit-586699/.

Linda Edwards Prehn. "Funding for Public Radio, TV Crucial for State Students." Madison.com, Madison, 11 Apr. 2015, host.madison.com/ct/news/opinion/column/linda-edwards-prehn-funding-for-public-radio-tv-crucial-for/article_031f6e9a-310a-53e7-9c7b-d95907a805c1.html.

Linkins, Jason. "PBS: We're Not the Ones Who Fired Juan Williams." *The Huffington Post*, TheHuffingtonPost.com, 25 May 2011, www.huffingtonpost. com/2010/10/27/pbs-reminds-people-that-t_n_774897.html.

McCauley, Michael, "NPR: The Trials and Tribulations of National Public Radio." Columbia University Press, 2005, pg 53

Mitchell, Jack W. "Listener Supported," Praeger, 2005, pg 99

Montgomery, David. "Meet Joshua Johnson, Diane Rehm's Successor–and a Bold Move for WAMU." The Washington Post, WP Company, 2 Feb. 2017, www.washingtonpost.com/lifestyle/magazine/meet-joshua-johnson-diane-rehms-successor—and-a-big-gamble-for-wamu/2017/02/01/6ad4eb26-d8d4-11e6-9f9f-5cdb4b7f8dd7_story.html?utm_term=.7f2cf1a6cd18.

Mullin, Benjamin. "Thomas Hjelm Will Be NPR's New Digital Chief." Poynter, 15 Mar. 2017, www.poynter.org/news/thomas-hjelm-will-be-nprs-new-digital-chief.

Niles, Robert. "Will NPR's Podcasts Birth a New Business Model for Public Radio?" Online Journalism Review, USC Annenberg School of Journalism, 27 Nov. 2005, www.ojr.org/will-nprs-podcasts-birth-a-new-business-model-for-public-radio/.

NPR Board Of Directors Welcomes New Chair. NPR, 4 Nov. 2015, www.npr. org/about-npr/454245951/npr-board-of-directors-welcomes-new-chair.

NPR Ethics Guide – "Impartiality." NPR, ethics.npr.org/category/f-impartiality/.

"NPR One." NPR, www.npr.org/about/products/npr-one/.

Propper, Ruth. "9/11 Television Viewing Linked To Dreams and Stress." ScienceDaily, Beth Israel Deaconess Medical Center, 16 Apr. 2007, www. sciencedaily.com/releases/2007/04/070413111636.htm.

PUBLIC RADIO MOUNTS EFFORT TO RAISE $1.8 MILLION BY JULY 29." , *The New York Times*, 16 July 1983, www.nytimes.com/1983/07/16/ arts/public-radio-mounts-effort-to-raise-1.8-million-by-july-29.html.

Read, Aaron. "The Problem with National-Level NPR Pledge Drives." Fried Bagels Broadcast Consulting, 30 Mar. 2009, friedbagels.blogspot.com/2009/.

Roberts, Michael. "WARNING: BAD AIR AHEAD." Westword, 2 Apr. 2016, www.westword.com/news/warning-bad-air-ahead-5055440.

Rupert Allman. Producer, WAMU, "*1A* with Joshua Johnson" phone conversation with author, Dec. 7, 2017

"Schiller Forced Out as NPR President Following Hidden-Camera Sting." FOX News Network, 9 Mar. 2011, www.foxnews.com/politics/2011/03/09/npr-president-schiller-resigns.html.

Siemering, William. "Bill Siemering's 'National *Public Radio Purposes*', 1970." *Current*, 22 Feb. 2017, current.org/2012/05/national-public-radio-purposes/.

Staff, "This is NPR: The First 40 Years," Chronicle Books, Aug 24, 2012, pg 196

Staff, "This is NPR: The First 40 Years," Chronicle Books, Aug 24, 2012, pg 230

Stampler, Laura." NPR Cuts 28 Jobs, Ends *Tell Me More* Broadcast." Time, 20 May 2014, time.com/106535/npr-layoffs-cancels-tell-me-more/.

"What Does the Public Radio Host of the Future Look and Sound like?" *Current*, 29 Sept. 2016, current.org/2016/09/what-does-the-public-radio-host-of-the-future-look-and-sound-like/.

Wildman, Sarah. "Tune In, Turn On, Fight Back." The American Prospect, 19 June 2005, prospect.org/article/tune-turn-fight-back.

Wilson, Benét J., et al. "Media & Diversity." All Digitocracy, 9 July 2015, alldigitocracy.org/michel-martin-tapped-to-host-nprs-weekend-all-things-considered/.

Worstall, Tim. "Yahoo Is The Number One US Website Again, Beating Google." *Forbes, Forbes* Magazine, 22 Aug. 2013, www.forbes.com/sites/timworstall/2013/08/22/yahoo-is-the-number-one-us-website-again-beating-google/#40c39a0a6280.

MPR/APR

"40th Anniversary Events, History and Arts Partner Discounts." Minnesota Public Radio." Minnesota Public Radio News, Minnesota Public Radio, minnesota.publicradio.org/about/features/2006/12/40th_anniversary/history.shtml.

"About Us." American Public Media, www.americanpublicmedia.org/about/.

"About." Marketplace, Marketplace, www.marketplace.org/about.

Adelson, Andrea. MEDIA;"The Business of National Public Radio." The New York Times, 5 Apr. 1999, www.nytimes.com/1999/04/05/business/media-the-business-of-national-public-radio.html?pagewanted=all.

PLEDGE: The Public Radio Fund Drive

American Public Media, "Organizational Structure." www.americanpublicme-dia.org/about/org-structure/.

Collins, Bob. "Live-Blogging: Bill Kling." NewsCut, 10 Sept. 2010, blogs. mprnews.org/newscut/2010/09/live-blogging_bill_kling/.

Crary, David. "For Red Cross, Hurricanes Bring Both Donations and Criticism." KWQC–Content–News, 14 Sept. 2017, www.kwqc.com/content/news/For-Red-Cross-hurricanes-bring-both-donations-and-criticism-444508643.html.

"David Brancaccio." Marketplace, www.marketplace.org/people/david-brancac-cio.

"David Brown." KUT, www.kut.org/people/david-brown.

Engelman, Ralph. "Public Radio and Television in America," Sage Publications, 1993, pg 125

Foster, Mark A. "Flagship Site of Music, Sounds and Video." Favorite Music, Sounds, and Videos, www.markfoster.net/mfn/music/.

"Founding Minnesota Public Radio." Wayback Machine Internet Archive, 2006, web.archive.org/web/20110719181730/http://www1.csbsju.edu/saint-johns150/information/MPRAnniversary.htm.

Greiff, Felicia. "Ira Glass: 'Public Radio Is Ready for Capitalism'." Ad Age, 30 Apr. 2015, adage.com/article/special-report-tv-upfront/ira-glass-public-ra-dio-ready-capitalism/298332/.

ibid, pg 87

ibid, pg 150

ibid, pg 155

"Kai Ryssdal." Marketplace, www.marketplace.org/people/kai-ryssdal.

Kerr, Euan. "Three Key Moments Define Bill Kling's Legacy in Public Radio." Minnesota Public Radio News, 29 June 2011, www.mprnews.org/sto-ry/2011/06/29/bill-kling-leaves-mpr.

Kerzman, Kris. "Throwback Thursday: When 'A Prairie Home Companion'

Got Its Name..." INFORUM, 10 Sept. 2015, www.inforum.com/news/3836153-throwback-thursday-when-prairie-home-companion-got-its-name-moor-head-cemetery.

Kling, William H. "MPR's Founder, Father Colman James Barry, O.S.B." MPR 50, www.mpr50.org/story/2017/09/08/mpr-founder-father-colman-james-barry-osb.

Lambert, Brian. "Anonymous Donor Gives $10 Million to MPR." MinnPost, www.minnpost.com/glean/2015/11/anonymous-donor-gives-10-million-mpr.

Lara, Isabel, and Andresen, Angie. "NPR AND AMERICAN PUBLIC MEDIA BRING 'MARKETPLACE MORNING REPORT' TO ALL 'MORNING EDITION' LISTENERS." American Public Media, 25 June 2014, www.americanpublicmedia.org/npr-and-american-public-media-bring-marketplace-morning-report-to-all-morning-edition-listeners/.

Lein, Deborah. Greater Public EDGE Blog, Greater Public, 4 Jan. 2018, go.greaterpublic.org/blog/topic/philanthropy.

McCauley, Michael P. "NPR: The Trials and Tribulations of National Public Radio," Columbia University Press, 2005, pg 8

ibid, pg 55

ibid, pg 54

ibid, pg 50

ibid, pg 74

ibid, pg 87

Miller, Amie. "The Overhead Myth: What Impact Really Costs." 11 Feb. 2015, pp. 1–3., www.pmbaonline.org/sites/default/files/2.11.15%20The%20Overhead%20Myth_Amie%20Miller.pdf.

Mitchell, Jack W. "Listener Supported," Praeger, 2005, pg 85

"MPR Brings Financial Talk Show to Rochester." Post Bulletin, 19 Oct. 1996, www.postbulletin.com/money-advice-was-sound—-mpr-brings-financial-talk/article_bfbb57c2-8094-5c75-99c9-233c65cf4951.html.

"MPR Stations." Minnesota Public Radio, www.mpr.org/listen/stations.

Owen, Laura Hazard. "Marketplace Doesn't 'Believe in the View from Nowhere,' but Still Fired a Reporter over a Blog Post." Nieman Lab, 2 Feb. 2017, www.niemanlab.org/2017/02/marketplace-doesnt-believe-in-the-view-from-nowhere-but-still-fired-a-reporter-over-a-blog-post/.

Phillis, James, and Chang, Victoria. "Minnesota Public Radio: Social Purpose Capitalism." *Harvard Business Review*, Nov. 1, 2016, hbr.org/product/minnesota-public-radio-social-purpose-capitalism/SI92-PDF-ENG.

"Service Agreement–American Public Media." 15 Oct. 2007, www.apmstations.org/files/station_tools/apm_streamagreement.pdf .

Sherman, Scott. "Good, Gray NPR." *The Nation*, 29 June 2015, www.thenation. com/article/good-gray-npr/.

"The MPR St. John's Story." St. Johns–Inspiring Lives for 150 Years, St. John's University, 25 Sept. 2007, www.srg.org/governance/resources/The%20 MPR%20St.%20John's%20Story.pdf.

"The Price of Commercial Success (SSIR)." Stanford Social Innovation Review: Informing and Inspiring Leaders of Social Change, ssir.org/articles/entry/ the_price_of_commercial_success.

"These Six Common Nonprofit IRS Audit Triggers Are No Laughing Matter." CRI Carr Riggs Ingram | Regional Accounting Firm, 14 Mar. 2016, www. cricpa.com/these-six-common-nonprofit-irs-audit-triggers-are-no-laughing-matter/.

"Welcome to the Sound Money Group!" Sound Money Group, www.soundmon-eygroup.com/.

"Yore to Depart as American Public Media Downsizes." *Current*, 16 Feb. 2015, current.org/2013/06/yore-to-depart-marketplace-as-american-public-me-dia-downsizes/.

APM/PRI

Buckley, Cara. "Ira Glass's 'This American Life' Leaves PRI." , *The New York Times*, 2 July 2014, www.nytimes.com/2014/07/06/arts/ira-glasss-this-american-life-leaves-pri.html.

Everett, Chris." PRI Affiliates–FY13," March 6, 2014, https://media.pri.org/ s3fs-public/PRI%20Affiliates%20FY13_March%206.pdf , pg 1-5

"Farewell to Steve." Stephen L. Salyer, President & CEO, Public Radio International, Aug. 2005, ssalyer.blogspot.com/2005/08/farewell-to-steve.html.

Janssen, Mike. "MPR to Rep Its Own Shows, Mainstays of PRI Catalog." *Current*, 22 Jan. 2018, current.org/2004/02/mpr-to-rep-its-own-shows-main-stays-of-pri-catalog/.

Janssen, Mike. "Suit Resolved, MPR and PRI Maintain Ties." *Current*, 19 Jan. 2018, current.org/2000/06/suit-resolved-mpr-and-pri-maintain-ties/.

Jensen, Dan. PRI press release, "Public Radio International and XM Satellite Radio to Launch Bob Edwards Weekend." PRI InfoSite, STATION TOOLS,

22 Sept. 2005, www2.pri.org/infosite/networknews/releases/bcw_launch.
cfm.

Lapin, Andrew. "Jesse Thorn's *Bullseye* Moving to NPR." *Current*, 16 Feb.
2015, current.org/2013/02/bullseye-moving-to-npr-jesse-thorn-hoping-for-
broader-station-push/.

McCauley, Michael. "NPR: The Trials and Tribulations of National Public Radio," Columbia University Press, 2005, pg. 54-55

ibid, pg. 76

Michaelson, Judith. "Minnesota Public Radio Buys 'Marketplace'." , Los Angeles Times, 14 Apr. 2000, articles.latimes.com/2000/apr/14/entertainment/
ca-19353.

Mitchell, Jack W, "Listener Supported: The Culture and History of Public Radio," Praeger, 2005, pg 87

"Mong Palatino – Contributor Profile." Global Voices, 26 Sept. 2013, global-
voices.org/author/mong/.

Mpr.org, "Traffic Statistics." SimilarWeb.com, 1 July, 2018, www.similarweb.
com/website/mpr.org.

Neyfakh, Leon. "An Antiquated Business Model. A Horde of Upstart Competitors. Does NPR Have a Future?" *Slate* Magazine, Slate, 10 Apr. 2016, www.
slate.com/articles/news_and_politics/cover_story/2016/04/the_fight_for_
the_future_of_npr_can_public_radio_survive_the_podcast_revolution.html.

"NPR Buys Interactive Arm of PRI." CBS News, CBS Interactive, 1 Aug. 2008,
www.cbsnews.com/news/npr-buys-interactive-arm-of-pri/.

"Npr.org Traffic Statistics." SimilarWeb.com, 1 July, 2018, www.similarweb.
com/website/npr.org.

"Organizational Structure." American Public Media, www.americanpublicme-
dia.org/about/org-structure/.

Peterson, Iver. "Rivalry Grows at Low End of Dial." , *The New York Times*, 2
Mar. 1998, www.nytimes.com/1998/03/02/business/rivalry-grows-at-low-
end-of-dial.html.

PRI press release, "PRI Sets Industry Record." PRI InfoSite, STATION TOOLS,
www2.pri.org/infosite/networknews/releases/700_affiliates.cfm.

PLEDGE: The Public Radio Fund Drive

PRI press release, "Public Radio International and XM Satellite Radio to Launch Bob Edwards Weekend." PRI InfoSite, STATION TOOLS, www2.pri.org/infosite/networknews/releases/bew_launch.cfm.

"Pri.org Traffic Statistics." SimilarWeb.com, 1 July 2018, www.similarweb.com/website/pri.org.

"PRI Fact Sheet." Public Radio International, PRI, www.pri.org/pri-fact-sheet.

"Public Radio International Acquired by Boston Public Broadcaster WGBH." Public Radio International, PRI, 26 July 2012, www.pri.org/stories/2012-07-26/public-radio-international-acquired-boston-public-broadcaster-wgbh.

"Public Radio International on Kickstarter." Kickstarter, www.kickstarter.com/pages/pri.

Taylor, Maggie. "PRX and PRI Announce Transformational Public Media Merger." Medium, 15 Aug. 2018, medium.com/prxofficial/prx-and-pri-announce-transformational-public-media-merger-dcb134dca29c.

PRX

Burbank, April. "How PRX Is Revolutionizing Public Radio by Making It (Really) Public." *Forbes, Forbes* Magazine, 14 Aug. 2012, www.forbes.com/sites/ashoka/2012/08/10/how-prx-is-revolutionizing-public-radio-by-making-it-really-public/.

Caygill, Sheelagh. "Podcasting Changes Face of Journalism and Audio Media." Communicate Influence, 12 Feb. 2018, communicateinfluence.com/podcasting-future-of-journalism/.

Cohen, Arthur. "WFMT to PRX from Content Depot." PRPD News for Programmers, 7 May 2014, prpd-news.blogspot.com/2014/05/wfmt-to-prx-from-content-depot.html.

Fast Company Staff. "The World's Top 10 Most Innovative Companies of 2015 In Media." , *Fast Company*, 2 May 2017, www.fastcompany.com/3041669/the-worlds-top-10-most-innovative-companies-of-2015-in-media.

Firestone, John D. Blog, "*The Moth Radio Hour* Wins Peabody Award." The Moth, themoth.org/dispatches/the-moth-radio-hour-wins-peabody-award.

Ha, Anthony. "Public Radio Marketplace PRX Spins out a New Mobile App Company," RadioPublic, TechCrunch, 19 May 2016, techcrunch. com/2016/05/19/prx-spins-out-radiopublic/.

Howard, Manny. "NPR Necromancers Finally Give 'The Best of *Car Talk*' a Rest." Salon, Salon.com, 1 July 2017, www.salon.com/2017/06/30/npr-best-of-car-talk-cancelled/.

Kirwan, Hope. "To Reduce Opioid Prescriptions, Tomah VA Looks To Acupuncture, Other Nontraditional Therapies." Wisconsin Public Radio, 13 Apr. 2018, wpr.org/reduce-opioid-prescriptions-tomah-va-looks-acupuncture-other-nontraditional-therapies.

Lichterman, Joseph. "How PRX and Radiotopia Are Rethinking the Public Radio Pledge Drive for the Podcast Era." Nieman Lab, 27 Oct. 2015, www. niemanlab.org/2015/10/how-prx-and-radiotopia-are-rethinking-the-public-radio-pledge-drive-for-the-podcast-era/.

Mills, Ken. The Ken Mills Agency. "PRX LAUNCHES FOR-PROFIT 'RADIOPUBLIC' & KEITH GOLDSTEIN PASSES AWAY IN LA." SPARK NEWS, 23 May 2016, acrnewsfeed.blogspot.com/2016/05/prx-launches-for-profit-radiopublic.html.

Mullin, Benjamin. "Radiotopia, an Early Podcast Network, Is Going Strong and Expanding." Poynter, 2 Mar. 2017, www.poynter.org/news/radiotopia-early-podcast-network-going-strong-and-expanding.

Murthy, Rekha. "Public Radio + IPhone = Public Radio Tuner." PRX, 12 Jan. 2009, blog.prx.org/2009/01/public-radio-iphone-public-radio-tuner/.

Pompeo, Joe. "Kinsey Wilson's Quick Rise at the Times." About Us, POLITICO, 28 Apr. 2015, www.politico.com/media/story/2015/04/kinsey-wilsons-quick-rise-at-the-times-003721.

"PRX – About." PRX–Public Radio Exchange, www.prx.org/company/about.

"PRX – Publishing Platform." PRX–Public Radio Exchange, www.prx.org/services/publishing-platform.

"PRX » Projects." PRX–Public Radio Exchange, exchange.prx.org/projects.

"PRX and PRI Announce Transformational Public Media Merger." Public Radio International, PRI, 15 Aug. 2018, www.pri.org/prx-and-pri-announce-transformational-public-media-merger.

"PRX Launches Radiotopia, New Podcast Network of Story-Driven Public Radio Shows by Industry's Best Emerging and Established Talent." Knight Foundation, 4 Feb. 2014, knightfoundation.org/press/releases/prx-launches-radiotopia-groundbreaking-podcast-net.

"PRX Wants To Redefine Radio." Radio Ink, 23 May 2016, radioink.com/2016/05/19/prx-wants-redefine-radio/.

"PRX Wins MacArthur Award for Creative and Effective Institutions ." Berkman Klein Center, 10 Apr. 2008, cyber.harvard.edu/node/94302.

"PRX » What Is Prx?" PRX–Public Radio Exchange, exchange.prx.org/about-us/what-is-prx.

"Reinventing Public Media for the Digital Age." MacArthur Award for Creative & Effective Institutions, www.macfound.org/maceirecipients/47/.

Reveal, "The VA's Opiate Overload." Peabody Awards, 2013, www.peabody-awards.com/award-profile/reveal-the-vas-opiate-overload-public-radio.

Shapiro, Jake. "CPB Extends SoundExchange Agreement, PRX Included." PRX, 11 Aug. 2009, blog.prx.org/2009/08/cpb-extends-soundexchange-agreement-prx-included/.

Shapiro, Jake. "Remix Radio Re-Imagines Public Radio as Interactive Collage." MediaShift, 12 Nov. 2010, mediashift.org/2010/11/remix-radio-re-imagines-public-radio-as-interactive-collage305/.

Shapiro, Jake. "Why PRX, Knight Created an Accelerator for Public Media." Knight Foundation, 19 Jan. 2012, knightfoundation.org/articles/why-prx-knight-created-accelerator-public-media.

Taylor, Maggie. "Ear Hustle Is the Winner of Radiotpia's Podquest Contest." PRX, 15 Nov. 2016, blog.prx.org/2016/11/your-podquest-winner-ear-hustle/.

Washenko, Anna. "RadioPublic Embarks on Equity Crowdfunding Campaign." RAIN News, 22 June 2018, rainnews.com/radiopublic-embarks-on-equity-crowdfunding-campaign/.

Community Radio & LPFM

Alquist, Ann. "The Problem(s) of Community Radio." Radio Survivor, 20 Sept. 2014, www.radiosurvivor.com/2014/09/16/problems-community-radio/.

Bibliography

Bailey, George. "*Journal of Broadcasting & Electronic Media*/December 2004 Free Riders, Givers, and Heavy Users: Predicting Listener Support for Public Radio." *Journal of Broadcasting & Electronic Media*, Dec. 2004, pp. 607–619.

"Changes in the Rules Relating to Noncommercial Educational FM Broadcast Stations," [Docket 20735, Second R&O, FCC 76-384].

Cockburn, Alexander. "NPR and NAB Ally to Crush Low Power Radio." The Columbus Freepress, 19 Apr. 2000, freepress.org/columns/display/2/2000/608.

Cohen, Elliot. "A Radio Station In Your Hands Is Worth 500 Channels of Mush: The Role of Community Radio in the Struggle Against Corporate Domination of Media." Startup Costs, Prometheus Radio Project, 2004, www.prometheusradio.org/radio-station-your-hands-worth-500-channels-mush-role-community-radio-struggle-against-corporate-dom.

Falk, Tyler. "Community Radio Stations Prepare Coordinated Year-End Fundraiser." *Current*, 17 Oct. 2016, current.org/2016/10/community-radio-stations-prepare-coordinated-year-end-fundraiser/.

FCC Fines Portland's Listener-Sponsored KBOO For Sarah Jones' 'Your Revolution'." ArtScope.net: Tony Fitzpatrick: Max and Gaby's Alphabet, 17 May 2001, www.artscope.net/NEWS/new0732001-3.shtml.

"FCC Reports LPFM Interference Findings to Congress," Radio Magazine, 1 Mar. 2004, web.archive.org/web/20080409100247/http://www.mediaaccess.org/programs/lpfm/RADIOmagazine.pdf.

Freed, Rachel. "KBOO Agrees to Change, a Little." *Current*, 16 Mar. 1998, https://current.org/wp-content/uploads/archive-site/cpb/cpb805k.html.

Gerry, Lyn. "Lynne Chadwick, Co-Founder of NFCB's 'Healthy Station Project' Named as New Manager for KPFA." Radio 4All, 3 July 1997, freepacifica.savegrassrootsradio.org/fp/healthystation.htm.

ibid

Harden, Blaine. "Religious and Public Stations Battle for Share of Radio Dial." *The New York Times*, 15 Sept. 2002, www.nytimes.com/2002/09/15/us/religious-and-public-stations-battle-for-share-of-radio-dial.html.

Hendrix, Steve. "A Station Is Born: Inside the High-Risk, Low-Watt, Quirky World of Community Radio." The Washington Post, WP Company, 5 Aug.

2016, www.washingtonpost.com/local/a-station-is-born-inside-the-high-risk-low-watt-quirky-world-of-community-radio/2016/08/05/12e98440-5444-11e6-bbf5-957ad17b4385_story.html?postshare.

Huntsberger, Michael. "The Emergence of Community Radio in the United States: A Historical Examination of the National Federation of Community Broadcasters, 1970 to 1990". Linfield College Faculty Publications, 2007 1 (1).

Kane, Sally. "About the National Federation of Community Broadcasters." National Arts Strategies, 30 Aug. 2016, http://www.artstrategies.org/down-loads/CEP/participant_directory_public.pdf.

Krauthammer, Charles, Time . "Limousine Liberal Hypocrisy." March 16, 2007.

Lasar, Matthew. "NPR's War on Low Power FM: the Laws of Physics vs. Politics." Ars Technica, 27 Apr. 2008, arstechnica.com/uncategorized/2008/04/nprs-war-on-low-power-fm-the-laws-of-physics-vs-politics/.

Law, Steve. "Embattled KBOO Manager Quits: New Board Slate Wins." Https://Joomlakave.com, 17 Sept. 2013, portlandtribune.com/pt/9-news/194825-embattled-kboo-manager-quits-new-board-slate-wins-.

"Low Power Radio–General Information." Federal Communications Commission, 11 Jan. 2017, www.fcc.gov/media/radio/low-power-radio-general-information.

McDonough, Ted. "Dead Air: KRCL Is Getting a Corporate Makeover. Is Community Radio Done for?" Salt Lake City Weekly, 1 July 2018, www.cityweekly.net/utah/feature-dead-air-krcl-is-getting-a-corporate-makeover-is-community-radio-done-for/Content?oid=2134992.

Moore, Nathan. "A Eulogy for Free Speech Radio News." Current, 8 May 2017,
current.org/2017/05/a-eulogy-for-free-speech-radio-news/. .

"NPR Offerings Expanded on WUTC FM 88.1." University of Tennessee–Chattanooga, 5 Jan. 2006, www.utc.edu/communications-marketing/news-center/archive/2006/wutcprogram06.php.

"NPR: Try Easing on LPFM. But Protect Reading Services," Radio World, 20 Oct, 2003, www.radioworld.com/news-and-business/npr-try-easing-on-lpfm-but-protect-reading-services.

Ornato, Ellen. "KBUT at Age 30 – A Three Part Series on the Valley's Radio Station." The Crested Butte News, crestedbuttenews.com/2016/07/kbut-at-age-30-a-three-part-series-on-the-valleys-radio-station-3/.

Reynolds, Glenn, "An Army of Davids: How Markets and Technology Empower Ordinary People to Beat Big Media, Big Government and Other Goliaths," Thomas Nelson, 4 February 2007, pg

Riismandel, Paul. "An Online Archive of the Fourth Community Radio Station: KRAB." *Radio Survivor*, 7 Nov. 2016, www.radiosurvivor.com/2016/11/06/online-archive-fourth-community-radio-station-krab/.

Robertson, Frank. "River FM Radio Station Changes Anger Volunteers in Perceived 'Coup D'etat'." Sonoma West Publishers, 20 Feb. 2013, www.sonomawest.com/sonoma_west_times_and_news/news/river-fm-radio-station-changes-anger-volunteers-in-perceived-coup/article_e1c5d5fe-7b9c-11e2-9c45-0019bb2963f4.html.

Stavisky, Alan G., et al, (2001). "From Class D to LPFM: The High-Powered Politics of Low-Power Radio". Journalism & Mass Communication Quarterly. 78: 340–54.

Walker, Jesse. "With Friends Like These: Why Community Radio Doesn't Need the Corporation for Public Broadcasting." Policy Analysis #277, 24 July 1997, pp. 1–18., object.cato.org/pubs/pas/pa277.pdf.

"Week at a Glance." 2017. KBOO, 8 June 2017, kboo.fm/file/70500/download?token=bPJl3zPY.

Zhao, Jijun, et al. "An agent based simulation methodology for analyzing public radio membership campaigns," *Information Technology for Economics and Management*, pg 32., www.item.woiz.polsl.pl/issue4.1/pdf/publicgoods_revised.pdf

Chapter 3 – Is There a Problem?

"A Network Engaged." NPR. 2016 Annual Report, 9 June 2017, pp. 1–48.

Belaska, John. "The 10 Richest Radio Personalities in the World." TheRichest, 17 Oct. 2014, www.therichest.com/expensive-lifestyle/money/the-10-richest-radio-personalities-in-the-world/.

Falk, Tyler. "As It Defines Relationship with Stations, NPR Gains Board Approval for Price Hike." *Current*, 24 Feb. 2017, current.org/2017/02/npr-proposes-new-dues-structure-strategy-for-stronger-future-with-stations/.

Falk, Tyler. "Program Directors Challenged to Think about Audience, Not Formats." *Current*, 2 Oct. 2015, current.org/2015/09/program-directors-chal-lenged-to-think-about-audience-not-formats/.

Farhi, Paul. "NPR Is Graying, and Public Radio Is Worried about It." The Washington Post, WP Company, 22 Nov. 2015, www.washingtonpost.com/lifestyle/style/npr-is-graying-and-public-radio-is-worried-about-it/2015/11/22/0615447e-8e48-11e5-baf4-bdf37355da0c_story.html.

Farhi, Paul. "NPR's New Headquarters Refuels Funding Debate." The Washington Post, WP Company, 21 June 2013, www.washingtonpost.com/lifestyle/style/nprs-new-headquarters-refuels-funding-debate/2013/06/21/bb53a64a-da00-11e2-a016-92547bf094cc_story.html?utm_term=.f05ddf244a88.

Garofalo, Pat. "Republicans' 'YouCut' Gimmick Leads Them To Propose Ending Successful Jobs Program.", ThinkProgress, 19 May 2010, thinkprogress.org/republicans-youcut-gimmick-leads-them-to-propose-ending-successful-jobs-program-9a2d18a231c9/.

Garofoli, Joe. "Public Broadcasting Stations Cut Staff, Budget." SFGate, San Francisco Chronicle, 9 Feb. 2012, www.sfgate.com/politics/article/Public-broadcasting-stations-cut-staff-budget-3174082.php.

Gerstein, Josh. "Josh Gerstein." NPR Salaries: Raw Data, 1 Jan. 1970, joshgerstein.blogspot.com/2008/12/npr-salaries-raw-data.html.

Jarvik, Elaine. "NPR: EXPOSED AND ENDANGERED?," Deseret News, 28 Apr. 1995, www.deseretnews.com/article/417799/NPR-EX-POSED-AND-ENDANGERED.html.

Jensen, Elizabeth. "NPR Gets $17 Million in Grants to Expand Coverage and Develop Digital Platform." *The New York Times*, 16 Dec. 2013, www.nytimes.com/2013/12/16/business/media/npr-gets-17-million-in-grants-to-expand-coverage-and-develop-digital-platform.html.

Molotsky, Irvin. "AUDIT SHOWS NPR HAS A DEFICIT OF $6.5 MILLION." *The New York Times*, 16 June 1983, www.nytimes.com/1983/06/16/arts/audit-shows-npr-has-a-deficit-of-6.5-million.html.

Mook, Ben, and Everhart, Karen. "NPR Board Appoints Haaga as Interim Chief, Announces 10-Percent Buy-out Plan." *Current,* 9 Oct. 2013, current. org/2013/09/npr-board-appoints-lay-leader-haaga-as-interim-president/.

"Radio Show Host Salary." www.payscale.com/research/US/Job=Radio_Show_Host/Salary.

Roderick, Kevin. "NPR's Budget Cuts Memo." Native Intelligence, 10 Dec. 2008, www.laobserved.com/archive/2008/12/nprs_budget_cuts.php.

Staff, "Nielsen 'People Meters' Draw Fire." Wired, Conde Nast, 5 June 2017, www.wired.com/2004/04/nielsen-people-meters-draw-fire/.

Taibi, Catherine. "NPR To Cut 28 Jobs." The Huffington Post, 20 May 2014, www.huffingtonpost.com/2014/05/20/npr-tell-me-more-jobs-lay-offs_n_5359343.html.

Weigel, David. "Republicans Pledge 'Full Audit' of NPR." *Slate* Magazine, *Slate*, 22 Oct. 2010, www.slate.com/content/slate/blogs/ weigel/2010/10/22/republicans_pledge_full_audit_of_npr.html.

Audience

"A Guide to Understanding and Using PPM Data." 21 Dec. 2010, pp. 1–24., www.arbitron.com/downloads/guide_to_using_ppm_data.pdf.

Bouryal, Kristie, and Kate Vanek. "Nielsen Acquires Arbitron; What People Watch, Listen To and Buy," 30 Sept. 2013, www.nielsen.com/us/en/press-room/2013/nielsen-acquires-arbitron.html.

Carney, Steve. "Don't Touch That Radio Dial–Arbitron Is Listening." Los Angeles Times, 24 Aug. 2011, articles.latimes.com/2011/aug/24/entertainment/ la-et-radio-ratings-20110824.

Cohen, Arthur. "MRC Withdraws PPM Accreditation in Five Markets." PRPD News for Programmers, 1 Feb. 2012, prpd-news.blogspot.com/search?q=ar-bitron#!/2012/02/mrc-withdraws-ppm-accreditation-in-five.html.

Elendil's Hair, et al. "Listening to NPR during Fund Drives." Straight Dope Message Board RSS, 3 June 2016, boards.straightdope.com/sdmb/show-thread.php?t=794755.

Falk, Tyler. "Program Directors Challenged to Think about Audience, Not Formats." *Current*, 2 Oct. 2015, current.org/2015/09/program-directors-chal-lenged-to-think-about-audience-not-formats/.

PLEDGE: The Public Radio Fund Drive

"FM and TV Propagation Curves." Federal Communications Commission, 7
Dec. 2015, www.fcc.gov/media/radio/fm-and-tv-propagation-curves.

Greenspan, Marc, and Sislen, Charlie. Hot Topics, "What Enhanced CBET
Means to Broadcasters." Research Director, Inc., 21 Oct. 2015, www.re-
searchdirectorinc.com/2015/10/what-enhanced-cbet-means-to-broadcasters/.

James, Meg. "Nielsen Confirms 'Inconsistencies' with Los Angeles Radio Ratings." Los Angeles Times, Los Angeles Times, 11 June 2014, beta.latimes.
com/entertainment/envelope/cotown/la-et-ct-nielsen-problems-los-angeles-
radio-ratings-20140611-story.html.

Lubove, Seth. "Bad Ratings For Arbitron." Forbes Magazine, 6 June 2013,
www.forbes.com/2003/03/11/cz_sl_0311arbitron.html#2dfa7761512c.

Nielsen Audio Ratings." RADIO ONLINE ®, Apr. 2018, ratings.radio-online.
com/cgi-bin/rol.exe/arb051.

Nielsen, "Terminology and Definitions." 15 May 2014, www.arbitron.com/
downloads/terms_brochure.pdf .

"Nielsen versus Arbitron: Why It Matters to Radio." Radio InSights, 23 Dec.
2008, www.radioinsights.com/2008/12/nielsen-versus-arbitron-why-it-mat-
ters-to-radio.html.

"Predicted Coverage Area for WVPB 88.5 FM, Charleston, WV.," radio-locator.
com/cgi-bin/patg?id=WVPB-FM.28. https://www.fcc.gov/media/radio/fm-
and-tv-propagation-curves

"Radio Market Survey Population, Survey Rankings & Information." 2015, pp.
1–30., www.nielsen.com/content/dam/corporate/us/en/docs/nielsen-audio/
market_populations_and_rankings_2015.pdf.

Radio Research Consortium, "Summer 2017 Quarter PPM ERanks." 12 Oct.
2017, pp. 1–4., www.rrconline.org/reports/pdf/Su17%20PPM%20eRanks.
pdf.

Radio-Locator.com. "Radio Stations in Salina, Kansas.," Radio-Locator.com,
radio-locator.com/.

RBR-TVBR." Radio & Television Business Report–The Financial + Regulatory
Voice of Electronic Media, RADIO+TELEVISION BUSINESS REPORT,
19 Jan. 2015, www.rbr.com/more-mostly-twenty-something-radio-rat-
ings-results/.

Robins, Ben. "Summary of Arbitron's Total Audience Measurement." NPR, 23 Jan. 2013, digitalservices.npr.org/post/summary-arbitrons-total-audience-measurement.

Simpson, April. "Generation Listen Aims to Bring Millennials into the NPR Family." *Current*, 5 July 2016, current.org/2016/07/generation-lis-ten-aims-to-bring-millennials-into-the-npr-family/.

"Summary of Arbitron's Total Audience Measurement." NPR, 23 Jan. 2012, digitalservices.npr.org/post/summary-arbitrons-total-audience-measurement.

Taylor, Dick. "What If the Problem Isn't PPM?" *RadioInsight*, 4 June 2015, radioinsight.com/blogs/93220/dick-taylor-what-if-the-problem-isnt-ppm/.

"Why Nielsen Comes Up Short in Radio Measurement." Insideradio.com, 12 Dec. 2016, http://www.insideradio.com/why-nielsen-comes-up-short-in-radio-measurement/article_5136c95e-c002-11e6-a72a-675bf13ae312.html

"West Virginia Public Broadcasting Merges Brands." Montgomery Herald, 7 Jan. 2015, www.montgomery-herald.com/news/west-virginia-public-broadcasting-merges-brands/article_eb3ddf3e-9623-11e4-84b7-93b9f8638b4d.html._.

Revenue

Adams, Guy. "Are TV Detector Vans Just a Cunning Con Trick? For Decades It's Been Claimed They Trap License Cheats. In Fact, They've Never Led to a Single Prosecution." Daily Mail Online, Associated Newspapers, 5 Oct. 2013, www.dailymail.co.uk/news/article-2445153/Are-TV-detector-vans-just-cunning-trick-For-decades-claimed-trap-licence-cheats-In-fact-theyve-led-single-prosecution.html.

Bullard, Gabe. "Crowdfunding the News." Nieman Reports, Sep. 27, 2016

Charney, Tamar, et al. "NPR One: One More Way to Reach Listeners during Pledge Drive." , NPR, 13 Sept. 2016, digitalservices.npr.org/post/npr-one-one-more-way-reach-listeners-during-pledge-drive.

CPB–Major Giving Initiative–Leadership for Philanthropy–LFP–Use Proven Resources–Success Stories–Capital Campaign, www.majorgivingnow.org/resources/stories_capital_campaign.html.

PLEDGE: The Public Radio Fund Drive

Cullinane, Mollie. "Who Owns a Nonprofit? No One!" Cullinane Law Group, Legal Counsel for Nonprofits + Associations, Austin Texas, 29 June 2017, cullinanelaw.com/nonprofit-law-basics-who-owns-a-nonprofit/.

"Fear and Courage Comments." 25 June 2013, niemanreports.org/articles/crowdfunding-the-news/.

Gonzalez, Mike." Stop Forcing Taxpayers to Fund Public Broadcasting." The Denver Post, 3 Nov. 2017, www.denverpost.com/2017/11/03/stop-forcing-taxpayers-to-fund-public-broadcasting/.

Janssen, Mike. "FCC Denies Stations' Bid for Looser Underwriting Language." Current, 23 May 2014, current.org/2014/05/fcc-denies-stations-bid-for-loos-er-underwriting-language/.

Murphy, Kate. "Bible Broadcast Corp. to Buy Radio Station WNKU." Cincinnati.com, Cincinnati Enquirer, 14 Feb. 2017, www.cincinnati.com/story/news/2017/02/14/wnku-sold-bible-broadcast-corp/97893994/.

Sefton, Dru. "For Some Pubcasters, State Funding Plays Valuable Role in Strengthening Service." Current, 23 May 2018, current.org/2018/05/for-some-pubcasters-state-funding-plays-valuable-role-in-strengthening-ser-vice/.

Silva, Ernesto. "President Johnson's Remarks." CPB, 30 Jan. 2015, www.cpb.org/aboutpb/act/remarks.

Silva, Ernesto. "CPB's Federal Appropriation Request & Justification." CPB, 12 Feb. 2018, www.cpb.org/funding.

Staff. "The History of Public Broadcasting." MPA@UNC, 21 Oct. 2013, onlinempa.unc.edu/history-of-public-broadcasting/.

USAspending.gov." www.usaspending.gov/#/keyword_search/WGBH.

Ydstie, John, and Kevin Klose. "Philanthropist Joan Kroc Leaves NPR $200 Million Gift." NPR, 6 Nov. 2003, www.npr.org/templates/story/story.php?storyId=1494600.

Funding Models

Ahmed, Sara. "It Would Only Cost Each American $1.37 a Year to Save PBS, But That Might Not Be Enough." Babble, Babble, 16 Mar. 2017, www.babble.com/entertainment/trumps-federal-spending-cuts-could-end-pbs/.

American Forces Network Online." MyAFN, myafn.dodmedia.osd.mil/.

Bleizffer, Dustin. "Wyoming Public Radio and Television Flirt with the End of Federal Funding." The Billings Gazette, 10 Apr. 2011, billingsgazette.com/news/state-and-regional/wyoming/wyoming-public-radio-and-television-flirt-with-the-end-of/article_17039561-99fc-5def-9164-9d930d7e330b.html.

Cord, David J. "Finland's Public Broadcaster under Pressure." Helsinki Times, 5 Sept. 2013, www.helsinkitimes.fi/business/7554-finland-s-public-broadcaster-under-pressure-2.html.

Dawson, Dennis, and Plett, Daniel Neil. "Time for Change: The CBC/Radio Canada in the Twenty-First Century." Report of the Standing Senate Committee, 14 July 2015, sencanada.ca/content/sen/Committee/412/trcm/rep/rep14jul15-e.pdf. pg 66

DeRienzo, Matt. "Industry Insight: 'Paywall' to 'Membership' Will Require a Massive Culture Shift for Newspapers." Editor & Publisher, 18 Mar. 2016, www.editorandpublisher.com/columns/industry-insight-paywall-to-membership-will-require-a-massive-culture-shift-for-newspapers/.

Fandos, Nicholas. "Nonprofit Journalism Groups Are Gearing Up With Flood of Donations." , The New York Times, 22 Dec. 2017, www.nytimes.com/2016/12/07/business/media/nonprofit-journalism-groups-are-gearing-up-with-flood-of-donations.html.

Foster, William Landis, et al. "Ten Nonprofit Funding Models (SSIR)." Stanford Social Innovation Review: Informing and Inspiring Leaders of Social Change, 2009, ssir.org/articles/entry/ten_nonprofit_funding_models.

Freire, Emma Elliott. "The BBC Is A Cross Between PBS And The IRS." The Federalist, 7 Aug. 2014, thefederalist.com/2014/08/07/the-bbc-is-a-cross-between-pbs-and-the-irs/.

Guth, Dana. "Subscription Is the New Sharing: The Rise of the 'Membership Economy'." Public Radio International, 1 Sept. 2015, pri.org/stories/2015-09-01/subscription-new-sharing-rise-membership-economy.

Janssen, Mike. "Spending of Kroc Gift Outlined," 2004. Fox News, 24 May 2004, web.archive.org/web/20110322154055/http://www.current.org/npr/npr0409krocgift.shtml.

Jeffrey Dvorkin," former NPR Ombudsman, email conversation with author, Jan. 9, 2018

Jones, Holly. "East: Thousands Caught Evading TV License." Heart, 4 Feb. 2012, www.heart.co.uk/suffolk/news/local/east-thousands-caught-evading-tv-licence/.

KRCU3 timestamp 7 Apr. 2016 1523 CST

Memmott, Mark. "In Video: NPR Exec Slams Tea Party, Questions Need For Federal Funds." NPR, 8 Mar. 2011, www.npr.org/sections/thetwo-way/2011/03/09/134358398/in-video-npr-exec-slams-tea-party-questions-need-for-federal-funds.

Merrill, Donald, "MyData," GoogleDocs Public Radio Survey, June 2017, Portland, OR

Moyers, Bil. "Prepared Remarks; Moyers Faith and Reason," Public Broadcasting Service, 18 May 2006, www.pbs.org/moyers/faithandreason/pbsaddress.html.

Oliphant, James. "NPR in Hot Water Again over Ron Schiller's Tea Party Remarks." Mcclatchydc, McClatchy Washington Bureau, 8 Mar. 2011, www.mcclatchydc.com/news/politics-government/article24615694.html.

OMB Circular A-122–The White House. OMB, 10 May 2004, https://www.whitehouse.gov/sites/whitehouse.gov/files/omb/circulars/A122/a122_2004.pdf.

Palmeri, Tara, et al. "Trump to Inherit State-Run TV Network with Expanded Reach." About Us, POLITICO, 12 Dec. 2016, www.politico.com/story/2016/12/donald-trump-voice-of-america-232442.

Plesser, Andy. (Video) "NPR's Problems with Money, 'Ownership' and Politicalization, Former CEO Speaks." The *Huffington Post*, 3 June 2013, www.huffingtonpost.com/andy-plesser/video-nprs-problems-with_b_1377378.html.

Radio Liberty Going off the Air in Russia.," NEPR.net Home, 18 Oct. 2012, digital.nepr.net/news/2012/10/18/radio-liberty-going-air-russia/.

Silverman, Lauren. "Web-Based Subscription Businesses Surf A New Wave." NPR, NPR, 5 Sept. 2012, www.npr.org/sections/alltechconsidered/2012/09/05/160397728/web-based-subscription-businesses-surf-a-new-wave.

"TV License Enforcement Review." Department for Culture, Media & Sport, 12 Feb. 2015, www.gov.uk/government/uploads/system/uploads/attachment_

data/file/403561/15_02_12_Consultation_document_-_TV_Licence_En-forcement_Review_2_.pdf

Turner, Zeke. "Interview: NPR's Dick Meyer Discusses NPR.org Redesign, Visual Vocabulary." Mediaite, 29 Oct. 2009, www.mediaite.com/online/in-terview-nprs-dick-meyer-discusses-npr-org-redesign-visual-vocabulary/.

"US Radio Marti: Still Transmitting Anti-Cuba Propaganda." Noticias, Tele-SUR, TeleSUR, 13 Feb. 2017, www.telesurtv.net/english/news/Radio-Mar-ti-A-Bastion-of-US-Anti-Cuba-Propaganda-20170213-0015.html.

Our Canadian Cousin

Ahmed, Sara. "It Would Only Cost Each American $1.37 a Year to Save PBS, But That Might Not Be Enough." Babble, Babble, 16 Mar. 2017, www.babble.com/entertainment/trumps-federal-spending-cuts-could-end-pbs/.

Broadcasting Decision CRTC 2013-263 and Broadcasting Orders CRTC 2013-264 and 2013-265." CRTC, Government of Canada, Canadian Radio-Tele-vision and Telecommunications Commission (CRTC), ARCHIVED 28 May 2013, crtc.gc.ca/eng/archive/2013/2013-263.htm.

"Canada CBC Radio Revenue 2016" Statista, www.statista.com/statis-tics/540635/cbc-radio-revenue-canada/.

"CBC President Defends Ad-Free Proposal, Asks Ottawa for $400M to 'Un-shackle' Broadcaster." CBC Radio." CBCnews, CBC/Radio Canada, 30 Nov. 2016, www.cbc.ca/radio/asithappens/as-it-happens-tuesday-edi-tion-1.3872769/cbc-president-defends-ad-free-proposal-asks-ottawa-for-400m-to-unshackle-broadcaster-1.3872770.

"CBC to Cut 657 Jobs, Will No Longer Compete for pro Sports Rights." CBC News. CBCnews, CBC/Radio Canada, 11 Apr. 2014, www.cbc.ca/news/canada/cbc-to-cut-657-jobs-will-no-longer-compete-for-professional-sports-rights-1.2605504.6.

CBC/Radio-Canada Annual Report 2014-2015. "Our History," 2014, www.cbc.radio-canada.ca/site/annual-reports/2014-2015/resources/people-leader-ship-en.html.15.

Ireland, Nicole. "CBC Asks for $400M to Go Ad-Free." CBC News." CBC-news, CBC/Radio Canada, 29 Nov. 2016, www.cbc.ca/news/canada/cbc-ra-dio-canada-ad-free-proposal-1.3871077.

PLEDGE: The Public Radio Fund Drive

"Justin Trudeau Goes One-on-One with CBC Host Andrew Chang." CBC News. CBCnews, CBC/Radio Canada, 23 Dec. 2014, www.cbc.ca/news/canada/ british-columbia/justin-trudeau-goes-one-on-one-with-cbc-host-andrew-chang-1.2878612.

Pitcher, Penny. "We Vote CBC in Victoria!" James Bay Beacon, Sept. 2015, jamesbaybeacon.ca/?q=node%2F1633.

Reid, Regan. "CBC Ad Revenue Spikes in 2016/2017." Media In Canada–Keeping Media and Marketing Execs up to Speed on the Canadian Media Scene, 20 Sept. 2017, mediaincanada.com/2017/09/20/cbc-ad-revenue-spikes-in-20162017/.

Rowland, Wade. "The CBC's a Service, Not a Business." The Globe and Mail, 26 June 2014, www.theglobeandmail.com/opinion/the-cbcs-a-service-not-a-business/article19354362/.

Taylor, Kate. "Ad-Free CBC Could Serve as a Rallying Point for Canadian Creativity." The Globe and Mail, 11 Apr. 2017, www.theglobeandmail.com/ arts/television/ad-free-cbc-could-act-as-a-rallying-point-for-canadian-creativity/article33138985/.

"Time for Change: The CBC/Radio-Canada in the Twenty-First Century." The Honourable Dennis Dawson, Chair; The Honourable Donald Neil Plett, Deputy Chair, Report of the Standing Senate Committee on Transport and Communications, July 2015, pp. 1–95., sencanada.ca/content/sen/Committee/412/trcm/rep/rep14jul15-e.pdf.

Waldie, Paul. "CBC to Boost Ads in Website Overhaul." Google News, 8 June 2005, https://www.friends.ca/news-item/3354.

Wong, Tony. "Who Says Canadian TV Is Dead? 2017 Was Best Year Ever for Drama." Thestar.com, Toronto Star, 24 Dec. 2017, www.thestar.com/entertainment/television/2017/12/24/who-says-canadian-tv-is-dead-2017-was-best-year-ever-for-drama.html.

Appropriated Funding in the U.S.

"10 Largest Budget Functions." Peter G. Peterson Foundation, 7 June 2018, www.pgpf.org/budget-basics/top-10-largest-budget-functions.

"A Brief Guide to the Federal Budget and Appropriations Process." American Council on Education, www.acenet.edu/news-room/Pages/A-Brief-Guide-to-the-Federal-Budget-and-Appropriations-Process.aspx.12.

Asturias, Jose. "Why Do Individuals Contribute to Public Radio?" University of Pennsylvania, 10 Oct. 2017, repository.upenn.edu/cgi/viewcontent.cgi?article=1032&context=wharton_research_scholars&usg=AOvVaw1a_JU5TPCx4eWbSdvavvgo.

"Budget Functions." House Budget Committee Democrats, 31 Jan. 2018, democrats-budget.house.gov/budgets/budget-functions.

Grove, Lloyd. "And Then They Came for Big Bird: Public Broadcasting Reels From Trump's Plan to Destroy It." *The Daily Beast*, 16 Mar. 2017, www.thedailybeast.com/and-then-they-came-for-big-bird-public-broadcasting-reels-from-trumps-plan-to-destroy-it.

Jacoby, Jeff. "What NPR Needs Is a Little Tough Love." Townhall, 14 Mar. 2011, townhall.com/columnists/jeffjacoby/2011/03/14/what-npr-needs-is-a-little-tough-love-n1075633.

Senter, Lerman, "Satellite Home Viewer Improvement Act." Lerman Senter Law Firm, 14 Mar. 2000, www.lermansenter.com/what-publications-45.html.

Silva, Ernesto. "Purpose & History of CPB's Advance Appropriations." CPB, 19 Feb. 2016, www.cpb.org/appropriation/purpose.

The American Presidency Project, www.presidency.ucsb.edu/ws/index.php.

"The Corporation for Public Broadcasting: Federal Funding and Issues." Congressional Research Service, 3 May 2017, fas.org/sgp/crs/misc/RS22168.pdf.

"The U.S. House of Representatives Committee On Appropriations, Chairman Rodney Frelinghuysen." Comprehensive Government Funding Bill Released, Committee on Appropriations, U.S. House of Representatives, 22 Mar. 2018, appropriations.house.gov/subcommittees/subcommittee/?IssueID=34777.

Weigel, David. "NPR Cans Ronald Schiller." *Slate* Magazine, *Slate*, 8 Mar. 2011, www.slate.com/content/slate/blogs/weigel/2011/03/08/npr_puts_ron_schiller_on_administrative_leave.html.

PLEDGE: The Public Radio Fund Drive

Zarroli, Jim. "Defunding Public Media: Disaster Or Opportunity?" WBUR
News, 24 Mar. 2011, www.wbur.org/npr/134830262/is-it-time-to-kill-fund-
ing-for-public-broadcasting.

Corporation for Public Broadcasting

"2018 Radio Community Service Grants–General Provisions and Eligibility
Criteria." CPB, 17 Dec. 2017, ttps://www.cpb.org/sites/default/files/stations/
radio/generalprovisions/FY-2018-Radio-General-Provisions.pdf.

"A Brief Guide to the Federal Budget and Appropriations Process," 23 Mar.
2018, www.acenet.edu/news-room/Pages/A-Brief-Guide-to-the-Federal-
Budget-and-Appropriations-Process.aspx.

Anonymous, and Myers, Kate. "Was 'Car Talk' Really the Most Expensive
Show on NPR?" What Is the Difference between SAP HANA and s4hana?–
Quora, 17 July 2012, www.quora.com/Was-Car-Talk-really-the-most-
expen-sive-show-on-NPR.

Beebe, Paul. "KCPW to Drop National Public Radio Programs." *The Salt Lake
Tribune*, 18 June 2013, archive.sltrib.com/article.php?id=56471604.

Boehlert, Eric. "Pushing PBS to the Right." Salon, 25 Sept. 2011, www.salon.
com/2005/05/10/cpb_bias_campaign/.

"Bylaws of National Public Radio Inc., 1999." *Current*, 19 Nov. 2012, current.
org/1999/01/bylaws-of-national-public-radio-inc-1999-2/.

Conciatore, Jacqueline. "Few Radio Stations Lose CPB Aid." *Current*, 16 Mar.
1998, current.org/wp-content/uploads/archive-site/cpb/cpb805d.html.

CPB, 20 June 2018, www.cpb.org/grants/archived.

Freed, Rachel. "KBOO Agrees to Change, a Little." *Current*, 16 Mar. 1998,
current.org/wp-content/uploads/archive-site/cpb/cpb805k.html.

Giovanonni, David. "Can Public Radio Replace Federal Funds with Audience
Sensitive Income?" CPB, May 1995, files.eric.ed.gov/fulltext/ED386148.
pdf.

Hart, Peter, and Rendall, Steve. "Time to Unplug the CPB." FAIR, 20 Feb. 2013,
fair.org/extra/time-to-unplug-the-cpb/.

Klopper, Hal. "Soundscapes: The Evolution and Challenges of National Public
Radio." Carnegie Results, 2006, pp. 1–12., www.carnegie.org/media/filer_

public/7c/09/7c09ca67-c0a3-4346-a8a5-f5fcbff10ca0/ccny_cresults_2006_
npr.pdf.

Korbelik, Jeff. "NET, KZUM Face Possible Cuts to Federal Funding." Jour-
nalStar.com, The Lincoln Journal Star, 9 Apr. 2017, journalstar.com/enter-
tainment/tv-radio/net-kzum-face-possible-cuts-to-federal-funding/article_
fc9e950d-9ae1-5e76-8ba1-ea9dd9cd1a69.html.20. https://www.csmonitor.
com/1987/0109/lfund.html

Kroll, John. "KCSN Seeks to Avert Loss of Federal Funds." California State
University, Northridge, 3 Sept. 1996, scholarworks.csun.edu/bitstream/han-
dle/10211.2/1152/atcsun96.09.03.pdf., pg 29

"Open Grants and RFPs." CPB, 19 July 2018, www.cpb.org/grants.

"Public Broadcasting Starts with You." Frequently Asked Questions, Nebraska
Educational Television, 24 Aug. 2012, d1vmz9r13e2j4x.cloudfront.net/
NET/misc/00027010.pdf.

"Public Radio Finances." , NPR, 20 June 2013, www.npr.org/about-
npr/178660742/public-radio-finances.32. ibid

"Radio Community Service Grants." FY2011, isis.cpb.org/ISIS_Help_Files/
SECTION_1_ELIGIBILITY.htm.

Sherman, Scott. "Press Watch." *The Nation*, 29 June 2015, www.thenation.com/
article/press-watch-2/.

Silva, Ernesto. "About Public Media." CPB, 11 May 2018, www.cpb.org/about-
pb/what-public-media.

Silva, Ernesto. "Community Service Grants." CPB, 6 June 2018, www.cpb.org/
stations.

Silva, Ernesto. "Content and Production Grants." CPB, 22 Mar. 2016, www.cpb.
org/grants/content-and-producers-grants.

Silva, Ernesto. "Corporate Officers and Senior Staff." CPB, 18 May 2018, www.
cpb.org/aboutcpb/leadership.

Silva, Ernesto. "CPB's Federal Appropriation Request & Justification." CPB, 12
Feb. 2018, www.cpb.org/funding/.

Stellman, Andrew. "KZUM Faces Federal Funding Cuts with Positive Momentum." Hear Nebraska, 10 Feb. 2016, hearnebraska.org/feature/kzum-fac-
es-federal-funding-cuts-with-positive-momentum/.

Public Radio's "Basket"

"2017 Instructions for Form 990 Return of Organization Exempt From Income Tax." IRS, 22 Jan. 2018, https://www.irs.gov/pub/irs-pdf/i990.pdf.

"A Network Engaged." 2016 Annual Report, NPR, 9 June 2017, https://www. npr.org/about/annualreports/2016_Annual_Report.pdf.

"About MPR." Minnesota Public Radio, www.mpr.org/about.

"Advance Ruling Process Elimination *Public Support Test*." Internal Revenue Service, www.irs.gov/charities-non-profits/charitable-organizations/advance-ruling-process-elimination-public-support-test.

Bond, Paul. "Fox News Slams Professors Who Claimed Its Viewers Were Ill-Informed." The Hollywood Reporter, 23 May 2012, www.hollywoodreporter. com/news/fox-news-slams-professors-ill-informed-viewers-fairleigh-dickinson-328771.

Collins, Bob. "Debating NPR Underwriting Announcements." NewsCut, 20 Apr. 2015, blogs.mprnews.org/newscut/2015/04/debating-npr-underwriting-announcements/.

Davis, Lisa Nachmias, Davis, O'Sullivan & Priest LLC, email conversation with author, 10 Nov 2016

"Exempt Organizations Annual Reporting Requirements Form 990 Schedules A and B Facts and Circumstances *Public Support Test*." Internal Revenue Service, www.irs.gov/charities-non-profits/exempt-organizations-annual-reporting-requirements-form-990-schedules-a-and-b-facts-and-circumstances-public-support-test.

Fishman, Stephen. "When Is a Nonprofit required to have an Independent Audit?" Www.nolo.com, Nolo, 2 Aug. 2013, www.nolo.com/legal-encyclopedia/when-is-nonprofit-required-have-independent-audit.html.

Fuerst, Mark. "Pubmedia Stations Foresee Decline of on-Air Pledge Drives, Cite Need for New Tactics." *Current*, 31 July 2014, current.org/2014/07/pubmedia-stations-foresee-decline-of-on-air-pledge-drives-cite-need-for-new-tactics/.

Greenspun, Phillip. "Public Radio Fund Drives Bill of Health," 22 June 2009, blogs.harvard.edu/philg/2009/06/22/public-radio-fund-drives/.

Jensen, Elizabeth. "Did Ploughshares Grant Skew NPR's Iran Deal Coverage?" NPR, 27 May 2016, www.npr.org/sections/ombudsman/2016/05/27/479588582/did-ploughshares-grant-skew-nprs-iran-deal-coverage.

McBride, Ashley. "With Budget Cuts at Bay (for Now) Public Media Are Searching for New Funding Sources." Poynter, 30 Aug. 2017, www.poynter.org/news/budget-cuts-bay-now-public-media-are-searching-new-funding-sources.

McCauley, Michael P., et al, "Public Broadcasting and the Public Interest," Routledge, 2016, pg 106

McLoughlin, Glenn J, and Lena A Gomez. "Federal Funding and Issues." fas.org/sgp/crs/misc/RS22168.pdf.

McRay, Greg. "Nonprofit Unrelated Business Income." Foundation Group®, 16 June 2015, www.501c3.org/nonprofit-unrelated-business-income/.

Merrill, Donald, "MyData," GoogleDocs Public Radio Survey, June 2017, Portland, OR

NPR Annual Report 2014. 6 Feb. 2015, www.npr.org/about/annualreports/FY14_annualreport.pdf.

Papish, Ross. "The Evolving Need for a Strong Firewall." Major Giving Now, 22 Apr. 2011, majorgivingnow.org/downloads/pdf/Evolving_Need_for_Firewall.pdf.

Philiss, James A, and Chang, Victoria. "The Price of Commercial Success (SSIR)." Stanford Social Innovation Review: Informing and Inspiring Leaders of Social Change, 2005, ssir.org/articles/entry/the_price_of_commercial_success.

"Public Broadcasting: Individual Giving and Underwriting Revenue for Public Radio (2016)." Pew Research Center's Journalism Project, 8 June 2016, www.journalism.org/chart/5630/.

"Public Radio Finances." NPR, 20 June 2013, www.npr.org/about-npr/178660742/public-radio-finances.

Rapoza, Kenneth. "Fox News Viewers Uninformed, NPR Listeners Not, Poll Suggests." *Forbes* Magazine, 15 July 2016, www.forbes.com/sites/kenrapo-za/2011/11/21/fox-news-viewers-uninformed-npr-listeners-not-poll-sug-gests/.

Romenesko, Jim. "Mike Pesca Quits NPR for *Slate* (so He Won't Be Getting an IPhone 5 Adapter Anniversary Gift)." JIMROMENESKO.COM, 11 Feb. 2014, jimromenesko.com/2014/02/11/mike-pesca-quits-npr-for-slate-so-he-wont-be-getting-an-iphone-5-adapter-anniversary-gift/.

Sexton, John. "NPR: We Probably Shouldn't Have Taken Funding from Ploughshares Fund to Cover Iran Deal." Hot Air, 31 May 2016, hotair.com/archives/2016/05/31/npr-we-probably-shouldnt-have-taken-funding-from-ploughshares-fund-to-cover-iran-deal/.

"State Budget Crises: Ripping the Safety Net Held by Nonprofits." National Council of Nonprofits, 16 Mar. 2010, www.councilofnonprofits.org/sites/default/files/documents/Special-Report-State-Budget-Crises-Ripping-the-Safety-Net-Held-by-Nonprofits_0.pdf., Pg 2.

Stine, Randy J. "PTFP Shutdown Leaves Pubcasters Scrambling." *Radio World*, 5 July 2011, www.radioworld.com/headlines/0045/ptfp-shut-down-leaves-pubcasters-scrambling/323115.

"Study Evaluates Strength of Public Radio's 'Halo' for Sponsors." *Current*, 12 July 2013, current.org/2013/07/study-evaluates-strength-of-public-radios-halo-for-sponsors/.

"The IRS and Nonprofit Media; Toward Creating a More Informed Public." Council on Foundations, 26 Mar. 2018, www.cof.org/sites/default/files/documents/files/Nonprofit-Media-Full-Report-03042013.pdf+.

"What We've Learned About Program-Related Investments." The Rockefeller Foundation, 8 Dec. 2016, www.rockefellerfoundation.org/blog/what-we-ve-learned-about-program-related/.

"Who Is the Millennial Generation?," Pew Research–Graphic Sociology. The Society Pages 4 Oct. 2011, thesocietypages.org/graphicsociology/2011/10/04/who-is-the-millennial-generation-pew-research/.

Direct Federal Grants

"Basic Memberships: More Trouble than They're Worth?" *Current*, 22 Apr. 2013, www.current.org/2012/12/basic-memberships-more-trouble-than-theyre-worth/.

CPB, 20 June 2018, www.cpb.org/grants/archived.

Falk, Tyler. "'Changing Business Realities' Shape Talks over NPR Programming Dues." *Current*, 12 Apr. 2016, current.org/2016/04/changing-business-realities-shape-npr-dues-talks/.

"Find. Apply. Succeed." GRANTS.GOV, www.grants.gov/learn-grants/grant-programs.html.

Goldfarb, Michael. "NPR Responds." The *Weekly Standard*, 13 Feb. 2009, www.weeklystandard.com/article/27801.

Jacoby, Jeff. "What NPR Needs Is a Little Tough Love." Townhall, 14 Mar. 2011, townhall.com/columnists/jeffjacoby/2011/03/14/what-npr-needs-is-a-little-tough-love-n1075633.

"New Rules on Costs, Reimbursement of Nonprofits Finalized." National Council of Nonprofits, 8 Jan. 2015, www.councilofnonprofits.org/article/new-rules-costs-reimbursement-of-nonprofits-finalized.

OMB Circular A-122–The White House. OMB, 10 May 2004, https://www.whitehouse.gov/sites/whitehouse.gov/files/omb/circulars/A122/a122_2004.pdf

Rickover, Hyram. "Hyram Rickover Quotes." BrainyQuote, Xplore, www.brainyquote.com/quotes/hyman_rickover_126493.

Rotenberg, Marc, et al. "Letter to NPR Ombudsman Alicia Shepard." 1 Dec. 2008, epic.org/news/DHS_NPR_ltr_12-08.pdf.

USAspending.gov.," www.usaspending.gov/.

Zhao, Jijun, et al. "An agent based simulation methodology for analyzing public radio membership." *Information Technology for Economics and Management*, pp 1-34, www.item.polsl.pl/issue4.1/pdf.publicgoods_revised.pdf

Corporate Underwriting

"About UPR." UPR Station Membership Brochure, 30 Aug. 2012, pp. 1–2., www.pradoweb.org/vertical/sites/%7BFFCC657E-D16A-4444-8CFE-FED-EFFFD712D%7D/uploads/UPR_Station_Membership_Brochure.pdf.

"Agency Authorization, Underwriter Purchase Agreement," South Carolina ETV and ETV Radio, 14 Feb. 2012, www.pradoweb.org/vertical/sites/%7BFF-CC657E-D16A-4444-8CFE-FEDEFFFD712D%7D/uploads/Agency_Authorization1. .pptx.

PLEDGE: The Public Radio Fund Drive

Bailey, George. "*Journal of Broadcasting & Electronic Media, D*ecember 2004 "Free Riders, Givers, and Heavy Users: Predicting Listener Support for Public Radio." Dec. 2004, pp. 1–14., www.walrusresearch.com/images/ Free-Riders_in_Journal_of_Broadcasting.pdf.

Bayliss, Gordon. "Six Ways to Cultivate Outstanding Underwriting Customer Relationships." Greater Public, 8 Dec. 2015, go.greaterpublic.org/ blog/2015/12/six-ways-to-cultivate-outstanding-underwriting-customer-relationships/.

Bodine, Larry. "NPR Ads by Law Firms Are Wasted Money." Larry Bodine Law Marketing Blog, 30 Dec. 2008, blog.larrybodine.com/2008/12/articles/advertising/npr-ads-by-law-firms-are-wasted-money/.

Brown, K. School of Library and Information Studies, University of Wisconsin–Madison, May 2002

Cohan, William D. "David Koch's Chilling Effect on Public Television." *Bloomberg*, 10 June 2013, www.bloomberg.com/view/articles/2013-06-09/ david-koch-s-chilling-effect-on-public-television.

"Commission Policy Concerning the Nature of Non-Commercial Nature of Educational Broadcasting Stations." 28 Mar. 1984, pp. 258., apps.fcc.gov/ edocs_public/attachmatch/FCC-84-105A1.pdf.

Everhart, Karen. "After Scandal, Fundraisers Debate Ethics." *Current*, 23 July 2012, current.org/2011/07/after-scandal-fundraisers-debate-ethics/.

Fortune, Gwendolyn Y. "Ad' vs. 'Underwriting.'" Keeping the Public in Public Radio, 27 July 2010, keeppublicradiopublic.com/2010/07/27/ad-vs-underwriting/.

Glover, Jerry. "FCC Fines Public Radio Station $12,500 For Broadcasting Advertisements – LSG Legal." LSG Legal, Leavens, Strand & Glover, 23 May 2012, lsglegal.com/fcc-fines-public-radio-station-12500-for-broadcasting-advertisements/.

"*Guidelines for National Program Service Programs.*" NPR Station Manager's Handbook, National Public Radio, 22 May 2000, www.nprstations.org/ handbook/36underwriting.pdf.

"INADMISSIBLE: Law Firms Drop Into Morning Mix on NPR," National Law Journal." Corporate Counsel, 4 Jan. 2016, www.law.com/nationallawjournal/almID/1202746130672/.

Bibliography

Janssen, Mike. "Arizona Radio Stations Ask FCC for Looser Underwriting Rules." *Current*, 18 Apr. 2013, current.org/2013/04/arizona-radio-stations-ask-fcc-for-looser-underwriting-rules/.

Janssen, Mike. "Insistent Sponsors Put Newsrooms on Alert." *Current*, 16 Feb. 2015, current.org/2012/08/insistent-sponsors-put-newsrooms-on-alert/.

Janssen, Mike. "Survey Finds 'Areas of Sensitivity' in Foundation Support for Nonprofit News." *Current*, 13 Dec. 2016, current.org/2016/04/survey-finds-areas-of-sensitivity-in-foundation-support-for-nonprofit-news/.

Laing, Lauren. "Ninth Circuit Upholds Law Prohibiting Corporate, Campaign Advertising on Public Stations." 3 Dec. 2013, www.jurist.org/news/2013/12/ninth-circuit-upholds-law-prohibiting-corporate-campaign-advertising-on-public-stations/.

Lewis, Jim, "If you pay commissions on underwriting sales, make them incentives for team behavior," *Current*, September 11, 2011

Moyers, Bill. "Bill Moyers: The Rightwing Attack on PBS." History News Network, 15 May 2005, historynewsnetwork.org/article/11969.

"National Public Radio Underwritten by Monsanto?" Bad Seed News, Natural News, 31 Aug. 2011, www.badseed.info/GMO-genetically-modified-crop-news/26687_national-public-radio-underwritten-by-monsanto.html.

PRI Underwriting Policy." PRI InfoSite, Station Tools, www2.pri.org/infosite/programsupport/underwriting_guidelines.cfm.

Siemering, William, phone conversation with the author, December 22, 2016

Schneider, Marlene, director of Enginuity Workshop talking with author Jim Lewis, *Current*, September 11, 2011

Staff. "Study Finds Most Listeners Don't Mind NPR's Embedded Underwriting Credits." *Current*, 15 May 2014, current.org/2014/05/study-finds-most-listeners-dont-mind-nprs-embedded-underwriting-credits/.

Siegel, Paul, "The 1992 PBS Funding Debate: How Much Diversity Is America Willing to Pay for?," February 1993, Western States Communication Association, https://eric.ed.gov/?id=ED373381

"Underwriting." PBS Program Underwriting Policy, 27 Aug. 2015, pp. 1–4., bento.cdn.pbs.org/hostedbento-prod/filer_public/PBS_About/Producing/Red%20Book/Underwriting%201.2011_1.pdf.

PLEDGE: The Public Radio Fund Drive

"Underwriting." Startup Costs, Prometheus Radio Project, www.prometheusra-dio.org/underwriting.

WBUR, *Here and Now*, timestamp 12 Nov. 2017 1108 EST

WSCL2 timestamp 13 Apr. 2016 1533 EST

WSDL3 timestamp 21 Apr. 2016 1505 EST

State Money

Avendano, John. "WKCC-FM to Shut Down By Year's End." Chicagoradioand-media.com, 18 June 2015, chicagoradioandmedia.com/news/7466-wkcc-fm-to-shut-down-by-year-s-end.

Bailey, George. *Journal of Broadcasting & Electronic Media*/December 2004 "Free Riders, Givers, and Heavy Users: Predicting Listener Support for Public Radio." Journal of Broadcasting & Electronic Media, Dec. 2004, pp. 1–14., www.walrusresearch.com/images/Free-Riders_in_Journal_of_Broad-casting.pdf.

Bleizeffer, Dustin. "Wyoming Public Radio and Television Flirt with the End of Federal Funding." The Billings Gazette, 10 Apr. 2011, billingsgazette.com/news/state-and-regional/wyoming/wyoming-public-radio-and-television-flirt-with-the-end-of/article_17039561-99fc-5def-9164-9d930d7e330b.html.

Dettro, Chris. "WUIS to Cut 'Science Friday,' 4 Other Programs amid State Budget Uncertainty." The State Journal, The State Journal-Register, 28 June 2015, www.sj-r.com/article/20150627/NEWS/150629562.

"Fair Labor Standards Act Advisor." Elaws–Employment Laws Assistance for Workers and Small Businesses, Department of Labor, webapps.dol.gov/elaws/whd/flsa/docs/volunteers.asp.

Granger, Erin. "Fairbanks Public Radio Station Cuts Programming, Staff Due to Funding Shortage." Fairbanks Daily News-Miner, 8 Aug. 2017, www.news-miner.com/news/local_news/fairbanks-public-radio-station-cuts-program-ming-staff-due-to-funding/article_adfb6cfe-7bdb-11e7-afff-7bd0a91412e9.html.

Harden, Blaine, and New York Times. "Religious Broadcasters Pushing Public Radio off Air / Secular Stations Rally, Battle to Save Their Frequencies from Wealthier Rivals." SFGate, San Francisco Chronicle, 28 Jan. 2012,

www.sfgate.com/news/article/Religious-broadcasters-pushing-public-ra-
dio-off-2769682.php.

Ley, Ana. "Vote on UNLV Radio Station Takeover Stalled." Las Vegas Re-
view-Journal, 3 Mar. 2017, www.reviewjournal.com/news/education/vote-
on-unlv-radio-station-takeover-stalled/.

Lichterman, Joseph. "As Oil Prices Sag, Nonprofit News Orgs Are Tightening
Their Belts and Watching Their Budgets." Nieman Lab, 21 July 2016, www.
niemanlab.org/2016/07/as-oil-prices-sag-nonprofit-news-orgs-are-tighten-
ing-their-belts-and-watching-their-budgets/.

McGlone, Peggy. "Gov. Christie Pushes Bill to Convert New Jersey Network
into Independent Entity." NJ.com, NJ.com, 3 Sept. 2010, www.nj.com/
news/index.ssf/2010/09/gov_christie_seeks_to_convert.html.

Merrill, Donald, "MyData," GoogleDocs Public Radio Survey, June 2017, Portland, OR

Murphy, Kate. "Bible Broadcast Corp. to Buy Radio Station WNKU." Cincin-
nati.com, Cincinnati Enquirer, 14 Feb. 2017, www.cincinnati.com/story/
news/2017/02/14/wnku-sold-bible-broadcast-corp/97893994/.

"New York Public Radio and Montclair State University Announce Joint Media
Partnership," WNYC, New York Public Radio, Podcasts, Live Streaming
Radio, News." WNYC, 15 May 2012, www.wnyc.org/press/njprmsu/.

Ohio Media Watch."'X-Star' Goes Dark in Cincy," 21 Aug. 2005, ohiomedia.
blogspot.com/2005/08/x-star-goes-dark-in-cincin.html.

OLA OFFICE OF THE LEGISLATIVE AUDITOR STATE OF MINNESOTA
EVALUATION REPORT, "State Grants to Nonprofit Organizations." 2 Jan.
2007, pp. 1–63., www.auditor.leg.state.mn.us/ped/pedrep/grants.pdf.

"Public Radio Finances." NPR, 20 June 2013, www.npr.org/about-
npr/178660742/public-radio-finances.

Resnick, Brian. "States Squeeze Funding for Public Media." The Atlantic,
Atlantic Media Company, 16 Nov. 2011, www.theatlantic.com/national/ar-
chive/2011/11/chart-states-squeeze-funding-for-public-media/248518/.

Simpson, April. "State Cuts Support to Mississippi Public Broadcasting."
Current, 19 May 2016, current.org/2016/05/state-cuts-support-to-
mississip-pi-public-broadcasting/.

Staff, "NKU to Explore Possibility of Sale of Radio Station, WNKU-FM, in Face of Looming State Budget Cuts." NKyTribune RSS, 6 Apr. 2016, www.nkytribune.com/2016/04/nku-to-explore-possibility-of-sale-of-radio-station-wnku-fm-in-face-of-looming-state-budget-cuts/.

"State Budget Cuts Will Reduce SDPB Staff, Programs." KELOLAND.com, Sioux Falls News & Weather, South Dakota News & Weather, Minnesota and Iowa News, 30 Mar. 2011, www.keloland.com/news/article/other/state-budget-cuts-will-reduce-sdpb-staff-programs.

Truman, Cheryl. "*Wait, Wait, Don't Tell Me*. Is Your Public Radio Station in Trouble?" Lexington Herald Leader, 12 Mar. 2017, www.kentucky.com/news/business/article138054288.html.

"U.S. Governors." National Governors Association, www.nga.org/governors/.

"WGTS License Likely for Sale." The Washington Times, 18 July 2007, www.washingtontimes.com/news/2007/jul/18/wgts-license-likely-for-sale-90-306/.

"WV Pubcasters Seeking Permission for Staffers to Work Pledge Drives." *Current*, 30 June 2010, current.org/2010/06/wv-pubcasters-seeking-permission-for-staffers-to-work-pledge-drives/.

Foundations and Philanthropy

Andruszka, Rebecca. The Daily Muse, "Career Advice and Articles From The Muse." Free Career Advice, The Muse, 30 Jan. 2014, www.themuse.com/advice/3-times-when-you-should-turn-down-a-donation-really?_escaped_fragment_=#!

"Angel Food Ministries Leaders Sentenced in Money Laundering." USA Today, Gannett Satellite Information Network, 30 Aug. 2013, www.usatoday.com/story/news/nation/2013/08/30/georgia-angel-food-ministries/2739077/.

"Charting New Ground: The Ethical Terrain of Nonprofit Journalism." 20 Apr. 2016, pp. 1–60., www.americanpressinstitute.org/wp-content/uploads/2016/04/The-ethical-terrain-of-nonprofit-journalism.pdf.

"Community Foundation Programs & Services." Council on Foundations, 17 Feb. 2016, www.cof.org/page/community-foundation-programs-services.

Conason, Joe. "The Coors campaign's deceptive advertising". Salon.com. Archived from the original on 2009-02-10. Retrieved 2009-05-05

CPB–*Major Giving Initiative*–Leadership for Philanthropy–"Use Proven Resources–Success Stories"–Capital Campaign, www.majorgivingnow.org/resources/stories_capital_campaign.html.

Deutsch, Lindsay. "Girl Scouts Rejects $100K Anti-Transgender Donation." USA Today, Gannett Satellite Information Network, 1 July 2015, www.usatoday.com/story/news/nation-now/2015/06/30/girl-scouts-raise-money-reject-donation-transgender/29543863/.

ECFA Standard 4 – "Use of Resources and Compliance with Laws," ECFA.org, www.ecfa.org/Content/Comment4.

Friedman, Barry D. "How nonprofit organizations fight off competition," Southern Politics, 7 July 2011, faculty.ung.edu/bfriedman/Studies/compete.htm.

"Grants." Melville Charitable Trust, melvilletrust.org/grants/.

Hyrwna, Mark. "Giving Estimated At $335.17 Billion For 2013." The Non-Profit Times, 17 June 2014, www.thenonprofittimes.com/news-articles/giving-usa-2013/.

Institute for Global Labour and Human Rights," www.facebook.com/iglhr.

Khan, Huma, and Wolf, Byron Z. "NPR CEO Vivian Schiller Resigns After Hidden Camera Sting Snares Top Fundraiser." ABC News Network, 9 Mar. 2011, abcnews.go.com/Politics/npr-ceo-vivian-schiller-resigns-james-okeefe-orchestrated/story?id=13092007.

Kling, William, phone conversation with author, 16 November 2016

Lewis, Jim. "'Restricted Unrestricted': a Productive New Flavor of Grants at KPBS." *Current*, 22 July 2012, current.org/2011/06/restricted-unrestricted-a-productive-new-flavor-of-grants-at-kpbs/.

Merrill, Donald, "MyData," GoogleDocs Public Radio Survey, June 2017, Portland, OR

"Private Foundations FAQ." Non-Profit Legal Center, www.nonprofitlegalcenter.com/faq/private-foundations-faq/.

"Push for Major Gifts Advances as NPR, Stations Work Together." *Current*, 20 July 2015, current.org/2015/07/push-for-major-gifts-advances-as-npr-stations-work-together/.

"Radio Show." Community Foundation Boulder County, 13 Jan. 2012, www.commfound.org/news-media/radio-show.

PLEDGE: The Public Radio Fund Drive

Rinallo, Diego and Basuroy, Suman., "Does Advertising Spending Influence
Media Coverage of the Advertiser," Journal of Marketing, v. 73, no. 6,
American Marketing Association, Nov. 2009, https://archive.ama.org/Ar-
chive/AboutAMA/Pages/AMA%20Publications/AMA%20Journals/Jour-
nal%20of%20Marketing/TOCs/SUM_2009.6/Does_Advertising_Spending.
aspx

Sabatier, Julie. "A Conversation with NPR's New President And CEO." Oregon
Public Broadcasting, 2 Apr. 2015, www.opb.org/radio/programs/thinkout-
loud/segment/a-conversation-with-nprs-new-president-and-ceo/.

Sawyer, Liz. "Unnamed Donor Gives $10 Million to MPR and American Public
Media." Star Tribune, 12 Nov. 2015, www.startribune.com/unnamed-donor-
gives-10-million-to-mpr-and-american-public-media/346387122/.

Soundscapes, "The Evolution and Challenges of National Public Radio." Carnegie Corporation of New York, Carnegie Results, 2006, www.carnegie.org/
publications/soundscapes-the-evolution-and-challenges-of-national-pub-
lic-radio/.

Stewart, Marshall. "Charities Get a Boost from a New Challenge Grant Program." Public Radio Tulsa, 11 Sept. 2012, publicradiotulsa.org/post/chari-
ties-get-boost-new-challenge-grant-program.

"The Rockefellers vs. Exxon, the Company That Made Them the Rockefellers."
New York Magazine, 8 Jan. 2018, nymag.com/daily/intelligencer/2018/01/
the-rockefellers-vs-exxon.html.

The Vincent Astor Foundation–Company Profile." Corporation Wiki, www.
corporationwiki.com/p/2ngs7p/the-vincent-astor-foundation.

Turner, Deb. "Strings Attached: What to Do When Donors Want to Restrict
Bequests." Mar. 2016, go.greaterpublic.org/blog/2016/03/strings-attached-
what-to-do-when-donors-want-to-restrict-bequests/.

"When Should Non-Profits Turn Down Donations?" Charity First, 1 July 2015,
www.charityfirst.com/archive/when-should-nonprofits-turn-down-dona-
tions/.

Ydstie, John, and Klose, Kevin. "Philanthropist Joan Kroc Leaves NPR $200
Million Gift." NPR, NPR, 6 Nov. 2003, www.npr.org/templates/story/story.
php?storyId=1494600.

Individual Giving

"Basic Memberships: More Trouble than They're Worth?" *Current*, 22 Apr. 2013, current.org/2012/12/basic-memberships-more-trouble-than-theyre-worth/.

Croson, Rachel, and Shang, Jen. "Social Influences in Giving." Non Profit News | *Nonprofit Quarterly*, 20 July 2015, nonprofitquarterly.org/2010/09/21/social-influences-in-giving/.

"Day Sponsors." WHQR, 1 Oct. 2017, whqr.org/day-sponsors#stream/0.

Dubner, Stephen J, and Mikemenn. "Question of the Day: Should I Feel Guilty About Not Supporting Public Radio?" Freakonomics, 30 Apr. 2013, freakonomics.com/2013/04/30/question-of-the-day-should-i-feel-guilty-about-not-supporting-public-radio/?c_page=3.

Fuerst, Mark. "Pubmedia Stations Foresee Decline of on-Air Pledge Drives, Cite Need for New Tactics." *Current*, 31 July 2014, current.org/2014/07/pubmedia-stations-foresee-decline-of-on-air-pledge-drives-cite-need-for-new-tactics/.

Giovanonni, David. "*Losing Our Grip*" Professional Papers and Publications, David Giovanonni, 9 May 2006, dgio.net/pubs.asp.

Sutton, John, "How Stations Can Stay Relevant as Listeners go Elsewhere for NPR Content," *Current*, August 12, 2014, https://current.org/2014/08/how-stations-can-stay-relevant-as-listeners-go-elsewhere-for-npr-content

Sutton, John. "Everybody but NPR." RadioSutton, 30 July 2009, radiosutton.blogspot.com/search?q=Everybody%2Bbut%2BNPR.

Sutton, John. "Public Radio's On-Air Fundraising Messaging Matrix." John Sutton and Associates, Sept. 2005, pp. 1–15., www.radiosutton.com/images/JSA-message-matrix-users.pdf.

Thomas, Thomas J, and Clifford, Theresa R. "Individual Giving to Public Radio Stations." pp. 1–40., www.srg.org/funding/IndividualGiving.pdf.

Other

Douban, Gigi. "Why Retailers Still Bother to Print Catalogs." Marketplace, 14 May 2014, www.marketplace.org/2014/05/14/business/why-retailers-still-bother-print-catalogs.

PLEDGE: The Public Radio Fund Drive

Kramer, Melody. "New Models for Public Media Membership: Melody Kramer's Nieman Report." Current, 13 July 2015, current.org/2015/07/new-models-for-public-media-membership-melody-kramers-nieman-report/.

"KSER Pledge Drive Pitch Playbook." Pledge Pitch Playbook KSER, pp. 1–22., www.kser.org/download/Pledge_Break_Playbook_KSER.pdf, pp. 2.

Lapin, Andrew. "*Planet Money* Crowdfunder Soars, PRI Campaign Falls Short of Goal." Current, 16 May 2013, current.org/2013/05/planet-money-crowdfunder-soars-pri-campaign-falls-short-of-goal/.

Lichterman, Joseph. "How PRX and Radiotopia Are Rethinking the Public Radio Pledge Drive for the Podcast Era." Nieman Lab, 27 Oct. 2015, www.niemanlab.org/2015/10/how-prx-and-radiotopia-are-rethinking-the-public-radio-pledge-drive-for-the-podcast-era/.

Miller, Paul. "Target Sells *Signals*, *Wireless* Catalogs." Multichannel Merchant, Multichannel Merchant, 13 Jan. 2013, multichannelmerchant.com/news/target-sells-signals-wireless-catalogs/.

"More Ways to Support WFUV." Domestic Violence Ad Campaign in NYC, WFUV, www.wfuv.org/ways.

Nashville Public Radio, WPLN, revenue_piechart.jpg, http://mediad.public-broadcasting.net/p/wpln/files/201609/revenue_piechart.jpg

Ozark Public Broadcasting's Funding. Mar. 2017, mediad.publicbroadcasting.net/p/ksmumain/files/styles/medium/public/201703/public_broadcasting_funding.png. -

"Percentage of Public Radio Station Revenue by Category (FY 08)." NPR and CPB, 2008, cjrarchive.org/img/posts/NPR2.jpg.

"SEC Adopts Rules to Permit Crowdfunding." SEC.gov, 30 Oct. 2015, www.sec.gov/news/pressrelease/2015-249.html.

Sutton, John. "Difficult Pledge Drive Days Ahead?" *RadioSutton*, John Sutton and Associates, 2 Feb. 2015, radiosutton.blogspot.com/search?q=More%2B-Spending%2C%2BMore%2BOn%2BAir%2BFundraising.

Wang, Shan. "Acast Wants to Get New Audiences 'in the Podcast Door' with More Diverse Shows and Better Data." Nieman Lab, 24 June 2016, www.niemanlab.org/2016/06/acast-wants-to-get-new-audiences-in-the-podcast-door-with-more-diverse-shows-and-better-data/.

WGBH, Media Access Group, "Caption Services," main.wgbh.org/wgbh/pages/mag/services/captioning/.

"Where Your Money Goes." Indiana Public Media, 25 June 2018, indianapublicmedia.org/support/radio/faq/where-your-money-goes/.

Sales and Investments

Bowman, Woods. "The Nonprofit Difference." Non Profit Quarterly, 9 May 2011, nonprofitquarterly.org/2011/05/09/the-nonprofit-difference/.

Brown, Jason. "Telemus Capital Acquires L.A.-Based Concentric Capital LLC ." *Bloomberg*.com, 25 Feb. 2014, www.businesswire.com/news/home/20140225005634/en/Telemus-Capital-Acquires-L.A.-Based-Concentric-Capital-LLC.

Eckel, Allison. "By Combining the Online Channels of Wireless, Seasons and Signals Catalogs, Target Corp. Serves up a Streamlined Shopping Experience." Total Retail, 1 Dec. 2001, www.mytotalretail.com/article/by-combining-online-channels-wireless-seasons-signals-catalogs-target-corp-serves-up-streamlined-shopping-experience-22169/all/.

Farhi, Paul. "NPR Taps Jarl Mohn as Eighth CEO in Eight Years." The Washington Post, WP Company, 9 May 2014, www.washingtonpost.com/lifestyle/style/npr-taps-jarl-mohn-as-new-ceo/2014/05/09/37382d9c-d78c-11e3-95d3-3bcd77cd4e11_story.html?utm_term=.9a7c455ecc16.

Fernandez, Gary J. Executive Profile & Biography–*Bloomberg." Bloomberg*.com, www.bloomberg.com/research/stocks/private/person.asp?personId=643716.

Govani, Mark. "QUARTERLY RETAIL E-COMMERCE SALES 1st Quarter 2018." U.S. Census Bureau News, U.S. Department of Commerce, 24 May 2018, www.census.gov/retail/mrts/www/data/pdf/ec_current.pdf.

Internet Archive Wayback Machine, 31 Dec. 2014, web.archive.org/details/shop.npr.org

Janssen, Mike, "Kroc Gift Lets NPR Expand News, Lower Fees," *Current*, May 24, 2004, https://web.archive.org/web/20110322154055/http://www.current.org/npr/npr0409krocgift.shtl

"Jarl Mohn." Harvard Graduate School Leadership Institute, hgsli.com/porftfolio/jarl-mohn/.

PLEDGE: The Public Radio Fund Drive

"Jarl Mohn: Executive Profile & Biography." *Bloomberg.*" *Bloomberg.* com, www.bloomberg.com/research/stocks/private/person.asp?person-Id=5377624.

Jensen, Elizabeth. "NPR Picks a New Leader with Lots of Commercial Experience.," www.nytimes.com/2014/05/10/business/media/npr-picks-a-new-leader-with-lots-of-commercial-experience.html.

Kravitz, Melissa. "NPR Launches Wine Club To Help Fund Public Radio." *Forbes* Magazine, 26 Sept. 2017, www.forbes.com/sites/melissakravitz/2017/09/26/npr-wine-club-fund-public-radio/#288e765078f0.

Lara, Isabel, Director of NPR Media Relations, email communication with author, Jan. 9, 2017

Miller, Paul. "Target Sells *Signals*, *Wireless* Catalogs." Multichannel Merchant, 13 Jan. 2013, multichannelmerchant.com/news/target-sells-signals-wireless-catalogs/.

Mitchell, Jack W., "Listener Supported–The Culture and History of Public Radio," Praeger, 2005, pg 155.

National Public Radio, Inc., Consolidated Financial Statements, "Supplemental Schedules and Independent Auditors' Report." BDO, 21 Dec. 2017, www.npr.org/about/statements/fy2017/National_Public_Radio_Consolidate_Financial_Statements_D1617_FINAL.pdf.

"NPR Shop: Where Your Purchase Supports NPR Programming." NPR, shop.npr.org/.

'Public Broadcasting Revenue Fiscal Year 2014." Annual Revenue Workbook FY14, CPB, 14 Dec. 2016, www.cpb.org/files/reports/revenue/2014PublicBroadcastingRevenuev2.pdf.

"Public Broadcasting Revenue Fiscal Year 2015." Annual Revenue Workbook FY 2015, CPB, 5 Dec. 2016, www.cpb.org/files/reports/revenue/2015PublicBroadcastingRevenue.pdf.

"Public Broadcasting Revenue Fiscal Year 2016." Annual Revenue Workbook FY 2016, 21 May 2018, www.cpb.org/files/reports/revenue/2016PublicBroadcastingRevenue.pdf.

Siempre Holdings LLC. Buzzfile, www.buzzfile.com/business/Siempre-Holdings-LLC-203-340-9855.

"Square Capital Is Expanding." *Business Insider*, 11 Aug. 2016, www.businessinsider.com/square-capital-is-expanding-2016-8.

"The Raine Group LLC: Private Company Information." *Bloomberg*. www.bloomberg.com/research/stocks/private/snapshot.asp?privcapId=59162559.

White, Ronald D. "The Old-Fashioned Mail-Order Catalog Is Making a Comeback." Los Angeles Times, 23 Nov. 2017, www.latimes.com/business/la-fi-catalogs-return-20171123-story.html.

Whois, npr.org." 8 July 2018, www.whois.com/whois/npr.org.

Wijnen, Renee. "Dayton Hudson Acquires Cataloger Rivertown Trading." Direct Marketing News , 30 Mar. 1998, www.dmnews.com/channel-marketing/multi-omnichannel/news/13103609/dayton-hudson-acquires-cataloger-rivertown-trading.

One Time Money

Atkinson, Rollie. "KRCB Reaps $72 Million Windfall." Sonoma West Publishers, 13 Feb. 2017, www.sonomawest.com/sonoma_west_times_and_news/news/krcb-reaps-million-windfall/article_260a205c-f24b-11e6-9b06-bf815dd61b65.html.

Common Ground, "Radio's Weekly Program on World Affairs." The Stanley Foundation, 3 May 2015, commongroundradio.org/index.html.

Denison, D C. "Court Ruling Could Lead to Political Ads on Public Radio and TV," Boston Globe, 19 Apr. 2012, www.bostonglobe.com/business/2012/04/19/court-ruling-could-lead-political-ads-public-radio-and/pYMzlYVmFSkTCyn15ENI5H/story.html?s_campaign=sm_tw.

Dolan, Maura, "Political ads on public Radio and TV." Los Angeles Times, December 2, 2013, http://articles.latimes.com/2013/dec/02/entertainment/la-et-ct-political-ads-on-public-radio-tv-20131202

Falk, Tyler. "'*Dinner Party Download*' to End Production." *Current*, 26 Oct. 2017, current.org/2017/10/dinner-party-download-to-end-production/.

Friedman, Wayne. "Midterm 2018 Political Advertising To See Small Rise Over 2014." Media Daily News, MediaPost, 30 Nov. 2017, www.mediapost.com/publications/article/310905/midterm-2018-political-advertising-to-see-small-ri.html.

PLEDGE: The Public Radio Fund Drive

Halim, Nadia. "Tobacco Settlement: Where's the Money?" The Scientist, 8 Nov. 1999, http://www.the-scientist.com/?articles.view/articleNo/19626/title/Tobacco-Settlement—Where-s-the-Money-/

Hand, Marc. "In Aftermath of Spectrum Auction, Even Stations That Sat out Could Still Benefit." Current, 12 May 2017, current.org/2017/05/in-after-math-of-spectrum-auction-even-stations-that-sat-out-could-benefit/.

James, Meg. "Political Ad Spending Estimated at $6 Billion in 2016." Los Angeles Times, Los Angeles Times, 18 Nov. 2015, www.latimes.com/entertainment/envelope/cotown/la-et-ct-political-ad-spending-6-billion-dollars-in-2016-20151117-story.html#.

Janssen, Mike. "Sale of Dozens of Noncommercial Signals in FCC Spectrum Auction Earns Minimum of $1.9 Billion." Current, 20 Apr. 2017, current. org/2017/04/final-fcc-auction-data-shows-sales-of-30-noncommercial-educational-tv-stations/.

"Justice Talking through the Years." Justice Talking, 23 June 2008, www.justicetalking.org/ShowPage.aspx?ShowID=669.

Kreiter, Suzanne. "Radio Talk Host Christopher Lydon Returns to WBUR-FM after 12-Year Absence." The Boston Globe, 20 Nov. 2013, www.boston-globe.com/lifestyle/style/2013/11/20/radio-talk-host-christopher-lydon-returns-wbur-after-year-absence/jLC042johF7aRALtnvWlNK/story.html.

Nielsen Scarborough Local Market Research, "Public radio anticipates political advertising revenue," http://dialog.scarborough.com/index.php/public-radio-anticipates-political-advertising-revenue/

Perrow, Charles. "The Disaster after 9/11: The Department of Homeland Security and the Intelligence Reorganization." HOMELAND SECURITY AFFAIRS, 16 Jan. 2015, www.hsaj.org/articles/174.

Post, Guest. "Go, Indie, Go. Will Networked Podcasts Get You There?" AIR, 15 Mar. 2015, airmedia.org/go-indie-go-will-networked-podcasts-get-you-there/.

Shear, Michael D. "Obama Lesson: 'Shovel Ready' Not So Ready." The New York Times, 15 Oct. 2010, thecaucus.blogs.nytimes.com/2010/10/15/obama-lesson-shovel-ready-not-so-ready/?mtrref=duckduckgo.com.

SHOW BIZ BUGS @ Warner Bros. Entertainment Inc. LOONEY TUNES and all related characters and elements are the property of Warner Bros. Entertainment, Inc.

"This Is the Third Wave of Podcasting," Jake Shapiro, Radioinfo, 30 Sept, 2015, www.radioinfo.com.au/news/third-wave-podcasting-jake-shapiro.

Vogel, Kenneth P., et al. "Obama, Romney Both Topped $1B." Politico, 7 Dec. 2012, www.politico.com/story/2012/12/barack-obama-mitt-romney-both-topped-1-billion-in-2012-084737.

Crowdfunding

Admin. "Indiegogo to the Rescue: KBBI Faces Equipment Crisis." Homer News, 25 June 2015, homernews.com/homer-features/backyard/2015-06-25/indiegogo-to-the-rescue-kbbi-faces-equipment-crisis.

Daks, Marty. "Pay-What-You-Can Concept Challenged By Thin Margins." The NonProfit Times, 31 Dec. 2013, www.thenonprofittimes.com/news-articles/pay-what-you-can-concept-challenged-by-thin-margins/.

Grech, Rose. "Keep KBBI on the Air, Literally." Indiegogo, 3 June 2015, www.indiegogo.com/projects/keep-kbbi-on-the-air-literally.

Holmes, David. "NPR's New Kickstarter Is a Clever Commentary on the Crowdfunding Reward System." Pando, 1 May 2013, pando.com/2013/04/30/nprs-new-kickstarter-is-a-clever-commentary-on-the-crowdfunding-reward-system/.

"Home." One World Everybody Eats, www.oneworldeverybodyeats.org/.

Ingram, Mathew. "Planet Money and Kickstarter: Is Web-Based Crowdfunding the Future of Public Media?" Gigaom, 7 May 2013, gigaom.com/2013/05/07/planet-money-and-kickstarter-is-web-based-crowdfunding-the-future-of-public-media/.

Lapin, Andrew. "Planet Money Crowdfunder Soars, PRI Campaign Falls Short of Goal." Current, 16 Feb. 2015, current.org/2013/05/planet-money-crowdfunder-soars-pri-campaign-falls-short-of-goal/.

Lapin, Andrew. "Podcast with Limited Radio Airplay Sets Kickstarter Record." Current, 2 Feb. 2017, current.org/2012/08/podcast-with-limited-radio-air-play-sets-kickstarter-record/.

Lee, Spike. Spike Lee Quotes." BrainyQuote, Xplore, www.brainyquote.com/ quotes/spike_lee_590066.

Lichterman, Joseph. "How PRX and Radiotopia Are Rethinking the Public Radio Pledge Drive for the Podcast Era." Nieman Lab, 27 Oct. 2015, www. niemanlab.org/2015/10/how-prx-and-radiotopia-are-rethinking-the-public-radio-pledge-drive-for-the-podcast-era/.

McPherson, Richard. "With Crowdfunding, Rethink Your Expectations for Engaging Public Media's Supporters." *Current*, 24 Dec. 2013, current. org/2013/12/with-crowdfunding-rethink-your-expectations-for-engaging-public-medias-supporters/.

"*Planet Money* T-Shirt." Kickstarter, NPR, 30 Apr. 2013, www.kickstarter.com/ projects/planetmoney/planet-money-t-shirt?ref=live.

Roettgers, Janko. "How Kickstarter Could Disrupt Public Radio." Gigaom, 18 July 2012, gigaom.com/2012/07/18/how-kickstarter-could-disrupt-public-radio/.

Sutton, John. *RadioSutton*, 1 May 2013, radiosutton.blogspot.com/2013_05_01_ archive.html.

"UM News." University Of Montana, 21 Oct. 2014, news.umt. edu/2014/10/102114mtpr.php.

Wolf, Michael. "Making Money With Podcasts No Longer Just About The Ads." *Forbes* Magazine, 12 Feb. 2014, www.forbes.com/sites/michael-wolf/2014/02/10/making-money-with-podcasts-no-longer-just-about-the-ads/.

The Cable TV Model

Anderson, Chris. "The Long Tail." About Me, 1 Feb. 2008, www.longtail.com/ the_long_tail/2008/02/narrower-is-bet.html.

Barron, Greg. "Radio Storytelling: Engaging Audiences in Long-Form Audio Stories-and Keeping Them Engaged. The Role of Surprise..." LinkedIn, 4 May 2017, www.linkedin.com/pulse/radio-storytelling-engaging-audiences-long-form-audio-greg-barron.

Chappell, Bill. "The Slants Win Supreme Court Battle Over Band's Name In Trademark Dispute." NPR, 19 June 2017, www.npr.org/sections/thetwo-way/2017/06/19/533514196/the-slants-win-supreme-court-battle-over-bands-name-in-trademark-dispute.

Chez Risque, https://thecage.co/podcasts/#/podcast/64

Dial, Minter. "How Many Podcasts Are There In 2015?" The State of the Podcast -. 27 Oct. 2015, myndset.com/2015/10/how-many-podcasts-are-there/.

Dockterman, Eliana. "Best Podcast Episodes of 2017 So Far." Time, 26 May 2017, time.com/4790406/best-podcasts-2017-so-far/.

Farhi, Paul. "Wait, Wait–Can You Say That on Air? There's a Debate on Cursing at NPR." The Washington Post, WP Company, 29 July 2015, www.washingtonpost.com/lifestyle/style/wait-wait—can-you-say-that-on-air-theres-an-internal-debate-on-cursing-at-npr/2015/07/29/61f7e4cc-3547-11e5-8e66-07b4603ec92a_story.html?utm_term=.fde5a17b1788.

Fryer, Bronwyn. "Storytelling That Moves People." *Harvard Business Review*, 1 Aug. 2014, hbr.org/2003/06/storytelling-that-moves-people.

garlic, et al, "Donating to Public Radio," *MetaFilter*, 25 Nov. 2013, ask.metafilter.com/252582/Donating-to-Public-Radio.

Gillies, Conor. "Podcasting and the Selling of Public Radio." The Awl, 12 May 2015, theawl.com/podcasting-and-the-selling-of-public-radio-243e7a5d63e0.

"Go, Indie, Go. Will Networked Podcasts Get You There?" AIR, 15 Mar. 2015, airmedia.org/go-indie-go-will-networked-podcasts-get-you-there/.

Griffin. "About." *RPPR* Actual Play, 9 Mar. 2011, actualplay.roleplayingpublicradio.com/about/.

Head, Tom. "Timeline and History of Television Censorship.," ThoughtCo, 17 Mar. 2017, www.thoughtco.com/can-fcc-censor-internet-radio-station-2843301.

"Interpreting the Recent FCC Fines." WFMU's Beware of the Blog, 4 Apr. 2006, blog.wfmu.org/freeform/2006/04/the_indecency_s.html.

Lane, Randy. "The Four Types Of Character Growth." Radio Ink, 5 July 2016, radioink.com/2016/07/05/four-types-character-growth/.

Lantz, Erika. "A Golden Age: How to Join the Podcast Revolution." PRX, 4 Sept. 2014, blog.prx.org/2014/09/golden-age-join-podcast-revolution/.

Martignoni, Miles. "Radiolab's Jad Abumrad on Podcasting's Uncertain Future: 'Supply Is Outstripping Demand'." *The Guardian*, Guardian News

and Media, 16 Nov. 2016, www.theguardian.com/media/2016/nov/16/
radiolabs-jad-abumrad-on-podcastings-uncertain-future-supply-is-outstrip-
ping-demand.

Niles, Robert. "Will NPR's Podcasts Birth a New Business Model for Public
Radio?" USCAnnenberg Online Journalism Review, 27 Nov. 2005, www.
ojr.org/will-nprs-podcasts-birth-a-new-business-model-for-public-radio/.

"Obscene, Indecent and Profane Broadcasts." Federal Communications Commission, 13 Sept. 2017, www.fcc.gov/consumers/guides/obscene-inde-
cent-and-profane-broadcasts.

Pacheco, Brian, and Trasandes, Monica. "'José Luis Sin Censura' Hit With
Historic FCC Fine As Result of NHMC, GLAAD Complaint." National
Hispanic Media Coalition, 18 Nov. 2013, www.nhmc.org/jose-luis-sin-cen-
sura-hit-with-historic-fcc-fine-as-result-of-nhmc-glaad-complaint/.

"Public Radio Audience Demographics–NPR Profiles." National Public Media,
nationalpublicmedia.com/npr/audience/.

Ryan, Joe. "Podcasts Try Dynamic Ad Insertion (But You Might Not Notice)."
AdExchanger, 8 Feb. 2016, adexchanger.com/platforms/podcasts-try-dy-
namic-ad-insertion-but-you-might-not-notice/.

Ryan, Joe. "With Podcasts Come Advertising: NPR Cultivates A Growing
Revenue Stream, Without Annoying Loyal Listeners." AdExchanger, 7
June 2016, adexchanger.com/digital-audio-radio/podcasts-come-advertis-
ing-npr-cultivates-growing-revenue-stream-without-annoying-loyal-listen-
ers/.

Staff. "'This American Life' Is Podcast Ad Gold." Insideradio.com, 17 Mar.
2016, www.insideradio.com/free/this-american-life-is-podcast-ad-gold/arti-
cle_c33b32ae-ec1a-11e5-bef1-033c5e08f263.html.

"The 1992 PBS Funding Debate: How Much Diversity Is America Willing to
Pay for?," Paul Siegel, February 1993, Western States Communication
Association, https://eric.ed.gov/?id=ED373381

Tan, Simon, Twitter conversation with the author, June 11-12, 2018

Wang, Amy X. "NPR Is Cutting Its Podcasts and Apps off at the Knees, and
Fans Are Livid." Quartz, Quartz, 18 Mar. 2016, qz.com/642682/npr-is-cut-
ting-its-podcasts-and-app-off-at-the-knees-and-fans-are-livid/.

Wang, Shan. "Acast Wants to Get New Audiences 'in the Podcast Door' with More Diverse Shows and Better Data." Nieman Lab, 24 June 2016, www.niemanlab.org/2016/06/acast-wants-to-get-new-audiences-in-the-podcast-door-with-more-diverse-shows-and-better-data/.

Williams, Mary Elizabeth. "Is This the End for a Homophobic Talk Show?" Salon, 25 Sept. 2011, www.salon.com/2011/06/03/homophobic_jose_luis_sin_censura_dropped/.

Pledge Free Streaming

Brown, Kelly Williams. "How to Survive a Public Radio Membership Drive." *The Daily Beast*, 11 May 2014, www.thedailybeast.com/how-to-survive-a-public-radio-membership-drive.

Chapman, Steve. "Escape the Pledge Drive." Globetrotting, Chicago Tribune, 24 June 2008, newsblogs.chicagotribune.com/steve_chapman/2008/06/escape-the-pled.html.

"Endless Public Radio Pledge Drives." [Archive]–Straight Dope Message Board." Straight Dope Message Board RSS, Oct. 2005, boards.straightdope.com/sdmb/archive/index.php/t-342099.html.

ERK. "KQED Discovers Excludability." 7 May 2011, www.educatedguesswork.org/2011/05/kqed_discovers_excludability.html.

"Got Questions about the Pledge-Free Stream? Here Are Some Answers!" Pledge Free Stream Frequently Asked Questions, WBEZ 91.5 Chicago, WBEZ, 2018, go.wbez.org/PFS_FAQ.

Kinney, Brendan. "Membership Drive FAQ." Vermont Public Radio, 2 Apr. 2018, digital.vpr.net/post/membership-drive-faq.

"KQED Pledge Free Stream." KQED, www.kqed.org/radio/pledge-free-stream.

"Pledge Free Stream Beta Survey." SurveyMonkey, New Hampshire Public Radio, www.surveymonkey.com/.

Robberson, Ted. "Another KERA Pledge Drive. Sigh." Dallas News, 14 Oct. 2011, www.dallasnews.com/opinion/opinion/2011/10/14/another-kera-pl.

Cantalano, Frank, Twitter correspondence with author, 12/19/17-1300 PST

Vinh, Kohl. "Radio Free Pledge Drives." Subtraction.com, 15 Feb. 2007, www.subtraction.com/2007/02/15/radio-free-p/.

PLEDGE: The Public Radio Fund Drive

"What's a Pledge Drive with No Pledge Drive?" NHPR Pledge Free Stream–
New Hampshire Public Radio, nhpr.convio.net/site/PageNavigator/Pledge-
FreeStream.html.

Spending

"A Network Engaged"–2016 Annual Report. NPR, 9 June 2017, www.npr.org/
about/annualreports/2016_Annual_Report.pdf. pg 1-48

admin. "CPB Report: Skyrocketing Content Costs, Small Stations Are Causes For Concern." The Top 22 RSS, 30 June 2013, www.thetop22.com/
news/2013/06/cpb-report-skyrocketing-content-costs-small-stations-are-
causes-for-concern/.

Arnold, Michael. "Public Radio Is Stronger, and Better, When Stations Invest in
National Shows." *Current*, 16 Feb. 2015, current.org/2013/09/public-radio-
is-stronger-and-better-when-stations-invest-in-national-shows/.

Aspan, Maria. "Public Radio Listeners Want Their Money Back." The New York
Times, 9 Jan. 2006, www.nytimes.com/2006/01/09/business/media/public-
radio-listeners-want-their-money-back.html?mtrref=undefined.

Bentley, Rick. "Public Radio Station KVPR Needs Matching Funds Now." Fres-
nobee, The Fresno Bee, 2 Dec. 2015, www.fresnobee.com/entertainment/
ent-columns-blogs/rick-bentley/article47596655.html.

Cheng, Jacqui. "NPR Fights Back, Seeks Rehearing on Internet Radio Royalty Increases." Ars Technica, 21 Mar. 2007, arstechnica.com/tech-poli-
cy/2007/03/npr-fights-back-seeks-rehearing-on-internet-radio-royalty-in-
creases/.

Day of Silence' for US Web Radio." BBC News, 26 June 2007, news.bbc.
co.uk/2/hi/technology/6240418.stm.

Falk, Tyler. "As It Defines Relationship with Stations, NPR Gains Board Approval for Price Hike." *Current*, 24 Feb. 2017, current.org/2017/02/npr-pro-
poses-new-dues-structure-strategy-for-stronger-future-with-stations/.

Falk, Tyler. "Program Directors Challenged to Think about Audience, Not Formats." *Current*, 2 Oct. 2015, current.org/2015/09/program-directors-
chal-lenged-to-think-about-audience-not-formats/.

Farhi, Paul. "NPR's New Headquarters Refuels Funding Debate." The Washington Post, WP Company, 21 June 2013, www.washingtonpost.com/lifestyle/

style/nprs-new-headquarters-refuels-funding-debate/2013/06/21/bb53a64a-da00-11e2-a016-92547bf094cc_story.html?utm_term=.f05ddf244a88.

"Federal Matching Funds Guidelines." National Endowment for the Humanities, 18 Mar. 2016, www.neh.gov/grants/manage/federal-matching-funds-guidelines.

"FY2015 Radio Station Collaboration Program: Grant Guidelines." CPB, 18 May 2016, https://www.cpb.org/sites/default/files/rfp/Radio-Station-Collaboration-Program-FY2015_0.pdf.

Lapin, Andrew. "WNYC, Takeaway Encourage Stations to Take It Apart." *Current*, 16 Feb. 2015, current.org/2013/09/wnyc-takeaway-encourage-stations-to-take-it-apart/.

Minnesota Public Radio American Public Media–July 2013 to June 2014. APM/PRI, 24 Nov. 2014, minnesota.publicradio.org/about/mpr/finance/Annual_Report_MPRAPM_FY14.pdf.

Moss, Brett. "PRSS Announces Station Fee Change." Radio World, 7 Mar. 2016, www.radioworld.com/business-and-law/0009/prss-announces-station-fee-change/337337.

National Public Radio, Inc. 2015 Form 990-T. NPR, 15 Aug. 2015, www.npr.org/about/statements/fy2016/NPR-990T.pdf.

Oxenford, David. "Noncommercial Webcasters Royalty Rate Proposals for 2016-2020." *Broadcast Law Blog*, 11 Nov. 2014, www.broadcastlawblog.com/2014/11/articles/noncommercial-webcasters-royalty-rate-proposals-for-2016-2020/.

"PRI Financials" FY13 6/30/2013. PRI, 28 Nov. 2017, media.pri.org/s3fs-public/PRI%20Financials%20FY13_March%206.pdf.

Public Radio International–FY16 Pricing. PRI, 31 Mar. 2015, www2.pri.org/Infosite/stationtools/FY16_fees.pdf.

Public Radio International, Inc.–EIN: 41-1425271. Guidestar, 13 July 2018, www.guidestar.org/ViewPdf.aspx?PdfSource=0&ein=41-1425271.

Shea, Bill. "WDET Apologizes to Donors after Complaint about Fund Drive's Ethics." Crain's Detroit Business, 31 Mar. 2017, www.crainsdetroit.com/article/20120923/SUB01/309239996/wdet-apologizes-to-donors-after-complaint-about-fund-drives-ethics.

Silva, Ernesto. "CPB's Federal Appropriation Request & Justification." CPB, 12 Feb. 2018, www.cpb.org/funding.

Programming and Carriage

APM Affiliate Agreement 2007.doc

Arnold, Michael. "Public Radio Is Stronger, and Better, When Stations Invest in National Shows." *Current*, 16 Feb. 2015, current.org/2013/09/public-radio-is-stronger-and-better-when-stations-invest-in-national-shows/.

Barrett, Grant. "How Stations Can Get the Show." *A Way with Words*, 7 Feb. 2018, www.waywordradio.org/about/broadcast-the-show/.

"Common Carriers Under the Communications Act." University of Chicago Law Review, 12 Jan. 2017, chicagounbound.uchicago.edu/cgi/viewcontent.cgi?article=4236&context=uclrev.

"CPB's Appropriation History," pp. 1–2., www.netadvisor.org/wp-content/uploads/2012/10/2012-00-00-CPBs-Appropriations-History-1969-2012.pdf.

Davidson, Randall. *"Non-Satellite Programming Resources for Radio Stations."* College Broadcasters, Inc., 2 Apr. 2018, www.askcbi.org/resources/non-satellite-programming-resources-for-radio-stations/.

Engelman, Ralph, "Public Radio and Television in America," SAGE Publications, 1996, pg 126

Ford. "Welcome to KRWG 90.7 FM's Membership Drive!" Properties of {4E08B085-5D3E-4250-A91B-69D6293301DE}.DOC, 24 Mar. 2009, http://www.pradoweb.org/vertical/sites/%7BFFCC657E-D16A-4444-8CFE-FEDEFFFD712D%7D/uploads/%7B4E08B085-5D3E-4250-A91B-69D6293301DE%7D.DOC

James, Meg. "'Marketplace' Is America's Most Popular Business Show. Now It Has Ambitious Plans to Expand." Los Angeles Times, 12 Apr. 2017, www.latimes.com/business/hollywood/la-fi-ct-marketplace-public-radio-20170412-story.html.

Jeffrey Dvorkin, former NPR Ombudsman, email conversation with author, Jan. 9, 2018

Joseph, Rebecca. "Loan Saves NPR From Bankruptcy." The Harvard Crimson, 29 July 1983, www.thecrimson.com/article/1983/7/29/loan-saves-npr-from-bankruptcy-pnational/.

June 18, 2013, "Salt Lake City's KCPW Cites Program Costs, Duplication in Canceling NPR Programs." *Current*, 16 Feb. 2015, current.org/2013/06/salt-lake-citys-kcpw-cites-program-costs-duplication-in-cancelling-npr-programs/.

McCauley, Michael P., "NPR: The Trials and Triumphs of National Public Radio," Columbia University Press, 2005, pg 75

Mitchell, Jack W. "Listener Supported," Praeger, 2005, pg 113

"National Public Radio – Carriage." Information Concepts, 5 Feb. 2013, www.infoconcepts.com/national-public-radio-carriage/.

NPR Stations Airing *Talk of the Nation*." NPR, www.npr.org/programs/totn/totn.a-c.carriage.html.

NPR Stations Airing *Talk of the Nation*." NPR, www.npr.org/programs/totn/totn.d-l.carriage.html.

NPR Stations Airing *Talk of the Nation*." NPR, www.npr.org/programs/totn/totn.m.carriage.html.

ibid

NPR Stations Airing Talk of the Nation." NPR, www.npr.org/programs/totn/totn.o-p.carriage.html.

NPR Stations Airing *Talk of the Nation*." NPR, www.npr.org/programs/totn/totn.r-w.carriage.html.

"NPR Stations and Public Media." NPR, 20 June 2013, www.npr.org/about-npr/178640915/npr-stations-and-public-media.

"Public Radio International FY16 Pricing (July 1, 2015–June 30, 2016)." Public Radio International, 31 Mar. 2015, www2.pri.org/Infosite/stationtools/FY16_fees.pdf.

"Radio Market Survey Population, Rankings & Information Fall 2015." Nielsen, 27 Aug. 2015, www.nielsen.com/content/dam/corporate/us/en/docs/nielsen-audio/populations-rankings-fall-2015.pdf.

"Science Guy Bill Nye Invites You to Air Planetary Radio!" The Planetary Society Blog, 31 Mar. 2015, www.planetary.org/multimedia/planetary-radio/broadcast-on-your-station.html.

Stelter, Brian. "After 21 Years, NPR Is Ending 'Talk of the Nation'." The New York Times, 30 Mar. 2013, www.nytimes.com/2013/03/30/business/media/npr-to-end-talk-of-the-nation.html.

ibid

Sutton, John. "NPR, Its Member Stations and Trust." *RadioSutton*, 23 May 2013, https://radiosutton.blogspot.com/search?q=NPR%2C+Its+member+stations

Walden, Eric. "Salt Lake City's KCPW Public Radio Station Erases $1.7M in Debt under New Financial Deal." *The Salt Lake Tribune*, 28 July 2017, archive.sltrib.com/article.php?id=5554108&itype=CMSID.

"Working Paper #2; CLASSICAL RADIO 101." CMI_0622_Brochure_main. Indd, 9 Oct. 2014, pp. 1–50., classicalmusicinitiative.publicradio.org/media/cmi_0622_brochure.pdf.

Salaries

Abudy, Mena, et al. "Do Contracts for Executive Compensation Maximize Firm Value?" CLS Blue Sky Blog, 26 July 2017, clsbluesky.law.columbia.edu/2017/07/26/do-executive-compensation-contracts-maximize-firm-value/.

"AMERICAN PUBLIC MEDIA." Jobs, Indeed, 1 June 2018, www.indeed.com/cmp/American-Public-Media/salaries.

Associated Press. "Minnesota Public Radio in Dispute over Salary Disclosure." 15 Feb. 2006, www.winonadailynews.com/news/state-and-regional/mn/minnesota-public-radio-in-dispute-over-salary-disclosure/article_5c50b339-d0d9-54b8-a19c-777dd46f1634.html.

Battenfeld, Joe. "Salary Hikes, Bonuses Abound at Taxpayer-Funded WGBH." Boston Herald, 30 June 2017, www.bostonherald.com/news/columnists/joe_battenfeld/2017/06/battenfeld_salary_hikes_bonuses_abound_at_taxpayer_funded.

Bebchuk, Lucian and Stulz, Rene', Executive Pay and the Financial Crisis," The Harvard Law School Forum, February 1, 2012, https://corpgov.law.harvard.edu/2012/02/01/executive-pay-and-the-financial-crisis/

Bergen, Jane M. Von. "What WHYY's Marrazzo Says about His Pay." Philly.com, 2 Oct. 2015, www.philly.com/philly/blogs/jobs/INQ_Jobbing_What-WHYYs-Marrazzo-says-about-his-pay-executive-compensation-nonprofit-media-radio-television.html.

Brauer, David. "Speaking of Pay: Just How Much Do MPR's Top National Hosts Make?" MinnPost, 11 Nov. 2009, www.minnpost.com/brau-blog/2009/11/speaking-pay-just-how-much-do-mprs-top-national-hosts-make.

DeMint, Jim. "Public Broadcasting Should Go Private." Wall Street Journal, 4 Mar. 2011, www.wsj.com/articles/SB1000142405274870355960457617666 3789314074.

Dent, Mark. "WHYY President Got a Massive Pay Raise Last Year: It's 'a Slap in the Face'." Billy Penn, 6 July 2017, billypenn.com/2017/07/06/whyy-president-got-a-massive-pay-raise-last-year-its-a-slap-in-the-face/.

Fortune, Gwendoline Y. "Unholy; *Keeping the Public in Public Radio*," 25 Apr. 2010, keeppublicradiopublic.com/unholy/.

Gerstein, Josh. "NPR Salaries: Raw Data." 11 Dec. 2008, joshgerstein.blogspot. com/2008/12/npr-salaries-raw-data.html.

Graham, Tim. "High NPR Star Salaries Curb the Appeal of Small-Dollar Donations." *NewsBusters*, Media Research Center, 23 July 2013, www.news-busters.org/blogs/nb/tim-graham/2013/07/23/high-npr-star-salaries-curb-appeal-small-dollar-donations.

Hill, Brad. "Do Public Radio Executives Make Too Much?" *RAIN News*, 24 Nov. 2015, rainnews.com/do-public-radio-executives-make-too-much/.

Janssen, Mike. "Anonymous Lender Saves Salt Lake Station from Default." Current, 26 July 2012, current.org/2011/11/anonymous-lender-saves-salt-lake-station-from-default/.

Marcotte, Michael V. "News Salaries by Market Size." Feb. 2011, www.mike-marcotte.com/newsroom-salaries/.

Marcotte, Michael V. "Weight Classes of Public Radio Newsrooms." Local NPR, 27 Jan. 2013, localnpr.org/2012/02/08/weight-classes-of-public-radio-newsrooms/.

Mook, Ben, and Janssen, Mike. "What Top Public Media Executives Are Earning." Current, 17 Nov. 2015, current.org/series/executive-compensation/.

Mook, Ben. "The Numbers: What Top Executives Are Making." Current, 14 Dec. 2016, current.org/2015/11/the-numbers-what-top-executives-are-making/.

PLEDGE: The Public Radio Fund Drive

November 1, 2011, "Atlanta Pubcasters' Salaries Scrutinized." *Current*, 1 Nov. 2011, current.org/2011/11/atlanta-pubcasters-salaries-scrutinized/.

NPR Salaries in Washington, DC." 8 June 2018, Glassdoor, www.glassdoor. co.in/Salary/NPR-Washington-DC-Salaries-EI_IE3965.0,3_IL.4,17_ IM911_IP2.htm.

Public Radio Finances, "Support Public Radio, "NPR, 20 June 2013, www.npr. org/about-npr/178660742/public-radio-finances.

Roose, Kevin. "In Defense of the Wall Street Bonus." New York Magazine, 12 Dec. 2012, nymag.com/daily/intelligencer/2012/12/defense-of-the-wall-street-bonus.html.

Roth, Michael. "WESU: Support College Radio at Its Best." Roth on Wesleyan, 6 May 2013, roth.blogs.wesleyan.edu/2013/05/06/wesu-support-college-ra-dio-at-its-best/.

Schlossberg, Mallory. "The Surprising Things Millennials Love–and Hate." *Business Insider*, 3 Oct. 2015, www.businessinsider.com/what-retailers-should-know-millennials-love-and-hate-2015-9/#hit-fast-casual-food-5.

Staff, Marketplace. "A Third of Millennials Share Their Salary Information with Co-Workers." 18 Oct. 2017, www.marketplace.org/2017/10/18/your-money/ millennials-sharing-salary-information-equal-pay.

Staff, The *Chronicle of Philanthropy*. "Auditors Investigate Salaries at Pub-lic-Radio Station." The *Chronicle of Philanthropy*, 1 May 2006, www. philanthropy.com/article/Auditors-Investigate-Salaries/197117.

Staff. "Wasatch Public Media Buys KCPW." Deseret News, 28 Sept. 2008, www.deseretnews.com/article/700262348/Wasatch-Public-Media-buys-KCPW.html.

Story, Louise, and Dash, Eric. "Bankers Reaped Lavish Bonuses During Bail-outs." *The New York Times*, 31 July 2009, www.nytimes.com/2009/07/31/ business/31pay.html.

"Your Coworkers Should Know Your Salary." *Harvard Business Review*, 10 Mar. 2016, hbr.org/ideacast/2016/03/your-coworkers-should-know-your-salary.html.

Fees

2017 Annual Report." fy2017_annual_report, pp. 1–7., static.wamu.org/d/about/
fy2017_annual_report.pdf.

"About Us." NPR, NPR, digitalservices.npr.org/about-us.

"Adams, Lauren,," GM KUCB, phone conversation with author, Jan. 15, 2018

"Annual Membership Dues." Public Radio Program Directors Association, prpd.
org/membership/dues.

"Become a Member–Society of Professional Journalists." Society of Professional Journalists–Improving and Protecting Journalism since 1909, www.spj.
org/whyjoin5.asp.

"Become A Member." Greater Public, www.greaterpublic.org/about/be-
come-member/.

"Before the COPYRIGHT ROYALTY BOARD in the Library of Congress.
Notice of Inquiry–Tom Worster-Spinitron," 27 May 2009, pp. 1–9., www.
crb.gov/comments/2008-7/noi/tom-worster-spinitron.pdf.

"Bylaws of National Public Radio Inc., 1999." Current, 19 Nov. 2012, current.
org/1999/01/bylaws-of-national-public-radio-inc-1999-2/.

"CPB Music Rights Main Page." CPB, www.cpb.org/musicrights.

"CPB, NPR, WRTI: Connecting the Dots to Understand Public Radio Funding."
WRTI, wrti.org/post/cpb-npr-wrti-connecting-dots-understand-public-ra-
dio-funding.

CPB. "SoundExchange Reporting," spinitron.com/doc/special-topics/web-
cast-reports/process-cpb/.

"CRB Sets Rates for Public Performance Royalties for Noncommercial Broadcast Stations for Over-the-Air Broadcasting – Rejects GMR Claim for
Royalties." *Broadcast Law Blog*, 22 Jan. 2018, www.broadcastlawblog.
com/2018/01/articles/crb-sets-rates-for-public-performance-royalties-for-
noncommercial-broadcast-stations-for-over-the-air-broadcasting-rejects-
gmr-claim-for-royalties/.

"Daebler, Danielle, and Jensen, Dan. PRI AND NPR ANNOUNCE DEAL."
NPR, 31 July 2008, www.npr.org/about/press/2008/073108.PublicInterac-
tive.html.

"Determination of Rates and Terms for Public Broadcasting (PB III)."
Federal Register, 7 Nov. 2017, www.federalregister.gov/documents/2017/11/07/2017-23991/determination-of-rates-and-terms-for-public-broadcasting-pb-iii.

Falk, Tyler. "As It Defines Relationship with Stations, NPR Gains Board Approval for Price Hike." *Current*, 24 Feb. 2017, current.org/2017/02/npr-proposes-new-dues-structure-strategy-for-stronger-future-with-stations/.

Falk, Tyler. "'Changing Business Realities' Shape Talks over NPR Programming Dues." *Current*, 12 Apr. 2016, current.org/2016/04/changing-business-reali-ties-shape-npr-dues-talks/.

Farhi, Paul. "NPR to End '*Tell Me More*' Program Aimed at Minorities." The Washington Post, WP Company, 20 May 2014, www.washingtonpost.com/lifestyle/style/npr-to-end-tell-me-more-program-aimed-at-minorities-eliminate-28-positions/2014/05/20/0593cc3a-e04f-11e3-8dcc-d6b7fede081a_story.html?utm_term=.e250a588c188.

"Fees, Federal Communications Commission." 1 Nov. 2017, www.fcc.gov/licensing-databases/fees.

Frequently Asked Questions about Public Broadcasting. "Public Broadcasting Starts with You," pp. 1–3., d1vmz9r13e2j4x.cloudfront.net/NET/misc/00027010.pdf.

Jeffrey Dvorkin," former NPR Ombudsman, email conversation with author, Jan. 12, 2018

"KUCO-FM Radio and KCSC Classical Radio Foundation Combined Financial Report June 30 2017 and 2016." Audit_2016-2017, pp. 1–15., www.kucofm.com/sites/kcsc/uploads/documents/Forms/Audit_2016-2017.pdf.

Lazarus, David. "Wireless Firms Make the Call to Nickel-and-Dime Customers." Los Angeles Times, 19 July 2009, articles.latimes.com/2009/jul/19/business/fi-lazarus19.

Martin, Garrett. "College Radio Is Dying–and We Need to Save It." Salon, 3 June 2014, www.salon.com/2014/06/02/college_radio_is_dying_and_we_need_to_save_it/.

"Membership." PRADO , 30 Jan. 2018, www.pradoweb.org/index.asp?SEC=BB3E6D9C-62FF-42B4-92F8-9C91A71F55A1&Type=B_EV.

Moss, Brett. "PRSS Announces Station Fee Change." Radio World, 7 Mar. 2016, www.radioworld.com/business-and-law/0009/prss-announces-station-fee-change/337337.

"Music Licensing for Noncommercial Broadcasters and Webcasters." Startup Costs | Prometheus Radio Project, www.prometheusradio.org/music-licensing-noncommercial-broadcasters-and-webcasters.

"NAB Membership." PublicStationMembershipForm, 20 Feb. 2017, pp. 1–1., www.nab.org/documents/membership/publicStationMembershipForm.pdf.

"Noncommercial Webcasters 2019 Rates." SoundExchange, www.soundexchange.com/service-provider/rates/noncommercial-webcasters-rates/.

"NPR Digital Services Composer Basic." ComposerBasic_Userguide, 27 Nov. 2012, pp. 1–7., mediad.publicbroadcasting.net/p/newnprdsblog/files/201211/ComposerBasic_Userguide.pdf.

"Oklahoma's Choice for Classical Music." KUCO Classical Radio, www.kucofm.com/membership/.

Oxenford, David. "CRB Announces Webcasting Royalty Rates for 2016-2020 – Lower Rates for Broadcasters Who Stream, Minimal Change for Pureplay Webcasters." Broadcast Law Blog, 17 Dec. 2015, www.broadcastlawblog.com/2015/12/articles/crb-announces-webcasting-royalty-rates-for-2016-2020-lower-rates-for-broadcasters-who-stream-minimal-change-for-pureplay-webcasters/.

Oxenford, David. "FCC Regulatory Fees for Broadcasters Proposed to Increase Significantly to Cover Cost of FCC Headquarters Move." Broadcast Law Blog, 2 June 2016, www.broadcastlawblog.com/2016/06/articles/fcc-regula-tory-fees-for-broadcasters-proposed-to-increase-significantly-to-cover-cost-of-fcc-headquarters-move/.

"Poynter Launches Membership Program to Support Career Success for Media Professionals and Educators." Poynter, 20 Oct. 2015, www.poynter.org/news/poynter-launches-membership-program-support-career-success-media-professionals-and-educators.

"Station Membership Calculator." PRX–Public Radio Exchange, www.prx.org/calculator.

"Resource Directory" NFCB, nfcb.org/directory/.

Sehgal, Kabir. "Spotify and Apple Music Should Become Record Labels so Musicians Can Make a Fair Living." CNBC, CNBC, 26 Jan. 2018, www.cnbc.com/2018/01/26/how-spotify-apple-music-can-pay-musicians-more-commentary.html.

Silva, Ernesto. "Public Media Organizations." CPB, 7 Feb. 2018, www.cpb.org/stations/pborganizations.

SoundExchange FAQs. NPR, 28 May 2009, digitalservices.npr.org/soundexchange-faqs#reporting_frequency.

SoundExchange "Artist & Copyright Owner." www.soundexchange.com/artist-copyright-owner/.

Spinitron. Philosophy, spinitron.com/about/philosophy/.

"Summary of Scales and Conditions." AFM Public Radio Agreement, 24 Oct. 2014, pp. 1–2., members.afm.org/uploads/file/AFM%20Public%20Radio%20Agrement%20Scale%20Summary%20and%20Conditions_020112%20thru013115.pdf.

Sutton, John. "NPR's Digital Services Proposal Is Really a Membership Issue." RadioSutton, 26 May 2011, radiosutton.blogspot.com/2011/05/nprs-digital-services-proposal-is.html.

"What Does That Mean? A Glossary of NPR Lingo." *NPR Station Manager's Handbook* IX. The Language of Public Radio, 22 May 2000, pp. 167–178., www.nprstations.org/handbook/91glossary.pdf.

Facilities and Infrastructure

Adams, Lauren, GM KUCB, phone conversation with the author, Jan. 15, 2018

"Aleutian Islands." Encyclopædia Britannica, 18 Dec. 2015, www.britannica.com/place/Aleutian-Islands.

Aleutian Peninsula Broadcasting, Inc. – "King Cove FM Radio Translator, Ground System, Studio Renovation, & Vehicle." proj54703, 5 May 2010, pp. 1–18., www.omb.alaska.gov/ombfiles/11_budget/CapBackup/proj54703.pdf.

Batzdorf, Nick. "The Great 'Marketplace' Studio Redesign of 2009-2014: American Public Media Updates Radio Facility for the 'Connected' World." Mixonline, 1 Apr. 2014, www.mixonline.com/sfp/great-marketplace-stu-

dio-redesign-2009-2014-american-public-media-updates-radio-facility-con-
nected-world-369369.

Collins, Glenn. "The Silence of the Alert System; Experts Urge Overhaul of Plan
Unused Even on Sept. 11". *The New York Times*, https://www.nytimes.
com/2001/12/21/nyregion/silence-alert-system-experts-urge-overhaul-plan-
unused-even-sept-11.html

Collins, Glenn. "WNYC's Planned Move Will Finish Its Breakup With the
City." *The New York Times*, 17 July 2006, www.nytimes.com/2006/07/17/
nyregion/17radio.html.

Deabler, Danielle. "NPR labs to Pilot Project of Radio Emergency Alerts for
Deaf and Hard of Hearing People in U.S. Gulf Coast," NPR, 22 Feb. 2013,
www.npr.org/about/press/2013/022213.NPRLabsPilot.html.

Editor. "New Delmarva Public Radio Transmitters Increase Sound Quality,
Reliability." Delmarva Public Radio, 10 Nov. 2016, delmarvapublicradio.
net/post/new-delmarva-public-radio-transmitters-increase-sound-quality-re-
liability.

Editor. "How To Make Broadcast Towers More Bird-Friendly: Turn Off Some
Lights." WUNC, 24 Jan. 2017, wunc.org/post/how-make-broadcast-towers-
more-bird-friendly-turn-some-lights#stream/0.

Fitch, Lynn, former Station Manager, KBOO, phone conversation Jan. 14, 2018

"FM Query Results." Federal Communications Commission, 8 June 2018, tran-
sition.fcc.gov/fcc-bin/fmq?call=WCVE.

Folkenflik, David. "Frederick Station Sold to WYPR." Tribunedigital-Bal-
timoresun, 13 Jan. 2004, articles.baltimoresun.com/2004-01-13/fea-
tures/0401130098_1_npr-station-frederick.

Fybush, Scott. "In Maintaining Towers, Stations Face Higher Costs, Lack of
Space." *Current*, 17 Sept. 2014, current.org/2014/09/in-maintaining-
towers-stations-face-higher-costs-lack-of-space/.

Kim, Ami. "WCVE Public Radio Has a New Transmitter." Community Idea Stations, 11 Jan. 2016, ideastations.org/wcve-public-radio-has-new-transmitter.

Kinney, Jim. "Public Radio Station WFCR-FM Plans Move from Amherst
to Springfield." Masslive.com, 13 May 2011, www.masslive.com/busi-
ness-news/index.ssf/2011/05/public_radio_station_wfcr_plans_move_to.ht-
ml.

Kordenbrock, Mike. "Yellowstone Public Radio Gets Interior Renovation." The Billings Gazette, 4 Apr. 2016, billingsgazette.com/news/local/yellowstone-public-radio-gets-interior-renovation/article_9dc43adc-2a21-545e-9360-dda4519324ea.html.

"Memorandum Opinion and Order." R.J.'s Late Night Entertainment Corporation, FCC, 8 Apr. 2015, apps.fcc.gov/edocs_public/attachmatch/DA-15-181A1.pdf.

Murray, Jon. "Colorado Public Radio Wins Rezoning OK for Possible New Studios, Tower on Ruby Hill Site." The Denver Post, 18 Mar. 2017, www.denverpost.com/2017/02/06/colorado-public-radio-wins-rezoning-ok-for-possible-new-studios-tower-on-ruby-hill-site/.

Murphy, Nancy email correspondence with author, January 18, 2018
OptimERA." OptimERA, optimera.us/.

Oxenford, David. "FAA Announces New Standards for Lighting Communications Towers." Broadcast Law Blog, 11 Dec. 2015, www.broadcastlawblog.com/2015/12/articles/faa-announces-new-standards-for-lighting-communications-towers/.

"Predicted Coverage Area for WCVE 88.9 FM, Richmond, VA." Radio Stations in Salina, Kansas., 7 June 2018, radio-locator.com/cgi-bin/patg?id=WCVE-FM.

"Products by Community." GCI, www.gci.com/gci-products-by-community.

"Public Notice–FCC Enforcement Advisory." Emergency Alert System, FCC, 6 Nov. 2013, apps.fcc.gov/edocs_public/attachmatch/DA-13-2123A1.pdf.

Radio Equipment List–Radio Station Construction Costs."A Nation Online: Entering the Broadband Age," National Telecommunications and Information Administration, 26 Jan. 2011, www.ntia.doc.gov/legacy/otiahome/ptfp/application/equipcost_Radio.html.

"Radio Market Survey Population, Rankings & Information." redbook_fa15–Population-Rankings-Fall-2015, www.nielsen.com/content/dam/corporate/us/en/docs/nielsen-audio/populations-rankings-fall-2015.pdf.

Radio Equipment List–Radio Station Construction Costs." A Nation Online: Entering the Broadband Age | National Telecommunications and Information Administration, 26 Jan. 2011, www.ntia.doc.gov/legacy/otiahome/ptfp/application/equipcost_Radio.html.

ibid

Read, Aaron. "The EC: RDS Text on the Radio." Rhode Island Public Radio, 24 Apr. 2015, ripr.org/post/theec-rds-text-radio.

Sheehan Nagle Hartray Architects. "WBEZ-FM – Sheehan Nagle Hartray Architects," www.sheehannaglehartray.com/projects/wbez-fm/.

Spitzer, Judith. "Public Radio Station to Start $5 Million Renovation." Spokane Journal of Business, 10 Apr. 2014, www.spokanejournal.com/special-report/public-radio-station-to-start-5-million-renovation/.

WAMU Gets New Digs." Washington *City Paper*, 2 Feb. 2012, www.washingtoncitypaper.com/news/city-desk/blog/13064962/wamu-gets-new-digs.

WSGE1 timestamp 30 Apr. 2016 1113 EST

Projects

"About Us." Localore, Association of Independents in Radio, 29 May 2018, localore.net/.

"Apply Now for the 2018 Challenge Fund – ONA Programs." Online News Association, journalists.org/programs/challenge-fund/.

Clark, Jessica, and Aufderheide, Pat. "Public Media 2.0: Dynamic, Engaged Publics." Center for Media and Social Impact, Feb. 2009, cmsimpact.org/resource/public-media-2-0-dynamic-engaged-publics/.

Dalton, Meg, and Hutchins, Corey. "Public Radio Rethinks Its Approach to Journalism." Columbia Journalism Review, 7 Nov. 2017, www.cjr.org/united_states_project/npr-corporation-public-broadcasting-collaboration.php.

Darville, Sarah. "For Public Radio and Television Stations, collaboration around the News Proves Challenging." Nieman Lab, 15 July 2013, www.niemanlab.org/2013/07/for-public-radio-and-television-stations-collaboration-around-the-news-proves-challenging/.

Deabler, Danielle. American Public Media, NPR, PBS, Public Radio International (PRI), and Public Radio Exchange (PRX) partner to create shared digital content platform. NPR, 14 June 2010, www.npr.org/about/press/2010/061410.PMPLaunch.html.

Finn, Scott. "W.Va. Public Broadcasting Receives Grant to Expand Regional Reporting." West Virginia Public Broadcasting, 9 Nov. 2015, wvpublic.org/post/wva-public-broadcasting-receives-grant-expand-regional-reporting.

PLEDGE: The Public Radio Fund Drive

"Five Reasons to Build on Public Media's Journalism Collaborations." Public Media Company, 10 Apr. 2018, www.publicmedia.co/pmc-portfolio/channel-x/.

"FROM AIRWAVES TO EARBUDS – Informed and Engaged." Medium, 26 Jan. 2017, medium.com/informed-and-engaged/from-airwaves-to-earbuds-8d42b52b7bc5.

Geisler, Erin. "22 Texas Public Radio Stations Air '*Texas Standard*' after First Six Months of Broadcasting." KUT, 8 Sept. 2015, kut.org/post/22-texas-public-radio-stations-air-texas-standard-after-first-six-months-broadcasting.

"Grant Announcements." Henry Luce Foundation, 2018, www.hluce.org/grantannouncements.aspx.

Habbak, Malak. "Social Relevance and Innovation in Public Radio." 13 Oct. 2017, broncoscholar.library.cpp.edu/bitstream/handle/10211.3/172771/HabbakMalak_JournalSubmission.pdf?sequence=6.

Hanley, Scott. "Technology and Public Media." 31 Aug. 2016, www.sehanley.com/technology.html.

Henderson, Mark, "Politics clouds blue-sky science," The London Times, September 19, 2005, http://www.timesonline.co.uk/tol/news/uk/article568223.ece

Janssen, Mike. "Currently Curious: Why Isn't There More Collaboration between TV and Radio?" Current, 22 Feb. 2016, current.org/2016/01/currently-curious-why-isnt-there-more-collaboration-between-tv-and-radio./

Kaplan, Lori. "A (Sort of) Farewell." NPR, 17 Aug. 2012, www.npr.org/sections/gofigure/2012/08/17/159005508/a-sort-of-farewell?ft=1.

Kretz, Chris. "What Can Libraries Learn from the Future of Public Media?" Urban Library Journal, SUNY Stony Brook, 2 Oct. 2017, academicworks.cuny.edu/cgi/viewcontent.cgi?article=1166&context=ulj.

Lyons, Nora, and Cooper, Meryl. "*The Moth* and The New York Public Library Team Up for Collaborative Audio Transcription Project, Together We Listen." The New York Public Library, 5 Apr. 2016, www.nypl.org/press/press-release/april-5-2016/moth-and-new-york-public-library-team-collaborative-audio.

Marcotte, Michael V. "Proposal: Innovation Labs in Local NPR Stations." www.mikemarcotte.com/innovation-labs-local-npr.html.

McKelvey, Karissa. "Sloan Funding Dat Development." Dat Project Blog, 9 May 2017, blog.datproject.org/2014/03/08/sloan-funding/.

"New York Public Radio Announces $10 Million Gift from The Jerome L. Greene Foundation; Launches New 'Discover' Feature on the WNYC App." WNYC, 10 Mar. 2014, www.wnyc.org/press/discover/031014/.

Newton, Eric. "Why We Need a Public Media Technology Transformation Fund." Searchlights & Sunglasses, 2011, www.searchlightsandsunglasses. org/why-we-need-a-public-media-technology-transformation-fund/.

"NPR One–On-Demand Digital Listening Platform." Knight Foundation, 31 Apr. 2013, knightfoundation.org/grants/201343177/.

Owen, Lauren Hazard. "6 Different Kinds of Collaborative Journalism and the Good and Bad Things about Each." IJNET/Nieman Labs, 29 Sept. 2017, ijnet.org/en/blog/6-different-kinds-collaborative-journalism-and-good-and-bad-things-about-each.

Pilhofer, Aron. "How DocumentCloud Bolsters Investigative Journalism and the Exchange of Public Information." Knight Foundation, 27 July 2017, knight-foundation.org/articles/how-documentcloud-bolsters-investigative-journal-ism-and-the-exchange-of-public-information.

Popham, Michael. "Innovation Interns Look Back Over Their Busy Summer." 50 Years Minnesota Public Radio, MPR, 2017, www.mpr50.org/sto-ry/2017/08/09/innovation-interns-look-back-over-their-busy-summer.

Project Argo, Knight Foundation, NPR, CPB, 3 Sept. 2015, argoproject.org/blog/page/2/learn.php.html.

"Radio Innovation Roundtable Reveals How Funders Partner With Public Music Stations to Rally Communities." Media Impact Funders, mediaim-pactfunders.org/radio-innovation-roundtable-reveals-how-funders-part-ner-with-public-music-stations-to-rally-communities/.

Radio Press Room. CPB, www.cpb.org/press-categories/radio.

"Radio Station and Regional Journalism Collaborations." CPB, 12 Aug. 2016, www.cpb.org/grants/archived?title=collaboration.

"RadioPublic." about.radiopublic.com/.

"Regional Journalism Collaborations." CPB, 26 Apr. 2016, www.cpb.org/sites/default/files/rfp/Regional-Journalism-Collaborations-Grant-Guide-lines-FY17.pdf.

Rosenberg, Gabriel. "How Public Media Collaborations Are Creating Opportunities for Local Reporting." *Columbia Journalism Review*, 22 July 2014, archives.cjr.org/united_states_project/local_journalism_centers_corpora-tion_public_broadcasting.php.

Silva, Ernesto. "CPB's Federal Appropriation Request & Justification." CPB, 12 Feb. 2018, www.cpb.org/funding.

Sonic Trace. KCRW, 27 Sept. 2012, www.kcrw.com/news-culture/shows/sonic-trace.

"Southern California Public Radio Received Irvine Foundation Grant for California Courts Collaborative." Press Release, SCPR, 6 Jan. 2016, www.scpr.org/about/press/2016-irvine-foundation-grant-for-california-counts.

Staff. NPR Research (@Nprresearch). Twitter, 2009-2012, twitter.com/nprresearch.

Tait, Richard, et al. "Five Successful Collaborations." PMBOnline.org, 2 June 2016, www.pmbaonline.org/sites/default/files/documents/2-%20Earth-Fix%20Summary_final_5_22.pdf.

"What We Do." Management Tools–Mission and Vision Statements–Bain & Company, www.bain.com/about/what-we-do/index.aspx.

Chapter 4 Whad' Ya Know

Alben W. Barkley Quotes." BrainyQuote, Xplore, www.brainyquote.com/quotes/alben_w_barkley_177030.

Aron, Hillel. "Left-Wing Darling Pacifica Radio Is Sliding Into the Abyss." L.A. Weekly, 5 Apr. 2016, www.laweekly.com/news/left-wing-darling-pacifica-radio-is-sliding-into-the-abyss-4521218.

Beaujon, Andrew. "Has WAMU Solved Public Radio's Diversity Problem?" Washingtonian, 30 May 2017, www.washingtonian.com/2017/05/25/wamu-solved-public-radios-diversity-problem/.

"Donors Demand Clearer View of Station Reality." Current, 8 Apr. 2012, current.org/2003/09/donors-demand-clearer-view-of-station-reality/.

Dubner, Stephen J. "Question of the Day: Should I Feel Guilty About Not Supporting Public Radio?" Freakonomics, 30 Apr. 2013, freakonomics.com/2013/04/30/question-of-the-day-should-i-feel-guilty-about-not-supporting-public-radio/.

Fraguada, Luis Edgardo. "I Want to Turn off NPR, but I Can't . . ." Archinect, 20 June 2005, archinect.com/forum/thread/20624/i-want-to-turn-off-npr-but-i-can-t.

Getler, Michael. "A Farewell to Viewers, and Readers, Like You." 24 Apr. 2017, www.pbs.org/ombudsman/blogs/ombudsman/2017/04/24/a-farewell-to-viewers-and-readers-like-you/.

Kling, William, founder of MPR, phone conversation with author, Nov. 16, 2016

Leek, Bill. "When It Comes to Wine." Wine Vertical Market Sheet, 6 Apr. 2016, pp. 1–1., mediad.publicbroadcasting.net/p/kwbu/files/wine_vertical_market_sheet.pdf.

Liptak, Adam. "In Supreme Court Opinions, Web Links to Nowhere." The New York Times, The New York Times, 24 Sept. 2013, www.nytimes.com/2013/09/24/us/politics/in-supreme-court-opinions-clicks-that-lead-nowhere.html.

Public Radio. Quora, www.quora.com/topic/Public-Radio.

"Public Radio." *Metafilter*, www.metafilter.com/contribute/search.mefi?site=ask&q=Public%2BRadio.

Smelser, Judith. "NPR-Themed Wines: Not Challenging, but Perfectly 'Drinkable'." *Current*, 7 Nov. 2017, current.org/2017/11/npr-themed-wines-not-challenging-but-perfectly-drinkable/.

Time

Barton, Julia. "The Broadcast Clock, the Diagram That Rules Public Radio." *Slate* Magazine, Slate, 12 Sept. 2013, www.slate.com/blogs/the_eye/2013/09/12/_99_invisible_on_npr_s_broadcast_clock_the_diagram_that_rules_public_radio.html.

"BBC Crafts Module to Take Advantage of NPR Clock Changes." Current, 16 Feb. 2015, current.org/2014/11/bbc-crafts-module-to-take-advantage-of-npr-clock-changes/.

Collins, Bob, "Debating NPR Underwriting Announcements." NewsCut, Minnesota Public Radio, 20 Apr. 2015, blogs.mprnews.org/newscut/2015/04/debating-npr-underwriting-announcements/.

Falk, Tyler. "With New Host Rachel Martin, '*Morning Edition*' Plans to Focus on Places 'We Haven't Paid Attention to'." Current, 5 Dec. 2016, current.

org/2016/12/with-new-host-rachel-martin-morning-edition-plans-to-focus-on-places-we-havent-paid-attention-to/.

Janssen, Mike. "Proposed NPR Clocks Would Add Morning Newscasts, Longer Underwriting Credits." Current, 16 Feb. 2015, current.org/2014/07/proposed-npr-clocks-would-add-morning-newscasts-longer-underwriting-credits/.

Jensen, Elizabeth. "'Morning Edition' Resets Its Clock (Again)." NPR, 16 Aug. 2018, www.npr.org/sections/ombudsman/2018/08/16/639209921/morning-edition-resets-its-clock-again.

Kinsella, Brent. "Are Broadcast Radio Ad Loads Sustainable?" XAPPmedia, 9 Feb. 2016, xappmedia.com/are-broadcast-radio-ad-loads-sustainable/. Merritt, Kathy. "Keeping the Morning Edition Audience." Grow the Audience for Public Radio, 20 Jan. 2004, www.srg.org/program/ME2findings.html.

Public Radio Audience Demographics–NPR Profiles." National Public Media, nationalpublicmedia.com/npr/audience/.

Shearer, Elisa. "Audio and Podcasting Fact Sheet." Pew Research Center's Journalism Project, 12 July 2018, www.journalism.org/fact-sheet/audio-and-podcasting/.

Staff. "As Podcast Revenues Climb, NPR Board Questions Effect on Radio Sales." Current, 13 May 2015, current.org/2015/05/as-podcast-revenues-climb-npr-board-questions-effects-on-radio-sales/.

Sutton, John. "How Stations Can Stay Relevant as Listeners Go Elsewhere for NPR Content." Current, 12 Aug. 2014, current.org/2014/08/how-stations-can-stay-relevant-as-listeners-go-elsewhere-for-npr-content/.

Tardif, Amy. "WGCU and NPR Reset the Clock." WGCU News, 12 Nov. 2014, news.wgcu.org/post/wgcu-and-npr-reset-clock.

Demographics

Ajzen, Icek (1991). "The Theory of Planned Behavior." Organizational Behavior and Human Decision Processes. 50 2. : 179–211.

Beaujon, Andrew. "Has WAMU Solved Public Radio's Diversity Problem?" Washingtonian, 30 May 2017, www.washingtonian.com/2017/05/25/wamu-solved-public-radios-diversity-problem/.

Consumer Neuroscience, Nielsen. "What People Watch, Listen To and Buy," www.nielsen.com/us/en/solutions/capabilities/consumer-neuroscience.html.

Garofoli, Joe. "Public Broadcasting Stations Cut Staff, Budget." SFGate, San Francisco Chronicle, 9 Feb. 2012, www.sfgate.com/politics/article/Public-broadcasting-stations-cut-staff-budget-3174082.php.

Giovannoni, David.–Home Page." David Giovannoni–Home Page, davidgiovannoni.com/pubs.asp.

Giovanonni, David. "*Audience 98* Public Service, Public Support." Audience 98–Doc-0100, 3 Oct. 2000, pp. 1–189., www.davidgiovannoni.com/pubs/doc-0100.pdf.

Gourville, John T. "Pennies-a-Day: The Effect of Temporal Reframing on Transaction Evaluation." JOURNAL OF CONSUMER RESEARCH, Inc., Mar. 1998, www.jstor.org/stable/10.1086/209517?seq=1#page_scan_tab_contents.

Greiff, Felicia. "Ira Glass: 'Public Radio Is Ready for Capitalism'." Crain's Chicago Business, 30 Apr. 2015, www.chicagobusiness.com/article/20150430/NEWS06/150439970/ira-glass-public-radio-is-ready-for-capitalism.

"How Many Listeners Donate? One in 12 or One in Three?" *Current*, 29 Jan. 2013, current.org/1998/08/how-many-listeners-donate-one-in-12-or-one-in-three/.

Hunter, D. "WBOI On-Air Fundraising Guide." 28 July 2012, niprfunddrive.tumblr.com/.

Kinnally, William, and Brinkerhoff, Bobbie. "Modeling the Members' Intentions to Give." Philosophy of the Social Sciences, Journal of Creative Communications, 4 Sept. 2013, journals.sagepub.com/doi/abs/10.1177/0973258613491665.

Kramer, Melody. "What, Exactly, Does It Mean to Be a Member of a Public Radio Station? Can That Definition Expand?" Nieman Lab, 15 May 2015, www.niemanlab.org/2015/05/what-exactly-does-it-mean-to-be-a-member-of-a-public-radio-station-can-that-definition-expand/.

"KSER *Pledge Drive Pitch Playbook*." Pledge_Pitch_Playbook_KSER, 4 June 2010, pp. 1–22., www.kser.org/download/Pledge_Break_Playbook_KSER.pdf.

Neyfakh, Leon. "An Antiquated Business Model. A Horde of Upstart Competitors. Does NPR Have a Future?" *Slate* Magazine, Slate, 10 Apr. 2016, www.slate.com/articles/news_and_politics/cover_story/2016/04/the_fight_for_the_future_of_npr_can_public_radio_survive_the_podcast_revolution.html.

"NPR ANNUAL REPORT 2014." FY14_annualreport, 6 Feb. 2015, www.npr.org/about/annualreports/FY14_annualreport.pdf+.

"Report Highlights Top Public Radio Stations." Public Radio Program Directors, July 2013, www.themediaaudit.com/press/archived-newsletters/the-media-audit-fyi/july-2013/report-highlights-top-public-radio-stations.

"Rhythms, Not Algorithms." WXPN 88.5, Public Radio from the University of Pennsylvania, www.xpn.org/.

Shang, Jen, and Croson, Rachel. "Limits of Social Influence on the Voluntary Provision of Public Goods: Evidence from Field Experiments." Social Comparison And Charitable Contribution, 2008, citeseerx.ist.psu.edu/viewdoc/download?doi=10.1.1.583.7541&rep=rep1&type=pdf, pg. 2

Sherman, Scott. "Good, Gray NPR." *The Nation*, 29 June 2015, www.thenation.com/article/good-gray-npr/.

SRI International. "*VALS* Market Research," www.sri.com/sites/default/timeline/timeline.php?timeline=business-entertainment#!&innovation=vals-market-research.

Staff. "Tough Economy Forces NPR to Address Unexpected Shortfall in Revenue." NPR, 10 Dec. 2008, www.npr.org/about/press/2008/121008.budget.html.

Sutton, John. "How Stations Can Stay Relevant as Listeners Go Elsewhere for NPR Content." Current, 12 Aug. 2014, current.org/2014/08/how-stations-can-stay-relevant-as-listeners-go-elsewhere-for-npr-content/.

"The 1992 PBS Funding Debate: How Much Diversity Is America Willing to Pay for?," Paul Siegel, February 1993, Western States Communication Association, https://eric.ed.gov/?id=ED373381

VALS™ Types, SBI. Strategic Business Insights, www.strategicbusinessinsights.com/vals/ustypes.shtml.

Diversity

"20 Years–420 Programs–1992." PBS Frontline, Public Broadcasting Service, 1992, www.pbs.org/wgbh/pages/frontline/twenty/programs/1992.html.

Bois, Jon. "'*A Prairie Home Companion*' Is Wretched and Awful." SBNation. com, 18 Oct. 2013, www.sbnation.com/2013/10/18/4848470/a-prairie-home-companion-is-wretched-and-unlistenable.

"Broadcasters Not Allowed to Refuse Political Ads for 'Nonstandard' Length." Reporters Committee for Freedom of the Press, 4 Oct. 1999, www.rcfp.org/browse-media-law-resources/news/broadcasters-not-allowed-refuse-political-ads-%E2%80%98nonstandard%E2%80%99-length.

Chen, David W. "WNYC Chief Pushed Growth at the Cost of Station's Culture." The New York Times, 22 Dec. 2017, www.nytimes.com/2017/12/22/nyregion/wnyc-chief-laura-walker-firing-hosts-misconduct.html.

Clander and Mylosh. "#20 Being an Expert on YOUR Culture." Stuff White People Like, 24 Jan. 2008, www.stuffwhitepeoplelike.com/2008/01/23/20-being-an-expert-on-your-culture/.

Danielle, Britni. "Sigh. Why Won't Rachel Dolezal Go Away?" EBONY, 10 May 2016, www.ebony.com/news-views/Rachel-dolezal-rasta.

DeVoe, Philip H. "Understanding Your Political Opponents Takes More than a Visit to Their Neck of the Woods." National Review, 16 Nov. 2017, www. nationalreview.com/2017/11/ken-stern-republican-like-me-entertaining-sociological-tourism-failed-bipartisan-appeal/.

Feder, Robert. "On Balance, WBEZ Removes '*Smiley & West*' from Lineup." Time Out Chicago, 9 Oct. 2012, www.timeout.com/chicago/tv/on-balance-wbez-removes-smiley-west-from-lineup.

Gabler, Jay. "Theater Review: 'Acting Black' Is a Reminder That We Have a Long Way to Go in Dismantling Racism." City Pages, 21 May 2018, www. citypages.com/arts/theater-review-acting-black-is-a-reminder-that-we-have-a-long-way-to-go-in-dismantling-racism/483214901.

"Hi, I'm Robert Seagull, and You're Listening to NPR," 7 Jan. 2018, www.meta-filter.com/171628/Hi-Im-Robert-Seagull-and-youre-listening-to-NPR.

Kimble, Julian. "Remembering Jennifer Lopez's N-Word Controversy, 15 Years Later." Genius, 18 July 2016, genius.com/a/remembering-jennifer-lopez-s-n-word-controversy-15-years-later.

Kitteh. "The Fight for the Future of NPR." Metafilter, 18 Apr. 2016, www.metafilter.com/158715/The-fight-for-the-future-of-NPR.

Krauthammer, Charles. "Limousine Liberal Hypocrisy." Time, 16 Mar. 2007, content.time.com/time/magazine/article/0,9171,1599714,00.html.

KUER timestamp 6 Apr. 2016 1525 MST

Mulvaney, Erin. "Inside the Morgan Lewis Investigation of Alleged Misconduct at NPR," National Law Journal." Corporate Counsel, 21 Feb. 2018, www.law.com/nationallawjournal/2018/02/21/inside-the-morgan-lewis-investigation-of-alleged-misconduct-at-npr/?slreturn=20180526164016.

"NPR Reporter Who Grilled Her Boss on Sexual Harassment, Gets Major Promotion." Women in the World, 19 Dec. 2017, womenintheworld.com/2017/12/19/mary-louise-kelly-npr-reporter-who-grilled-her-boss-on-sexual-harassment-gets-major-promotion/.

Papper, Bob. "RTDNA Research: Women and Minorities in Newsrooms." RTDNA, 3 July 2017, rtdna.org/article/rtdna_research_women_and_minorities_in_newsrooms_2017.

Pulver, Andrew. "David Oyelowo: 'People of Colour Have Been Expunged from British History'." The Guardian, 6 Oct. 2016, www.theguardian.com/film/2016/oct/06/david-oyelowo-a-united-kingdom-people-of-colour-film.

Roosa, Sadie. "Public Broadcasting Act of 1967." American Archive of Public Broadcasting, americanarchive.org/exhibits/station-histories/public-broadcasting-act.

Sailer, Steve. "How Many Hispanics Listen to NPR?" Isteve.blogspot, 7 Dec. 2011, isteve.blogspot.com/2011/12/how-many-hispanics-listen-to-npr.html.

Schumacher-Matos, Edward. "Taking Stock: NPR's Ferguson Coverage So Far." NPR, 22 Sept. 2014, www.npr.org/sections/ombudsman/2014/09/22/348763573/taking-stock-npr-s-ferguson-coverage-so-far.

Simpson, April. "CPB-Backed Diversity Project Draws Close Scrutiny." Current, 25 Sept. 2017, current.org/2017/09/cpb-backed-diversity-project-draws-close-scrutiny/.

Staff. "Letters: Should Listeners Pay for Public Radio?" Marketplace, 20
    Apr. 2012, www.marketplace.org/2012/04/20/life/letters-should-listen-
    ers-pay-public-radio.

Staff. "An account of the Ferguson shooting, from the man standing beside
    Brown." NPR, 18 Aug. 2014, www.npr.org/2014/08/18/341426635/an-ac-
    count-of-the-ferguson-shooting-from-the-man-standing-beside-brown.

Stancill, Jane. "Radio Station Refuses to Broadcast ECU Game after Band
    Protest." News Observer, 4 Oct. 2016, www.newsobserver.com/news/local/
education/article105917537.html.

Stern, Ken. "Ken Stern: Don't Deny an Obvious Truth about the Media." *Cur-
    rent,* 26 Oct. 2017, current.org/2017/10/ken-stern-dont-deny-an-
    obvious-truth-about-the-media/.

Siegel, Paul, "The 1992 PBS Funding Debate: How Much Diversity Is America
    Willing to Pay for?" February 1993, Western States Communication Associ-
    ation, https://files.eric.ed.gov/fulltext/ED373381.pdf

WBHM timestamp 13 Apr. 2016 1517 CST

In the House

Admin. "NPR Hires New Ombudsman," Elizabeth Jensen. IMediaEthics, 7 Oct.
    2015, www.imediaethics.org/npr-hires-new-ombudsman-elizabeth-jensen/.

Bartlett, Sarah Hayley, and Nn, Oscar. "Latinx: The Ungendering of the Spanish
    Language." *Latino USA,* 30 Jan. 2016, latinousa.org/2016/01/29/latinx-un-
    gendering-spanish-language/.

Siemering, William telephone conversation with the author, Dec 22, 2016

Chioke I'Anson – "NPR's New Voice for Funding Credits." Reddit, June 2017,
    https://www.reddit.com/r/NPR/comments/5i5doe/chioke_ianson_nprs_new_
    voice_for_funding_credits/

Collins, Bob. "NPR Pushes Back, Says It's Not Demoting Ombudsman Job."
    NewsCut, Minnesota Public Radio, 17 July 2014, blogs.mprnews.org/news-
    cut/2014/07/npr-pushes-back-says-its-not-demoting-ombudsman-job/.

Cox, Patrick. "Why We Are so Drawn to the Letter 'X'." Public Radio Interna-
    tional, 3 Apr. 2018, www.pri.org/stories/2018-04-03/why-we-are-so-drawn-
    letter-x.

PLEDGE: The Public Radio Fund Drive

"Demographics and Political Views of News Audience." Pew Research Center's
Journalism Project, 27 Sep. 2012, http://www.people-press.org/2012/09/27/
section-4-demographics-and-political-views-of-news-audiences/.

Evans, Anthony. "Letter to Jarl Mohn." National Black Church Initiative, 21
May 2014, www.naltblackchurch.com/pdf/npr-letter.pdf.

Farhi, Paul. "NPR Taps Jarl Mohn as Eighth CEO in Eight Years." The Washington Post, WP Company, 9 May 2014, www.washingtonpost.com/lifestyle/
style/npr-taps-jarl-mohn-as-new-ceo/2014/05/09/37382d9c-d78c-11e3-
95d3-3bcd77cd4e11_story.html.

Fox, Justin. "Here's Who Isn't Listening to Public Radio." Chicagotribune.com,
23 Nov. 2015, www.chicagotribune.com/news/opinion/commentary/ct-npr-
public-radio-listeners-old-20151123-story.html.

Fung, Katherine. "NPR CEO Talks Public Funding, Diversity On First Day."
The Huffington Post, 7 Dec. 2017, www.huffingtonpost.com/2011/12/02/
npr-ceo-gary-knell-public-funding-diversity_n_1125619.html.

Jilani, Zaid. "Radio Show Distributed By NPR Fires Host After She Takes Part
In Protests." ThinkProgress, 20 Oct. 2011, thinkprogress.org/radio-show-
distributed-by-npr-fires-host-after-she-takes-part-in-protests-8868e5fa7b3.

Khalid, Asma. "Reporter's Notebook: What It Was Like As A Muslim To Cover
The Election." NPR, 7 Dec. 2016, www.npr.org/2016/12/07/504486620/
reporters-notebook-what-a-muslim-on-the-campaign-trail-in-2016.

Kim, Queena Sook. "Why the Heck Do Latino Reporters on Public Radio Say
Their Names That Way?" KQED Education, 29 Feb. 2016, ww2.kqed.org/
news/2015/02/15/why-the-heck-do-mexican-reporters-on-public-radio-say-
their-names-that-way/.

Malatia, Torey. "Op-Ed: WBEZ's Malatia Says Public Media Must Revi-
talize Open, Civic Discourse in Our Communities." Current, 16 Feb.
2015, current.org/2012/11/public-media-must-revitalize-open-civic-dis-
course-in-our-communities/.

Martin, Marty E. "Taking the Unitarian Universalist Diversity Crisis Seriously,"
University of Chicago Divinity School, The Marty Martin Center, 15 May
2017, divinity.uchicago.edu/sightings/taking-unitarian-universalist-diversi-
ty-crisis-seriously.

"Michel Martin Named Weekend Host for '*All Things Considered*.'" Radio
Syndication Talk, 1 Oct. 2015, radiosyndicationtalk.com/2015/10/01/mi-
chel-martin-named-weekend-host-for-all-things-considered/.

Montgomery, David. "Meet Joshua Johnson, Diane Rehm's Successor–and a
Bold Move for WAMU." The Washington Post, WP Company, 2 Feb. 2017,
www.washingtonpost.com/lifestyle/magazine/meet-joshua-johnson-di-
ane-rehms-successor—and-a-big-gamble-for-wamu/2017/02/01/6ad4eb26-
d8d4-11e6-9f9f-5cdb4b7f8dd7_story.html?noredirect=on.

Oppenheimer, Mark. "NPR's Great Black Hope." *The Atlantic*, Atlantic Media
Company, 19 Feb. 2014, www.theatlantic.com/magazine/archive/2013/07/
nprs-great-black-hope/309394/.

Peralta, Eyder. NPR, '*World of Opera*' Split Over Host's Role In Protests."
NPR22 Oct. 2011, www.npr.org/sections/thetwo-way/2011/10/21/141603820/
npr-world-of-opera-split-over-hosts-role-in-protests.

Prince, Richard. "Was *Tell Me More* NPR's Last Attempt to Target Blacks?"
Journal-Isms, Journalisms.theroot.com, 12 Jan. 2017, journalisms.theroot.
com/was-tell-me-more-npr-s-last-attempt-to-target-blacks-1790885434.

Roush, Chris. "Transgender 'Marketplace' Reporter Fired over Blog Post."
Talking Biz News, 31 Jan. 2017, talkingbiznews.com/1/transgender-market-
place-reporter-fired-over-blog-post/.

Ryan, Charlotte. "A Study of National Public Radio." FAIR, 28 Apr. 1993, fair.
org/extra/a-study-of-national-public-radio/.

Schlossberg, Mallory. "The Surprising Things Millennials Love–and Hate."
Business Insider, 3 Oct. 2015, www.businessinsider.com/what-retailers-
should-know-millennials-love-and-hate-2015-9/.

Schumacher-Matos, Edward. "S. Dakota Indian Foster Care 1: Investigative
Storytelling Gone Awry." NPR, 9 Aug. 2013, www.npr.org/sections/om-
budsman/2013/08/09/186943929/s-dakota- indian-foster-care-1-investiga-
tive-storytelling-gone-awry.

Silva, Ernesto. "Public Media Organizations." CPB, 7 Feb. 2018, www.cpb.org/
stations/pborganizations.

Sullivan, Margaret. Perspective, "How One Reporter's Rejection of Objectivity
Got Him Fired." The Washington Post, WP Company, 1 Feb. 2017, www.
washingtonpost.com/lifestyle/style/how-one-reporters-rejection-of-objectiv-

ity-got-him-fired/2017/02/01/bc5cc9c6-e7ef-11e6-80c2-30e57e57e05d_story.html?utm_term=.e1b55c2f0956.

Zurawik, David. "Lisa Simeone Confirms Her Firing from Public Radio's '*Soundprint*' Show." Baltimoresun.com, 21 Oct. 2011, www.baltimoresun.com/entertainment/tv/z-on-tv-blog/bal-npr-lisa-simeone-fired-soundprint-occupy-dc-20111020-story.html.

In the Streets

"2015 Turnover Rates by Industry." Compensation Force, www.compensation-force.com/2016/04/2015-turnover-rates-by-industry.html.

Conway, Madeline. "U.S. Ethics Chief Who Pressured Trump Resigns." POLITICO, 6 July 2017, www.politico.com/story/2017/07/06/us-office-of-government-ethics-director-resigns-240263.

Gamerman, Ellen. "Public Radio's Existential Crisis." The Wall Street Journal, Dow Jones & Company, 16 June 2016, www.wsj.com/articles/radios-existential-crisis-1466111586.

Hall, KC. "Employer-Reported Turnover Rates by Industry." Trends in 2017, 14 Jan. 2016, blog.compdatasurveys.com/turnover-trends-by-industry-2015.

Jensen, Elizabeth. "NPR's Online Source Diversity: New Data to Help Guide Newsroom." NPR, 17 July 2018, www.npr.org/sections/ombudsman/2018/07/17/629533978/nprs-online-source-diversity-new-data-to-help-guide-newsroom.

Jensen, Elizabeth. "NPR's Staff Diversity Numbers," 2016. NPR, 21 Apr. 2017, www.npr.org/sections/ombudsman/2017/04/21/508381413/nprs-staff-diversity-numbers-2016.

"NPR Reviews." Glassdoor, www.glassdoor.com/Reviews/NPR-Reviews-E3965.htm.

O'Donnell, J.T. "Is It Ever Okay to 'Diss' a Former Employer?" LinkedIn, 9 Jan. 2014, www.linkedin.com/pulse/20140109134712-7668018-is-it-ever-okay-to-dis-a-former-employer/.

Quah, Nicholas. Hot Pod, "Is This American Life Violating the Public Radio Mission by Straying to Platforms like Pandora?" Nieman Lab, 17 May 2016, www.niemanlab.org/2016/05/hot-pod-is-this-american-life-violating-the-public-radio-mission-by-straying-to-platforms-like-pandora/.

Ragusea, Adam. "Tess Vigeland on Her New Book and Leaving '*Marketplace Money*'." *Current*, 25 Aug. 2015, current.org/2015/08/tess-vigeland-on-her-new-book-and-leaving-marketplace-money/.

Resler, Seth. "Write Digital Instructions to Help With Radio Station Staff Turnover." Jacobs Media Strategies, 26 Jan. 2018, jacobsmedia.com/write-digital-instructions-to-help-with-radio-station-staff-turnover/.

Rubin, Robert, and Laser, Stephen. "When an Ex-Employee Wrote a Stinging Commentary about His Former Employer." SIOP in the News, Society for Industry and Organizational Psychology, 12 July 2017, www.siop.org/tip/july12/37boutelle.aspx

Staff. "Why People Quit Their Jobs." *Harvard Business Review*, 23 Aug. 2016, hbr.org/2016/09/why-people-quit-their-jobs.

Svoboda, Elizabeth. "What Makes Whistleblowers Speak out While Others Stay Silent about Wrongdoing.," 13 July 1970, jessiepowell.blogspot.com/2017/07/what-makes-whistleblowers-speak-out.html.

"Why Do Former Employees Talk so Much More Freely after They Quit? MetaFilter, 26 Apr. 2018, ask.metafilter.com/321599/Why-do-former-employees-talk-so-much-more-freely-after-they-quit.

Content

Arnold, Michael. "Public Radio Is Stronger, and Better, When Stations Invest in National Shows." *Current*, 16 Feb. 2015, current.org/2013/09/public-radio-is-stronger-and-better-when-stations-invest-in-national-shows/.

Brustein, Joshua. "We Now Spend More Time Staring at Phones Than TVs."*Bloomberg*.com, 19 Nov. 2014, www.bloomberg.com/news/articles/2014-11-19/we-now-spend-more-time-staring-at-phones-than-tvs.

"Coming of Public Radio to Rural Areas Can Be Rough on Both Listeners and Broadcasters." *Current*, 14 Mar. 1994, current.org/1994/03/coming-of-public-radio-to-rural-areas-can-be-rough-on-both-listeners-and-broadcasters/.

Johnson, Nicholas. FromDC2Iowa. "Public Radio's Self-Inflicted Wounds," 11 Nov. 2008, fromdc2iowa.blogspot.com/2008/11/public-radios-self-inflicted-wounds.html.

Kramer, Staci D. "NPR.org Relaunches; Video Doesn't Play A Big Role.,"
Gigaom, 26 July 2009, gigaom.com/2009/07/26/419-npr-org-relaunches-
video-doesnt-play-a-big-role/.

McClintock, Pamela. Box Office 2014: "Moviegoing Hits Two-Decade Low."
The Hollywood Reporter, 31 Dec. 2014, www.hollywoodreporter.com/
news/box-office-2014-moviegoing-hits-760766.

Riley, David. "Mobile Gaming Consumer Trends in 2014." NPD Group, 27 Jan.
2015, www.npd.com/wps/portal/npd/us/news/press-releases/2015/average-
time-spent-playing-games-on-mobile-devices-has-increased-57-percent-
since-2012/.

Silva, Ernesto. "Local Content and Service Report." CPB, 17 Jan. 2018, www.
cpb.org/stations/localcontent/.

Takahashi, Dean. "*Call of Duty*: Advanced Warfare by the (Big) Numbers."
VentureBeat, 25 Nov. 2014, venturebeat.com/2014/11/24/call-of-duty-ad-
vanced-warfare-by-the-big-numbers/.

"UNESCO Designates Iowa City as the World's Third City of Literature." 20
Nov. 2008, www.news-releases.uiowa.edu/2008/november/112008unesco.
html.

"WPSU-FM's Local Content and Services." CPB-Radio-Report, 24 Feb. 2015,
pp. 1–2., wpsu.psu.edu/pdf/public/CPB-Radio-Report.pdf.

News

Arria, Michael. "NPR Workers Just Showed Us Why Journalists Need to Organize." Salon, 26 July 2017, www.salon.com/2017/07/27/npr-workers-just-
showed-us-why-journalists-need-to-organize_partner/.

BDO USA, LLP. "Consolidated Financial Statements, and Supplemental Schedules, and Independent Auditor's Report." National Public Radio, Inc., 15
Dec. 2016, pp. 1–45.

Berrier, Ralph. "Public Radio Makes Programming Changes." The Roanoke
Times, 8 July 2014, www.roanoke.com/arts_and_entertainment/public-ra-
dio-makes-programming-changes/article_84a94558-1bab-581a-a1cf-
a98c76d85baa.html.

Brady, Jim. "Local News Isn't Dead. We Just Need to Stop Killing It." *Columbia Journalism Review*, 17 June 2016, www.cjr.org/analysis/local_news_newspaper_print_business_model.php.

CISION, et al. "National Survey Finds Majority of Journalists Now Depend on Social Media for Story Research." Cision, 20 Jan. 2010, www.cision.com/us/about/news/2010-press-releases/national-survey-finds-majority-of-journalists-now-depend-on-social-media-for-story-research/.

Cockburn, Alexander. "NPR and NAB Ally to Crush Low Power Radio." The Columbus Freepress, 19 Apr. 2000, freepress.org/columns/display/2/2000/608.

Dinges, Gary. "KUT Aims to Set the 'Standard' with New Show," TV & Radio." Austin 360, 6 Feb. 2016, tvradio.blog.austin360.com/2015/02/06/kut-aims-to-set-the-standard-with-new-show/.

Editor. "NPR and On-Air Credits: The End Of A Thank You." WVXU/WMUB, 30 Aug. 2013, wvxu.org/post/npr-and-air-credits-end-thank-you#stream/.

"Facebook Live Audio-Opportunity/Challenge for Stations." Insideradio.com, 22 Dec. 2016, www.insideradio.com/free/facebook-live-audio-opportunity-challenge-for-stations/article_18c8e7ac-c820-11e6-b7cd-1f46af36f873.html.

Garber, Megan. "Vivian Schiller on NPR's New Public Media Platform, the Argo Project, and the Org's Reporting Priorities." Nieman Lab, 19 Apr. 2010, www.niemanlab.org/2010/04/vivian-schiller-on-nprs-new-public-media-platform-the-argo-project-and-the-orgs-reporting-priorities/.

Geisler, Erin. "'*Texas Standard*' to Connect Texans to Stories around the State and Globe," 9 Feb. 2015, kut.org/post/texas-standard-connect-texans-stories-around-state-and-globe.

Henry, Mike. "News Stations Should Watch for Competition from Low-Power Upstarts." *Current*, 21 Oct. 2016, current.org/2016/10/news-stations-should-watch-for-competition-from-low-power-upstarts/.

Israel, Shel. "The Great Facebook Employee Password Non-Issue." *Forbes* Magazine, 7 June 2012, www.forbes.com/sites/shelisrael/2012/03/25/the-great-facebook-employee-password-nonissue/#4edd7a0265a7.

PLEDGE: The Public Radio Fund Drive

IU Survey: "U.S. Journalists Say They Are Less Satisfied and Have Less Autonomy." IU Bloomington Newsroom, 1 May 2014, archive.news.indiana.edu/releases/iu/2014/05/american-journalist-in-the-digital-age.shtml.

Kramer, Melody. "Why Does Local Matter? Let's Ask Our Audience." Poynter, 15 Mar. 2017, www.poynter.org/2015/why-does-local-matter-lets-ask-our-audience/352419/.

Kramer, Staci D. "NPR Hires Key Staff For Local News Effort; Finalizes Station List." Gigaom, 24 Dec. 2009, gigaom.com/2009/12/24/419-npr-hires-key-staff-for-local-news-effort-finalizes-station-list/.

Lapin, Andrew. "As Newsrooms Expand, Employees at Several Stations Push to Unionize." *Current*, 27 Aug. 2014, current.org/2014/07/as-newsrooms-ex-pand-employees-at-several-stations-push-to-unionize/.

Levy, Steven. "Can an Algorithm Write a Better News Story Than a Human Reporter?" *Wired*, Conde Nast, 7 Mar. 2018, www.wired.com/2012/04/can-an-algorithm-write-a-better-news-story-than-a-human-reporter/.

MacAdam, Alison. "Understanding Story Structure with the 'Three Little Pigs.'" NPR Training, 24 Mar. 2015, training.npr.org/audio/understanding-story-structure-with-the-three-little-pigs/.

Marcotte, Michael V. "Attributes of Local NPR Stations: On Air Content." Local NPR, 2 May 2015, localnpr.org/2013/05/24/attributes-of-local-npr-stations-on-air-content/.

McLellan, Michelle, and Porter, Tim. "Investing-in-the-Future-of-News-Survey_KeyFindings." Issuu, 7 Apr. 2011, issuu.com/knightfoundation/docs/investing-in-the-future-of-news-survey_keyfindings.

"National Public Radio Consolidated Financial Statements," Year Ended September 30, 2009." 2009_LA-NPR_cons, 22 Dec. 2009, www.npr.org/about/statements/fy2009/2009_LA_NPR_Cons.pdf.

"Online Etymology Dictionary." News, www.etymonline.com/word/news.

"Pew Research Center's Journalism Project." 6 June 2018, www.journalism.org/.

"Public Radio Finances." NPR, 20 June 2013, www.npr.org/about-npr/178660742/public-radio-finances.

"Radio Facts and Figures," Broadcast Media Relations, News Generation, Inc., www.newsgeneration.com/broadcast-resources/radio-facts-and-figures/.

Silva, Ernesto. "CPB's Federal Appropriation Request & Justification." 12 Feb. 2018, www.cpb.org/appropriation.

Sokol, Brett. "FM Stations That Don't Reach Far, but Reach Deep." *The New York Times*, 14 Oct. 2016, www.nytimes.com/2016/10/15/business/media/fm-stations-that-dont-reach-far-but-reach-deep.html.

Spinner, Jackie. "How Journalists Are Using Social Media Monitoring to Support Local News Coverage." *Columbia Journalism Review*, 13 Oct. 2015, www.cjr.org/united_states_project/social_media_geotagging_local_journalists.php.

Staff. "The 60-Second Interview: Jennifer Brandel, Co-Founder and C.E.O. of Hearken." About Us, POLITICO, 23 June 2015, www.politico.com/media/story/2015/06/the-60-second-interview-jennifer-brandel-co-founder-and-ceo-of-hearken-003893.

Sutton, John. "How Stations Can Stay Relevant as Listeners Go Elsewhere for NPR Content." *Current*, 12 Aug. 2014, current.org/2014/08/how-stations-can-stay-relevant-as-listeners-go-elsewhere-for-npr-content/.

Torres, Ben Fong. "Radio Waves." SFGate, 12 Mar. 2006, www.sfgate.com/entertainment/radiowaves/article/RADIO-WAVES-2502221.php.

Vail, Bruce. "After Public Radio Station Hires Notorious Union Buster, Employees Likely to Lose Union Vote." In These Times, 6 Nov. 2014, inthesetimes.com/working/entry/17324.

Walrus Research. "Strategic Differentiation of NPR News Formats." Mar. 2004, pp. 1–16., walrusresearch.com/images/Strategic_Differentiation_of_NPR_News_Formats.pdf.

Wilson, Josh. "Survey Results: #Newsroom #Engagement Programs among Nonprofit Newsrooms, October 2016." https://T.co/WmXtOomuVd Pic.twitter.com/SXKXD0zlxH." Twitter, 25 Oct. 2016, twitter.com/MrJoshuaWilson/status/790707115736244224.

Wilson, Josh, "Survey of Newsroom Public Engagement," http://watershedmediaproject.net/2016/10/24/survey-of-newsroom-public-engagement-programs-october-2016/

Music

Association of Music Personnel in Public Radio (AMPPR). 12 June 2018, www.facebook.com/amppr.

Benson, Kristina. "Public Radio Music under Attack." L.A. Weekly, 5 Apr. 2016, www.laweekly.com/music/public-radio-music-under-attack-2168951.

Brown, Jeffrey. "Embracing Classical Music and Its Potential for 'Sonic Salvation'." PBS, Public Broadcasting Service, 8 Mar. 2019, www.pbs.org/newshour/show/embracing-classical-music-and-its-potential-for-sonic-salvation.

Budmen, Lawrence. "South Florida Classical Review." 11 July 2015, southfloridaclassicalreview.com/2015/07/south-florida-to-lose-sole-classical-radio-outlet/.

Cheng, Jacqui. "NPR Fights Back, Seeks Rehearing on Internet Radio Royalty Increases." Ars Technica, 21 Mar. 2007, arstechnica.com/tech-policy/2007/03/npr-fights-back-seeks-rehearing-on-internet-radio-royalty-increases/.

Christman, Ed. "'Fair Play, Fair Pay Act' Introduced, Seeks Cash from Radio Stations." Billboard, 23 Apr. 2015, www.billboard.com/articles/business/6531693/fair-play-fair-pay-act-performance-royalty-radio.

Commercial VS. Non-Commercial Radio." Planetary Group, 2016, www.planetarygroup.com/music-promotion-guide/stations-right/.

Crotzer, Carrie. "Budget to Cause Tuition Increases." The Northerner, 19 Apr. 2016, www.thenortherner.com/news/2016/04/19/budget-to-cause-tuition-increases/.

Falk, Tyler. "NPR's Tiny Desk Concert Searches for New Acts." Current, 16 Feb. 2015, current.org/2014/12/nprs-tiny-desk-concert-searches-for-new-acts/.

Fast, Austin. "Northern Kentucky University Rejects $5 Million Bid to 'Save' WNKU, Louisville Public Media Says." WCPO, 5 May 2017, www.wcpo.com/news/local-news/campbell-county/highland-heights/northern-kentucky-university-rejects-louisville-public-medias-5-million-bid-to-save-wnku?page=2.

Ferguson, Andrew. "Radio Silence." The Weekly Standard, 5 June 2004, www.weeklystandard.com/article/5410.

George, Patrick. "Nonprofit KDRP Radio in Dripping Springs Gains Following." Statesman, Associated Press, 22 Sept. 2012, www.statesman.com/
news/local/nonprofit-kdrp-radio-dripping-springs-gains-following/WkBub-
Hhd4P7BcW40jR0d5M/.

Giovanonni, David. "Format Flavors." Audience 98, 1 Sept. 2000, www.ara.net/
a98/sidebars/a98-s60.htm.

Henry, Mike. "'DISCOVERING MUSIC: WNKU Targets More Listeners
with New Format.'" Paragon Media Strategies, 10 Nov. 2015, www.
paragonmediastrategies.com/discovering-music-wnku-targets-more-listen-
ers-with-new-format.

Hill, Brad. "Pew Study Tracks Generational Use of Mobile Music." *RAIN
News*, 6 Apr. 2015, rainnews.com/pew-study-tracks-generational-use-of-
mobile-music/.

Kamenetz, Anya. "Will NPR Save the News?" Fast Company, 28 Mar. 2014,
www.fastcompany.com/1208947/will-npr-save-news.

Koon, Samantha. "After Time of Turmoil, WTJU Reprograms, Increases
Fundraising." The Daily Progress, 22 July 2012, www.dailyprogress.com/
entertainment/after-time-of-turmoil-wtju-reprograms-increases-fundraising/
article_d7772d9e-cfba-5de5-ad4e-a3a8792a5e29.html.

"Leaked Internal Email from NPR's Policy and Representation Division Explaining NPR Membership on McCoalition." The Trichordist,
11 May 2015, thetrichordist.com/2015/05/10/breaking-leaked-in-
ternal-email-from-nprs-policy-and-representation-division-explain-
ing-npr-membership-on-mccoalition/.

Lefford, Nyssim. "ACM–Computers in Entertainment." History & Evolution of
Video Games : ACM–Computers in Entertainment, 18 June 2012, cie.acm.
org/articles/afropop-worldwide-radio-hip-deep-social-media-and-web/.

Mandel, Howard, et al. "Jazz Audience Surveyed, Segmented." Jazz Beyond
Jazz, Arts Journal, 17 Aug. 2011, www.artsjournal.com/jazzbeyond-
jazz/2011/08/jazz-audience-surveyed-segmented.html.

McKay, Nellie. "The Last Oasis of Free and Independent Music." *The Huffington Post*, TheHuffingtonPost.com, 5 June 2012,
www.huffingtonpost.com/nellie-mckay/public-radio_b_1406791.html.

PLEDGE: The Public Radio Fund Drive

Memmott, Mark. "Don Voegeli, Composer Of The '*All Things Considered*' Theme, Has Died." NPR, 23 Nov. 2009, www.npr.org/sections/thetwo-way/2009/11/voegeli_all_things_considered.html.

Merzbach, Scott. "WMUA Radio Station Turmoil Continues as More Jazz Hosts Quit, Annual Fund Drive Falls Short of Goal." Daily Hampshire Gazette, 4 Dec. 2015, www.gazettenet.com/Archives/2015/12/wmuaupdate-hg-120315.

Michaelson, Judith. "Drop in Core KUSC Listeners Led to Fiscal Woes, Study Says." Los Angeles Times, 27 Nov. 1996, articles.latimes.com/1996-11-27/entertainment/ca-3271_1_core-kusc-listeners.

"Multi-Platform Options." STATION TOOLS, PRI InfoSite, www2.pri.org/infosite/stationtools/multiplatform_options.cfm.

New York Radio Guide. Radio Station Format Guide, nyradioguide.com/formats.htm.

"NPR Offerings Expanded on WUTC FM 88.1." UTC Wordmark, University of Tennessee Chattanooga, 5 Jan. 2006, www.utc.edu/communications-marketing/news-center/archive/2006/wutcprogram06.php.

Owsley, Dennis. "There Are Now Fewer than 400 Jazz DJs on the Air-and Yes, There Are Cultural Consequences." *St. Louis Magazine*, 19 June 2012, www.stlmag.com/arts/There-Are-Now-Fewer-than-400-Jazz-DJs-on-the-Airand-Yes-There-Are-Cultural-Consequences/.

Oxenford, David. "Music in Podcasts – Reminder That ASCAP, BMI, SESAC and SoundExchange Licenses Don't Cover Music Use in Podcasts." *Broadcast Law Blog*, 25 May 2017, www.broadcastlawblog.com/2017/05/articles/music-in-podcasts-reminder-that-ascap-bmi-sesac-and-soundexchange-li-censes-dont-cover-music-use-in-podcasts/.

Paul Farhi, Washington Post, "NPR Reassessing Jazz, Classical Music Programs." Los Angeles Times, 1 Mar. 2002, articles.latimes.com/2002/mar/01/entertainment/et-farhi1.

"PRPD." Public Radio Program Directors Association, www.prpd.org/resources/digital-music-rights-and-public-media.

"Public Radio Today 2013–How America Listens to Radio." Executive Summary, pp. 1–8., www.arbitron.com/downloads/PublicRadioToday2013_ExecutiveSummary.pdf.

"Public Radio/Television Survey; Report 1: Public Awareness, Listening and Programming," Corporation for Public Broadcasting, Washington D.C.; Statistical Research, Inc. Westfield, N.J. Jun 1978, pg 1-41, http://eric.ed.gov/?id=ED159746

Ramsey, Doug. "It's Public Radio, If You Can Keep It." Field Notes, 26 June 2012, www.artsjournal.com/rifftides/2012/06/its-public-radio-if-you-can-keep-it.html.

Ronish, Marty, et al. "WGCU: Another Classical Station Bites the Dust." Joe Goetz on Classical Music Broadcasting, 28 Aug. 2008, www.insidethearts.com/scanningthedial/wgcu-another-classical-station-bites-the-dust/.

Srebnik, David. "When Classical Music Programmers Go Bad." LinkedIn, June 2016, www.linkedin.com/groups/69651/69651-6023847499846995972.

Staff, NPR. "Brilliance In Bumps And Bruises, On Air And On Screen." NPR, 15 Nov. 2014, www.npr.org/2014/11/15/363541820/brilliance-in-bumps-and-bruises-on-air-and-on-screen.

Staff. "An Upbeat Trend for Classical Pubradio despite Audience Slide." Current, 16 Feb. 2015, current.org/2013/02/an-upbeat-trend-for-classical-pubra-dio-despite-audience-slide/.

Staff. "Casady & Greene Discontinues SoundJam MP At Developer's Request ."The Mac Observer." 7 May 2001, www.macobserver.com/article/2001/05/07.10.shtml.

Staff. "Houston Public Media Completes Sale Of Classical Station KUHA 91.7 FM To KSBJ." Houston Public Media, 14 July 2016, www.houstonpublicmedia.org/articles/news/2016/07/15/160454/houston-public-media-completes-sale-of-classical-station-kuha-91-7-fm-to-ksbj/.

Staff. "KSBJ Educational Foundation to Acquire KUHA-FM from the University of Houston System." Houston Chronicle, 27 Feb. 2016, www.chron.com/neighborhood/kingwood/news/article/KSBJ-Educational-Foundation-to-acquire-KUHA-FM-9698889.php.

Staff. "News 101: When a Story Is 'News'." Redlands Daily Facts, 7 May 2013, www.redlandsdailyfacts.com/article/ZZ/20070421/NEWS/704219944.

Swohio75. "Bye Bye Locally Owned WPFB..." Middletown Forum, 19 Jan. 2011, www.middletownusa.com/forum/forum_posts.asp?TID=3612&title=bye-bye-locally-owned-wpfb.

"The Aging Audience." 2009, pp. 1–13., www.walrusresearch.com/images/Aging_Public_Radio_Audience_-_Walrus_Research.pdf.

Turner, Zeke. "Interview: NPR's Dick Meyer Discusses NPR.org Redesign, Visual Vocabulary." Mediaite, 29 Oct. 2009, www.mediaite.com/online/interview-nprs-dick-meyer-discusses-npr-org-redesign-visual-vocabulary/.

Washburn, Mark. "What's Put WDAV among Nation's Top Classical Stations?" Charlotteobserver, Charlotte Observer, 20 Apr. 2017, www.charlotteobserver.com/entertainment/tv/media-scene-blog/article145715614.html.

Weesner, Matt. "'Music Forward,' CPR Classical's Newest Show, Explores Modern Classical." Colorado Public Radio, 25 May 2016, www.cpr.org/classical/story/music-forward-cpr-classical-s-newest-show-explores-modern-classical.

"WFUV Focuses on Music Discovery, Drops NPR Newscasts." PRPD News for Programmers, Oct. 2013, prpd-news.blogspot.com/2013/10/wfuv-focuses-on-music-discovery-drops.html#!/2013/10/wfuv-focuses-on-music-discovery-drops.html.

"What Is Vuhaus?" VuHaus, www.vuhaus.com/about.

Entertainment

"About 'Ask Me Another.'" NPR, 30 Apr. 2012, www.npr.org/templates/story/story.php?storyId=5058.

Ahlgrim, Callie. "Popular Boston-Born Radio Show 'Best of Car Talk' Announces an End Date." Boston.com, The Boston Globe, 28 July 2016, www.boston.com/culture/cars/2016/07/28/best-car-talk-will-end-september.

"America.gov–Engaging the World." Wayback Machine Internet Archive, U.S. Department of State, 16 Dec. 2007, web.archive.org/web/20091113070938/http://www.america.gov/st/pubs-english/2007/December/20071216153045esnamfuak0.6855432.html.

Arnold, Michael. "Public Radio Needs More Weekend Hits, and Fast." Current, 16 June 2015, current.org/2015/06/public-radio-needs-more-weekend-hits-and-fast/.

Brenna, Susan. "NPR's 'Wait, Wait ... Don't Tell Me!' You Can't Make This Stuff Up. Or Can You?" The New York Times, 4 June 2006, www.nytimes.

com/2006/06/04/arts/television/04brenn.html?_r=0&mtrref=en.wikipedia. org&gwh=7C4142C071CA14CF9AC52F5D6B496A60&gwt=pay.

Carlton, Bob. "Birmingham Public Radio Station WBHM 90.3 FM Shuffles Lineup, Cancels Several Shows." AL.com, 15 May 2018, www.al.com/entertainment/index.ssf/2016/09/birmingham_public_radio_statio_2.html.

Carone, Angela. "Let's Talk: Are NPR Listeners Snooty?" KPBS Public Media, 3 Mar. 2011, www.kpbs.org/news/2011/mar/03/letters-npr-are-snooty/. Derby, Samara Kalk. Wisconsin Public Radio, "*Whad'Ya Know* Announcer Jim Packard Dies." Wisconsin State Journal, 19 June 2012, host.madison. com/ct/news/local/retired-whad-ya-know-announcer-jim-packard-dies/article_01b7be24-ba17-11e1-b71e-001a4bcf887a.html.

Dockterman, Eliana. "Podcast: NPR's Sam Sanders Has *It's Been a Minute.*" Time, Time, 21 June 2017, time.com/4824307/sam-sanders-podcast-npr-its-been-a-minute/.

Farhi, Paul. "NPR Is Graying, and Public Radio Is Worried about It." The Washington Post, WP Company, 22 Nov. 2015, www.washingtonpost. com/lifestyle/style/npr-is-graying-and-public-radio-is-worried-about-it/2015/11/22/0615447e-8e48-11e5-baf4-bdf37355da0c_story.html?utm_ term=.5af0a5045765.

Hapsis, Emmanuel. "Kim Kardashian Appears on '*Wait Wait...Don't Tell Me,*' NPR Fans Go Postal." KQED Education, 16 June 2015, ww2.kqed.org/ pop/2015/06/15/kim-kardashian-appears-on-wait-wait-dont-tell-me-fans-go-postal/.

Jensen, Elizabeth. "What's All The 'Kommotion' About Kim Kardashian On 'Wait Wait'?" NPR, 17 June 2015, www.npr.org/sections/ombudsman/2015/06/17/415203751/what-s-all-the-kommotion-about-kim-kardashian-west-on-wait-wait.

Justin, Neal. "Public Radio's '*Wits*' Has Been Canceled." Star Tribune, 27 July 2015, www.startribune.com/public-radio-s-wits-has-been-canceled/318654571/.

Justin, Neal. "Sun Is Setting on Garrison Keillor's Time on Lake Wobegon." Star Tribune, 6 July 2016, www.startribune.com/sun-is-setting-on-garrison-keillors-time-on-lake-wobegon/382713261/.

"Michael Feldman Will End Production." WPR, 30 June 2016, www.wpr.org/
wpr-michael-feldman-will-end-production-michael-feldmans-whadya-
know-june-30-2016.

Moore, Jerry. "The Snobby Listeners of NPR." Watertown Daily Times, 26 June
2015, www.watertowndailytimes.com/blogs16/the-snobby-listeners-of-
npr-20150626.

Niles, Robert. "Will NPR's Podcasts Birth a New Business Model for Public
Radio?" Online Journalism Review, USC Annenberg, 27 Nov. 2005, www.
ojr.org/will-nprs-podcasts-birth-a-new-business-model-for-public-radio/.

"Not My Job: Kim Kardashian Gets Quizzed On Kim Jong Un." NPR, 13 June
2015, www.npr.org/2015/06/13/413926893/not-my-job-kim-kardashian-
gets-quizzed-on-kim-jong-un.

Phelps, Andrew. "Love Me, Love My NPR: Public Radio Listeners Can
Show off Their Loyalty." Nieman Lab, 14 Apr. 2011, www.niemanlab.
org/2011/04/love-me-love-my-npr-public-radio-listeners-can-show-off-
their-loyalty/.

Ramsey, Mark. "How to Disrupt Public Radio." Mark Ramsey Media LLC, 2
Apr. 2015, www.markramseymedia.com/2015/04/how-to-disrupt-public-
radio/.

Says You! A Game of Bluff and Bluster." www.saysyouradio.com/.

Shows, Public Radio International, PRI, http://www2.pri.org/Infosite/program-
support/prog_direct.cfm

Staff. "Manjoo Joins Wall Street Journal as Technology Columnist." The Wall
Street Journal, Dow Jones & Company, 4 Sept. 2013, blogs.wsj.com/dig-
its/2013/09/04/manjoo-joins-wall-street-journal-as-technology-columnist/.

"WBOI Listens–Talk/Interview Shows." Google Slides, 13 June 2018, docs.
google.com/forms/d/e/1FAIpQLSfdqV-WVnZPQjXmLfVJVP5Azf4ojYaK-
k0pthHYOE335Hp6nXg/viewform.

"WBOI Listens Survey–Talk/Entertainment Programming." Northeast Indiana
Public Radio, 9 May 2017, wboi.org/post/wboi-listens-survey-talkentertain-
ment-programming#stream/0.

"Wisconsin Public Radio Michael Feldman's *Whad'Ya Know*? Welcomes New Show Announcer, Stephanie Lee." Facebook, 15

Sept. 2015, www.facebook.com/wisconsinpublicradio/photos
/a.155254922803.118475.122951382803/10153220069127804/.

Sports

"CBC to Cut 657 Jobs, Will No Longer Compete for pro Sports Rights," CBC
News. CBCnews, CBC/Radio Canada, 11 Apr. 2014, www.cbc.ca/news/
canada/cbc-to-cut-657-jobs-will-no-longer-compete-for-professional-sports-
rights-1.2605504.

Draper, Kevin. "Why Is NPR's Sports Coverage so Bad?" *The Diss.*, 9 Apr.
2014, thedissnba.com/2014/04/09/why-is-nprs-sports-coverage-so-bad/.

Druckenbrod, Andrew. "Name This Tune: You Sing 'Take Me Out,' It's 100
Years Old." Post-Gazette.com, Pittsburgh Post Gazette, 23 June 2008, old.
post-gazette.com/pg/08175/891968-63.stm.

Kang, Cecilia. "Podcasts Are Back–and Making Money." The Washington Post,
WP Company, 25 Sept. 2014, www.washingtonpost.com/business/technol-
ogy/podcasts-are-back—and-making-money/2014/09/25/54abc628-39c9-
11e4-9c9f-ebb47272e40e_story.html?utm_term=.12da2d698200.

Lyons, Jessica. "College Coaches Can Earn Over 10X More Than College Presidents." Study.com, 13 Sept. 2011, study.com/articles/Who_Should_Earn_
More_Money_College_Coaches_or_Administrators.html.

Manjoo, Farhad. "NPR Letters: The Tedious, Annoying Complaints of Public
Radio Listeners." *Slate* Magazine, 2 Mar. 2011, www.slate.com/articles/
life/a_fine_whine/2011/03/we_listen_to_npr_precisely_to_avoid_this_sort_
of_stupidity.html.

"Mike Pesca Quits NPR for *Slate* (so He Won't Be Getting an IPhone 5 Adapter
Anniversary Gift)." JIMROMENESKO.COM, 11 Feb. 2014, jimromenes-
ko.com/2014/02/11/mike-pesca-quits-npr-for-slate-so-he-wont-be-getting-
an-iphone-5-adapter-anniversary-gift/.

"NPR Audience Profile." MRI , 2002, cache.trustedpartner.com/docs/li-
brary/000316/NPR%20Jazz%20Demographics.pdf.

Pesca, Mike, phone conversation with the author, June 9, 2017

Pesca, Mike, text message to the author, June 10, 2017

Public Radio/Television Survey; Report 1: "Public Awareness, Listening and
Programming," Corporation for Public Broadcasting, Washington D.C.;

Statistical Research, Inc. Westfield, N.J. Jun 1978, pg 1-41, http://eric.
ed.gov/?id=ED159746

Siemering, William, conversation with the author, December 22, 2016

"Sports." Public Radio International,13 June 2018, www.pri.org/sections/sports.

"The Power of Trash Talk For Bhutanese Archers." NPR, 2 Aug. 2012, www.
npr.org/2012/08/02/157764140/the-power-of-trash-talk-for-bhutanese-ar-
chers.

Blogs

Andrews, Paul. "Is Blogging Journalism?" Neiman Reports, 15 Sept. 2003,
niemanreports.org/articles/is-blogging-journalism/.

Combs, Marianne. "Why Blog about Art?" NewsCut, 6 Aug. 2009, blogs.
mprnews.org/state-of-the-arts/2009/08/why-blog-about-art/.

"Cumulative Total of Tumblr Blogs from May 2011 to April 2018 (in Millions)."
Tumblr: Total Number of Blogs 2018, Statista, Apr. 2018, www.statista.
com/statistics/256235/total-cumulative-number-of-tumblr-blogs/.

Dekmezian, Gary. "Why Do People Blog? The Benefits of Blogging." The
Huffington Post, 23 Sept. 2016, www.huffingtonpost.com/gary-
dekmezian/why-do-people-blog-the-be_b_8178624.html.

DeMers, Jayson. "The 6 Main Types Of Blog Posts And How To Use
Them." *Forbes* Magazine, 23 Sept. 2014, www.forbes.com/sites/
jayson-demers/2014/09/23/the-6-main-types-of-blog-posts-and-how-to-
use-them/#5033d2afc732.

Dodge, Amanda. "4 Statistics Every Blogger Should Know About Content Word
Count." Copypress, 16 Apr. 2013, www.copypress.com/blog/4-statistics-ev-
ery-blogger-should-know-about-content-word-count/.

eliskt-ga. "NY Times Newspaper Article (Average Word Count)." Google Answers, 20 Mar. 2006, answers.google.com/answers/threadview/id/709596.
html.

Gordon, Jon. "Study: Liberal Blogs More Participatory, Conservative Blogs
More Hierarchical." *Future Tense*, 29 Apr. 2010, blogs.publicradio.org/fu-
turetense/2010/04/study-liberal-b.html.

Hug, Kira. "Your Blog vs Medium. Copywriting for Startups and Marketers," 4
Aug. 2016, copyhackers.com/2016/02/publish-on-medium/.

Huver, Joshua. "'Mayday, M'aidez!: Santa Cruz-Based 88.9 KUSP in Danger of Shutting Down." The Bay Bridged–San Francisco Bay Area Indie Music, 20 Apr. 2016, thebaybridged.com/2016/04/20/kusp-shutting-down/.

Krulwich, Robert. "This Blog Is Ending Soon." NPR, 24 Sept. 2014, www.npr.org/sections/krulwich/2014/09/24/350888287/this-blog-is-ending-soon.

Lowrey, Wilson, and Mackey, Jenn Burleson. "Journalism and Blogging." University of Alabama, Feb. 2008, www.researchgate.net/publication/249032832_JOURNALISM_AND_BLOGGING.

Meyer, Robinson. "U.S. Court: Bloggers Are Journalists." *The Atlantic*, Atlantic Media Company, 22 Jan. 2014, www.theatlantic.com/technology/archive/2014/01/us-court-bloggers-are-journalists/283225/.

mitatur. "Minimum (Realistic) Word Count of Non-Fiction Book." Writing Stack Exchange, 16 Sept. 2011, writers.stackexchange.com/questions/3983/minimum-realistic-word-count-of-non-fiction-book#3986.

Nielsen, Jakob. "How Little Do Users Read?" Nielsen Norman Group, 6 May 2008, www.nngroup.com/articles/how-little-do-users-read/.

Public Radio Archives. protectmypublicmedia.org/blog/tag/public-radio-2/.

Rampton, John. "Blogging Stats 2012 (Infographic). "Guide to Start a Blog in 3 Simple Steps [Updated for 2018], Blogging.org, 13 July 2012, blogging.org/blog/blogging-stats-2012-infographic/.

"Real Data from 4,000 Businesses." Lead Generation Lessons from 4,000 Businesses, pp. 1–24., cdn2.hubspot.net/hub/53/file-13221878-pdf/docs/ebooks/lead-generation-lessons-from-4000-businesses.pdf.

Schmidt, Christine. "The Wall Street Journal Shutters Eight Blogs: 'The Tools for Telling' Stories Have Changed." Nieman Lab, 3 July 2017, www.niemanlab.org/2017/07/the-wall-street-journal-shutters-eight-blogs-the-tools-for-telling-stories-have-changed/.

Taylor, Maggie, PRX, 22 May 2017, blog.prx.org/author/maggie/.

Whitehill, Nate. "Top 5 Reasons Most Blogs Don't Last." 15 May 2007, natewhitehill.com/top-5-reasons-most-blogs-dont-last/.

Platforms

Ala-Fossi, Marko, et al. "The Future of Radio Is Still Digital-But Which One? Expert Perspectives and Future Scenarios for Radio Media in 2015."

Journal of Radio & Audio Media, 28 May 2008, www.tandfonline.com/doi/
abs/10.1080/19376520801971337?journalCode=hjrs20.

Collins, Bob, "NPR Reporter Quits to cure What Ails It." NewsCut, 4 Jan. 2016,
blogs.mprnews.org/newscut/2016/01/npr-reporter-quits-to-cure-what-ails-
it/.

Cunningham, Wayne. "Chevrolet App Shop Replicates a Smartphone in the
Dashboard–Roadshow." CNET, 7 Jan. 2014, www.cnet.com/roadshow/
news/chevrolet-app-shop-replicates-a-smartphone-in-the-dashboard/.

Directories. podCast411–Learn about Podcasting and Podcasters, 4 Oct. 2004,
podcast411.libsyn.com/directories.

Falk, Tyler. "NPR Tech Reporter Quits to Build a New Kind of Radio'." *Current*,
4 Jan. 2016, current.org/2016/01/npr-tech-reporter-quits-to-build-a-new-
kind-of-radio/.

Gamerman, Ellen. "Public Radio's Existential Crisis." The Wall Street Journal,
Dow Jones & Company, 16 June 2016, www.wsj.com/articles/radios-exis-
tential-crisis-1466111586.

Grehn, Kim. "Digital News Users Not Buying." LinkedIn, 28 June 2015, www.
linkedin.com/pulse/digital-news-users-buying-kim-grehn.

Hollis. "NPR App on Chevy Dash." PRPD News for Programmers, 6 Jan. 2014,
prpd-news.blogspot.com/2014/01/npr-app-on-chevy-dash.html#!/2014/01/
npr-app-on-chevy-dash.html.

Moradi, Javaun. "How Can You Increase Listenership in Public Radio?" Quora,
4 Jan. 2011, www.quora.com/How-can-you-increase-listenership-in-public-
radio.

Phelps, Andrew. "Schiller to Public Radio: Don't Just Sit There, Take Risks."
Nieman Lab, 21 Apr. 2011, www.niemanlab.org/2011/04/schiller-to-public-
radio-dont-just-sit-there-take-risks/.

Quah, Nicholas. "Hot Pod: Is This American Life Violating the Public Radio
Mission by Straying to Platforms like Pandora?" Nieman Lab, 17 May
2016, www.niemanlab.org/2016/05/hot-pod-is-this-american-life-violating-
the-public-radio-mission-by-straying-to-platforms-like-pandora/.

Staff. "Station Dropping NPR Program Because Of Pandora." Radio Ink, 17
May 2016, radioink.com/2016/05/16/station-dropping-npr-program-pando-
ra/.

Staff. "Summer Chaos Prompts NAB's Gordon Smith To Push FM Chips In Mobile Phones." All Access, 3 July 2012, www.allaccess.com/net-news/ archive/story/107832/summer-chaos-prompts-nab-s-gordon-smith-to-push-fm.

"State of the News Media." Pew Research Center RSS, 11 Jan. 2018, www. stateofthemedia.org/2011/audio-essay/#hd-radio-falters-as-broadcast-ers-look-for-new-technologies.

Sutton, John. "Use Plays from Radio's Winning Gamebook to Connect with Mobile, Online Listeners." Current, 18 Sept. 2015, current.org/2015/09/ use-plays-from-radios-winning-gamebook-to-connect-with-mobile-online-listeners/.

Thompson, Derek. "The Most Popular Social Network for Young People? Texting." The Atlantic, Atlantic Media Company, 11 Nov. 2014, www. theatlantic.com/technology/archive/2014/06/facebook-texting-teens-insta-gram-snapchat-most-popular-social-network/373043/.

Walker, Laura. "Radio's Next Incarnation: Join the Creative Disruption." Medium, Augmenting Humanity, 22 June 2016, medium.com/@lwalker/radi-os-next-incarnation-join-the-creative-disruption-a527ec2a364.

Welcome to PublicRadioFan.com. 14 June 2018, publicradiofan.com/.

"What Is the Public Media Platform and How Does It Work?" PRX – Help Desk, 3 May 2018, help.prx.org/hc/en-us/articles/211591557-What-is-the-Public-Media-Platform-and-how-does-it-work-.

Satellite

ContentDepot: For Stations. PRSS, 14 June 2018, www.prss.org/sta-tions-0#node-34.

Evans, Siriol. "World Radio Network from NPR Brings China Radio International to America." NPR, 17 Apr. 2000, www.npr.org/about/press/000417. wrn.html.

"Eutelsat Hot Bird 13B at 13.0°E–LyngSat." Worldwide Satellites, Channel–LyngSat, www.lyngsat.com/Eutelsat-Hot-Bird-13B.html.

"Free to Air Receivers." Tech-FAQ, www.tech-faq.com/free-to-air-receivers. html.

"How to Listen to Satellite Radio." WikiHow, 10 Apr. 2017, www.wikihow.com/Listen-to-Satellite-Radio.

Kalish, Jon. "SiriusXM Cancels 'Bob Edwards Show', but Weekly Public Radio Show Will Continue." *Current*, 27 Oct. 2016, current.org/2014/09/siriusxm-cancels-bob-edwards-show-but-weekly-public-radio-show-will-continue/.

Laukkonen, Jeremy. "What's the Big Deal With Satellite Radio?" Lifewire, 4 Mar. 2018, www.lifewire.com/what-is-satellite-radio-534582.

Lefkowitz, Jason A. "Why XM Doesn't Carry NPR." Just Well Mixed, 1 June 2004, jasonlefkowitz.net/2004/06/why_xm_doesnt_c/.

Musil, Steven. "FCC Approves Sirius-XM Satellite Radio Merger." CNET, 26 July 2008, www.cnet.com/news/fcc-approves-sirius-xm-satellite-radio-merger/.

"Predicted Coverage Area for KAUD 90.5 FM, Mexico, MO." Radio Stations in Salina, Kansas., 14 June 2018, radio-locator.com/cgi-bin/patg?id=KAUD-FM.

Shuster, David. "David Shuster Quotes." BrainyQuote, Xplore, www.brainyquote.com/quotes/david_shuster_516611.

Siklos, Richard, and Sorkin, Andrew Ross. "Merger Would End Satellite Radio's Rivalry." *The New York Times*, 20 Feb. 2007, www.nytimes.com/2007/02/20/business/media/20radio.html?pagewanted=all.

"State of the News Media." Pew Research Center RSS, 11 Jan. 2018, www.stateofthemedia.org/2010/audio-summary-essay/satellite/.

Sullivan, Mark. "This New Wave Of Satellite Broadband Could Challenge Cable And Fiber." *Fast Company*, 14 Mar. 2018, www.fastcompany.com/40542241/this-new-wave-of-satellite-broadband-could-challenge-cable-and-fiber.

"Vehicle Availability." SiriusXM, 14 June 2018, www.siriusxm.com/vehicleavailability.

Internet

"6 Private Companies That Could Launch Humans Into Space." Space.com, 16 Mar. 2012, www.space.com/8541-6-private-companies-launch-humans-space.html.

Adams, Richard. "*Huffington Post* to Be Sold to AOL for $315m." *The Guardian*, Guardian News and Media, 7 Feb. 2011, www.theguardian.com/world/ richard-adams-blog/2011/feb/07/huffington-post-sale-aol-ariana.

American Public Media: Audio Help, 14 June 2018, americanpublicmedia.publicradio.org/audio_help/.

Audrey. "PRX Listening Goes Mobile." PRX, 26 Mar. 2012, blog.prx. org/2012/03/new-player-new-ways-to-listen/.

Benton, Joshua. "NPR Decides It Won't Promote Its Podcasts or NPR One on Air." Nieman Lab, 17 Mar. 2016, www.niemanlab.org/2016/03/npr-decides-it-wont-promote-its-podcasts-or-npr-one-on-air/.

Brumfiel, Geoff. "Can You Hear Me Now? Cellphone Satellites Phone Home." NPR, 26 Apr. 2013, www.npr.org/2013/04/26/178846158/can-you-hear-me-now-cellphone-satellites-phone-home.

Charron, Kristin. "Press Release–NPR Digital Services Selects Triton Digital® for Online Audio Delivery, Monetization and Measurement." Triton Digital, 25 July 2016, www.tritondigital.com/press-releases/npr-digital-services-selects-triton-digital-for-online-audio-delivery-monetization-and-measurement.

"Checklist of Requirements for Federal Websites and Digital Services." DigitalGov, 9 Jan. 2014, www.digitalgov.gov/resources/checklist-of-requirements-for-federal-digital-services/.

Curry, Adam. "NPR Can't Promote Podcasts." 18 Mar. 2016, adam.curry.com/ html/NPRandPodcasts-1458316248.html.

Eggerton, John. "NAB 2017: Gordon Smith Says Broadcasters Poised to Be Digital Convergence Players." Broadcasting & Cable, 24 Apr. 2017, www. broadcastingcable.com/news/washington/nab-2017-gordon-smith-says-broadcasters-poised-be-digital-convergence-players/165175.

Ellett, John. "Alexa's Latest Magic Trick: Turning Millennials into NPR Listeners." *Forbes, Forbes* Magazine, 20 July 2017, www.forbes.com/sites/ johnellett/2017/07/20/alexas-latest-magic-trick-turning-millennials-into-npr-listeners/#fd5800bcffc0. http://peconicpublicbroadcasting.org/post/ note-our-listeners-and-donors

Falk, Tyler. "NPR, Members Look Ahead to Reinvention of Station Websites." *Current*, 1 Dec. 2017, current.org/2017/12/npr-members-look-ahead-to-reinvention-of-station-websites/.

Fenton, William. "The NPR Radio by Livio." PCMAG, 7 Feb. 2011, www.pcmag.com/article2/0,2817,2378995,00.asp.

Folkenflik, David. "In Forcing Out Senior Executive, New CEO Mohn Puts Stamp On NPR." 17 Oct. 2014, www.npr.org/2014/10/17/356998435/in-forcing-out-senior-executive-new-ceo-mohn-puts-stamp-on-npr.

"Free Podcasts." RadioPublic, 14 June 2018, www.radiopublic.com/.

Fuerst, Mark." *Grow the Audience* for Public Radio," 24 Nov. 2008, www.srg.org/GTA/FuerstComments.html.

Golgher, Paulo. "Tchau Orkut–Orkut Blog." 30 June 2014, web.archive.org/web/20140723220408/http://en.blog.orkut.com/2014/06/tchau-orkut.html.

Home. Pass Time, 14 June 2018, www.passtimesoftware.com/.

Home. Public Media Apps, 14 June 2018, www.publicmediaapps.com/#whatwe-do.

"Internet Users by Country (2016)." Google Search Statistics–Internet Live Stats, 2016, www.internetlivestats.com/internet-users-by-country/.

Ion, Florence. "NPR One Review: A Step Forward for Public Radio, a Step Back for Affiliates." Greenbot, 1 Aug. 2014, www.greenbot.com/article/2459867/npr-one-review-a-step-forward-for-public-radio-a-step-back-for-affiliates.html.

"Is Terrestrial Radio Destined to Die?" NPR, 30 Nov. 2007, www.npr.org/templates/transcript/transcript.php?storyId=16771846.

Jacobson, Daniel. "NPR, the API and OSCON 2009." NPR, 11 Aug. 2009, www.npr.org/blogs/inside/2009/08/npr_the_api_and_oscon_2009.html.

"Join Us." Chartbeat, Dashboards, 14 June 2018, chartbeat.com/careers/?gh_jid=61134.

Kiesow, Damon. "NPR Releases Android App Code to the Public." Poynter, 2 Mar. 2017, www.poynter.org/2010/npr-releases-android-app-code-to-the-public/103056/.

Kramer, Melody. "Today's Public Media Fight Misses The Point." Medium. 11 Apr. 2016, medium.com/@mkramer/today-s-public-media-fight-misses-the-point-1383b4ef8a71.

"KSBR's Digital Future." KSBR, 12 Sept. 2017, www.ksbr.nct/ksbrs-digital-future-1.

Laukkonen, Jeremy. "The 6 Biggest Problems with HD Radio." Lifewire, 21 Mar. 2017, www.lifewire.com/problem-with-hd-radio-534510.

Lavey-Heaton, Megan. "NPR Debuts Official IPhone App." Engadget, 14 July 2016, www.engadget.com/2009/08/18/npr-debuts-official-iphone-app/.

"Listening on NPR.org: How We Designed a Persistent Audio Player." Design at NPR, 22 June 2016, npr.design/listening-on-npr-org-how-we-designed-a-persistent-audio-player-85c33e21fb04.

"Mobile Listening." Minnesota Public Radio, 14 June 2018, www.mpr.org/listen/mobile.

Moradi, Javaun. "Why Does NPR Not Offer *All Things Considered* as a Podcast through ITunes? Other Popular Programs like Fresh Air Are Available as Podcasts." Quora, 10 Feb. 2011, www.quora.com/Why-does-NPR-not-offer-*All-Things-Considered*-as-a-podcast-through-iTunes-Other-popular-programs-like-Fresh-Air-are-available-as-podcasts.

"Mutiny Radio–Broadcasting from San Francisco's Mission District." Mutiny Radio, pcrcollective.org/.

"NPRbackstory," Twitter, 8 July 2011, twitter.com/NPRbackstory.

Peckham, Matt. "RIP Google Reader, Hello Four Best RSS-Reader Replacements." Time, 1 July 2013, techland.time.com/2013/07/01/r-i-p-google-reader-hello-four-best-rss-reader-replacements/.

Phelps, Andrew. "NPR's Infinite Player: It's like a Public Radio Station That Only Plays the Kinds of Pieces You like, Forever." Nieman Lab, 16 Nov. 2011, www.niemanlab.org/2011/11/nprs-infinite-player-its-like-a-public-radio-station-that-only-plays-the-kinds-of-pieces-you-like-forever/.

Phelps, Andrew. "NPR's Todd Mundt Says Public Radio Needs to Innovate or Die." Nieman Lab, 17 Sept. 2012, www.niemanlab.org/2012/09/nprs-todd-mundt-says-public-radio-needs-to-innovate-or-die/.

"Podcast."–Definition of Podcast, Merriam-Webster, 7 June 2018, www.merriam-webster.com/dictionary/podcast.

PRI–Apps on Google Play. Google, Google, 16 Apr. 2018, play.google.com/store/apps/details?id=org.pri.android.

Public Radio Player on the App Store. Apple Music, Apple Inc, 25 Apr. 2009, itunes.apple.com/us/app/public-radio-player/id312880531?mt=8.

Quantcast Measurement. ProgrammableWeb, 14 June 2018, www.programmableweb.com/api/quantcast-measurement.

Silverman, Dwight. "Public Radio Endangered by an IPhone App?" SciGuy, 21 July 2009, blog.chron.com/techblog/2009/07/public-radio-endangered-by-an-iphone-app/.

Smith, Wally. "A Note to Our Listeners and Donors." WPPB, June 2017, peconicpublicbroadcasting.org/post/note-our-listeners-and-donors.

Staff. "Nielsen: On-Demand Streaming Grows by 93%." Radio Ink, 7 Jan. 2016, radioink.com/2016/01/07/nielsen-on-demand-streaming-grows-by-93/.

Staff. "NPR One Available On Apple's CarPlay." Radio Ink, 25 Jan. 2016, radioink.com/2016/01/24/npr-one-available-on-apples-carplay/.

Staff. "IHeartRadio and National Public Radio Announce Streaming Partnership." Billboard Magazine, 14 July 2016, www.billboard.com/articles/news/7438264/iheartradio-national-public-radio-join-news-talk.

Statt. "How NPR Increased Podcasting Ad Sales by 10 Times in 2 Years." Adweek, 27 Oct. 2016, www.adweek.com/digital/how-npr-increased-podcasting-ad-sales-10-times-2-years-174267/.

Stroud, Scott. "Listening on NPR.org: How We Designed a Persistent Audio Player." Design at NPR, NPR, 22 June 2016, npr.design/listening-on-npr-org-how-we-designed-a-persistent-audio-player-85c33e21fb04.

Thorn, Jesse. "What's the Problem with NPR?" Interview on *The Sound of Young America*, Maximum Fun, 13 Mar. 2008, www.maximumfun.org/blog/2008/03/whats-problem-with-npr.html.

Tompkins, Al. "NPR Now Allows Users to Embed 800,000 Pieces of Audio." Poynter, 2 Mar. 2017, www.poynter.org/2015/npr-now-allows-users-to-embed-800000-pieces-of-audio/340547/.

"Video on Demand." What People Watch, Listen To and Buy, 16 Mar. 2016, www.nielsen.com/us/en/insights/reports/2016/video-on-demand.html.

Washenko, Anna. "Jacobs Media Survey Reviews Top Trends among Public Radio Listeners." *RAIN News*, 17 Sept. 2015, rainnews.com/jacobs-media-survey-reviews-top-trends-among-public-radio-listeners/.

"Ways to Listen to NPR." NPR, 9 Aug. 2013, www.npr.org/about-npr/187046089/ways-to-listen-to-npr.

Wilson, Tracy V. "How Streaming Video and Audio Work." HowStuffWorks, 12 Oct. 2007, computer.howstuffworks.com/internet/basics/streaming-video-and-audio.htm.

Terrestrial Radio

Anderson, John. "HD Radio's Next Bling Things." DIYmedia.net, 28 Nov. 2016, diymedia.net/hd-radios-next-bling-things/8627.

Behrens, Steve. "More Power for HD Radio, More Buzz on Analog." *Current*, 2   Sept. 2008, current.org/wp-content/uploads/archive-site/tech/tech0815hdradio.shtml

Brand, Madeleine, and Chadwich, Alex. "Is Terrestrial Radio Destined to Die?" NPR, 30 Nov. 2007, www.npr.org/templates/transcript/transcript.php?storyId=16771846.

Cerillo, Vanessa. "HD Radio FAQ." New England Public Radio, 18 Mar. 2017, mediad.publicbroadcasting.net/p/wfcr/files/hd_reception_faq_pdf.pdf?_ga=2.21031739.1429933805.1534705546-1014418097.1534705546.

Farhi, Paul. "NPR Is Graying, and Public Radio Is Worried about It." The Washington Post, WP Company, 22 Nov. 2015, www.washingtonpost.com/lifestyle/style/npr-is-graying-and-public-radio-is-worried-about-it/2015/11/22/0615447e-8e48-11e5-baf4-bdf37355da0c_story.html?utm_term=.fbd593c12268.

"FM Chip & Streaming." NextRadio, 14 June 2018, nextradioapp.com/supported-devices/.

Fortune, Gwendoline Y. "HD Scam." *Keeping the Public in Public Radio*, 25 Apr. 2010, keeppublicradiopublic.com/the-hd-radio-scam-2/.

Francis, Daniel. "The FCC Wants Smartphones' FM Chips Activated." Pulse Headlines, 19 Feb. 2017, www.pulseheadlines.com/fcc-smartphones-fm-chips-activated/59454/.

"Free Radio on My Phone." 15 June 2018, freeradioonmyphone.org/?__hstc=183552953.93d48a2327c57e41ba2a0019319c98b2.1499741474728.1499741474728.1499741474728.1&__hssc=183552953.1.1499741474728&__hsfp=1026658539.

PLEDGE: The Public Radio Fund Drive

Groves, Paul. "Opinion: The Future of FM Radio–England, Scotland, Wales and Northern Ireland." 26 May 2018, www.frequencyfinder.org.uk/Opinion_FM.pdf.

Hercher, James. "OOH Is Becoming A Measurement Tool For Digital Marketers." AdExchanger, 30 June 2016, adexchanger.com/digital-out-of-home/ooh-becoming-measurement-tool-digital-marketers/.

Hesseldahl, Arik. "Public Radio Goes Begging," *Forbes* Magazine, 6 June 2013, www.forbes.com/2001/03/30/0330pubradio.html#7a8d4873e9c1.

"How Can Radio Stations Convert Listeners Into Donors." MobileCause, 8 Aug. 2016, www.mobilecause.com/mobile-donations-on-radio/.

Huntsberger, Michael. "HD Radio vs. Public Radio Player." Linfield College, 6 Dec. 2016, digitalcommons.linfield.edu/cgi/viewcontent.cgi?article=1001&-context=mscmfac_pres.

"IBiquity: HD Radio Receiver Sales Double Last Year." *Radio World,* 16 Dec. 2009, www.radioworld.com/business-and-law/0009/ibiquity-hd-radio-receiver-sales-double-last-year/303255.

Jacobs, Fred. "*Business Insider* Survey Neglects to Include Radio." Jacobs Media Strategies, 12 Apr. 2016, jacobsmedia.com/wheres-radio-3/#comment-31131.

"More Music. More Stations. More Features. Digital Sound. No Subscription." HD Radio, 15 June 2018, hdradio.com/broadcasters.

Oxenford, David. "FCC Releases Instructions for Window for AM Stations to File for FM Translators and Announces Translator Filing Freeze – Pay Attention to the Details!" *Broadcast Law Blog*, 7 June 2017, www.broad-castlawblog.com/2017/06/articles/fcc-releases-instructions-for-window-for-am-stations-to-file-for-fm-translators-and-announces-translator-filing-freeze-pay-attention-to-the-details/.

Oxenford, David. "FM Translators for AM Stations – Now That the Filing Window Is Done, What's Next?" *Broadcast Law Blog*, 3 Aug. 2017, www.broadcastlawblog.com/2017/08/articles/fm-translators-for-am-stations-now-that-the-filing-window-is-done-whats-next/.

Peterson, Elizabeth. "National Public Radio Embraces Advertising ... Itself." Business News Daily, 7 Feb. 2013, www.businessnewsdaily.com/3915-npr-advertising.html.

Ragusea, Adam. "Stations Have a Future in Local Appeal, Distinct Program-
     ming." *Current*, 31 Mar. 2016, current.org/2016/03/stations-have-a-
future-in-local-appeal-distinct-programming/.

Reader, Bill. "Air Mail: NPR Sees 'Community' in Letters from Listeners."
     VLex, 4 Dec. 2007, law-journals-books.vlex.com/vid/air-mail-npr-sees-let-
ters-listeners-56258298.

"Revision of Part 15 of the Commission's Rules Regarding Operation in the 57-
     64 GHz Band." Report and Order, p. 32., apps.fcc.gov/edocs_public/attach-
match/FCC-13-112A1_Rcd.pdf.

Reynolds, John, and Plunkett, John. "Analogue Radio Listeners Resisting
     Switch to Digital, New Survey Suggests." *The Guardian*, Guardian
     News and Media, 25 Sept. 2013, www.theguardian.com/media/2013/
     sep/25/ra-dio-listeners-resist-digital.

Riismendel, Paul. "Website Campaigns to Keep the Public in Public Radio."
     Radio Survivor, 26 Apr. 2010, www.radiosurvivor.com/2010/04/26/website-
     campaigns-to-keep-the-public-in-public-radio/.

Shearer, Elisa. "Audio and Podcasting Fact Sheet." Pew Research Center's
     Journalism Project, 16 June 2017, www.journalism.org/fact-sheet/au-
     dio-and-podcasting/.

Staff. "FCC's Wheeler Rebuffs FM Chips Request." Insideradio.com, 29 Apr.
     2015, www.insideradio.com/free/fcc-s-wheeler-rebuffs-fm-chips-request/
     article_cc275c38-ee43-11e4-af69-939420e218f2.html.

Staff. "Jacobs Media, PRPD Release 8th Annual Public Radio Tech Survey." All
     Access, 18 Oct. 2016, www.allaccess.com/net-news/archive/story/158765/
     jacobs-media-prpd-release-8th-annual-public-radio-.

Staff. "NPR's Vivian Schiller: Net Will Replace Broadcast In 5-10 Years." All
     Access, 3 June 2010, www.allaccess.com/net-news/archive/story/76125/
     npr-s-vivian-schiller-net-will-replace-broadcast-i.

"State of the News Media." Pew Research Center RSS, 11 Jan. 2018, www.
     stateofthemedia.org/2011/audio-essay/#hd-radio-falters-as-broadcast-
     ers-look-for-new-technologies.

Suhay, Lisa. "Norway to End FM Radio Broadcasts. Will US Follow?" The
     Christian Science Monitor, 20 Apr. 2015, www.csmonitor.com/World/Glob-

al-News/2015/0420/Norway-to-end-FM-radio-broadcasts.-Will-US-follow-video.

Venta, Lance. "Boston University Sells Cape Cod Signal." RadioInsight, 5 Aug. 2013, radioinsight.com/headlines/84502/boston-university-ty-sells-cape-cod-signal/.

Vestberg, Hans. "Hans Vestberg Quotes." BrainyQuote, Xplore, 31 Aug. 2006, www.brainyquote.com/quotes/quotes/h/hansvestbe719948.html.

Washenko, Anna. "NAB and NPR Pitch FCC for FM Chip Activation." *RAIN News*, 15 Jan. 2016, rainnews.com/nab-and-npr-pitch-fcc-for-fm-chip-activation/.

Washenko, Anna. "NAB Study Finds 44% of Top U.S. Smartphones Have FM Chips Activated." *RAIN News*, 1 Feb. 2017, rainnews.com/nab-study-finds-44-of-top-u-s-smartphones-have-fm-chips-activated/.

Conflicts

Battaglio, Stephen. "NPR Union Members Will Ask SAG-AFTRA to Authorize a Strike Vote." Los Angeles Times, 14 July 2017, www.latimes.com/business/hollywood/la-fi-ct-npr-strike-20170714-story.html.

"Communication Conflicts in America: The Case of National Public Radio," Tom McCourt, Praeger, 1999, p 98

"*Grow the Audience*. Public Radio in the New Network Age," CPB, 12 Jan. 2010, www.srg.org/GTA/Public_Radio_in_the_New_Network_Age.pdf+.

Mikelionis, Lukas. "Russian Troll Farm Created Fake City Newspaper Twitter Accounts ... to Spread Real Local Stories: Report." Fox News, FOX News Network, 13 July 2018, www.foxnews.com/tech/2018/07/13/russian-troll-farm-created-fake-city-newspaper-twitter-accounts-to-spread-real-local-stories-report.html.

Roe, Mike. "*Radiolab*, This American Life Try to Kneecap Each Other in Public Radio Brackets." Southern California Public Radio, 8 Apr. 2013, www.scpr.org/blogs/newmedia/2013/04/06/13194/radiolab-this-american-life-try-to-kneecap-each-ot/.

Staff. "Why Would NPR Do This?" Radio Ink, 22 Mar. 2016, radioink.com/2016/03/21/why-would-npr-do-this/.

Station vs. Network

Adelson, Andrea. "The Business of National Public Radio." *The New York Times*, 5 Apr. 1999, www.nytimes.com/1999/04/05/business/media-the-business-of-national-public-radio.html.

Charney, Tamar. "How NPR One Data Points to New Ways of Thinking about Local Content." *Current*, 15 Dec. 2016, current.org/2016/12/how-npr-one-data-points-to-new-ways-of-thinking-about-local-content/.

"*Conflicting Communication Interests in America*: The Case of National Public Radio," Tom McCourt, Praeger, October 1999, p. 97,

Cyberweavers. "Lynne Chadwick, Co-Founder of NFCB's 'Healthy Station Project' Named as New Manager for KPFA." Radio 4All, 3 July 1997, free-pacifica.savegrassrootsradio.org/fp/healthystation.htm.

December 16, 2013 "Flatow Finds More Traction for 'Science Friday' in PRI Distribution." *Current*, 16 Feb. 2015, current.org/2013/12/flatow-finds-more-traction-for-science-friday-in-pri-distribution/.

Dechter, Gadi. "Locally Grown." Baltimore *City Paper*, 13 July 2005, web.archive.org/web/20120902092613/http://www2.citypaper.com/news/story.asp?id=10286.

Everhart, Karen. "News Leaders Draw Hard Line on Employees' Public Comments." *Current*, 26 July 2012, current.org/2011/11/news-leaders-draw-hard-line-on-employees-public-comments/.

Everhart, Karen. "NPR, Greater Public Team up to Create Pledge Campaign Built on Spark Promotions." *Current*, 10 July 2015, current.org/2015/07/npr-greater-public-team-up-to-create-pledge-campaign-built-on-spark-promotions/.

Finn, Scott. "We Learn More from Our Mistakes. So Why Don't We Talk about Them?" *Current*, 5 Nov. 2015, current.org/2015/11/we-learn-more-from-our-mistakes-so-why-dont-we-talk-about-them/.

Fuerst, Mark. "Localism Emphasis Poses Risk." *Current*, 16 Feb. 2015, current.org/2013/09/localism-emphasis-poses-risk/.

Gervin, Cari Wade. "Public Radio Reporter Suing UTC Over Firing." Nashville Scene, 30 Mar. 2017, www.nashvillescene.com/news/pith-in-the-wind/article/20856772/fired-public-radio-reporter-suing-utc-over-firing.

Goldberg, Bernard. "NPR and the Nina Totenberg Problem." BernardGoldberg. com, 29 Oct. 2010, bernardgoldberg.com/npr-and-the-nina-totenberg-problem/.

Graves, Ralph. "Finding Beauty in Ephemera." Non-NPR Public Radio, 28 Mar. 2008, the-unmutual.blogspot.com/2008/03/non-npr-public-radio.html.

Janssen, Mike. "Science Friday Producer Settles with Government over Alleged Misuse of NSF Funds." *Current*, 16 Feb. 2015, current.org/2014/09/science-friday-producer-settles-with-government-over-alleged-misuse-of-nsf-funds/.

Jilani, Zaid. "Radio Show Distributed By NPR Fires Host After She Takes Part In Protests." *ThinkProgress*, 20 Oct. 2011, thinkprogress.org/radio-show-distributed-by-npr-fires-host-after-she-takes-part-in-protests-8868e5fa7b3. ibid.

Kaplan, Joel. "Dialing for Radio Dollars." CPB, 21 Mar. 2016, www.cpb.org/ombudsman/dialing-radio-dollars.

Kasten, Roy. "Media & Diversity." All Digitocracy, 31 Aug. 2016, alldigitocracy.org/hyper-local-community-podcast-finds-national-audience/#.V8cJF-vo-iS0.linkedin.

Kaul, Greta, and Andrea Schug. "New Funding Process Frustrates Small Public Radio Stations." MinnPost, 11 Jan. 2012, www.minnpost.com/politics-policy/2012/01/new-funding-process-frustrates-small-public-radio-stations.

Kramer, Melody. "Putting the Public into Public Media Membership." Nieman Lab, 13 July 2015, www.niemanlab.org/2015/07/putting-the-public-into-public-media-membership/#footnote_3_110647.

Kramer, Melody. "Why Does Local Matter? Let's Ask Our Audience." Poynter, 15 Mar. 2017, www.poynter.org/2015/why-does-local-matter-lets-ask-our-audience/352419/.

Lindsay, Drew. "Has Success Spoiled NPR?" Washingtonian, 1 Mar. 2007, www.washingtonian.com/2007/03/01/has-success-spoiled-npr/.

Margolick, David. "What's Wrong with NPR?" The Hive, Vanity Fair, 17 Apr. 2018, www.vanityfair.com/news/business/2012/01/National-Public-Rodeo.

Moradi, Javaun. "Why Does NPR Not Offer *All Things Considered* as a Podcast through ITunes? Other Popular Programs like Fresh Air Are Available as Podcasts." Quora, 10 Feb. 2011, www.quora.com/Why-does-NPR-not-offer-*All-Things-Considered*-as-a-podcast-through-iTunes.

Morley, Jefferson. "Fired NPR Host Sees 'McCarthyism.'" Salon, Salon.com, 24 Oct. 2011, www.salon.com/2011/10/20/fired_npr_host_sees_mccarthyism/.

Mueller, Angela. "KWMU, KETC, KDHX Face Threat of Funding Cuts ." Bizjournals.com, The Business Journals, 16 Mar. 2011, www.bizjournals.com/stlouis/news/2011/03/16/kwmu-ketc-face-threat-of-funding-cuts.html.

"NPR Ethics Handbook." NPR, 14 June 2018, ethics.npr.org/.

"NPR Host Ira Flatow & Affiliated Charity Settle False Claims Act Allegations." Berger Montague, 26 Mar. 2018, bergermontague.com/npr-host-ira-flatow-affiliated-charity-settle-false-claims-act-allegations/.

Olson, Steve. "Radio Stations Have Ample Opportunity to Boost Listening." Current, 25 Feb. 2016, current.org/2016/02/radio-stations-have-ample-opportunity-to-boost-listening/.

Ostrow, Joanne. "At CPR, What You Don't Hear Also Matters." The Denver Post, 7 May 2016, www.denverpost.com/2008/09/25/at-cpr-what-you-dont-hear-also-matters/.

Phelps, Andrew. "Location, Location, Location: NPR Customizes the News with Local Content." Nieman Lab, 23 Mar. 2012, www.niemanlab.org/2012/03/location-location-location-npr-customizes-the-news-with-local-content/.

"Public Radio Programming Performance." Grow the Audience for Public Radio, Station Resource Group, May 2003, www.srg.org/program/pgmperf.html.

Rehm, Dana. "NPR and Science Friday–What's the Deal?" NPR, 7 Oct. 2010, www.npr.org/sections/npr-extra/2010/10/07/130398131/npr-and-science-friday-what-s-the-deal.

Robinson, Frank S. "'Public' Broadcasting and Partisan WAMC Radio." The Rational Optimist, 19 Oct. 2012, rationaloptimist.wordpress.com/2012/10/11/public-broadcasting-and-partisan-wamc-radio/.

Roush, Chris. "Transgender 'Marketplace' Reporter Fired over Blog Post." Talking Biz News, 31 Jan. 2017, talkingbiznews.com/1/transgender-marketplace-reporter-fired-over-blog-post/.

Shepard, Alicia. "Albany Gets a Lot of Chartock, but How Much Is Too Much?" Current, 3 Feb. 2017, current.org/2011/12/albany-gets-a-lot-of-chartock-but-how-much-is-too-much/.

Shuster, David. David Shuster Quotes." BrainyQuote, Xplore, www.brainy-quote.com/quotes/david_shuster_516610.

Staff. "KUNC Launches *The Colorado Sound.*" Radio Ink, 1 Mar. 2016, radio-ink.com/2016/02/29/kunc-launches-the-colorado-sound/.

Staff. "NPR's Mohn Points to Early Success with 'Spark Initiative'." *Current*, 7 Apr. 2015, current.org/2015/03/nprs-mohn-points-to-early-success-with-spark-initiative/.

Staff. "Public Stations Spread Thinly in Funding War." OregonLive.com, 22 Mar. 2011, www.oregonlive.com/opinion/index.ssf/2011/03/public_sta-tions_spread_thinly.html.

Staff. "Study of NPR's Spark Initiative Shows Stations Getting Morning Edition Boost." Current, 23 Apr. 2015, current.org/2015/04/study-of-nprs-spark-ini-tiative-shows-stations-getting-morning-edition-boost/.

Staff. "Top NPR News Executive Mike Oreskes Resigns Amid Al-legations Of Sexual Harassment." NPR, 1 Nov. 2017, www.npr.org/2017/11/01/561427869/top-npr-new-executive-mike-oreskes-re-signs-amid-allegations-of-sexual-harassment..

Stone, Ben. "Why National Public Radio Canceled Mara Liasson's Speech in Portland." *Willamette Week*, 14 June 2016, www.wweek.com/news/2016/06/15/why-national-public-radio-cancelled-mara-liassons-speech-in-portland/.

Sutton, John. "A Mixed Bag of Thoughts." *RadioSutton*, 6 Feb. 2006, radiosut-ton.blogspot.com/search?q=mixed%2Bbag%2Bof%2Bthoughts.

Tompkins, Al. "Across the United States, NPR Is Reorganizing Its Member Stations around Regional Hubs." Poynter, 27 June 2017, www.poynter.org/2017/across-the-united-states-npr-is-reorganizing-its-member-stations-around-regional-hubs/464570/.

"WNYC Studios and 'Science Friday' Announce New Partnership." WNYC, New York Public Radio, Podcasts, Live Streaming Radio, News." 11 Jan. 2018, www.wnyc.org/press/science-friday/11118/.

Station vs. Station

Arsenault, Mark. "In Well-Mannered Public Radio, an Airwaves War." The Boston Globe, 4 June 2017, www.bostonglobe.com/metro/2017/06/03/

well-mannered-public-radio-airwaves-war/4tmVpry89f7ZN1RFwNwjJO/
story.html.

Ashby, Charles. "Some Public Radio Stations Cry Foul over CPR Fundraising." The Daily Sentinel, 3 Mar. 2011, www.gjsentinel.com/news/west-
ern_colorado/some-public-radio-stations-cry-foul-over-cpr-fundraising/
article_5976342f-679b-534f-bd25-e66bc4d36d14.html.

Blake, Casey. "Answer Woman: WCQS Ghost Stations, Men in Dresses."
The Citizen-Times, 5 Sept. 2014, www.citizen-times.com/story/news/
local/2014/09/05/answer-woman-wcqs-ghost-stations-men-dress-
es/15157743/.

Eiseman, Lee. "One Year After Change: Is WGBH/WCRB Working?"
The Boston Musical Intelligencer, 7 Nov. 2010, www.classical-scene.
com/2010/11/07/one-year/.

Feder, Robert. "WBEZ Buys Kankakee Public Station." Robertfeder.com, 16
Dec. 2015, www.robertfeder.com/2015/12/16/wbez-buys-kankakee-public-
radio-station/.

Fortune, Gwendoline Y. "Bad Beans." Keeping the Public in Public Radio, 23
Apr. 2011, keeppublicradiopublic.com/2011/04/23/bad-beans/.

Grehn, Kim. "Public Radio Partnerships: Strength in Numbers." LinkedIn, 26
Dec. 2015, www.linkedin.com/pulse/public-radio-partnerships-strength-
numbers-kim-grehn.

Ho, Rodney. "WABE Chairman Blasts GSU/GPB Partnership with WRAS."
Radio and TV Talk, AJC, 2 July 2014, radiotvtalk.blog.ajc.com/2014/07/02/
wabe-chairman-blasts-gsugpb-partnership-with-wras/.

Ho, Rodney. "Georgia Public Broadcasting Takes over Georgia State's WRAS-
FM/Album 88 Daytime Programming." Radio and TV Talk, 6 May 2014,
radiotvtalk.blog.ajc.com/2014/05/06/georgia-public-broadcasting-takes-
over-georgia-states-wras-fmalbum-88/.

Hollis. "Public Radio Acquisitions Reported." PRPD News for Programmers, 17
June 2014, prpd-news.blogspot.com/2014/06/public-radio-aquisitions-re-
ported.html#!/2014/06/public-radio-aquisitions-reported.html.

Interview between Heather Clayborn, John Avendano and Wendy Turner, WKCC, Dec. 17, 2015, https://www.facebook.com/wkccradio/
posts/1098676846823222

PLEDGE: The Public Radio Fund Drive

Mass, Cliff. "KUOW: A Major Public Radio Station Stumbles." Cliff Mass
   Weather and Climate Blog, 18 June 2014, cliffmass.blogspot.com/2014/06/
kuow-major-public-radio-station-stumbles.html.

Meyer, Robinson. "Map: The Nation's Public Radio Stations." *The Atlantic*,
   Atlantic Media Company, 22 Nov. 2013, www.theatlantic.com/technology/
   archive/2013/11/map-the-nations-public-radio-stations/281716/.

Nugent, Kari. "Chicago Public Media Purchases WKCC." Kankakee Community College, 17 Dec. 2015, kcc.edu/news/Pages/Chicago-Public-Media-Pur-
   chases-WKCC.aspx.

Radil, Amy. "Uncertainty At KPLU Over KUOW Acquisition." KUOW
   News and Information, 12 Nov. 2015, kuow.org/post/uncertainty-kp-
   lu-over-kuow-acquisition.

Ragusea, Adam. "KUOW's GM Discusses the 'Jaw-Dropping' Offer to Purchase
   KPLU." Current, 28 July 2016, current.org/2016/07/kuows-gm-discusses-
   the-jaw-dropping-offer/.

Ryan, John. "Campaign To Save KPLU Launches; Needs At Least $7M In 6
   Months." KUOW News and Information, 11 Jan. 2016, kuow.org/post/cam-
   paign-save-kplu-launches-needs-least-7m-6-months.

Staff, Associated Press. "Station May Lose Funding." Amarillo Globe-News,
   30 Mar. 2011, amarillo.com/news/local-news/2011-03-30/station-may-lose-
   funding.

"The Melian Dialogue–HISTORY OF THE PELOPONNESIAN WAR–by Thucydides." CHAPTER XVII–Sixteenth Year of the War–The Melian Conference–Fate of Melos, www.mtholyoke.edu/acad/intrel/melian.htm.

Waits, Jennifer. "College Radio Watch: Protests over Future of WRAS Continue, With WABE Critiquing the Deal as Well." *Radio Survivor*, 12 July
   2014, www.radiosurvivor.com/2014/07/11/college-radio-watch-protests-fu-
   ture-wras-continue-lpfm-dismissals-news/.

"WKCC Is Ending Its on-Air Run." Chicago Public Media Purchases WKCC,
   kcc.edu/news/Lists/KCCAnnouncements/DispForm2.aspx?ID=84.

Station vs. Itself

Careaga, Andrew, et al. "St. Louis Public Radio to Assume Operations of KMST." Press Release, pp. 1–2., www.stlpublicradio.org/info/press/2017/stlpr-kmst.pdf.

Falk, Tyler. "KUSP License, Assets, Wine Sold off to Religious Broadcaster." *Current*, 28 Oct. 2016, current.org/2016/10/kusp-license-assets-wine-sold-off-to-religious-broadcaster/.

Finn, Scott. "We Learn More from Our Mistakes. So Why Don't We Talk about Them?" *Current*, 5 Nov. 2015, current.org/2015/11/we-learn-more-from-our-mistakes-so-why-dont-we-talk-about-them/.

Forfeiture Order." DA 12-1205A1.Pdf, FCC, 27 July 2012, apps.fcc.gov/edocs_public/attachmatch/DA-12-1205A1.pdf.

Glover, Jerry. "FCC Fines Public Radio Station $10,000 for Public File Violations – LSG Legal." LSG Legal, 1 July 2016, lsglegal.com/fcc-fines-public-radio-station-10000-for-public-file-violations/.

Haddadin, Jim. "FCC Fines Student Radio Station at Framingham State." MetroWest Daily News, Framingham, MA, 13 Jan. 2015, www.metrowest-dailynews.com/article/20150113/NEWS/150119167.

KMST 88.5 Rolla, 96.3 Lebanon." RSS, 14 June 2018, stlpublicradio.org/kmst/.

Marcus, William. "Montana Public Radio Facing Deficit, Reaches to Supporters for Help." Missoulian, 13 Apr. 2015, missoulian.com/butte/news/opinion/editorial/montana-public-radio-facing-deficit-reaches-to-supporters-for-help/article_a8aac2c3-7393-55ab-ab71-1b6ae3b7f3ce.html.

Martin, Harry. "FCC Plans Crack-down on Silent Stations." Radio Magazine, 1 Nov. 2010, www.radiomagonline.com/misc/0082/fcc-plans-crackdown-on-silent-stations/32695.

Miller, Margaret L., et al. "FCC'S $10,000 fines against College Radio Stations: Playing Bad Records may be Legal; Keeping Bad Records is not." *NA-CUNotes,* 4 Dec. 2012, pp. 1–6., www.higheredcompliance.org/resources/resources/CollegeRadio.pdf.

"Olsen, Jerry," Chief Engineer for KOMQ and KPBG, phone conversation with the author, April 25, 2016.

Oxenford, David. "$540,000 FCC Penalty for Cumulus Station Missing Formal Sponsorship Identification on Issue Ad Campaign." *Broadcast Law Blog*, 8 Jan. 2016, www.broadcastlawblog.com/2016/01/articles/540000-fcc-pen-alty-for-cumulus-station-missing-formal-sponsorship-identification-on-is-sue-ad-campaign/.

Oxenford, David. "Broadcast Stations Going Dark–Issues to Think About." *Broadcast Law Blog*, 24 Oct. 2013, www.broadcastlawblog.com/2009/07/articles/broadcast-stations-going-dark-issues-to-think-about/.

Reed, Eve K. "Beware: Higher Fines for FCC Violations Coming July 1, 2016." WileyonMedia, 30 June 2016, www.wileyonmedia.com/2016/06/be-ware-higher-fines-for-fcc-violations-coming-july-1-2016/.

Russo, Michelle. "FCC fines 28 Radio Stations for Public Radio file Violations." 8 Oct. 2003, press release, pp. 1–1., apps.fcc.gov/edocs_public/attachmatch/DOC-239705A1.pdf.

Sandomir, Richard. "Affectionate Scorn for '62 Mets." *The New York Times*, 8 Apr. 2012, www.nytimes.com/2012/04/08/sports/baseball/breslin-chroni-cler-of-62-mets-recalls-their-appeal.html.

"Silent AM Broadcast Stations List." Federal Communications Commission, 12 June 2018, www.fcc.gov/media/radio/silent-am-list#block-menu-block-4.

Staff. "KQED SF Still Feels Aftershocks Of June Cyberattack." Insideradio.com, 20 July 2017, www.insideradio.com/free/kqed-sf-still-feels-aftershocks-of-june-cyberattack/article_244347de-6d21-11e7-9a55-c76e3575e236.html.

Tannenwald, Peter. "Student-Run College Radio: A Species Endangered by FCC Fines?" CommLawBlog, 25 June 2015, www.commlawblog.com/2012/07/articles/broadcast/student-run-college-radio-a-species-endangered-by-fcc-fines/.

Thrust, Paul. "Copper Theft and How to Avoid It." Engineering Radio RSS, 26 Apr. 2010, www.engineeringradio.us/blog/2010/04/copper-theft-and-how-to-avoid-it/#comment-518.

Wayne Heinan," AM Radiolog Editor, National Radio Club, email conversation with the author, July 17, 2016.

Wayne Heinan," AM Radiolog Editor, National Radio Club, email conversation with the author, July 16, 2016.

WDVH-AM 980 Gainesville, Central Florida Radio, www.cflradio.net/980_wdvh_am.htm.

Station vs. Anonymous

Anderson, John. "Radio Stations Fall Victim to Cyberattack (Again)." DIYmedia.net, 27 Oct. 2014, diymedia.net/radio-stations-fall-victim-to-cyberattack-again/7345.

Brantley, Max. "KUAR: On-Air, but Fire Mystery Remains." Arkansas Blog, 3 Apr. 2011, www.arktimes.com/ArkansasBlog/archives/2011/04/03/kuar-on-air-but-fire-mystery-remains#more.

Eddington, Sarah. "Damages to 2 NPR Stations Not Likely Related." *The Victoria Advocate*, 13 Apr. 2011, www.victoriaadvocate.com/news/2011/apr/13/bc-ar-npr-stations-damaged/.

Eisenbaum, Joel. "Local Radio Station Says Hack Causes Slur to Appear on Display." KPRC, 23 Nov. 2015, www.click2houston.com/news/local-radio-station-says-hack-causes-slur-to-appear-on-display.

Mackiel, Kurt. "April 8 Support Deadline Affected More than Windows XP." Redmond Channel Partner, 8 Apr. 2014, rcpmag.com/articles/2014/04/08/april-8-deadline-more-than-xp.aspx.

Moye, David. "WATCH: TV Station Hacked To Broadcast Fake Zombie Apocalypse Alert." The *Huffington Post*, 16 Feb. 2013, www.huffingtonpost.com/2013/02/11/krtv-fake-zombie-alert_n_2665469.html.

Shepherd, Katie. "Portland Community Radio Station KBOO Had Its Computer Servers Hacked by Cryptocurrency Miners." *Willamette Week*, 10 May 2018, www.wweek.com/news/business/2018/05/10/portland-community-radio-station-kboo-had-its-computer-servers-hacked-by-cryptocurrency-miners/.

Soderberg, Jenka. "Our Website Is Back!" KBOO, 15 June 2018, kboo.fm/hack2018.

Staff. "Broadcast Engineers Offer Necessary Anti-Hacking Tips." Insideradio.com, 28 Apr. 2017, www.insideradio.com/free/broadcast-engineers-offer-necessary-anti-hacking-tips/article_18214f62-2be7-11e7-8e3a-bb1d-48c2357f.html.

Staff. "KQED SF Still Feels Aftershocks Of June Cyberattack." 20 July 2017, www.insideradio.com/free/kqed-sf-still-feels-aftershocks-of-june-cyberattack/article_244347de-6d21-11e7-9a55-c76e3575e236.html.

Staff. Alarms Sound on Cyberattacks. InsiderRadio, 29 May 2015, www.insideradio.com/alarm-sounded-for-stations-to-step-up-cyberattack-preparations/article_c45462c2-05cb-11e5-a4fb-4799d.

Thurst, Paul. "Copper Theft and How to Avoid It." Engineering Radio RSS, 26 Apr. 2010, www.engineeringradio.us/blog/2010/04/copper-theft-and-how-to-avoid-it/#comment-518.

Thurst, Paul. "How Stupid Do You Have to Be?" Engineering Radio RSS, 8 Sept. 2009, www.engineeringradio.us/blog/2009/09/how-stupid-do-you-have-to-be/.

Chapter 5 – Big Pimpin'

Barboza, David. "The 'Enhanced Underwriting' of Public Broadcasting Is Taking a More Commercial Flair." *The New York Times*, 27 Dec. 1995, www.nytimes.com/1995/12/27/business/media-business-advertising-enhanced-underwriting-public-broadcasting-taking-more.html.

Battaglio, Stephen. "NPR President Jarl Mohn Is Betting on Smart, Addictive Podcasts to Hook Millennials." Los Angeles Times, 29 June 2016, www.latimes.com/entertainment/envelope/cotown/la-et-ct-jarl-mohn-npr-on-the-record-20160629-snap-story.html.

Elizabeth, Karen. "Pimp, #19." Urban Dictionary, 19 Mar. 2004, www.urbandictionary.com/define.php?term=pimp.

"Pretentious Amex Branding Does Not Entice Millennials." *Host Merchant Services*, 16 May 2017, www.hostmerchantservices.com/2017/04/pretentious-amex-branding-not-entice-millennials/.

Staff. "Basic Memberships: More Trouble than they're Worth?" *Current*, 13 Apr. 2012, current.org/2012/12/basic-memberships-more-trouble-than-theyre-worth/.

Staff. "Donors Demand Clearer View of Station Reality." Current, 8 Apr. 2012, current.org/2003/09/donors-demand-clearer-view-of-station-reality/.

Sutton, John. "How Stations Can Stay Relevant as Listeners Go Elsewhere for NPR Content." *Current*, 12 Aug. 2014, current.org/2014/08/how-stations-can-stay-relevant-as-listeners-go-elsewhere-for-npr-content.

The Public Radio "sound"

Audio Superfreak. "Shure sm7b vs. Neumann u87Ai." SoundCloud, 2011, soundcloud.com/audio-superfreak/sm7b_then_u87ai.

Bradley, Bill. "Photos: The Faces of NPR." The Hive, *Vanity Fair*, 29 Sept. 2014, www.vanityfair.com/culture/photos/2010/12/npr-slide-show-201012.

Chávez-Peón, Mario E. "Non-Modal Phonation in Quiaviní Zapotec: Universidad Nacional Autónoma De México," 6 Oct. 2011, web.archive.org/web/20140826115820/http://www.ailla.utexas.org/site/cilla5/Chavez_CILLA_V.pdf.

Dreher, Rod. "'Does NPR Sound Too White?'." The American Conservative, 31 Jan. 2015, www.theamericanconservative.com/dreher/does-npr-sound-too-white/.

Dvorkin, Jeffrey A. "Why Doesn't NPR Sound More Like the Rest of America?" NPR, 18 May 2005, www.npr.org/templates/story/story.php?storyId=4656584.

Farhi, Paul. "NPR Is Graying, and Public Radio Is Worried about It." The Washington Post, 22 Nov. 2015, www.washingtonpost.com/lifestyle/style/npr-is-graying-and-public-radio-is-worried-about-it/2015/11/22/0615447e-8e48-11e5-baf4-bdf37355da0c_story.html?utm_term=.aa70be326b5a.

Fitzpatrick, Jason. "Geek Trivia: NPR Radio Shows Have A Very Crisp And Bright Sound Profile That Is Optimized For?" How-To Geek, 5 July 2016, www.howtogeek.com/trivia/npr-radio-shows-have-a-very-crisp-and-bright-sound-profile-that-is-optimized-for/.

Gallardo, Adrianno, and O'Donovan, Betsy. "Media Criticism: Public Radio and the Sound of America." 21 Nov. 2015, betsyodonovan.com/work/media-criticism-public-radio-and-the-sound-of-america/.

Graham, Tim. "Ouch: AP Says ISIS Radio Station for European Recruits 'Sounds Like NPR'." *NewsBusters*, MRC, 9 June 2015, www.newsbusters.org/blogs/tim-graham/2015/06/09/ouch-ap-says-isis-radio-station-european-recruits-sounds-npr.

Holohan, Meghan. "Listening to Soft Voices Can Cause 'Brain Orgasms.'" Mental Floss, 2 Dec. 2013, mentalfloss.com/article/53220/listening-soft-voices-can-cause-brain-orgasms.

Kane, Sally. "Public Radio's Distribution Superhighway: the Public Radio Satellite System." NFCB, nfcb.org/public-radios-distribution-superhighway-the-public-radio-satellite-system/.

Kautz, R L, and Huggard, Brent M. "Tilt-a-whirl_physics_huggard.Pdf." Google, Jan. 1994, drive.google.com/file/d/0BytVpJaWhqkjTGdHWU-9WOVRXU2M/view.

Lahey, Jessica. "Why Middle-School Girls Sometimes Talk Like Babies." The Atlantic, Atlantic Media Company, 19 Feb. 2014, www.theatlantic.com/education/archive/2014/02/why-middle-school-girls-sometimes-talk-like-babies/283894/.

MacAdam, Allison. "Getting beyond 'Public Radio Voice': Finding and Decoding Identity on the Air." Nieman Lab, 22 Apr. 2015, www.niemanlab.org/2015/04/getting-beyond-public-radio-voice-finding-and-decoding-identity-on-the-air/.

Manjoo, Farhad. "NPR Letters: The Tedious, Annoying Complaints of Public Radio Listeners." Slate Magazine, 2 Mar. 2011, www.slate.com/articles/life/a_fine_whine/2011/03/we_listen_to_npr_precisely_to_avoid_this_sort_of_stupidity.html.

Ochona. "I Want to Turn off NPR, but I Can't . . ." Archinect, 5 Jan. 2007, archinect.com/forum/thread/20624/i-want-to-turn-off-npr-but-i-can-t.

Radke, Heather. "The Old, Weird Days of National Public Radio." The Paris Review, 8 Aug. 2017, www.theparisreview.org/blog/2017/07/26/american-sounds/.

Ragusea, Adam. "The Pub, Episode 5: End of the Vocal Fry Debate, Jacki Lyden on Fashion, and Lessons from Commercial Media." Current, 17 Nov. 2017, current.org/2015/02/the-pub-episode-5-end-of-the-vocal-fry-debate-jacki-lyden-on-fashion-and-lessons-from-commercial-media/.

Sally. "I Love NPR/I Hate NPR." The What, 30 Jan. 2007, heysally.wordpress.com/2007/01/30/i-love-npri-hate-npr/.

Barnhurst, Kevin, The New Long Journalism, https://kgbcomm.people.uic.edu/longnews/pdf/barnljch2.pdf

Seaton, Matt. "Speech Habits: Uptalk." *The Guardian*, Guardian News and Media, 21 Sept. 2001, www.theguardian.com/books/2001/sep/21/reference-andlanguages.mattseaton.

Seitz-Brown, Marybeth. "Young Women Shouldn't Have to Talk Like Men to Be Taken Seriously." Slate Magazine, 16 Dec. 2014, www.slate.com/blogs/lexicon_valley/2014/12/16/uptalk_is_okay_young_women_shouldn_t_have_to_talk_like_men_to_be_taken_seriously.html.

Wayne, Teddy. "'NPR Voice' Has Taken Over the Airwaves." The New York Times, 21 Dec. 2017, www.nytimes.com/2015/10/25/fashion/npr-voice-has-taken-over-the-airwaves.html.

Yuasa, Ikuko Patricia. "Creaky Voice: A New Feminine Voice Quality for Young Urban-Oriented Upwardly Mobile American Women?" American Speech, Duke University Press, 1 Aug. 2010, read.dukeupress.edu/american-speech/article-abstract/85/3/315/5885/Creaky-Voice-A-New-Feminine-Voice-Quality-for?redirectedFrom=fulltext.

Snob Factors

"A Lot Happened While You Were Busy Watching Washington." Marketplace, 1 Aug. 2017, www.marketplace.org/shows/marketplace/08012017.

"A Quote by George Burns." Goodreads, www.goodreads.com/quotes/128348-sincerity—-if-you-can-fake-that-you-ve-got-it.

Blundell, Anneli. "The 7 Reasons People Talk over the Top of Others." Linkedin, 1 Feb. 2015, www.linkedin.com/pulse/7-reasons-people-talk-over-top-others-anneli-blundell/.

Brady, Jeff. "Heading to Florida to Help Cover This Terrible Crime with My NPR & WLRN Colleagues... Heart Breaking on a Day Meant to Celebrate Love." https://Lnkd.in/DRvaAZJ. LinkedIn, 14 Feb. 2018, www.linkedin.com/feed/update/urn:li:activity:6369710446655598592/.

"Cup of Joe," Interview by Joe Donilon of Portland, OR KGW Channel 8 with Peter Sagel and Bill Kurtis, July 1, 2016

"Family Of Muslim Marine Recruit Speaks Out About His Death. Broad Jurisdiction of U.S. Border Patrol Raises Concerns about Racial Profiling" WBUR News, WBUR, 1 Aug. 2017, www.wbur.org/hereand-now/2017/08/01/raheel-siddiqui-marine-death.

PLEDGE: The Public Radio Fund Drive

"Guidance on The Use Of 'Disturbing' Videos And Audio." NPR Ethics Handbook, 11 Aug. 2015, ethics.npr.org/memos-from-memmott/guidance-on-the-use-of-disturbing-videos-and-audio-2/.

Kern, Jonathan, "*Sound Reporting*: The NPR Guide to Journalism and Production," University of Chicago Press, 2008, pg. 122

Lickteig, Steve. "Voice-Recognition Technology Will Kill All Things Considered. Here's What Will Take Its Place." *Slate* Magazine, 2 June 2016, www.slate.com/articles/technology/technology/2016/06/voice_recognition_technology_will_kill_all_things_considered_here_s_what.html.

McCauley, Michael P., "NPR: The Trials and Triumphs of National Public Radio" Columbia University Press, 2005, pg 128

"Pledge Drive Training for Public Radio and Television." Prezi.com, Goal-Busters Consulting, 30 Aug. 2017, prezi.com/qnwidgkpnpf7/pledge-drive-training-for-public-radio-and-television/.

Sabatier, Julie. "Brooke Gladstone on '*The Trouble with Reality*'." Oregon Public Broadcasting, 9 Nov. 2017, www.opb.org/radio/programs/thinkoutloud/segment/brooke-gladstone-interview-trouble-with-reality/.

Stamberg, Susan, "Every Night at 5," National Public Radio, Random House, 1982

"This Community Reporter Has Covered 3 Mass Shootings In 3 Years." NPR, 15 Feb. 2018, www.npr.org/2018/02/15/586172079/this-community-reporter-has-covered-3-mass-shootings-in-3-years.

Triscut. "Do You Think That Most TV Talk Show Hosts and News Reporters Interrupt Their Guests Too Often ?" Yahoo! Answers, 2008, answers.yahoo.com/question/index?qid=20090117135909AAAbnCD.

Van den Abeele, Christiane. "Pitch Training Manual. KPFT," 25 Jan. 2016, www.kpft.org/documents/15pitchbook.pdf, pg 19

Wayne, Teddy. "'NPR Voice' Has Taken Over the Airwaves." The New York Times, 21 Dec. 2017, www.nytimes.com/2015/10/25/fashion/npr-voice-has-taken-over-the-airwaves.html

Engagement

Donor Development Strategies, 16 June 2018, donordevo.com/.

Greenspun, Philip. "Public Radio Fund Drives." Philip Greenspun's Weblog, 22 June 2009, blogs.harvard.edu/philg/2009/06/22/public-radio-fund-drives/.

IRS 990, "Return or Organization Exempt from Income Tax." Oregon Public Broadcasting, Guidestar, 2013, pp. 26., www.guidestar.org/FinDocuments/2014/930/814/2014-930814638-0b226ec9-9.pdf.

Jensen, Elizabeth. "Show Producers at WNYC Turn to Digital Platforms to Add Fresh Voices, Engage Younger Audiences." *Current*, 16 Feb. 2015, current.org/2014/04/show-producers-at-wnyc-turn-to-digital-platforms-to-add-fresh-voices-engage-younger-audiences/.

KERA timestamp 18 Apr. 2016 1158 CST

Kerr, Antionette. "How NPR and PBS Engage Digital Audiences (An #Npcomm Showdown)." Kivi's Nonprofit Communications Blog, 20 July 2016, www.nonprofitmarketingguide.com/blog/2016/07/20/how-npr-and-pbs-engage-digital-audiences-an-npcomm-showdown/.

Kramer, Melody. "Putting the Public into Public Media Membership." Nieman Lab, 13 July 2015, www.niemanlab.org/2015/07/putting-the-public-in-to-public-media-membership/.

Kramer, Melody. "What, Exactly, Does It Mean to Be a Member of a Public Radio Station? Can That Definition Expand?" Nieman Lab, 15 May 2015, www.niemanlab.org/2015/05/what-exactly-does-it-mean-to-be-a-member-of-a-public-radio-station-can-that-definition-expand/.

LaBarre, Suzanne. "Why We're Shutting Off Our Comments." Popular Science, 24 Sept. 2013, www.popsci.com/science/article/2013-09/why-were-shutting-our-comments.

Merrill, Donald, "MyData," GoogleDocs Public Radio Survey, June 2017, Portland, OR

NPR's David Green generally promoting station support, run by KSKA, timestamp 13 Apr. 2016 0659 AKST

NPR's Peter Sagel's announcing the legal station ID for KRCU, timestamp 7 Apr. 2016 2359 CST

O'Shea, Chris. "NPR Is Closing Its Comments Section." *Adweek*, 17 Aug. 2016, www.adweek.com/digital/npr-is-closing-its-comments-section/.

Public Insight Network. American Public Media, www.publicinsightnetwork.org/.

Rayner, Ken, and Cridland, James. "When Radio Stations Take Calls, Who Takes Responsibility for Dumping Calls." Quora, 12 Jan. 2011, www.quora. com/When-radio-stations-take-listener-calls-who-takes-responsibility-for-dumping-calls-when-caller-statements-might-contravene-broadcasting-laws-and-regulations.

Reed, Americus, et al. "How to Convince People to Donate Time." Knowledge@Wharton, 8 June 2015, knowledge.wharton.upenn.edu/article/how-to-convince-people-to-donate-time/.

Schneider, Marlene. "Public Broadcasting Major Giving Initiative Direct Mail Sample Letters."" CPB, 14 Dec. 2007, majorgivingnow.org/downloads/doc/letter_templates.doc.

Schneider, Marlene. "Q&A: Greater Public Board Chair Paul Jacobs on the Future of Public Radio." Greater Public, 28 Apr. 2015, go.greaterpublic.org/blog/2015/04/qa-greater-public-board-chair-paul-jacobs-on-the-future-of-public-radio/.

Staff. "Door To Door." Wisconsin Public Radio, 11 Mar. 2016, www.wpr.org/door-door.

The Top 25 Wealthiest Zip Codes in Wisconsin–Map (2015). Zipdatamaps.com, 2015, www.zipdatamaps.com/top-25-wealthiest-zipcodes-in-wisconsin.php.

Wendt, Ann Phi. "Online Engagement: the Savior of Public Radio?" Ann Phi-Wendt Marketing Communications Manager Public Radio International (PRI)–Ppt Download." SlidePlayer, Public Radio International, 2007, slideplayer.com/slide/4743856/.

"WGBH Deploys the RedPoint Convergent Marketing Platform ™ to Engage Its next Generation of Donors and Transform Public Media Marketing Nationwide." RedPoint Case Study, 11 Oct. 2016, pp. 1–4.

"What does the public think about public radio," www.colemaninsights.com/wp-content/uploads/2017/06/What-Does-The-Public-Think-About-Public-Radio-Coleman-Insights-2017.pdf

Wilson, Josh. "Survey Results: #Newsroom #Engagement Programs among Nonprofit Newsrooms," October 2016.... Https://T.co/WmXtOomuVd Pic. twitter.com/SXKXD0zlxH." Twitter, Twitter, 25 Oct. 2016, twitter.com/MrJoshuaWilson/status/790707115736244224. Original link–http://watershed-

mediaproject.net/2016/10/24/survey-of-newsroom-public-engagement-pro-
grams-october-2016/–Rotted

Zomorodi, Manoush. "Self-Help as a Publishing Strategy." Nieman Lab, Dec.
2017, www.niemanlab.org/2017/12/self-help-as-a-publishing-strategy/.

Chapter 6 – Drives and Elements

Bell, Robert Platt. "Does Public Broadcasting Need Your Tote Bag Money?" 10
May 2012, livingstingy.blogspot.com/2012/05/does-public-broadcasting-
need-your-tote.html.

Beth Bowsky," Policy Specialist, Council of Non Profits, email conversation
with the author, 9 Dec. 2016

Brooks, Jeff. "Those Awful Public Radio Pledge Drives: Self-Fulfilling
Prophecy?" *Future Fundraising Now*, 5 Nov. 2009,
www.futurefund-raisingnow.com/future-fundraising/2009/11/those-
awful-public-ra-dio-pledge-drives-selffulfilling-prophecy.html.

Brown, Kelly Williams. "How to Survive a Public Radio Membership Drive."
The Daily Beast, 11 May 2014, www.thedailybeast.com/how-to-survive-a-
public-radio-membership-drive.

Bunting, Sarah D. "Pledge-Driving Me Nuts." Tomato Nation, 15 May 2007,
tomatonation.com/culture-and-criticism/pledge-driving-me-nuts/.

Colvin, Leonard E. "The New Journal and Guide Newspaper." 14 Apr. 2016,
www.kolumnmagazine.com/2016/04/14/nsu-station-hosts-first-membership-
drive/.

"Commission Policy Concerning the Nature of Non-Commercial Nature of
Educational Broadcasting Stations." 28 Mar. 1984, pp. 261., apps.fcc.gov/
edocs_public/attachmatch/FCC-84-105A1.pdf.

"Donors Demand Clearer View of Station Reality." Current, 8 Apr. 2012, cur-
rent.org/2003/09/donors-demand-clearer-view-of-station-reality/.

Eddy, Max. "Is Max Alive? Have Ira Glass Confront Your Friends!" July 2008,
ismaxalive.blogspot.com/2008/07/have-ira-glass-confront-your-friends.
html.

"Enterprising Non-Profits: A Toolkit for Social Entrepreneurs," j. Gregory Dees,
Jed Emerson, Peter Economy, Wiley & Sons, 2002, pg 215

PLEDGE: The Public Radio Fund Drive

Gaskin, Kendra. "Making Pledge Drives Not Just Bearable, But Memorable Too." NPR, 19 Oct. 2013, www.npr.org/sections/npr-extra/2013/10/19/237652158/making-pledge-drives-not-just-bearable-but-memorable-too.

Glass, Ira. "Ira Glass Quotes." BrainyQuote, Xplore, www.brainyquote.com/quotes/ira_glass_686377.

Grehn, Kim. "Ebbing Loyalty," 19 Feb. 2015, kgrehnblog.blogspot.com/2015/02/ebbing-loyalty.html.

Hodgson, Jim. "Fifteen Dead in WABE Public Radio Pledge Drive." The Atlanta Banana, 1 May 2014, www.atlbanana.com/fifteen-dead-in-wabe-public-radio-pledge-drive/.

Holp, Karen. "Voting Is Open To Support KGOU." KGOU, 27 Mar. 2016, kgou.org/post/voting-open-support-kgou.

Hood, Michael. "Without Your Support." The Stranger, Index Newspapers LLC, 11 Oct. 2007, www.thestranger.com/seattle/Content?oid=413441.

"Introduction to PledgeDriver." PledgeDriver®, On Air Fundraising, 16 June 2018, www.onairfundraising.com/pledgedriver/.

Johnson, Megan. "Not Another @*$! Pledge Drive." NPR, 22 Oct. 2013, www.npr.org/sections/npr-extra/2013/10/22/236245578/not-another-pledge-drive.

Merlan, Anna. "WNYC's Drunk Fundraising Pledge Drive Was Delightful." Village Voice, 28 Feb. 2014, www.villagevoice.com/2014/02/28/wnycs-drunk-fundraising-pledge-drive-was-delightful/.

Merrill, Donald, "MyData," GoogleDocs Public Radio Survey, June 2017, Portland, OR

"Public Radio Association of Development Officers." Membership–PRADO , 25 May 2018, www.pradoweb.org/.

Sefton, Dru. "Pet-Themed Fund Drives Spur Pledges from Animal-Loving Listeners." Current, 1 Dec. 2014, current.org/2013/12/pet-themed-fund-drives-spur-pledges-from-animal-loving-listeners/.

Staff. "LOOK: KPCC Hosts Lose Their Damn Minds Over Pledge Drive." The Huffington Post, 7 Dec. 2017, www.huffingtonpost.com/2013/10/16/kpcc-pledge-drive-parody-_n_4111547.html.

Staff. "NPR Network Pledge Drive Proposed; Schiller Says No." All Access, 30
Mar. 2009, www.allaccess.com/net-news/archive/story/55408/npr-network-
pledge-drive-proposed-schiller-says-no.

Stein, Michael. "Solving the Riddle of Donor Fatigue for Nonprofit Organizations." Community, TechSoup, 21 Mar. 2017, forums.techsoup.org/cs/com-
munity/b/tsblog/archive/2017/03/21/solving-the-riddle-of-donor-fatigue.
aspx.

Sutton, John. "Listener Perceptions of Telemarketing." *RadioSutton*, 18
July 2007, radiosutton.blogspot.com/search?q=listener%2Bpercep-
tions%2Bof%2Btelemarketing.

Sutton, John. "More Expense, Less On-Air Fundraising?" *RadioSutton*, 2 Aug.
2007, radiosutton.blogspot.com/search?q=More%2BExpense%2C%2B-
Less%2BOn-Air%2BFundraising%3F%2B.

Sutton, John. "Public Radio 2018: The Inevitability of NPR Raising Money
Directly from Listeners ." *RadioSutton*, 8 Apr. 2013, radiosutton.blogspot.
com/search?q=Public%2BRadio%2B2018%3A%2BThe%2BInevitabili-
ty%2Bof%2BNPR%2BRaising%2BMoney%2BDirectly%2Bfrom%2BLis-
teners%2B.

Thomas, June. "The 10 Cunning Ways Public Radio Stations Convince You to
Give Them Money." *Slate* Magazine, *Slate*, 2 Mar. 2009, www.slate.com/
articles/arts/culturebox/2009/03/lets_get_those_phones_ringing.html.

"Wisconsin Public Radio Listener Survey." pp. 1–30., 2013, www.markettrends-
research.com/wisconsin_public_radio_listener_survey.htm.

The Long and Short of It

Boyce, Cary. "Thank You for Adding a 'Power Hour' to Spring Pledge Drive!"
Spokane Public Radio, 26 Apr. 2017, spokanepublicradio.org/post/thank-
you-adding-power-hour-spring-pledge-drive.

Burdett, Bruce. "Fund Drive Saves WMVY Radio; Will Stream Live for Now."
EastBayRI.com, 30 Jan. 2013, eastbayri.com/stories/fund-drive-saves-wm-
vy-radio-will-stream-livNWPR 2100 $268-thousand dollars.e-for-now,3491.

Callahan, Robert. "Donate Now to End Our Torment." Capecodtimes.
com, 23 Dec. 2015, www.capecodtimes.com/article/20151228/OPIN-
ION/151229729.

PLEDGE: The Public Radio Fund Drive

Chinn, Becky. "Public Radio and TV Donors Expect to Give at Year-End." Greater Public, 10 Nov. 2015, go.greaterpublic.org/blog/2015/11/public-radio-and-tv-donors-expect-to-give-at-year-end/.

Clayton, Jay. "The Long and Short of Eliminating Pledge Drives." Greater Public, 20 May 2015, go.greaterpublic.org/blog/2015/05/the-long-and-short-of-eliminating-pledge-drives/.

Conner, Molly. "89.1 WBOI's Spring Warp Drive." Northeast Indiana Public Radio, 23 Feb. 2017, wboi.org/post/891-wbois-spring-warp-drive#stream/0.

"Delmarva Public Radio Hosts 'A Little More' Fund Drive June 25-26." Salisbury University–Academics @ SU–Academics @ SU, 25 June 2015, www.salisbury.edu/news/article.html?id=6354.

Emerson, Patrick. "Economic Science of Charitable Giving." Oregon Business Report, 19 May 2010, oregonbusinessreport.com/2010/05/economic-science-of-charitable-giving/.

Falk, Tyler. "Community Radio Stations Prepare Coordinated Year-End Fundraiser." *Current*, 17 Oct. 2016, current.org/2016/10/community-radio-stations-prepare-coordinated-year-end-fundraiser/.

Falk, Tyler. "WBUR's New Twist on Shorter Pledge Drives Pays Off." Current, 22 Apr. 2016, current.org/2016/04/wburs-new-twist-on-shorter-pledge-drives-pays-off/.

Gullickson, Jim. "It's Pledge Drive Time!" KSMU, pp. 1–7., www.mnsu.edu/kmsufm/newsletter/kmsu_apr_14.pdf.

Hoover, Carl. "Waco Public Radio Station KWBU Looking for 'Power Morning' Boost Thursday." WacoTrib.com, 22 Feb. 2017, www.wacotrib.com/blogs/entertainment_in_waco/waco-public-radio-station-kwbu-looking-for-power-morning-boost/article_a7008031-ff07-5bfd-92d8-57eef8acb9ba.html.

Jeffery, Michelle. "Three-Day Pledge Drive Will Fight Hunger And Promote Nutrition Education," vprblog.blogspot.com/2012/08/three-day-pledge-drive-will-fight.html.

Jensen, Elizabeth. "In Tight Times, PBS Leans on Pledge Drives." The New York Times, 14 Mar. 2011, www.nytimes.com/2011/03/14/business/media/14pledge.html?_r=0.

Johnson, Kelly. "Capital Public Radio Capitalizes on Spirit of Giving for Pledge Drive ." Bizjournals.com, The Business Journals, 13 Dec. 2012, www.

bizjournals.com/sacramento/blog/kelly-johnson/2012/12/capital-public-radio-short-pledge-drive.html.

Johnson, Steve. "Low-Key Pledge Drive Finds Success At Wbez." Tribunedigital-Chicagotribune, 6 Mar. 2000, articles.chicagotribune.com/2000-03-06/features/0005190062_1_pledge-public-radio-hillside-strangler.

Keenan, Michelle. "1-Day Drive: Help WCQS Stay on Track and Win an IPad!" Blue Ridge Public Radio, 21 May 2014, bpr.org/post/1-day-drive-help-wcqs-stay-track-and-win-ipad.

KRCU4 timestamp 7 Apr. 2016 2200 CST

KTTZ timestamp 15 Apr. 2016 1519 CST

KUSP1 timestamp 15 Apr. 2016 1512 PST

KVNF timestamp 15 Apr. 2016 1600 MST

KWGS1a timestamp 6 Apr. 2016 1618 CST

"MPBN Nets 475 New Members during One-Day Pledge Drive." Bangor Daily News, 15 Feb. 2016, bangordailynews.com/bdn-maine/community/2135478/.

"NET Radio Trailblazer." Netnebraska.org/Basic-Page/Foundations/Net-Radio-Trailblazer, 16 June 2018, netnebraska.org/basic-page/foundations/net-radio-trailblazer.

"NWPR Launches Super Thursday Campaign." WSU Insider, Washington State University, 20 Oct. 2009, news.wsu.edu/2009/10/20/nwpr-launches-super-thursday-campaign/.

"Programs Available through Automated Delivery." PRX – Help Desk, 8 June 2018, help.prx.org/hc/en-us/articles/202988670-List-of-programs-delivered-via-SubAuto.

Rodriguez, Rosa Salter. "NIPR Unveils New Digs," The Journal Gazette, 12 Apr. 2017, www.journalgazette.net/news/local/20170412/nipr-unveils-new-digs.

"Salt Lake City's KCPW Cites Program Costs, Duplication in Canceling NPR Programs." Current, 16 Feb. 2015, current.org/2013/06/salt-lake-citys-kcpw-cites-program-costs-duplication-in-cancelling-npr-programs/.

Staff. "Do Those Pledge Drives on PBS Seem Longer to You? That's Because They Are." TVWeek, 14 May 2011, www.tvweek.com/broadcast/2011/03/do-those-pledge-drives-on-pbs/.

Staff. "The Next Standard, the Campaign for Minnesota Public Radio Fact Sheet." 22 June 2004, pp. 1–2., access.minnesota.publicradio.org/features/040622_capcampaign/press/capital_campaign_fact_sheet.pdf.

Stoltz, Helen. "KMST Spring Membership Drive to Coincide with NPR." News and Events, 28 Mar. 2016, news.mst.edu/2016/03/kmst-spring-membership-drive-to-coincide-with-npr/.

Sutton, John. "Difficult Pledge Drive Days Ahead?" *RadioSutton*, 2 Feb. 2015, radiosutton.blogspot.com/search?q=Difficult%2BPledge%2BDrive%2B-Days%2BAhead.

"The Bringing Music to Life Instrument Drive." Colorado Public Radio, www.cpr.org/community/instrument-drive.

WCBE timestamp 9 Apr. 2016 1319 EST

Wilke, Phil. "KPR Fall Membership Drive Falls Short of $250,000 Goal." The University of Kansas, 27 Oct. 2015, today.ku.edu/kpr-fall-membership-drive-falls-short-250000-goal.

"Year-End Giving Trends." Charity Navigator, 1 Nov. 2011, www.charitynavigator.org/index.cfm?bay=content.view&cpid=1302.

Breaks and Pitches

"*Annoyance with Fundraising.*" The Public Radio Tracking Study, 2004, pp. 7., walrusresearch.com/images/Annoyance_with_Fund_Raising.pdf.

bluedaniel. "What the Sharing Economy Takes," Metafilter, 6 Nov. 2003, www.metafilter.com/29412/McNewsFilter.

Coulson, Melanie. "Post-Election Year-End Scripts and Pitch Points." 18 Nov. 2016, go.greaterpublic.org/blog/post-election-year-end-scripts-and-pitch-points.

"History: On Again, Off Again." Spokane Public Radio, www.spokanepublicradio.org/history-again-again.

"How about Sharing Your Favorite Pledge Drive Pitch Script? What Do You Do to Make the Phones Ring?" r/NPR." Reddit, 2015, www.reddit.com/r/NPR/comments/2ecuau/how_about_sharing_your_favorite_pledge_drive/.

"Introduction to PledgeDriver." PledgeDriver®, On Air Fundraising, 16 June 2018, www.onairfundraising.com/pledgedriver/.

KEMC timestamp 11 Apr. 2016 0736 MST

Bibliography

KEMC timestamp 11 Apr. 2016 1530 MST

KHSU–Diverse Public Radio, 26 Apr. 2014, www.pradoweb.org/vertical/
sites/%7BFFCC657E-D16A-4444-8CFE-FEDEFFFD712D%7D/uploads/
French_Press_-_Pitch_Points.docx.

McClanahan, Kristie. "Drinking With St. Louis Public Radio's Spring Pledge
Drive." Riverfront Times, 2 Apr. 2016, www.riverfronttimes.com/music-
blog/2012/03/20/drinking-with-st-louis-public-radios-spring-pledge-drive.

Merrill, Donald, "MyData," GoogleDocs Public Radio Survey, June 2017, Portland, OR

Moore, John. "Public Radio Pledge Drive Don'ts." *Brand Autopsy*, Feb. 2016,
brandautopsy.com/2004/03/public_radio_pl.html.

"Pledge Drive Training for Public Radio and Television." Issuu, 17 May 2016,
issuu.com/goalbusters/docs/pledge_training_manual.

"PRI InfoSite, ON-AIR FUNDRAISING and PROMOTIONS." PRI InfoSite |
STATION TOOLS, 16 June 2018, www2.pri.org/infosite/fundraising/tim-
ingscues.cfm.

Sutton, John. "The Well-Chosen Word Matters in Pledge Drives Too ." *RadioSutton*, 22 Apr. 2015, radiosutton.blogspot.com/search?q=The%2B-
Well%2BChosen%2BWord.

Thomas, Thomas J, and Clifford, Theresa R. "Individual Giving to Public Radio
Stations." pp. 15.

Goals

Berman, Jillian. "Public Media CEO's Salary Pales Compared to Million-Dol-
lar Packages at Other Nonprofits." *MarketWatch*, 11 July 2017, www.
marketwatch.com/story/public-media-ceos-salary-is-modest-com-
pared-to-these-million-dollar-packages-at-other-nonprofits-2017-07-11.

Croson, Rachel, and Shang, Jen. "Limits of Social Influence on the Voluntary
Provision of Public Goods : Evidence from Field Experiments." Social
Comparison and Charitable Contribution, Indiana University, citeseerx.ist.
psu.edu/viewdoc/download?doi=10.1.1.583.7541&rep=rep1&type=pdf, pg
2

Desloge, Rick. Bizjournals.com, The Business Journals, 17 Aug. 2008, www.
bizjournals.com/stlouis/stories/2008/08/18/story6.html.

Emerson, Patrick. "Economic Science of Charitable Giving." Oregon Business Report, 19 May 2010, oregonbusinessreport.com/2010/05/economic-science-of-charitable-giving/.

Falk, Tyler. "As It Defines Relationship with Stations, NPR Gains Board Approval for Price Hike." *Current*, 24 Feb. 2017, current.org/2017/02/npr-pro-poses-new-dues-structure-strategy-for-stronger-future-with-stations/.

Figueroa, Alyssa. "Why Some Public Radio Supporters Won't Be Donating to NPR This Year." Alternet, 3 Jan. 2013, www.alternet.org/media/why-some-public-radio-supporters-wont-be-donating-npr-year.

Frame, Randy. "CT Classic: Did Oral Roberts Go Too Far?" Christian History, Learn the History of Christianity & the Church, 15 Dec. 2009, www.christianitytoday.com/ct/2009/decemberweb-only/151-21.0.html.

Garrison, Chad. "Radio Active: What Has Patty Wente Done to Create Such a Meltdown at KWMU?" Riverfront Times, 14 July 2018, www.riverfronttimes.com/stlouis/radio-active-what-has-patty-wente-done-to-create-such-a-meltdown-at-kwmu/Content?oid=2481926.

Graham, Tim. "High NPR Star Salaries Curb the Appeal of Small-Dollar Donations." *NewsBusters*, 23 July 2013, www.newsbusters.org/blogs/nb/tim-graham/2013/07/23/high-npr-star-salaries-curb-appeal-small-dollar-donations.

Hawaii Public Radio (HPR) – "Fall Fund Drive Surpasses Million Dollars in Pledges." Hawaii Meals On Wheels (HMoW)–Kaimuki–Honolulu, Hawaii News, 25 Oct. 2013, www.kaimukihawaii.com/news/201311/5075.html.

Hendrix, Steve. "Public Radio Fundraisers Dial It Back." The Washington Post, WP Company, 14 Feb. 2009, www.washingtonpost.com/wp-dyn/content/article/2009/02/13/AR2009021303270.html.

Hoover, Carl. "KWBU Radio Station Prepares for Pledge Drive Blitz." WacoTrib.com, 14 Feb. 2014, www.wacotrib.com/entertainment/accesswaco/tv_and_radio/kwbu-radio-station-prepares-for-pledge-drive-blitz/article_fb-c896ea-24f7-5cf3-8986-f63ccfa8144c.html.

Johnson, Kelly. "Capital Public Radio Falls Short of Pledge Goal." Bizjournals.com, The Business Journals, 19 Dec. 2012, www.bizjournals.com/sacramento/blog/kelly-johnson/2012/12/capital-public-radio-pledge-drive-goal.html.

KFAE timestamp 19 Apr. 2016 0506 PST

Kickstarter, 17 June 2018, www.kickstarter.com/help/search?ut-f8=%E2%9C%93&term=what%2Bare%2Bstretch%2Bgoals%3F.

Merrill, Donald, "MyData," GoogleDocs Public Radio Survey, June 2017, Portland, OR

Public Radio Today 2013 – "How America Listens to Radio." Public Radio Today, pp. 1–8., www.arbitron.com/downloads/PublicRadioToday2013_ExecutiveSummary.pdf.

Shang, Jen, and Croson, Rachel. "A Field Experiment in Charitable Contribution; The impact of social information on the voluntary provision of public goods." The Economic Journal, 2 Aug. 2014, econweb.ucsd.edu/~jandreon/PhilanthropyAndFundraising/Volume%202/27%20Shang%20Croson%202009.pdf,+pg+1428.

Staff. "Basic Memberships: More Trouble than they're Worth?" Current, 22 Apr. 2013, current.org/2012/12/basic-memberships-more-trouble-than-theyre-worth/.

Staff. "Community Service Grant (CSG) Eligibility." SECTION 1. ELIGIBILITY, CPB, 25 Jan. 2011, isis.cpb.org/ISIS_Help_Files/SECTION_1_ELIGIBILITY.htm.

Staff. "Michigan Radio Pledge Drive Sets Spring Record." Ann Arbor News, 26 Mar. 2010, www.annarbor.com/entertainment/michigan-radio-pledge-drive-sets-spring-record/.

Staff. "Salt Lake City's KCPW Hits Fundraising Goal to Keep Programming." Current, 3 July 2014, current.org/2014/07/salt-lake-citys-kcpw-hits-fund-raising-goal-to-keep-programming/.

"State's Public Radio Stations Meet, Surpass Fund-Raising Goals." Plainview Daily Herald, 3 Nov. 2003, www.myplainview.com/news/article/State-s-public-radio-stations-meet-surpass-8857263.php.

"Support Capital Public Radio." Donate to Capital Public Radio–Capital Public Radio, 17 June 2018, community.capradio.org/site/Donation2;jsessionid=00000000.app216a?df_id=1520&1520.donation=form1&mfc_pref=T&NONCE_TOKEN=EFA291CDC6A256557C2CBABFCA506E23.

Sutton, John. "Fundraising Puzzler." RadioSutton, 7 Jan. 2007, radiosutton.blogspot.com/search?q=fundraising%2Bpuzzler.

Sutton, John. "Quiz #4 Answers." RadioSutton, 16 May 2006, radiosutton.blogspot.com/search?q=someone%2Belse.

Sutton, John. "Renewal or Resurrection." RadioSutton, 13 Apr. 2006, radiosutton.blogspot.com/search?q=renewal%2Bor%2Bresurrection.

Sutton, John. "Transition for NPR Highlights Major Industry Issues–Part 1: Financial ." RadioSutton, 3 Oct. 2013, radiosutton.blogspot.com/search?q=salaries.

Wilke, Phil. "KPR Fall Membership Drive Falls Short of $250,000 Goal." The University of Kansas, 27 Oct. 2015, today.ku.edu/kpr-fall-membership-drive-falls-short-250000-goal.

Wilke, Phil. "KPR Wraps up Spring Membership Drive with More than $270K in Pledges." The University of Kansas, 19 Apr. 2016, today.ku.edu/kpr-wraps-spring-membership-drive-more-270000-pledges.

Zhao, Jijun, et al. "An Agent Based Simulation Methodology for Analyzing Public Radio Membership Campaigns." *Information Technology for Economics and Management*, pp. 1–34., www.item.woiz.polsl.pl/issue4.1/pdf/public-goods_revised.pdf. pg 4

Language

albionwood. "Effective Pledge Drive Techniques." Publicradio, 3 Oct. 2007, publicradio.livejournal.com/13911.html.

Ballard, Ford. "Welcome to KRWG 90.7 FM's Membership Drive!" PRADO, 24 Mar. 2009, www.pradoweb.org/vertical/sites/%7BFFCC657E-D16A-4444-8CFE-FEDEFFFD712D%7D/uploads/%7B4E08B085-5D3E-4250-A91B-69D6293301DE%7D.DOC.

"Bene Gesserit–The Voice." Wikipedia, the Free Encyclopedia, taggedwiki.zubiaga.org/new_content/9a834edfba4681245e617d96e0b37559#The_ Voice.

Bobek, Patricia. "KCSB Fundraiser Falls Short of Goal." The *Daily Nexus*, 23 Nov. 2004, dailynexus.com/2004-11-23/kcsb-fundraiser-falls-short-of-goal/. Cooper, Joseph, et al. "'Members Only' Call-In: Tell Us Why You Support WLRN April 2016 Edition." WLRN, 13 Apr. 2016, wlrn.org/post/members-only-call-tell-us-why-you-support-wlrn-april-2016-edition.

Clinton, William, *Washington Post*, Grand Jury Testimony, Part 4, Sept 9, 1998

"Effective use of premiums." PRI InfoSite, STATION TOOLS, 17 June 2018, www2.pri.org/Infosite/fundraising/use_of_premiums.cfm.

Fisher, Robert J. "An Empathy Helping Perspective on Consumers' Responses to Fundraising Appeals." 1 Oct. 2008, www.jstor.org/stable/10.1086/586909?seq=1#page_scan_tab_contents.

Folkenflik, David. "Totenberg On Helms Comment: 'It Was A Stupid Remark.'" NPR, 26 Oct. 2010, www.npr.org/sections/thetwo-way/2010/10/26/130838719/totenberg-on-helms-remark-stupidest-thing-she-s-said-on-tv.

Fortune, Gwendoline. "KUT." *Keeping the Public in Public Radio*, 17 Apr. 2010, keeppublicradiopublic.com/kut-austin/.

Fortune, Gwendoline. "WGBH." *Keeping the Public in Public Radio*, 17 Apr. 2010, keeppublicradiopublic.com/wgbh/.

Gibbs, Constance. "Robin Roberts' 'Bye, Felicia' Is the Ultimate Way to Dismiss Omarosa." NY Daily News." Nydailynews.com, New York Daily News, 14 Dec. 2017, www.nydailynews.com/life-style/robin-roberts-bye-felicia-peak-dismiss-omarosa-article-1.3698767.

Goalbusters Consulting. "Pledge Drive Training for Public Radio and Television." Prezi.com, 30 Aug. 2017, prezi.com/qnwidgkpnpf7/pledge-drive-training-for-public-radio-and-television/.

Grehn, Kim. "Eliminating Seams (Building Audience)." LinkedIn, 25 July 2015, www.linkedin.com/pulse/eliminating-seams-building-audience-kim-grehn.

Grehn, Kim. "Working Together in Public Radio: Does It Matter?" LinkedIn, 16 June 2016, www.linkedin.com/pulse/working-together-public-radio-does-matter-kim-grehn.

Heinze, Jamey. "More Fundraising Lessons from NPR's 'Membership' Drives–CDS Global." CDS Global Canada, 5 Feb. 2015, www.cdsglobal.ca/blog/more-fundraising-lessons-from-nprs-membership-drives/.

Hendrix, Steve. "Public Radio Fundraisers Dial It Back." The Washington Post, WP Company, 14 Feb. 2009, www.washingtonpost.com/wp-dyn/content/article/2009/02/13/AR2009021303270.html.

Herstein, Olivia. "CSUN Today." California State University, Northridge, 3 Apr. 2017, csunshinetoday.csun.edu/arts-and-culture/kcsns-own-radio-legend-promotes-the-legendary-and-the-new/.

Hingsbergen, John. "Feedback on Music Segment and 'Begging, Begging, Begging.'" WEKU, 6 Mar. 2017, weku.fm/post/feedback-music-segment-and-begging-begging-begging.

"Is There a Word or Term to Describe a Statement That Implies a Question so Sufficiently That the Question Is Not Actually Included?" English Language & Usage Stack Exchange, Nov. 2013, english.stackexchange.com/questions/138488/is-there-a-word-or-term-to-describe-a-statement-that-implies-a-question-so-suffi.

"Jimmy Kimmel Live! Celebrities Read Mean Tweets #11." ABC, 25 Sept. 2017, abc.go.com/shows/jimmy-kimmel-live/video/mean-tweets/VDKA4077416.

Kernis, Jay. "Jay Kernis' 2006 Advice to NPR: 'I Want the Air to Sing.'" Current, 25 Aug. 2015, current.org/2015/08/jay-kernis-2006-advice-to-npr-i-want-the-air-to-sing/.

La Rose, Lauren. "CBC Rebrands Radio Program 'Q' as 'q'." The Globe and Mail, 14 May 2018, www.theglobeandmail.com/arts/cbc-rebrands-radio-program-q-as-q/article23969246/.

Merrill, Donald, "MyData," GoogleDocs Public Radio Survey, June 2017, Portland, OR

Morales, Fernando. "Diamond Shreddies, an Unbelievable Rebranding Case Study." Fameable Online Marketing, 30 Aug. 2016, fameable.com/diamond-shreddies-rebranding-case-study/144/.

Paul, Sonia. "Pew: Older Adults Show Faster Adoption of Internet." MediaShift, 2 July 2015, mediashift.org/2015/07/pew-older-adults-show-faster-adoption-of-internet/.

"Pitch Training Manual." 1-15 pitchbook, 25 Jan. 2016, pp. 1–39., kpft.org/documents/15pitchbook.pdf.

Plato, "The Republic." translated by Benjamin Jowett, Catharine Maria Sedgwick (Sedgwick, Catharine Maria, 1789-1867), The Online Books Page, Project Gutenberg, 22 May 2008, onlinebooks.library.upenn.edu/webbin/gutbook/lookup?num=150.

"Pledge Drive Training for Public Radio and Television." Issuu, 17 May 2016, issuu.com/goalbusters/docs/pledge_training_manual.

Rehm, Dana Davis. "What's In A Name?" NPR, 12 July 2010, www.npr.org/sections/inside/2010/07/12/128475395/npr-what-s-in-a-name.

Searls, Doc. "An Open Source Approach to Fixing Public Media Funding," Home, Linux Journal, 29 May 2007, www.linuxjournal.com/node/1000231.

Simpson, April. "KPCC Case Study: Using the 'Dark Arts of Digital Marketing' to Convert Donors." *Current*, 3 Aug. 2016, current.org/2016/08/kpcc-case-study-using-the-dark-arts-of-digital-marketing-to-convert-donors/.

Sutton, John. "Cliches R Us." *RadioSutton*, 20 Mar. 2009, radiosutton.blogspot.com/search?q=every%2Bdollar%2Bmatters.

Sutton, John. "The Impact of Sustaining Givers on Public Radio Fund Drives ." *RadioSutton*, 17 Feb. 2015, radiosutton.blogspot.com/2015/02/the-impact-of-sustaining-givers-on.html.

Thomas, June. "The 10 Cunning Ways Public Radio Stations Convince You to Give Them Money." Slate Magazine, Slate, 2 Mar. 2009, www.slate.com/articles/arts/culturebox/2009/03/lets_get_those_phones_ringing.html.

thora55. "The Fight for the Future of NPR." 18 Apr. 2016, 1327, www.metafilter.com/158715/The-fight-for-the-future-of-NPR#6487455.

WSGE timestamp 30 Apr. 2016 1112 EST

Listener Comments

"*Annoyance with Fundraising*." Walrus Research, 8 Oct. 2009, The Public Radio Tracking Study, 2004, pp. 7., walrusresearch.com/images/Annoyance_with_Fund_Raising.pdf.

Bode, Karl. "NPR, The Latest Website To Prevent You From Commenting Because It Simply Adores 'Relationships' And 'Conversation.'" Techdirt., 17 Aug. 2016, www.techdirt.com/articles/20160817/09172335265/npr-latest-website-to-prevent-you-commenting-because-it-simply-adores-relationships-conversation.shtml/.

"Brickbat Definition and Meaning." Collins English Dictionary, www.collinsdictionary.com/dictionary/english/brickbat.

Christel, Frank. *Kudos & Brickbats* Received From Listeners [Fall 2014 Edition]." Public Radio Tulsa, 24 Sept. 2014, publicradiotulsa.org/post/kudos-brickbats-received-listeners-fall-2014-edition.

Christel, Frank. "*Kudos & Brickbats* Received from Listeners During This
Spring Fund Drive." Public Radio Tulsa, 7 Apr. 2015, publicradiotulsa.org/
post/kudos-brickbats-received-listeners-during-spring-fund-drive.

Ellis, Justin. "What Happened after 7 News Sites Got Rid of Reader Comments." Nieman Lab, 16 Sept. 2015, www.niemanlab.org/2015/09/what-
happened-after-7-news-sites-got-rid-of-reader-comments/.

Folkenflik, David. "Journalists Ask Questions, Then Refuse to Answer Them."
15 Sept. 2001, niemanreports.org/articles/journalists-ask-questions-then-re-
fuse-to-answer-them/.

Hallahan, Kirk. "Strategic Framing." International Encyclopedia of Communication, 15 May 2007, pp. 1–5., www.pitt.edu/~mitnick/MESM10/HallahanS-
trategicFramingHallahan_ICE_051507.pdf.

Hedgpeth, Dana, and Jouvenal, Justin. "Suspect in Slaying of Two TV Station
Employees in SW Virginia Shoots Himself and Dies." The Washington
Post, WP Company, 26 Aug. 2015, www.washingtonpost.com/news/local/
wp/2015/08/26/tv-camera-crew-caught-in-active-shooter-situation-in-south-
west-virginia/?utm_term.

Manjoo, Farhad. "NPR Letters: The Tedious, Annoying Complaints of Public
Radio Listeners." *Slate* Magazine, 2 Mar. 2011, www.slate.com/articles/
life/a_fine_whine/2011/03/we_listen_to_npr_precisely_to_avoid_this_sort_
of_stupidity.html.

Merrill, Donald, "MyData," GoogleDocs Public Radio Survey, June 2017, Portland, OR

"*Open to the Public* 2014." Programming Comments, pp. 1–27., www.cpb.org/
files/reports/yourfeedback/2014_your_feedback.pdf.

O'Shea, Chris. "NPR Is Closing Its Comments Section." *Adweek*, 17 Aug. 2016,
www.adweek.com/fishbowlny/npr-is-closing-its-comments-section/383389.

Oxenford, David. "FCC Releases Order on Online Public Inspection File –
Answering Questions about Compliance with Radio's New Obligations."
Broadcast Law Blog, 21 Sept. 2017, www.broadcastlawblog.com/2016/02/
articles/fcc-releases-order-on-online-public-inspection-file-answering-ques-
tions-about-compliance-with-radios-new-obligations/.

Oxenford, David. "FCC To Consider Abolition of Requirement That Broadcasters Maintain Letters From the Public in Their Public Files – Moving Toward

the End of the Physical Public File?" *Broadcast Law Blog*, 5 May 2016, www.broadcastlawblog.com/2016/05/articles/fcc-to-consider-abolition-of-requirement-that-broadcasters-maintain-letters-from-the-public-in-their-public-files-moving-toward-the-end-of-the-physical-public-file/.

Pan, Zhongdang, and Kosicki, Gerald M. "Framing Analysis: An Approach to News Discourse." Political Communication, 1993, pp. 1–22., pdfs.semanticscholar.org/d356/ad4a6146fba5193fbdea2b1afdbbce8c8d39.pdf.

Reader, Bill, "Audience Feedback in the News Media," Routledge, Taylor & Francis, 2015, pg 3

Reader, Bill. "Air Mail: NPR Sees 'Community' in Letters from Listeners." VLex, *Journal of Broadcasting and Electronic Media*, 4 Dec. 2007, law-journals-books.vlex.com/vid/air-mail-npr-sees-letters-listeners-56258298.

Staff. "Two Police Wounded In Shoot-Out." Pew Research Center's Journalism Project, 11 Jan. 2010, www.journalism.org/2010/01/11/two-police-wounded-shootout/.

"*The Public and Broadcasting* (July 2008 Edition)." Federal Communications Commission, 3 Oct. 2017, www.fcc.gov/media/radio/public-and-broadcasting#CONTENTS.

Wahl-Jorgensen, Karin. "The Construction of the Public in Letters to the Editor." Philosophy of the Social Sciences, SAGE Journals, 1 Aug. 2002, journals.sagepub.com/doi/abs/10.1177/146488490200300203.

Welsh, Madeline. "Can Comment Sections Contain (Gasp!) Rational, Coherent, Civil Debate? Maybe? Sometimes?" Nieman Lab, 24 June 2015, www.niemanlab.org/2015/06/can-comment-sections-contain-gasp-rational-coherent-civil-debate-maybe-sometimes/?relatedstory.

WVAS-FM Public Radio Station Station Compliance: Certification Requirements." Open Meeting Requirements, 6 Nov. 2015, pp. 1–10., mediad.publicbroadcasting.net/p/wvas/files/wvas_cpb_compliance_documentation.pdf.

"Your Feedback Archive." CPB, 2015, www.cpb.org/open/.

Zamora, Amanda. "Comments Are Changing. Our Commitment to Audiences Shouldn't." Poynter, 15 Mar. 2017, www.poynter.org/2016/comments-are-changing-our-commitment-to-audiences-shouldnt/428399/.

Ziglar, Zig."Zig Ziglar Quotes." BrainyQuote, Xplore, www.brainyquote.com/quotes/zig_ziglar_173504.

The Human Touch

albionwood. "Effective Pledge Drive Techniques." Publicradio, 3 Oct. 2007, publicradio.livejournal.com/13911.html.

Aleksander, Irina. "Have Female Journalists Ended the Boys-on-the-Bus Era of Campaign Reporting?" Vogue, 26 May 2017, www.vogue.com/article/campaign-reporting-politics-female-journalists.

Greenspun, Philip. "Public Radio Fund Drives." Philip Greenspun's Weblog, Harvard University, 22 June 2009, blogs.harvard.edu/philg/2009/06/22/public-radio-fund-drives/.

KGLT timestamp 27 Mar. 2016 1730 MST

KUFM timestamp 18 Apr. 2016 1206 MST

Staff. "WUWM, WMSE Work Hard to Attract Cash, Listeners." Journal Sentinel, 25 May 2010, archive.jsonline.com/entertainment/tvradio/94888354.html.

WEAA timestamp 16 Apr. 2016 1532 EST

"WGBH TV & Radio Schedule." 18 June 2018, www.wgbh.org/schedule?-date=2018-06-18&type=radio&channel=89.7%2BWGBH.

Cheerleading

Baer, April. Twitter conversation with the author, 30 Sept, 2016

backseatpilot, "Public Radio Fundraising Changeup." *MetaFilter*, 1 Oct. 2012, ask.metafilter.com/225695/Public-Radio-Fundraising-Changeup.

clearlynuts, et al, "Is NPR Practicing Moral Hazard or Am I Freerider?," MetaFilter, 8 Apr. 2008, ask.metafilter.com/88258/Is-NPR-practicing-moral-hazard-or-am-I-freerider#1299487.

Greer, Jordan. "Chandler Parsons Calls out Trail Blazers on Twitter, Gets Torched by C.J. McCollum." Sporting News, 28 Jan. 2017, www.sportingnews.com/nba/news/chandler-parsons-cj-mccollum-twitter-trail-blazers-grizzlies-damian-lillard/nyn1xl5l388j1k3469d1fzis0.

Jackson, Josh. "The 40 Best Little Radio Stations in the U.S." Pastemagazine.com, 23 Sept. 2010, www.pastemagazine.com/blogs/lists/2010/09/the-best-little-radio-stations-in-the-us.html.

Kamenetz, Anya. "Will NPR Save the News?" *Fast Company*, 28 Mar. 2014, www.fastcompany.com/1208947/will-npr-save-news.

"KSER *Pledge Drive Pitch Playbook*." Pledge Pitch Playbook KSER, pp. 1–22., www.kser.org/download/Pledge_Break_Playbook_KSER.pdf, pp. 2.

Marcotte, Michael V. "Which Is the Best Local Public Radio Station and Why?" Quora, 13 Oct. 2010, www.quora.com/Which-is-the-best-local-public-radio-station-and-why.

Merrill, Donald, "MyData," GoogleDocs Public Radio Survey, June 2017, Portland, OR

Reals, Tucker. "God save National Public Radio." CBS News, CBS Interactive, 13 Feb. 2009, www.cbsnews.com/news/god-save-national-public-radio/.

Staff. "The 10 Best College Radio Stations." The Huffington Post, 14 Dec. 2012, www.huffingtonpost.com/2012/12/14/the-10-best-college-radio_n_2301281.html.

Zjestika, et al. "Am I Stealing? [Archive]–Straight Dope Message Board." Straight Dope Message Board RSS, 6 Nov. 2004, boards.straightdope.com/sdmb/archive/index.php/t-285268.html.

The Money Shot

Bailey, George. "Free Riders, Givers, and Heavy Users: Predicting Listener Support for Public Radio." Dec. Journal of Broadcasting and Electronic Media, 2004, http://walrusresearch.com/images/Free-Riders_in_Journal_of_Broadcasting.pdfr.

"Gambling Laws and Regulation in the United States." GamblingSites.com, Oct. 2015, www.gamblingsites.com/online-gambling-jurisdictions/us/.

Kronstadt, Sylvia. "The Beggar Wears Prada — or Why I Stopped Giving to Public Radio." The Economic Populist, 16 Aug. 2014, www.economicpopulist.org/content/beggar-wears-prada-or-why-i-stopped-giving-public-radio-5558.

Mamet, David. "David Mamet: Why I Am No Longer a 'Brain-Dead Liberal.'" *Village Voice*, 11 Mar. 2018, www.villagevoice.com/2008/03/11/david-mamet-why-i-am-no-longer-a-brain-dead-liberal/.

Ravenelle, Alyssa. "What Are Matches and Challenges?" GiveGab Non-Profit Giving Platform, 15 July 2018, support.givegab.com/highlight-your-fundraising-efforts-through-your-giving-day/motivate-your-donors-with-match-es-and-challenges/what-are-matches-and-challenges.

Shannon, Chelsea. "Bitch Don't Kill My Vibe; or, Why I Stopped Listening to NPR." Now Is Magic, Mar. 2014, nowismagic.blogspot.com/2014/03/bitch-dont-kill-my-vibe-or-why-i.html.

Stockton, Sean Stannard. "Why Do People Really Give to Charity? (SSIR)." Stanford Social Innovation Review: Informing and Inspiring Leaders of Social Change, 25 June 2008, ssir.org/articles/entry/why_do_people_really_give_to_charity.

Sutton, John. "Public Radio's On-Air Fundraising Message Matrix." 21 Jan. 2018, www.radiosutton.com/images/JSA-message-matrix-users.pdf.

Tuschman, Richard. "Using Volunteers and Interns: Is It Legal?" Forbes, 28 Aug. 2012, www.forbes.com/sites/richardtuschman/2012/08/24/using-volunteers-and-interns-is-it-legal/.

Wong, Kristin. "Track Your Happiness Helps You Understand What Makes You Happy." Lifehacker, 19 Oct. 2015, lifehacker.com/track-your-happiness-helps-you-understand-what-makes-yo-1737038850.

Gifts, Premiums and "Leverage"

Bailey, George. "Free Riders, Givers, and Heavy Users: Predicting Listener Support for Public Radio." *Journal of Broadcasting & Electronic Media*, Dec. 2004, pp. 1–14., www.walrusresearch.com/images/Free-Riders_in_Journal_of_Broadcasting.pdf.

Coast Community Radio Spring 2016 Pledge Drive, KMUN, timestamp – 20 Mar. 2016 0833 PST

"During a Single Hour of a Pledge Drive for a Public Radio." GMAT Club Forum, 2009, gmatclub.com/forum/during-a-single-hour-of-a-pledge-drive-for-a-public-radio-92544.html.

Greenspun, Philip. "Public Radio Fund Drives." Philip Greenspun's Weblog, Harvard University, 22 June 2009, blogs.harvard.edu/philg/2009/06/22/public-radio-fund-drives/.

Hrywna, Mark. "T Shirt Premium Jazzes Up Public Radio Fundraising." The *NonProfit Times*, 15 Sept. 2009, www.thenonprofittimes.com/news-arti-cles/t-shirt-premium-jazzes-up-public-radio-fundraising/.

Kramer, Melody. "Putting the Public into Public Media Membership." Nieman Lab, 13 July 2015, www.niemanlab.org/2015/07/putting-the-public-into-public-media-membership/.

Lipschultz, Jeremy Harris, and Hilt, Michael. "Public Radio Listener Data Analysis: Mass Communication Research Course Student Projects." University of Nebraska–Omaha, 4 Apr. 2017, digitalcommons.unomaha.edu/cgi/viewcontent.cgi?article=1054&context=commfacpub, pg 5

"New Service Gives Station Donors Choice of Digital Music Premiums." Current, 4 Aug. 2014, current.org/2014/08/new-service-gives-station-donors-choice-of-digital-music-premiums/.

"Online Pledge Form WVXU/WUMB," Cincinnati Public Radio, secure2.convio.net/cpr/site/Donation2.

"Plane Truth." E*Trade TV Commercial, ISpot.TV, 17 June 2018, www.ispot.tv/ad/wpUX/etrade-plane-truth-song-by-tony-bennett.

"Premiums." PRI InfoSite, STATION TOOLS, 2005, www2.pri.org/Infosite/fundraising/premiums.shtml.

Sefton, Dru. "Public Radio Tattoos Make a Comeback." Current, 16 Feb. 2015, current.org/2013/04/public-radio-tattoos-make-a-comeback/.

Sefton, Dru. "WHYY Finds Interest in PBS Passport Premium among Radio Audience as Well." Current, 11 May 2016, current.org/2016/05/whyy-finds-interest-in-pbs-passport-premium-among-radio-audience-as-well/.

Seligson, Susan. "WBUR Has Rosy Offer for BU Community, BU Today, Boston University." Boston Hospitality Review RSS, 6 Feb. 2016, www.bu.edu/today/2016/wbur-has-rosy-offer-for-bu-community/.

Simpson, April. "Stations Try Different Approaches with Food Bank Partnerships." Current, 2 June 2016, current.org/2016/05/stations-try-different-approaches-with-food-bank-partnerships/.

Staff. "What Is PBS Passport?" PBS, 3 May 2018, help.pbs.org/support/solutions/articles/5000692392-what-is-pbs-passport.

Steinhoff, Barbara. "Feed Public Radio...Feed a Family Helps WGCU and the Food Bank." Harry Chapin Food Bank of Southwest Florida, 18 June 2018, harrychapinfoodbank.org/blog/recent-posts/feed-public-radio-feed-a-family-helps-wgcu-and-the-food-bank.

Steves, Rick. "Scenes from the Great American Pledge Drive." Rick Steves'
    Travel Blog, 12 Dec. 2010, blog.ricksteves.com/blog/scenes-from-the-great-
    american-pledge-drive-2/.

Sutton, John. " It's Taking More Leverage to Generate Pledge Drive Con-
    tributions." *RadioSutton*, 12 Feb. 2015, radiosutton.blogspot.com/
    search?q=leverage.

Sutton, John. "Listener Focused Fundraising–System Report." 2000, pp. 1–9.

Sutton, John. "Planned Giving," *RadioSutton*, 12 Feb. 2015, radiosutton.blog-
    spot.com/search?q=planned%2Bgiving.

"Thank You Gifts." Nevada Public Radio, 18 June 2018, knpr.org/support/mem-
    ber-benefits/thank-you-gifts.

Thorpe. "I Hate NPR's Valentine's Day Pledge Drive." *eNotAlone*. 12 Feb.
    2009, www.enotalone.com/forum/showthread.php?t=271520.

Waters, Joe. "Urban Outfitters' Cause Marketing for NPR Is a Poor Fit." The
    Huffington Post, 16 July 2011, www.huffingtonpost.com/joe-waters/ur-
    ban-outfitters-cause-ma_b_862213.html.

Zachary, Adrienne. "Dear Sponsorship Partners." Prado, 2009, pp. 1–1., www.
    pradoweb.org/vertical/sites/%7BFFCC657E-D16A-4444-8CFE-FED-
    EFFFD712D%7D/uploads/%7BEC0EFA37-9658-4DAC-AA8D-A6F-
    92FA6A15E%7D.PDF.

Challenges and Matches

carmicha. "Comments on Public Radio Fundraising Changeup," Monday, Octo-
    ber 01, 2012

"Challenge and Matching Gifts," www.ecfa.org/Content/TopicChallengeMatch-
    ingGifts+.

Dutra, Ana. "A More Effective Board of Directors." *Harvard Business Review*, 7
    Aug. 2014, hbr.org/2012/11/a-more-effective-board-of-dire.

Karlan, Dean, and List, John A. "Does Price Matter in Charitable Giving?"
    American Economic Review, 24 Aug. 2017, http://econweb.ucsd.edu/~jan-
    dreon/PhilanthropyAndFundraising/Volume%202/14%20KarlanList.pdf.

King, Nicholas. "Corporate Philanthropy Report." Wiley Online Library, 13
    June 2018, www.corporatephilanthropyreport.com/Article-Detail/cecp-re-
    port-shows-corporate-giving-levels-on-the-rise.aspx.

Leonhardt, David. "What Makes People Give?" home.uchicago.edu/~jlist/press/ NYTimes3908.pdf.

List, John A, and Reiley, David Lucking. "The Effects of Seed Money and Refunds on Charitable Giving: Experimental Evidence from a University Capital Campaign." The University of Chicago Press Journals, 1 Feb. 2002, www.jstor.org/stable/10.1086/324392?seq=1#page_scan_tab_contents.

Pagnoni, Laurence. "Challenge Gift Drives and Corporate Matching Gifts." Non Profit News, *Nonprofit Quarterly*, 20 Dec. 2017, nonprofitquarterly. org/2017/10/09/challenge-gift-drives-and-corporate-matching-gifts/.

Poderis, Tony. "Challenge/Matching Gift Programs For Your Fund-Raising Campaigns," Fundraising Magazine, 2010, www.fundsraiser.com/may07/ challenge-matching-gift-programs.html.

Poderis, Tony. "How Board Members Can Become Effective Fund-Raisers." Raise-Funds.com, 18 June 2018, www.raise-funds.com/how-board-mem- bers-can-become-effective-fund-raisers/.

Roisman, Deborah, and Murillo, Ruben Hernandez. "The Economics of Charita- ble Giving: What Gives?" Federal Reserve Bank of St. Louis, 13 Jan. 2015, www.stlouisfed.org/publications/regional-economist/october-2005/the-eco- nomics-of-charitable-giving-what-gives.

"Small Matches and Charitable Giving: Evidence from a Natural Field Ex- periment" 2010, Journal of Public Economics, Dean Karlan, John List, Eldar Shafir – https://www.sciencedirect.com/science/article/abs/pii/ S0047272710001842

Staff. "Challenge Grants." KJZZ, 18 Apr. 2018, kjzz.org/challenge-grants.

Staff. "Member Challenges." Colorado Public Radio, 18 June 2018, www.cpr. org/support/individual-giving/member-challenges.

Sullivan, Nina. "Matching Gift Eligibility: Which Nonprofits Qualify?" Dou- ble the Donation, Adam Weinger, 13 Dec. 2017, doublethedonation.com/ blog/2015/06/matching-gift-nonprofit-eligibility/.

Sutton, John. " It's Taking More Leverage to Generate Pledge Drive Con- tributions." *RadioSutton*, 12 Feb. 2015, radiosutton.blogspot.com/ search?q=leverage.

Thomas, June. "The 10 Cunning Ways Public Radio Stations Convince You to Give Them Money." *Slate* Magazine, 2 Mar. 2009, www.slate.com/articles/arts/culturebox/2009/03/lets_get_those_phones_ringing.html.

Zhao, Jijun, et al. "An Agent Based Simulation Methodology for analyzing Public Radio Membership Campaigns." *Information Technology for Economics and Management*, pp. 1–34., www.item.woiz.polsl.pl/issue4.1/pdf/public-goods_revised.pdf. pg 4

Games

"Artist Tee Shirt Contest." Texas Public Radio, 2018, www.tpr.org/shirtcontest

"Broadcast–Contests." Federal Communications Commission, 21 Oct. 2014, www.fcc.gov/general/broadcast-contests.

Carmody, Bill. "Online Promotions; Wining Strategies and Tactics ," Black Forest Press, 2004

Chandler, Kim. "Which States Don't Have a Lottery? One Might Surprise You." AL.com, 31 Dec. 2013, blog.al.com/wire/2013/12/which_states_dont_have_a_lotte.html.

"Contest Rules of Entry." Iowa Public Radio, 19 June 2018, iowapublicradio.org/contest-rules-entry#stream/0.

"Contest Rules." Rhode Island Public Radio, 18 June 2018, ripr.org/contest-rules#stream/0.

Flick, Lauren Lynch. "The FCC Has Written Good Contest Rules, Now You Should Too." Comm Law Center, 16 Feb. 2016, www.commlawcenter.com/2016/02/fcc-written-good-contest-rules-now.html.

"Focus on Nevada Photo Contest–Rules." Nevada Public Radio, 2018, knpr.org/desert-companion/focus-nevada-photo-contest/focus-nevada-photo-contest-rules.

Godin, Seth. *Small is the New Big*, Penguin Random House, 2006, pg 203 .

Halley, William H. "Back to the Negotiating Table: Designing a Tribal-State Compact for Alabama." 30 May 2017, scholars.law.unlv.edu/cgi/viewcontent.cgi?article=1119&context=glj, Pg 160

Lasar, Matthew. "Big Radio to FCC: Stop Making Us Explain Contest Rules over the Air." *Radio Survivor*, 21 Dec. 2012, www.radiosurvivor.

com/2012/12/21/big-radio-to-fcc-stop-making-us-explain-contest-rules-over-the-air/.

Neyfakh, Leon. "Gross! Contest Attracts Public Radio Amateurs." *Gawker*, 28 Apr. 2007, gawker.com/256161/gross-contest-attracts-public-radio-amateurs.

"*Notice of Apparent Liability* for Forfeiture." Policies and Rules Concerning Children's Television Programming, MM Docket No. 93-48, FCC, 13 Nov. 2003, transition.fcc.gov/eb/Orders/2003/DOC-241846A2.html.

Opinion. "Alabama Needs Statewide Gaming Commission." Tuscaloosa News, 16 Dec. 2008, www.tuscaloosanews.com/article/DA/20081216/Opinion/606127912/TL/. .

Slocum, Joyce, et al. "Statement of National Public Radio, Inc." Amendment of Sec. 73.1216 of the Commission's Rules Concer Ning Contest RM-11684 Rules Disclosures by Radio Stations, 20 Dec. 2012, pp. 1–4., www.stateofthemedia.org/2011/audio-essay/#hd-radio-falters-as-broadcasters-look-for-new-technologies.

Staff. "Florida Man Dies after Eating Roaches and Worms in Contest." 9 Oct. 2012, www.reuters.com/article/us-usa-florida-roach/florida-man-dies-after-eating-roaches-and-worms-in-contest-idUSBRE8980QH20121009.

Staff. "Why Are Some National Contests Invalid in Certain States and Other Countries?" HowStuffWorks, 2 Jan. 2001, money.howstuffworks.com/question541.htm.

The Basics." Sweepstakes and Skill contests – The Basics, Enns & Archer LLP, 22 July 2003, www.ennsandarcher.com/s_basics.html.

People Like You

Anonymous. "I'm Fed up with Being Asked for Money by the Charity I Work For." *The Guardian*, 5 July 2015, www.theguardian.com/voluntary-sec-tor-network/2015/jul/05/im-fed-up-of-being-asked-for-money-by-the-chari-ty-i-work-for.

"Basic Memberships: More Trouble than they're Worth?" Current, 22 Apr. 2013, current.org/2012/12/basic-memberships-more-trouble-than-theyre-worth/.

Gage, Marisue. OPB Membership Center Representative, email correspondence with author, 15 Dec. 2017

Klein, Kim. "Are Small Gifts a Waste of Time?" Grassroots Institute for Fundraising Training, 10 Mar. 2015, www.grassrootsfundraising.org/2015/03/are-small-gifts-a-waste-of-time/.

Merrill, Donald, "MyData," GoogleDocs Public Radio Survey, June 2017, Portland, OR

Myler, Larry. "Acquiring New Customers Is Important, But Retaining Them Accelerates Profitable Growth." *Forbes*, 8 June 2016, www.forbes.com/sites/larrymyler/2016/06/08/acquiring-new-customers-is-important-but-retaining-them-accelerates-profitable-growth/#3a4ba6db6671.

Ni, Jian, et al. "Upselling versus Upsetting Customers? A Model of Intrinsic and Extrinsic Incentives." June 2015, pp. 1–34., marketing.wharton.upenn.edu/wp-content/uploads/2015/04/Ni-Jian-01-19-2017-CarRental_2015.pdf.

"Planned Giving." Tri States Public Radio, tspr.org/planned-giving.

"Push for Major Gifts Advances as NPR, Stations Work Together." *Current*, 20 July 2015, current.org/2015/07/push-for-major-gifts-advances-as-npr-stations-work-together/.

Simpson, April. "What's a Major Gift in Public Media? Depends on Who You Ask." *Current*, 23 Mar. 2017, current.org/2017/03/whats-a-major-gift-in-public-media-depends-on-who-you-ask/.

Simpson, April. "While Sustainers Are Growing, Experts Say Public Radio Still Needs New Donors." *Current*, 5 June 2017, current.org/2016/09/while-sus-tainers-are-growing-experts-say-public-radio-still-needs-new-donors/.

"Sustainers, Allegiance Fundrasing Group." Allegiance Software, www.allegiancesoftware.com/solutions/fundraising-donor-relationship-management/sustainers/.

Sutton, John. "Eliminating Pledge Drives." RadioSutton, 25 Feb. 2007, radiosutton.blogspot.com/search?q=eliminating%2Bpledge%2Bdrives.

Sutton, John. "Eliminating Pledge Drives II." RadioSutton, 5 Mar. 2007, radiosutton.blogspot.com/search?q=eliminating%2Bpledge%2Bdrive%2BII.

Sutton, John. "It's Taking More Leverage to Generate Pledge Drive Contributions." Radio Sutton, 12 Feb. 2015, radiosutton.blogspot.com/search?q=It%E2%80%99s+Taking+More+Leverage+to+Generate+Pledge+Drive+Contributions+.

Teresa, Mary (Mother), National Prayer Breakfast, Wash. D.C., 3 Feb, 1997.

Thomas, Thomas J, and Clifford, Theresa R. "Individual Giving to Public Radio Stations." 12 June 2008, pp. 1–40., www.srg.org/funding/IndividualGiving.pdf.

"Upsell and Cross-Sell Strategies That Work," OnDemand Webinar, LORMAN Education Services, 19 June 2018, www.lorman.com/training/sales/upsell-and-cross-sell-strategies-that-work.

New and Renew

Allen, David. "The Trouble with Transactional Giving." Development for Conservation, Development for Conservation, 14 Mar. 2017, www.developmentforconservation.com/2017/the-trouble-with-transactional-giving/.

"Basic Memberships: More Trouble than They're Worth?" *Current*, 22 Apr. 2013, current.org/2012/12/basic-memberships-more-trouble-than-theyre-worth/.

Chinn, Becky. "Get Them and Keep Them: The TWO Pillars of Successful Membership." Greater Public, 24 July 2015, go.greaterpublic.org/blog/2015/07/get-them-and-keep-them-the-two-pillars-of-successful-membership/.

Clayton, Jay. "New Year's Resolutions for Your Membership Team." Greater Public, 15 Dec. 2015, go.greaterpublic.org/blog/2015/12/new-years-resolutions-for-your-membership-team/.

Gallo, Amy. "The Value of Keeping the Right Customers." *Harvard Business Review*, 5 Nov. 2014, hbr.org/2014/10/the-value-of-keeping-the-right-customers.

Kramer, Melody. "Putting the Public into Public Media Membership." Nieman Lab, 13 July 2015, www.niemanlab.org/2015/07/putting-the-public-into-public-media-membership/.

Lichterman, Joseph. "How PRX and Radiotopia Are Rethinking the Public Radio Pledge Drive for the Podcast Era." Nieman Lab, 27 Oct. 2015, www.niemanlab.org/2015/10/how-prx-and-radiotopia-are-rethinking-the-public-radio-pledge-drive-for-the-podcast-era/.

Simpson, April. "What's a Major Gift in Public Media? Depends on Who You Ask." *Current*, 23 Mar. 2017, current.org/2017/03/whats-a-major-gift-in-public-media-depends-on-who-you-ask/.

Simpson, April. "While Sustainers Are Growing, Experts Say Public Radio Still Needs New Donors." *Current*, 5 June 2017, current.org/2016/09/while-sustainers-are-growing-experts-say-public-radio-still-needs-new-donors/.

"Sustaining Membership." Spokane Public Radio, spokanepublicradio.org/sustaining-membership.

Thomas, Thomas J, and Clifford, Theresa R. "Individual Giving to Public Radio Stations." 12 June 2008, pp. 1–40., www.srg.org/funding/IndividualGiving.pdf., pgs 6, 9 & 20

Waits, Jennifer. "NFCB Sessions' Fundraising Tips for Radio: Celebrity Smackdowns, 1-Day Drives and the Philanthropist Next Door." *Radio Survivor*, 22 June 2011, www.radiosurvivor.com/2011/06/21/nfcb-sessions-fundraising-tips-for-radio-celebrity-smackdowns-1-day-drives-and-the-philanthropist-next-door/.

Young, Liz. "Federal Tax Reform Could Affect Donations to Nonprofits." The Business Journals, 21 Dec. 2017, www.bizjournals.com/albany/news/2017/12/21/federal-tax-reform-could-affect-donations-to.html.

Sustain and Upsell

Arganbirght, Valarie, et al. "Clarifying the Sustainer Message for TV." July 2015, pp. 1–38., greaterpublic.org/wp-content/uploads/2016/05/bd-42d0afd33d47dcb18079a96186fa22.pdf, pg 21

Arganbright, Valerie, and Barbara Appleby. "Results–Minnesota Public Radio." Appleby Arganbright LLC, 2012, www.applebyarganbright.com/results/.

Asturias, Jose. "Why Do Individuals Contribute to Public Radio? The Wharton School of Economics, May 2006, repository.upenn.edu/cgi/viewcontent.cgi?referer=http://www.google.com/url. pg 20

Blancharski, Dave. "*Superior Customer Service*." Atlantic Publishing Group, 30 Jan. 2006, pg. 126

Blum, Debra E. "When Shrinking a Donor Pool Means Bigger Gifts." The *Chronicle of Philanthropy*, 29 Feb. 2016, www.philanthropy.com/article/When-Shrinking-a-Donor-Pool/235474.

Chen, Raymond. "Answering Phones at KUOW for Their Fall 2006 Pledge Drive." PowerShell Team Blog, Microsoft Developer, 17 Oct. 2006, blogs.msdn.microsoft.com/oldnewthing/20061017-08/?p=29353.

Chinn, Becky. "Get Them and Keep Them: The TWO Pillars of Successful Membership." Greater Public, 24 July 2015, go.greaterpublic.org/
blog/2015/07/get-them-and-keep-them-the-two-pillars-of-successful-mem-
bership/.

Clayton, Jay. "The Imbalanced State of Public Radio Sustainer Programs."
Greater Public, 25 Mar. 2016, go.greaterpublic.org/blog/2016/03/the-imbal-
anced-state-of-public-radios-sustainers-programs/.

Crane, Michael. "Make a Simple and Powerful Change to Your WPR Gift."
EFTConversion2015, Wisconsin Public Radio, 1 Sept. 2015, www.prad-
oweb.org/vertical/sites/%7BFFCC657E-D16A-4444-8CFE-FEDEFFFD-
712D%7D/uploads/EFTConversion2015_Final.pdf+.

Emerson, Patrick. "Economic Science of Charitable Giving." Oregon Business
Report, 19 May 2010, oregonbusinessreport.com/2010/05/economic-sci-
ence-of-charitable-giving/.

Falk, Tyler. "Joint Licensees Breaking down TV, Radio Barriers." Current, 12
Apr. 2016, current.org/2016/04/joint-licensees-breaking-down-tv-radio-bar-
riers/.

Gage, Marisue. OPB Membership Center Representative, email correspondence
with author, Dec 15, 2017-1343PST

Ginsberg, Johanna, and Goldberg, Sheila. "Synagogues Adopt Voluntary Dues
Model." *New Jersey Jewish News*, 3 June 2015, njjewishnews.com/arti-
cle/27423/synagogues-adopt-voluntary-dues-model#.WmLQtk3SkjI.

Guettler, Ellen. "The Hidden Cost of Sustainers." go.greaterpublic.org/
blog/2015/01/the-hidden-costs-of-sustainers/.

Hoggatt, Leslie M. "Thank You for Your Membership Support." 90.3 FM
WBHM Birmingham, 15 Mar. 2010, www.pradoweb.org/vertical/
sites/%7BFFCC657E-D16A-4444-8CFE-FEDEFFFD712D%7D/up-
loads/%7BD7BEEA14-EB46-4D8A-B3D6-F325A5CAF422%7D.DOC.

KERA timestamp 19 Apr. 2016 1527 CST

KOPB timestamp 8 Oct. 2014 0619 PST

KOPB timestamp 4 Oct. 2014 1427 PST

Lapin, Andrew. "Podcast with Limited Radio Airplay Sets Kickstarter Record."
Current, 2 Feb. 2017, current.org/2012/08/podcast-with-limited-radio-
air-play-sets-kickstarter-record/.

Lichterman, Joseph. "How PRX and Radiotopia Are Rethinking the Public
     Radio Pledge Drive for the Podcast Era." Nieman Lab, 27 Oct. 2015, www.
     niemanlab.org/2015/10/how-prx-and-radiotopia-are-rethinking-the-public-
     radio-pledge-drive-for-the-podcast-era/.

Markidan, Len. "How to Use Upselling to Increase Customer Happiness, Re-
     tention and Revenue." Blog, Groove, 20 July 2018, www.groovehq.com/
     support/upsells.

Ni, Jian, et al. "Upselling versus Upsetting Customers? A Model of Intrinsic and
     Extrinsic Incentives." June 2015, pp. 1–34., marketing.wharton.upenn.edu/
     wp-content/uploads/2015/04/Ni-Jian-01-19-2017-CarRental_2015.pdf.

"NPR DS Marketing Forms." Powerpoint Presentation, NPR Digi-
     tal Services, Aug. 2016, mediad.publicbroadcasting.net/p/newn-
     prdsblog/files/201608/Marketing-Forms-Intro-8.2016.pdf?_
     ga=2.223069913.356172353.1513243214-1992214127.1483921645.

"Our Capabilities." Stenocall Call Center Our Capabilities, stenocall.com/
     our-capabilities.

Resler, Seth. "Can Your Radio Station Generate Revenue with a Membership
     Website?" Jacobs Media Strategies, 29 Oct. 2016, jacobsmedia.com/ra-
     dio-station-generate-revenue-membership-website/.

Rieck, Dean. "P.S. Don't Forget to Include a Sales Letter Postscript." Pro Copy
     Tips–Copywriting Tips for Professional Copywriters, 2 Nov. 2009, www.
     procopytips.com/post-scripts.

Roisman, Deborah. "The Economics of Charitable Giving: What Gives?"
     Federal Reserve Bank of St. Louis, 13 Jan. 2015, www.stlouisfed.org/publi-
     cations/regional-economist/october-2005/the-economics-of-charitable-giv-
     ing-what-gives.

Snodgrass, Sheldon. "WFCR National Public Radio." Steadysales.com, www.
     steadysales.com/wfcr-national-public-radio/.

Staff. "Hawaii Public Radio–Welcome! Thank You for Volunteering at HPR.
     Gifts in All Amounts Are Greatly Appreciated." 16 Sept. 2015, pp. 1–20.,
     files.hawaiipublicradio.org/pdf/volunteer/F15-ScriptSet.pdf.

Stewart, Tessa. "WNYC Doesn't Need Your Money: NY Public Radio Announc-
     es $10 Million Grant Barely A Week After Pledge Drive Ends." Village
     Voice, 11 Mar. 2014, www.villagevoice.com/2014/03/11/wnyc-doesnt-need-

your-money-ny-public-radio-announces-10-million-grant-barely-a-week-after-pledge-drive-ends/.

Sutton, John. "A Mixed Bag of Thoughts." *RadioSutton*, 6 Feb. 2006, radiosutton.blogspot.com/search?q=mixed%2Bbag%2Bof%2Bthoughts.

Sutton, John. "The Impact of Sustaining Givers on Public Radio Fund Drives." *RadioSutton*, 17 Feb. 2015, radiosutton.blogspot.com/2015/02/the-impact-of-sustaining-givers-on.html.

"The Psychology of Color and What It Means for Fundraising." Network for Good, 11 June 2014, www.networkforgood.com/nonprofitblog/the-psychology-of-color-and-what-it-means-for-fundraising/.

Thomas, Thomas J, and Clifford, Theresa R. "Individual Giving to Public Radio Stations." 12 June 2008, pp. 1–40., www.srg.org/funding/IndividualGiving.pdf, pg 6

Major Giving and Bequests

"A Donor Bill or Rights." 4 Mar. 2015, www.afpnet.org/files/contentdocuments/donor_bill_of_rights.pdf.

Bayliss, Gordon. "The Right Words When Rates Go Up." Greater Public, 22 Apr. 2015, go.greaterpublic.org/blog/2015/04/the-right-words-when-rates-go-up/.

Bergsma, Stephanie. "A Major Donor Checklist." Greater Public, 23 Feb. 2015, go.greaterpublic.org/blog/2015/02/a-major-donor-checklist/.

Bergsma, Stephanie. "Everybody Talks! (A Major Giving Cautionary Tale)." Greater Public, 15 Oct. 2015, go.greaterpublic.org/blog/2015/10/a-major-giving-cautionary-tale/.

Flandez, Raymund. "NPR Gets $17-Million for Expanded Coverage and New Media Platform." The *Chronicle of Philanthropy*, 16 Dec. 2013, www.philanthropy.com/article/NPR-Gets-17-Million-for/153895.

Grace, Francie. "Joan Kroc Dies of Brain Cancer." CBS News, 13 Oct. 2003, www.cbsnews.com/news/joan-kroc-dies-of-brain-cancer/.

"Guidelines for Ethical Fundraising." CPB *Major Giving Initiative*, Leadership for Philanthropy LFP–Design Your Program–2012, majorgivingnow.org/design/guidelines_ethical_fundraising.html.

Lewis, Jim. "'Restricted Unrestricted': a Productive New Flavor of Grants at KPBS." *Current*, 22 July 2012, current.org/2011/06/restricted-unrestricted-a-productive-new-flavor-of-grants-at-kpbs/.

Mook, Ben. "Donated Cars Bring Big Bucks to Public Stations." *Current*, 31 July 2018, current.org/2013/07/donated-cars-bring-big-bucks-to-public-stations/.

Orman, Suze. "Suze Orman Quotes." BrainyQuote, Xplore, www.brainyquote.com/quotes/suze_orman_173484.

"Push for Major Gifts Advances as NPR, Stations Work Together." *Current*, 20 July 2015, current.org/2015/07/push-for-major-gifts-advances-as-npr-stations-work-together/.

Simpson, April. "What's a Major Gift in Public Media? Depends on Who You Ask." *Current*, 23 Mar. 2017, current.org/2017/03/whats-a-major-gift-in-public-media-depends-on-who-you-ask/.

Sutton, John. "Big Money." *RadioSutton*, 12 Apr. 2005, radiosutton.blogspot.com/search?q=big%2Bmoney.

Thomas, Thomas J, and Clifford, Theresa R. "Individual Giving to Public Radio Stations." 12 June 2008, pp. 1–40., www.srg.org/funding/IndividualGiving.pdf, pg 25

Turner, Deb. "12 Planned Giving Action Steps." Greater Public, 9 Apr. 2015, go.greaterpublic.org/blog/2015/04/12-planned-giving-action-steps/.

Turner, Deb. "Raising the Bar: Reaching for Major Gifts." Greater Public, 18 Aug. 2015, go.greaterpublic.org/blog/2015/08/raising-the-bar-reaching-for-major-gifts/.

Ydstie, John, and Klose, Kevin. "Philanthropist Joan Kroc Leaves NPR $200 Million Gift." NPR, 6 Nov. 2003, www.npr.org/templates/story/story.php?storyId=1494600.

Ydstie, John. "Philanthropist Joan Kroc Leaves NPR $200 Million Gift." Kroc Leaves NPR Record Gift, NPR, 6 Nov. 2003, go.greaterpublic.org/blog/2015/02/a-major-donor-checklist/.

Keeping Track

Bowsky, Beth. "Policy Specialist, Council of Non-Profits, email correspondence with author, Dec. 9, 2016

Chinn, Becky. "Get Them and Keep Them: The TWO Pillars of Succ
ful Membership." Greater Public, 24 July 2015, go.greaterpublic
blog/2015/07/get-them-and-keep-them-the-two-pillars-of-success
bership/.

Coulson, Melanie. "The Seven Habits of Highly Effective Mail Campaigns."
Greater Public, 25 Aug. 2015, go.greaterpublic.org/blog/2015/08/the-seven-
habits-of-highly-effective-mail-campaigns/.

Creedon, Aine. "How Nonprofits Use Social Media to Engage with Communi-
ties." Non Profit News | Nonprofit Quarterly, 16 Sept. 2015, nonprofitquar-
terly.org/2014/03/13/social-media-nonprofits-engaging-with-community/.

Ford, Robert. "Special Report: Online Giving Is More than the 'Donate Now'
Button." The NonProfit Times, 1 Apr. 2005, www.thenonprofittimes.com/
news-articles/special-report-online-giving-is-more-than-the-donate-now-
button/.

Hawkins-Gaar, Katie. "5 Ways Newsrooms Can Make the Most of Instagram."
Poynter, 2 Mar. 2017, www.poynter.org/news/5-ways-newsrooms-can-
make-most-instagram#.VP9DBama9BA.linkedin.

Jayy, Mikey, et al. "Do Donation Buttons for Radio Stations, Really Work?"
Quora, 5 Jan. 2017, www.quora.com/Do-Donation-buttons-for-radio-sta-
tions-really-work5.

Matney, Lucas. "Facebook Rolls Out Its 'Donate Now' Button To Nonprofits."
TechCrunch, 24 Aug. 2015, techcrunch.com/2015/08/24/facebook-rolls-
out-its-donate-now-button-to-non-profits/.

Miller, Merton. "Investment Gurus: A Roadmap to Wealth from the World's
Best Money Managers," Peter J. Tanous, NY Institute of Finance, 1999, pg 267

"Partner Development Software for Missionaries." Donor Manager Software,
Home, 18 June 2018, donormanager.com/.

Old Dogs

Anderson, Nate. "Public Radio Remakes Itself by Entering the IPhone Age." Ars
Technica, 5 Mar. 2010, arstechnica.com/tech-policy/2010/03/public-radio-
remakes-itself-by-entering-the-iphone-age/.

Bickham, Imelda, et al. "Face to Face Communication vs Other Types of Communication." People Communicating at Work, www.people-communicating. com/face-to-face-communication.html.

Chinn, Becky. "Finish Strong with a Fiscal Year-End Campaign." Greater Public, 13 Mar. 2015, go.greaterpublic.org/blog/2015/03/effective-fiscal-year-end-fundraising/.

Chinn, Becky. "Get Them and Keep Them: The TWO Pillars of Successful Membership." Greater Public, 24 July 2015, go.greaterpublic.org/ blog/2015/07/get-them-and-keep-them-the-two-pillars-of-successful-membership/.

College of Fine Arts and Communication. MobileCause, app.mobilecause. com/f/8z6/n.

Cooke, Harriet. "SMS SOS! Text Messages Mark 20-Year Anniversary but Have ALREADY Been Overtaken by Twitter and Instant Messaging." Daily Mail Online, Associated Newspapers, 3 Dec. 2012, www.dailymail.co.uk/news/ article-2241743/Text-messages-mark-20-year-anniversary-overtaken-Twitter-instant-messaging.html.

Coulson, Melanie. "The Seven Habits of Highly Effective Mail Campaigns." Greater Public, 25 Aug. 2015, go.greaterpublic.org/blog/2015/08/the-seven-habits-of-highly-effective-mail-campaigns/.

Donor Development Strategies, donordevo.com/.

Egner, Jeremy. "Fundraiser's Past a Red Flag No One Saw." *Current*, 6 May 2012, current.org/2005/08/fundraisers-past-a-red-flag-no-one-saw/.

Griffin, Jonathan. "Google Voice Searches Double Year on Year." 60 Percent of Searches Are from Mobile Devices, The Webmaster, 15 Feb. 2016, www. thewebmaster.com/seo/2016/feb/15/google-voice-searches-doubled-past-year/.

Janssen, Mike. "Who's Taking Your Donation When You Call in a Pledge?" *Current*, 17 May 2016, current.org/2016/05/whos-taking-your-donation-when-you-call-in-a-pledge/.

"Just Launched, out 'Text to Donate' Program! Text 'Kpfk' to 41444 to Support Your Favorite Public Radio Station! Pic.twitter.com/WrSgCOJFVg." Twitter, 1 Apr. 2017, twitter.com/KPFK/status/847978803418636288.

Kan, Paul, and Whitt, Jacqueline E. "Sun Tzu and the Art of War – Great Strategists (Episode 2)." US Army War College War Room, 26 Oct. 2017, warroom.armywarcollege.edu/special-series/great-strategists/sun-tzu-art-war-great-strategists-episode-2/.

Kitty, P. "Oregon Public Broadcasting." Yelp, 18 Sept. 2010, www.yelp.com/biz/oregon-public-broadcasting-portland.

"KSER *Pledge Drive Pitch Playbook*." Pledge Pitch Playbook KSER, pp. 1–22., www.kser.org/download/Pledge_Break_Playbook_KSER.pdf, pp. 2.

Levey, Richard. "The Check's In the Mail." The *NonProfit Times*, 3 Nov. 2015, www.thenonprofittimes.com/news-articles/the-checks-in-the-mail.

McIntyre, Erin. "Come Visit the NPR DC Headquarters; Daily Tours Begin In June." NPR, 30 May 2013, www.npr.org/sections/npr-ex-tra/2013/05/30/185850828/come-visit-the-npr-dc-headquarters-daily-tours-begin-in-june.

Merrill, Donald, "MyData," GoogleDocs Public Radio Survey, June 2017, Portland, OR

"National Public Radio Pledge-a-Thon." MobileCause, 12 May 2011, www.mobilecause.com/radio-mobile-donations/.

"OPB Sustainer Declined Charge & EFT Recapture and EFT Conversion Efforts." OPB, 12 July 2016, www.pradoweb.org/vertical/sites/%7BFF-CC657E-D16A-4444-8CFE-FEDEFFFD712D%7D/uploads/OPB_Sustain-er_Declined_Charge_Recapture_and_EFT_Conversion_Efforts.docx.

Peter, Ian. "The History of Email." www.nethistory.info, 2004, www.nethistory.info/History%20of%20the%20Internet/email.html.

Plunkett, John. "Decline of the Phone Call: Ofcom Shows Growing Trend for Text Communication." *The Guardian*, Guardian News and Media, 17 July 2012, www.theguardian.com/technology/2012/jul/18/ofcom-report-phone-calls-decline.

Purdy, Michael W. "The Limits to Human Contact: How Communication Technology Mediates Relationships." Academia.edu, 13 Mar. 1997, www.academia.edu/603616/The_limits_to_human_contact_How_communica-tion_technology_mediates_relationships

"r/Atlanta–GPB Soliciting Door-to-Door." Reddit, 2016, www.reddit.com/r/At-lanta/comments/3ia339/gpb_soliciting_doortodoor/.

Rosenwald, Michael S. "Your IPhone's Secret Past: How Cadaver Ears and a Talking Dog Led to the Telephone." The Washington Post, WP Company, 3 Nov. 2017, www.washingtonpost.com/news/retropolis/wp/2017/11/03/ how-alexander-graham-bells-talking-dog-led-to-the-iphone-x/?utm_term=. a914219b53c5.

Simpson, April. "Pubcasters Refine Tactics for Acquiring Donors through Canvassing." Current, 9 Aug. 2016, current.org/2016/08/pubcasters-refine-tac-tics-for-acquiring-donors-through-canvassing/.

Simpson, April. "WNYC Boosts Podcast Income with Text-to-Donate Efforts." Current, 1 Sept. 2016, current.org/2016/09/wnyc-boosts-podcast-income-with-text-to-donate-efforts/.

Staff. "GPB's Door to Door Membership Campaign." Georgia Public Broadcasting, 19 June 2018, www.gpb.org/support/door-to-door.

Stenocall. Stenocall Call Center "Our Capabilities," www.stenocall.com/our-capabilities.

Thomas, June. "The 10 Cunning Ways Public Radio Stations Convince You to Give Them Money." Slate Magazine, Slate, 2 Mar. 2009, www.slate.com/ articles/arts/culturebox/2009/03/lets_get_those_phones_ringing.html.

Thompson, Derek. "The Most Popular Social Network for Young People? Texting." The Atlantic, Atlantic Media Company, 11 Nov. 2014, www. theatlantic.com/technology/archive/2014/06/facebook-texting-teens-insta-gram-snapchat-most-popular-social-network/373043/.

Waits, Jennifer. "My Visit to Public Radio Station KEXP in Seattle." Radio Survivor, 14 Jan. 2015, www.radiosurvivor.com/2015/01/14/visit-public-ra-dio-station-kexp-seattle/.

"When Telemarketers Pocket Money Meant For Charity." WGBH, 13 Sept. 2012, news.wgbh.org/post/when-telemarketers-pocket-money-meant-charity.

"WPR Membership FAQ." Wisconsin Public Radio, 27 Mar. 2018, www.wpr. org/support/wpr-membership-faq.

Yaeger, Ross. "The Two Biggest Ad Trends in Public Radio and TV Right Now (And What to Watch Out For)." Greater Public, 3 Nov. 2015, go.greaterpub-lic.org/blog/2015/11/the-two-biggest-ad-trends-in-public-radio-and-tv-right-now-and-what-to-watch-out-for/.

Yu, Roger. "Voice Mail in Decline with Rise of Text, Loss of Patience." USA Today, Gannett Satellite Information Network, 3 Sept. 2012, usatoday30. usatoday.com/tech/news/story/2012-09-03/voicemail-decline/57556358/1.

New Tricks

"6 Ways Nonprofits Can Use Instagram for Fundraising." Nonprofit Tech for Good, 2 Aug. 2017, www.nptechforgood.com/2014/02/06/6-ways-nonprofits-can-use-instagram-for-fundraising/.

Anderson, Nate. "Public Radio Remakes Itself by Entering the IPhone Age." Ars Technica, 5 Mar. 2010, arstechnica.com/tech-policy/2010/03/public-radio-remakes-itself-by-entering-the-iphone-age/.

Bayliss, Gordon. "Working Ahead of the Curve: Your Digital Revenue Budget." Greater Public, 19 Jan. 2015, go.greaterpublic.org/blog/2015/01/working-ahead-of-the-curve-your-digital-revenue-budget/.

Brooke, Heather. "Writing in the Digital Revolution," The Huffington Post, August 12, 2011

Ciobanu, Madalina. "NPR's Facebook Live Strategy Focuses on Getting the Audience to Participate in the Broadcasts." Journalism.co.uk, newswired. com, Journalism.UK, 2 Aug. 2016, www.journalism.co.uk/news/npr-s-facebook-live-strategy-focuses-on-getting-the-audience-to-participate-in-the-broadcasts/s2/a661028/.

Creedon, Aine. "How Nonprofits Use Social Media to Engage with Communities." Non Profit News, *Nonprofit Quarterly*, 16 Sept. 2015, nonprofitquarterly.org/2014/03/13/social-media-nonprofits-engaging-with-community/.

Drizin, Julie. "Why Is *Current* Launching a Paywall? And Other Questions." *Current*, 12 Apr. 2018, current.org/2017/05/why-is-current-launching-a-pay-wall-and-other-questions/.

"Facebook Live Audio-Opportunity/Challenge for Stations." Insideradio.com, 22 Dec. 2016, www.insideradio.com/free/facebook-live-audio-opportunity-challenge-for-stations/article_18c8e7ac-c820-11e6-b7cd-1f46af36f873. html.

Fiegerman, Seth, and Segall, Laurie. "Facebook's News Feed to Show More Content from Friends, Less from Publishers and Brands." CNNMoney, 11

Jan. 2018, money.cnn.com/2018/01/11/technology/facebook-news-feed-change/index.html.

Gauger, Carol. "Are Websites Still Relevant? The Importance of Business Sites in a Mobile World." LinkedIn, 28 June 2016, www.linkedin.com/pulse/websites-still-relevant-importance-business-sites-mobile-carol-gauger/.

Grehn, Kim. "When to Post (Using Social Media)." LinkedIn, 27 Jan. 2016, www.linkedin.com/pulse/when-post-using-social-media-kim-grehn.

Guettler, Ellen. "Make the Most of Social Media During Drives." Greater Public, 8 May 2015, go.greaterpublic.org/blog/2015/05/make-the-most-of-social-media-during-drives/.

Holmes, Ryan. "How to Turn Your Entire Staff Into A Social Media Army." Fast Company, 6 Nov. 2015, www.fastcompany.com/3053233/how-to-turn-your-entire-staff-into-a-social-media-army.

Kallas, Priit. "Top 15 Most Popular Social Networking Sites and Apps [June 2018]." DreamGrow, 19 June 2018, www.dreamgrow.com/top-15-most-popular-social-networking-sites/?utm_content=buffereb63e&utm_medium=buffer_social&utm_source=twitter&utm_campaign=buffer_updates.

Koetsier, John. "How Google Searches 30 Trillion Web Pages, 100 Billion Times a Month." VentureBeat, 16 Jan. 2018, venturebeat.com/2013/03/01/how-google-searches-30-trillion-web-pages-100-billion-times-a-month/.

Leinbach-Reyhle, Nicole. "3 Reasons Websites Are Vital for Small Businesses." Forbes, 28 Mar. 2016, www.forbes.com/sites/nicoleleinbachreyhle/2014/09/29/websites-for-small-businesses/#17ec155c2026.

Mansfield, Healther. "Ten Best Practices for Your Station's Facebook Page." Greater Public, 14 May 2015, go.greaterpublic.org/blog/2015/05/ten-best-practices-for-your-stations-facebook-page/.

Mansfield, Heather. "Nine Must-Know Best Practices for Distributing Your Station's Content on Social Networks." Greater Public, 17 July 2015, go.greaterpublic.org/blog/2015/07/9-must-know-best-practices-for-distributing-your-nonprofits-content-on-social-networks/.

Matney, Lucas. "Facebook Rolls Out Its 'Donate Now' Button To Nonprofits." TechCrunch, 24 Aug. 2015, techcrunch.com/2015/08/24/facebook-rolls-out-its-donate-now-button-to-non-profits/.

Merrill, Donald, "MyData," GoogleDocs Public Radio Survey, June 2017, Portland, OR

Oppenheimer, David M, and Olivola, Christopher Y. *The Science of Giving*: Experimental Approaches to the Study of Charity. Psychology Press, 19 Jan. 2011, pg 73, books.google.com/books?id=yx55AgAAQBAJ&vq=-public+radio+fund+pledge+membership+drive&dq=public+radio+fund+-pledge+membership+drive&lr=&source=gbs_navlinks_s.

Palmer, Charis. "Media Companies May No Longer Control Distribution, But They Do Control Trust." MediaShift, 25 Oct. 2016, mediashift.org/2016/10/media-companies-may-no-longer-control-distribution-control-trust/.

Patel, Sahil. "Two Months in: Four Things NPR Has Learned Using Facebook Live." Digiday, 7 July 2016, digiday.com/media/two-months-four-things-npr-learned-using-facebook-live/?sthash_aESshMxi_mjjo.

Perlberg, Steven. "Podcasts Experiment with Paid Subscriptions." The Wall Street Journal, Dow Jones & Company, 23 May 2016, www.wsj.com/articles/podcasts-experiment-with-paid-subscriptions-1463997601.

"Privacy Policy." Oregon Public Broadcasting, 1 Dec. 2017, www.opb.org/about/privacypolicy/.

Renner, Nausicaa. "NPR Rides Facebook Wave to Traffic Record." Columbia *Journalism Review*, 2 Oct. 2016, www.cjr.org/tow_center/npr_facebook_traffic.php.

Robles, Patricio. "What Non-Profits Need to Know about Facebook's New Fundraising Tools." Econsultancy, 19 Nov. 2015, econsultancy.com/blog/67223-what-non-profits-need-to-know-about-facebook-s-new-fundraising-tools/.

Shahani, Aarti. "Facebook Wants Great Power, But What About Responsibility?" NPR, 19 Feb. 2017, www.npr.org/sections/alltech-considered/2017/02/19/516094134/facebook-wants-great-power-but-what-about-responsibility.

Shastry, Anjali. "The Growing Power of Tumblr–For News." American Journalism Review, 4 Mar. 2015, ajr.org/2014/12/22/growing-power-tumblr-news/.

Simpson, April. "NPR One Will Test in-App Donations with U.S., U.K. Users." *Current*, 11 May 2017, current.org/2017/05/npr-one-will-test-in-app-dona-tions-with-u-s-u-k-users/.

Theisen, Stephanie. "Are Banner Ads Worth It on Radio Station Websites?" Leighton Broadcasting, 5 Oct. 2016, blog.leightonbroadcasting.com/blog/ are-banner-ads-worth-it-on-radio-station-websites.

Wang, Shan. "Out of Many, NPR One: The App That Wants to Be the 'Netflix of Listening' Gets More Local." Nieman Lab, 11 Jan. 2016, www.niemanlab. org/2016/01/out-of-many-npr-one-the-app-that-wants-to-be-the-netflix-of- listening-gets-more-local/.

Freeriders and Moral Hazard

Bailey, George. "*Journal of Broadcasting & Electronic Media*/December 2004 Free Riders, Givers, and Heavy Users: Predicting Listener Support for Public Radio." *Journal of Broadcasting & Electronic Media*, Dec. 2004, pp. 1–14., www.walrusresearch.com/images/Free- Riders_in_Journal_of_Broad-casting.pdf, pg 609

Bentley, Joshua. "Best Practices in Noncommercial Radio Fundraising: A Prac- titioner Perspective." Texas Christian University, Oct. 2014, www.research- gate.net/publication/265689684_Best_practices_in_noncommercial_radio_ fundraising_a_practitioner_perspective.

Burgo, Joseph. "The Difference between Guilt and Shame." Psychology To- day, Sussex Publishers, 30 May 2013, www.psychologytoday.com/blog/ shame/201305/the-difference-between-guilt-and-shame.

"Consider All Things, Stations Ask." Las Vegas Sun, 20 Oct. 2006, lasvegassun. com/news/2006/oct/20/consider-all-things-stations-ask/.

Croson, Rachel, and Shang, Jen. "Limits of Social Influence on the Voluntary Provision of Public Goods : Evidence from Field Experiments." Social Comparison and Charitable Contribution, Indiana University, citeseerx.ist. psu.edu/viewdoc/download?doi=10.1.1.583.7541&rep=rep1&type=pdf, pg 2

Diez, Maria Sanchez. "A Dutch City Is Giving Money Away to Test the 'Basic Income' Theory." Quartz, 30 June 2015, qz.com/437088/utrecht-will-give- money-for-free-to-its-citizens-will-it-make-them-lazier/.

Effective use of Premiums, " Station Tools, PRI, 19 June 2018, www2.pri.org/ Infosite/fundraising/use_of_premiums.cfm.

Ellen King-Rodgers, GM of KGLT, email correspondence with the author, October 26, 2017

Friess, Steve. "Two Things That Shocked Me Yesterday." Las Vegas Blog: Steve Friess' VEGAS HAPPENS HERE, 24 Oct. 2008, thestrippodcast.blogspot. com/2008/10/two-things-that-shocked-me-yesterday.html.

Garland, Eric. "The '*In Rainbows*' Experiment: Did It Work?" NPR, 17 Nov. 2009, www.npr.org/sections/monitormix/2009/11/the_in_rainbows_experiment_did.html.

Gentry, Carol. "Don't Turn Me into Ira Glass. Please Donate!" Health News Florida, 17 Oct. 2011, health.wusf.usf.edu/post/don-t-turn-me-ira-glass-please-donate#stream/0.

Hardin, Garrett. "Extensions of 'The Tragedy of the Commons.'" Science, American Association for the Advancement of Science, 1 May 1998, science.sciencemag.org/content/280/5364/682.full.

"Home" One World Everybody Eats, www.oneworldeverybodyeats.org/.

Jacquet, Jennifer. "*Is Shame Necessary?*" Google Books, Random House, 12 Jan. 2016, books.google.com/books?id=D33ZCwAAQBAJ&pg=PA110&lpg=PA110&dq=public%2Bradio%2Bshame&source=bl&ots=7dXfW-7WHRp&sig=nE0SQr_zwfnyMDfBOQz8D9gSokk&hl=en&sa=X-&ved=0ahUKEwiS3Kvx0YLYAhUIKpQKHfEsChYQ6AEIdDAR#v=onepage&q=public%20radio%20shame&f=false.

KGLT timestamp, 15 Apr. 2016 1651 MST

KNPR timestamp 15 Apr. 2016 0836 PST

Matt. "About *Mortified*: Share the Shame," getmortified.com/about/.

Rosenberg, Ross A. "Shame Excavation: Unearthing Toxic Shame." The *Huffington Post*, 23 Jan. 2014, www.huffingtonpost.com/ross-a-rosenberg/shame_b_4168571.html.

Strainchamps, Anne, and Paulson, Steve. "*To the Best of Our Knowledge–*Shame (Repeat)." Wisconsin Public Radio, 14 Dec. 2016, www.wpr.org/shows/shame-repeat.

Thomas, June. "The 10 Cunning Ways Public Radio Stations Convince You to Give Them Money." *Slate* Magazine, 2 Mar. 2009, www.slate.com/articles/arts/culturebox/2009/03/lets_get_those_phones_ringing.html.

Jung, Carl G., *Memories, Dreams & Reflections*, Random House, 1963

Weltman, Josh. "Seducing Strangers: How to Get People to Buy What You're Selling," Workman Publishing, March 2015, pg 14

Word of Mouth. "The Shame Show." New Hampshire Public Radio, 29 July 2015, nhpr.org/post/shame-show#stream/0.

WPR timestamp 29 Feb. 2016 1525 CST

Zaretsky, Robert. "Public Radio's Fund Drive: an Inevitable Rite of Spring," Houston Chronicle, 27 Mar. 2012, www.chron.com/opinion/outlook/article/Public-radio-s-fund-drive-an-inevitable-rite-of-3439200.php.

Zhao, Jijun, et al. "An Agent Based Simulation Methodology for analyzing Public Radio Membership Campaigns." *Information Technology for Economics and Management*, pp. 1–34., www.item.woiz.polsl.pl/issue4.1/pdf/public-goods_revised.pdf. pg 4

Interns, Volunteers & Temps

Anderson, John. "Wrath of Interns Reaches Clear Channel." DIYmedia.net, 15 July 2014, diymedia.net/wrath-of-interns-reaches-clear-channel/5687.

Arria, Michael, In These Times, Jul 24, 2017, inthesetimes.com/working/entry/20355/NPR-Workers-Unions-Journalism-Media-Strike.

Bergsma, Stephanie. "Seeds in the Community: How to Use Station Volunteers." Greater Public, 23 June 2015, go.greaterpublic.org/blog/2015/06/seeds-in-the-community-how-to-use-station-volunteers/.

Collins, Bob, and Minnesota Public Radio. "NPR, Temporary Workers, and Survival of the Fittest Journalists." State of the Arts, 11 Dec. 2018, blogs.mprnews.org/newscut/2018/12/npr-temporary-workers-and-survival-of-the-fittest-journalists/.

Couch, Christina. "Know Your Internship Rights." *Get In Media*, 2013, getinmedia.com/articles/film-tv-careers/know-your-internship-rights.

Farhi, Paul. "At NPR, an Army of Temps Faces a Workplace of Anxiety and Insecurity." The Washington Post, WP Company, 9 Dec. 2018, www.washingtonpost.com/lifestyle/style/at-npr-an-army-of-temps-resents-a-workplace-full-of-anxiety-and-insecurity/2018/12/07/32e49632-f35b-11e8-80d0-f7e1948d55f4_story.html?utm_term=.37b3fa9a4a14.

"FCC Fines Portland's Listener-Sponsored KBOO For Sarah Jones' 'Your Revolution,'" ArtScope.net: Tony Fitzpatrick: Max and Gaby's Alphabet, 3 July 2001, www.artscope.net/NEWS/new0732001-3.shtml.

"Find Volunteer Opportunities in over 400 Communities," Volunteers of America." Volunteers of America: National, www.voa.org/volunteer.

Fitch, Lynn, former KBOO Station Manager, phone conversation with author, Dec. 24, 2017

Frey, Jennifer. "After Crisis, WAMU Mobilizes Volunteers." 6 Mar. 2004, www.washingtonpost.com/archive/lifestyle/2004/03/06/after-crisis-wamu-mobilizes-volunteers/d4fbb99e-a45d-4c87-a92c-ef7994592afb/?utm_term=.6229a4fec5ea.

Fritz, Joanne. "Never Take a Volunteer for Granted." *The Balance*, 16 Nov. 2016, www.thebalance.com/why-fundraisers-should-never-take-a-volunteer-for-granted-2501855.

Greenhouse, Steven. "'Charlie Rose' Show Agrees to Pay Up to $250,000 to Settle Interns' Lawsuit." *The New York Times*, 20 Dec. 2012, mediadecoder.blogs.nytimes.com/2012/12/20/charlie-rose-show-agrees-to-pay-up-to-250000-to-settle-interns-lawsuit/.

Grynbaum, Michael M. "Unpaid Interns Gain the Right to Sue." The New York Times, 20 Dec. 2017, www.nytimes.com/2014/04/16/nyregion/unpaid-interns-gain-the-right-to-sue.html.

Hirschfeld, Peter. "Union Looks To Curb State's Use Of Temp Workers." Feb 28, 2014, Vermont Public Radio, www.vpr.org/post/union-looks-curb-states-use-temp-workers.

Janssen, Mike. "With Board Support Gone, KBOO Leader Calls It Quits." Current, 16 Feb. 2015, current.org/2013/11/with-board-support-gone-kboo-leader-calls-it-quits/.

KBOO Weekly Schedule. June 2017, kboo.fm/file/70500/download?token=bPJl3zPY.

Kramer, Melody. "What, Exactly, Does It Mean to Be a Member of a Public Radio Station? Can That Definition Expand?" Nieman Lab, 15 May 2015, www.niemanlab.org/2015/05/what-exactly-does-it-mean-to-be-a-member-of-a-public-radio-station-can-that-definition-expand/.

Lapin, Andrew. "Public Media Wrestles with Legality of Unpaid Internships." *Current*, 14 Apr. 2016, current.org/2013/07/public-media-wrestles-with-legality-of-unpaid-internships/.

Lasar, Matthew. "Is Pacifica Radio Worth Saving?" *The Nation*, 29 June 2015, www.thenation.com/article/pacifica-radio-worth-saving/.

Loretto, Penny. "Here Are the New Rules for Interns from the Department of Labor." *The Balance*, 17 Aug. 2017, www.thebalance.com/new-department-of-labor-guidelines-on-internships-1986582.

Merrill, Donald, "MyData," GoogleDocs Public Radio Survey, June 2017, Portland, OR

"Minnesota Public Radio Volunteer Network Confidentialty Agreement." pp. 1–2., webcache.googleusercontent.com/search?q=cache:BukhtzP1vn-4J:https://www.shiftboard.com/mpr/docs/4ce4178e5246e409.pdf+&cd=1&hl=en&ct=clnk&gl=us.

Miller, Jody Greenstone and Miller, Matt. "The Rise of the Supertemp." *Harvard Business Review*, 1 Aug. 2014, hbr.org/2012/05/the-rise-of-the-supertemp.

Pattillo, Natalie. "One More Media Organization Just Admitted: Unpaid Internships Have to Go." The Nation, 11 Aug. 2016, www.thenation.com/article/one-more-media-organization-just-admitted-unpaid-internships-have-to-go/.

"Pay WNYC Interns a Living Wage." Sign the Petition, Change.org, 2016, www.change.org/p/new-york-public-radio-pay-wnyc-interns-a-living-wage.

Rall, Ted. "Romney's Silly but Salient Point on PBS." MSNBC, NBCUniversal News Group, 10 Oct. 2012, www.msnbc.com/msnbc/romneys-silly-salient-point-pbs.

Scopellitini, Vince. "Liability for Volunteers: The Question of Workers Compensation." LinkedIn, 21 Dec. 2016, www.linkedin.com/pulse/liability-volunteers-question-workers-compensation-vince-scopelliti/.

Sefton, Dru. "WJFF Manager Resigns after Public Controversy." *Current*, 12 Apr. 2013, current.org/2013/04/wjff-manager-resigns-after-public-controversy/.

Shepherd. "Balancing Community Obligations with Operational Needs in a Public Org." *MetaFilter*, 26 Oct. 2016, ask.metafilter.com/301929/Balanc-ing-community-obligations-with-operational-needs-in-a-public-org.

Smith, Jacquelyn. "How To Turn Your Temp Job Into A Permanent One." *Forbes, Forbes* Magazine, 28 Sept. 2012, www.forbes.com/sites/jacquelynsmith/2012/09/28/how-to-turn-your-temp-job-into-a-permanent-one/#310e731469af.

Spera, Christopher, et al. "Volunteering as a Pathway to Employment." The Corporation for National & Community Service, June 2013, pp. 1–36., www.nationalservice.gov/sites/default/files/upload/employment_research_report.pdf.

Staff. "'Black Swan' Interns Sue Fox Searchlight After Working for Free." The Hollywood Reporter, 28 Nov. 2012, www.hollywoodreporter.com/news/black-swan-interns-sue-fox-241739.

Staff. "Former Interns Are Suing *Gawker*." The *Huffington Post*, 24 June 2013 www.huffingtonpost.com/2013/06/22/interns-sue-gawker-unpaid-no-pay_n_3483706.html.

Staff. "Paying Thousands to Find Unpaid Internships." Public Radio International, PRI, 13 Sept. 2010, www.pri.org/stories/2010-09-13/paying-thousands-find-unpaid-internships.

"Volunteer Statement of Confidentiality." Prairie Public Broadcasting, Inc., 4 Feb. 2010, pp. 1–1., www.pradoweb.org/vertical/sites/%7BFFCC657E-D16A-4444-8CFE-FEDEFFFD712D%7D/uploads/%7B0757AC02-35C7-4DF8-A152-AF761624DF09%7D.PDF.

Warfield, Samantha Jo. "New Report: Service Unites Americans; Volunteers Give Service Worth $184 Billion." *Corporation for National and Commu-nity Service*, 15 Nov. 2016, www.nationalservice.gov/newsroom/press-re-leases/2016/new-report-service-unites-americans-volunteers-give-service-worth-184.

Wattles, Jackie, National Public Radio workers could go on strike. "NPR Radio Workers Threaten to Strike." July 14, 2017, CNNMoney, Cable News Network, money.cnn.com/2017/07/14/media/npr-workers-strike/index.html.

"WLRN Public Radio and Television." WLRN Public Radio, Facebook, 20 July 2015, www.facebook.com/WLRNmedia/posts/10153353530710202.

Stein, Matthew, and Swarthmore College. "VIDEO: Student Radio Hosts Yanked from Air, Suspended after using the word Tranny.' The College Fix, 21 Nov 2017

Conclusion

"§396. Corporation for Public Broadcasting." 47 U.S.C. United States Code, 2011 Edition , U.S. Government Publishing Office, 2011, https://www.gpo.gov/fdsys/pkg/USCODE-2011-title47/html/USCODE-2011-title47-chap5-subchapIII-partIV-subpartd-sec396.htm

"A Quote by Maya Angelou." Goodreads, www.goodreads.com/quotes/5934-i-ve-learned-that-people-will-forget-what-you-said-people.

Grehn, Kim. "Public Radio Partnerships: Strength in Numbers." LinkedIn, 26 Dec. 2015, www.linkedin.com/pulse/public-radio-partnerships-strength-numbers-kim-grehn.

Howard Nemerov in Conversation with Studs Terkel." The WFMT Studs Terkel Radio Archive | A Living Celebration, 12 Apr. 1960, studsterkel.wfmt.com/programs/howard-nemerov-conversation-studs-terkel.

Humphries, Matthew. "Samsung's Galaxy J2 Pro Phone Can't Access the Internet." PCMAG, 16 Apr. 2018, www.pcmag.com/news/360447/samsungs-galaxy-j2-pro-phone-cant-access-the-internet.

Kogan, Rick. "Studs Terkel Radio Archive Is a Wealth of American History in the Making." Chicagotribune.com, 25 Jan. 2016, www.chicagotribune.com/entertainment/music/ct-studs-terkel-radio-archive-ae-0124-20160121-column.html.

Kramer, Melody, and O'Donovan, Betsy. "F Is for Future: How to Think about Public Media's next 50 Years." Knight Foundation, 2017, www.knightfoundation.org/public-media-white-paper-2017-kramer-o-donovan.

Kronstadt, Sylvia. "The Beggar Wears Prada — or Why I Stopped Giving to Public Radio." The Economic Populist, 16 Aug. 2014, www.economicpopulist.org/content/beggar-wears-prada-or-why-i-stopped-giving-public-radio-5558.

Lakin, Derek. "The Problems with Online People Searches, & How You Can Find the Same Information for Free." HighYa, 4 Sept. 2015, www.highya.com/articles-guides/the-problems-with-online-people-searches-and-how-you-can-find-the-same-information-for-free.

Lopez, Linette. "How Baby Boomers Became the Most Selfish Generation." *Business Insider, Business Insider*, 30 Nov. 2016, www.businessinsider. com/how-baby-boomers-became-the-most-selfish-generation-2016-11.

Perry, Suzanne. "NPR's Uneven Climb to Attract More Big Gifts." The Chronicle of Philanthropy, 9 May 2014, www.philanthropy.com/article/NPR-s-Uneven-Climb-to/153133.

Pierce, David. "Turn Off Your Push Notifications. All of Them." *Wired*, Conde Nast, 21 July 2017, www.wired.com/story/turn-off-your-push-notifications/.

Russell, Mark and Wheeler, Shannon, "*God Is Disappointed in You*, 9781603090988: Amazon.com: Books." Amazon, 27 Aug. 2013, www. amazon.com/God-Disappointed-You-Mark-Russell/dp/1603090983.

Tarter, Steve. "Future of WCBU Public Radio Appears Questionable." Journal Star, 23 May 2018, www.pjstar.com/news/20180522/future-of-wcbu-public-radio-appears-questionable.

Worsham, Sabrina. "Cindy Sheehan." Encyclopedia Britannica, 29 Aug. 2017, www.britannica.com/biography/Cindy-Sheehan.

PLEDGE: The Public Radio Fund Drive

Index

An index is a great leveler."

—George Bernard Shaw

PLEDGE: The Public Radio Fund Drive

674

N

O

P

CPSIA information can be obtained
at www.ICGtesting.com
Printed in the USA
FFHW020704190619
53073464-58708FF